IF FOUND, please notify and arrange return to owner. This text is an important study guide for the owner's career and/or exam preparation.

Name: ______________________________

Address: ______________________________

City, State, ZIP: ______________________________

Telephone: (____) ________________ Email: ______________________________

Groundwood Paper and Highlighters — All Gleim books are printed on high-quality groundwood paper. We recommend you use a non-bleed-through (dry) highlighter (e.g., the Avery *Glidestick*™ – ask for it at your local office supply store) when highlighting page items within these books.

REVIEWERS AND CONTRIBUTORS

Garrett W. Gleim, B.S., CPA (not in public practice), is a graduate of The Wharton School at the University of Pennsylvania. Mr. Gleim coordinated the production staff, reviewed the manuscript, and provided production assistance throughout the project.

Grady M. Irwin, J.D., is a graduate of the University of Florida College of Law and has taught in the University of Florida College of Business. Mr. Irwin provided substantial editorial assistance throughout the project.

Scott Lawton, B.S., is a graduate of Brigham Young University-Idaho and Utah Valley University. He has passed the EA exam and has been employed by the Utah State Tax Commission.

John F. Rebstock, B.S.A., is a graduate of the Fisher School of Accounting at the University of Florida. He has passed the CIA and CPA exams. Mr. Rebstock reviewed portions of the manuscript.

Stewart B. White, B.M., *Cum Laude*, University of Richmond, B.S., Virginia Commonwealth University, has passed the CPA and CISA exams and has worked in the fields of retail management, financial audit, IT audit, COBOL programming, and data warehouse management.

A PERSONAL THANKS

This manual would not have been possible without the extraordinary effort and dedication of Jacob Brunny, Kyle Cadwallader, Julie Cutlip, Mumbi Ngugi, Eileen Nickl, Teresa Soard, and Joanne Strong, who typed the entire manuscript and all revisions, and drafted and laid out the diagrams and illustrations in this book.

The author also appreciates the production and editorial assistance of Daniel Fisher, Katherine Goodrich, James Harvin, Jean Marzullo, Shane Rapp, Katie Wassink, and Martha Willis.

The author also appreciates the critical reading assistance of Ellen Buhl, Will Clamons, Matthew Milner, Selden Ross, and Jeremy Wright.

Finally, we appreciate the encouragement, support, and tolerance of our families throughout this project.

FOURTEENTH EDITION

CIA REVIEW

PART III

BUSINESS ANALYSIS AND INFORMATION TECHNOLOGY

by

Irvin N. Gleim, Ph.D., CPA, CIA, CMA, CFM

with the assistance of
Grady M. Irwin, J.D.

ABOUT THE AUTHOR

Irvin N. Gleim is Professor Emeritus in the Fisher School of Accounting at the University of Florida and is a member of the American Accounting Association, Academy of Legal Studies in Business, American Institute of Certified Public Accountants, Association of Government Accountants, Florida Institute of Certified Public Accountants, The Institute of Internal Auditors, and the Institute of Management Accountants. He has had articles published in the *Journal of Accountancy*, *The Accounting Review,* and *The American Business Law Journal* and is author/coauthor of numerous accounting and aviation books and CPE courses.

Gleim Publications, Inc.
P.O. Box 12848
University Station
Gainesville, Florida 32604
(800) 87-GLEIM or (800) 874-5346
(352) 375-0772
FAX: (352) 375-6940
Internet: www.gleim.com
Email: admin@gleim.com

This is the first printing of the fourteenth edition of ***CIA Review: Part III, Business Analysis and Information Technology***. Please email update@gleim.com with **CIA III 14-1** included in the subject or text. You will receive our current update as a reply. Updates are available until the next edition is published.

EXAMPLE:

To:	update@gleim.com
From:	*your email address*
Subject:	**CIA III 14-1**

ISSN: 1547-8068

ISBN: 978-1-58194-760-1

First Printing: May 2009

ACKNOWLEDGMENTS FOR PART III

The author is grateful for permission to reproduce the following materials copyrighted by The Institute of Internal Auditors: Certified Internal Auditor Examination Questions and Suggested Solutions (copyright © 1980 - 2008), excerpts from *The Practice of Modern Internal Auditing* and from *Sawyer's Internal Auditing* (5th ed.), parts of the 2008 *Candidate Handbook*, The IIA Code of Ethics, *International Standards for the Professional Practice of Internal Auditing*, and Practice Advisories.

The author also appreciates and thanks the Institute of Certified Management Accountants for permission to use questions from past CMA examinations, copyright © 1982 - 2007 by the Institute of Management Accountants.

Visit our website (www.gleim.com) for the latest updates and information on all of our products.

TABLE OF CONTENTS

PREFACE

The purpose of this book is to help **you** prepare **yourself** to pass Part III of the CIA examination. The overriding consideration is to provide an inexpensive, effective, and easy-to-use study program. This manual

1. Defines topics tested on Part III of the CIA examination.
2. Includes all recent changes in Part III of the CIA program.
3. Explains how to optimize your grade by analyzing how the CIA exam is constructed and graded.
4. Suggests exam-taking techniques to help you maximize your exam score.
5. Outlines all of the subject matter tested on Part III of the CIA exam in 10 easy-to-use study units, including all relevant authoritative pronouncements.
6. Reorganizes past exam questions according to the subunits within each of the study units and presents an intuitively appealing explanation of each objective question answer.

The outline format and spacing and the question and answer formats are designed to facilitate learning, understanding, and readability. Please read the Introduction of this book carefully.

Even though the Gleim four-volume *CIA Review* constitutes a complete self-study program for the CIA exam, candidates may consider enrolling in a formal review program. Local IIA chapters throughout the world have, in the past, coordinated their CIA review programs with our materials. All candidates should invest in the Gleim *CIA Review System*, which is designed to maximize your limited studying time. Our *System* includes our *CIA Test Prep* CD-Rom and Test Prep for Pocket PC, which are powerful supplemental study aids. Also, our *System* includes our Audio CDs, books, and Gleim Online. If you have not already purchased the Gleim *CIA Review System*, you may call us at (800) 874-5346 to purchase the remaining components at a reduced price.

Thank you for your interest in our materials. We deeply appreciate the thousands of letters and suggestions we have received from CIA, CMA, CPA, and EA candidates and accounting students and professors during the last four decades.

Please send us your suggestions, comments, and corrections concerning *CIA Review: Part III*. The last two pages in this book have been designed to help you note corrections and suggestions throughout your study process. It is imperative that we receive your feedback after you take the CIA exam. We pledge to continue to improve the product (with your suggestions, we hope) in subsequent editions.

To continue providing our customers with first-rate service, we request that questions about our materials be sent to us via mail, email, or fax. The appropriate staff member will give each question thorough consideration and a prompt response. Questions concerning orders, prices, shipments, or payments will be handled via telephone by our competent and courteous customer service staff.

Good Luck on the Exam,

Irvin N. Gleim

May 2009

PREPARING FOR AND TAKING THE CIA EXAM

ABOUT THE CIA EXAM

Introduction

CIA is the acronym for Certified Internal Auditor. The CIA designation is international, with the examination administered in numerous countries. The CIA exam has been administered by The Institute of Internal Auditors (The IIA) since 1974. The exam consists of four 3-hour parts that are given on demand throughout the year. Each part consists of 100 four-answer multiple-choice questions.

Computer-Based Testing

The CIA exam is computerized to facilitate easier testing. The computerized environment allows you more freedom in choosing when and where to take the test and ensures that your score is available to you immediately at the conclusion of your test. Additionally, the risk of committing mistakes when transferring answers to a booklet is eliminated with computer-based testing.

Part I	The Internal Audit Activity's Role in Governance, Risk, and Control	3 hours
Part II	Conducting the Internal Audit Engagement	3 hours
Part III	Business Analysis and Information Technology	3 hours
Part IV	Business Management Skills	3 hours
		12 hours

Each part consists of 100 questions, and testing lasts 2 hours and 45 minutes with 15 minutes given for tutorials and a survey. Pearson VUE, the testing company that The IIA contracts to proctor the exams, has over 400 testing centers worldwide, and candidates can choose test dates throughout the year. The Gleim Test Prep CD-Rom and Gleim Online provide tutorials and exact exam emulations of the Pearson VUE computer screens and procedures to prepare you to PASS. The one-time exam application fee is US $60 for members and US $75 for nonmembers (US $30 for students). The price to register per part is US $130 for members and US $160 for nonmembers (US $85 for students).

Please note as you read through this introduction that CIA program rules and prices are subject to change. Please visit the Gleim CIA Candidate Forum at www.gleim.com/account/forum/CIA for the most up-to-date information.

Development of Internal Auditing

Internal auditing is a management-oriented discipline that has evolved rapidly since World War II. Once a function primarily concerned with financial and accounting matters, internal auditing now addresses the entire range of operating activities. Thus, it performs a correspondingly wide variety of **assurance** and **consulting** services. The development of internal auditing was fostered by the increased size and decentralization of organizations and the greater complexity and sophistication of their operations. The result is a need for an independent, objective means of evaluating and improving risk management, control, and governance processes. Accordingly, The IIA's **definition of internal auditing** is

> *Internal auditing is an independent, objective assurance and consulting activity designed to add value and improve an organization's operations. It helps an organization accomplish its objectives by bringing a systematic, disciplined approach to evaluate and improve the effectiveness of risk management, control, and governance processes.*

Public policy considerations have contributed to the improved status and broadened scope of internal auditing. For example, the Sarbanes-Oxley Act of 2002 requires management and external auditors to report on the effectiveness of internal controls over financial reporting. Internal auditors provide assurance of the effectiveness of internal controls to management that must sign the annual reports. These activities align the internal auditor with the **monitoring** and **risk assessment** processes of the COSO internal control framework. The internal auditors may also reduce the review of internal controls required by external auditors, effectively saving the company significant costs in audit fees.

The Institute of Internal Auditors (The IIA)

The IIA is an international professional association that was organized in 1941 to develop the professional status of internal auditing. The organization's international headquarters is in Altamonte Springs, about 5 miles north of Orlando, Florida.

The IIA has over 160,000 members in more than 165 countries working in the fields of internal auditing, risk management, governance, internal control, IT audit, education, and security. Presently, over 70,000 individuals have attained The IIA's CIA designation. The approximately 250 chapters and affiliated institutes around the world hold regular meetings, seminars, and conferences that encourage members to network with peers, develop professional contacts, and stay informed about current issues and practices in internal auditing.

The IIA's mission is to be the global voice of the internal audit profession and to provide dynamic leadership. The IIA is committed to

- Advocating and promoting the value that internal audit professionals add to their organizations.
- Providing comprehensive professional educational and development opportunities, standards and other professional practice guidance, and certification programs.
- Researching, disseminating, and promoting to practitioners and stakeholders knowledge concerning internal auditing and its appropriate role in control, risk management, and governance.
- Educating practitioners and other relevant audiences on best practices in internal auditing.
- Bringing together internal auditors from all countries to share information and experiences.

The IIA's annual dues in the United States, Canada, and Caribbean nations:

1.	Regular Member	US $145*	4.	Life Member	US $2,100
2.	Government Audit Program	US $75	5.	Retired Member	US $35
3.	Educational Member	US $75	6.	Student Member	US $35

Specialty (gaming audit, CAE services, and financial services auditor) and group (government audit and standard audit) memberships are also available. Visit www.theiia.org/membership for details.

Individuals outside the United States, Canada, and Caribbean nations may become members of The IIA by joining the nearest IIA institute. Institutes charge their own membership fees and offer local programs and services. Contact the institute directly to obtain specific information regarding fees and membership conditions. Visit www.theiia.org/chapters to find the nearest IIA institute.

Member-at-large (non-Chapter) classification is available to those without a chapter or institute in the area. Dues are US $145 annually, plus a US $25 application fee. These members are also required to pay US 30 to cover bank collection charges for drafts drawn on banks outside the United States and Canada.

*New Regular Members must also pay a one-time membership application fee of US $25.

CIA Board of Regents

The Board of Regents is a special committee of The Institute of Internal Auditors established to direct the certification program for internal auditors as established or modified by The IIA's Board of Directors.

The Board of Regents consists of at least nine regents. The regents are appointed by the Chairman of the Board of Directors to serve 3-year terms. Membership on the Board of Regents rotates, with two or three regents being appointed each year. The responsibilities of the Board of Regents include

a. Defining the common body of knowledge for the Certified Internal Auditor examination and other Institute certification examinations
b. Defining the education, experience, character, examination, and other program requirements relating to The Institute certifications
c. Defining continuing professional education (CPE) requirements for Institute certifications
d. Maintaining the quality and security of examinations
e. Promoting The Institute's certifications globally

CIA Program

The following is the official statement of The IIA Board of Directors regarding the CIA program:

> ***Professional Qualifications***
>
> *To assist in achieving the goals and objectives of The Institute, the Certified Internal Auditor (CIA) Program was established. The Board of Directors will develop, approve and modify as necessary, such policies and procedures as may be required to stimulate and encourage this program.*
>
> *While "Certified Internal Auditor" is intended to be the worldwide designation of qualified internal audit professionals, it is recognized for various reasons other professional organizations of internal auditors may develop similar designations. The Board of Directors will develop, approve and modify as necessary, such procedures as may be deemed desirable to recognize those designations.*
>
> *The Board may also approve additional certifications as appropriate.*

The IIA Certification Department

The Vice Presidents of the Learning Center and the Certification Department staff, who are located in The IIA's Florida offices, administer the program. They undertake all of the day-to-day work with respect to the Board of Regents' responsibilities.

The chair of the Board of Regents divides the members into subcommittees. Each subcommittee is responsible for one part of the exam; i.e., each subcommittee makes the initial recommendations concerning the content and grading of its part of the examination to the Board of Regents as a whole.

Well-Planned Evolution Rather than Abrupt Change

One of the responsibilities of The IIA Board of Regents is to continually update and enhance the sources of exam questions, which in their entirety constitute the **common body of knowledge**.

At the same time, the scope and content of the CIA exam appear to evolve so as to be predictable to CIA candidates. Addition of new topics and deletion of currently tested topics are announced at least one year in advance so that candidates may plan and prepare accordingly. The **common body of knowledge**, referred to in The IIA's materials, is reflected in this edition of *CIA Review*.

Objectives and Content of the CIA Examination

The CIA exam tests a candidate's knowledge and ability regarding the current practice of internal auditing. It enables candidates and prospective managers to adapt to professional changes and challenges by

- Addressing nearly all management skills
- Focusing on the principles of management control
- Measuring a candidate's understanding of risk management and internal controls

THE IIA'S CIA CONTENT SPECIFICATION OUTLINES

Part I: The Internal Audit Activity's Role in Governance, Risk, and Control

A.	Comply with The IIA's Attribute Standards	20%
B.	Establish a risk-based plan to determine the priorities of the internal audit activity	20%
C.	Understand the internal audit activity's role in organizational governance	15%
D.	Perform other internal audit roles and responsibilities	5%
E.	Governance, risk, and control knowledge elements	20%
F.	Plan Engagements	20%

Part II: Conducting the Internal Audit Engagement

A.	Conduct Engagements	30%
B.	Conduct Specific Engagements	30%
C.	Monitor Engagement Outcomes	10%
D.	Fraud Knowledge Elements	10%
E.	Engagement Tools	20%

Part III: Business Analysis and Information Technology

A.	Business Processes	20%
B.	Financial Accounting and Finance	20%
C.	Managerial Accounting	15%
D.	Regulatory, Legal, and Economics	10%
E.	Information Technology (IT)	35%

Part IV: Business Management Skills

A.	Strategic Management	25%
B.	Global Business Environments	20%
C.	Organizational Behavior	20%
D.	Management Skills	25%
E.	Negotiating	10%

See Appendix A for complete details and cross-references to this book.

The IIA publishes a Content Specification Outline (CSO), also known as a Content Syllabus, to outline topics covered on each part of the CIA exam. The percentage coverage of each exam part is indicated to the right of each topic. (Note that The IIA "percentage coverage" is given in ranges, e.g., 15-25%, as presented in Appendix A. Above, we present the midpoint of each range to simplify and provide more relevant information to CIA candidates, e.g., 20% instead of 15-25%.) In other words, the percentages listed are plus or minus 5% of the percentage coverages you can expect to encounter during the actual exam. We continually adjust the content of our materials to changes in The IIA's CSOs and changes to CIA exam questions.

Appendix A contains the CSOs in their entirety as well as cross-references to the subunits in our text where topics are covered. Remember that we have studied and restudied the CSOs in developing our *CIA Review* materials. Accordingly, you do not need to spend time with Appendix A. Rather, it should give you confidence that Gleim *CIA Review* is the best review source available to help you PASS the CIA exam. The CSOs refer to proficiency and awareness levels. The IIA definitions of these levels are presented below.

> **Proficiency** -- *Candidates must exhibit proficiency (thorough understanding and ability to apply concepts) in these topic areas.*
>
> **Awareness** -- *Candidates must exhibit awareness (knowledge of terminology and fundamentals) in these topic areas.*

Gleim Study Unit Listing

We believe our 10 study unit titles better describe the content of each part of the CIA exam. Our study unit titles and content also reflect feedback from CIA candidates. Please use the last two pages in this book to give us feedback after each exam. Thank you.

LISTING OF GLEIM STUDY UNITS

Part I: Internal Audit's Role in Governance, Risk, and Control

1. Standards and Proficiency
2. Charter, Independence, and Objectivity
3. Internal Audit Roles I
4. Internal Audit Roles II
5. Control Knowledge Elements
6. Control Aspects of Management
7. Planning and Supervising the Engagement
8. Managing the Internal Audit Activity I
9. Managing the Internal Audit Activity II
10. Engagement Procedures, Ethics, and Fraud

Part II: Conducting the Internal Audit Engagement

1. Engagement Information
2. Communicating Results and Monitoring Progress
3. Specific Engagements I
4. Specific Engagements II
5. Information Technology I
6. Information Technology II
7. Specific IT Engagements
8. Statistics and Sampling
9. Other Engagement Tools
10. Ethics and Fraud

Part III: Business Analysis and Information Technology

1. Business Performance
2. Managing Resources and Pricing
3. Financial Accounting I
4. Financial Accounting II
5. Finance
6. Managerial Accounting
7. Regulatory, Legal, and Economic Issues
8. Information Technology I
9. Information Technology II
10. Information Technology III

Part IV: Business Management Skills

1. Structural Analysis and Strategies
2. Industry and Market Analysis
3. Industry Environments
4. Strategic Decisions
5. Global Business Issues
6. Motivation and Communications
7. Organizational Structure and Effectiveness
8. Managing Groups
9. Influence and Leadership
10. Time Management, Conflict, and Negotiation

Requirements to Attain the CIA Designation

The CIA designation is granted only by The IIA. Candidates must complete the following steps to become a CIA:

1. Complete the appropriate certification application form online and register for the part(s) you are going to take. See Subunit 1.10 of the *CIA Review: A System for Success* booklet for concise instructions on the application/registration process. This booklet also contains a useful worksheet to help you keep track of your process and organize what you need for exam day.
2. Pass all four parts of the CIA exam or pass Parts I, II, and III and gain approval for Professional Recognition Credit for Part IV (see page 8).
3. Fulfill or expect to fulfill the education and experience requirements (see next page).
4. Provide a character reference proving you are of good moral character.
5. Comply with The IIA's Code of Ethics.

Credits can be retained as long as the requirements are fulfilled. Once a designation is earned, the CIA must comply with the program's CPE requirement. Contact Gleim for all of your CPE needs.

Education and Experience Requirements

Anyone who satisfies these character, educational, and professional requirements may sit for the examination.

1. **Bachelor's degree or equivalent.** Candidates must have an undergraduate (4-year) degree or its equivalent from an accredited college-level institution.
   a. Educational programs outside the United States and the qualifications of candidates who have completed most but not all of a degree program are evaluated by The IIA's Board of Regents to determine equivalency.
   b. The IIA's affiliates have been given the authority to recommend educational and experience criteria for their countries to ensure adequate consideration of cultural and societal differences around the world. In addition, certain international professional designations (such as Chartered Accountant) may be accepted as equivalent to a bachelor's degree.
   c. Full-time university students who are in their senior (final) year may sit for the CIA exam before completing their education requirement as long as they complete the Student/Professor Application Form and submit the Full-Time Student Status Form.
2. **Character reference.** CIA candidates must exhibit high moral and professional character and must submit a character reference from a responsible person such as a CIA, supervisor, manager, or educator. The character reference must accompany the candidate's exam application.
3. **Work experience.** Candidates are required to have 24 months of internal auditing experience (or the equivalent) prior to receiving the CIA certificate. A candidate may sit for the exam before completing the work experience requirements, but (s)he will not be certified until the experience requirement is met.
   a. An advanced academic degree beyond the Bachelor's (e.g., a Master's degree) or work experience in related business professions (such as accounting, law, finance) can be substituted for one year of work experience (1-year maximum).
   b. Equivalent work experience means experience in audit/assessment disciplines, including external auditing, quality assurance, compliance, and internal control.
   c. Full-time college or university-level teaching in the subject matter of the examination is considered equivalent to work experience. Two years of teaching equals one year of internal auditing work experience.
   d. Work experience must be verified by a CIA or the candidate's supervisor. An Experience Verification Form is available on The IIA's website and in the CIA *Candidate Handbook* for use in verifying professional experience. This may accompany the candidate's application or be submitted later when criteria have been met.

If you have questions about the acceptability of your work experience, contact The IIA Certification Department at certification@theiia.org or by fax at (407) 937-1108. If you do not possess a Bachelor's degree and are unsure whether your educational achievements or professional designation qualify as equivalents to a Bachelor's degree, you should check "Other" in the Education section of the application and submit required documentation with the application. Include a complete description of your situation. Submit documentation as an attachment to your application via email (certification@theiia.org) or by fax (407-937-1108).

The IIA will typically review all submitted documents within 5 business days of receipt. You may confirm approval of a document through your online CCMS (Certification Candidate Management System) account. Applicants for equivalency may be registered for the exam pending review but should expect a separate letter regarding the outcome of the review. Applicants who do not receive an equivalency status letter within 4 weeks of submission of the application and equivalency request should contact The IIA.

Professional Recognition Credit for Part IV

The IIA offers a Part IV Professional Recognition Credit for qualified professional certifications. Registered candidates and new CIA candidates who have successfully completed the examination requirements for many designations are eligible to receive credit for Part IV of the CIA exam. Hence, candidates who attain the credit for Part IV and pass Parts I, II, and III satisfy the examination requirement for the CIA designation.

In the U.S., the designations that qualify for the credit include

CBA	CCSA	CFIRS	CISA	CPEA
CBM	CDFM	CGAP	CISSP	CPA
NCCO	CFSA	CGFM	CIDA	CRCM
CCBIA	CFE	CHFP	CMA	CRP

Please visit The IIA's website (www.theiia.org/certification/certified-internal-auditor; click on Professional Recognition Credit in the right toolbar) for a complete list of certifications approved for credit in other countries. See Subunit 1.11 in the *CIA Review: A System for Success* booklet for detailed instructions.

Nondisclosed Exam

The CIA exam is a **nondisclosed** exam. **Nondisclosed** means that exam questions and solutions are NOT released after each examination. You will be asked to read and sign The IIA's "Non-Disclosure Agreement and General Terms of Use" prior to taking the CIA exam.

In order to keep our materials up to date and relevant to CIA candidates, we request feedback after each CIA exam. We need to know what topics need to be added or enhanced in our *CIA Review* materials. Note that we are not asking for information about CIA questions. Rather, we are asking for feedback on our outlines, questions, and answer explanations. This approach has been approved by The IIA.

CIA Exam Fees

Fees	IIA Members	Nonmembers	Professors/ Full-Time Students
Exam Application (initial nonrefundable fee)	US $60	US $75	US $30
Exam Parts Registration (per part/per sitting)	US $130	US $160	US $85
Part IV Professional Recognition Credit (PRC-IV) (nonrefundable fee; waived for CCSAs, CGAPs, and CFSAs)	US $130	US $160	US $85
Canadian Exam Site Tax (*percent of total exam part fees paid, including PRC-IV credit)	GST 6%* HST 14%*	GST 6%* HST 14%*	GST 6%* HST 14%*
Deferrals/Cancelations/Changes			
...by the application deadline (without exam fee refund)	US $0	US $0	US $0
...by the application deadline (with exam fee refund)	US $25	US $25	US $25
...after the application deadline	US $35	US $35	US $35
...beginning Wednesday of week before exam or no-shows	US $85	US $110	US $35

Special Professor and Student Examination Fee

The exam application fee is the charge for enrolling candidates in the CIA program. The CIA examination is available to professors and full-time students at reduced fees. For them, the exam application fee is US $30 (instead of US $60), plus an exam registration fee of US $85 (instead of US $130) per part. Professors and students may sit for each part at this special rate one time only.

1. To be eligible for the reduced rate, a student must
   a. Be enrolled as a senior in an undergraduate program or as a graduate student
   b. Be a full-time student as defined by the institution in which the student is enrolled (a minimum of 12 semester hours or its equivalent for senior-level undergraduate students and 9 semester hours for graduate students)
   c. Register for and take the CIA exam while enrolled in school
2. To be eligible for the reduced rate, a professor must
   a. Work full-time as a professor with an accredited educational institution
   b. Provide a letter from the local IIA chapter verifying his/her eligibility for professor status for pricing
3. In addition to the requirements above, the following items should be submitted to the Certification Department of The Institute of Internal Auditors:
   a. A Certified Internal Auditor Examination Registration/Application-Student/Professor Form
   b. A completed and signed Full-Time Student/Professor Status Form
   c. A completed and signed Character Reference Form
   d. Payment for the US $30 exam application fee and the US $85 exam registration fee for each part
4. IIA approval of full-time student or professor status is valid for 180 days. Exam parts must be completed within that time period for candidates to use the discounted prices.

Maintaining Your CIA Designation

After certification, CIAs are required to maintain and update their knowledge and skills. Practicing CIAs must complete and report 80 hours of Continuing Professional Education (CPE) every 2 years. Every February, CIAs who are required to report in the current year will receive reporting forms and instructions from The IIA. Completed forms should be filed with The IIA by May 31 of the required reporting year. Each July, participants in the current year's CPE program will receive an acknowledgment of compliance. Those with even-numbered identification numbers report in even years and those with odd-numbered identification numbers report in odd years. Nonmembers must submit a US $50 processing fee with their report. Contact Gleim for all of your CPE needs.

Examination Sites

The CBT CIA examinations are administered at Pearson VUE testing centers, which are located in over 165 countries across the world. A complete list of these test centers, addresses, and driving directions can be found at www.pearsonvue.com. Click on the "locate - Find a test center" link at the right of the screen, choose the CIA testing program (Institute of Internal Auditors), and then choose the country and region in which you would like to take your exam.

If you require testing accommodations because of a special need, call a Pearson VUE agent at the time of registration for assistance.

PREPARING TO PASS THE CIA EXAM

Control: How To Be In

You have to be in control to be successful during exam preparation and execution. Control can also contribute greatly to your personal and other professional goals. The objective is to be confident that the best possible performance is being generated. Control is a process whereby you

1. Develop expectations, standards, budgets, and plans
2. Undertake activity, production, study, and learning
3. Measure the activity, production, output, and knowledge
4. Compare actual activity with expected and budgeted activity
5. Modify the activity, behavior, or study to better achieve the desired outcome
6. Revise expectations and standards in light of actual experience
7. Continue the process or restart the process in the future

Every day you rely on control systems implicitly. For example, when you groom your hair, you use a control system. You have expectations about the desired appearance of your hair and the time required to style it. You monitor your progress and make adjustments as appropriate. The control process, however, is applicable to all of your endeavors, both professional and personal. You should refine your personal control processes specifically toward passing the CIA exam.

In this book, we suggest explicit control systems for

1. Preparing to take the CIA exam
2. Studying an individual Gleim study unit
3. Answering individual multiple-choice questions

Most endeavors will improve with explicit control. This is particularly true of the CIA examination.

1. Develop an explicit control system over your study process.
2. Practice your question-answering techniques (and develop control) as you prepare solutions to recent CIA questions during your study program.
3. Prepare a detailed plan of steps you will take at the CIA exam.

How Many Parts to Take

The CIA examination consists of four parts: Parts I and II cover internal auditing subject matter, whereas Part III, Business Analysis and Information Technology, and Part IV, Business Management Skills, cover a wide variety of material.

According to The IIA, you may choose to take only one part at each sitting, which is what Gleim recommends for the CBT exam. Unless you have a strong preference to do otherwise, it is best to take the parts in numerical order, from Part I to Part IV. Also, be sure to investigate whether you qualify to receive the Professional Recognition Credit for Part IV and, if you do, submit your application and documentation for it immediately.

Candidates have an initial eligibility period of 2 years from the first exam after their registration is approved. In addition, each time a candidate sits for an exam part, the candidate's eligibility period is extended 2 years from the date of the last exam part taken. A candidate's eligibility expires only if the candidate does not take a single exam part within any 2-year period. If a candidate's eligibility expires, the candidate loses credit for any part or parts passed and must submit a new CIA Exam Application Form and appropriate fees in order to take future examinations.

Study Plan, Time Budget, and Calendar

Complete one ***CIA Review*** study unit at a time. Initially, budget 3 to 4 hours per study unit (1 to 2 hours studying the outline and 1 to 2 minutes each on all the multiple-choice questions). Depending on your background, your time to prepare will vary.

This Introduction	2	hours
10 study units at 3.5 hours each	35	
Review	10	
Total	47	hours

Each week, you should evaluate your progress and review your preparation plans for the time remaining prior to the exam. Marking a calendar will facilitate your planning. Note the exam dates and the weeks to go before the exam. Review your commitments, e.g., out-of-town assignments, personal responsibilities, etc., and note them on your calendar to assist you in keeping to your schedule.

How to Study a Study Unit Using the Gleim *CIA Review System*

To ensure that you are using your time effectively, we recommend that you follow the steps listed below when using all of the materials together (books, CD-Rom, Audio CDs, Gleim Online, and Test Prep for Pocket PC):

1. (25-30 minutes) In the *CIA Gleim Online* course, complete Multiple-Choice Quiz #1 in 20-25 minutes (excluding the review session). It is expected that your scores will be low on the first quiz.
   a. Immediately following the quiz, you will be prompted to review the questions you marked and/or answered incorrectly. For each question, analyze and understand why you marked it or answered it incorrectly. This step is an essential learning activity.
2. (15-30 minutes) Use the audiovisual presentation for an overview of the study unit. The Gleim *CIA Review Audio CDs* can be substituted for audiovisual presentations and can be used while driving to work, exercising, etc.
3. (30-45 minutes) Complete the 30-question True/False quiz. It is interactive and most effective if used prior to studying the Knowledge Transfer Outline.
4. (60 minutes) Study the Knowledge Transfer Outline, specifically the troublesome areas identified from the multiple-choice questions in the Gleim Online course. The Knowledge Transfer Outlines can be studied either online or from the books.
5. (25-30 minutes) Complete Multiple-Choice Quiz #2 in the Gleim Online course.
   a. Immediately following the quiz, you will be prompted to review the questions you marked and/or answered incorrectly. For each question, analyze and understand why you marked it or answered it incorrectly. This step is an essential learning activity.
6. (40-50 minutes) Complete two 20-question quizzes while in Test Mode from the *CIA Test Prep* CD-Rom or Test Prep for Pocket PC.

When following these steps, you will complete all 10 units in about 30-50 hours. Then spend about 5-10 hours using the *CIA Test Prep* CD-Rom or Test Prep for Pocket PC to create customized tests for the problem areas that you identified. To review the entire part before the exam, use the *CIA Test Prep* CD-Rom or Test Prep for Pocket PC to create 20-question quizzes that draw questions from all 10 study units. Continue taking 20-question quizzes until you approach your desired proficiency level, e.g., 75%+.

CIA Gleim Online

CIA Gleim Online is a versatile, interactive, self-study review program delivered via the Internet. With *CIA Gleim Online,* Gleim guarantees that you will pass the CIA exam on your first sitting. It is divided into four courses (one for each part of the CIA exam) and emulates the CIA CBT exam.

Each course is broken down into 10 individual, manageable study units. Completion time per study unit will vary from 3-5 hours. Each study unit in the course contains an audiovisual presentation, 30 true/false study questions, 10-20 pages of Knowledge Transfer Outlines, and two 20-question multiple-choice quizzes.

CIA Gleim Online provides you with a Personal Counselor, who will provide support to ensure your competitive edge. Gleim Online is a great way to get confidence as you prepare with Gleim. This confidence will continue during and after the exam.

Gleim Books and Test Prep CD-Rom

Twenty-question tests in the ***CIA Test Prep*** CD-Rom or Test Prep for Pocket PC will help you focus on your weaker areas. Make it a game: How much can you improve?

Our *CIA Test Prep* forces you to commit to your answer choice before looking at answer explanations; thus, you are preparing under true exam conditions. It also keeps track of your time and performance history for each study unit, which is available in either a table or graphical format.

Simplify the exam preparation process by following our suggested steps listed below and on the next page. DO NOT omit the step in which you diagnose the reasons for answering questions incorrectly; i.e., learn from your mistakes while studying so you avoid making similar mistakes on the CIA exam.

1. In test mode, answer a 20-question diagnostic test from each study unit before studying any other information.
2. Study the Knowledge Transfer Outline for the corresponding study unit in your Gleim book.
   a. Place special emphasis on the weaker areas that you identified with the initial diagnostic quiz in Step 1.
3. Take two or three 20-question tests in test mode after you have studied the Knowledge Transfer Outline.
4. Immediately following the quiz, you will be prompted to review the questions you marked and/or answered incorrectly. For each question, analyze and understand why you answered it incorrectly. This step is an essential learning activity.
5. Continue this process until you approach a predetermined proficiency level, e.g., 75%+.
6. Modify this process to suit your individual learning process.
   a. Learning from questions you answer incorrectly is very important. Each question you answer incorrectly is an **opportunity** to avoid missing actual test questions on your CIA exam. Thus, you should carefully study the answer explanations provided to understand why you chose the incorrect answer so you can avoid similar errors on your exam. This study technique is clearly the difference between passing and failing for many CIA candidates.

b. You **must** determine why you answered questions incorrectly and learn how to avoid the same error in the future. Reasons for missing questions include:
   1) Misreading the requirement (stem)
   2) Not understanding what is required
   3) Making a math error
   4) Applying the wrong rule or concept
   5) Being distracted by one or more of the answers
   6) Incorrectly eliminating answers from consideration
   7) Not having any knowledge of the topic tested
   8) Employing bad intuition when guessing
c. It is also important to verify that you answered correctly for the right reasons. Otherwise, if the material is tested on the CIA exam in a different manner, you may not answer it correctly.
d. It is imperative that you complete your predetermined number of study units per week so you can review your progress and realize how attainable a comprehensive CIA review program is when using the Gleim *CIA Review System*. Remember to meet or beat your schedule to give yourself confidence.

> Avoid studying Gleim questions to learn the correct answers. Use Gleim questions to help you learn how to answer CIA questions under exam conditions. Expect the unexpected and be prepared to deal with it. Become an educated guesser when you encounter questions in doubt; you will outperform the inexperienced exam taker.

Gleim Audio CDs

Gleim *CIA Review* Audio CDs provide a 20- to 50-minute introductory review for each study unit. Each review provides a comprehensive overview of the outline in the *CIA Review* book. The purpose is to get candidates "started" so they can relate to the questions they will answer before reading the study outlines in each study unit.

The audios are short and to the point, as is the entire Gleim System for Success. We are working to get you through the CIA exam with minimum time, cost, and frustration.

Core Concepts

Core concepts are included at the beginning of each study unit. The core concepts provide an overview of the key points that serve as the foundation for learning. In many cases, the core concepts are concise statements of attribute, performance, and implementation standards. As part of your review, you should make sure that you understand each of them.

Study Unit Summaries

Study unit summaries also are included in each study unit. These summaries are similar to the core concepts, but they provide more in-depth synopses of the material. They should help reinforce the main points within each of the study units.

Practice Advisory Summaries

Gleim *CIA Review* also provides the summarization of practice advisories (PA). Each PA is followed by a synopsis of its crucial aspects. The PA summaries provide the reinforcement of key issues that The IIA expects CIA candidates to know.

Multiple-Choice Question-Answering Technique

The following suggestions are to assist you in maximizing your score on each part of the CIA exam. Remember, knowing how to take the exam and how to answer individual questions is as important as studying/reviewing the subject matter tested on the exam.

1. **Budget your time.**
    a. We make this point with emphasis. Just as you would fill up your gas tank prior to reaching empty, so too should you finish your exam before time expires.
    b. You have 165 minutes to answer 100 questions, i.e., 1.65 minutes per question. We suggest you attempt to answer eight questions every 10 minutes, which is 1.25 minutes per question. This would result in completing 100 questions in 125 minutes to give you almost 40 minutes to review questions that you have flagged.
    c. Use the wipeboard provided by Pearson VUE for your Gleim Time Management System at the exam. List the question numbers for every 20 questions (i.e., 1, 21, 41, etc.) in a column on the left side of the wipeboard. The right side of the wipeboard will have your start time at the top and will be used for you to fill in the time you have remaining at each question checkpoint. Stay consistent with 1.25 minutes per question.
2. **Answer the items in numerical order.**
    a. Do **not** agonize over any one item. Stay within your time budget.
    b. Note any items you are unsure of by clicking the "Flag for Review" button in the upper-right corner of your screen, and return to them later if time allows. Plan on going back to all the questions you flagged.
3. **For each item,**
    a. **Read the question** stem carefully (the part of the question that precedes the answer choices) to determine the precise requirement.
        1) Focusing on what is required enables you to ignore extraneous information and to proceed directly to determining the correct answer.
            a) Be especially careful to note when the requirement is an **exception**; e.g., "Which of the following is **not** an indication of fraud?"
    b. **Determine the correct answer** before reading the answer choices. The objective is to avoid allowing the answer choices to affect your reading of the question.
        1) **Cover up the answer choices** by scrolling to view only the question or, if necessary, with your hand. Do not allow the answer choices to affect your reading of the item stem.
        2) When four answer choices are presented, three of them are incorrect. They are called distractors for a very good reason.
        3) Read each answer choice with close attention.
            a) Even if the first answer appears to be the correct choice, do not skip the remaining answer choices. The second, third, or fourth choice may be better.
            b) Treat each answer choice as a true/false question.
    c. **Select the best answer.** Select the most likely or best answer choice. If you are uncertain, make an educated guess.
        1) The CIA exam does not penalize guessing, because your score is determined by the number of correct responses. Thus, you should answer every question.

If You Don't Know the Answer

Guess, but make it an educated guess, which means select the best possible answer. First, rule out answers that you feel are obviously incorrect. Second, speculate on The IIA's purpose and/or the rationale behind the question. These steps may lead you to the correct answer. Third, select the best answer, or guess between equally appealing answers. Flag the question in case you have time to return to it for further analysis. However, unless you made an obvious mistake or computational error, try to avoid changing answers at the last minute. Your first guess is usually the most intuitive.

If you cannot make an educated guess, read the item and each answer and pick the best or most intuitive answer. Never leave a question unanswered.

Do **not** look at the previous answer to try to detect an answer. The answers are random, but it is possible to have four or more consecutive questions with the same answer letter, e.g., answer (B).

NOTE: Do not waste time beyond the amount budgeted. Move ahead and stay on or ahead of schedule.

If You Failed One or More Parts

The pass rate on each part of the CIA exam averages 44%. Thus, you may not pass all parts attempted. If you failed a part, you must wait at least 90 days to retake it.

1. Once you have put the reaction to the bad news behind you, you should regroup and begin implementing the suggestions in this introduction. The Gleim system really works! Avoid thinking "I knew that" or "I don't have to study that again." What you knew and how you took the exam last time did NOT work. Develop new and improved perspectives.
2. Avoid failure on the next exam by **identifying**, **correcting**, and **understanding** your mistakes as you practice answering multiple-choice questions during your study sessions. Use the Gleim system as described on the previous pages. This methodology applies to all CIA candidates. Understand your mistakes while you study so you can avoid them on the exam.

As you practice answering multiple-choice questions under exam conditions, it is imperative that you re-study each question you answer incorrectly.

CBT Exam Components

- Time and Progress

The upper-right corner of the screen will continuously display the time you have remaining in your exam. Below the time remaining, the question number you are currently working on is displayed in contrast to how many total questions there are on the exam (e.g., 14 of 100).

You can choose to allow these reminders to show during the exam, or you can minimize them by clicking on their icons. If you minimize the time remaining, it will automatically reappear when you have 5 minutes left.

- Navigation

The following Navigation buttons will be available at the bottom of every screen during your exam:

Previous – Moves you back to the preceding screen
Next – Moves you forward to the following screen

- Using the Scroll Bar

If you encounter a question that does not fit on the screen in its entirety, use the scroll bar that will appear along the side of the screen. To scroll down, you can either click on the scroll bar and drag it down or click on the arrow at the bottom of the scroll bar. To show the top part of the question again, either click and drag the scroll bar back up or click on the arrow at the top of the scroll bar.

Make certain that you have seen the entire question by always checking to see if the scroll bar appears. If you attempt to complete a question without scrolling to the bottom of the screen, a prompt may appear to remind you to scroll down.

English Display Screen

If you are taking the CIA exam in a language other than English, you may choose to view an English translation of any question on the exam.

To view the translation, click on the English button below the question. A separate screen will open and display the English translation of the current question. Close the translation when you are finished with it by clicking on the X in the lower-right corner of the translation screen.

Calculator

There will be an online calculator available for every question on the CIA exam. To use the calculator, click on the Calculator button in the upper-left corner of the screen. To enter numbers, you can either use your mouse to click the numbers on the calculator display or use the number keypad on your keyboard. Close the calculator when you are finished with it by clicking on the X in the upper-right corner of the calculator display screen.

Flag for Review

To flag a question so you can go back and review it later, click the Flag for Review button in the upper-right corner of the question screen. A flag image will appear in the flag icon on the question screen and to the left of that question number on the review screen. You can flag both answered and unanswered questions for review, but you must complete your review of flagged questions (and answer any unanswered questions) in the allotted exam time.

To unflag a flagged question, click on the Flag for Review button again.

Review Screen

When you have flagged for review or answered all 100 questions, the Review Screen will be displayed. Each question is displayed with the status of that question: answered, flagged for review, or incomplete (unanswered).

You will be able to review your questions by choosing to either

Review All questions and answers
Review Incomplete questions and answers only
Review Flagged questions and answers only

The computer will then generate your review based on which questions you chose to be included. During this review, you will be able to go back to your main Review Screen by selecting the Review Screen button. Once you are done with your review, you will click on the End Review button and then confirm that you are, in fact, done with the review, which means you are also done with the exam. Once you have clicked Yes on this screen, you will no longer be able to return to your exam.

TAKING THE CIA EXAM

CIA Examination Preparation Checklist

1. Acquire your study materials. Rely on the Gleim *CIA Review System* as your primary study source.
2. Communicate with your Personal Counselor to design a study plan that meets your needs.
3. **Apply online** to the exam program (see page 6).
4. **Register online** for the desired part or file the reapplication form.
   a. As soon as your examination location is confirmed, contact Pearson VUE to schedule an appointment to take the exam. Make travel and lodging reservations if necessary.
5. Locate a suitable place to study.
6. Implement your study program.
7. Periodically review, reassess, and revise your study program as needed.
8. Recognize that an orderly, controlled study program builds confidence, reduces anxiety, and produces success!
9. **Pass the examination!**

Exam Psychology

Plan ahead for the exam and systematically prepare for it. Go to the exam and give it your best. Neither you nor anyone else can expect more. If you have undertaken a systematic preparation program, you will do well.

Maintain a positive attitude and do not become anxious or depressed if you encounter difficulties before or during the exam. An optimist will usually do better than an equally well-prepared pessimist. Remember, you are not in a position to be objective about your results during the exam. Many well-prepared examination candidates have been pleasantly surprised by their scores. Indeed, you should be confident because you are competing with many less-qualified persons who have not prepared as well as you. Optimism and a fighting spirit are worth points on every exam; fear, anxiety, and depression tend to impair performance.

Proper exercise, diet, and rest during the weeks before the exam are very important. High energy levels, reduced tension, and a positive attitude are among the benefits. A good aerobic fitness program, a nutritious and well-balanced diet, and a regular sleep pattern will promote your long-term emotional and physical well-being as well as contribute significantly to a favorable exam result. Of course, the use of health-undermining substances should be avoided.

CBT Preparation

Your examination will be taken on a computer at the Pearson VUE testing center. You do not need any computer experience or typing skills to take your examination. Before you start the examination, you will be able to take a tutorial on the testing system if you wish. If you have used the Gleim *CIA Test Prep* CD-Rom and Gleim Online, you will be completely familiar and comfortable with the CBT format. You can also access a tutorial/demo on the CBT experience at Pearson VUE on their website (www.vue.com/athena).

Examination Tactics Emphasized by Gleim

1. Dressing for exam success means emphasizing comfort, not appearance. Be prepared to adjust for changes in temperature, e.g., remove a sweater or put on a coat. Do not bring notes, this text, other books, etc., to the exam. You will only make yourself nervous and confused by trying to cram during the last 5 minutes before the exam. Books are not allowed in the exam room, and there is limited on-site storage space anyway.
2. Arrive 30 minutes before your scheduled appointment. If you arrive less than 30 minutes before your scheduled time, you may be denied the ability to take your exam on that day and forfeit your registration fee. This early check-in allows time for you to sign in and for staff to verify your identification.
3. Bring your Authorization to Test notification from The IIA, your appointment confirmation letter from Pearson VUE, and at least one valid form of identification with you.
4. Read the exam instructions carefully. View the tutorial to ensure that you are familiar with how to navigate through the exam.
5. Answer the 100 questions in chronological order. Flag any questions that you are leaving for later or you wish to review.
6. You have 165 minutes (2 hours 45 minutes) to answer 100 questions. If you allocate 1.25 minutes per question, you will use only 125 minutes, leaving 40 minutes to complete Step 7. If you use the Gleim Time Management System (see Subunit 4.4 of *CIA Review: A System for Success*) to pace yourself during the exam, you will have adequate time to complete each part.
7. After you worked through all 100 questions, you should return to the questions you flagged and make a final selection, i.e., your best answer.
   a. Review each question carefully. If you made an obvious mistake, e.g., misread the question, make the correction. **Do not**, however, begin changing answers and second-guessing yourself. Your first answer to each question should be based on the systematic question-answering technique that you have practiced throughout your preparation program.
8. Upon exiting the testing room, you will receive a print out of your unofficial exam results. Your score will become official once The IIA publishes the score to the CCMS within a few days.
9. As soon as you return home from your exam, please email, fax, or write to us (use the last two pages of this book) with your comments on our materials. We are particularly interested in which topics need to be added or expanded. We are **not** asking about specific CIA questions. Rather, we are asking for feedback on our materials. This approach is approved by The IIA.
10. When you are ready to take another part of the exam, re-review this tactics list and be confident in maximizing your score.

CIA Testing Procedures at Pearson VUE

The following procedures for taking the CIA exam at Pearson VUE were adapted from The IIA's 2008 *Candidate Handbook.*

1. Arrive 30 minutes early and bring your Authorization to Test notification, your appointment confirmation letter, and your identification (see below).
2. The test center administrator will show you where to store your personal items. You must place all personal belongings, including purses, wallets, watches, jewelry, cell phone, etc., in the storage lockers (or other secured location) provided by the test center. You will be given the key to your locker, which must be returned to the test center staff when you leave. The lockers are very small and are not intended to hold large items. Do not bring anything to the test center unless it is absolutely necessary. Neither test center personnel, Pearson VUE, nor The IIA will be responsible for lost or stolen items.
3. The administrator will provide you with a copy of the Candidate Rules Agreement. You must accept the terms of this agreement in order to take an exam at a Pearson VUE testing center.
4. You must provide one form of acceptable identification (e.g., driver's license, passport, military identification, etc.). The administrator will verify that the name on the identification matches the name on the exam registration. You must keep this identification with you at all times during the exam. If you leave the testing room for any reason, you will be required to show your identification to be re-admitted.
   a. Identification must contain your name exactly as you provided it during your registration process, have a permanently-affixed photo of your face, and be current (non-expired). Employee or student IDs will not be accepted.
5. The administrator will capture your signature and verify that your signature matches that on your identification (if any).
6. Your fingerprint will be captured, and a digital photograph of your face will be made.
7. If you have brought a translation dictionary, the administrator will check it to be certain that it is acceptable and does not contain any markings or inserted material.

   (Please note that the only item that a candidate may bring to the test that is allowed in the testing room is a language translation dictionary. This dictionary may not contain definitions of terms. It cannot have anything written or highlighted in the book nor can it contain any added notes or documents inserted into the book.)
8. You will be offered an erasable note board and pen on which you can take notes during the exam. You must return this to the administrator prior to leaving the test center. You cannot take any notes from the test center.
9. An onscreen calculator will be available during the exam. If you prefer a hand-held calculator and the test center has one available, you may request to be provided with one. You will not be allowed to bring a personal calculator or any other such device with you into the testing room.
10. You will be required to sign the test center log and you will be admitted to the test. Your test will start within 30 minutes of the scheduled start time. If circumstances arise, other than candidate error, which delay your session more than 30 minutes, you will be given the choice of continuing to wait or rescheduling your appointment.

11. If you leave the testing room for any reason, you will be required to sign the test center log and show your identification. You may also be required to provide a fingerprint when leaving or re-entering the testing room.
12. You will not be allowed to bring any food or drink into the testing room.
13. You will be escorted to a workstation by the exam proctor. You must remain in your seat during the exam, except when authorized to leave the testing room.
14. After you are logged into your exam, proceed through the introductory screens without delay. You will have the opportunity to view a tutorial that shows you how to navigate through the exam. It is recommended that you review the tutorial, but you will have the option to skip it. [There is a 10-minute time limit on the initial screens and, if that time limit is exceeded, the exam session will automatically begin.]
15. If you encounter ANY computer problem, report it immediately to the exam proctor.
16. When you finish the exam, leave the testing room quietly, turn in your note board, and sign the test center log. The test center staff will provide you with a printed "unofficial" score report and dismiss you after completing all necessary procedures.

    NOTE: Your score will become official once The IIA publishes the score to The IIA Certification Candidate Management System. This normally takes a few days. Exam scores may be suspended, voided, or otherwise invalidated after becoming official if The IIA discovers errors or evidence of cheating or other improper activity.

STUDY UNIT ONE
BUSINESS PERFORMANCE

(36 pages of outline)

This study unit addresses the analysis of performance by business organizations. A pervasive consideration is the pursuit of **quality** in all aspects of the organization's activities. The importance of quality management has been recognized by the **International Organization for Standardization**, which has issued quality assurance standards. Also crucial to successful business performance is effective planning. The aspect of planning covered in this study unit is **forecasting**, including a variety of mostly quantitative forecasting models. The study unit continues with **project management**, a topic of growing importance to all types of organizations in a technology-based society. The next subunit describes **business process reengineering** and its implications, concluding with an approach to the persistent problem of bottleneck management.

Core Concepts

- TQM is the continuous pursuit of quality in every aspect of organizational activities through (1) a philosophy of doing it right the first time, (2) employee training and empowerment, (3) promotion of teamwork, (4) improvement of processes, and (5) attention to satisfaction of internal and external customers.
- The total cost of quality (conformance and nonconformance costs) should be minimized.
- Benchmarking involves analysis and measurement of key outputs against those of the best organizations. This procedure also involves identifying the underlying key actions and causes that contribute to the performance difference.
- The balanced scorecard is a means of implementing an organization's strategy. It connects critical success factors determined in a strategic analysis to performance measures that may be financial or nonfinancial.
- ISO 9000 is a series of voluntary generic standards for establishing and maintaining a quality management system (QMS) within a company.
- Forecasts are the basis for business plans. They attempt to answer questions about the outcomes of events, the timing of events, or the future value of a statistic (e.g., sales).
- Project management techniques are designed to aid the planning and control of large-scale projects having many interrelated activities. A project is a temporary undertaking with specified objectives that often involves a cross-functional team and working outside customary organizational lines.
- One approach to business process analysis is reengineering (also called business process reengineering). It involves process innovation and core process redesign. Instead of improving existing procedures, it finds new ways of doing things.
- The theory of constraints (TOC) is a short-term approach to managing bottlenecks (binding constraints) in production and distribution processes.

1.1 TOTAL QUALITY MANAGEMENT

Process Quality and Product Quality

1. **Deming management.** The work of W. Edwards Deming was influential worldwide in gaining acceptance of the principle that quality improvement generates economic advances. Better quality means lower costs, higher productivity, increased market share, more business, and more employment. According to Deming, education and self improvement are essential components of total quality management.
2. The fundamental areas of quality are process quality and product quality.
   a. **Process quality** is the effectiveness and efficiency of the organization's internal operations. **Product quality** is the conformance of the organization's output with customer expectations. Product quality is best analyzed from **multiple perspectives**: (1) attributes of the product (performance, serviceability, durability, etc.), (2) customer satisfaction, (3) conformity with specifications, and (4) value (relation of quality and price).
      1) One of the dimensions of quality is **conformance**, or how well a product and its components meet applicable standards. Traditionally, conforming products were deemed to be those with characteristics that lie within an acceptable specified **range of values** that includes a target value. This approach also regards a certain percentage of defective (nonconforming) units as acceptable.
         a) The traditional approach was superseded by the **zero-defects (goalpost conformance)** approach. It seeks to eliminate nonconforming output.
         b) An extension of this approach is the **robust quality (absolute quality conformance)** concept. Its goal is to reach the target value in every case. The purpose is to eliminate the hidden quality costs that occur when output varies from the target even though the units are within specifications.

Total Quality Management (TQM)

3. The total quality management approach, also frequently called **total quality (TQ)**, was a very significant development.
   a. **TQM** can increase revenues and decrease costs substantially. The following are TQM's **core principles** or **critical factors**:
      1) Emphasis on the **customer**
         a) Satisfaction of external customers
         b) Satisfaction of internal customers
         c) Requirements for external suppliers
         d) Requirements for internal suppliers
      2) **Continuous improvement** as a never-ending process, not a destination.
      3) **Engaging every employee** in the pursuit of total quality because avoidance of defects in products or services and satisfaction of external customers requires that all internal customers be satisfied.
4. TQM is a **comprehensive approach**. It treats the pursuit of quality as a **basic organizational function** that is as important as production or marketing. Accordingly, TQM is a strategic weapon. Because it affects every aspect of the organization, it permeates the organizational culture. Thus, the cumulative effect of TQM's continuous improvement process can attract and hold customers and cannot be duplicated by competitors.

a. **Definition.** TQM is the continuous pursuit of quality in every aspect of organizational activities through

1) A philosophy of doing it right the first time,
2) Employee training and empowerment,
3) Promotion of teamwork,
4) Improvement of processes, and
5) Attention to satisfaction of internal and external customers.

a) TQM emphasizes the **supplier's relationship with the customer** and identifies customer needs. It recognizes that everyone in a process is at some time a customer or supplier of someone else, either inside or outside of the organization.

b) Thus, TQM begins with external customer requirements, identifies internal customer-supplier relationships and requirements, and establishes requirements for external suppliers.

b. Organizations tend to be vertically organized, but TQM requires strong **horizontal linkages**.

Implementation

5. Implementation of **TQM** cannot be accomplished by application of a formula, and the process is lengthy and difficult. The following phases are typical:

a. Establishing an executive-level **quality council** of senior managers with strong involvement by the CEO
b. Providing **quality training** programs for senior managers
c. Conducting a **quality audit** to identify improvement opportunities and identify strengths and weaknesses compared with competitors
d. Preparing a **gap analysis** to determine what is necessary to bridge the gap between the organization and the quality leaders in its industry and to establish a database for the development of the strategic quality improvement plan
e. Developing **strategic quality improvement plans** for the short and long term
f. Conducting **employee communication and training** programs
g. Establishing **quality teams** to ensure that goods and services conform to specifications

1) Hierarchal structure is replaced with teams of people from different specialties. This change follows from an emphasis on empowering employees and teamwork. Employees should (a) have proper training, necessary information, and the best tools; (b) be fully engaged in the decision process; and (c) receive fair compensation. If empowered employees are assembled in teams of individuals with the required skills, they will be more effective than people performing their tasks separately in a rigid structure. Moreover, a team is a vehicle for idea sharing, which results in process improvement.

h. Creating a **measurement system** and setting goals
i. Revising **compensation, appraisal, and recognition systems**
j. **Reviewing and revising** the entire effort periodically

Processes, Tools, and Measures

6. Various management processes, tools, and measures should be adopted.

a. **Policy deployment** systematically plans organizational objectives and how subunits will approach their accomplishment. Objectives should be consistent across the entity.

b. **Quality function deployment** ensures that customer requirements are translated into design requirements at each step in **product development**. It is an umbrella concept most useful in an environment in which the **Plan-Do-Check-Act (PDCA) Cycle** (the Deming Cycle) is used at all levels.

   1) PDCA is a "management by fact" or scientific method approach to continuous improvement. PDCA creates a **process-centered environment** because it involves (a) studying the current process, (b) collecting and analyzing data to identify causes of problems, (c) planning for improvement, and (d) deciding how to measure improvement **(Plan)**.
   2) The plan is then implemented on a small scale if possible **(Do)**.
   3) The next step is to determine what happened **(Check)**.
   4) If the experiment was successful, the plan is fully implemented **(Act)**.
   5) The cycle is then repeated using what was learned from the preceding cycle.

c. **Kaizen** is the Japanese word for the continuous pursuit of improvement in every aspect of organizational operations.

   1) For example, a **kaizen budget** projects costs based on future improvements. The possibility of such improvements must be determined, and the cost of implementation and the savings must be estimated.

d. **Employee involvement** means training and empowering employees to harness their creativity for problem solving. **Quality control circles** are used to obtain input from employees and to locate the best perspective on problem solving.

e. **Suppliers' management** is the careful selection of suppliers and the cultivation of long-term relationships based on the consistent ability to meet mutual expectations.

f. **Competitive benchmarking** involves continuously evaluating the practices of the best organizations and adapting processes to incorporate the best of these practices.

g. **Quality training** familiarizes all employees with the means for preventing, detecting, and eliminating nonquality. The educational processes are tailored to each group.

h. **Reward and recognition** for quality improvement should be group oriented. They should be based on quality measures.

i. **Customer retention** is a vitally important measure of **service quality**. Loyal customers spend more, refer new customers, and are less costly to service.

<u>**Measures**</u>

j. Examples of **nonfinancial measures of internal performance** are (1) manufacturing cycle efficiency (value-added production time ÷ total manufacturing lead or cycle time), (2) ratio of good output to total output, (3) defects per product line, (4) the half-life method (time required to reduce the defect ratio by 50%), (5) new product development time, and (6) shipments per period.

k. Examples of **nonfinancial measures of customer satisfaction** are (1) percentage of defective goods shipped, (2) customer complaints, (3) customer response time, (4) on-time deliveries, (5) survey data, and (6) market share.

<u>**Quantitative Methods**</u>

l. Statistical and other quantitative methods are used to identify quality problems.

   1) The **Taguchi quality loss function** is a measure of the departure from absolute quality conformance (robust quality). It is based on the principle that quality losses occur even when items are within specified limits or tolerances. Thus, any variation from a quality target for a characteristic results in **hidden quality costs**.
   2) **Statistical quality control** is a method of determining whether a process, e.g., a shipment or production run of units, lies within acceptable limits.

      a) It also is used to determine whether production processes are out of control.

b) **Statistical control charts** are graphic aids for monitoring the status of any process subject to random variations. Originally developed to control the quality of production processes, they also have applications of direct interest to auditors and accountants, for example, (1) unit cost of production, (2) direct labor hours used, (3) ratio of actual expenses to budgeted expenses, (4) number of calls by sales personnel, and (5) total accounts receivable.

   i) The chart consists of three horizontal lines plotted on a horizontal **time scale**.

   ii) The **center line** represents the average or mean value for the process being controlled.

   iii) The other two lines are the **upper control limit (UCL)** and the **lower control limit (LCL)**.

   iv) The processes are measured periodically, and the values are plotted on the chart (X). If the value falls within the control limits, no action is taken. If the value falls outside the limits, the process is considered **out of control**, and an investigation is made for possible corrective action. An advantage of the chart is that it makes **trends** and **cycles** visible.

   v) EXAMPLE:

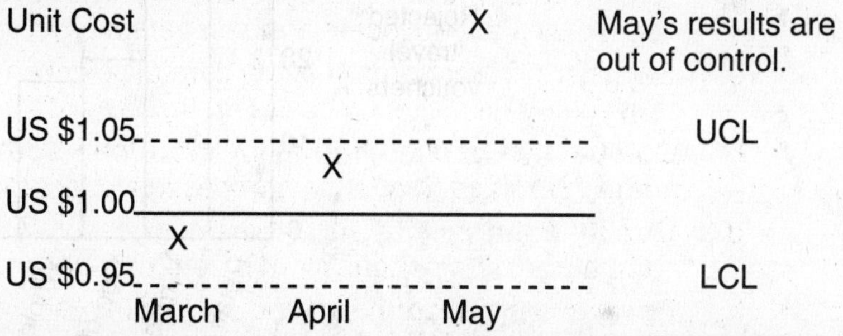

   vi) A **P chart** is based on an attribute (acceptable/not acceptable) rather than a measure of a variable. Specifically, it shows the percentage of defects in a sample.

   vii) A **C chart** also is an attribute control chart. It shows defects per item.

   viii) An **R chart** shows the range of dispersion of a variable, such as size or weight.

   ix) An **X-bar chart** shows the sample mean for a variable.

c) Variations in a **process parameter** may have several causes.

   i) **Random variations** occur by chance. Present in virtually all processes, they are not correctable because they will not repeat themselves in the same manner. Excessively narrow control limits will result in many investigations of what are simply random fluctuations.

   ii) **Implementation deviations** occur because of human or mechanical failure to achieve target results.

   iii) **Measurement variations** result from errors in the measurements of actual results.

   iv) **Model fluctuations** can be caused by errors in the formulation of a decision model.

   v) **Prediction variances** result from errors in forecasting data used in a decision model.

3) A **Pareto diagram** is a bar chart that assists managers in what is commonly called 80:20 analysis.

   a) The **80:20 rule**, formulated by management theorist Joseph M. Juran, states that 80% of all effects are the result of only 20% of all causes.

   b) In the context of quality control, managers optimize their time by focusing their effort on the sources of most problems.

      i) The independent variable, plotted on the X axis, is the factor selected by the manager as the area of interest: department, time period, geographical location, etc. The frequency of occurrence of the defect (dependent variable) is plotted on the Y axis.

      ii) The occurrences of the independent variable are ranked from highest to lowest, allowing the manager to see at a glance which areas are of most concern.

      iii) EXAMPLE: The chief administrative officer wants to know which departments are generating the most travel vouchers that have to be returned to the submitter because of incomplete documentation.

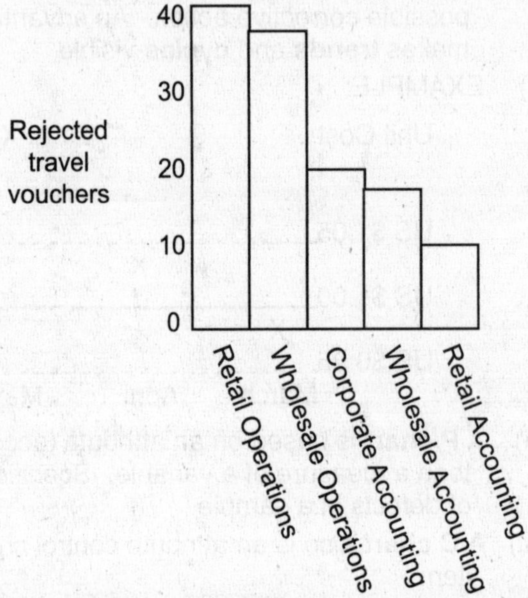

4) A **histogram** displays a continuum for the frequency distribution of the independent variable.

   a) EXAMPLE: The CAO wants to know the amount of the travel reimbursement delayed by a typical returned travel voucher.

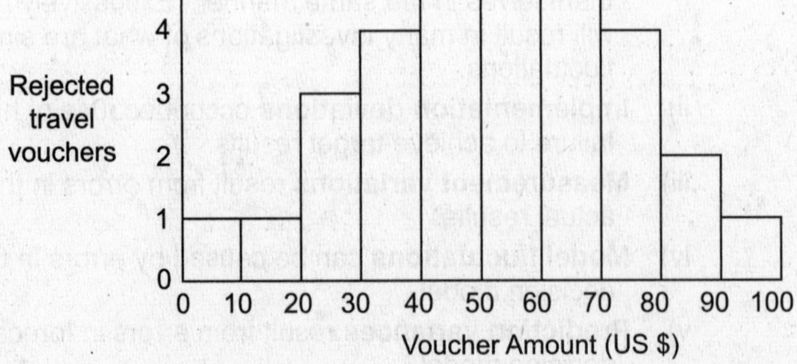

5) A **fishbone diagram** (also called a **cause-and-effect diagram** or an **Ishikawa diagram**) is a total quality management process improvement technique that is useful in studying **causation** (why the actual and desired situations differ).

a) This format organizes the analysis of causation and helps to identify possible interactions among causes.

b) The head of the skeleton represents the statement of the problem.

c) The principal classifications of causes are represented by lines (bones) drawn diagonally from the heavy horizontal line (the spine).

d) Smaller horizontal lines are added in their order of probability in each classification.

e) EXAMPLE:

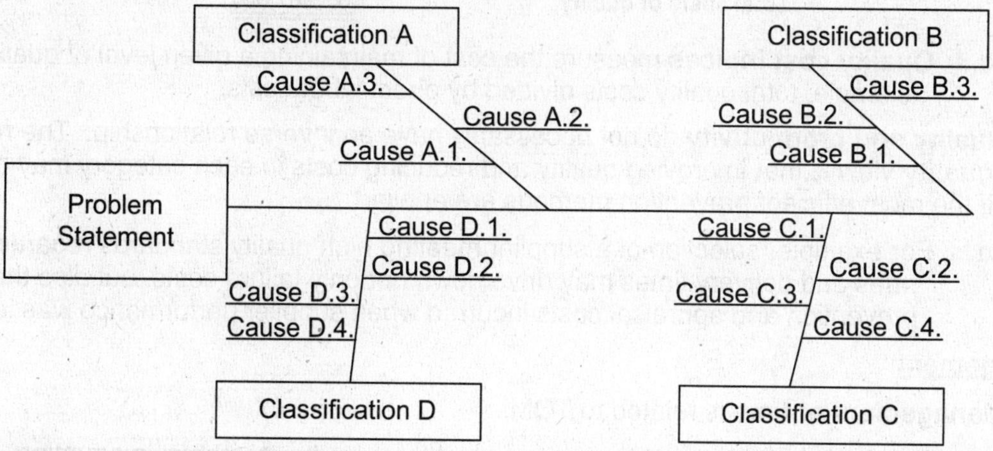

Costs of Quality

7. The costs of quality must be assessed in terms of relative costs and benefits. Thus, an organization should attempt to **minimize its total cost of quality**. Moreover, nonquantitative factors also must be considered. For example, an emphasis on quality improves competitiveness, enhances employee expertise, and generates goodwill.

a. **Conformance costs** include costs of prevention and costs of appraisal, which are financial measures of internal performance.

1) **Prevention** attempts to avoid defective output. These costs include (a) preventive maintenance, (b) employee training, (c) review of equipment design, and (d) evaluation of suppliers.

2) **Appraisal** embraces such activities as statistical quality control programs, inspection, and testing.

b. **Nonconformance costs** include internal failure costs (a financial measure of internal performance) and external failure costs (a financial measure of customer satisfaction).

1) **Internal failure** costs occur when defective products are detected before shipment. Examples are scrap, rework, tooling changes, and downtime.

2) The costs of **external failure**, e.g., warranty costs, product liability costs, and loss of customer goodwill, arise when problems occur after shipment.

a) They are even more important in **service** enterprises than in **manufacturing** environments. Faulty goods sometimes may be reworked or replaced to a customer's satisfaction, but poor service tends to result in a loss of customers.

3) **Environmental costs** also are external failure costs, e.g., fines for nonadherence to environmental law and loss of customer goodwill.

c. A **cost-of-quality report** includes most costs related to quality. However, some items often are not reported, for example, lost contribution margins from poor product quality. They are opportunity costs and are not usually recorded by the accounting system. The result is understatement of the costs of poor quality.

1) Lost contribution margins from reduced sales, market share, and sales prices are external failure costs that also are not usually included in a cost-of-quality report.

2) An example of a **cost of quality report** is presented below:

Prevention costs	US $35,000
Appraisal costs	5,000
Internal failure costs	17,500
External failure costs	9,500
Total costs of quality	**US $67,000**

d. **Quality cost indices** measure the cost of maintaining a given level of quality, for example, total quality costs divided by direct labor costs.

8. **Quality and productivity** do not necessarily have an inverse relationship. The **robust quality** view is that improving quality and reducing costs in each category may be possible if the most efficient prevention methods are applied.

a. For example, selection of a supplier meeting high quality standards regarding defect rates and delivery times may drive down not only failure costs, but also the prevention and appraisal costs incurred when supplier performance was less reliable.

Time Management

9. **Management of time** is related to TQM.

a. **Product development time** is a crucial factor in the competitive equation. An entity that is first in the market with a new product has obvious advantages.

1) One financial measure of product development is **breakeven time.** It is the time from management approval of the project to the time when the **cumulative present value of cash inflows equals the cumulative present value of cash outflows.**

a) The most popular method of determining breakeven time calculates the time required for the **present value of the cumulative cash flows to equal zero.**

i) An alternative that results in a longer breakeven time is to consider the time required for the present value of the cumulative cash inflows to equal the present value of **all the expected future cash outflows.**

b. **Customer response time** is the delay between order placement and delivery of the good or service.

Benchmarking

10. Benchmarking involves analysis and measurement of key outputs against those of the **best organizations**. This procedure also involves identifying the underlying key actions and causes that contribute to the performance difference.

a. **Best practices** are recognized by authorities in the field and by customers for generating outstanding results. They are generally innovative technically or in their management of human resources.

b. Benchmarking is an ongoing process that requires **quantitative and qualitative measurement** of the difference between the performance of an activity and the performance by the benchmark. This entity need not be a competitor.

11. The following are kinds of benchmarking:
    a. **Competitive benchmarking** studies an organization in the same industry.
    b. **Process (function) benchmarking** studies operations of organizations with similar processes regardless of industry. Thus, the benchmark need not be a competitor or even a similar entity.
    c. **Strategic benchmarking** is a search for successful competitive strategies.
    d. **Internal benchmarking** is the application of best practices in one part of the organization to its other parts.
12. Use of **benchmarking teams** permits (a) an equitable division of labor, (b) participation by those responsible for implementing changes, and (c) inclusion of a variety of functional expertise and work experience.
13. **Selecting and prioritizing** benchmarking projects involves understanding **critical success factors** and the **business environment** so as to identify **key business processes and drivers** and to develop parameters defining what processes to benchmark.
14. Researching and **identifying best-in-class performance** is often the most difficult phase of the process.
15. **Data analysis** identifies performance gaps, obtains an understanding of the reasons they exist, and prioritizes the key activities that will facilitate the behavioral and process changes needed. Sophisticated statistical and other methods may be needed when the study involves many variables, testing of assumptions, or quantified results.
16. **Leadership** is most important in the **implementation phase** because the team must be able to justify its recommendations. Moreover, the process improvement teams must manage the implementation of approved changes.

Stop and review! You have completed the outline for this subunit. Study multiple-choice questions 1 through 10 beginning on page 56.

1.2 BALANCED SCORECARD

<u>Performance Measurement</u>

1. Internal auditors may conduct a **performance audit** to provide assurance about the organization's **key performance indicators**. They also may conduct a **consulting engagement** to design such a performance measurement system.
    a. Effective **management control** requires **performance measurement** and feedback. This process affects allocation of resources to organizational subunits. It also affects decisions about managers' compensation, advancement, and future assignments.
2. The trend in performance measurement is the **balanced scorecard approach** to managing the implementation of the firm's strategy. It connects the firm's **critical success factors (CSFs)** to measurements of its performance. CSFs are **financial and nonfinancial measures** of the elements of firm performance vital to competitive advantage. **SWOT analysis** (strengths, weaknesses, opportunities, and threats) is used to identify CSFs.
    a. **Problems in implementation** of the balanced scorecard approach include
        1) Using too many measures, with a consequent loss of focus on CSFs
        2) Failing to evaluate personnel on nonfinancial as well as financial measures
        3) Including measures that will not have long-term financial benefits
        4) Not understanding that subjective measures (such as customer satisfaction) are imprecise
        5) Trying to achieve improvements in all areas at all times
        6) Not observing when current nonfinancial measures no longer relate to ultimate financial success

b. A typical balanced scorecard includes measures in four categories:

1) **Financial**

a) The **CSFs** may be sales, fair value of the firm's stock, profits, and liquidity.

b) **Measures** may include (1) sales, (2) projected sales, (3) accuracy of sales projections, (4) new product sales, (5) stock prices, (6) operating earnings, (7) earnings trend, (8) revenue growth, (9) gross margin percentage, (10) cost reductions, (11) economic value added (EVA), (12) return on investment (or any of its variants), (13) cash flow coverage and trends, (14) turnover (assets, receivables, and inventory), and (15) interest coverage.

2) **Customer**

a) The **CSFs** may be (1) customer satisfaction, (2) customer retention rate, (3) dealer and distributor relationships, (4) marketing and selling performance, (5) prompt delivery, and (6) quality.

b) **Measures** may include (1) returns, (2) complaints, (3) survey results, (4) coverage and strength of distribution channels, (5) market research results, (6) training of marketing people, (7) sales trends, (8) market share and its trend, (9) on-time delivery rate, (10) service response time and effectiveness, and (11) warranty expense.

3) **Internal Business Processes**

a) The **CSFs** may be (1) quality, (2) productivity (an input-output relationship), (3) flexibility of response to changing conditions, (4) operating readiness, and (5) safety.

b) **Measures** may include (1) rate of defects, (2) amounts of scrap and rework, (3) returns, (4) survey results, (5) field service reports, (6) warranty costs, (7) vendor defect rate, (8) cycle (lead) time, (9) labor and machine efficiency, (10) setup time, (11) scheduling effectiveness, (12) downtime, (13) capacity usage, (14) maintenance, and (15) accidents and their results.

4) **Learning, Growth, and Innovation**

a) The **CSFs** may be (1) development of new products, (2) promptness of their introduction, (3) human resource development, (4) morale, and (5) competence of the workforce.

b) **Measures** may include (1) new products marketed, (2) amount of design changes, (3) patents and copyrights registered, (4) R&D personnel qualifications, (5) actual versus planned shipping dates, (6) hours of training, (7) skill set levels attained, (8) personnel turnover, (9) personnel complaints and survey results, (10) financial and operating results, (11) technological capabilities, (12) organizational learning, and (13) industry leadership.

c. EXAMPLE:

1) Each **objective** is associated with one or more **measures** that permit the organization to gauge progress toward the objective.

2) Achievement of the objectives in each **perspective** makes it possible to achieve the organization's objectives.

Balanced Scorecard

Financial Perspective	
Objective: Increase shareholder value	**Measures:** Increase in ordinary (common) stock price Reliability of dividend payment
Customer Perspective	
Objective: Increase customer satisfaction	**Measures:** Greater market share Higher customer retention rate Positive responses to surveys
Internal Business Process Perspective	
Objective: Improve product quality	**Measures:** Achievement of zero defects
Objective: Improve internal processes	**Measures:** Reduction in delivery cycle time Smaller cost variances
Learning, Growth, and Innovation Perspective	
Objective: Increase employee confidence	**Measures:** Number of suggestions to improve processes Positive responses to surveys
Objective: Increase employee competence	**Measures:** Attendance at internal and external training seminars

Stop and review! You have completed the outline for this subunit. Study multiple-choice question 11 on page 59.

1.3 ISO FRAMEWORK

Overview

1. In 1987, the **International Organization for Standardization (ISO)** introduced **ISO 9000**, a "family" of 11 voluntary standards and technical reports that provide guidance for establishing and maintaining a **quality management system (QMS)**. The ISO's rules specify that its standards be revised every 5 years in light of technological and market developments. (NOTE: ISO is not an acronym. It means equal, suggesting that entities certified under ISO 9001:2000 have equal quality.)
   a. The current standards **(ISO 9000:2008)** were issued in November 2008. For specific and up-to-date information, see www.iso2008.org; the standards can be purchased at the ISO's website, www.iso.org.
   b. The intent of the standards is to ensure the quality of the **process, not the product**. The marketplace determines whether a product is good or bad.
      1) For this reason, the ISO deems it unacceptable for phrases referring to ISO certification to appear on individual products or packaging.
   c. Only one of the standards is a certification standard.
      1) **ISO 9001:2008,** *Quality Management Systems – Requirements*, is the standard that provides a model for quality assurance programs.
      2) For this reason, "ISO 9001:2008 certified" is the only acceptable formulation. There is no such thing as "ISO 9000 certification."
      3) **ISO 9000:2005** applies to (a) entities implementing a QMS, (b) entities seeking assurance about products provided by suppliers, (c) users of the products, (d) everyone needing an understanding of quality terminology, (e) those who assess QMSs, (f) those who provide advice or training relative to a QMS, and (g) standard setters.

Environmental Standards

2. The ISO also has issued a set of **environmental standards** known as **ISO 14000**. These standards are comparable in purpose to ISO 9000 but concern **environmental quality** systems. Although they have not been as widely adopted as the ISO 9000 standards, they may become a necessity for conducting international business. Some European countries already have environmental systems standards in place, and how these single-country standards will mesh with ISO 14000 is not clear. However, individual countries' standards are typically more strict.
3. The scope of **ISO 19011:2002** extends to (a) the principles of auditing, (b) managing audit programs, (c) conducting QMS audits and **environmental management system (EMS)** audits, and (d) the competence of QMS and **EMS** auditors.
   a. It applies to all entities that must perform internal or external audits of QMSs or environmental management systems or manage an audit program.
   b. ISO 19011 may apply to other types of audits if due consideration is given to identifying the competencies required of the auditors.
4. **ISO 10012:2003** is a generic standard. It addresses the management of measurement processes and confirmation of measuring equipment used to support compliance with required measures.
   a. It states quality management requirements of a **measurement management system (MMS)** that can be used as part of the overall management system.
   b. It is not to be used as a requirement for demonstrating conformance with other standards. Interested parties may agree to use ISO 10012:2003 as an input for satisfying MMS requirements in certification activities. However, other standards apply to specific elements affecting measurement results, e.g., details of measurement methods, competence of personnel, or comparisons among laboratories.
5. **ISO 14063:2006** states principles, policies, strategies, and activities for **environmental communications**, whether external or internal. It addresses the unique circumstances of environmental communications and applies to every entity regardless of whether it has an EMS.
6. **ISO Guide 64:2008** applies to environmental questions arising in the setting of **product standards**. Its purpose is to help standard setters to minimize negative environmental effects at each step in the **product life cycle**.
7. **ISO 14050:2009** is a glossary of **environmental management vocabulary**.
8. **ISO 9001-2008** is a generic standard that states requirements for a QMS. It applies when an entity needs to demonstrate its ability to (a) sell a product that meets customer and regulatory requirements and (b) increase customer satisfaction through improving the QMS and ensuring conformity with requirements.

Stop and review! You have completed the outline for this subunit. Study multiple-choice question 12 on page 60.

1.4 FORECASTING

1. Forecasts are the basis for **business plans**, including budgets. They attempt to answer questions about the **outcomes** of events (e.g., the effect of a war involving a producer of oil on the oil market), the **timing** of events (e.g., when will unemployment fall), or the **future value of a statistic** (e.g., sales). In addition to intuition (informed judgment), many quantitative methods are useful in projecting the future from past experience.
   a. Examples of forecasts include sales projections, inventory demand, cash flow, and future capital needs.
      1) Most **models** are used in the forecasting process. They are used to make decisions that optimize future results.
      2) The **reliability** of the forecast should be determined before using it. No objective method can determine the reliability of judgmental forecasts. When quantitative methods are used, however, measurement of reliability is usually possible, e.g., by calculating the standard error of the estimate.

<u>**Correlation**</u>

2. **Correlation analysis** is used to measure the strength of the linear relationship between two or more random variables. Correlation between two variables can be seen by plotting their values on a single graph to form a scatter diagram. If the points tend to form a **straight line**, correlation is high. Otherwise, correlation is low. Correlation measures only linear relationships.
   a. If the points form a curve, several possibilities exist.
      1) A linear relationship (a straight line) may be used to approximate a portion of the curve.
      2) A linear relationship exists between some other function of the independent variable x (e.g., log x) and the dependent variable y.
      3) No relationship exists.
   b. The **coefficient of correlation (r)** measures the relative strength of the linear relationship. It has the following properties:
      1) The magnitude of r is independent of the scales of measurement of x and y.
      2) $-1.0 \leq r \leq 1.0$
         a) A value of –1.0 indicates a perfectly inverse linear relationship between x and y.
         b) A value of zero indicates no linear relationship between x and y.
         c) A value of +1.0 indicates a direct relationship between x and y.
   c. **Scatter diagrams** may be used to demonstrate correlations. Each observation creates a dot that pairs the x and y values. The collinearity and slope of these observations are related to the coefficient of correlation by the above-stated rules.

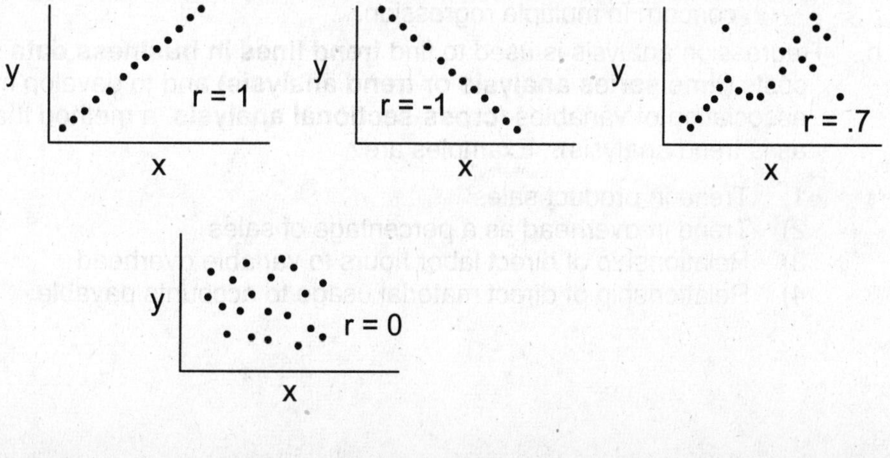

d. The **coefficient of determination (r^2)**, or the coefficient of correlation squared, may be interpreted as the proportion of the total variation in y that is explained or accounted for by the regression equation.

1) It is approximately equal to 1 minus the quotient of the unexplained variation divided by the total variation when the sample is large. The following is the formula:

$$r^2 = 1 - \frac{\sum (y_i - \hat{y})^2}{\sum (y_i - \bar{y})^2}$$

If: r^2 = the coefficient of determination
Σ = summation
y_i = an actual data point
$\hat{y}$ = a point on the regression line calculated from the sample linear regression equation
$\bar{y}$ = the mean of the observed data points

2) EXAMPLE: The assertion that new car sales are a function of disposable income with a coefficient of correlation of .8 is equivalent to stating that 64% ($.8^2$) of the variation of new car sales (from average new car sales) can be explained by the variation in disposable income (from average disposable income).

3) Because r^2 increases as the number of **independent variables** increases, regardless of whether the additional variables are actually correlated with the dependent variable, r^2 may be adjusted (reduced) to allow for this effect. If k is the number of independent variables and n is the number of observations, the formula for adjusted r^2 is

$$r^2 - \frac{(k - 1)}{(n - k)} \times (1 - r^2)$$

Regression Analysis

3. Regression **(least squares)** analysis extends correlation to find an equation for the linear relationship among variables. The behavior of the dependent variable is explained in terms of one or more independent variables. Thus, regression analysis determines functional relationships among quantitative variables.

a. **Simple regression** has one independent variable, and **multiple regression** has more than one.

1) EXAMPLE: A dependent variable such as sales is dependent on advertising, consumer income, availability of substitutes, and other independent variables.

2) **Multicollinearity** is the condition in which two or more independent variables are strongly correlated. The effect is greater uncertainty regarding the coefficient of the variables; that is, their standard errors increase. Multicollinearity is a concern in multiple regression.

b. Regression analysis is used to find **trend lines in business data** such as sales or costs **(time series analysis or trend analysis)** and to develop models based on the association of variables (**cross-sectional analysis**, a method that is not time related as is trend analysis). Examples are

1) Trend in product sales
2) Trend in overhead as a percentage of sales
3) Relationship of direct labor hours to variable overhead
4) Relationship of direct material usage to accounts payable

c. Some **reasonable basis** should exist for expecting the variables to be related.

1) If they are obviously independent, any association found by regression is mere coincidence.

2) Regression does not determine causality, however. Although x and y move together, the apparent relationship may be caused by some other factor.

a) EXAMPLE: A strong negative correlation exists between the decline in infant mortality and the increase in the number of senior citizens. Both are likely to be primarily caused by a factor such as better medical care.

3) The statistical relationships revealed by regression and correlation analysis are valid **only** for the range of the data in the sample.

d. The **simple regression equation** is

$$y = a + bx + e$$

If: y = the dependent variable
a = the y-axis intercept (the fixed cost in cost functions)
b = the slope of the regression line (the variable portion of the total cost in cost functions)
x = the independent variable
e = the error term

1) **Assumptions of the model** are that

a) For each value of x, there is a distribution of values of y. The means of these distributions form a straight line. Hence, x and y are linearly related.

b) The error term (e) is normally distributed with a mean or expected value equal to zero.

i) The y-intercept (a) and the slope of the regression line (b) also have normal distributions.

c) Errors in successive observations are statistically independent.

i) Thus, the estimators are unbiased.

ii) **Autocorrelation (serial correlation)** occurs when the observations are not independent; in other words, later observations may be dependent on earlier ones.

d) The distribution of y around the regression line is constant for different values of x.

i) Thus, the observations are characterized by **homoscedasticity** or **constant variance**. The deviation of points from the regression line does not vary significantly with a change in the size of the independent variable.

- **Heteroscedasticity** is the condition in which the variance of the error term is not constant.

ii) Graphically, the model is represented by a series of normal distributions (subpopulations of y) around the regression line. As noted on the previous page, these subpopulations have the same variance.

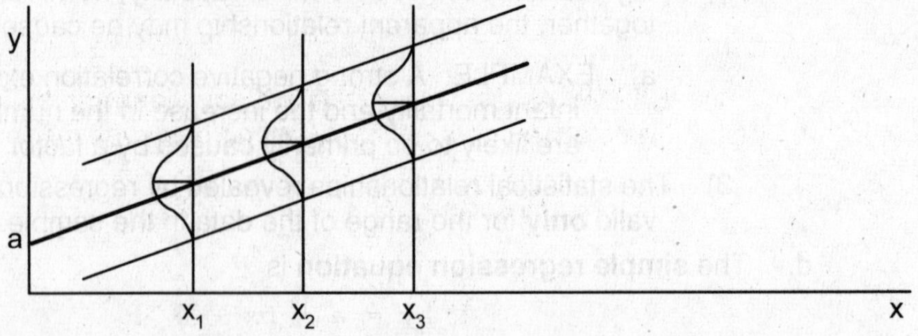

e. From linear algebra, the **equation for a straight line** may be stated as follows:

$$y = a + bx$$

If: a = the y-axis intercept
b = the slope of the line

1) Regression analysis uses the **method of least squares**, which minimizes the sum of the squares of the vertical distance between each observation point and the regression line.

2) EXAMPLE: Observations are collected on advertising expenditures and annual sales for a firm.

Sales (US $000,000s)	Advertising (US $000s)
28	71
14	31
19	50
21	60
16	35

a) According to the regression equation that results from using least squares computations, expected sales equal 4.2 plus .31 times the advertising expenditure.

$$y = 4.2 + .31(x)$$

b) The observations are graphed as follows:

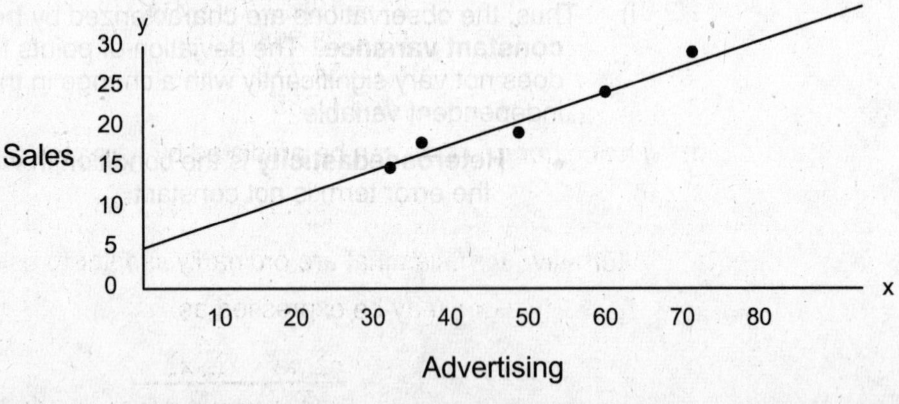

f. Regression analysis is particularly valuable for **budgeting** and **cost accounting** purposes. For instance, it is almost a necessity for computing the fixed and variable portions of mixed costs for flexible budgeting.

g. The following **equations** can be used to determine the equation for the least squares regression line (the equation for the line is in the form of $y = a + bx$):

$$\sum y = na + b(\sum x)$$

$$\sum xy = a(\sum x) + b(\sum x^2)$$

1) EXAMPLE: The use of the two equations can be illustrated with the following data based on a set of six paired observations (n = 6):

y	x
US \$ 6	2
7	3
5	2
4	1
8	3
6	2
Σy = US \$36	Σx = 13

Σxy	Σx^2
6 × 2 = 12	4
7 × 3 = 21	9
5 × 2 = 10	4
4 × 1 = 4	1
8 × 3 = 24	9
6 × 2 = 12	4
83	31

a) Substituting into the two equations gives

$$36 = 6a + 13b$$
$$83 = 13a + 31b$$

b) Solving simultaneously for the two unknowns,

$$1116 = 186a + 403b$$
$$1079 = 169a + 403b$$
$$37 = 17a$$

c) Thus, $a = 2.176$. Solving for b in the second original equation gives

$$83 = 13(2.176) + 31b$$
$$83 = 28.288 + 31b$$
$$31b = 54.712$$
$$b = 1.765$$

d) Hence, future costs can be predicted by using the following equation:

$$y = \text{US }\$2.176 + \$1.765x$$

e) Alternative formulas that are ordinarily simpler to use are given below:

i) The slope may be expressed as

$$b = \frac{n\sum xy - \sum x \sum y}{n\sum x^2 - (\sum x)^2}$$

ii) The value of the y-intercept may be expressed as

$$a = \bar{y} - b(\bar{x})$$

h. A **scattergraph** is a diagram of a set of paired observations. This method entails drawing a line to approximate the relationship suggested by the data.

1) The scattergraph method suffers from being reliant on the judgment of the person visualizing the line.

2) Once the line has been drawn, the equation of the line can be determined from any two points on the line.

i. The **high-low method** is used to generate a regression line by basing the equation on only the highest and lowest of a series of observations.

1) EXAMPLE: A regression equation covering electricity costs could be developed by using only the high-cost month and the low-cost month. If costs were US $400 in April when production was 800 machine hours and US $600 in September when production was 1,300 hours, the equation would be determined as follows:

High month	US $600	for	1,300	hours
Low month	400	for	800	hours
Increase	US $200		500	hours

Because costs increased US $200 for 500 additional hours, the variable cost is US $.40 per machine hour. For the low month, the total variable portion of that monthly cost is US $320 ($.40 × 800 hours). Given that the total cost is US $400 and US $320 is variable, the remaining US $80 must be a fixed cost. The regression equation is $y = 80 + .4x$.

2) The major criticism of the high-low method is that the high and low points may be abnormalities not representative of normal events.

Time Series

4. Time series or **trend analysis** relies on past experience. Changes in the value of a variable (e.g., unit sales of a product) over time may have several possible components.

a. In time series analysis, the dependent variable is regressed on time (the independent variable).

b. The **secular trend** is the long-term change that occurs in a series. It is represented by a straight line or curve on a graph.

c. **Seasonal variations** are common in many businesses. A variety of analysis methods includes seasonal variations in a forecasting model, but most methods make use of a seasonal index.

d. **Cyclical fluctuations** are variations in the level of activity in business periods. Although some of these fluctuations are beyond the control of the firm, they need to be considered in forecasting. They are usually incorporated as index numbers.

e. **Irregular** or **random variables** are any variations not included in the categories above. Business can be affected by random happenings (e.g., weather, strikes, fires, etc.).

f. The **percentage-of-sales** method is the most widely used for sales forecasting. It adjusts the current level of sales by a specified percentage increase or decrease. This method is a form of trend analysis that is convenient and easy to apply and intuitively appealing to managers. It is also useful for developing **pro forma financial statements** by estimating items that vary directly with sales as percentages of expected sales.

1) This method is based on the assumptions that most items directly correlate with sales and that current levels of all assets are optimal for current sales.

Exponential Smoothing

5. Exponential smoothing levels or smooths variations encountered in a forecast. This technique also adapts the forecast to changes as they occur.

   a. The simplest form of smoothing is the **moving average**, in which each forecast is based on a fixed number of prior observations. Exponential smoothing is similar to the moving average.

   b. Exponential means that greater weight is placed on the most recent data, with the weights of all data falling off exponentially as the data age. The selection of **alpha** (α), the smoothing factor, is important because a high alpha places more weight on recent data.

   c. The equation for the forecast (F) for period t + 1 is

$$F_{t+1} = \alpha(x_t) + (1 - \alpha)F_t$$

If: x_t = the observation for period t
t = the most recent period
α = the smoothing factor ($0 \le \alpha \le 1$)
F_t = the forecast for period t

      1) This method weights the observation for period t by α and the forecast for period t by $(1 - \alpha)$.

Learning Curves

6. **Learning curves** reflect the increased rate at which people perform tasks as they gain experience. The time required to perform a given task becomes progressively shorter, but this technique is applicable only to the early stages of production or of any new task.

   a. Ordinarily, the curve is expressed as a percentage of reduced time to complete a task for each doubling of cumulative production. Research has shown learning curve percentages to be between 60% and 80%. In other words, the time required is reduced by 20% to 40% each time cumulative production is doubled, with 20% being common.

      1) One common assumption made in a learning curve model is that the **cumulative average time per unit** is reduced by a certain percentage each time production doubles.

         a) The alternative assumption is that **incremental unit time** (time to produce the last unit) is reduced when production doubles.

      2) EXAMPLE: An 80% learning curve would result in the following performance for the lots shown, when run in sequence (top to bottom).

Cumulative Number of Tasks	Cumulative Average Time per Unit
100	3.0
200	2.4 (3.0 × 80%)
400	1.92 (2.4 × 80%)
800	1.536 (1.92 × 80%)
1,600	1.228 (1.536 × 80%)

b. **Graphical Presentation**

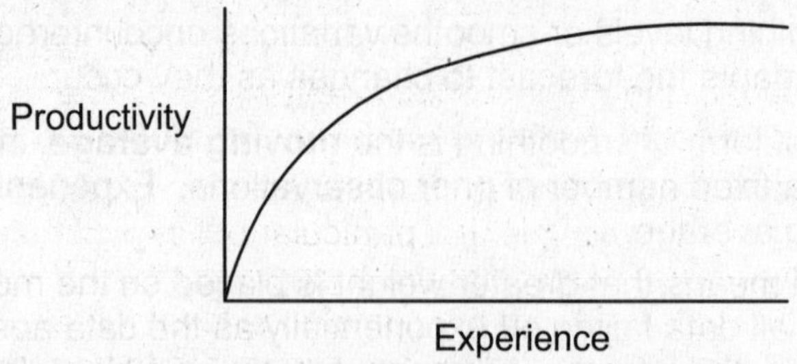

c. If the average time for 100 units in the example were 3 minutes per unit, the total time would be 300 minutes. At an average time of 2.4 minutes for 200 units, the total time would be 480 minutes. In other words, the additional 100 units required only 180 minutes (480 – 300), or 1.8 minutes per unit.

Simulation Models

7. Simulation is a technique for experimenting with logical and mathematical models using a computer.

   a. Despite the power of mathematics, many problems cannot be solved by known analytical methods because of the behavior of the variables and the complexity of their interactions, e.g.,

      1) Corporate planning models
      2) Financial planning models
      3) New product marketing models
      4) Queuing system simulations
      5) Inventory control simulations

   b. **Experimentation** is neither new nor uncommon in business. Building a mockup of a new automobile, having one department try out new accounting procedures, and test-marketing a new product are all forms of experimentation. In effect, experimentation is organized trial and error using a model of the real world to obtain information prior to full implementation.

   c. **Models** can be classified as either physical or abstract.

      1) Physical models include automobile mockups, airplane models used for wind-tunnel tests, and breadboard models of electronic circuits.
      2) Abstract models may be pictorial (architectural plans), verbal (a proposed procedure), or logical-mathematical. Experimentation with logical-mathematical models can involve many time-consuming calculations. Computers have eliminated much of this costly drudgery and have led to the growing interest in simulation for management.

   d. The **simulation procedure** has five steps:

      1) **Define the objectives.** The objectives serve as guidelines for all that follows. The objectives may be to aid in the understanding of an existing system (e.g., an inventory system with rising costs) or to explore alternatives (e.g., the effect of investments on the firm's financial structure). A third type of objective is estimating the behavior of some new system, such as a production line.
      2) **Formulate the model.** The variables to be included, their individual behavior, and their interrelationships must be defined in precise logical-mathematical terms. The objectives of the simulation serve as guidelines in deciding which factors are relevant.

3) **Validate the model.** Some assurance is needed that the results of the experiment will be realistic. This assurance requires validation of the model -- often using historical data. If the model gives results equivalent to what actually happened, the model is historically valid. Some risk remains, however, that changes could make the model invalid for the future.
4) **Design the experiment.** Experimentation is sampling the operation of a system. For example, if a particular policy is simulated on an inventory model for two years, the results are a single sample. With replication, the sample size can be increased and the confidence level raised. The number of runs to be made, length of each run, measurements to be made, and methods for analyzing the results are all part of the design of the experiment.
5) **Conduct the simulation -- evaluate results.** The simulation should be conducted with care. The results are analyzed using appropriate statistical methods.

e. The **Monte Carlo technique** is often used in simulation to generate the individual values for a random variable. A random number generator is used to produce numbers with a uniform probability distribution (equal likelihoods of occurrence). The second step is to transform these numbers into values consistent with the desired distribution.

1) The performance of a quantitative model may be investigated by randomly selecting values for each of the variables in the model (based on the probability distribution of each variable) and then calculating the value of the solution. If this process is performed a large number of times, the distribution of results from the model will be obtained.
2) EXAMPLE: A new marketing model includes a factor for a competitor's introduction of a similar product within 1 year. Management estimates a 50% chance that this event will happen. For each simulation, this factor must be determined, perhaps by flipping a coin or by putting two numbers in a hat and selecting one number. Random numbers between 0 and 1 could be generated. Numbers under .5 would signify introduction of a similar product; numbers over .5 would indicate the nonoccurrence of this event.

f. The **advantages of simulation** are as follows:

1) Time can be compressed. A corporate planning model can show the results of a policy for 5 years into the future, using only minutes of computer time.
2) Alternative policies can be explored. With simulations, managers can ask what-if questions to explore possible policies, providing management with a powerful new planning tool.
3) Complex systems can be analyzed. In many cases, simulation is the only possible quantitative method for analyzing a complex system such as a production or inventory system, or the entire firm.

g. The **limitations of simulation** are as follows:

1) Cost. Simulation models can be costly to develop. They can be justified only if the information to be obtained is worth more than the costs to develop the model and carry out the experiment.
2) Risk of error. A simulation results in a prediction of how an actual system would behave. As in forecasting, the prediction may be in error.

h. **Sensitivity analysis.** After a problem has been formulated into any mathematical model, it may be subjected to sensitivity analysis.

1) A trial-and-error method may be adopted in which the sensitivity of the solution to changes in any given variable or parameter is calculated.

a) The risk of the project being simulated may also be estimated.

b) The best project may be one that is least sensitive to changes in probabilistic (uncertain) inputs.

2) In **linear programming** problems, sensitivity is the range within which a constraint value, such as a cost coefficient or any other variable, may be changed without changing the optimal solution. Shadow price is the synonym for sensitivity in that context.

Markov Analysis

8. Markov processes are useful in decision problems in which the probability of the occurrence of a future state depends only on the current state.

a. A characteristic of the Markov process is that the initial state matters less and less as time goes on because the process will eventually reach its steady state.

b. EXAMPLE: A machine tool may be in one of two states, in adjustment or out of adjustment. The machine moves from one state to the other in 1 day with the following probabilities:

From \ To	In adjustment	Out of adjustment
In adjustment	.8	.2
Out of adjustment	.6	.4

c. If the machine is in adjustment on day 1, the probabilities of it being in or out of adjustment are as follows:

		IN	OUT	Pr
On day 2	(1.0) × (.8)	= .8	(1 – .8)	= .2
On day 3	(.8) × (.8) + (.2) × (.6)	= .76	(1 – .76)	= .24
On day 4	(.76) × (.8) + (.24) × (.6)	= .752	(1 – .752)	= .248
On day 5	(.752) × (.8) + (.248) × (.6)	= .7504	(1 – .7504)	= .2496

1) The process approaches a probability of .75 on day n of being in adjustment.

Queuing Theory

9. Models based on queuing theory determine the operating characteristics of a **waiting line.**

a. These models have the following variables:

1) Probability that no units are in the system
2) Average units in the line or system
3) Average time a unit waits or is in the system
4) Probability that a unit must wait
5) Probability of a given number of units in the system

b. **Examples** of queuing systems include

1) Bank teller windows
2) Grocery checkout counters
3) Highway toll booths
4) Docks for ships
5) Airport holding patterns

c. The structure of queuing systems depends on the **number of lines and service facilities** and how they are coupled. Grocery stores usually have multiple-line, multiple-server systems. Some banks have single-line, multiple-teller systems. Job shops can be conceived of as multistage systems in which each machine is a server with its own queue.

d. Mathematical solutions are available for simple systems having **unscheduled random arrivals**. For other systems, simulation must be used to find a solution.

e. The **arrivals** in a queuing model occur in accordance with a **Poisson process**.

1) The model has the following **assumptions**:

a) The probability of occurrence of an event is constant,

b) The occurrence of an event is independent of any other,

c) The probability of an occurrence is proportional to the length of the interval, and,

d) If the interval is small enough, the probability of more than one occurrence approaches zero.

2) The **Poisson probability distribution** is used to predict the probability of a specified number of occurrences of an event in a specified time interval, given the expected number of occurrences per time unit.

3) The related **exponential distribution** is used to approximate service times. This distribution gives the probability of zero events in a given interval. Accordingly, it gives the probability that service time will not exceed a given length of time.

Game Theory

10. Game theory classifies games according to how many players participate and the sum of the results.

a. In a two-person game, if the payoff is given by the loser to the winner, the algebraic sum is zero and the game is called a **zero-sum game**.

1) If it is possible for both players to profit, however, it is called a **positive-sum game**.

b. Mathematical models have been developed to select optimal strategies for certain simple games.

1) For example, labor negotiations can be viewed as a two-person, nonzero-sum game.

c. Game theorists have developed various **decision rules**.

1) The **maximax criterion** is a decision rule adopted by **risk-seeking**, optimistic players who desire the largest possible payoff and are willing to accept high risk. The player determines (a) the payoff for each state of nature expected to arise after each possible decision, (b) the maximum payoff for each decision, and (c) the decision with the maximum payoff.

2) A player who uses the **minimax criterion** determines the **maximum loss** for each decision possibility and then chooses the decision with the minimum maximum loss. This rule produces the same result as the **maximin** technique, which determines the minimum payoff for each decision and then chooses the decision with the maximum minimum payoff.

a) Minimax and maximin are conservative criteria used by **risk-averse** players for whom the utility of a gain is less than the disutility of an equal loss.

3) The **minimax regret criterion** is used by a player who wishes to minimize the effect of a bad decision in either direction. It chooses the decision that has the **lowest maximum opportunity cost** (profit forgone).

4) The **insufficient reason (Laplace) criterion** may be used when the decision maker cannot assign probabilities to the states of nature arising after a decision.

a) The reasoning is that, if no probability distribution can be assigned, the probabilities must be equal, and the **expected value** is calculated accordingly. For each decision, the payoffs for the various states of nature are simply added, and the decision with the highest total is chosen. This criterion is **risk-neutral**.

5) An **expected value criterion** might be used by a risk-neutral player, that is, one for whom the utility of a gain is the same as the disutility of an equal loss.

Expected Value

11. For decisions involving **risk**, expected value provides a rational means for selecting the best alternative. The expected value of an action is found by multiplying the probability of each outcome by its payoff and adding the products. It is the **long-term average payoff** for repeated trials. The best alternative has the highest expected value.

a. EXAMPLE: A dealer in yachts may order 0, 1, or 2 yachts for this season's inventory. The cost of carrying each excess yacht is US $50,000, and the gain for each yacht sold is US $200,000.

State of Nature = Actual Demand	Decision = Order 0	Decision = Order 1	Decision = Order 2
0 yachts	US $0	US $(50,000)	US $(100,000)
1 yacht	0	200,000	150,000
2 yachts	0	200,000	400,000

1) The probabilities of the season's demand are

Demand	Pr
0	.10
1	.50
2	.40

2) The dealer may calculate the expected value of each decision as follows:

Order 0		Order 1		Order 2	
US $0 × .1	= US $0	US $(50,000) × .1 =	US $ (5,000)	US $(100,000) × .1 =	US $ (10,000)
0 × .5 =	0	200,000 × .5 =	100,000	150,000 × .5 =	75,000
0 × .4 =	0	200,000 × .4 =	80,000	400,000 × .4 =	160,000
EV(0)	= US $0	EV(1)	= US $175,000	EV(2)	= US $225,000

a) The decision with the greatest expected value is to order two yachts. Absent additional information, the dealer should order two.

b. **Perfect information** is the knowledge that a future state of nature will occur with certainty, i.e., being sure of what will occur in the future. The **expected value of perfect information (EVPI)** is the difference between the expected value without perfect information and the return if the best action is taken given perfect information.

1) EXAMPLE (continued):

State of Nature	Pr	Best Action	Best Action Payoff	Expected Value (Pr × Payoff)
Demand = 0	.1	Buy 0	US $ 0	US $ 0
Demand = 1	.5	Buy 1	200,000	100,000
Demand = 2	.4	Buy 2	400,000	160,000
				US $260,000

a) The dealer expects to make US $260,000 with perfect information about future demand and US $225,000 if the choice with the best expected value is made. EVPI is

Expected value with perfect information	US $260,000
Expected value without perfect information	(225,000)
	US $ 35,000

b) The dealer will not pay more than US $35,000 for perfect information.

Qualitative Forecasting

12. In the absence of historical information, or when conditions have changed significantly, qualitative forecasting approaches are used.
    a. The **Delphi technique** is an approach in which the manager solicits opinions on a problem from experts, summarizes the opinions, and feeds the summaries back to the experts (without revealing any of the participants to each other). The process is reiterated until the opinions converge on an optimal solution.
    b. Forecasts based on **scenario writing** depend on defined sets of assumptions. Different future scenarios are written based on different assumptions. The decision maker then chooses the most likely scenario.
    c. **Brainstorming** in a group setting is an intuitive approach. Individuals are encouraged to offer ideas spontaneously, and no criticism is allowed.

Stop and review! You have completed the outline for this subunit. Study multiple-choice questions 13 through 23 beginning on page 60.

1.5 PROJECT MANAGEMENT TECHNIQUES

Fundamentals

1. Project management techniques, including **software** packages, are designed to aid the planning and control of large-scale projects having many interrelated activities.
    a. A **project** is a temporary undertaking with **specified objectives** that often involves a **cross-functional team** and working outside customary organizational lines. Hence, **interpersonal skills** are at a premium in project management because a manager may not have line authority over some team members.
    b. The **project life cycle** consists of
        1) **Conceptualization** (setting overall objectives, budgets, and schedules)
        2) **Planning** (obtaining resources, assigning duties, and coordinating activities)
        3) **Execution** (monitoring, correcting, meeting expectations, and finishing the project within time and budgetary limits)
            a) The largest amount of resources are used during this stage.
        4) **Termination** (turning the project over to the user and redistributing project resources)
    c. The following are **basic planning guides** for projects:
        1) The schedule and results are more important than the process.
        2) A manager must simultaneously consider the overall objective, the deadline, and operational details.
        3) Planning is essential.
        4) A challenging deadline is a strong motivator.

d. The project management triangle represents the basic constraints of a project:

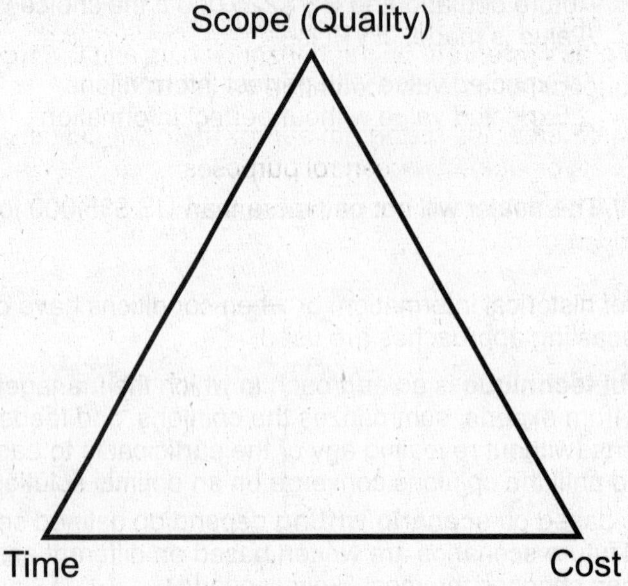

1) The **scope** is what is to be achieved. The **quality performance** of the intended result are elements of the scope.
2) **Time** is the permitted duration of the project.
3) **Cost** is the amount of resources that may be expended.
4) Changing one component affects at least one of the others.
5) One component is usually held constant. The effect is that the other components depend on each other. Thus, if the cost is fixed, quality will vary directly with the resources available.

e. **Enterprise resource planning (ERP)** is relevant to project management. For a detailed outline, see Study Unit 10.

f. Example applications of project management:

1) Building construction
2) Research and development projects
3) New product planning
4) Feasibility studies
5) Audit studies
6) Movie production
7) Conversion to a new computer information system

Bar Charts

2. **Bar charts** (bar graphs) are two-dimensional (variables plotted on x and y axes) graphic means of quantitative comparison. They use bars or rectangles with lengths proportional to the measure of the data or things being compared.

a. Bar charts may be vertical (column charts) or horizontal.

b. **Pareto analysis** is based on the concept that about 80% of results or effects are caused by about 20% of people or events. Thus, managers should concentrate on the relatively few people or events that have the most significant effects. **Pareto diagrams** are bar charts in which the frequencies of the various types of adverse conditions that may occur in a given process are depicted.

1) For example, an auditor might construct a Pareto diagram of the types and numbers of control deviations found in the receiving department. The tallest (or longest) bar signifies the most common type of problem.

c. A **histogram** is a bar chart used to depict a frequency distribution.

1) It is a graph of the results of repeated measurements of a single variable, with the **class intervals** on the horizontal axis and the **frequency** (or relative frequency) of occurrence on the vertical axis.

a) Whether the histogram approximates or deviates from a normal distribution is of interest for control purposes.

2) EXAMPLE: A histogram of the number of occurrences of various net cash flows is given below.

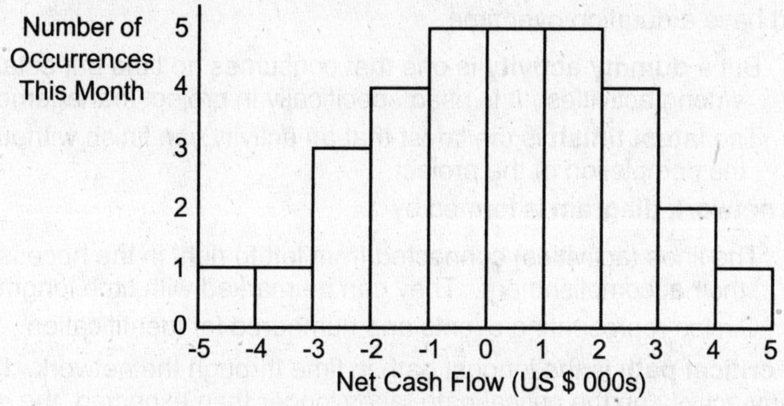

a) Cash flows between US $0 and US $1,000 occurred on 5 days; cash flows between US $1,000 and US $2,000 also occurred on 5 days; cash flows between –US $2,000 and –US $3,000 occurred on 3 days, etc.

3. **Gantt charts** are simple to construct and use. A Gantt chart divides the project into logical subprojects, called activities or tasks, estimates the start and completion times for each activity, and shows each activity as a horizontal bar along a time scale. A traditional Gantt chart is given below. However, a chart also may be drawn that displays work completed as of a given date.

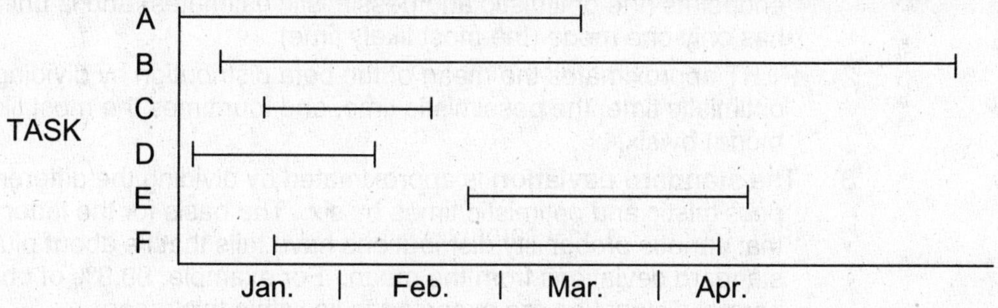

a. The **major advantage** of the Gantt chart is its simplicity. It forces the planner to think ahead and define logical activities. As the project progresses, actual completion times can be compared with planned times. Furthermore, the technique requires no special tools or mathematics and can be used on small projects.

b. The **major disadvantage** is that interrelationships among activities are not shown. Several special methods have been developed to show these on a Gantt chart, but they are feasible only for simple relationships.

Program Evaluation and Review Technique (PERT)

4. PERT was developed to aid managers in controlling large-scale, complex projects. PERT diagrams are free-form networks showing each activity as a line between events. A sequence of lines shows interrelationships among activities. PERT diagrams are more complex than Gantt charts, but they have the advantages of incorporating probabilistic time estimates and identifying the critical path.
   a. **Events** are discrete moments in time representing the start or finish of an activity. They consume no resources.
   b. **Activities** are tasks to be accomplished. They consume resources (including time) and have a duration over time.
      1) But a **dummy activity** is one that consumes no time but establishes precedence among activities. It is used specifically in project management.
      2) The **latest finish** is the latest that an activity can finish without causing delay in the completion of the project.
   c. The **network diagram** is formed by
      1) The lines (activities) connected from left to right in the necessary sequence of their accomplishment. They can be marked with time lengths.
      2) Circles representing events and numbered for identification.
   d. The **critical path** is the longest path in time through the network. It is critical because, if any activity on the critical path takes longer than expected, the entire project will be delayed. Every network has at least one critical path. Some have more than one.
   e. Paths that are not critical have **slack time**. One advantage of PERT is that it identifies slack time, which represents unused resources that can be diverted to the critical path.
   f. PERT analysis includes probabilistic estimates of activity completion times. **Three time estimates** are made – optimistic, most likely, and pessimistic.
      1) The time estimates for an activity are assumed to approximate a beta probability distribution. In contrast with the normal distribution, this distribution has finite endpoints (the optimistic and pessimistic estimates) and is unimodal; that is, it has only one mode (the most likely time).
      2) PERT approximates the mean of the beta distribution by dividing the sum of the optimistic time, the pessimistic time, and four times the most likely time (the mode) by six.
      3) The **standard deviation** is approximated by dividing the difference between the pessimistic and optimistic times by six. The basis for the latter approximation is that various probability distributions have tails that lie about plus or minus three standard deviations from the mean. For example, 99.9% of observations in the normal distribution are expected to lie within this range.
   g. EXAMPLE: If an activity can be completed in 6 days (optimistic time), 10 days (most likely time), or 20 days (pessimistic time), the expected duration is 11 days {[6 + (4 × 10) + 20] ÷ 6}.
      1) Thus, the most likely time is weighted the most heavily.
      2) The standard deviation is 2.33 [(20 – 6) ÷ 6].

h. EXAMPLE:

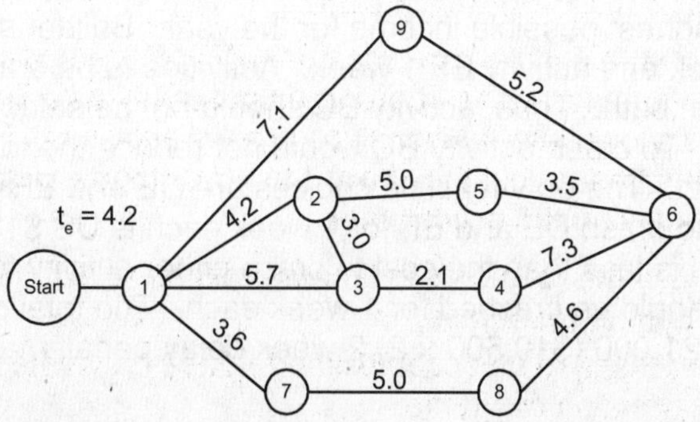

1) For the network above, the following are the paths and path times:

Path	Time (hours)
Start-1-9-6	16.5
Start-1-2-5-6	16.9
Start-1-2-3-4-6	20.8
Start-1-3-4-6	19.3
Start-1-7-8-6	17.4

2) Path Start-1-2-3-4-6 is the **critical path** because it has the longest time.

3) Path 1-3 takes only 5.7 hours, but the critical path events (1-2-3) take 7.2 hours. The slack time represented by path 1-3 is thus 7.2 – 5.7, or 1.5. People assigned to path 1-3 have an extra 1.5 hours to help elsewhere.

Critical Path Method (CPM)

5. This method was developed independently of PERT and is widely used in the construction industry. CPM may be thought of as a subset of PERT. Like PERT, it is a network technique. Unlike PERT, it uses deterministic time and cost estimates. Its advantages include cost estimates plus the concept of "crash" efforts and costs.
   a. Activity times are estimated for normal effort and crash effort. **Crash time** is the time to complete an activity, assuming that all available resources were devoted to the task (overtime, extra crew, etc.).
   b. Activity costs are also estimated for normal and crash efforts.
   c. These estimates allow the project manager to estimate the costs of completing the project if some of the activities are completed on a crash basis.
   d. The **network diagram** is constructed in the same manner as PERT diagrams. Once the diagram is constructed, the critical paths are found for normal and crash times. More than one critical path may exist for each diagram.
   e. **Crashing the network** means finding the minimum cost for completing the project in minimum time.
      1) EXAMPLE (*CMA, adapted*): Builder uses the critical path method to monitor jobs. It is currently 2 weeks behind schedule on Job #181, which is subject to a US $10,500-per-week completion penalty. Path A-B-C-F-G-H-I has a normal completion time of 20 weeks, and critical path A-D-E-F-G-H-I has a normal completion time of 22 weeks. The following activities can be crashed:

Activities	Cost to Crash 1 Week	Cost to Crash 2 Weeks
BC	US $ 8,000	US $15,000
DE	10,000	19,600
EF	8,800	19,500

Builder desires to reduce the normal completion time of Job #181 and report the highest possible income for the year. Builder should crash Activity DE 1 week and activity EF 1 week. Activities to be crashed should be on the critical path. Thus, activity BC should not be selected. It is not on the critical path. To crash activity BC would not reduce the total time to complete the project. The only feasible choices are DE and EF on the critical path. The total cost to crash DE and EF for 1 week each is US $18,800 ($10,000 + $8,800), which is less than the cost to crash either activity for 2 weeks. Thus, DE and EF should be crashed for 1 week each. The total cost is less than the US $21,000 ($10,500 × 2) 2-week delay penalty.

Network Models

6. **Network models** are used to solve managerial problems pertaining to project scheduling, information systems design, and transportation systems design. Networks consisting of nodes and arcs may be created to represent in graphic form problems related to transportation, assignment, and transshipment. The shortest-route, minimal spanning tree, and maximal flow problems are other applications of network models.
   a. A **shortest-route algorithm** minimizes total travel time from one site to each of the other sites in a transportation system.
   b. The **maximal flow algorithm** maximizes throughput in networks with distinct entry (source node) and exit (sink node) points. Examples of applications are highway transportation systems and oil pipelines. Flows are limited by capacities of the arcs (e.g., highways or pipes).
   c. The **minimal spanning tree algorithm** identifies the set of connecting branches having the shortest combined length. A spanning tree is a group of branches (arcs) that connects each node in the network to every other node. An example problem is the determination of the shortest telecommunications linkage among users at remote sites and a central computer.

Flowcharting

7. **Flowcharting** is a pictorial method of analyzing and understanding the processes and procedures involved in operations, whether manual or computerized. It is commonly used in computer programming and total quality management.
   a. Flowcharting is therefore useful in describing the **sequence** of a project's planned activities and decisions.
   b. Flowcharting is based on standardized symbols.
      1) However, different systems of symbols have been devised, so care must be taken that the usage is consistent.
   c. **Software** has simplified the flowcharting task.
   d. One **drawback** of flowcharting is that it is not feasible for a complicated project with many simultaneous activities. A second drawback is that a flowchart does not display the time needed for each activity and decision.

Stop and review! You have completed the outline for this subunit. Study multiple-choice questions 24 through 27 beginning on page 64.

1.6 BUSINESS PROCESS ANALYSIS

1. **Process analysis** studies the means of producing a product or service for the purpose of lowering costs and increasing **effectiveness** (accomplishment of objectives) and **efficiency** (economical, timely, and accurate accomplishment of objectives) while producing items of appropriate quality.
   a. It differs from product (or service) quality control, which involves inspection during production to eliminate unacceptable results.

Reengineering

2. One approach to business process analysis is **reengineering** (also called **business process reengineering**). It involves process innovation and core process redesign. Instead of improving existing procedures, it finds new ways of doing things.

   a. The emphasis is on simplification and **elimination of nonvalue-adding activities**. Thus, reengineering is not continuous improvement or simply downsizing or modifying an existing system. It should be reserved for the most important processes.

      1) In the modern highly competitive business environment, an organization may need to **adapt quickly** and radically to change. Accordingly, reengineering will usually be a cross-departmental process of innovation requiring substantial investment in information technology and retraining. Successful reengineering may bring dramatic improvements in **customer service** and the speed of **new product introductions**.

   b. A reengineered organization may use **work flow process** departmentation. Such a **horizontal organization** focuses on the flow of work between identifying and satisfying **customer needs**.

      1) For example, sales, billing, and service might be combined in one account management process department.

   c. Reengineering and TQM techniques eliminate many traditional **controls**. They exploit modern technology to improve productivity and decrease the number of clerical workers. Thus, controls should be automated and self-correcting and require minimal human intervention. Moreover, auditors must be prepared to encounter (and use) new technologies.

      1) The emphasis therefore shifts to **monitoring** so management can determine when an operation may be out of control and corrective action is needed.

         a) **Monitoring** assesses the quality of internal control over time. Management considers whether internal control is properly **designed** and **operating as intended** and modifies it to reflect changing conditions. Monitoring may be in the form of separate, periodic evaluations or of ongoing monitoring.

            i) **Ongoing monitoring** occurs as part of routine operations. It includes management and supervisory review, comparisons, reconciliations, and other actions by personnel as part of their regular activities.

      2) Most reengineering and TQM techniques also assume that humans will be **motivated** to work actively in improving operations when they are full participants in the process. However, these techniques may be met by resistance from employees who are insecure because of lack of skills, fear of failure, breakup of work groups, and other factors.

Theory of Constraints (TOC)

3. When a production process consists of interdependent operations, for example, when one part must be manufactured before another operation can continue, **bottlenecks** result in idle time. Thus, the items waiting in line to be processed and the items waiting for the output of the bottleneck are idle.

   a. TOC is a short-term approach to managing bottlenecks **(binding constraints)** in production and distribution processes. Its basic principle is that short-term profit maximization requires maximizing the contribution margin of the binding constraint (the throughput contribution).

b. TOC analysis defines all costs as **fixed** in the short-term except direct materials costs. Accordingly, the **throughput contribution** equals sales dollars minus direct materials costs, which include materials handling costs as well as raw materials and purchased components. This approach is a type of **supervariable costing** because only direct materials costs are inventoried.

1) The objective of TOC analysis is to **maximize throughput contribution** and to **minimize investments** (defined as materials costs of all inventories, plus R&D costs, plus fixed assets) and **other operating costs** (defined as all operating costs other than direct materials costs necessary to earn the throughput contribution).

c. TOC analysis **identifies the bottleneck operation** that determines the throughput contribution. This operation has large inventories waiting to be processed.

1) The bottleneck operation establishes the **processing schedule** for nonbottleneck operations. Hence, nonbottleneck production should not exceed what can be processed by the bottleneck operation.

2) In the longer term, actions should be undertaken to improve the **capacity of the bottleneck operation** so that the increase in the throughput contribution exceeds the additional costs.

3) Production flow is managed using a **drum-buffer-rope (DBR)** system.

a) The **drum** (or drummer providing the beat to which a production process marches) is the bottleneck operation or binding constraint.

b) The **buffer** is a minimal amount of work-in-process input to the drum that is maintained to ensure that it is always in operation.

c) The **rope** is the sequence of activities preceding and including the bottleneck operation that must be coordinated to avoid inventory buildup. Analysis of the rope includes consideration of lead times.

d. The **optimal strategy** to avoid bottleneck problems is to (1) redesign processes, (2) apply improved technology, (3) redesign products to make them easier to manufacture, or (4) possibly eliminate some products that are difficult to manufacture. **Value engineering** is useful for this purpose because it explicitly balances product cost and the needs of potential customers (product functions).

e. To summarize, the steps in a **TOC analysis** include

1) Determining the bottleneck operation or binding constraint, that is, the one that restricts output to less than the amount demanded.

2) Discovering the best use of the bottleneck operation, for example, by choosing the optimal product mix or by enhancing product flow through (a) minimizing setups, (b) ascertaining the appropriate lot size, (c) improving the quality of units produced, and (d) focusing on the throughput contribution instead of efficiency.

3) Using the DBR system to manage production through the bottleneck operation.

4) Increasing the bottleneck operation's capacity after the foregoing procedures are complete, provided that the throughput contribution exceeds the cost.

5) Redesigning the process or product(s) for greater flexibility and faster throughput.

f. A **TOC report** should present relevant performance measures, for example, of (1) throughput contribution, (2) elimination of bottlenecks, (3) reduction of average lead times, and (4) number of unfilled orders.

g. TOC analysis complements **activity-based costing (ABC)** because it has a **short-term**, materials-related perspective on product profitability. ABC has a **long-term** perspective with a focus on all product costs, including driver analysis and unit costing as a basis for strategic pricing and product mix decisions. Moreover, TOC analysis, unlike ABC, addresses the issues of **resource constraints** and **operational capacity**. Also unlike ABC, it can determine the optimal product mix in the short run.

Linear Programming (LP)

4. LP **maximizes a revenue or profit function**, or minimizes a cost function, subject to constraints, e.g., limited (scarce) resources or minimum/maximum levels of production, performance, etc. In business, linear programming is used for planning the most profitable or least costly allocation of resources.

   a. EXAMPLE: A manufacturer should minimize production costs while satisfying production requirements, maintaining required inventory levels, staying within production capacities, and using available employees. The objective function is the production cost to be minimized. The constraints are production requirements, inventory levels, production capacity, and available employees.

   b. The **objective** of LP is to choose the best solution from a potentially infinite number of possibilities.

   c. Several methods are available to solve LP problems.

      1) The **graphical method** is limited to problems with two variables.
      2) The **algebraic method** is a trial-and-error method. Pairs of constraints are solved algebraically to find their intersection. The values of the decision variables are then substituted into the objective function and compared to find the best combination.
         a) The optimal solution is at the intersection of two or more constraint equations.
         b) All intersections can be computed and each solution evaluated in the objective function to determine which solution is optimal.
      3) The **simplex method** is an algorithm to move from one corner solution to a better corner solution. When a better solution cannot be found, the optimal solution has been reached.

   d. EXAMPLE: A company produces products G and J. Product G contributes profits of US $5,000 per unit sold, and product J contributes US $4,000 per unit.

      1) The company seeks to maximize profits, so the **objective function** is

         Maximize $5G + 4J$ (the maximum profit in thousands of dollars)

      2) The objective function is subject to the following **constraints**:
         a) The minimal production requirement: $G + J \geq 5$
         b) The market balance requirement: $G \leq 3J$
         c) The production capacity constraint: $10G + 15J \leq 150$
         d) The nonnegativity constraint: $G, J \geq 0$

3) **Graphical solution.** To plot this set of constraints,

   a) Change inequalities to equalities,
   b) Plot the equalities, and
   c) Identify the correct side of the line for the original inequalities.

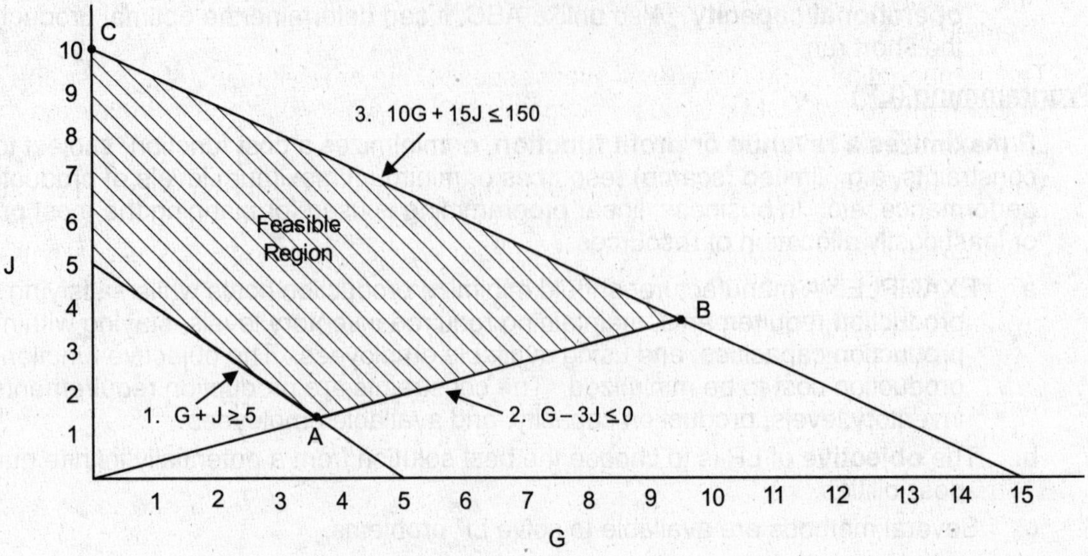

4) **Algebraic solution.** The combination of G and J that maximizes the objective function will occur at one of the extreme points or corners of the feasible region.

   a) Simultaneously solving the constraints intersecting at those corners and substituting into the objective function,

      i) At point A:

      $$\begin{array}{r} G + J = 5 \\ \underline{-G + 3J = 0} \\ 4J = 5 \end{array}$$

      J = 1.25 and G = 3.75

      Profit = US $5,000(3.75) + $4,000(1.25) = <u>US $23,750</u>

      ii) At point B:

      $$\begin{array}{r} G - 3J = 0 \\ \underline{10G + 15J = 150} \end{array} \longrightarrow \begin{array}{r} 5G - 15J = 0 \\ \underline{+\ 10G + 15J = 150} \\ 15G \quad = 150 \end{array}$$

      G = 10 and J = 3.333

      Profit = US $5,000(10) + $4,000(3.333) = <u>US $63,333</u>

      iii) At point C:

      $$\begin{array}{r} G \qquad = 0 \\ \underline{10G + 15J = 150} \end{array}$$ (from nonnegativity constraint)

      J = 10 and G = 0

      Profit = US $5,000(0) + $4,000(10) = <u>US $40,000</u>

      iv) Point D does not lie in the feasible region.

   b) The firm should choose to produce at point B (10 of product G and 3.333 of product J). This solution assumes that partial units of J may be produced. If product J is produced in single units, the answer may be interpreted to be to produce at a rate of 3-1/3 units in a given period.

Stop and review! You have completed the outline for this subunit. Study multiple-choice questions 28 through 30 beginning on page 65.

1.7 SUMMARY

1. Quality is best viewed from multiple perspectives: (a) attributes of the product (performance, serviceability, durability, etc.), (b) customer satisfaction, (c) conformity with specifications, and (d) value (relation of quality and price). TQM is a comprehensive approach. It treats the pursuit of quality as a basic organizational function that is as important as production or marketing.
2. The management of quality affects every aspect of the organization. Moreover, the implementation of TQM cannot be accomplished by application of a formula, and the process is lengthy and difficult.
3. Various management processes, tools, and measures should be adopted to promote quality: (a) policy deployment, (b) quality function deployment, (c) kaizen, (d) employee involvement, (e) supplier management, (f) competitive benchmarking, (g) quality training, (h) reward and recognition, (i) customer retention, and (j) quantitative methods.
4. The costs of quality include conformance costs (prevention and appraisal) and nonconformance (internal and external failure).
5. Benchmarking is an ongoing process that requires quantitative and qualitative measurement of the difference between the performance of an activity and the performance by the benchmark. This entity need not be a competitor. An organization must understand its critical success factors and business environment to identify key business processes and drivers and to develop parameters defining what processes to benchmark. The criteria for selecting what to benchmark relate to the reasons for the existence of a process and its importance to the entity's mission, values, and strategy. These reasons relate in large part to satisfaction of end user or customer needs.
6. The trend in performance measurement is the balanced scorecard approach to managing the implementation of the firm's strategy. It connects the firm's critical success factors (CSFs) to measurements of its performance. CSFs are financial and nonfinancial measures of the elements of firm performance vital to competitive advantage. Once the firm has identified its CSFs, it must establish specific measures for each CSF that are both relevant to the success of the firm and reliably stated. These measures provide a basis for implementing the firm's competitive strategy. A typical balanced scorecard includes measures in four categories: (a) financial; (b) customer; (c) internal business process; and (d) learning, growth, and innovation.
7. ISO 9000 is a series of voluntary generic standards for establishing and maintaining a quality management system (QMS) within a company.
8. Correlation analysis is used to measure the strength of the linear relationship between two or more variables. The coefficient of correlation (r) measures the relative strength of the linear relationship. The coefficient of determination (r^2), or the coefficient of correlation squared, may be interpreted as the proportion of the total variation in y that is explained or accounted for by the regression equation.
9. Regression (least squares) analysis extends correlation to find an equation for the linear relationship among variables. The behavior of the dependent variable is explained in terms of one or more independent variables. Thus, regression analysis determines functional relationships among quantitative variables. The simple regression equation is $y = a + bx + e$.
10. Time series or trend analysis relies on past experience. Changes in the value of a variable (e.g., unit sales of a product) over time may have several possible components: (a) secular trend, (b) seasonal variations, (c) cyclical fluctuations, and (d) random variables.
11. Exponential smoothing is a technique used to level or smooth variations encountered in a forecast. This technique also adapts the forecast to changes as they occur.

12. Learning curves reflect the increased rate at which people perform tasks as they gain experience. The time required to perform a given task becomes progressively shorter, but this technique is applicable only to the early stages of production or of any new task.
13. Simulation is a technique for experimenting with logical and mathematical models using a computer.
14. After a problem has been formulated into any mathematical model, it may be subjected to sensitivity analysis. A trial-and-error method may be adopted in which the sensitivity of the solution to changes in any given variable or parameter is calculated.
15. Markov processes are useful in decision problems in which the probability of the occurrence of a future state depends only on the current state.
16. Models based on queuing theory determine the operating characteristics of a waiting line.
17. Project management techniques include (a) bar charts, (b) Gantt charts, (c) PERT, (d) CPM, (e) network models, and (f) flowcharting.
18. One approach to business process analysis is reengineering (also called business process reengineering). It involves process innovation and core process redesign. Instead of improving existing procedures, it finds new ways of doing things. The emphasis is on simplification and elimination of nonvalue-adding activities.
19. The theory of constraints (TOC) is a short-term approach to managing bottlenecks (binding constraints) in production and distribution processes. Its basic principle is that short-term profit maximization requires maximizing the contribution margin of the binding constraint (the throughput contribution).

QUESTIONS

1.1 Total Quality Management

1. A traditional quality control process in manufacturing consists of mass inspection of goods only at the end of a production process. A major deficiency of the traditional control process is that

A. It is expensive to do the inspections at the end of the process.

B. It is not possible to rework defective items.

C. It is not 100% effective.

D. It does not focus on improving the entire production process.

Answer (D) is correct. *(CIA, adapted)*

REQUIRED: The major deficiency of a traditional quality control process.

DISCUSSION: The process used to produce the goods is not thoroughly reviewed and evaluated for efficiency and effectiveness. Preventing defects and increasing efficiency by improving the production process raises quality standards and decreases costs.

Answer (A) is incorrect. Other quality control processes can also be expensive. Answer (B) is incorrect. Reworking defective items may be possible although costly. Answer (C) is incorrect. No quality control system will be 100% effective.

2. In which of the following organizational structures does total quality management (TQM) work **best**?

A. Hierarchal.

B. Teams of people from the same specialty.

C. Teams of people from different specialties.

D. Specialists working individually.

Answer (C) is correct. *(CIA, adapted)*

REQUIRED: The structure in which TQM works best.

DISCUSSION: TQM advocates replacement of the traditional hierarchal structure with teams of people from different specialties. This change follows from TQM's emphasis on empowering employees and teamwork. Employees should have proper training, necessary information, and the best tools; be fully engaged in the decision process; and receive fair compensation. If such empowered employees are assembled in teams of individuals with the required skills, TQM theorists believe they will be more effective than people performing their tasks separately in a rigid structure.

Answer (A) is incorrect. Hierarchal organization stifles TQM. Answer (B) is incorrect. TQM works best with teams of people from different specialties. Answer (D) is incorrect. Teamwork is essential for TQM.

3. The four categories of costs associated with product quality costs are

A. External failure, internal failure, prevention, and carrying.

B. External failure, internal failure, prevention, and appraisal.

C. External failure, internal failure, training, and appraisal.

D. Warranty, product liability, training, and appraisal.

Answer (B) is correct. *(CMA, adapted)*

REQUIRED: The categories of product quality costs.

DISCUSSION: The following are the four categories of quality costs: prevention, appraisal, internal failure, and external failure (lost opportunity). Costs of prevention include attempts to avoid defective output, including employee training, review of equipment design, preventive maintenance, and evaluation of suppliers. Appraisal costs include quality control programs, inspection, and testing. Internal failure costs are incurred when detection of defective products occurs before shipment, including scrap, rework, tooling changes, and downtime. External failure costs are incurred after the product has been shipped, including the costs associated with warranties, product liability, and customer ill will.

Answer (A) is incorrect. Carrying cost is not one of the elements of quality costs. Answer (C) is incorrect. Training cost is not a category of quality costs. Answer (D) is incorrect. Warranty, product liability, and training are not quality cost categories.

4. Listed below are selected line items from the cost-of-quality report for Company B for last month.

Category	Amount
Rework	US $ 725
Equipment maintenance	1,154
Product testing	786
Product repair	695

What is Company B's total prevention and appraisal cost for last month?

A. US $786

B. US $1,154

C. US $1,940

D. US $2,665

Answer (C) is correct. *(CMA, adapted)*

REQUIRED: The total prevention and appraisal costs.

DISCUSSION: The costs of prevention and appraisal are conformance costs that serve as financial measures of internal performance. Prevention costs are incurred to prevent defective output. These costs include preventive maintenance, employee training, review of equipment design, and evaluation of suppliers. Appraisal costs are incurred to detect nonconforming output. They embrace such activities as statistical quality control programs, inspection, and testing. The equipment maintenance cost of US $1,154 is a prevention cost. The product testing cost of US $786 is an appraisal cost. Their sum is US $1,940.

Answer (A) is incorrect. US $786 is the appraisal cost. Answer (B) is incorrect. US $1,154 is the prevention cost. Answer (D) is incorrect. US $2,665 includes rework, an internal failure cost.

5. The Plan-Do-Check-Act (PDCA) cycle is a quality tool devised by W.E. Deming. How is PDCA **best** described?

A. A "management by fact" approach to continuous improvement.

B. An ongoing evaluation of the practices of best-in-class organizations.

C. The translation of customer requirements into design requirements.

D. The responsibility of every employee, work group, department, or supplier to inspect the work.

Answer (A) is correct. *(Publisher, adapted)*

REQUIRED: The best description of PDCA.

DISCUSSION: PDCA is a "management by fact" or scientific method approach to continuous improvement. PDCA creates a process-centered environment because it involves studying the current process, collecting and analyzing data to identify causes of problems, planning for improvement, and deciding how to measure improvement (Plan). The plan is then implemented on a small scale if possible (Do). The next step is to determine what happened (Check). If the experiment was successful, the plan is fully implemented (Act). The cycle is then repeated using what was learned from the preceding cycle.

Answer (B) is incorrect. Competitive benchmarking is an ongoing evaluation of the practices of best-in-class organizations. Answer (C) is incorrect. Quality deployment is the translation of customer requirements into design requirements. Answer (D) is incorrect. The "quality at the source" concept emphasizes the responsibility of every employee, work group, department, or supplier to inspect the work.

6. Quality costing is similar in service and manufacturing organizations. Nevertheless, the differences between these organizations have certain implications for quality management. Thus,

A. Direct labor costs are usually a higher percentage of total costs in manufacturing organizations.

B. External failure costs are relatively greater in service organizations.

C. Quality improvements resulting in more efficient use of labor time are more likely to be accepted by employees in service organizations.

D. Poor service is less likely to result in loss of customers than a faulty product.

Answer (B) is correct. *(Publisher, adapted)*

REQUIRED: The true statement distinguishing quality considerations in service and manufacturing organizations.

DISCUSSION: External failure costs arise when problems occur after delivery. They occur because products or services are nonconforming or otherwise do not satisfy customers. External failure costs in service enterprises are even more important than in manufacturing environments. Faulty goods sometimes may be reworked or replaced to a customer's satisfaction, but poor service tends to result in a loss of customers.

Answer (A) is incorrect. Direct labor costs are usually a higher percentage of total costs in service organizations. Answer (C) is incorrect. Service activities are usually more labor intensive than in modern manufacturing environments. Thus, more efficient labor usage is more likely to be viewed as a threat to employee job security in service organizations. Answer (D) is incorrect. The badwill resulting from poor service may be even more likely than a defective product to result in loss of customers.

7. In Year 2, a manufacturing company instituted a total quality management (TQM) program producing the following report:

Summary Cost of Quality Report (000s)

	Year 1	Year 2	% Change
Prevention costs	US $ 200	US $ 300	+50
Appraisal costs	210	315	+50
Internal failure costs	190	114	–40
External failure costs	1,200	621	–48
Total quality costs	US $1,800	US $1,350	–25

On the basis of this report, which one of the following statements is **most** likely true?

A. An increase in conformance costs resulted in a higher quality product and therefore resulted in a decrease in nonconformance costs.

B. An increase in inspection costs was solely responsible for the decrease in quality costs.

C. Quality costs, such as scrap and rework, decreased by 48%.

D. Quality costs, such as returns and repairs under warranty, decreased by 40%.

Answer (A) is correct. *(CMA, adapted)*

REQUIRED: The true statement about a report prepared by a company using a TQM program.

DISCUSSION: TQM emphasizes the supplier's relationship with the customer and recognizes that everyone in a process is at some time a customer or supplier of someone else, either within or outside the organization. The costs of quality include costs of conformance and costs of nonconformance. Costs of conformance include prevention costs and appraisal (inspection) costs. Nonconformance costs are composed of internal failure costs and external failure costs, such as lost opportunity. Conformance costs (prevention and appraisal) increased substantially, whereas the nonconformance costs (internal and external failure) decreased. Hence, the increase in conformance costs resulted in a higher-quality product.

Answer (B) is incorrect. Prevention costs also increased substantially, which could also have led to higher-quality products. Answer (C) is incorrect. Scrap and rework are internal failure costs, which decreased by 40%. Answer (D) is incorrect. Returns and repairs are external failure costs, which decreased by 48%.

8. Which of the following statements regarding benchmarking is false?

A. Benchmarking involves continuously evaluating the practices of best-in-class organization and adapting company processes to incorporate the best of these practices.

B. Benchmarking, in practice, usually involves a company's formation of benchmarking teams.

C. Benchmarking is an ongoing process that entails quantitative and qualitative measurement of the difference between the company's performance of an activity and the performance by the best in the world or the best in the industry.

D. The benchmarking organization against which a firm is comparing itself must be a direct competitor.

Answer (D) is correct. *(Publisher, adapted)*

REQUIRED: The false statement about benchmarking.

DISCUSSION: Benchmarking is an ongoing process that entails quantitative and qualitative measurement of the difference between the company's performance of an activity and the performance by a best-in-class organization. The benchmarking organization against which a firm is comparing itself need not be a direct competitor. The important consideration is that the benchmarking organization be an outstanding performer in its industry.

9. One of the main reasons that implementation of a total quality management program works better through the use of teams is

A. Teams are more efficient and help an organization reduce its staffing.

B. Employee motivation is always higher for team members than for individual contributors.

C. Teams are a natural vehicle for sharing ideas, which leads to process improvement.

D. The use of teams eliminates the need for supervision, thereby allowing a company to reduce staffing.

Answer (C) is correct. *(CIA, adapted)*

REQUIRED: The reason that implementation of a TQM program works better through the use of teams.

DISCUSSION: TQM promotes teamwork by modifying or eliminating traditional (and rigid) vertical hierarchies and instead forming flexible groups of specialists. Quality circles, cross-functional teams, and self-managed teams are typical formats. Teams are an excellent vehicle for encouraging the sharing of ideas and removing process improvement obstacles.

Answer (A) is incorrect. Teams are often inefficient and costly. Answer (B) is incorrect. High motivation does not directly affect the process improvement that is the key to quality improvement. Answer (D) is incorrect. The use of teams with less supervision and reduced staffing may be by-products of TQM, but they are not ultimate objectives.

10. One of the main reasons total quality management (TQM) can be used as a strategic weapon is that

A. The cumulative improvement from a company's TQM efforts cannot readily be copied by competitors.

B. Introducing new products can lure customers away from competitors.

C. Reduced costs associated with better quality can support higher shareholder dividends.

D. TQM provides a comprehensive planning process for a business.

Answer (A) is correct. *(CIA, adapted)*

REQUIRED: The reason TQM can be used as a strategic weapon.

DISCUSSION: TQM is a comprehensive approach to quality. It treats the pursuit of quality as a basic organizational function that is as important as production or marketing. Because TQM affects every aspect of the organization's activities, it permeates the organizational culture. Thus, the cumulative effect of TQM's continuous improvement process can attract and hold customers and cannot be duplicated by competitors.

Answer (B) is incorrect. New products can be quickly copied by competitors and therefore do not provide a sustained competitive advantage. Answer (C) is incorrect. TQM does not focus solely on cost reduction. Answer (D) is incorrect. TQM is only one tool of strategic management.

1.2 Balanced Scorecard

11. Using the balanced scorecard approach, an organization evaluates managerial performance based on

A. A single ultimate measure of operating results, such as residual income.

B. Multiple financial and nonfinancial measures.

C. Multiple nonfinancial measures only.

D. Multiple financial measures only.

Answer (B) is correct. *(Publisher, adapted)*

REQUIRED: The nature of the balanced scorecard approach.

DISCUSSION: The trend in managerial performance evaluation is the balanced scorecard approach. Multiple measures of performance permit a determination as to whether a manager is achieving certain objectives at the expense of others that may be equally or more important. These measures may be financial or nonfinancial and usually include items in four categories: (1) financial; (2) customer; (3) internal business processes; and (4) learning, growth, and innovation.

Answer (A) is incorrect. The balanced scorecard approach uses multiple measures. Answer (C) is incorrect. The balanced scorecard approach includes financial measures. Answer (D) is incorrect. The balanced scorecard approach includes nonfinancial measures.

1.3 ISO Framework

12. Why have many European Union countries **not** adopted ISO 14000 standards?

A. Adhering to ISO 14000 standards will not reduce monitoring and inspection by regulatory agencies.

B. Individual European Union countries' standards are typically more strict than ISO 14000 standards.

C. Regulators are permitted to use voluntary audits as a basis for punitive action.

D. ISO 14000 standards will not make it easier to do business across borders.

Answer (B) is correct. *(Publisher, adapted)*

REQUIRED: The reason many European Union countries have not adopted ISO 14000 standards.

DISCUSSION: Many European countries already have environmental systems in place, and many individual countries' standards are typically more strict than the ISO 14000 standards.

Answer (A) is incorrect. Many believe adhering to ISO 14000 standards will reduce monitoring or inspection by regulatory agencies. Answer (C) is incorrect. Many countries in the European Union have adopted measures similar to the ones in the US to prevent self-incrimination during voluntary ISO audits. Answer (D) is incorrect. ISO 14000 establishes internationally recognized standards that are intended to diminish trade barriers and make it easier to do business across borders.

1.4 Forecasting

13. What coefficient of correlation results from the following data?

X	Y
1	10
2	8
3	6
4	4
5	2

A. 0

B. –1

C. +1

D. Cannot be determined from the data given.

Answer (B) is correct. *(CIA, adapted)*

REQUIRED: The coefficient of correlation.

DISCUSSION: The coefficient of correlation (in standard notation, r) measures the strength of the linear relationship. The magnitude of r is independent of the scales of measurement of X and Y. Its range is –1.0 to 1.0. A value of –1.0 indicates a perfectly inverse linear relationship between X and Y. A value of zero indicates no linear relationship between X and Y. A value of +1.0 indicates a perfectly direct relationship between X and Y. As X increases by 1, Y consistently decreases by 2. Hence, a perfectly inverse relationship exists, and r must be equal to –1.0.

Answer (A) is incorrect. A perfect negative correlation exists. Answer (C) is incorrect. An inverse, not a direct, relationship exists. Answer (D) is incorrect. A linear relationship exists between X and Y.

14. An internal auditor for a large automotive parts retailer wishes to perform a risk analysis and wants to use an appropriate statistical tool to help identify stores that would be out of line compared to the majority of stores. The **most** appropriate statistical tool to use is

A. Linear time series analysis.

B. Cross-sectional regression analysis.

C. Cross tabulations with chi-square analysis of significance.

D. Time series multiple regression analysis to identify changes in individual stores over time.

Answer (B) is correct. *(CIA, adapted)*

REQUIRED: The best statistical tool for identifying stores that deviate from the majority.

DISCUSSION: Time series data pertain to a given entity over a number of prior time periods. Cross-sectional data, however, pertain to different entities for a given time period or at a given time. Thus, cross-sectional regression analysis is the most appropriate statistical tool because it compares attributes of all stores' operating statistics at one moment in time.

Answer (A) is incorrect. Linear time series analysis is inapplicable. It is a simple model that compares data for an individual store over time. Answer (C) is incorrect. Cross tabulations have to be built on a model of expectations. Unless the model is built, the analysis is not useful. Answer (D) is incorrect. The objective is to compare stores at one moment in time. Multiple regression time series analysis compares the performance of an individual store over a period of time.

15. A division uses a regression in which monthly advertising expenditures are used to predict monthly product sales (both in millions of US dollars). The results show a regression coefficient for the independent variable equal to 0.8. This coefficient value indicates that

A. The average monthly advertising expenditure in the sample is US $800,000.

B. When monthly advertising is at its average level, product sales will be US $800,000.

C. On average, every additional dollar of advertising results in US $.80 of additional sales.

D. Advertising is not a good predictor of sales because the coefficient is so small.

Answer (C) is correct. *(CIA, adapted)*

REQUIRED: The significance of the regression coefficient for the independent variable.

DISCUSSION: The regression coefficient represents the change in the dependent variable corresponding to a unit change in the independent variable. Thus, it is the slope of the regression line.

Answer (A) is incorrect. A regression coefficient is unrelated to the means of the variables. Answer (B) is incorrect. To predict a specific value of sales, the value of the independent variable is multiplied by the coefficient. The product is then added to the y-intercept value. Answer (D) is incorrect. The absolute size of the coefficient bears no necessary relationship to the importance of the variable.

16. Quality control programs employ many tools for problem definition and analysis. A scatter diagram is one of these tools. The objective of a scatter diagram is to

A. Display a population of items for analysis.

B. Show frequency distribution in graphic form.

C. Divide a universe of data into homogeneous groups.

D. Show the vital trend and separate trivial items.

Answer (A) is correct. *(CIA, adapted)*

REQUIRED: The objective of a scatter diagram.

DISCUSSION: The objective of a scatter diagram is to demonstrate correlations. Each observation is represented by a dot on a graph corresponding to a particular value of X (the independent variable) and Y (the dependent variable).

Answer (B) is incorrect. The objective of a histogram is to show frequency distribution in graphic form. Answer (C) is incorrect. The objective of stratification is to divide a universe of data into homogeneous groups. Answer (D) is incorrect. Regression analysis is used to find trend lines.

17. As part of a risk analysis, an auditor wishes to forecast the percentage growth in next month's sales for a particular plant using the past 30 months' sales results. Significant changes in the organization affecting sales volumes were made within the last 9 months. The **most** effective analysis technique to use would be

A. Unweighted moving average.

B. Exponential smoothing.

C. Queuing theory.

D. Linear regression analysis.

Answer (B) is correct. *(CIA, adapted)*

REQUIRED: The most effective analysis technique to forecast the percentage growth in next month's sales.

DISCUSSION: Under exponential smoothing, each forecast equals the sum of the last observation times the smoothing constant, plus the last forecast times one minus the constant. Thus, exponential means that greater weight is placed on the most recent data, with the weights of all data falling off exponentially as the data age. This feature is important because of the organizational changes that affected sales volume.

Answer (A) is incorrect. An unweighted average will not give more importance to more recent data. Answer (C) is incorrect. Queuing theory is used to minimize the cost of waiting lines. Answer (D) is incorrect. Linear regression analysis determines the equation for the relationship among variables. It does not give more importance to more recent data.

18. A firm is attempting to estimate the reserves for doubtful accounts. The probabilities of these doubtful accounts follow a transition process over time. They evolve from their starting value to a changed value. As such, the **most** effective technique to analyze the problem is

A. Markov chain analysis.

B. Econometric theory.

C. Monte Carlo analysis.

D. Dynamic programming.

Answer (A) is correct. *(CIA, adapted)*

REQUIRED: The most effective technique to analyze a problem involving changing probabilities.

DISCUSSION: A Markov chain is a series of events in which the probability of an event depends on the immediately preceding event. An example is the game of blackjack in which the probability of certain cards being dealt is dependent upon what cards have already been dealt. In the analysis of bad debts, preceding events, such as collections, credit policy changes, and writeoffs, affect the probabilities of future losses.

Answer (B) is incorrect. Econometrics forecasts the impact of different economic policies and conditions. Answer (C) is incorrect. Monte Carlo analysis is a simulation technique that uses random-number procedures to create values for probabilistic components. Answer (D) is incorrect. Dynamic programming is a problem-solving approach that breaks a large mathematical model into a number of smaller, manageable problems.

19. A company has several departments that conduct technical studies and prepare reports for clients. Recently, there have been long delays in having these reports copied at the company's centralized copy center because of the dramatic increase in business. Management is considering decentralizing copy services to reduce the turnaround and provide clients with timely reports. An appropriate technique for minimizing turnaround time and the cost of providing copy services is

A. Queuing theory.

B. Linear programming.

C. Regression analysis.

D. Game theory.

Answer (A) is correct. *(CIA, adapted)*

REQUIRED: The appropriate method for minimizing turnaround time and the cost of providing copy services.

DISCUSSION: Two basic costs are involved in queuing (waiting-line) models: (1) the cost of providing service (including facility costs and operating costs), and (2) the cost of idle resources waiting in line. The latter may be a direct cost if paid employees are waiting, or an opportunity cost in the case of waiting customers. The objective of queuing theory is to minimize the total cost of the system, including both service and waiting costs, for a given rate of arrivals. This minimization occurs at the point at which cost of waiting is balanced by the cost of providing service. This company wishes to reduce the total of waiting costs (turnaround time) and the cost of copy services.

Answer (B) is incorrect. Linear programming is a mathematical technique for optimizing a given objective function subject to constraints. Answer (C) is incorrect. Regression analysis is a statistical procedure for estimating the relation between variables. Answer (D) is incorrect. Game theory is a mathematical approach to decision-making in which each decision-maker takes into account the courses of action of competitors.

20. Only two companies manufacture Product A. The finished product is identical regardless of which company manufactures it. The cost to manufacture Product A is US $1, and the selling price is US $2. One company considers reducing the price to achieve 100% market share but fears the other company will respond by further reducing the price. Such a scenario would involve a

A. No-win strategy.

B. Dual-win strategy.

C. One win-one lose strategy.

D. Neutral strategy.

Answer (A) is correct. *(CIA, adapted)*

REQUIRED: The effect of a price war.

DISCUSSION: If both firms reduce the selling price of Product A, neither will gain sales and the resultant price war will cause both firms to earn lower profits. This outcome is inevitable when reduced profit margins do not result in a significant increase in sales. The effect is a no-win strategy.

Questions 21 and 22 are based on the following information.

A bank has two drive-in lanes to serve customers: one attached to the bank itself and one on an island. One teller serves both stations. The bank is interested in determining the average waiting times of customers and has developed a model based on random numbers. The two key factors are the time between successive car arrivals and the time customers wait in line.

Assume that the analysis begins with cars just arriving at both service windows, both requiring 3 minutes of service time. Car 1 is at the attached window and car 2 at the island window. A car will always go to the window attached to the bank unless that window has more cars waiting than the island window. The lone teller will always serve the car that arrived first. If two cars arrive simultaneously, the one at the attached window will be served before the one at the island.

Based on a known probability distribution, the bank assigns random numbers to arrival and service times:

Random #	Time between Arrivals	Random #	Service Time
1	1 minute	1, 2	1 minute
2, 3	2 minutes	3	2 minutes
4, 5, 6	3 minutes	4, 5, 6	3 minutes
7, 8	4 minutes	7, 8, 9	4 minutes

The bank then selects random numbers for the next two cars as follows:

	Arrival	Service
Car 3	#3	#7
Car 4	#7	#8

21. The arrival time follows which probability distribution?

A. Binomial.

B. Chi-square.

C. Poisson.

D. Exponential.

Answer (C) is correct. *(CIA, adapted)*

REQUIRED: The distribution of the arrival time.

DISCUSSION: Queuing models assume that arrivals follow a Poisson process: the events (arrivals) are independent, any number of events must be possible in the interval of time, the probability of an event is proportional to the length of the interval, and the probability of more than one event is negligible if the interval is sufficiently small. If λ is the average number of events in a given interval, k is the number of events, and e is the natural logarithm (2.71828...), the probability of k is

$$f(k) = \frac{\lambda^k e^{-\lambda}}{k!}$$

Answer (A) is incorrect. The binomial distribution is a discrete distribution in which each trial has just two outcomes. Answer (B) is incorrect. The chi-square distribution is a continuous distribution used to measure the fit between actual data and the theoretical distribution. Answer (D) is incorrect. Service time has an exponential distribution. This distribution gives the probability of zero events in a given interval, i.e., the probability of a specified time between arrivals.

22. The time that car 3 will have to wait to be serviced (**not** including its own service time) is

A. 0-2 minutes.

B. 3 minutes.

C. 4 minutes.

D. 5+ minutes.

Answer (C) is correct. *(CIA, adapted)*

REQUIRED: The time that car 3 will have to wait to be serviced (not including its own service time).

DISCUSSION: Car 1 is at the attached window and will require 3 minutes to service. Car 2 must wait for car 1 to be serviced (3 *minutes in the queue* + 3 *minutes to be serviced* = 6 *minutes*). Car 3 arrived at the attached window 2 minutes after cars 1 and 2. It must wait 1 minute for car 1 to be serviced and 3 minutes for car 2 to be serviced, a waiting time of 4 minutes.

23. Philip Enterprises, distributor of compact disks (CDs), is developing its budgeted cost of goods sold for 1998. Philip has developed the following range of sales estimates and associated probabilities for the year:

Sales Estimate	Probability
US $ 60,000	25%
85,000	40
100,000	35

Philip's cost of goods sold averages 80% of sales. What is the expected value of Philip's 1998 budgeted cost of goods sold?

A. US $85,000

B. US $84,000

C. US $68,000

D. US $67,200

Answer (D) is correct. *(CMA, adapted)*

REQUIRED: The expected value of cost of goods sold.

DISCUSSION: The expected value is calculated by weighting each sales estimate by the probability of its occurrence. Consequently, the expected value of sales is US $84,000 [$60,000 × .25) + ($85,000 × .40) + ($100,000 × .35)]. Cost of goods sold is therefore US $67,200 (80% × $84,000).

Answer (A) is incorrect. US $85,000 is the sales estimate with the highest probability. Answer (B) is incorrect. US $84,000 is the expected value of sales. Answer (C) is incorrect. US $68,000 is 80% of the sales estimate with the highest probability.

1.5 Project Management Techniques

24. A Gantt chart

A. Shows the critical path for a project.

B. Is used for determining an optimal product mix.

C. Shows only the activities along the critical path of a network.

D. Does not necessarily show the critical path through a network.

Answer (D) is correct. *(CMA, adapted)*

REQUIRED: The true statement about a Gantt chart.

DISCUSSION: A Gantt or bar chart is sometimes used in conjunction with PERT or CPM to show the progress of a special project. Time is shown on the horizontal axis, the length of a bar equals the length of an activity, and shading indicates the degree of completion. However, the Gantt chart is not as sophisticated as PERT or CPM in that it does not reflect the relationships among the activities or define a critical path.

Answer (A) is incorrect. The critical path is not shown on a Gantt chart. Answer (B) is incorrect. Linear programming is used to determine an optimal product mix. Answer (C) is incorrect. A Gantt chart shows the activities to be completed but not their sequencing.

25. As of week 8, the Gantt chart shows that the project is

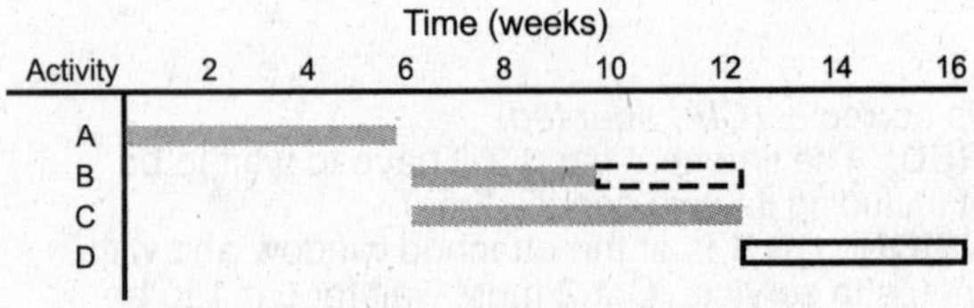

A. Complete.

B. Ahead of schedule.

C. On schedule.

D. Behind schedule.

Answer (B) is correct. *(CIA, adapted)*

REQUIRED: The status of a project according to the Gantt chart.

DISCUSSION: Assuming that (1) each of the bars represents the expected time necessary to complete an activity and (2) the shaded regions represent the portions completed, activity A has been completed as scheduled and activities B and C are ahead of schedule. Consequently, the project is ahead of schedule.

26. The network below describes the interrelationships of several activities necessary to complete a project. The arrows represent the activities. The numbers between the arrows indicate the number of months to complete each activity.

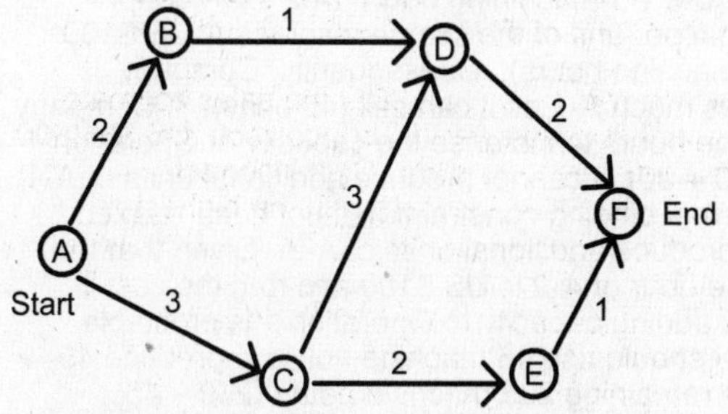

The shortest time to complete the project is

A. 5 months.

B. 6 months.

C. 8 months.

D. 14 months.

Answer (C) is correct. *(CIA, adapted)*

REQUIRED: The shortest time to complete the project.

DISCUSSION: The longest, or critical, path in the network from node (A) to node (F) is path A-C-D-F. All other paths are shorter than path A-C-D-F, so the activities along those paths can be completed before the activities along path A-C-D-F. Thus, the shortest time to complete the project is 8 months (3 + 3 + 2).

Answer (A) is incorrect. The project cannot be completed in less than 8 months. Answer (B) is incorrect. The project cannot be completed in less than 8 months. Answer (D) is incorrect. No path through the network requires 14 months.

27. Which of the following project scheduling techniques is commonly used in total quality management for simplifying work processes?

A. Gantt charts.

B. Flowcharting.

C. Program evaluation and review technique.

D. Critical path method.

Answer (B) is correct. *(Publisher, adapted)*

REQUIRED: The description of flowcharting.

DISCUSSION: Flowcharting is commonly used in computer programming for determining program logic and in total quality management for simplifying work processes. However, they are also used for establishing the desirable sequence of activities and decisions.

Answer (A) is incorrect. Gantt charts divide projects into subprojects and then estimate start and completion times for them. Answer (C) is incorrect. Program evaluation and review technique helps managers in planning and controlling large-scale projects. Answer (D) is incorrect. The critical path method is a network technique widely used in the construction industry that uses deterministic time and cost estimates.

1.6 Business Process Analysis

28. Business process reengineering is **most** likely to

A. Implement modern information systems technology to eliminate some controls.

B. Be applied within individual departments.

C. Improve existing procedures.

D. Apply a continuous improvement model.

Answer (A) is correct. *(Publisher, adapted)*

REQUIRED: The statement about business process engineering most likely to be true.

DISCUSSION: Reengineering and TQM techniques eliminate many traditional controls. They exploit modern technology to improve productivity and decrease the number of clerical workers. Thus, controls should be automated and self-correcting and require minimal human intervention. Moreover, auditors must be prepared to encounter (and use) new technologies. The emphasis therefore shifts to monitoring so management can determine when an operation may be out of control and corrective action is needed.

Answer (B) is incorrect. Reengineering will usually be a cross-departmental process of innovation requiring substantial investment in information technology and retraining. Answer (C) is incorrect. Reengineering (also called business process reengineering) involves process innovation and core process redesign. Instead of improving existing procedures, it finds new ways of doing things. Answer (D) is incorrect. The emphasis is on simplification and elimination of nonvalue-adding activities. Thus, reengineering is not continuous improvement or simply downsizing or modifying an existing system. Therefore, it should be reserved for the most important processes.

29. Company J produces two components: A-1 and A-2. The unit throughput contribution margins for A-1 and A-2 are US $150 and US $300, respectively. Each component must proceed through two processes: Operation 1 and Operation 2. The capacity of Operation 1 is 180 machine hours, with A-1 and A-2 requiring 1 hour and 3 hours, respectively. Furthermore, Company J can sell only 45 units of A-1 and 100 units of A-2. However, Company J is considering expanding Operation 1's capacity by 90 machine hours at a cost of US $80 per hour. Assuming that Operation 2 has sufficient capacity to handle any additional output from Operation 1, how much should Company J produce?

	Units of A-1	Units of A-2
A.	180	0
B.	45	100
C.	45	75
D.	0	60

Answer (C) is correct. *(Publisher, adapted)*

REQUIRED: The optimal product mix given expanded capacity.

DISCUSSION: A-1's throughput contribution margin per unit of the scarce resource (the internal binding constraint) is US $150 ($150 UCM ÷ 1 machining hour). A-2's throughput contribution margin per unit of the scarce resource is US $100 ($300 UCM ÷ 3 machine hours). Consequently, Company J should produce as much A-1 as it can sell (45 units). If Company J adds 90 machine hours to increase the capacity of Operation 1 to 270 hours (180 + 90), it cannot produce additional units of A-1 because the external binding constraint has not been relaxed. However, it can produce additional units of A-2. Given that the UCM per machine hour of A-2 is US $100 and that the cost is US $80 per hour, adding capacity to Operation 1 is profitable. Thus, Company J should use 45 machine hours to produce 45 units of A-1. The remaining 225 machine hours (270 – 45) should be used to produce 75 units (225 ÷ 3 hours) of A-2. The latter amount is within the external binding constraint.

Answer (A) is incorrect. Company J can sell only 45 units of A-1. Answer (B) is incorrect. Company J can produce only 75 units of A-2 if it produces 45 units of the more profitable A-1. Answer (D) is incorrect. Company J should produce as much of A-1 as it can sell.

30. One drawback of business process reengineering (BPR), sometimes referred to as business process analysis, is

A. Improved efficiency in the business processes analyzed.

B. Excess of cost over the benefit.

C. Reduction of operational efficiency.

D. Employee resistance to change.

Answer (D) is correct. *(Publisher, adapted)*

REQUIRED: The drawbacks of business process reengineering.

DISCUSSION: Business process reengineering (BPR), or business process analysis, involves process innovation and process redesign. Instead of improving existing procedures, it finds new ways of doing things. One major drawback of BPR is that employees may be resistant due to fear of layoffs, being replaced, or insecurity about new required skills or tasks that the employee now has to perform.

Answer (A) is incorrect. Improved efficiency in the business processes analyzed is an advantage of BPR. Answer (B) is incorrect. The cost of reengineering business processes should never exceed the benefit. If the costs are greater than the potential benefit, management should not undertake the project. Answer (C) is incorrect. Reengineering business processes should be done to increase the company's chances of success as a whole.

STUDY UNIT TWO
MANAGING RESOURCES AND PRICING

(26 pages of outline)

This study unit continues the treatment of business processes that began in the first study unit. The first two subunits concern the management of resources in the supply chain, particularly inventory. The third subunit addresses the objectives and factors that influence the pricing of the organization's products and services. The last subunit covers the management of human capital.

Core Concepts

- Inventory management applies to the acquisition, use, and distribution of inventory.
- Purchasing is the inventory management function that concerns the acquisition process. It encompasses choice of suppliers, contract negotiation, the decision whether to purchase centrally or locally, and value analysis.
- The basic EOQ model minimizes the sum of ordering (setup) costs and carrying costs.
- The just-in-time (JIT) inventory model limits output to the demand of the next operation. JIT systems are based on a manufacturing philosophy popularized by the Japanese that combines purchasing, production, and inventory control. Minimization of inventory is a goal because many inventory-related activities are viewed as nonvalue-added.
- In a JIT system, the dependability of suppliers is crucial. Organizations that adopt JIT systems therefore have strategic teaming agreements with a few carefully chosen suppliers who are extensively involved in the buyer's processes.
- Modern manufacturing environments impose control and improve quality through automation, whether involving one piece of equipment, a cell, or an integrated plant.
- The supply chain consists of flows from sources of (1) raw materials, (2) components, (3) finished goods, (4) services, or (5) information through intermediaries to ultimate consumers. These flows occur across the value chain.
- Distribution is the transfer of goods (and, in other contexts, services and information) from producers to customers or from distribution centers to merchandisers.
- The objectives of pricing are maximization of profit and target margins, achievement of sales volume objectives, enhancement of firm image, and market stability.
- Many factors affect price, for example, (1) supply and demand, (2) marketing strategy, (3) costs, (4) capacity usage, (5) nature of the market, and (6) competitor's actions.
- Pricing policies vary with the stage of the product life cycle.
- Managing human resources means acquiring, retaining, and developing employees.

2.1 INVENTORY MANAGEMENT

1. Inventory management applies to the acquisition, use, and distribution of inventory.
   a. An entity carries inventories because of the difficulty in predicting the amount, timing, and location of **supply and demand**. Thus, one purpose of **inventory control** is to determine the optimal level of inventory necessary to minimize costs.
   b. Many entities use inventory as a hedge against **inflation** as well as a guarantee of future **availability**.
   c. Inventory carrying costs are sometimes transferred to **suppliers or customers**.
      1) If a manufacturer knows exactly when materials are needed, orders can be placed so that they arrive no earlier than actually needed **(just-in-time, or JIT)**.
         a) This practice relies on a supplier who takes the responsibility for storing the needed inventory and shipping it to arrive on time.
         b) Suppliers with strong competition are more likely to provide JIT delivery.
      2) Customers sometimes carry large quantities of inventory when given special **quantity discounts or extended credit terms**.
      3) If customers are willing to accept **long lead times**, inventory can be manufactured to order to avoid storing large quantities.
      4) Reducing carrying costs may result in **shortage (stockout) costs**. These include the lost contribution margin on sales, customer ill will, and production interruptions.
   d. **Order costs** include all costs associated with purchasing and receiving inventory other than the costs initially recognized in the balance sheet.
   e. **Carrying costs** include rent, insurance, taxes, security, depreciation, and opportunity cost (i.e., the pretax return forgone by investing capital in inventory rather than the best alternative). Carrying costs also may include a charge for shrinkage, e.g., from spoilage of perishable items, obsolescence, theft, or waste.
      1) **Opportunity cost** equals average inventory (economic order quantity ÷ 2) times the cost of capital.

<u>Inventory Policies</u>

   f. The cost of holding safety stock and the cost of stockouts should be minimized.
      1) **Safety stock** is the amount of extra stock that is kept to guard against stockouts. It is the inventory level at the time of reordering minus the expected usage during the **lead time** (time from order placement to its receipt).
         a) EXAMPLE (adapted from CMA 1293 4-9): A company sells 60,000 units per year. The average purchase lead time is 20 working days. Maximum lead time is 27 working days. The company operates 240 days per year. Thus, safety stock should be 1,750 units. Daily usage is 250 units (60,000 per year ÷ 240 days), and a safety stock for 7 days (27 – 20) should be maintained. Hence, safety stock is 1,750 units (250 units × 7).
      2) **Stockout costs** are lost sales, production, customer goodwill, etc.

3) The problem may be diagrammed as follows:

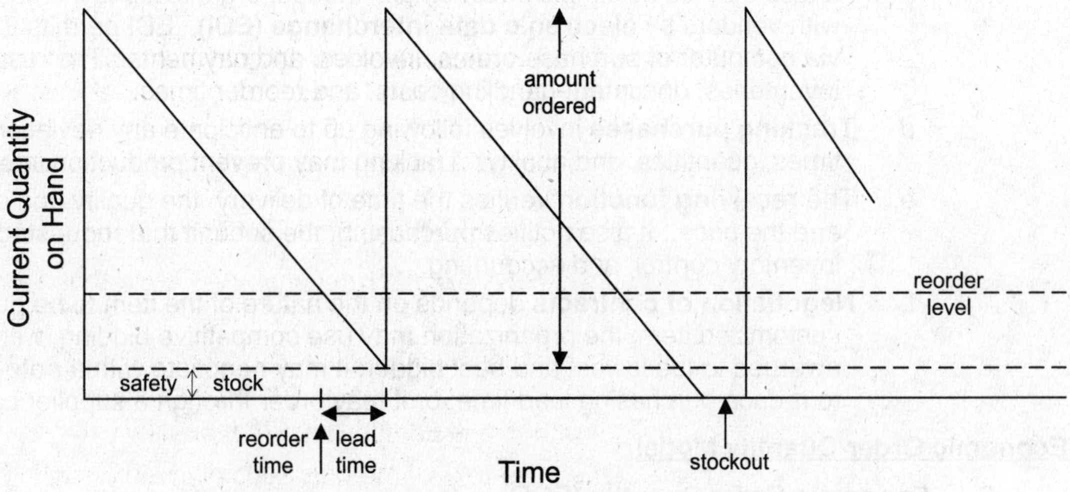

a) The **economic order quantity (EOQ)** determines order size.

b) The **reorder point** is the intersection of the reorder level and the downward-sloping total inventory line that allows sufficient lead time for an order to be placed and received.

4) EXAMPLE (adapted from CMA 1288 5-22): Annual demand is 50,000 units, and the optimal lot size is 6,250 units. Per-unit carrying costs and stockout costs are US $13 and US $3, respectively. The following data relate to the appropriate safety stock level:

Units Short During the Lead Time	Number of Shortages in Last 40 Reorder Cycles
200	6
300	12
400	6

The annual cost of establishing a 200-unit safety stock is expected to be US $5,200.

The annual cost is the carrying cost of safety stock (200 units × US $13 = US $2,600), plus the stockout costs incurred. Excess demand has been 100 units (300 – 200) greater than the safety stock 30% of the time (12 ÷ 40). The cost per stockout was US $300 (100 × $3). Demand has exceeded the safety stock by 200 units (400 – 200) 15% of the time (6 ÷ 40). The cost per stockout was US $600 (200 × $3). Thus, the expected stockout cost is US $180 per reorder cycle [($300 × 30%) + ($600 × 15%)]. Given 8 cycles (50,000 units ÷ 6,250 EOQ), the annual cost is therefore US $4,040 [$2,600 + (8 × $180)].

Purchasing

2. **Purchasing** is the inventory management function that concerns the acquisition process. It encompasses choice of suppliers, contract negotiation, the decision whether to purchase centrally or locally, and value analysis.

   a. The process is initiated by **purchase requisitions** issued by the production control function. Purchase requisitions ultimately result from **make-or-buy decisions** made when production processes were designed. For a **retailer**, the purchase decision is the same as the decision about what to sell.

   b. The **choice of suppliers** depends on price, quality, delivery performance, shipping costs, credit terms, and service.

c. **Ordering** may be a complicated task when a one-time, expensive purchase is made. It also may be as simple as an email. Indeed, organizations increasingly are linked with vendors by **electronic data interchange (EDI)**. EDI permits the transmission via computer of purchase orders, invoices, and payments. The result is reduced inventories, document-handling costs, and reorder times.

d. **Tracking purchases** involves following up to anticipate any deviations from delivery times, quantities, and quality. Tracking may prevent production interruptions.

e. The **receiving function** verifies the time of delivery, the quality and quantity received, and the price. It also notifies purchasing, the subunit that requested the delivery, inventory control, and accounting.

f. **Negotiation of contracts** depends on the nature of the item to be purchased. For a customized item, the organization may use competitive bidding, with the contract awarded to the lowest and best bidder; it may negotiate with a **sole-source supplier** to reduce purchasing lead time; or it may order through a supplier catalog.

<u>Economic Order Quantity Model</u>

3. **Economic Order Quantity (EOQ)**

a. **Inventory models** are quantitative models designed to control inventory costs by determining the optimal time to place an order (or begin production) and the optimal order quantity (production run).

1) The timing of an order can be periodic (placing an order every X days) or perpetual (placing an order whenever the inventory declines to X units).

a) **Periodic order systems** place minimal emphasis on record keeping. However, a risk of substantial overstock or understock may arise unless inventories are checked for assurance that the model is still appropriate.

b) **Perpetual systems** detect an inventory decline to the reorder point by entering every withdrawal on a perpetual record that shows the balance.

i) An alternative is to use the **two-bin method** for physical storage. In this system, the reorder level amount is stored separately from the balance of the items. When the stock clerk removes the last item from the balance bin, an order should be placed. The reorder level bin is then used until the order is received.

c) Physical inventories should be taken to reconcile records and verify models in either a periodic or a perpetual system.

b. The **basic EOQ model** minimizes the sum of ordering (setup) costs and carrying costs.

1) The following are the **assumptions** of this model:

a) Demand is known and uniform throughout the period.

b) The fixed costs of ordering are excluded.

c) Cost per order (setup) and unit carrying cost are constant.

i) Thus, the model is based on variable costs.

d) Full replenishment occurs instantly when the last item is used, stockout costs are zero, and no safety stock is held. Thus, average inventory is 50% of the EOQ.

i) For example, if the EOQ is 500, the basic model predicts that the average inventory level will be 250. The company will have 500 units immediately after a purchase and zero immediately before the receipt of the next purchase (replenishment is assumed to be instantaneous).

ii) However, safety stock increases the average inventory level by the amount of the safety stock. The **modified EOQ model** assumes that safety stock will never be used. Thus, if a safety stock of 100 is carried by the company in the example, the average inventory level will increase to 350. Inventory will be 600 units immediately upon receipt of a purchase and 100 units immediately before the receipt of the next purchase.

e) The model is relatively insensitive to error. A given percentage error in a value results in a lower percentage change in the EOQ.

i) An EOQ **sensitivity analysis** involves varying the holding costs per unit or the order costs to determine how much the changes affect the optimal EOQ.

2) The EOQ results from using **differential calculus** to determine the **minimum point** on the total cost curve. It also corresponds to the intersection of the variable carrying cost and variable ordering (setup) cost curves. The basic EOQ model is based on variable costs. The reason is that fixed costs are eliminated when the total cost equation is differentiated with regard to order/production quantity. (This calculation is not given.) The following is the basic formula:

$$X = \sqrt{\frac{2aD}{k}}$$

If: X = EOQ
a = variable cost per order (setup)
D = periodic demand in units
k = unit periodic carrying cost

3) EXAMPLE: If periodic demand is uniform at 1,000 units, the cost to place an order is US $4, and the cost to carry one unit in inventory for a period is US $2, the EOQ is 63.25 units.

$$EOQ = \sqrt{\frac{2(\text{US } \$4)(1{,}000)}{\$2}} = 63.25 \text{ units}$$

4) The **average level of inventory** for this model will be one-half of the EOQ. The formula shows that the EOQ varies directly with demand and order (setup) costs, but inversely with carrying costs. Thus, if demand quadruples, the EOQ will only double.

5) The EOQ is a **periodic model**. The number of orders (production runs) per period is given by the periodic demand divided by the EOQ.

c. Variations of the EOQ model are numerous.

1) The **effects of quantity discounts** can be considered by using trial and error. If the EOQ is below the discount level, the total cost equals the sum of the purchase cost plus annual carrying and order costs. Next, the minimum order quantity needed to obtain the discount is considered, and total cost is found for this level. This process is repeated for multiple levels of discount. The optimal order quantity is the one giving the **lowest periodic total cost**.

2) **Lead time** is accounted for by simply placing orders in advance. If back ordering is acceptable to customers, it can be incorporated into the model.
3) The **limitations of the EOQ model** are its restrictive assumptions, especially that of constant demand. But it can be combined with **probability concepts** to form an effective **perpetual system.**

d. **Probabilistic models** have been developed for the situation in which demand is random yet has a known distribution.

1) In a perpetual system, the possibility of running out of stock exists only during the reorder period, the time between placing and receiving the order. The reorder point is found by using the probability distribution for demand during the period.
   a) The order quantity is found by using the basic EOQ model and average demand.
   b) If stockout costs are known, an optimal reorder point can be found.
      i) If these costs are unknown, management can select a service level or probability of being in stock that can be used to find the reorder point.

e. Among the **limitations of inventory models for control** are that they are restricted to one item at a time and consider each item to be of equal importance.

1) If a firm has 10,000 line items, 10,000 calculations must be made. Computer programs are available to perform the computations, but they still need periodic review.
2) The importance of items can vary from essential to immaterial. The priority of an item needs to be considered in establishing controls.
3) A third limitation is that demand is often more variable than expected. Seasonal variations, as well as unexpected changes, can be provided for by including a forecasting model to estimate the demand to be used in the inventory model.

ABC Inventory Management

4. **The ABC system** is a simple inventory management technique.

a. This method controls inventories by dividing items into three groups:

1) **Group A** consists of high-monetary-value items, which account for a small portion (perhaps 10%) of the total inventory usage.
2) **Group B** consists of medium-monetary-value items, which may account for perhaps 20% of the total inventory items.
3) **Group C** consists of low-monetary-value items, which account for the remaining 70% of sales or usage.

b. The ABC system permits the proper **degree of managerial control** to be exercised over each group. The level of control reflects cost-benefit concerns.

1) Group A items are reviewed on a regular basis.
2) Group B items may not need review as often as group A items, but they may need review more often than group C items.
3) For group C, extensive use of models and records is not cost effective. It is cheaper to order large quantities infrequently.

Materials Requirement Planning

5. **Materials requirements planning (MRP)** is an integrated computer-based system designed to plan and control materials used in production. It is a **push-through system**. Production is activated by forecasts of demand, not actual needs.
   a. MRP is also a **dependent-demand system**. It assumes that demand for materials typically depends on some other factor that can be programmed, e.g., demand for the product.
   b. The timing of deliveries is vital to avoid production delays.
   c. EXAMPLE: An auto manufacturer need only decide how many autos of each type to make. The system determines the amount of each component and generates a complete list (a **bill of materials**).
   d. MRP, in effect, **schedules** when inventory will be needed for production. If parts are not in stock, the computer automatically generates a purchase order on the proper date (considering **lead times**) so that deliveries will arrive on time.
   e. As in other computer-based production systems, **bar coding** is used to track the movement of items.

Just-in-Time

6. Modern inventory control favors the **just-in-time (JIT)** model. Companies have traditionally built parts and components for subsequent operations on a preset schedule. Such a schedule provides a cushion of inventory so that the next operation will always have parts to work with -- a **just-in-case method**.
   a. In contrast, JIT limits output to the demand of the next operation. **Reductions in inventory levels** result in less money invested in idle assets; reduction of storage space requirements; and lower inventory taxes, pilferage, and obsolescence risks.
      1) High inventory levels often mask **production problems** because defective parts can be overlooked when plenty of good parts are available. If only enough parts are made for the subsequent operation, however, any defects will immediately halt production.
      2) The focus of **quality control** under JIT shifts from the discovery of defective parts to the prevention of quality problems, so **zero machine breakdowns** (achieved through preventive maintenance) and **zero defects** are ultimate goals. Higher quality and lower inventory go together.
   b. JIT is a reaction to the **trends** of global competition and rapid technological progress that have resulted in shorter product life cycles and greater consumer demand for product diversity.
      1) The **objectives** of JIT methods are (a) higher productivity, (b) reduced order costs as well as carrying costs, (c) faster and cheaper setups, (d) shorter manufacturing cycle times, (e) better due date performance, (f) improved quality, and (g) more flexible processes. The ultimate objectives are increased competitiveness and higher profits.
   c. JIT systems are based on a **manufacturing philosophy** that combines purchasing, production, and inventory control. It also treats many inventory-related activities as **nonvalue-added**. Carrying inventory is regarded as indicating problems, such as poor quality, long cycle times, and lack of coordination with suppliers.
      1) A JIT system reduces **carrying costs** by eliminating inventories and increasing supplier deliveries. Ideally, shipments are received just in time to be part of the manufacturing process. This system increases the risk of **stockout costs** because inventory is reduced or eliminated.

d. However, JIT also encompasses changes in the **production process** itself. JIT is a **pull system**. Items are pulled through production by **current demand**, not pushed through by anticipated demand. Thus, one operation produces only what is needed by the next operation, and components and raw materials arrive just in time to be used. To implement this approach and to eliminate waste of materials, labor, factory space, and machine usage, the factory is reorganized to permit what is often called **lean production**.

   1) In a **pull system**, workers might often be idle if they were not multiskilled. Hence, (a) central support departments are reduced or eliminated, (b) space is saved, (c) fewer and smaller factories may be required, and (d) materials and tools are brought close to the point of use. **Manufacturing cycle time** and **setup time** are also reduced. As a result, on-time delivery performance and response to changes in markets are enhanced, and production of customized goods in **small lots** becomes feasible.

e. The Japanese term **kanban** and JIT have often been confused. JIT is the total system of purchasing, production, and inventory control. Kanban is one of the many elements in the JIT system as it is used in Japan. Kanban means **ticket**. Tickets (also described as cards or markers) control the flow of production or parts so that they are produced or obtained in the needed amounts at the needed times.

f. Another feature of the lower inventory levels in a JIT system is elimination of the need for several traditional **internal controls**. Frequent receipt of deliveries from suppliers often means less need for a sophisticated inventory control system and for control personnel.

   1) JIT also may eliminate central receiving areas, hard copy receiving reports, and storage areas. A **central warehouse** is not needed because deliveries are made by suppliers directly to the area of production.

   2) The **quality of parts** provided by suppliers is verified by use of statistical controls rather than inspection of incoming goods. Storage, counting, and inspecting are eliminated in an effort to perform only value-adding work.

g. In a JIT system, the dependability of **suppliers** is crucial. Organizations that adopt JIT systems therefore have **strategic teaming agreements** with a few carefully chosen suppliers who are extensively involved in the buyer's processes.

   1) Long-term contracts are typically negotiated to reduce order costs.

   2) Buyer-supplier relationships are further facilitated by **electronic data interchange (EDI)**, a technology that allows the supplier access to the buyer's online inventory management system. Thus, electronic messages replace paper documents (purchase orders and sales invoices), and the production schedules and deliveries of the parties can be more readily coordinated.

7. Modern manufacturing environments impose control and improve quality through **automation**, whether involving one piece of equipment, a cell, or an integrated plant.

Computer-Integrated Manufacturing

8. A **computer-integrated manufacturing (CIM)** system involves (a) designing products using computer-aided design (CAD), (b) testing the design using computer-aided engineering (CAE), (c) manufacturing products using computer-aided manufacturing (CAM), and (d) integrating all components with a computerized information system.

   a. CIM entails a holistic approach to manufacturing in which design is translated into product by **centralized processing and robotics**. The concept also includes materials handling. The advantages of CIM include increased productivity, flexibility, integration, synergism, and cost minimization because of decreased waste, scrap, rework, and spoilage.

1) **Flexibility** is a key advantage. A traditional manufacturing system might become disrupted from an emergency change, but CIM will reschedule everything in the plant when a priority requirement is inserted into the system. The areas of flexibility include the following:

a) Varying production volumes during a period
b) Handling new parts added to a product
c) Changing the proportion of parts being produced
d) Adjusting to engineering changes of a product
e) Adapting the sequence in which parts come to the machinery
f) Adapting to changes in materials

<u>**Manufacturing Resource Planning**</u>

9. **Manufacturing resource planning (MRP-II)** is a closed-loop computerized manufacturing system that integrates all facets of a manufacturing business, including production, sales, inventories, schedules, and cash flows.

a. The same system is used for both financial reporting and management of operations (both use the same transactions and numbers).

b. MRP-II uses a **master production schedule (MPS)**, which is a statement of the anticipated manufacturing schedule for selected items for selected periods.

1) MRP also uses the MPS. Thus, MRP is a component of an MRP-II system.

Stop and review! You have completed the outline for this subunit. Study multiple-choice questions 1 through 10 beginning on page 92.

2.2 SUPPLY CHAIN MANAGEMENT

1. The relationship of an organization with its suppliers has already been described in the sections on **purchasing and JIT**. This subunit concentrates on the distribution element of the supply chain.

2. The **supply chain** consists of flows from sources of (a) raw materials, (b) components, (c) finished goods, (d) services, or (e) information through intermediaries to ultimate consumers.

a. These flows and the related activities may occur across the functions in an organization's **value chain** (R&D, design, production, marketing, distribution, and customer service). These flows and the related activities also may occur across separate organizations.

b. The activities in the supply chain, wherever they occur, should be **integrated and coordinated** for optimal cost management.

c. Sharing of information and coordination among the organizations in the supply chain can avoid the **bullwhip, or whiplash, effect** on inventories. This phenomenon begins when retailers face **uncertain demand from consumers** caused by randomness in buying habits. However, the **variability of retailers' orders to manufacturers** is affected by factors in addition to consumer demand. In turn, manufacturers' orders to suppliers may reflect a still greater variability because those orders depend on factors in addition to retailer demand.

1) **Causes.** The bullwhip effect, that is, a cascade of demand variability throughout the supply chain, may be caused by
   a) Difficulties of predicting demand and derived demand at each link in the supply chain
   b) The need to purchase or manufacture goods in cost-efficient batches
   c) Changes in price that may encourage purchases in anticipation of future increases
   d) Shortages that may lead to rationing by suppliers or manufacturers and hoarding by manufacturers or retailers

d. **Sharing of information** about sales, inventory, pricing, advertising campaigns, and sales forecasts by all functions and organizations in the supply chain moderates demand uncertainty for all parties. The desired results are
   1) Minimization of inventories held by suppliers, manufacturers, and retailers
   2) Avoidance of stockouts
   3) Fewer rush orders
   4) Production as needed by retailers

e. Supply-chain inventory management faces certain **difficulties**, for example,
   1) Incompatibility of the information systems of the parties
   2) Refusal of some parties to share information, possibly because of security concerns
   3) Devoting insufficient resources to the task
   4) Fear that others will not meet their obligations

<u>Distribution Channels</u>

3. **Distribution** is the transfer of goods (and, in other contexts, services and information) from producers to customers or from distribution centers to merchandisers. Thus, distribution manages outflows, and purchasing manages inflows. Among the interrelated issues involved in distribution are selection of (a) distribution channels, (b) inventory placement, (c) means of transportation, (d) shipment schedules, (e) routes, and (f) carriers.

4. A **distribution channel** is a series of interdependent marketing institutions that facilitate the transfer of a product from producer to ultimate consumer or industrial user. A distribution channel creates **place, time, and possession utility** by bringing sellers and buyers together.
   a. The following are **intermediaries** between sellers and buyers:
      1) **Merchant middlemen** buy the goods outright and necessarily take title to them. They include merchant wholesalers (distributors or jobbers) and most retailers.
      2) An **agent** represents a principal in negotiating purchases, sales, or both, but does not take title to the goods.
      3) A **broker** serves as a go-between. Unlike an agent, a broker ordinarily does not maintain a relationship with a particular buyer or seller. A broker also does not assume title risks. An example is a travel agency.
      4) A **consignee** merely sells the consignor's goods for a fee. Title remains with the consignor until the goods are sold and title passes to the buyer.
      5) **Facilitating intermediaries** are persons or entities outside the channel that perform some services (inventory control, financial services, risk management, information services, promotions) more effectively and efficiently than the channel members.

b. **Channel structure.** Conventional distribution systems consist of one or more independent producers, wholesalers, and retailers, each of which is a separate profit-maximizing business. The profit objective of each independent channel member may result in actions that are not profit maximizing for the system as a whole, and the system offers no means for defining roles and controlling **channel conflict**.

1) In **vertical distribution systems**, producers, wholesalers, and retailers act as a unified system. Channel conflict is managed through common ownership, contractual relationships, or administration by one or a few dominant channel members.

a) Conflict is between levels, e.g., when a manufacturer tries to enforce resale price agreements with dealers.

2) **Horizontal distribution systems** consist of two or more entities at one level of the channel working together to exploit new opportunities, such as the introduction of ATMs in supermarkets. The joint nature of horizontal distribution efforts is the tool for managing channel conflict.

a) Conflict occurs at the same level, e.g., when service standards vary.

3) In a **multichannel system**, a single entity sets up two or more channels to reach one or more customer segments. Because such a system is managed by a single firm, channel conflicts can be evaluated and managed internally.

a) Conflict is between channels, e.g., when the manufacturer's stores compete with other retailers.

<u>Inventory Placement</u>

5. **Inventory placement** concerns the location of finished goods.

a. **Forward placement** puts inventory close to final customers at a distribution center (warehouse), wholesaler, or retailer. This option minimizes transportation costs and delivery times.

1) Forward placement is typical for **convenience goods**. These are consumer goods and services that are usually low-priced and widely available. Consumers buy them often and with a minimum of comparison and effort. Examples are soap and newspapers. Producers of convenience goods ordinarily use intensive distribution to sell their products through a large number of retail or wholesale units.

b. **Backward placement** involves keeping inventory at a factory or maintaining no inventory at all. This option is indicated when products are customized or when regional demand fluctuates unpredictably. Centralizing the inventory helps to smooth the effects of changes in regional demand.

6. **Scheduling movements of freight** balances purchasing, production, customer response times, shipping costs, and selection of routes and carriers.

Stop and review! You have completed the outline for this subunit. Study multiple-choice questions 11 through 13 beginning on page 95.

2.3 PRICING

1. **Pricing Objectives**
   a. **Profit maximization.** Classical economic theory assumes all firms always select the price that results in the highest profit.
   b. **Target margin maximization.** This is stated as a percentage ratio of profits to sales.
   c. **Volume-oriented objectives** set prices to meet target sales volumes or market shares.
   d. **Image-oriented objectives** set prices to enhance the consumer's perception of the firm's merchandise mix.
   e. **Stabilization objectives** set prices to maintain a stable relationship between the firm's prices and the industry leader's prices.
2. **Price-Setting Factors**
   a. **Supply** of and **demand** for products and services are determined by customers' impact on demand, the actions of competitors, and costs.
   b. **Internal Factors**
      1) **Marketing objectives** may include survival, current profit maximization, market-share leadership, or product-quality leadership.
      2) **Marketing-mix** strategy.
      3) All **relevant costs** (variable, fixed, and total costs) in the value chain from R&D to customer service affect the amount of a product that the company is willing to supply. Thus, the lower costs are in relation to a given price, the greater the amount supplied.
      4) Organizational **location of pricing decisions**.
      5) **Capacity.**
         a) For example, under **peak-load pricing**, prices vary directly with capacity usage. Thus, when idle capacity is available, that is, when demand falls, the price of a product or service tends to be higher given a peak-load pricing approach.
   c. **External Factors**
      1) The **type of market** (pure competition, monopolistic competition, oligopolistic competition, or pure monopoly) affects the price. For example, a monopolist is usually able to charge a higher price because it has no competitors. However, a company selling a relatively undifferentiated product in a highly competitive market may have no control over price.
      2) **Customer perceptions** of price and value.
      3) The **price-demand relationship**.
         a) The **demand curve for normal goods** is ordinarily downward sloping to the right. Thus, quantity demanded usually increases as the price decreases.
         b) However, over some intermediate range of prices, the reaction to a price increase for **prestige goods** is an increase in the quantity demanded. Within this range, the demand curve is upward sloping. Consumers interpret the higher price to indicate a better or more desirable product. Above some price, the relation between price and quantity demanded will again be negatively sloped.
         c) **Price elasticity of demand.** If demand is price elastic (inelastic), the ratio of the percentage change in quantity demanded to the percentage change in price is greater (less) than 1.0. For example, if customer demand is price elastic, a price increase will result in the reduction of the seller's total revenue.

4) **Competitors'** products, costs, prices, and amounts supplied.

3. **Pricing Approaches**

a. **Cost-based pricing** involves setting a price that will recover the value chain costs and provide the desired return on investment.

b. **Market-based pricing** involves basing prices on the product's perceived value and competitors' actions rather than on the seller's cost. **Nonprice variables** in the marketing mix augment the perceived value. For example, a cup of coffee may have a higher price at an expensive restaurant than at a fast-food outlet. Market-based pricing is typical when there are many competitors and the product is undifferentiated, as in many commodities markets, e.g., agricultural products or natural gas.

c. **Competition-Based Pricing**

1) **Going-rate pricing** bases price largely on competitors' prices.

2) **Sealed-bid pricing** bases price on a company's perception of its competitors' prices.

d. **New Product Pricing**

1) **Price skimming** is the practice of setting an introductory price relatively high to attract buyers who are not concerned about price and to recover R&D costs.

2) **Penetration pricing** is the practice of setting an introductory price relatively low to gain deep market penetration quickly.

e. **Product-Mix Pricing**

1) **Product-line pricing** sets price steps among the products in the line based on costs, consumer perceptions, and competitors' prices.

2) **Optional-product pricing** requires the firm to choose which products to offer as accessories and which as standard features of a main product.

3) **Captive-product pricing** involves products that must be used with a main product, such as razor blades with a razor. Often the main product is relatively cheap, but the captive products have high markups.

4) **By-product pricing** usually sets prices at any amount in excess of storing and delivering by-products. Such prices allow the seller to reduce the costs and therefore the prices of the main products.

5) **Product-bundle pricing** involves selling combinations of products at a price lower than the combined prices of the individual items. This strategy promotes sales of items consumers might not otherwise buy if the price is low enough. An example is season tickets for sports events.

f. **Illegal pricing.** For example, pricing products below cost to destroy competitors **(predatory pricing)** may be illegal.

1) **Price discrimination among customers** also may be illegal.

2) **Collusive pricing** results when companies conspire to restrict output and set artificially high prices.

a) A **cartel** is an organization of sellers (e.g., the oil cartel OPEC) who undertake joint action to maximize profits by controlling the **supply**, and therefore the **price**, of their product. In many nations, such collusive conduct is illegal. The reason is that, as a result of the monopolistic and anticompetitive practices of cartels, (1) supply is lower, (2) prices are higher, (3) competition is restrained, and (4) the relevant industry is less efficient.

3) **Dumping** is a trade practice that violates international agreements. It occurs when a firm charges a price (a) lower than that in its home market or (b) less than the cost of product. Dumping is done to **penetrate a market** or as a result of **export subsidies.**

Cost-Based Pricing

4. **Cost-based pricing** begins with a cost determination followed by setting a price that will recover the value chain costs and provide the desired return on investment. When an industry is characterized by significant product differentiation, e.g., automobiles, cost-based and market-based pricing approaches are combined.

   a. A **cost-plus price** equals the cost plus a markup. Cost may be defined in many ways. Most companies use either absorption manufacturing cost or total cost when calculating the price. Variable costs may be used as the basis for cost, but then fixed costs must be covered by the markup.

      1) Following are four commonly used **cost-plus pricing formulas**:

         a) $$\text{Price} = \text{Total cost} + (\text{Total cost} \times \text{Markup percentage})$$

         b) $$\text{Price} = \text{Absorption manufacturing cost} + (\text{Absorption manufacturing cost} \times \text{Markup percentage})$$

         c) $$\text{Price} = \text{Variable manufacturing cost} + (\text{Variable manufacturing cost} \times \text{Markup percentage})$$

         d) $$\text{Price} = \text{Total variable cost} + (\text{Total variable cost} \times \text{Markup percentage})$$

      2) The preferred formula is

         a) $$\text{Price} = \frac{\text{Average unit cost}}{1 - \text{Markup percentage}}$$

      3) The costs of **unused capacity** in production facilities, distribution channels, marketing organizations, etc., are ordinarily not assignable to products or services on a cause-and-effect basis, so their inclusion in **overhead rates** may distort pricing decisions. Including the fixed costs of unused capacity in a cost-based price results in higher prices and in what is known as the **downward (black hole) demand spiral**.

         a) As higher prices depress demand, unused capacity costs increase, the **fixed costs** included in prices increase, and demand will continue to spiral downward. One way to avoid this problem is not to assign unused capacity costs to products or services. The result should be better operating decisions and better evaluation of managerial performance.

Target Pricing

5. A **target price** is the expected market price for a product or service, given the company's knowledge of its consumers' perceptions of value and competitors' responses.

   a. The company's contacts with its customers and its market research studies provide information about **consumers' perceptions of value**.

b. The company also must gain information about **competitors' potential responses** by learning about their technological expertise, products, costs, and financial positions. This information may be obtained from competitors' customers, suppliers, employees, and financial reports. Reverse engineering of their products is also possible.

c. **Value engineering** is a means of reaching targeted cost levels. It is a systematic approach to assessing all aspects of the **value chain** cost buildup for a product: (1) R&D, (2) design of products, (3) design of processes, (4) production, (5) marketing, (6) distribution, and (7) customer service. The purpose is to minimize costs without sacrificing customer satisfaction.

1) Value engineering requires identifying value-added and nonvalue-added costs. **Value-added costs** are costs of activities that cannot be eliminated without reducing the quality, responsiveness, or quantity of the output required by a customer or the organization.

2) Value engineering also requires distinguishing between cost incurrence and locked-in costs. **Cost incurrence** is the actual use of resources, and **locked-in** (designed-in) costs will result in use of resources in the future as a result of past decisions. Traditional cost accounting focuses on budget comparisons, but value engineering emphasizes controlling costs at the design stage before they are locked in.

<u>**Product Life Cycle**</u>

6. The **product life cycle** begins with **precommercialization** (product development), proceeds through the **introduction and growth** stages, continues into the product's maturity stage, and finally ends with the **harvest or decline** stage and the final provision of customer support.

a. Life-cycle costing is sometimes used as a basis for **cost planning** and **product pricing**. Life-cycle costing estimates a product's revenues and expenses over its expected life cycle. The result is to highlight **upstream and downstream costs** in the cost planning process that often receive insufficient attention. Emphasis is on the need to price products to cover **all costs**, not just production costs.

1) A concept related to life-cycle cost that is relevant to pricing is **whole-life cost**, which equals **life-cycle costs** plus **after-purchase costs** (operating, support, repair, and disposal) incurred by customers. Reduction of whole-life costs is a strong competitive weapon. Customers may pay a premium for a product with low after-purchase costs.

b. **Pricing Policies**

1) During **precommercialization**, the strategy is to innovate by conducting R&D, marketing research, and production tests. The firm has no sales and therefore **no pricing policy**, but it has high investment costs.

2) The **introduction stage** is characterized by slow sales growth and lack of profits because of the high expenses of promotion. Competitors are few, basic versions of the product are produced, and higher-income customers are usually targeted. **Cost-plus prices** are charged. They may initially be high to permit cost recovery when unit sales are low.

3) In the **growth stage**, sales and profits increase rapidly, cost per customer decreases, customers are early adopters, new competitors enter an expanding market, new product models and features are introduced, and promotion spending declines or remains stable. **Prices are set to penetrate the market.**

4) Some writers identify a separate stage between growth and maturity. During the **shakeout period**, the overall growth rate falls, price cutting occurs, industry profits decrease, and weaker firms leave the market. The growth phase tends to result in too many competitive entrants, brands, and models; greater intensity of competition; and too much capacity.
   a) The firm eliminates weak products and product lines, strengthens R&D and engineering efforts, **reduces prices** through effective promotions, and improves relationships with other firms in the distribution channel (e.g., by reducing inventory carrying costs).
   b) The firm also must ensure that it has a sustainable competitive advantage. For example, an early quality advantage may disappear as competing products improve and customers focus more on **price and service**.
5) In the **maturity stage**, sales peak but growth declines, competitors are most numerous but may begin to decline in number, and per-customer cost is low. Profits are high for large market-share firms. For others, profits may fall because of **competitive price-cutting** and increased R&D spending to develop improved versions of the product.
6) During the **decline stage**, sales and profits drop as **prices are cut**, and some firms leave the market. Customers include late adopters, and per-customer cost is low. Weak products and unprofitable distribution media are eliminated, and advertising budgets are pared to the level needed to retain the most loyal customers.

Strategies

7. Pricing and Generic Competitive Strategies

a. Michael E. Porter's **generic strategies model** is based on the concept that each of a firm's **competitive advantages** ultimately may be categorized as either a **cost** or a **differentiation** advantage.

b. Using the variables of **competitive advantage** (cost and differentiation) and **competitive scope** (broad and narrow), Porter described four generic strategies to be applied by business units.

1) **Cost leadership** is the generic strategy favored by a firm that seeks competitive advantage through **lower costs**. This strategy has a **broad competitive scope**. Such a firm can earn higher profits than its competitors at the **industry average price** or charge a **lower price** to increase market share.
2) **Differentiation** is the generic strategy that seeks competitive advantage through providing a **unique product or service**. This strategy has a **broad competitive scope**. Such a firm may earn higher profits because consumers are willing to pay a **higher price** than that charged by competitors. However, that price difference must exceed the additional cost of the differentiated product or service.
   a) A successful differentiation strategy creates a buyer perception that few, if any, **substitutes** are available. Thus, the firm may have the additional advantage of being able to **increase price** by passing supplier **cost increases** to buyers.
3) **Cost focus** is the generic strategy favored by a firm that seeks competitive advantage through **lower costs** but with a **narrow competitive scope** (e.g., a regional market or a specialized product line). The rationale for a cost-focus strategy is that the narrower market can be better served because the firm knows it well.

4) **Focused differentiation** is the generic strategy favored by a firm that seeks competitive advantage through providing a **unique product or service** but with a **narrow competitive scope**, e.g., a regional market or a specialized product line.

8. **Pricing and Market-Based Competitive Strategies**

a. The dominant firm in a market pursues a **market-leader strategy**. The leader should attempt to **increase total demand** in the market because it will gain the most. Demand will increase if the firm uses pricing to attract **new users** by employing a

1) **Market-penetration strategy** to focus on customers who might use the product or service.
2) **New-market segment strategy** to pursue customers who have never used the product or service.
3) **Geographical expansion strategy** to target users in previously unserved localities

b. The leader may attempt to obtain a **greater market share**. In general, a firm that increases its market share in its **served (target) market**, as opposed to the total market, will increase profits if it adopts an appropriate strategy.

1) The **economic cost** of the strategy must be acceptable. Beyond a certain **optimal market share**, profits may decline, for example, because prices may need to be lowered and costs (e.g., legal and lobbying costs) may increase.
2) The leader must adopt the right **marketing mix** (the marketing methods used). For example, market share should be earned, not bought by **lower profit margins**.

c. Trailing (runner-up) firms may choose a **market challenger strategy**.

1) The challenger may attack the leader, for example, by across-the-board innovation or by better serving the market. The attack may be directed at firms of similar size that are not serving the market, e.g., those that are failing to introduce new products or are **overpricing**.

d. **Market-follower strategies** are adopted by firms that do not wish to challenge the leader.

1) These firms believe that **product imitation** may be preferable to **product innovation**. Because the innovator has already incurred the expenses of bringing the new product to market, the imitator may be profitable selling at or below the market price charged by the leader.

e. **Market-nicher strategies** are followed by small or mid-size firms that compete in small (niche) markets that may be overlooked by large firms.

1) Successful niche marketers often have higher rates of return than firms in large markets. They often (a) sell high-quality products at **premium prices**, (b) have low costs, and (c) excel in need satisfaction because they know their markets well.
2) Successful niche marketers have high profit margins. By contrast, mass marketers sell at low prices in high volume.
3) Niche marketers must create, expand, and protect their niches. The risk is that a niche may evaporate or be entered by a large firm.
4) The essence of niche marketing is **specialization**, but success often depends on **multiple niching**. Creating new niches diversifies risk and increases the firms's probability of survival.

Stop and review! You have completed the outline for this subunit. Study multiple-choice questions 14 through 24 beginning on page 96.

2.4 MANAGING HUMAN RESOURCES

1. Managing human resources means **acquiring, retaining, and developing employees.** These functions should be consistent with the strategy and structure of the organization. The essential activities include
   a. Developing a **human resource strategy**. Such a strategy at its broadest is a systems approach that treats employees and future employees as **human capital**, that is, as intangible assets whose fullest potential should be developed.
   b. Recruitment and selection.
   c. Evaluation of performance.
   d. Training and development.
2. Research indicates that a **people-centered** human resource strategy improves employee retention and profits. Jeffrey Pfeffer (see Kreitner, *Management*, 9th ed., page 357) suggests the following practices:
   a. A job security policy
   b. Stringent hiring procedures
   c. Employee empowerment (e.g., use of self-managed teams)
   d. Basing compensation on performance
   e. Comprehensive training
   f. Reduction of status differences
   g. Information sharing
3. **Human resource planning** consists of forecasting future employment requirements. It includes the hiring, training, and monitoring of employees. Planning includes scanning the **external environment** to understand the area's labor supply, workforce composition, and work patterns. Companies often perform such analysis before building a new plant in a new geographic area, but **regular analyses** at established locations is sometimes overlooked. Companies must forecast future employee needs to ensure adequate resources when needed. Labor resources are not always as mobile as raw materials.

<u>**Job Analysis**</u>

4. **Job analysis** is the first step. It entails interviewing superior employees about the way they accomplish their tasks, analyzing work flows, and studying the methods used to achieve work-unit objectives.
   a. Has the nature of the job changed? If so, the job description should be rewritten.
   b. If the job's nature remains the same, the job specifications should be written from the job description and sent to personnel to be advertised.
   c. A **job description**, based on job analysis, should list basic duties. For higher-level positions, reporting relationships may also be included.
      1) EXAMPLE: For an accounting clerk, the job description might include
         a) Preparing payroll checks
         b) Maintaining inventory ledgers
         c) Preparing invoices

Job Specifications

d. **Job specifications**, based on the job description, should list the abilities needed by a person hired for that job.

1) EXAMPLE: Job specifications for an accounting clerk may list
   a) 10-key facility
   b) Typing ability at a specified number of correct words per minute
   c) Experience in a similar position for a specified number of years
   d) Bondability
   e) Education to a specified level and, perhaps, in specified courses
2) For other jobs, other factors may be pertinent:
   a) Physical characteristics, e.g., strength and stamina
   b) Personal characteristics, e.g., personality and communication skills
3) Some sources include job specifications within the definition of job description.

5. **Recruitment**

a. Many countries have laws that prohibit employment discrimination with regard to any employment action, for example, hiring, training, compensation, retention, or promotion. Prohibited bases of discrimination may be race, color, religion, sex, national origin, age, or disability.

1) The law may prohibit doing the following in **recruiting interviews**:
   a) Making notation of sex
   b) Asking marital status (may ask after hiring for insurance purposes)
   c) Asking for number of children (may ask after hiring for insurance purposes)
   d) Asking for height and weight
   e) Asking for criminal record (only for security clearance)
   f) Asking type of military discharge
   g) Asking age
2) The modern trend, reinforced not only by legal requirements but also by the need for fresh viewpoints, is to **recruit for diversity**.
   a) In this context, diversity may be defined to include not only legally protected categories but also other differences such as background and personality. Genuine diversity is an absence of any form of intolerance and the creation of a heterogeneous culture.
   b) Recruiting for diversity includes an emphasis on **retention**.

6. Using **temporary or part-time workers** gives management the flexibility to adjust quickly to changing market conditions.

Selection

7. **Employee selection.** Requirements should come from job specifications developed from each job description and include education, experience, physical characteristics, and personal characteristics.

a. All requirements, including selection tests, must be based on their relationship to the ability to perform successfully in a specific job category.

b. Employee information preferably should be verified.

c. According to Del J. Still (see Kreitner, pp. 359-360), the **selection process** involves

1) Preparation by developing job descriptions and job specifications and writing interview questions
2) Reviewing those questions for fairness and conformity with the law
3) Organizing by defining the roles and methods of interviewers
4) Collecting information from applicants
5) Evaluating
6) Meeting to discuss information about applicants
7) Deciding whether to offer employment

d. **Interviewing** is the most frequently used selection method. Because the unstructured interview is subject to cultural and other forms of bias, the **structured interview** is preferable. It consists of written questions related to the job that have standard answers. The questions are created and scored by a committee so as to minimize bias. Types of questions address

1) Job situations
2) Job-related knowledge
3) Simulation of job activity
4) Employee requirements

<u>**Testing**</u>

8. **Applicant testing.** Testing applicants for jobs with quantifiable output (e.g., jobs requiring clerical skills or manual dexterity) is easier than testing for positions with a less tangible work product (e.g., public relations director or human resource manager).

a. All tests must be **validated** in each organization and for minority and nonminority groups before they can be predictive of successful performance.

b. Tests must be given to **all applicants** for the same job category.

c. It is not easy or inexpensive to validate a test.

d. Test **validity** is the capacity of a test to measure accurately what it was designed to measure.

e. Test **reliability** is the ability of a test to obtain the same scores in repeated administrations, regardless of validity.

f. Lie detector tests, drug tests, DNA screening, AIDS tests, and personality tests are significant and controversial matters.

9. **Training and Development**

a. **Training** consists of organizational programs to prepare employees to perform currently assigned tasks.

1) **On-the-job or experiential training**, for example, by job rotation, apprenticeships, and mentoring arrangements, is usually less costly than off-the-job training. However, it may disrupt the workplace and result in increased errors. It is suited to acquisition of technical skills.
2) **Off-the-job training** is provided, for example, in classroom lectures, film study, and simulations. It is well suited to development of problem solving and interpersonal abilities and to teaching of complex skills.
3) **Computer-based** training is expected to become more common.

b. **Development** includes programs to prepare people to perform future tasks and acquire new skills.

1) The focus is mostly on management and organizational development of human relations skills. Management **coaching and mentoring** enhance the development process.

c. Kreitner (p. 373) defines **training** broadly as "using guided experience to change employee behavior or attitude."

d. The **evaluation and appraisal** process helps identify individual strengths and weaknesses as the basis for **training and development opportunities**. Also, jobs and markets change, leading to a need for workers with different skills. Organizations thrive when workers value lifelong learning.

   1) Viewing performance evaluation as a training and developmental process can foster a culture in which evaluation is sought out.
   2) A **training needs assessment** should be conducted to (a) determine what training is relevant to employees' jobs, (b) determine what training will improve performance, (c) determine whether training will make a difference, (d) distinguish training needs from organizational problems, and (e) link improved job performance with the organization's objectives and bottom line.
   3) **Self-assessment** normally yields shorter-term training needs and often has more to do with employees' personal career goals than with strategic business needs. Thus, self-assessment often may be used only as a supplement to other approaches.

e. Training and development programs are successful when they achieve the greatest **retention (learning) of skills and knowledge** that are transferred to the job. The following is a model for the process of learning:

   1) Establishing objectives
   2) Modeling the skills or making a meaningful presentation of facts
   3) Practicing the skills
   4) Obtaining feedback

10. **Evaluation**

a. An important aspect of management is the evaluation of **employees**.

   1) Evaluations are important to employees, the employer, and the organization.
   2) Evaluations provide an opportunity for **growth** and may prevent disputes.
   3) Evaluations tend to focus on who did the job, how it was done, or what was done.

      a) **Behavior-oriented** evaluation rewards the behavior desired by management. Behavior control involves examining work processes rather than work output.
      b) **Goal-oriented** evaluation measures how well the employee attained the objectives set by management.
      c) **Trait-oriented** evaluation tends to reward what the supervisor thinks of the employee rather than the job the employee did.
      d) **Employee-oriented** evaluation focuses on who did the job.

b. **Purposes of Evaluation**

   1) Performance criteria identify necessary job-related abilities.
   2) Performance objectives help employees direct their energies toward achieving the organization's objectives without constant supervision.
   3) Performance outcomes promote employee satisfaction by acknowledging when jobs are completed and done well.
   4) Evaluation distinguishes effective from ineffective job performance.
   5) The employer and the organization develop employee strengths and identify weaknesses.

6) Evaluation sets compensation.

   a) But separating performance evaluations from compensation decisions may be beneficial. An advantage is that more emphasis is placed on long-term objectives. It also emphasizes other rewards, such as feelings of achievement and the recognition of superiors. Another advantage is that the employee's good performance can be separated from the overall company's bad financial performance.

      i) A disadvantage is that the employee may not be motivated immediately by a good appraisal because of the delay in receipt of any monetary reward. The evaluation also may not be taken as seriously by the employee if compensation is not correlated with performance.

7) Evaluation identifies promotable employees.

   a) Internal promotions motivate employees and are less difficult and expensive than external hiring.

      i) Many firms look to external candidates for certain jobs because they bring a fresh perspective to the organization's problems and may have more up-to-date training or education.

c. **Problems of Evaluation**

1) **Halo effect.** A manager's judgment on one positive trait affects rating on other traits. The converse is the **horn effect**, that is, allowing one negative trait to influence the evaluation of other traits.
2) **Central tendency.** All personnel are rated within the same narrow range, e.g., "All my people are good." In a sense, all employees are rated average.
3) **Recency effect.** Most recent behavior overshadows overall performance.
4) **Differing standards.** Some managers have stricter standards than others, making cross-departmental comparisons difficult.
5) **Personal bias.** Traits may not reflect actual job performance, so appraisal can be biased by the degree to which the manager likes the subordinate.
6) **Leniency error** occurs when a manager fails to give a negative evaluation because of fear of damaging a good working relationship with a worker.
7) **Contrast error** is the tendency to rate people relative to other people rather than performance standards. If most employees are mediocre, a person performing at an average level is rated as "outstanding." That same person might be rated as "poor" if most workers perform at an above-average level. Although such comparisons may be appropriate at times, the normal rating process should be based on job requirements.
8) The **once-a-year process** tends to affect the usefulness and accuracy of any job-related information.

d. **Major Types of Appraisals**

1) **Management by objectives (MBO)** is a participative process in which supervisors and subordinates mutually establish objectives. A rating is based on achievement of the objectives.
2) **Behaviorally anchored rating scales (BARS)** contain descriptions of good and bad performance. They are developed through job analysis for a number of specific job-related behaviors and then used for evaluation of employees.

3) Check off the box provides a list of **categories for rating** performance for the supervisor to check off. Methods using check the box evaluations include

a) **Graphic scale**, which provides a list of job duties and a scale to grade them, i.e., 1 = Excellent, etc.

b) A **checklist**, which provides statements relating to job performance, and the evaluator checks the statements that apply.

c) A method similar to the checklist method in that it provides statements for the evaluator to choose from but requires the evaluator to choose the one that most resembles the employee's performance and the one that least resembles the employee's performance, which is called **forced choice**.

4) Comparing an employee's performance to the work of others is known as the **comparative method**. Comparative methods include

a) **Ranking**, which ranks all employees from highest to lowest. This method can lend itself to bias on the part of the evaluator.

b) Pairing an employee with other employees and ranking him or her compared to the other employee(s), which is known as **paired comparison**.

c) The **forced normal distribution**. This method distributes employees along a bell-shaped curve. It compels evaluators to rate some employees in the tails of the curve even though their performance levels are not normally distributed.

5) The **narrative method** includes **essays** and the **critical incidents method**, both of which consume large amounts of time and effort.

a) **Field reviews** require human resources personnel to prepare the evaluation for each employee based on the supervisor's input.

i) The supervisor has the ability to veto or modify.

6) A **360° performance appraisal** is a multirater model for employee assessment. It provides anonymous feedback by peers, customers, supervisors, and subordinates.

a) Appraisal is subjective and may be affected by popularity.

b) Evaluations do not include copies of job descriptions or performance goals.

e. **Characteristics of Effective Evaluation Systems**

1) **Relevant.** Criteria should be reliable and valid. They should relate to employee functions, that is, to activities over which the employees exert control.

2) **Unbiased.** Systems should be based on performance, not on unrelated personal characteristics.

3) **Significant.** The focus should be on the important part of the job, not what is convenient to evaluate.

4) **Practical.** Systems should be as objective, easy to use, clearly understood, and efficient as possible.

11. **Human Resource Planning**

a. A **human resource audit** evaluates compliance with laws and regulations, determines whether operations are efficient, and considers the company's recruitment and salary and benefit programs.

b. **Human resource or human asset accounting** attempts to measure the value, and the changes in value, of the organization's investment in human capital.

1) Although this "asset" is enormously valuable (sometimes estimated at two or three times the annual payroll), it is not shown in balance sheets or accounted or in earnings statements.

a) One experimental measurement approach is a "present value" of human resources.

b) Another is a "cost" approach, with financial investments (training, customer goodwill, etc.) offset by reductions (e.g., retirement).

12. **Safety.** Employers may have responsibilities to their employees under local and national law. Employers may have to comply with, among other things,

a. Standards regulating the **workplace environment** and the safety of equipment.

1) Employers may have a **general duty** to provide a safe workplace for employees.
2) Employers may be required to inform employees about legal requirements.

b. Laws that may prohibit employers from discriminating on the basis of a **disability**.

c. **Workers' compensation** laws that provide payments to employees injured at work, including lost wages, medical expenses, and, in some cases, training for employment in a different field.

Stop and review! You have completed the outline for this subunit. Study multiple-choice questions 25 through 30 beginning on page 100.

2.5 SUMMARY

1. Although traditional inventory management minimizes inventory and the related holding costs, many companies use inventory as a hedge against inflation as well as a guarantee of future availability. Moreover, inventory carrying costs are sometimes transferred to suppliers or customers.

2. Inventory policy considers, among other things, (a) the types of ordering and carrying costs, (b) stockout costs, (c) safety stock, and (d) reorder points.

3. The purchasing process is initiated by purchase requisitions issued by the production control function. Purchase requisitions ultimately result from make-or-buy decisions made when production processes were designed. For a retailer, the purchase decision is the same as the decision about what to sell. The choice of suppliers depends on price, quality, delivery performance, shipping costs, credit terms, and service. Ordering is increasingly done by EDI. Other purchasing issues are (a) negotiation of contracts, (b) tracking, and (c) receiving.

4. Inventory models are quantitative models designed to control inventory costs by determining the optimal time to place an order (or begin production) and the optimal order quantity (production run). The timing of orders may be periodic or perpetual.

5. The basic EOQ model minimizes the sum of ordering (setup) costs and carrying costs. The EOQ is the square root of twice the periodic demand times the order (setup cost), divided by the periodic unit carrying cost.

6. In the ABC system of inventory management, the level of control of each group reflects cost-benefit concerns.

7. Materials requirements planning (MRP) is an integrated computer-based information system designed to plan and control raw materials used in a production setting. MRP is characterized as a push-through system because production is activated by forecasts of demand, not actual customer needs.

8. The just-in-time (JIT) model of inventory control limits output to the demand of the next operation. Reductions in inventory result in less investment in idle assets; reduction of storage space requirements; and lower inventory taxes, pilferage, and obsolescence risks. JIT also encompasses changes in the production process. JIT is a pull system. Items are pulled through production by current demand, not pushed through by anticipated demand. Thus, one operation produces only what is needed by the next operation, and components and raw materials arrive just in time to be used. To implement this approach and to eliminate waste, the factory is reorganized to permit lean production.
9. In a JIT system, the buyer-supplier relationship is critical. It is often facilitated by EDI. Thus, long-term contracts are typically negotiated to reduce order costs.
10. A computer-integrated manufacturing (CIM) system involves (a) designing products using computer-aided design (CAD), (b) testing the design using computer-aided engineering (CAE), (c) manufacturing products using computer-aided manufacturing (CAM), and (d) integrating all components with a computerized information system.
11. Manufacturing resource planning (MRP-II) is a closed-loop, computerized manufacturing system that integrates all facets of a manufacturing business, including production, sales, inventories, schedules, and cash flows.
12. The supply chain consists of flows from sources of (a) raw materials, (b) components, (c) finished goods, (d) services, or (e) information through intermediaries to ultimate consumers. These flows and the related activities may occur across the functions in an organization's value chain (R&D, design, production, marketing, distribution, and customer service). These flows and the related activities also may occur across separate organizations. The activities in the supply chain should be integrated.
13. Distribution is the transfer of goods (and, in other contexts, services and information) from producers to customers or from distribution centers to merchandisers. Thus, distribution manages outflows, and purchasing manages inflows. Among the interrelated issues involved in distribution are selection of (a) distribution channels, (b) inventory placement, (c) means of transportation, (d) shipment schedules, (e) routes, and (f) carriers.
14. Price-setting factors include supply and demand. Supply of and demand for products and services are determined by customers' impact on demand, the actions of competitors, and costs. Internal factors include (a) marketing objectives, (b) the marketing-mix strategy, (c) all relevant costs in the value chain, (d) the organizational location of pricing decisions, and (e) capacity. External factors include (a) the type of market; (b) customer perceptions of price and value; (c) the price-demand relationship; and (d) competitors' products, costs, prices, and amounts supplied.
15. Prices may be cost-, market-, or competition-based.
16. Pricing may depend on the sellers' place in the distribution channel and whether a product is new. Price also reflects geographical factors, various discounts and allowances, promotional considerations, and the product mix.
17. Predatory and collusive pricing are illegal in the U.S., and price discrimination among customers may be. Moreover, international cartels engage in monopolistic and anticompetitive practices.
18. A target price is the expected market price for a product or service, given the company's knowledge of its consumers' perceptions of value and competitors' responses. Subtracting the unit target operating income determines the long-term unit target cost. Relevant costs are all future value-chain costs, whether variable or fixed.
19. Life-cycle costing is a basis for cost planning and product pricing. It estimates a product's revenues and expenses over its expected life cycle.
20. Pricing policies should be appropriate to the stage of the product life cycle: (a) introduction, (b) growth, (c) shakeout, (d) maturity, and (e) decline.

21. Using the variables of **competitive advantage** (cost and differentiation) and **competitive scope** (broad and narrow), Porter described four generic business strategies: (a) cost leadership, (b) differentiation, (c) cost focus, and (d) focused differentiation.

22. The dominant firm in a market pursues a **market-leader strategy**. The leader should attempt to **increase total demand** because it will gain the most. Demand will increase if the firm uses pricing to attract new users by employing a market penetration, new-market-segment, or geographical-expansion strategy.

23. Managing human resources means acquiring, retaining, and developing employees. These functions should be consistent with the strategy and structure of the organization. The essential activities include (a) development of a human resource strategy that treats employees as human capital, (b) recruitment and selection, (c) evaluation of performance, and (d) training and development.

QUESTIONS

2.1 Inventory Management

1. The order costs associated with inventory management include

A. Insurance costs, purchasing costs, shipping costs, and obsolescence.

B. Obsolescence, setup costs, quantity discounts lost, and storage costs.

C. Quantity discounts lost, storage costs, handling costs, and interest on capital invested.

D. Purchasing costs, shipping costs, setup costs, and quantity discounts lost.

Answer (D) is correct. *(CMA, adapted)*

REQUIRED: The items included in order costs.

DISCUSSION: Order costs include purchasing costs, shipping costs, setup costs for a production run, and quantity discounts lost.

Answer (A) is incorrect. Insurance costs are a carrying cost. Answer (B) is incorrect. Obsolescence and storage costs are carrying costs. Answer (C) is incorrect. Storage costs, handling costs, and interest on capital invested are all carrying costs.

2. The carrying costs associated with inventory management include

A. Insurance costs, shipping costs, storage costs, and obsolescence.

B. Storage costs, handling costs, capital invested, and obsolescence.

C. Purchasing costs, shipping costs, setup costs, and quantity discounts lost.

D. Obsolescence, setup costs, capital invested, and purchasing costs.

Answer (B) is correct. *(CMA, adapted)*

REQUIRED: The items included in carrying costs.

DISCUSSION: Carrying costs include storage costs, handling costs, insurance costs, interest on capital invested, and obsolescence.

Answer (A) is incorrect. Shipping costs are ordering costs, not carrying costs. Answer (C) is incorrect. Purchasing costs, shipping costs, setup costs, and quantity discounts lost are ordering or manufacturing costs. Answer (D) is incorrect. The setup costs for a production run are equivalent to ordering costs. Additionally, purchasing costs are considered costs of ordering.

3. The calculation of an economic order quantity (EOQ) considers

A. The purchasing manager's salary.

B. A corporate charge for advertising expenses.

C. The shipping costs to deliver the product to the customer.

D. Capital costs.

Answer (D) is correct. *(CMA, adapted)*

REQUIRED: The true statement about the calculation of the economic order quantity.

DISCUSSION: The determination of the economic order quantity balances the variable costs of ordering and carrying inventory. Factors in the equation include the cost of placing an order, unit carrying cost, and annual demand in units. Carrying costs include storage costs, handling costs, insurance, property taxes, obsolescence, and the opportunity cost of investing capital in inventory. Thus, the return on capital that is forgone when it is invested in inventory should be considered.

Answer (A) is incorrect. The purchasing manager's salary is a fixed cost. The EOQ model includes variable costs only. Answer (B) is incorrect. Advertising is not an ordering or carrying cost. Answer (C) is incorrect. The cost of shipping to customers is a selling expense.

4. Companies that adopt just-in-time purchasing systems often experience

A. An increase in carrying costs.

B. A reduction in the number of suppliers.

C. A greater need for inspection of goods as the goods arrive.

D. Less need for linkage with a vendor's computerized order entry system.

Answer (B) is correct. *(CMA, adapted)*

REQUIRED: The true statement about companies that adopt just-in-time (JIT) purchasing systems.

DISCUSSION: The objective of JIT is to reduce carrying costs by eliminating inventories and increasing the deliveries made by suppliers. Ideally, shipments of raw materials are received just in time to be incorporated into the manufacturing process. The focus of quality control under JIT is the prevention of quality problems. Quality control is shifted to the supplier. JIT companies typically do not inspect incoming goods; the assumption is that receipts are of perfect quality. Suppliers are limited to those who guarantee perfect quality and prompt delivery.

Answer (A) is incorrect. Carrying costs typically decline in JIT companies. Less inventory is on hand. Answer (C) is incorrect. In a JIT system, materials are delivered directly to the production line ready for insertion in the finished product. Answer (D) is incorrect. The need for communication with the vendor is greater. Orders and deliveries must be made on short notice, sometimes several times a day.

Questions 5 and 6 are based on the following information. The diagram presented represents the economic order quantity (EOQ) model.

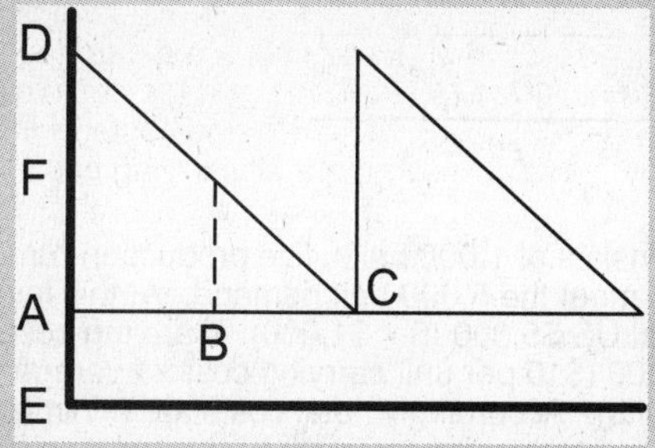

5. Which line segment represents the reorder lead time?

A. AB.

B. AE.

C. AF.

D. BC.

Answer (D) is correct. *(CMA, adapted)*

REQUIRED: The line segment representing the reorder lead time.

DISCUSSION: The quantity of inventory on hand is represented by the y axis and time by the x axis. The reorder lead time is represented by the line segment BC.

Answer (A) is incorrect. AB is the time between receipt of the last order and the placing of the next order. Answer (B) is incorrect. AE is the safety stock. Answer (C) is incorrect. AF represents the quantity of inventory that will be used during the reorder lead time.

6. Which line segment represents the length of time to consume the total quantity of materials ordered?

A. DE.

B. BC.

C. AC.

D. AE.

Answer (C) is correct. *(CMA, adapted)*

REQUIRED: The line representing the time to consume all the materials ordered.

DISCUSSION: Time is shown along the x axis. The line segment AC depicts the time to consume an entire order (to reduce the inventory to the safety stock).

Answer (A) is incorrect. DE represents the total inventory on hand just after an order has been received. Answer (B) is incorrect. BC is the reorder lead time. Answer (D) is incorrect. AE is the safety stock.

Questions 7 and 8 are based on the following information. Ned Ryerson Computer Furniture, Inc. (RCF) manufactures a line of office computer chairs. The annual demand for the chairs is estimated to be 5,000 units. The annual cost to hold one unit in inventory is US $10 per year, and the cost to initiate a production run is US $1,000. There are no computer chairs on hand, and RCF has scheduled four equal production runs of computer chairs for the coming year, the first of which is to be run immediately. RCF has 250 business days per year, sales occur uniformly throughout the year, and production start-up is within one day. RCF is considering using the following formula for determining the economic order quantity (EOQ):

$$EOQ = \sqrt{\frac{2AD}{K}}$$

If: A = cost to initiate a production run per purchase order
D = annual unit demand
K = cost of carrying one unit per year

7. What is the number of production runs per year of computer chairs that would minimize the sum of carrying and setup costs for the coming year?

A. 1

B. 2

C. 4

D. 5

Answer (D) is correct. *(CMA, adapted)*

REQUIRED: The number of production runs that minimizes the sum of setup and carrying costs.

DISCUSSION: The EOQ minimizes the sum of carrying and setup costs. The EOQ is the amount at which carrying costs are equal to setup costs. Thus, plugging the data into the EOQ formula results in the following:

$$EOQ = \sqrt{\frac{2\,(US\ \$1{,}000)\,(5{,}000)}{\$10}} = 1{,}000\ units$$

Thus, if each lot consists of 1,000 units, five production runs per year are needed to meet the 5,000-unit demand. At this level, setup costs will total US $5,000 (5 × $1,000). Carrying costs will also equal US $5,000 ($10 per unit carrying cost × average inventory of 500 units). Accordingly, total costs are minimized at US $10,000.

Answer (A) is incorrect. A single production run indicates an EOQ of 5,000 units. The carrying costs of US $25,000 [$10 × ($5,000 ÷ 2)] would exceed the US $1,000 of setup costs. Answer (B) is incorrect. Two production runs correspond to an EOQ of 2,500 units and an average inventory of 1,250 units. The resulting US $12,500 of carrying costs would exceed the US $2,000 of setup costs. Answer (C) is incorrect. Four production runs correspond to an EOQ of 1,250 units and an average inventory of 625 units. The resulting US $6,250 of carrying costs would exceed the US $4,000 of setup costs.

8. If RCF does **not** maintain a safety stock, the estimated total carrying costs for the computer chairs for the coming year based on their current schedule is

A. US $4,000

B. US $5,000

C. US $6,250

D. US $12,500

Answer (C) is correct. *(CMA, adapted)*

REQUIRED: The estimated total annual carrying costs, assuming no safety stock is held.

DISCUSSION: Given four production runs and an annual demand of 5,000 units, each production run must generate 1,250 units. Inventory will total 1,250 units at the completion of each run but will decline to zero just prior to the next run. Thus, the average inventory is 625 units (1,250 ÷ 2), and the total carrying cost is US $6,250 (625 units × $10).

Answer (A) is incorrect. The cost of maintaining an average inventory of 625 units is US $6,250. Answer (B) is incorrect. US $5,000 is based upon an EOQ of 1,000 units and an average of 500 units. Answer (D) is incorrect. US $12,500 is based on the maximum inventory level.

9. Each stockout of a product sold by Company K costs US $1,750 per occurrence. The carrying cost per unit of inventory is US $5 per year, and the company orders 1,500 units of product 24 times a year at a cost of US $100 per order. The probability of a stockout at various levels of safety stock is

Units of Safety Stock	Probability of a Stockout
0	.50
100	.30
200	.14
300	.05
400	.01

What is the optimal safety stock level for the company?

A. 0 units.

B. 100 units.

C. 300 units.

D. 400 units.

Answer (D) is correct. *(CMA, adapted)*

REQUIRED: The optimal level of safety stock.

DISCUSSION: The total expected cost of safety stock equals the sum of the expected annual stockout cost and the expected annual carrying cost. Annual expected stockout cost equals the cost per occurrence (US $1,750), times the probability of a stockout per cycle, times the number of cycles (24). Annual expected carrying cost of a safety stock equals the unit carrying cost (US $5) times the number of units. Hence, a safety stock of 400 units has the lowest total expected cost.

Units Held	Carrying Cost	Expected Stockout Cost Per Cycle	Expected Stockout Cost for 24 Cycles	Total Expected Cost
0	US $ 0	US $875.00	US $21,000	US $21,000
100	500	525.00	12,600	13,100
200	1,000	245.00	5,880	6,880
300	1,500	87.50	2,100	3,600
400	2,000	17.50	420	2,420

Answer (A) is incorrect. A safety stock of 0 units has a total expected cost of US $21,000. Answer (B) is incorrect. A safety stock of 100 units has a total expected cost of US $13,100. Answer (C) is incorrect. A safety stock of 300 units has a total expected cost of US $3,600.

10. A major justification for investments in computer-integrated manufacturing (CIM) projects is

A. Reduction in the costs of spoilage, reworked units, and scrap.

B. Lower carrying amount and depreciation expense for factory equipment.

C. Increased working capital.

D. Stabilization of market share.

Answer (A) is correct. *(CIA, adapted)*

REQUIRED: The major justification for investments in CIM.

DISCUSSION: Automating and computerizing production processes requires a substantial investment in fixed assets and an increase in risk because of greater fixed costs. CIM also necessitates an increase in software costs and extensive worker retraining. However, the costs of spoilage, rework, and scrap are reduced along with labor costs. The qualitative advantages of CIM are increased flexibility, shorter manufacturing lead time, quicker development of new products, better product delivery and service, faster response to market changes, and improved competitiveness.

Answer (B) is incorrect. An increase in fixed assets results in a higher carrying amount and depreciation expense. Answer (C) is incorrect. Working capital normally is reduced as investments shift from current to fixed assets. Answer (D) is incorrect. Actual or potential market share changes may trigger investments in CIM.

2.2 Supply Chain Management

11. The bullwhip, or whiplash, effect on inventories begins when retailers face uncertain demand from consumers caused by randomness in buying habits. It can be avoided by

A. The need to purchase or manufacture goods in cost-efficient batches.

B. Changes in price that may encourage purchases in anticipation of future increases.

C. Shortages that may lead to rationing by suppliers or manufacturers and hoarding by manufacturers or retailers.

D. Sharing of information and coordination among the organizations in the supply chain.

Answer (D) is correct. *(Publisher, adapted)*

REQUIRED: The means of preventing the bullwhip, or whiplash, effect.

DISCUSSION: Sharing information about sales, inventory, pricing, advertising campaigns, and sales forecasts by all functions and organizations in the supply chain moderates demand uncertainty for all parties. The desired results are (a) minimization of inventories held by suppliers, manufacturers, and retailers; (b) avoidance of stockouts; (c) fewer rush orders; and (d) production as needed by retailers.

Answer (A) is incorrect. The need to purchase or manufacture goods in cost-efficient batches is a cause of the bullwhip, or whiplash, effect. Answer (B) is incorrect. Purchases in anticipation of future price increases cause the bullwhip, or whiplash, effect. Answer (C) is incorrect. Rationing by suppliers or manufacturers and hoarding by manufacturers or retailers cause the bullwhip, or whiplash, effect.

12. Which of the following are intermediaries between sellers and buyers?

I. Agent
II. Broker
III. Consignee
IV. Consumer

A. I and II only.

B. I and III only.

C. I, II, and III only.

D. I, II, III, and IV.

Answer (C) is correct. *(Publisher, adapted)*

REQUIRED: The intermediaries between sellers and buyers.

DISCUSSION: A distribution channel is a series of interdependent marketing institutions that facilitate the transfer of a product from producer (seller) to consumer (buyer). Intermediaries include merchant middlemen, agents, brokers, consignees, and facilitating intermediaries.

Answer (A) is incorrect. A consignee is also an intermediary between sellers and buyers. Answer (B) is incorrect. A broker is an intermediary. Answer (D) is incorrect. A consumer is a buyer, not an intermediary.

13. Which of the following channel structures have the **best** means of managing channel conflict?

I. Conventional
II. Vertical
III. Horizontal
IV. Multichannel

A. I and II.

B. II, III, and IV.

C. I, III, and IV.

D. II and III.

Answer (B) is correct. *(Publisher, adapted)*

REQUIRED: The channel structures that offer the best means of managing conflict.

DISCUSSION: In vertical distribution systems, channel conflict is managed through common ownership, contractual relationships, or administration by one or a few dominant channel members. The joint nature of horizontal distribution efforts is the tool for managing channel conflict. In a multichannel system, because such a system is managed by a single entity, channel conflicts can be evaluated and managed internally. Conventional distribution systems consist of one or more independent producers, wholesalers, and retailers, each of which is a separate profit-maximizing business. The profit objective of each independent channel member may result in actions that are not profit-maximizing for the system as a whole, and the conventional distribution system offers no means for controlling channel conflict.

Answer (A) is incorrect. A conventional distribution system offers no inherent means of controlling channel conflict. Horizontal and multichannel systems also offer effective means of managing channel conflict. Answer (C) is incorrect. A conventional distribution system offers no inherent means of controlling channel conflict. Vertical systems also offer effective means of managing channel conflict. Answer (D) is incorrect. Multichannel distribution systems also offer effective means of managing channel conflict.

2.3 Pricing

14. Buyer-based pricing involves

A. Adding a standard markup to the cost of the product.

B. Determining the price at which the product will earn a target profit.

C. Basing prices on the product's perceived value.

D. Basing prices on competitors' prices.

Answer (C) is correct. *(CIA, adapted)*

REQUIRED: The definition of buyer-based pricing.

DISCUSSION: Buyer-based pricing involves basing prices on the product's perceived value rather than on the seller's cost. Nonprice variables in the marketing mix augment the perceived value. For example, a cup of coffee may have a higher price at an expensive restaurant than at a fast-food outlet.

Answer (A) is incorrect. Adding a standard markup to the cost of the product is cost-plus pricing. Answer (B) is incorrect. Determining the price at which the product will earn a target profit is target profit pricing. Answer (D) is incorrect. Basing prices on competitors' prices is going-rate pricing.

15. Which one of the graphs depicts the demand curve for prestige goods?

A.

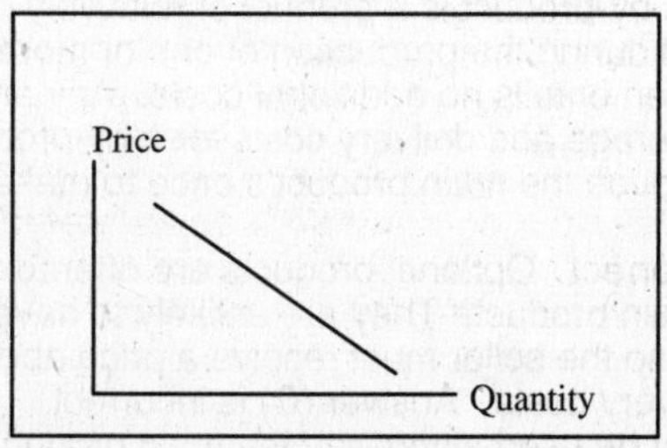

B.

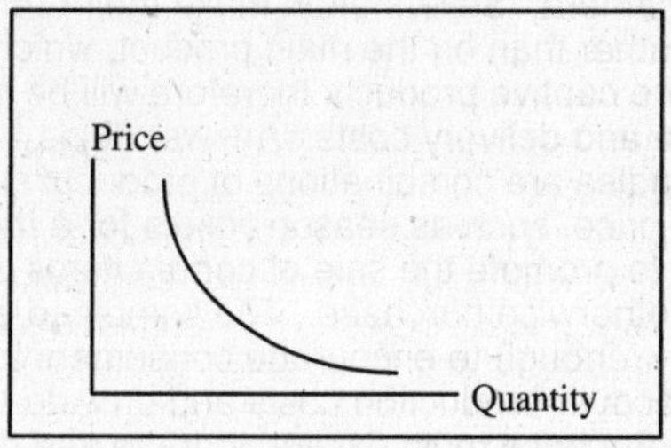

C.

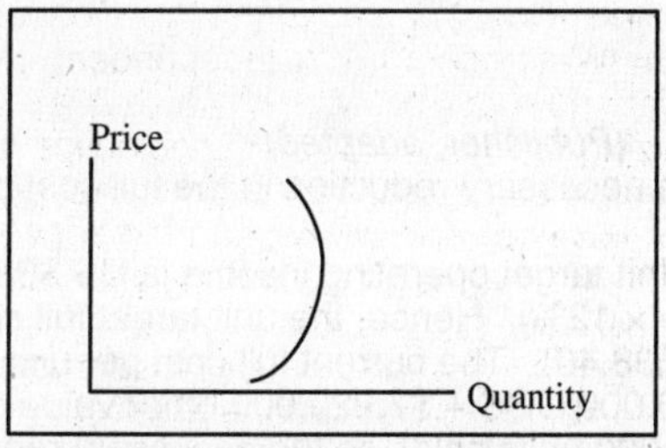

D.

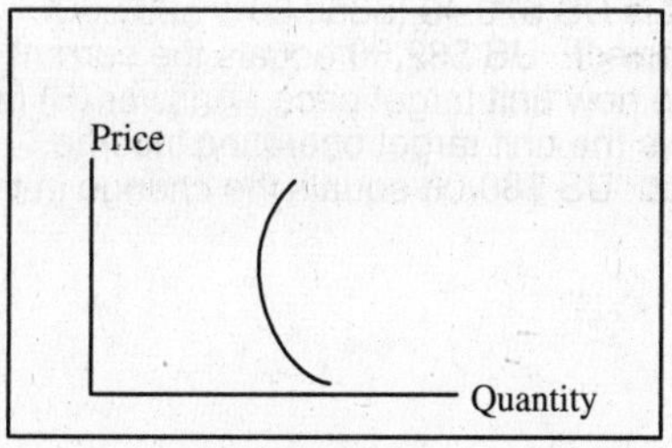

Answer (C) is correct. *(CIA, adapted)*

REQUIRED: The graph depicting the demand curve for prestige goods.

DISCUSSION: Over some intermediate range of prices, the reaction to a price increase for prestige goods is an increase, not a decrease, in the quantity demanded. Within this range, the demand curve is upward sloping. The reason is that consumers interpret the higher price to indicate a better or more desirable product. Above some price level, the relation between price and quantity demanded will again become negatively sloped.

Answer (A) is incorrect. This graph describes the familiar, negatively sloped relation between price charged and the resulting demand level for normal goods. Answer (B) is incorrect. The demand curve can be linear or curvilinear. Answer (D) is incorrect. This demand curve has the same basic shape as the demand curve for prestige goods, but it bends the wrong way. As prices increase, quantity demanded first falls and then rises in this graph.

16. A seller's price is below an appropriate measure of costs. Moreover, the seller has a reasonable prospect of recovering the resulting loss in the future through higher prices or a greater market share. Accordingly, the seller has engaged in

A. Collusive pricing.

B. Dumping.

C. Predatory pricing.

D. Price discrimination.

Answer (C) is correct. *(Publisher, adapted)*

REQUIRED: The effect of charging a price below an appropriate measure of costs, given a reasonable expectation of recovering the loss.

DISCUSSION: Predatory pricing is intentionally pricing below cost to eliminate competition and reduce supply. Federal statutes and many state laws prohibit the practice. The U.S. Supreme Court has held that pricing is predatory when two conditions are met: (1) the seller's price is below "an appropriate measure of its costs," and (2) it has a reasonable prospect of recovering the resulting loss through higher prices or greater market share.

Answer (A) is incorrect. Collusive pricing involves a conspiracy to set higher prices. Answer (B) is incorrect. Dumping is defined under U.S. law as sale by a non-U.S. company in the U.S. market of a product below its market value in the country where it was produced. Such sale is illegal if it threatens material injury to a U.S. industry. Answer (D) is incorrect. Price discrimination involves charging different prices to different customers for essentially the same product without a legal justification.

17. In which product-mix pricing strategy is it appropriate for the seller to accept any price that exceeds the storage and delivery costs for the product?

A. By-product pricing.

B. Optional-product pricing.

C. Captive-product pricing.

D. Product-bundle pricing.

Answer (A) is correct. *(CIA, adapted)*

REQUIRED: The pricing strategy that accepts any price greater than storage and delivery costs.

DISCUSSION: A by-product is a product of relatively minor importance generated during the production of one or more other products. Its production entails no additional costs. Any amount received above the storage and delivery costs for a by-product allows the seller to reduce the main product's price to make it more competitive.

Answer (B) is incorrect. Optional products are offered for sale along with the main product. They are unlikely to have a zero production cost, so the seller must receive a price above their storage and delivery costs. Answer (C) is incorrect. Captive products must be used along with the main product, such as film for use with a camera. Sellers often make their profits on the captive products rather than on the main product, which is sold at a low price. The captive products therefore will be priced well above the storage and delivery costs. Answer (D) is incorrect. Product bundles are combinations of products sold together at a reduced price, such as season tickets for a theater. Products are bundled to promote the sale of certain items that consumers might not otherwise purchase. The combined price of the bundle must be low enough to encourage consumers to buy the bundle but must recover production costs and provide some profit for the seller, so the price must exceed storage and delivery costs.

18. Fulford Company applies the target pricing and costing approach. The following information about costs and revenues of Fulford's product are available for the year just ended:

Unit sales	60,000
Unit selling price	US $400
Cost of goods sold	US $13,200,000
Value-chain operating costs excluding production	US $7,920,000

Fulford plans to increase unit sales to 80,000 by reducing the product's unit price to US $320. If Fulford desires a unit target operating income of 12%, by what amount must it reduce the full cost per unit?

A. US $32.00

B. US $38.40

C. US $70.40

D. US $80.00

Answer (C) is correct. *(Publisher, adapted)*

REQUIRED: The necessary reduction in the full cost per unit.

DISCUSSION: Unit target operating income is US $38.40 ($320 unit target price × 12%). Hence, the unit target full cost is US $281.60 ($320 – $38.40). The current full cost per unit is US $352.00 [($13,200,000 CGS + $7,920,000 other value chain operating costs) ÷ 60,000 units sold], so the necessary reduction in the full cost per unit is US $70.40 ($352.00 – $281.60).

Answer (A) is incorrect. US $32.00 equals the current full cost per unit minus the new unit target price. Answer (B) is incorrect. US $38.40 is the unit target operating income. Answer (D) is incorrect. US $80.00 equals the change in the unit price.

19. A manufacturing company produces plastic utensils for a particular segment at the lowest possible cost. The company is pursuing a cost

A. Leadership strategy.

B. Focus strategy.

C. Differentiation strategy.

D. Containment strategy.

Answer (B) is correct. *(CIA, adapted)*

REQUIRED: The cost strategy pursued by the manufacturing company.

DISCUSSION: A cost focus strategy aims at cost leadership in a particular segment, such as a regional market or a specialty product line. The rationale for a focus strategy is that the narrower market can be better served.

Answer (A) is incorrect. A cost leader is the lowest cost producer in the industry as a whole. Answer (C) is incorrect. Cost differentiation aims at providing a product at different costs in different market segments. Answer (D) is incorrect. Cost containment aims at controlling costs related to a particular product/market but not necessarily producing at the lowest possible cost.

20. During the growth stage of a product's life cycle,

A. The quality of products is poor.

B. New product models and features are introduced.

C. There is little difference between competing products.

D. The quality of the products becomes more variable and products are less differentiated.

Answer (B) is correct. *(CIA, adapted)*

REQUIRED: The true statement regarding the growth stage of a product's life cycle.

DISCUSSION: In the growth stage, sales and profits increase rapidly, cost per customer decreases, customers are early adopters, new competitors enter an expanding market, new product models and features are introduced, and promotion spending declines or remains stable. The firm enters new market segments and distribution channels and attempts to build brand loyalty and achieve the maximum share of the market. Thus, prices are set to penetrate the market, distribution channels are extended, and the mass market is targeted through advertising. The strategy is to advance by these means and by achieving economies of productive scale.

Answer (A) is incorrect. Poor product quality is evident during the introduction stage of the product life cycle. Answer (C) is incorrect. Competitors are most numerous and products become less differentiated during the maturity stage of the product life cycle. In this stage, imitators have entered the market and competitors have learned which technologies and features are successful. Answer (D) is incorrect. The quality of the products becomes more variable and products are less differentiated during the decline stage of the product life cycle.

21. While auditing a marketing department, the internal auditor discovered that the product life cycle model was used to structure the marketing mix. Under such a philosophy, the price charged on a consistent basis for a specific product would probably be lowest during which life cycle stage?

A. Introduction stage.

B. Growth stage.

C. Maturity stage.

D. Decline stage.

Answer (C) is correct. *(CIA, adapted)*

REQUIRED: The product life cycle stage during which the price charged on a consistent basis for a specific product is likely to be the lowest.

DISCUSSION: During the maturity stage, competition is at its greatest and costs are at their lowest. Moreover, firms are engaged in competitive price-cutting measures, resulting in some of the lowest prices seen during a product's life cycle.

Answer (A) is incorrect. During the introduction stage, per-unit costs of production are high and little competition exists. Hence, prices are at their highest. Answer (B) is incorrect. During the growth stage, prices will be lower than during the introduction stage, but not as low as during the maturity stage. In the growth stage, costs are dropping and competitors are being added, but costs are not at their minimum and competitors are not at their maximum. Answer (D) is incorrect. During the decline stage, price-cutting predominates as firms struggle to maintain sales volume in the face of a permanent decrease in demand. However, late in the decline stage, there are few competitors, so prices can be raised. In addition, per-unit costs are on the rise because volume is declining, resulting in higher prices.

22. A firm buys like-new computer equipment from bankrupt companies and resells it in foreign markets at prices significantly below those charged by competitors. The firm is

A. Engaged in dumping.

B. Engaged in price discrimination.

C. Operating in a gray market.

D. Operating in a black market.

Answer (C) is correct. *(Publisher, adapted)*

REQUIRED: The term for sale in a higher-price market of goods acquired cheaply in another market.

DISCUSSION: In a gray market, products imported from one country to another are sold by persons trying to make a profit from the difference in retail prices between the two countries. In essence, the seller firm in this case was exploiting a price difference between markets.

Answer (A) is incorrect. Dumping is sale below cost or at less than the price charged in the home market. Answer (B) is incorrect. Price discrimination involves illegally selling the same products at different prices to different customers. Answer (D) is incorrect. Black market operations are illegal.

23. A firm ships its product to a foreign subsidiary and charges a price that may increase import duties but lower the income taxes paid by the subsidiary. The **most** likely reason for these effects is that the

A. Price is an arm's-length price.

B. Price is a cost-plus price.

C. Transfer price is too low.

D. Transfer price is too high.

Answer (D) is correct. *(Publisher, adapted)*

REQUIRED: The reason that sale to a subsidiary results in high import duties.

DISCUSSION: A transfer price is the price charged by one subunit of a firm to another. When the subsidiary-buyer is in a foreign country, the higher the transfer, the higher the potential tariffs. However, the tax levied on a subsequent sale by the subsidiary will be lower because of its higher acquisition cost.

Answer (A) is incorrect. An arm's-length price is what a competitor would charge in that market. Answer (B) is incorrect. A cost-plus price does not necessarily trigger higher import duties. Answer (C) is incorrect. If the transfer price is too low, import duties would be lower and taxes would be higher.

24. A firm sells its product in a foreign market for a much higher price than in its home market. The reason is **most** likely

A. Price elasticity of demand.

B. Dumping.

C. Gray market activity.

D. Price escalation.

Answer (D) is correct. *(Publisher, adapted)*

REQUIRED: The most likely reason for disparate prices in different national markets.

DISCUSSION: Price escalation is caused by an accumulation of additional costs, e.g., currency fluctuations; transportation expenses; profits earned by importers, wholesalers, and retailers; and import duties.

Answer (A) is incorrect. Price elasticity of demand is the relationship of total revenue to a change in price. If demand is price elastic, a price increase results in lower revenue. Answer (B) is incorrect. Dumping is sale at a price below cost or below the price in the home country. Answer (C) is incorrect. In a gray market, products imported from one country to another are sold by persons trying to make a profit from the difference in retail prices between the two countries.

2.4 Managing Human Resources

25. Evaluating performance is **not** done to

A. Determine the amount of nondiscriminatory benefits that each employee deserves.

B. Assess the available human resources of the firm.

C. Motivate the employees.

D. Determine which employees deserve salary increases.

Answer (A) is correct. *(Publisher, adapted)*

REQUIRED: The statement that is not a purpose of performance evaluations.

DISCUSSION: Evaluations reinforce accomplishments, help in assessing employee strengths and weaknesses, provide motivation, assist in employee development, permit the organization to assess its human resource needs, and serve as a basis for wage increases. Nondiscriminatory benefits are given to everyone in the organization in equal amounts, regardless of title, pay, or achievement of objectives.

26. A company allows each of its departments to develop its own system for evaluating performance. How should the personnel director communicate appraisal information to a new employee?

A. Presenting anything that is pertinent to the listener's situation.

B. Providing an overview of all systems within the company.

C. Describing how her own performance is evaluated.

D. Discussing each department's evaluation system in detail.

Answer (A) is correct. *(Publisher, adapted)*

REQUIRED: The best method of discussing performance evaluations with a new employee.

DISCUSSION: The personnel director should tailor the discussion to the listener by describing how the employee's department evaluates performance and what is expected of him/her. The director should also obtain feedback from the employee to determine if everything is clearly understood. Discussing information that is irrelevant to the new employee's appraisal information would confuse the new employee.

27. A disadvantage of separating performance evaluations from compensation-increase decisions is that

A. Not enough emphasis is placed on short-run performance.

B. Financial rewards may lose their motivational effect.

C. Employees may not be motivated by good appraisals.

D. The employee's performance evaluation does not consider the financial status of the company overall.

Answer (C) is correct. *(Publisher, adapted)*

REQUIRED: The disadvantage of separating performance appraisals from compensation increases.

DISCUSSION: The employee may not be motivated immediately by a good appraisal because of the delay in receipt of any monetary reward. The evaluation also may not be taken as seriously by the employee if compensation is not correlated with performance.

Answer (A) is incorrect. An advantage of separating appraisals from compensation increases is that more emphasis is placed on long-term objectives. Answer (B) is incorrect. This separation does not deprive money of its motivational power, but it does emphasize other rewards, such as feelings of achievement and the recognition of superiors. Answer (D) is incorrect. An advantage of separating performance evaluations from compensation-increase decisions is that the employee's good performance can be separated from the overall company's bad financial performance.

28. If a supervisor fails to give an employee a negative evaluation because of fear of damaging a good working relationship, this is known as the

A. Leniency error.

B. Recency effect.

C. Halo effect.

D. Contrast error.

Answer (A) is correct. *(Publisher, adapted)*

REQUIRED: The term referring to the avoidance of giving a negative evaluation because of fear of damaging a good working relationship.

DISCUSSION: A leniency error is a manager's failure to give a negative evaluation because of fear of damaging a good working relationship with an employee.

Answer (B) is incorrect. The recency effect means that the employee's most recent behavior overshadows overall performance. Answer (C) is incorrect. The halo effect means the manager's judgment on one positive trait affects the rating on other traits. Answer (D) is incorrect. A contrast error is the tendency to rate people relative to other people, without consideration of performance standards.

29. An evaluator is rating 100 employees on a bell curve. She is instructed to label five employees "extraordinary" and five employees "unsatisfactory." The evaluator also is instructed to label 10 employees "above average" and 10 employees "below average." All of the other employees will be in the "average" category.

Which of the following is the major drawback of using this method?

A. The process of using the method is too time consuming

B. An employee's evaluation will depend on who the evaluator is.

C. Different evaluators have different standards.

D. The evaluator must place some employees in the lowest and highest tails of a bell-shaped curve.

Answer (D) is correct. *(Publisher, adapted)*

REQUIRED: The major drawback of using the forced normal distribution method

DISCUSSION: The forced normal distribution method forces evaluators to label employees with ratings that fall along the normal distribution of a bell-shaped curve. The major drawback of this method is that the employees will be labeled with an evaluation regardless of their abilities. No matter what, some people will be evaluated at the bottom of the normal distribution and some people will be evaluated at the top of the normal distribution.

Answer (A) is incorrect. The forced normal distribution method is not necessarily more time consuming than other means of evaluation. Answer (B) is incorrect. Bias is a factor in many appraisal methods. Answer (C) is incorrect. Cross-departmental comparisons are difficult because different evaluators have different standards. But this problem is not unique to the forced normal distribution method.

30. An organization has a compensation system for its managers based on a management-by-objectives (MBO) approach. The essential premise of MBO is that

A. Compensation should be based on qualitative factors.

B. Employees should be concerned with routine matters, and managers should attend to exceptions.

C. Employees should participate in setting objectives.

D. Managers should establish objectives for their employees.

Answer (C) is correct. *(Publisher, adapted)*

REQUIRED: The essential premise of MBO.

DISCUSSION: MBO involves mutual setting of objectives by the superior and the subordinate as a basis for performance evaluation. Based on the Theory Y philosophy that employees want to work hard if they know what is expected, MBO requires (1) senior management participation and commitment to the program, (2) integration of the objectives for all subunits into a compatible system directed toward accomplishment of organizational objectives, (3) provision for regular reporting of performance, and (4) free and honest communication between superior and subordinates. Subordinates must make careful assessments of their abilities and their interests, and managers must "coach" subordinates rather than dictate their proper objectives. Both sides must maintain flexibility to accommodate unforeseen changes, and the review and analysis of results before setting the next round of objectives is a vital part of the process.

Answer (A) is incorrect. MBO objectives may be set in terms of quantitative measures (such as sales) or qualitative ones (such as improved service). Answer (B) is incorrect. The essence of management by exception is that employees should be concerned with routine matters, and managers should attend to exceptions. Answer (D) is incorrect. Setting of objectives should be participative.

STUDY UNIT THREE
FINANCIAL ACCOUNTING I

(44 pages of outline)

Financial accounting provides the information reported in a complete set of financial statements. The **balance sheet** presents financial position, and the **income statement** presents performance. The other two basic financial statements are the **statement of cash flows** and the **statement of changes in equity**. Financial statements may be prepared for any entity, e.g., a business, school, government, or fraternal organization. This study unit outlines the international sources of the body of knowledge regarding financial statement preparation for business entities and the underlying accounting theory. It also covers the procedural aspects of financial reporting, the main categories of assets, and financial liabilities.

Study Units 3 and 4 cover **International Financial Reporting Standards (IFRSs)**. **International Accounting Standards (IASs)**, related Interpretations, and the framework for the preparation and presentation of financial statements were issued by the predecessor to the current standard setter, the **International Accounting Standards Board (IASB)**. They will be effective until amended or superseded. The IASB issues IFRSs, which is also the collective term for IASs and IFRSs. See Appendix C for a list of current IASs and IFRSs.

Core Concepts

- Business entities should provide information about financial position, performance, and changes in financial position that is helpful to many users in making economic decisions. However, these statements do not provide all necessary information.
- The principal qualitative characteristics of information in financial statements are understandability, relevance, reliability, and comparability.
- The elements of financial statements are (1) assets, (2) liabilities, (3) equity, (4) income, (5) expenses, and (6) capital maintenance adjustments.
- Recognition is the inclusion in the balance sheet or income statement of an item that satisfies the definition of an element and the recognition criteria.
- The following are recognition criteria: (1) Any future economic benefit associated with the item will probably flow to or from the entity, and (2) the cost or value of the item is measurable with reliability.
- Recognition of income occurs at the same time as recognition of increases in assets or decreases in liabilities.
- Recognition of expenses occurs at the same time as recognition of increases in liabilities or decreases in assets.
- Measurement is the determination of the amounts at which the elements are to be recognized. Different measurement bases are used.
- Accrual accounting recognizes the financial effects of transactions and other events in the periods when they occur and records and reports them in the periods to which they relate.
- Financial statements are the output of the accrual accounting cycle.

- IAS 18 defines revenue as "the gross inflow of economic benefits during the period arising in the course of the ordinary activities of an entity when those inflows result in increases in equity, other than increases relating to contributions from equity participants."
- Fair value is "the amount for which an asset could be exchanged, or a liability settled, between knowledgeable, willing parties in an arm's-length transaction."
- Revenue is recognized for a sale of goods if certain conditions are met.
- If the outcome of a services transaction can be reliably estimated, revenue is recognized based on the stage of completion.
- A complete set of financial statements includes statements of (1) financial position, (2) comprehensive income, (3) changes in equity, and (4) cash flows. It also includes notes and a presentation of accounting policies.
- Separate classifications on the balance sheet of current and noncurrent assets and liabilities should be presented unless a presentation by order of liquidity is reliable and more relevant.
- All nonowner changes in equity may be presented in one statement or two (e.g., an income statement and a statement of comprehensive income.
- Comprehensive income for a period consists of (1) profit or loss and (2) other comprehensive income.
- All recognized income and expense items are included in profit or loss unless a pronouncement requires otherwise.
- In a statement of changes in equity, changes from transactions with owners are presented separately from changes from nonowner transactions.
- A cash flow statement is presented for each period for which financial statements are presented because users need to assess the entity's ability to generate cash and cash equivalents. Cash flows are classified and separately disclosed as from operating, investing, or financing activities.
- Notes describe the basis of preparation and the significant policies applied, make required disclosures not presented on the face of the statements, and provide additional information needed for a fair presentation.
- An interim period is shorter than a full year. An interim financial report contains either a complete set of financial statements or a set of condensed financial statements.
- A financial instrument is a contract that results in a financial asset of one entity and a financial liability or equity instrument of another entity.
- A financial asset or liability is initially recognized only when the entity is a party to the contract. Thus, rights and obligations pertaining to derivatives are recognized as assets and liabilities, respectively.
- A derivative is a financial instrument whose value changes with the change in the underlying (a specified interest rate, security price, exchange rate, price index, etc.). A derivative requires little or no initial net investment compared with contracts having similar responses to changing market conditions. It is settled in the future.
- The following are the kinds of designated hedging relationships: a fair value hedge, a cash flow hedge, and a hedge of a net investment in a foreign operation.
- Inventories are measured at the lower of cost or net realizable value.
- Use of LIFO is not allowed.
- The cost of an item of property, plant, and equipment (PPE) meets the recognition criteria if (1) it is probable that the entity will receive future economic benefits, and (2) the costs are reliably measurable. Such items are initially measured at cost.
- Measurement after recognition of an item of PPE is at cost minus any accumulated depreciation and impairment losses.
- An asset is impaired when its carrying amount exceeds its recoverable amount.
- Held-for-sale assets or disposal groups are reported at the lower of their carrying amount or fair value minus costs to sell.
- An intangible asset is "an identifiable nonmonetary asset without physical substance." It is initially recognized at cost. It is amortized only if it has a finite useful life.

3.1 FRAMEWORK FOR THE PREPARATION & PRESENTATION OF FINANCIAL STATEMENTS

Conceptual Framework

1. The Framework states the concepts that underlie general-purpose financial statements. It concerns
   a. The objective of financial statements
   b. Qualitative characteristics that make financial information useful
   c. Elements of financial statements
   d. Concepts of capital maintenance

Objective of Financial Statements

2. Business entities should provide information about financial position, performance, and changes in financial position that is helpful to many users in making **economic decisions**. However, these statements do not provide all necessary information.
3. Financial statements should show the results of management's stewardship or its **accountability** for assets.
4. Users need to evaluate the ability of the entity to generate **cash** and the timing and certainty of its generation.
5. An entity's **financial position** is determined by its economic resources, financial structure, liquidity and solvency, and adaptability.
6. Information about **performance** and its variability helps to predict (a) changes in the resources the entity may control, (b) how effectively it will use additional resources, and (c) its capacity to generate cash from existing resources.
7. Information about **changes in financial position** is useful in assessing financing, investing, and operating activities. For this purpose, funds may be defined differently.
8. Information about financial position is primarily provided in a **balance sheet**. Information about performance is primarily provided in an **income statement**. Information about changes in financial position is provided in a separate statement, such as a **cash flow statement** or a funds flow statement.
9. The components of financial statements **interrelate** because they present different aspects of the same transactions and other events.
10. **Notes and supplementary schedules** are included in the financial statements. Examples of disclosures are (a) relevant additional information about reported items, (b) risks and uncertainties, (c) off-balance-sheet resources and obligations, (d) segment information, and (e) the effects of changing prices.

Underlying Assumptions

11. The accrual basis of accounting is used. For a full outline, see Subunit 3.2.
12. The entity is assumed to be a going concern that (a) will operate indefinitely and (b) has no need or intent to liquidate or materially reduce its operations.
    a. Given this need or intent, **another basis of accounting**, e.g., liquidation value, must be used and disclosed.
13. **Economic-entity assumption.** The reporting entity is separately identified for the purpose of economic and financial accountability. Thus, the economic affairs of owners and managers are kept separate from those of the reporting entity.
    a. The legal entity and the economic entity are not necessarily the same. For example, consolidated reporting is permitted, if not required, even though the parent and its subsidiaries are legally distinct entities.

14. **Monetary-unit (unit-of-money) assumption.** Accounting records are kept in terms of money. Using money as the unit of measure is the best way of providing economic information to users of financial statements.
    a. The changing **purchasing power** of the monetary unit is assumed not to be significant.
15. **Periodicity (time period) assumption.** Even though the most accurate way to measure an entity's results of operations is to wait until it liquidates, this method is not followed. Instead, financial statements are prepared periodically throughout the life of an entity to ensure the timeliness of information.
    a. The periodicity assumption necessitates the use of **estimates** in the preparation of financial statements. It sacrifices some reliability of information for increased relevance.

<u>**Qualitative Characteristics**</u>

16. The principal qualitative characteristics of information in financial statements are understandability, relevance, reliability, and comparability.
    a. **Understandability.** Information should be readily understandable by reasonably knowledgeable users, but relevant information should not be excluded because of its complexity.
    b. **Relevance.** Useful information is relevant to **user decision making**. Information has relevance if users are able to predict the outcome of future events or confirm or correct their prior expectations.
        1) **Materiality** is a threshold or cut-off point. The issue is whether a given item or error is large enough so that its omission or misstatement will influence users.
    c. **Reliability.** Information is reliable if it is **free of material error and bias**. Users should be able to depend upon it to represent faithfully the economic transactions or events it purports to represent or could reasonably be expected to represent.
        1) **Substance over form.** To be **representationally faithful**, transactions and other events must be accounted for in accordance with their substance and economic reality, not their legal form.
        2) **Neutrality.** Reliable information must be free of bias intended to produce a predetermined result or induce certain behavior.
        3) **Prudence** is a reaction to the uncertainty arising from estimates. It includes caution in the exercise of judgment. Prudence does not approve introducing bias through deliberate understatement of assets and income or overstatement of liabilities and expenses.
        4) **Completeness.** Reliable information is complete within the limits of materiality and cost.
    d. **Comparability.** Financial statements must be comparable for the same entity over time. They also should be comparable among different entities.
        1) Thus, measurement and display should be **consistent** throughout an entity over time and for different entities.
        2) **Compliance with standards**, including disclosure of accounting policies, promotes comparability.
        3) Financial statements should report information for preceding periods.

Constraints

17. Certain constraints on **relevant and reliable information** limit the process of recognition in the financial statements.

    a. **Timeliness.** Reliability and timeliness must be balanced. **Undue delay** may cause a loss of relevance. The primary criterion for determining this balance is how best to serve economic decision makers.

    b. **Balance between benefit and cost.** This balance is a **pervasive constraint** that requires a judgment as to whether the benefits of information exceed its cost. The judgment may be difficult because, for example, costs are not necessarily incurred by the users who receive the benefits.

    c. **Balance of characteristics.** Professional judgment is needed to determine the appropriate tradeoffs among qualitative characteristics that will achieve the objective of financial statements.

    d. **True and fair view.** Applying the qualitative characteristics and appropriate accounting standards should result in financial statements that reflect a true and fair view, or fair presentation, of financial position, performance, and changes in financial position.

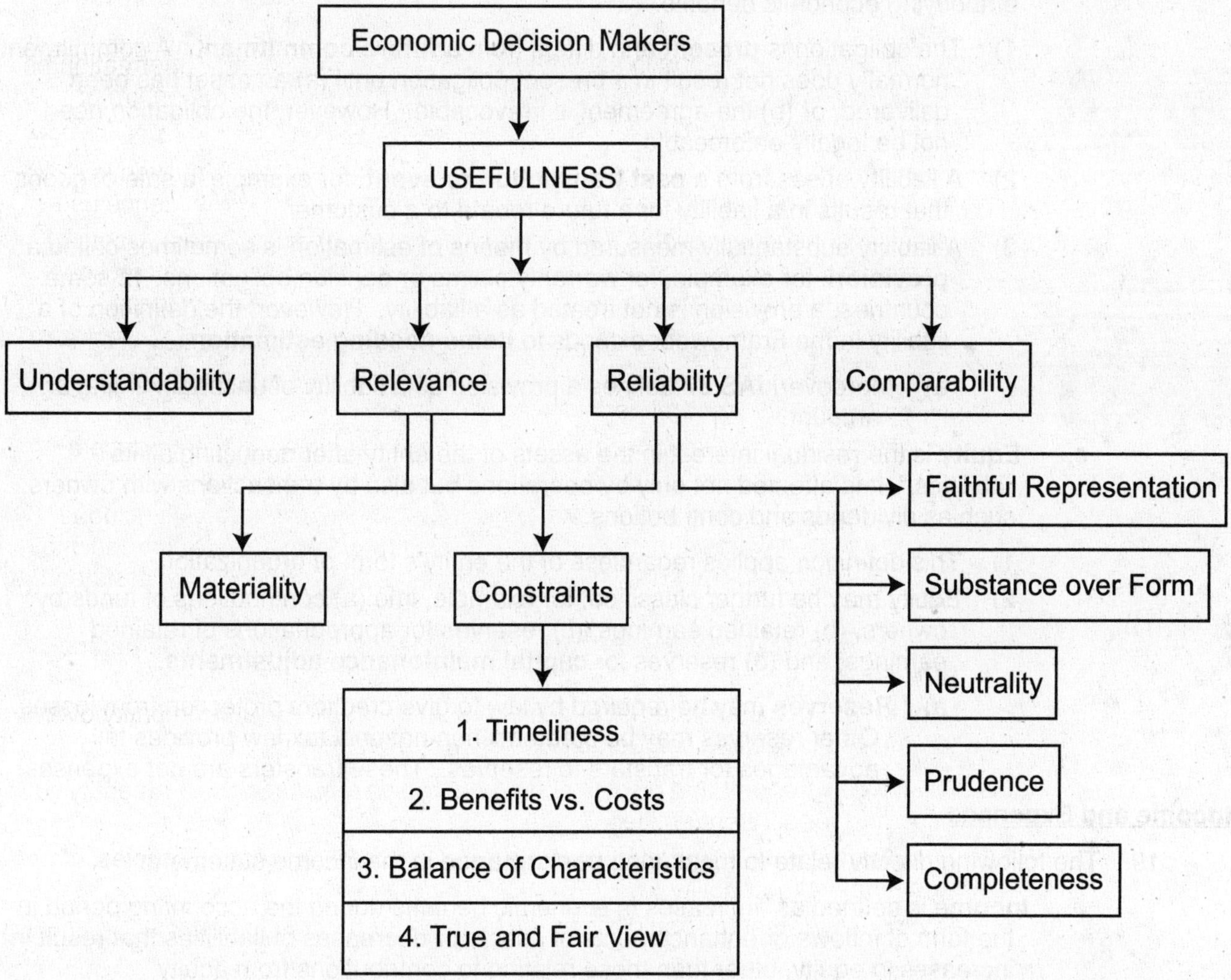

Elements of Financial Statements

18. The elements are groups of transactions and other events classified based on their economic characteristics. The following directly relate to the measurement of **financial position** in the balance sheet:
    a. **Assets** are resources "controlled by the entity as a result of past events and from which future economic benefits are expected to flow to the entity."
        1) The **benefit** is the potential for a direct or indirect contribution to the inflow of cash in the future.
        2) **Neither legal ownership nor legal control** is essential to the existence of an asset.
        3) The essence of assets is that, singly or together, they can be **controlled by the entity** so that they contribute to the generation of future net cash inflows. However, many common characteristics of assets are not shared by all assets. Thus, **not all assets** are acquired, tangible, legally enforceable, or exchangeable.
    b. **Liabilities** are present obligations "of the entity arising from past events, the settlement of which is expected to result in an outflow from the entity of resources embodying economic benefits."
        1) The obligation is **present** and differs from a **future commitment**. A commitment normally does not result in a present obligation until (a) an asset has been delivered, or (b) the agreement is irrevocable. However, the obligation need not be legally enforceable.
        2) A liability arises from a **past transaction or event**, for example, a sale of goods that results in a liability for a future rebate to a customer.
        3) A liability substantially measured by means of estimation is sometimes called a **provision**, for example, for warranty claims or pension obligations. In some countries, a provision is not treated as a liability. However, the definition of a liability in the Framework extends to **items needing estimation**.
            a) Moreover, **IAS 37** defines a provision as a liability of uncertain timing or amount.
    c. "**Equity** is the residual interest in the assets of the entity after deducting all its liabilities." It is affected not only by operations but also by transactions with owners, such as dividends and contributions.
        1) This definition applies regardless of the entity's form of organization.
        2) Equity may be further classified, for example, into (a) contributions of funds by owners, (b) retained earnings, (c) reserves for appropriations of retained earnings, and (d) reserves for **capital maintenance adjustments**.
            a) **Reserves** may be required by law to give creditors protection from losses. Other reserves may be created when national tax law provides tax advantages for transfers to reserves. These transfers are not expenses.

Income and Expenses

19. The following directly relate to measuring **performance** in the income statement:
    a. **Income** is defined as "increases in economic benefits during the accounting period in the form of inflows or enhancements of assets or decreases of liabilities that result in increases in equity, other than those relating to contributions from equity participants." **Income includes revenues and gains.** Thus, revenues and gains are not treated as separate elements.
        1) **Revenues** occur in the course of ordinary activities.

2) **Gains** meet the definition of income but may not occur in the course of ordinary activities. For example, gains may result from the sale of noncurrent assets.
   a) Gains may be unrealized.
   b) Gains are usually reported separately.

b. **Expenses** are "decreases in economic benefits during the accounting period in the form of outflows or depletions of assets or incurrences of liabilities that result in decreases in equity, other than those relating to distributions to equity participants." **Expenses include losses.** Thus, losses are not treated as separate elements.
   1) Expenses include items arising in the course of ordinary activities.
   2) **Losses** meet the definition of expenses but may not occur in the course of ordinary activities. For example, losses may result from the sale of noncurrent assets or from natural disasters.
      a) Losses may be unrealized.
      b) Losses are usually reported separately and often net of related income.

Recognition of Elements of Financial Statements

20. Recognition is the inclusion in the balance sheet or income statement of an item that satisfies the definition of an element and the recognition criteria. Disclosure of accounting policies used in the notes or explanatory matter is not a satisfactory alternative to recognition.
21. **Criteria.** Recognition of an element should occur if the following criteria are met:
   a. Any **future economic benefit** associated with the item will probably flow to or from the entity.
      1) **Probability** is the degree of uncertainty regarding the future flow of economic benefits.
   b. The **cost or value** of the item is measurable with reliability.
      1) **Reliability** is not impaired if reasonable estimates are used.
22. Recognition of an **asset** occurs when (a) a benefit will probably **flow to** the entity, and (b) the item's cost or value is reliably measurable.
23. Recognition of a **liability** occurs when (a) a benefit will probably **flow from** the entity as a result of settling a present obligation, and (b) the settlement amount is reliably measurable.
24. Recognition of **income** occurs at the same time as recognition of increases in assets or decreases in liabilities.
   a. The usual procedures for income recognition, such as that **revenue be earned**, reflect the recognition criteria, that is, (1) reliable measurement and (2) a sufficient probability. Thus, income is recognized when an increase in future economic benefits associated with an increase in an asset or a decrease in a liability has arisen that can be reliably measured.
25. Recognition of **expenses** occurs at the same time as recognition of increases in liabilities or decreases in assets.
   a. Expenses are recognized if the costs are **directly associated** with the earning of particular income items. This process is often called **matching**. Matching is simultaneous or combined recognition of the revenues and expenses that result directly and jointly from the same transactions or other events.
   b. Expenses also are recognized when they are broadly or indirectly associated with income. In these cases, a **systematic and rational allocation** procedure, such as depreciation or amortization, is used.
   c. **Immediate recognition** of expenses is appropriate when an expenditure results in no future economic benefit or when that benefit does not qualify or ceases to qualify as an asset.

Measurement

26. Measurement is the determination of the amounts at which the elements are to be recognized. Different measurement bases are used. The following are examples:
    a. **Historical cost** is the most common basis. Assets are recorded at the cash paid or the fair value of other assets given. Liabilities are recorded at the amount of proceeds received or, in some cases, at the amount of cash expected to be paid to satisfy the obligation. Examples are property, plant, and equipment and some inventories.
    b. **Realizable (settlement) value.** Assets are recorded at the amount of cash currently obtainable by sale in an orderly disposal. Liabilities are recorded at the undiscounted amount of cash expected to be paid for settlement in the normal course of business. Examples are accounts receivables, some inventories, and trade payables.
    c. **Present value.** Assets (liabilities) are recorded at the discounted amount of the future net cash inflows (outflows) that are expected to be generated (required for settlement) in the normal course of business. Examples are bonds receivable or payable.
    d. **Current cost.** Assets are recorded at the amount of cash to be paid if the same or an equivalent asset were currently obtained. An example is a liability recorded at the undiscounted amount of cash needed for current settlement.

Stop and review! You have completed the outline for this subunit. Study multiple-choice questions 1 through 3 on page 147.

3.2 ACCRUAL ACCOUNTING AND TIME VALUE OF MONEY

Cash-Basis Accounting

1. Under this basis, income is recognized when cash is received.
    a. Expense is recognized when paid.
    b. Cash-basis accounting is subject to manipulation by arranging payments or receipts before or after the end of an accounting period.
    c. The cash basis cannot properly reflect transactions in which cash payments or receipts relate to several financial reporting periods.

Accrual-Basis Accounting

2. Accrual accounting applies to an item that meets (a) the definition of an element of financial statements and (b) the criteria for recognition and measurement. It recognizes the financial effects of transactions and other events **when they occur** rather than when their direct cash consequences occur. It records these effects in the accounting records and reports them in the financial statements of the periods **to which they relate**.
    a. Accordingly, accrual accounting also considers (1) noncash exchanges of goods or services, (2) credit transactions, (3) nonreciprocal transfers, (4) price changes, (5) changes in fair values, (6) changes in form of assets or liabilities, etc.
    b. Accrual accounting embraces both accruals and deferrals.
        1) **Accruals** anticipate future cash flows. They recognize assets or liabilities and the related liabilities, assets, revenues, expenses, gains, or losses. Sales or purchases on account, interest, and taxes are common accruals.
        2) **Deferrals** reflect past cash flows. They recognize liabilities (for receipts) and assets (for payments), with deferral of the related revenues, expenses, gains, and losses. The deferral ends when the obligation is satisfied or the future economic benefit is used up. Prepaid insurance is a typical deferral.

c. **Allocation** assigns or distributes an amount according to a plan or formula. **Depreciation (amortization)** is a form of allocation. It is the "systematic allocation of the depreciable amount of an asset over its useful life." The term amortization is applied to, for example, intangible assets. More specifically, it is an allocation process for deferrals. It involves reducing a liability (asset) recorded as a result of a cash receipt (payment) by recognizing revenues (expenses).

1) Examples of allocation are the apportionment of a lump-sum purchase price among the assets acquired or the assignment of manufacturing costs to products.
2) Examples of amortization are depreciation and depletion expenses and the recognition of earned subscriptions revenue.

Accounting Cycle

3. Financial statements are the output of the accrual accounting cycle. The order of steps in the accounting cycle is as follows:

a. Identification and measurement of transactions and events required to be recognized,
b. Journalization,
c. Posting from the journals to the ledgers,
d. Development of a trial balance,
e. Adjustments to produce an adjusted trial balance,
f. Statement presentation,
g. Closing,
h. Taking a post-closing trial balance (optional), and
i. Making reversing entries (optional).

Time Value of Money

4. Time value of money concepts have many applications. For example, they affect the accounting for noncurrent receivables and payables (bonds and notes), leases, and certain employee benefits.
5. A quantity of money to be received or paid in the future is worth less than the same amount now. The difference is measured in terms of interest calculated using the appropriate **discount rate**. Interest is the payment received by holders of money from the current consumer to forgo current consumption.
6. Standard tables have been developed to facilitate the calculation of present and future values. Each entry in one of these tables represents the factor by which any monetary amount can be modified to obtain its present or future value.
7. The **present value (PV) of an amount** is the value today of some future payment.

a. It equals the future payment times the present value of 1 (a factor found in a standard table) for the given number of periods and interest rate.

EXAMPLE

	Present Value		
No. of Periods	6%	8%	10%
1	0.943	0.926	0.909
2	0.890	0.857	0.826
3	0.840	0.794	0.751
4	0.792	0.735	0.683
5	0.747	0.681	0.621

The present value of US $1,000, to be received in 3 years and discounted at 8%, is US $794 ($1,000 × 0.794).

8. The **future value (FV) of an amount** is the amount available at a specified time in the future based on a single investment (deposit) today. The FV is the amount to be computed if one knows the present value and the appropriate discount rate.

   a. It equals the current payment times the future value of 1 (a factor found in a standard table) for the given number of periods and interest rate.

EXAMPLE

	Future Value		
No. of Periods	6%	8%	10%
1	1.0600	1.0800	1.1000
2	1.1236	1.1664	1.2100
3	1.1910	1.2597	1.3310
4	1.2625	1.3605	1.4641
5	1.3382	1.4693	1.6105

The future value of US $1,000 invested today for 4 years at 10% interest will be US $1,464 ($1,000 × 1.464).

Annuities

9. An annuity is usually a series of equal payments at equal intervals of time, e.g., US $1,000 at the end of every year for 10 years.

   a. An **ordinary annuity (annuity in arrears)** is a series of payments occurring at the end of each period. In an **annuity due (annuity in advance)**, the payments are made (received) at the beginning of each period.

      1) **Present value.** The first payment of an ordinary annuity is discounted. The first payment of an annuity due is not discounted.

      2) **Future value.** Interest is not earned for the first period of an ordinary annuity. Interest is earned on the first payment of an annuity due.

   b. The **PV of an annuity**. A typical present value table is for an ordinary annuity, but the factor for an annuity due can be easily derived. Select the factor for an ordinary annuity for one less period (n – 1) and add 1.000 to it to include the initial payment (which is not discounted).

EXAMPLE

	Present Value		
No. of Periods	6%	8%	10%
1	0.943	0.926	0.909
2	1.833	1.783	1.736
3	2.673	2.577	2.487
4	3.465	3.312	3.170
5	4.212	3.993	3.791

To calculate the present value of an **ordinary annuity** of four payments of US $1,000 each discounted at 10%, multiply US $1,000 by the appropriate factor (US $1,000 × 3.170 = US $3,170).

Using the same table, the present value of an **annuity due** of four payments of US $1,000 each also may be calculated. This value equals US $1,000 times the factor for one less period (4 – 1 = 3), increased by 1.0. Thus, the present value of the annuity due for four periods at 10% is US $3,487 [$1,000 × (2.487 + 1.0)].

The present value of the annuity due (US $3,487) is greater than the present value of the ordinary annuity (US $3,170) because the payments occur 1 year sooner.

c. The **FV of an annuity** is the value that a series of equal payments will have at a certain moment in the future if interest is earned at a given rate.

EXAMPLE

	Future Value		
No. of Periods	6%	8%	10%
1	1.0000	1.0000	1.0000
2	2.0600	2.0800	2.1000
3	3.1836	3.2464	3.3100
4	4.3746	4.5061	4.6410
5	5.6371	5.8667	6.1051

To calculate the FV of a 3-year **ordinary annuity** with payments of US $1,000 each at 6% interest, multiply US $1,000 by the appropriate factor (US $1,000 × 3.184 = US $3,184).

The FV of an **annuity due** also may be determined from the same table. Multiply the US $1,000 payment by the factor for one additional period (3 + 1 = 4) decreased by 1.0 (4.375 – 1.0 = 3.375) to arrive at a FV of US $3,375 ($1,000 × 3.375).

The future value of the annuity due (US $3,375) is greater than the future value of an ordinary annuity (US $3,184). The deposits are made earlier.

Stop and review! You have completed the outline for this subunit. Study multiple-choice questions 4 through 6 on page 148.

3.3 REVENUE RECOGNITION

Revenue Definition

1. The **Framework** defines revenue as income arising in the ordinary course of an entity's activities. The timing of recognition is the principal issue in accounting for revenue.
2. **IAS 18**, *Revenue*, is the pronouncement with the widest applicability to revenue recognition. It concerns revenue resulting from sales of goods, rendering of services, and others' use of entity assets that provides returns of interest, royalties, and dividends.
   a. **Goods** include not only items produced for sale but also merchandise, land, and other property held for resale.
   b. **Services** involve "the performance by the entity of a contractually agreed task over an agreed period."
   c. Other standards apply to certain **other revenues**, for example, those from leases, equity-based investments, and changes in fair value of financial assets and liabilities.
3. IAS 18 defines **revenue** as "the gross inflow of economic benefits during the period arising in the course of the ordinary activities of an entity when those inflows result in increases in equity, other than increases relating to contributions from equity participants."
   a. Thus, amounts collected on behalf of a principal or otherwise on behalf of third parties, such as sales or value-added taxes, are not revenue.

Measuring Revenue

4. Revenue is measured at the fair value of the consideration received or receivable by the entity. This amount is ordinarily determined by the parties to the transaction after due allowance for trade discounts and volume rebates.
   a. **Fair value** is "the amount for which an asset could be exchanged, or a liability settled, between knowledgeable, willing parties in an arm's-length transaction."

b. When the cash inflow is deferred, the fair value may be less than the nominal amounts of cash received or receivable, for example, when the seller accepts a note with a below-market rate.

1) **Imputed interest.** If the transaction is effectively a financing arrangement, future receipts are discounted at an imputed rate to determine the fair value. This rate is the more clearly determinable of either (a) the prevailing rate for a similar instrument given the issuer's credit standing or (b) the rate that discounts the nominal amount to the cash sales price.

a) The difference between the nominal amount of consideration and the fair value is **interest revenue**.

Revenue Recognition – Sales of Goods

5. Revenue is recognized when **five conditions** are met:

a. The entity has transferred the significant **risks and rewards** of ownership.

1) This usually occurs with the passage of title or possession.
2) However, retention of significant risks of ownership may occur in many ways. For example, (a) a sale may be contingent upon resale; (b) the buyer may rescind for a reason stated in the contract, and the probability of return may be uncertain; or (c) the seller may be obligated for unsatisfactory performance beyond the normal warranty.

b. The entity has neither continuing **managerial involvement** to an extent associated with ownership nor effective **control** over the goods.

c. The amount of the transaction can be **reliably measured**.

d. It is probable that the **economic benefits** will flow to the entity.

1) In some cases, this criterion may be met only when the consideration (money) is received or when an uncertainty is eliminated.

a) For example, if collection is certain, the amount involved is recognized as an **expense** (e.g., bad debt expense), not as an adjustment of revenue.

i) This principle applies to revenue from services, interest, royalties, and dividends, as well as sales of goods.

e. **Transaction costs** can be reliably measured.

1) Revenues and expenses related to the same transaction or other event should be matched. But if expenses cannot be reliably measured, revenues are not recognized, and any consideration already received is recorded as a liability.

Revenue Recognition – Rendering of Services

6. If the outcome of a services transaction can be reliably estimated, revenue is recognized based on the stage of completion (the **percentage-of-completion** method). The outcome can be reliably estimated when four conditions are met:

a. Revenue can be **reliably measured**.
b. It is probable that the **economic benefits** will flow to the entity.
c. The **stage of completion** can be reliably measured.
d. The **costs incurred** and the **costs to complete** can be reliably measured.

7. **Reliable estimates** of the stage of completion ordinarily are possible under an agreement among the parties that defines the enforceable rights of each party, the consideration, and the terms of settlement.

a. As services are performed, **revisions of estimates** are customary. They do not necessarily indicate that reliable measurement of revenue is not feasible.

8. The stage of completion of services should be estimated using the method that results in a reliable measurement of the particular transaction. Examples are surveys of work performed, services performed to date divided by total services, or costs incurred to date divided by total costs.
   a. **Progress payments and advances** are not necessarily correlated with the services performed.
9. In practice, if the number of acts to be performed over a defined period cannot be determined, the **straight-line method** of revenue recognition ordinarily is used.
10. If the outcome of a **services transaction** cannot be reliably estimated, recognized revenue equals recognized recoverable expenses.

EXAMPLE: Construction Contracts

If the outcome of the contract can be **estimated reliably**, revenue, expense, and profit are recognized based on the **stage of completion** at the balance sheet date (the percentage-of-completion method).

An **expected loss** (total costs > total revenue) is always **expensed immediately**.

The **stage of completion** is estimated using the method that reliably measures the work. (But **progress payments** by customers may not indicate the extent of work.) Possible methods include

a. Determining the ratio of costs incurred to total costs
b. Surveying work done
c. Measuring the physical proportion of work done

Costs incurred related to **future activity** are recorded as an asset if it is **probable** they will be **recovered**. The entity may use a construction in progress account to record costs and profit.

Construction in progress	XXX	
Cash or accounts payable		XXX
Construction in progress	XXX	
Construction profit		XXX

Ordinarily, **progress billings** are made and payments are received during the term of the contract.

Accounts receivable	XXX	
Progress billings		XXX

As cash is received, cash is debited and accounts receivable is credited. Neither billing nor the receipt of cash affects profit.

The difference between construction in progress (costs and recognized profit) and progress billings to date is a **current asset** if construction in progress is greater or as a **current liability** if billings are greater.

The **closing entry** is to debit progress billings and to credit construction in progress.

A variation on the preceding entries is to credit periodic revenue for the gross amount. This practice requires a **debit to a nominal account** (a cost of revenue earned account similar to cost of goods sold) that equals the costs incurred in the current period.

Construction in progress (profit)	XXX	
Construction expenses (a nominal account)	XXX	
Gross revenue		XXX

Revenue Recognition – Interest, Royalties, and Dividends

11. These amounts result from the use by others of entity assets. Revenue from these sources is recognized if two conditions are met:
    a. It is probable that the economic benefits will flow to the entity.
    b. Revenue can be reliably measured.
12. **Interest** is recognized using the **effective interest method**.
13. **Royalties**, for example, fees for use of patents, copyrights, or software, are recognized in accordance with the relevant agreement on the accrual basis. Royalties accrue according to the relevant agreement unless, based on its substance, another systematic and rational basis is more appropriate.

14. **Dividends** are recognized when the shareholder has the right to be paid. Dividends from pre-acquisition profit are a recovery of the cost of the equity securities. However, dividends are revenue unless they clearly represent such a recovery.
15. IAS 18 provides for **disclosures** that include accounting policies related to revenue recognition, such as the method for determining the stage of completion. It also provides for disclosure of the amounts of the significant categories of revenue for the period and the amount of revenue from exchanges included in each significant category.

Stop and review! You have completed the outline for this subunit. Study multiple-choice questions 7 through 9 on page 149.

3.4 FINANCIAL STATEMENTS

1. Under **IAS 1**, *Presentation of Financial Statements*, a **complete set of general-purpose financial statements** includes a statement of financial position at the **end of the period**. The complete set also includes the following reported **for the period**: (a) a statement of comprehensive income, (b) a statement of changes in equity, (c) a cash flow statement, (d) notes, and (e) a presentation of accounting policies.
    a. The statement of changes in equity shows either all such changes or all changes except those from transactions with equity holders.
    b. The **accrual basis** should be used to prepare all financial statements except the cash flow statement.

Fair Presentation

2. Financial position, financial performance, and cash flows should be fairly presented, ordinarily in statements prepared at least annually. Properly applying IFRSs almost always results in **fair presentation**.
    a. Notes describe the **basis of preparation** and the **significant policies** applied, make required disclosures not presented on the face of the statements, and provide additional information needed for a fair presentation.
    b. **Compliance with IFRSs** should be explicitly stated provided all requirements of relevant pronouncements are met.
    c. The **notes** and **disclosure of accounting policies** cannot be used to compensate for inappropriate accounting.
    d. In rare cases, compliance with a pronouncement may be misleading. Departure from it is permitted when necessary for a fair presentation if full disclosure is made.
3. **Accounting policies** and valuation methods are specific bases, conventions, rules, and practices adopted to prepare and present financial statements. They should be selected and applied to meet all requirements of standards and interpretations. Absent a requirement, management must use its judgment to provide relevant and reliable information.
    a. A **change** in an accounting policy requires disclosure in the notes as well as an explanation for the change.
    b. **Consistency** of presentation and classification, including consistent application of accounting policies, should be retained unless a change in presentation is justified by operational circumstances or the issuance of a new pronouncement.
4. Financial statements are prepared on a **going concern basis** unless management, based on an assessment of information for at least the next 12 months, expects to liquidate the entity or cease trading.
    a. Disclosure should be made of **material uncertainties** relating to circumstances that may create significant doubt about the entity's ability to continue.

5. **Comparative information** ordinarily should be disclosed regarding the previous period for all numerical information in the financial statements.
   a. Comparative, descriptive, or narrative information also should be presented if it is relevant to understanding the current statements.
   b. The **presentation or classification** of information may have changed. In this case, **comparative amounts** are reclassified if feasible. The improvement in comparability helps users to assess trends.

Statement of Financial Position (Balance Sheet)

6. Separate classifications on the balance sheet of **current and noncurrent** assets and liabilities should be presented unless a presentation by **order of liquidity** is reliable and more relevant. In either case, however, amounts expected to be recovered or settled in more than 12 months should be disclosed.
   a. **Current assets** are expected to be realized, or are held for sale or consumption, in the normal course of the operating cycle. Assets also are current if they are unrestricted cash items or cash equivalents, are held for trading purposes, or are expected to be realized within 12 months.
      1) All other assets are **noncurrent**, including long-term tangible, intangible, and financial assets.
      2) The **operating cycle** extends from the acquisition of assets for processing to realization in cash or cash equivalents.
         a) Inventories and trade receivables that enter into the normal operating cycle are current even though they are expected to be realized in more than 12 months.
         b) Assets **held primarily for trading** and the current portion of noncurrent assets are classified as current.
   b. **Current liabilities** are (1) expected to be settled in the normal course of the operating cycle, (2) due to be settled within 12 months after the balance sheet date, (3) held primarily to be traded, or (4) obligations for which the entity does not have an unconditional right to defer payment for 12 months after the balance sheet date.
      1) All other liabilities are **noncurrent**, including obligations the entity expects and has **discretion to refinance or roll over** for at least 12 months after the balance sheet date under **an existing loan agreement**. However, a **breach** of a long-term loan agreement that causes an obligation to be **due on demand** at the balance sheet date results in current classification.
      2) Certain liabilities, such as trade payables and accruals for various operating costs, are part of working capital. They are current even if they are due to be settled in more than 12 months after the balance sheet date. Other liabilities, such as the **current portion of long-term debt**, are not settled as part of the current operating cycle but are classified as current because they are due within 12 months after the balance sheet date.
7. **Additional items** should be separately presented based on judgments about (a) the nature and liquidity of assets; (b) the function of assets within the entity; and (c) the amounts, nature, and timing of liabilities.
8. **Deferred tax amounts** are not classified as current.
9. Total **assets held for sale** and assets in disposal groups held for sale are reported in line items. Liabilities in disposal groups held for sale also are reported in a line item.

Statement of Comprehensive Income

10. **All nonowner changes in equity** may be presented in one statement or two (e.g., an income statement and a statement of comprehensive income in which the first item is profit or loss).
    a. The **statement of changes in equity** must **not** report the components of comprehensive income.
    b. Comprehensive income for a period consists of (1) **profit or loss** (the bottom line of the income statement) and (2) **other comprehensive income.**
    c. The following are possible **components of other comprehensive income**:
        1) The effective portion of a gain or loss on a hedging instrument in a **cash flow hedge** (Subunit 3.5).
        2) A gain or loss on remeasurement of an **available-for-sale financial asset** (Subunit 3.5).
        3) **Translation** gains and losses for financial statements of foreign operations (Subunit 4.10).
        4) Changes in **revaluation surplus** for property, plant, and equipment (Subunit 3.7) and intangible assets (Subunit 3.8).
        5) Certain actuarial gains and losses of **defined employee benefit plans** (Subunit 4.1).

EXAMPLE

Statement of Comprehensive Income

Profit after taxes (or net income)		US $24,000
Other comprehensive income (net of tax):		
Changes in revaluation surplus	US $ 1,200	
Actuarial loss on defined benefit plans	(2,000)	
Gains on foreign currency translation	4,500	
Gains on remeasuring available-for-sale financial assets	1,100	
Effective portion of losses on cash flow hedges	(800)	(4,000)
Total comprehensive income		US $20,000

Income Statement

11. IFRSs do not require a particular income statement format, although, at a minimum, certain line items must be presented.
12. All recognized income and expense items are included in profit or loss unless a pronouncement requires otherwise.
13. Under the IFRSs, **no** items are classified as extraordinary, either on the statement or in the notes.
14. On the face of the income statement, profit or loss must be apportioned between (a) the equity holders of the **parent** and (b) the **noncontrolling interest**.
15. The nature and amount of **material items of income and expense** must be disclosed separately. Examples are (a) writedowns or disposals of property, plant, and equipment; (b) writedowns of inventory; (c) restructurings; (d) discontinued operations; and (e) disposals of investments.

16. An **analysis of expenses** should be presented, preferably on the face of the income statement. One of two classifications is used, based on which method provides information that is reliable and more relevant.

   a. The **nature-of-expense method** involves classifying items based on their inherent character, regardless of the organizational purposes served.

Nature-of-Expense Classification

Sales		US $400,000
Other income		20,000
Cost of materials	US $155,000	
Salaries, wages, and benefits	125,000	
Depreciation expense	20,000	
Advertising expense	15,000	
Other expense	10,000	
Finance costs	30,000	
Total expenses		(355,000)
Profit before tax		US $ 65,000

   b. The **function-of-expense method** (also called the cost-of-sales method) involves classifying items based on the organizational purpose served by the expense.

Function-of-Expense Classification

Sales	US $400,000
Cost of sales	(215,000)
Gross profit	US $185,000
Other income	20,000
Selling costs	(60,000)
Administrative expenses	(40,000)
Other expenses	(10,000)
Finance costs	(30,000)
Profit before tax	US $ 65,000

      1) If the function-of-expense method is used, additional information about the nature of expenses must be provided, including (a) depreciation, (b) amortization, and (c) staff costs (salaries and wages).

17. **Dividends** recognized as distributions and **dividends per share** should be disclosed on the face of the income statement, the statement of changes in equity, or in the notes. Declared but undistributed dividends, the per-share amount, and unrecognized cumulative preference (preferred) dividends are disclosed in the notes.

18. A **discontinued operation (DO)** is a component of an entity that has been disposed of or meets the criteria for classification as held for sale. It is (a) a separate major line of business or geographical operating area, (b) part of a single plan to dispose of such a line or area, or (c) a subsidiary acquired solely for resale.

   a. A **component of an entity** consists of operations and cash flows that are clearly distinguishable from the rest of the entity for financial reporting as well as operationally.

   b. A **single amount** is disclosed on the face of the income statement equal to the sum of

      1) After-tax **profit or loss** of the DO
      2) After-tax **gain or loss** on

         a) Measurement at **fair value minus cost to sell** or
         b) **Disposal** of the assets or disposal groups that constitute the DO.

   c. An **analysis of the single amount** is disclosed in the notes or on the face of the income statement.

   d. Net operating, investing, and financing **cash flows** of DOs are disclosed in the notes or on the face of the income statement. These items are explained later in Subunit 3.4.

Statement of Changes in Equity

19. Changes in equity resulting from **transactions with owners** must be presented separately from changes resulting from **nonowner transactions**.
20. Each of the following components must be **reported on the face of the statement**:
    a. Total comprehensive income, with separate subtotals for the parent and noncontrolling interest
        1) The components of comprehensive income are not presented in the statement.
    b. The effects of retrospective application of accounting policies or restatement of errors, with separate subtotals for each component of equity
    c. Contributions from and distributions to owners
    d. A reconciliation of the beginning balance for each component of equity to the ending balance that separately discloses each change

	Share Capital	Retained Earnings	Available-for-Sale Financial Assets	**Total Owners**	Noncontrolling Interest	**Total Equity**
Beginning balance	US $1,000,000	US $240,000	US $160,000	**US $1,400,000**	US $150,000	**US $1,550,000**
Total comprehensive income	--	110,000	15,000	**125,000**	15,000	**140,000**
Changes in accounting policy	--	(25,000)	--	**(25,000)**	--	**(25,000)**
Dividends distributed	--	(180,000)	--	**(180,000)**	--	**(180,000)**
Issue of share capital	200,000	--	--	**200,000**	--	**200,000**
Ending balance	US $1,200,000	US $145,000	US $175,000	**US $1,520,000**	US $165,000	**US $1,685,000**

Statement of Cash Flows

21. A cash flow statement is presented for each period for which financial statements are presented. Users need to assess the entity's ability to generate cash and cash equivalents.
    a. **Cash equivalents** are short-term, highly liquid investments readily convertible to known amounts of cash. Their risk of changes in value is insignificant. Usually, only investments with short maturities, e.g., 3 months or less, qualify.
22. Cash flows are **classified** and separately disclosed as from operating, investing, or financing activities.
23. **Operating activities.** These are the principal revenue-producing activities of the entity. They also include any other activities that are not investing or financing activities. Examples are
    a. Cash inflows from sales of goods and services, royalties, fees, commissions, refunds of taxes, and contracts held for dealing or trading
        1) Securities and loans held for dealing or trading are similar to inventory. Thus, the related cash flows are deemed to be from operating activities.
    b. Cash outflows to suppliers, employees, and governments
24. **Investing activities.** These include acquiring, or disposing of, long-term assets and other investments that are not cash equivalents. Examples are
    a. Cash inflows from sales and cash outflows from purchases of (1) property, plant, and equipment; (2) intangibles; (3) other long-term assets; (4) equity or debt of other entities; and (5) interests in joint ventures.
    b. Cash inflows from repayments of advances and loans made to others and from futures, forward, option, and swap contracts.
    c. Cash outflows from advances and loans made to others and from futures, forward, option, and swap contracts.

25. **Financing activities.** These result from changes in contributed equity and borrowing. Examples are
    a. Cash inflows from issuing equity instruments and long- or short-term debt.
    b. Cash outflows from purchases and redemptions of the entity's own shares and from repayments of debt. These outflows include a lessee's payments that reduce the liability arising from a finance lease.

Cash Flows from Operating Activities

26. They are reported using the direct method or the indirect method.
    a. The **direct method** discloses major classes of gross cash flows. It is the preferable (but not required) method because it provides more information than the indirect method. This information may be obtained from the accounting records or by adjusting sales, cost of sales, and other income statement items for
        1) Changes in inventories and in operating receivables and payables
        2) Other noncash items
        3) Investing or financing cash flows
    b. The **indirect method** adjusts profit or loss for (1) noncash transactions, (2) deferrals or accruals of past or future operating cash flows, and (3) income or expense related to investing or financing cash flows. The result is net cash flow from (used by) operating activities.
        1) The adjustments are similar to those for the direct method.

Other Statement of Cash Flow Issues

27. Major classes of gross **cash flows from investing and financing activities** are reported separately.
28. A **transaction in a foreign currency** is recorded using the exchange rate at the date of the cash flow between the entity's functional currency and the foreign currency.
    a. **Translation** of a foreign subsidiary's cash flows also is at current rates.
    b. However, **IAS 21**, *The Effects of Changes in Foreign Exchange Rates*, permits use of a **weighted-average rate** that approximates the actual rate for recording foreign currency transactions and for translation purposes.
        1) The effects of exchange rate fluctuations on cash and cash equivalents is separately reported as a reconciling item after operating, investing, and financing activities.
29. Cash flows from **interest and dividends** should be separately disclosed and consistently classified.
    a. Total interest paid is disclosed whether it was expensed or capitalized.
    b. A **financial institution** customarily classifies interest paid or received and dividends received as operating items.
30. For **entities other than financial institutions**, the following are the appropriate classifications:

	Operating	Financing	Investing
Interest paid	Yes	Yes	No
Interest received	Yes	No	Yes
Dividends paid	Yes	Yes	No
Dividends received	Yes	No	Yes

31. A cash flow associated with **income taxes** is separately disclosed. It is classified as an operating item unless specifically and practicably identified with investing or financing activities.
32. Aggregate cash flows from **acquisitions and disposals of business units** are separately disclosed and classified as investing items.
33. **Noncash investing and financing transactions** are not reported in the cash flow statement. They are disclosed elsewhere in the financial statements in a manner that conveys all relevant information. Examples are acquisition of a business unit by issuing equity instruments, a finance lease, and the conversion of debt to equity.
34. The policy for determining the **components of cash and cash equivalents** should be disclosed.
    a. The amounts in the cash flow statement and the balance sheet should be reconciled.

<u>**Notes**</u>

35. Notes describe the basis of preparation and the significant policies applied, make required disclosures not presented on the face of the statements, and provide additional information needed for a fair presentation.

<u>**Interim Financial Reporting**</u>

36. An **interim period** is shorter than a full year. An **interim financial report** contains either a **complete set** of financial statements or a set of **condensed** financial statements.
37. The **minimum content** of an interim financial report includes condensed versions of the balance sheet, income statement, statement of changes in equity, and cash flow statement. It also includes selected notes.
38. If the interim report includes a **complete set of statements**, they should meet the requirements for annual statements. If **condensed** statements are published, they should include the headings and subtotals in the annual statements.
    a. **Other line items or notes** are included if necessary to prevent the interim report from being misleading.
    b. **Basic and diluted earnings per share (EPS)** are presented on the face of the income statement.
    c. The **notes** should contain information about (1) use of accounting policies and computational methods, (2) the seasonality of operations, (3) unusual items, (4) changes in estimates, (5) debt and equity transactions, (6) dividends, (7) segment data, (8) material subsequent events, (9) changes in the entity's composition, and (10) changes in contingencies.
    d. The interim report should contain various comparative and cumulative statements.
39. **Materiality** is determined in relation to the interim data.
40. If an **estimate** in an interim report changes significantly in the final interim period, but no interim report is published for that period, disclosures should be made in the notes to the annual statements.
41. **Accounting policies** are the same in interim and annual statements.
    a. Frequency of measurement should not affect annual results, so interim measurements are made on a **year-to-date basis**. Thus, if an item is recognized and measured in an earlier interim period and the estimate changes in a later interim period, the earlier estimate is adjusted in the later interim report.
42. **Revenues received** and **costs incurred unevenly** over the year should not be anticipated or deferred at the end of an interim period unless such treatment is appropriate at year-end.
43. Interim reports ordinarily require a **greater use of estimates** than annual reports.

44. **Financial Statement Interrelationships**

a. Financial statements **complement each other**. They describe different aspects of the same transactions, and more than one statement will be necessary to provide information for a specific economic decision.

1) Moreover, the **elements** of one statement **articulate** (interrelate) with those of other statements.

b. Among the interrelationships are those listed below.

1) Accrual-basis **profit or loss** from the statement of income is reported in

a) A statement of cash flows prepared using the indirect method of presenting cash flows from operating activities.

b) Retained earnings, a component of the statement of financial position.

2) The components of cash and equivalents from the statement of financial position are reconciled with the corresponding items in the statement of cash flows.

3) Items of equity from the statement of financial position are reconciled with the beginning balances on the statement of changes in equity.

4) When an entity has **material ending inventories**, these amounts are reported in current assets on the statement of financial position and are reflected in the calculation of cost of goods sold on the statement of income.

5) **Amortization** and **depreciation** reported in the statement of income also are reflected in asset and liability balances in the statement of financial position.

45. The following are the 2008 financial statements of Total System Services, Inc. (TSYS), a U.S. corporation. The points of articulation are lettered. (See pages 124 through 127.)

a. Ending-balance **cash and equivalents** from the statement of financial position are also reported in the statement of cash flows [letters (a) and (b)].

b. Items of **shareholder's equity** from the statement of financial position are also reported in the statement of changes in equity and the statement of other comprehensive income [letters (c) through (j)].

c. **Retained earnings** from the statement of financial position is also reported in the statement of changes in equity and the statement of other comprehensive income [letters (k) and (l)].

d. Accrual-basis **profit or loss** (net income) from the statement of income is also reported in a statement of cash flows prepared using the indirect method of presenting cash flows from operations [letters (m) through (o)].

e. When an entity has **material ending inventories**, these amounts are reported in current assets on the statement of financial position and are reflected in the calculation of cost of goods sold on the statement of income.

Consolidated Balance Sheets

(in thousands, except per share data)	December 31, 2008	2007
Assets		
Current assets:		
Cash and cash equivalents (includes US $136.4 million on deposit with a related party at 2007) (Notes 2 and 3)	**US $ 220,018 (a)**	**US $ 210,518 (b)**
Restricted cash (includes US $8.2 million on deposit with a related party at 2007) (Note 2)	35,821	29,688
Accounts receivable, net of allowance for doubtful accounts and billing adjustments of US $8.3 million and US $10.1 million at 2008 and 2007, respectively (includes US $331 from related parties at 2007) (Note 2)	257,721	256,970
Deferred income tax assets (Note 18)	22,851	17,152
Prepaid expenses and other current assets (Note 4)	88,690	72,250
Total current assets	625,101	586,578
Property and equipment, net of accumulated depreciation and amortization (Notes 5 and 20)	280,174	283,138
Computer software, net of accumulated amortization (Note 6)	202,927	205,830
Contract acquisition costs, net of accumulated amortization (Note 7)	137,402	151,599
Goodwill (Note 8)	165,995	142,545
Equity investments (Note 9)	85,928	80,905
Other intangible assets, net of accumulated amortization (Note 10)	17,452	13,462
Other assets	35,273	14,963
Total assets	US $1,550,252	US $1,479,020
Liabilities and Shareholders' Equity		
Current liabilities:		
Accrued salaries and employee benefits	US $ 59,844	US $ 85,142
Accounts payable (includes US $12 and US $281 payable to related parties at 2008 and 2007, respectively) (Note 2)	32,318	41,817
Current portion of long-term debt (Note 11)	8,575	8,648
Current portion of obligations under capital leases (Note 11)	6,344	3,080
Other current liabilities (includes US $11.2 million payable to related parties at 2007) (Notes 2 and 12)	141,630	135,108
Total current liabilities	248,711	273,795
Long-term debt, excluding current portion (Note 11)	196,294	252,659
Deferred income tax liabilities (Note 18)	60,610	67,428
Obligations under capital leases, excluding current portion (Note 11)	13,576	3,934
Other long-term liabilities	30,212	28,151
Total liabilities	549,403	625,967
Noncontrolling interests in consolidated subsidiaries	9,901	8,580
Shareholders' equity (Notes 13, 14, 15 and 16):		
Common stock – US $0.10 par value. Authorized 600,000 shares; 200,356 and 199,660 issued at 2008 and 2007, respectively; 196,703 and 197,965 outstanding at 2008 and 2007, respectively	**20,036 (c)**	**19,966 (d)**
Additional paid-in capital	**126,888 (e)**	**104,762 (f)**
Accumulated other comprehensive (loss) income, net	**(6,627) (g)**	**28,322 (h)**
Treasury stock (shares of 3,652 and 1,695 at 2008 and 2007, respectively)	**(69,641) (i)**	**(34,138) (j)**
Retained earnings	**920,292 (k)**	**725,561 (l)**
Total shareholders' equity	990,948	844,473
Commitments and contingencies (Note 17)		
Total liabilities and shareholders' equity	US $1,550,252	US $1,479,020

Consolidated Statements of Income

(in thousands, except per share data)	Years Ended December 31, 2008	2007	2006
Revenues:			
Electronic payment processing services (includes US $5.6 million and US $5.1 million from related parties for 2007 and 2006, respectively)	US $ 976,852	US $ 955,926	US $ 989,062
Merchant acquiring services	261,427	254,069	260,275
Other services (includes US $9.0 million and US $7.8 million from related parties for 2007 and 2006, respectively)	253,779	218,128	185,096
Revenues before reimbursable items	1,492,058	1,428,123	1,434,433
Reimbursable items (includes US $2.5 million and US $1.8 million from related parties for 2007 and 2006, respectively)	446,550	377,713	352,738
Total revenues (Notes 2 and 20)	1,938,608	1,805,836	1,787,171
Expenses:			
Salaries and other personnel expense (Notes 14 and 19)	598,573	576,655	522,244
Net technology and facilities expense	298,701	273,154	327,254
Spin related expenses (Note 23)	11,140	13,526	—
Other operating expenses (includes US $9.5 million and US $9.6 million to related parties for 2007 and 2006, respectively)	212,094	211,277	227,853
Expenses before reimbursable items	1,120,508	1,074,612	1,077,351
Reimbursable items	446,550	377,713	352,738
Total expenses (Note 2)	1,567,058	1,452,325	1,430,089
Operating income	371,550	353,511	357,082
Nonoperating income (includes US $16.5 million and US $7.5 million from related parties for 2007 and 2006, respectively) (Note 2)	5,850	24,180	14,772
Income before income taxes, noncontrolling interests and equity in income of equity investments	377,400	377,691	371,854
Income taxes (Note 18)	131,795	143,668	126,182
Income before noncontrolling interest and equity in income of equity investments	245,605	234,023	245,672
Noncontrolling interest in consolidated subsidiaries' net income	(1,576)	(1,976)	(752)
Equity in income of equity investments (Note 9)	6,071	5,396	4,243
Net income	**US $ 250,100 (m)**	**US $ 237,443 (n)**	**US $ 249,163 (o)**
Basic earnings per share	US $ 1.28	US $ 1.21	US $ 1.27
Diluted earnings per share	US $ 1.27	US $ 1.20	US $ 1.26
Weighted average common shares outstanding	196,106	196,759	196,744
Increase due to assumed issuance of shares related to common equivalent shares	599	406	333
Weighted average common and common equivalent shares outstanding	196,705	197,165	197,077

Consolidated Statements of Cash Flows

(in thousands)	Years Ended December 31, 2008	2007	2006
Cash flows from operating activities:			
Net income	**US $250,100 (m)**	**US $237,443 (n)**	**US $249,163 (o)**
Adjustments to reconcile net income to net cash provided by operating activities:			
Noncontrolling interests in consolidated subsidiaries' net income, net of tax	1,576	1,976	752
Net gain on foreign currency translation	(10,481)	(41)	(1,232)
Equity in income of equity investments, net of tax	(6,071)	(5,396)	(4,243)
Dividends received from equity investments (Note 2)	6,421	2,994	2,371
Share-based compensation	24,733	18,620	9,157
Excess tax benefit from share-based payment arrangements	(90)	(8,507)	(2,984)
Depreciation and amortization	159,690	152,468	184,894
Amortization of debt issuance costs	154	–	–
Asset impairments	–	1,158	–
Provisions for (recoveries of) bad debt expenses and billing adjustments	618	1,231	1,614
Charges for transaction processing provisions	3,172	35	10,981
Deferred income tax (benefit) expense	(4,439)	(10,052)	(23,288)
Loss on disposal of equipment, net	182	500	147
(Increase) decrease in:			
Accounts receivable	(15,490)	(10,796)	(47,056)
Prepaid expenses, other current assets and other long-term assets	(48,024)	(14,870)	12,342
Increase (decrease) in:			
Accounts payable	4,550	10,080	673
Accrued salaries and employee benefits	(25,267)	4,445	(5,416)
Other current liabilities and other long-term liabilities	12,411	(46,426)	(2,116)
Net cash provided by operating activities	353,745	334,862	385,759
Cash flows from investing activities:			
Purchases of property and equipment, net	(47,969)	(55,274)	(26,506)
Additions to licensed computer software from vendors	(31,499)	(33,382)	(11,858)
Additions to internally developed computer software	(21,777)	(17,785)	(13,972)
Cash acquired in acquisitions	899	–	8,150
Cash used in acquisitions and equity investments	(51,826)	(12,552)	(77,541)
Subsidiary repurchase of noncontrolling interest	(343)	–	–
Additions to contract acquisition costs	(41,456)	(22,740)	(42,452)
Net cash used in investing activities	(193,971)	(141,733)	(164,179)
Cash flows from financing activities:			
Proceeds from borrowings	18,575	263,946	–
Excess tax benefit from share-based payment arrangements	90	8,507	2,984
Principal payments on long-term debt borrowings and capital lease obligations	(67,631)	(4,816)	(2,691)
Dividends paid on common stock (includes US $528.4 million and US $41.5 million to a related party for 2007 and 2006, respectively) (Note 2)	(55,449)	(655,246)	(51,269)
Subsidiary dividends paid to noncontrolling shareholders	(241)	–	–
Proceeds from exercise of stock options	268	11,672	4,253
Debt issuance costs	–	(767)	–
Repurchase of common stock	(35,698)	–	(22,874)
Net cash used in financing activities	(140,086)	(376,704)	(69,597)
Effect of exchange rate changes on cash and cash equivalents	(10,188)	4,970	(429)
Net (decrease) increase in cash and cash equivalents	9,500	(178,605)	151,554
Cash and cash equivalents at beginning of year	210,518	389,123	237,569
Cash and cash equivalents at end of year	**US $220,018 (a)**	**US $210,518 (b)**	US $389,123
Cash paid for interest	US $ 11,299	US $ 2,670	US $ 573
Cash paid for income taxes, net of refunds	US $151,165	US $176,141	US $144,880
Significant noncash transactions (Note 21)			

Consolidated Statements of Shareholders' Equity and Comprehensive Income

(in thousands, except per share data)	Common Stock Shares	Common Stock Dollars	Additional Paid-in Capital	Accumulated Other Comprehensive Income (Loss)	Treasury Stock	Retained Earnings	Total Shareholders' Equity
Balance as of December 31, 2005	197,975	US $19,797	US $ 50,666	US $ 5,685	US $(12,841)	US $ 949,465	US $1,012,772
Comprehensive income:							
Net income	–	–	–	–	–	**249,163 (o)**	249,163
Other comprehensive income	–	–	–	–	–	–	14,956
Comprehensive income	–	–	–	–	–	–	264,119
Common stock issued from treasury shares for exercise of stock options (Note 15)	–	–	117	–	482	–	599
Common stock issued for exercise of stock options (Note 14)	275	28	3,595	–	–	–	3,623
Common stock issued for nonvested awards (Note 14)	426	43	(43)	–	–	–	–
Share-based compensation (Note 14)	–	–	9,150	–	–	–	9,150
Cash dividends declared (US $0.27 per share)	–	–	–	–	–	(53,221)	(53,221)
Purchase of treasury shares (Note 15)	–	–	–	–	(22,874)	–	(22,874)
Tax benefits associated with share based payment arrangements	–	–	3,192	–	–	–	3,192
Balance as of December 31, 2006	198,676	19,868	66,677	20,641	(35,233)	1,145,407	1,217,360
Cumulative effect of change in accounting policy	–	–	–	–	–	(1,969)	(1,969)
Comprehensive income:							
Net income	–	–	–	–	–	**237,443 (n)**	237,443
Other comprehensive income	–	–	–	–	–	–	7,681
Comprehensive income	–	–	–	–	–	–	245,124
Common stock issued from treasury shares for exercise of stock options (Note 15)	–	–	314	–	1,095	–	1,409
Common stock issued for exercise of stock options (Note 14)	752	75	10,188	–	–	–	10,263
Common stock issued for nonvested awards (Note 14)	225	22	(22)	–	–	–	–
Common stock issued under commitment to charitable foundation	7	1	99	–	–	–	100
Difference in carrying value of asset transferred from related party	–	–	371	–	–	–	371
Share-based compensation (Note 14)	–	–	18,430	–	–	–	18,430
Cash dividends declared (US $3.31 per share)	–	–	–	–	–	(655,320)	(655,320)
Tax benefits associated with share based payment arrangements	–	–	8,705	–	–	–	8,705
Balance as of December 31, 2007	199,660	**19,966 (d)**	**104,762 (f)**	**28,322 (h)**	**(34,138) (i)**	**725,561 (l)**	844,473
Comprehensive income:							
Net income	–	–	–	–	–	**250,100 (m)**	250,100
Other comprehensive (loss) income, net of tax (Note 16)							
Foreign currency translation	–	–	–	(35,060)	–	–	(35,060)
Certain actuarial gains and losses on defined benefit postretirement healthcare plans	–	–	–	111	–	–	111
Other comprehensive (loss) income	–	–	–	–	–	–	(34,949)
Comprehensive income	–	–	–	–	–	–	215,151
Common stock issued from treasury shares for exercise of stock options (Note 15)	–	–	30	–	195	–	225
Common stock issued for exercise of stock options (Note 14)	2	1	42	–	–	–	43
Common stock issued for nonvested awards (Note 14)	692	69	(69)	–	–	–	–
Share-based compensation (Note 14)	–	–	24,583	–	–	–	24,583
Cash dividends declared (US $0.28 per share)	–	–	–	–	–	(55,369)	(55,369)
Purchase of treasury shares (Note 15)	–	–	–	–	(35,698)	–	(35,698)
Pre-spin tax benefits adjustment	–	–	(1,820)	–	–	–	(1,820)
Tax shortfalls associated with share based payment arrangements	–	–	(640)	–	–	–	(640)
Balance as of December 31, 2008	200,354	**US $20,036**	**US $126,888**	**US $ (6,627)**	**US $(69,641)**	**US $ 920,292**	US $ 990,948
		(c)	**(e)**	**(g)**	**(i)**	**(k)**	

Stop and review! You have completed the outline for this subunit. Study multiple-choice questions 10 through 15 beginning on page 150.

3.5 FINANCIAL ASSETS AND LIABILITIES

1. **IAS 39**, *Financial Instruments: Recognition and Measurement*, applies to most financial instruments and entities.

Definitions

2. **IAS 32**, *Financial Instruments: Disclosure and Presentation*
   a. A **financial instrument** is a contract that results in a financial asset of one entity and a financial liability or equity instrument of another entity.
   b. **Financial assets** include
      1) Cash
      2) Equity instruments of other entities (e.g., preference shares)
      3) Contract rights to receive cash or other financial assets from other entities (e.g., accounts receivable)
      4) Contract rights to exchange financial instruments under potentially favorable conditions (e.g., held options)
      5) Certain contracts to be settled in the entity's own equities.
   c. **Financial liabilities** include
      1) Contract obligations to deliver cash or another financial asset (e.g., accounts payable)
      2) Contract obligations to exchange financial instruments under potentially unfavorable conditions (e.g., written options)
      3) Certain contracts to be settled in the entity's own equities.
   d. An **equity instrument** is a contract that is evidence of a residual interest in an entity's net assets.

Recognition

3. A financial asset or liability is **initially recognized** only when the entity is a party to the contract. Thus, contract rights and obligations under **derivatives** are recognized as assets and liabilities, respectively.
   a. A **firm commitment** to buy or sell goods or services ordinarily does not result in recognition until at least one party has performed.
      1) However, certain contracts to buy or sell a nonfinancial item may result in recognition of an **asset or liability**.
         a) For example, a firm commitment to buy a commodity in the future that (1) can be settled in cash and (2) is not held for the purpose of receiving the commodity is treated as a **financial instrument**. Accordingly, its net fair value is recognized at the commitment date.
         b) If an **unrecognized** firm commitment is hedged in a **fair value hedge**, a change in its net fair value related to the hedged risk is recognized as an asset or liability.
4. An issuer of a **financial guarantee** initially recognizes a liability and measures it at fair value (unless the issuer qualifies to elect insurance accounting). **Subsequent measurement** is at the greater of (a) the amount based on accounting for provisions or (b) the amortized amount.

Derivatives

5. A **derivative** is a financial instrument whose value changes with the change in the **underlying**. Examples are futures, forward, swap, or option contracts. The underlying is a specified interest rate, security price, foreign currency exchange rate, price index, commodity price, etc. A derivative requires **little or no initial net investment** compared with contracts having similar responses to changing market conditions. It is **settled in the future**.
6. The categories of **financial instruments** include the following:
   a. Financial assets or liabilities **at fair value through profit or loss** satisfy one of the two following criteria:
      1) **Financial assets or liabilities held for trading** are intended to be sold or repurchased in the near term. Regardless of intent, however, a financial asset or liability is held for trading if it is included in a **portfolio** with a recent pattern of short-term profit taking. **Derivatives** also are deemed to be held for trading unless they are designated and effective as hedging instruments.

   b. **Held-to-maturity investments** are nonderivatives that have fixed or determinable payments and a fixed maturity. Moreover, the entity must have a positive intent and ability to hold such investments to maturity. However, this classification excludes items in the other categories.

   c. **Available-for-sale financial assets** are nonderivatives that (1) are designated as such or (2) do not fall within one of the other classifications.

Hedge Accounting

7. An entity can mitigate a possible loss by using derivatives or other hedging instruments to offset risk. Thus, an entity is said to hedge its financial positions.
   a. The following are the kinds of designated **hedging relationships**:
      1) A **fair value hedge** is a hedge of the exposure to changes in fair value of a **recognized asset or liability** or **unrecognized firm commitment**. The exposure must be due to a given risk and be able to affect profit or loss.
      2) A **cash flow hedge** is a hedge of the exposure to variability in cash flows that (a) is due to a given risk associated with a **recognized asset or liability** (e.g., interest on variable rate debt) or a **highly probable forecast transaction** and (b) could affect profit or loss.
         a) The hedge of the **foreign currency risk** of a firm commitment also may be accounted for as a cash flow hedge.
      3) A hedge of a **net investment in a foreign operation**.

   b. **Criteria for Hedge Accounting**
      1) The hedge is formally **designated and documented** at its inception, along with the risk management objective and strategy.
      2) The hedge is expected to be **highly effective** and can be **reliably measured**.
      3) A **forecast transaction** subject to a cash flow hedge must be highly probable and be able to affect profit or loss.
      4) The hedge is **continually assessed** and determined to have been effective.

Accounting for Receivables

8. The **net method** records receivables net of any applicable sales discount offered as an incentive for early payment. If the payment is not received during the discount period, **sales discounts forfeited** is credited at the end of the discount period or when the payment is received.
9. The **gross method** accounts for receivables at their face amount. If a discount is taken, a sales discount is recorded and classified as an offset to sales in the income statement to yield net sales.

Bad Debt Expense

10. When an entity records sales on account, it expects that some customers will pay late or not at all.
    a. The **allowance method** is the most common method of accounting for bad debt expense. It records the **impairment or bad debt loss** systematically. It is usually based on a percentage of either sales or the level of accounts receivable on an annual basis.
        1) The credit is to a **contra account**.
        2) As accounts receivable are written off, they are debited to the allowance. The **write-off** has no effect on working capital or total assets. The asset and the allowance are reduced by equal amounts.
        3) If the loss is a **percentage of sales**, the impairment is considered a function of sales on account. This approach is **income-statement oriented**.
        4) If the allowance is adjusted to reflect a **percentage of accounts receivable**, the impairment is a function of both sales and collections. This approach is **balance-sheet oriented**.
        5) A common method of estimating the loss is an analysis of accounts receivable known as an **aging schedule**. Stratifying the receivables according to the time they have been outstanding permits the use of different percentages for each category. The result should be a more accurate estimate of the recoverable amount than if a single rate is used.

Other Revenue Recognition Methods

11. The **installment method** recognizes profit on a sale when cash is collected rather than when the sale occurs. This method is used only when collection of the sales price is not reasonably assured.
    a. Revenues and cost of sales are recognized in the period of sale. The **gross profit** is deferred to the periods in which cash is collected.
    b. Special deferred gross profit and installment receivable accounts must be established for **each year**. The gross profit rate usually changes yearly.
12. The **cost-recovery method** may be used when (a) receivables are collected over an extended period, (b) considerable doubt exists as to collectibility, and (c) a reasonable estimate of the loss cannot be made. Profit is recognized only **after collections exceed cost**. Subsequent receipts are treated entirely as revenues.

Reducing Accounts Receivable Risk

13. Entities may transfer accounts receivable to third parties that assume the risk of nonpayment.
    a. **Pledging.** A pledge (a general assignment) uses receivables as collateral for a loan. The borrower agrees to use collections to repay the loan. Upon default, the lender can sell the receivables to recover the loan proceeds.
        1) A pledge is a relatively informal arrangement not reflected in the accounts, but disclosure should be made. The loan is recorded normally.

b. **Assignment.** An assignment (a specific assignment) is a more formal borrowing arrangement in which the receivables are used as **security**. The assignor (borrower) signs a promissory note and financing agreement, and specific receivables serve as collateral. The assignee (lender) reduces its risk by accepting only accounts with a high probability of collection.

1) Occasionally, the **debtors may be notified** to make payments to the assignee, but most assignments are not on a notification basis.
2) The loan is at a **specified percentage** of the face amount of the collateral. Interest and service fees are charged to the assignor.
3) **Assigned accounts** should be segregated from other accounts (debit accounts receivable assigned, credit accounts receivable), and a liability should be recognized. If the creditor may sell or repledge the collateral, it should recognize an asset and a liability.

c. **Factoring arrangements** discount receivables on a nonrecourse, notification basis. The receivables are sold outright, usually to a transferee (the factor) that assumes the full risk of collection, even in the event of a loss. When the conditions for loss of control are met, a factoring arrangement is accounted for as a sale of financial assets.

1) The **transferor** receives money that can be immediately reinvested into new inventories. It can offset the fee charged by the factor by eliminating its bad debts, credit department, and accounts receivable staff.
2) The **factor** usually receives a high financing fee plus a fee for performing the collection. Furthermore, the factor can often operate more efficiently than its clients because of the specialized nature of its services.

EXAMPLE

Assume a factor charges a 2% fee plus an interest rate of 18% on all monies advanced to the company. Monthly sales are US $100,000, and the factor advances 90% of the receivables submitted after deducting the 2% fee and the interest. Credit terms are net 60 days. What is the **cost to the transferor** of this arrangement?

Amount of receivables submitted	US $100,000
Minus: 10% reserve	(10,000)
Minus: 2% factor's fee	(2,000)
Amount accruing to the transferor	US $ 88,000
Minus: 18% interest for 60 days (on US $88,000)	(2,640)
Amount to be received immediately	US $ 85,360

The transferor also will receive the US $10,000 reserve at the end of the 60-day period if it has not been absorbed by sales returns and allowances. Thus, the total cost to factor the sales for the month is US $4,640 ($2,000 factor fee + interest of $2,640). Assuming that the factor has approved the customer's credit in advance, the seller will not absorb any bad debts.

The **journal entry** to record the preceding transaction is

Cash	US $85,360	
Equity in factored receivables	10,000	
Factor fee expense	2,000	
Prepaid interest	2,640	
Accounts receivable		US $100,000

Notes Receivable – Discounting

14. When a note receivable is **discounted** (sold), usually at a bank, the gain or loss on disposition of the note must be calculated.
15. The **holder** of the note receives the maturity amount (principal + interest at maturity) of the note minus the bank's discount. The bank usually collects the maturity amount from the **maker of the note**.

16. **Process of discounting.** The steps in discounting are to compute the
    a. Total interest receivable on the note (face amount × stated rate × note term).
    b. Maturity amount (face amount + total interest receivable).
    c. Accrued interest receivable (face amount × stated rate × note term elapsed).
    d. Bank's discount (maturity amount × bank's discount rate × note term remaining).
    e. Cash proceeds (maturity amount – bank's discount).
    f. Carrying amount of the note (face amount + accrued interest receivable).
    g. Gain or loss (proceeds – carrying amount).
        1) If a gain results, the entry is

Cash	XXX	
Gain on sale of note receivable		XXX
Note receivable		XXX
Interest receivable		XXX

        2) If a loss results, the entry is

Cash	XXX	
Loss on sale of note receivable	XXX	
Note receivable		XXX
Interest receivable		XXX

17. If a note is discounted **with recourse**, the note must be reported as a **new financial liability**.
    a. The credit in the previous entry is sometimes made to **notes receivable discounted**, a contra-asset account.
18. When computing yearly interest, the day the note is received, made, etc., is not included, but its maturity date is counted.

EXAMPLE

A 30-day note dated January 17 matures on February 16. Because 14 days (31 – 17) remain in January, 16 days must be counted in February.

Disclosures

19. **IFRS 7**, *Financial Instruments: Disclosures*, requires instruments to be grouped into classes, with disclosures by class about their significance and risk.
    a. **Qualitative** disclosures describe (1) risk exposures, (2) risk management, and (3) periodic changes.
    b. **Quantitative** disclosures include information summarizing exposure to each risk and detailed information about (1) credit risk, (2) liquidity risk, (3) market risk, and (4) concentrations of risk.
    c. When **financial assets are reclassified** from the **fair-value-through-profit-or-loss** or **available-for-sale** category, disclosures must be made about carrying amounts, fair values, gains and losses recognized in profit or loss or other comprehensive income, interest rates, and cash flows.
    d. Disclosures must be made based on a three-tier **hierarchy of fair value measurements.**
        1) Unadjusted quoted prices
        2) Other observable inputs for the asset or liability
        3) Unobservable inputs

e. Other disclosures address changes in the methods of determining fair value and a maturity analysis for **derivative liabilities**.

> **EXAMPLE**
>
> A firm commitment for a future transaction should be disclosed even if the transaction is not recognized.

Stop and review! You have completed the outline for this subunit. Study multiple-choice questions 16 through 22 beginning on page 152.

3.6 INVENTORY

1. **IAS 2**, *Inventories*, applies to most inventories.
2. **Inventories** are assets consisting of (a) items held for sale in the ordinary course of business, (b) work in progress, or (c) materials or supplies to be used in production.
   a. Inventories also include land or other property held for resale and costs of services for which the related revenues have not been recognized.
3. Inventories are measured at the **lower of cost or net realizable value**.
   a. **Cost** includes **purchase** costs (after subtraction of trade discounts), **conversion** costs, and other costs of bringing inventories to their current location and condition, such as taxes, transport, labor, utility fees, and handling.
      1) **Conversion costs** include costs directly related to units of production, e.g., **direct labor**, and systematically allocated fixed and variable production overheads.
      2) **Fixed overheads** are indirect costs that are relatively uncorrelated with production volume, e.g., depreciation, maintenance, and administration.
         a) Fixed overheads are allocated based on **normal capacity**, an expected average use of facilities under normal conditions. Unallocated overheads are expensed. If production is unusually high, fixed overhead per unit is decreased to avoid measurement above cost. Variable overheads are allocated based on actual use.
      3) **Variable overheads** are indirect costs that are nearly directly correlated with production volume, e.g., indirect materials and labor.
      4) **Joint products** or a main product and a **by-product** may be produced simultaneously. **Joint conversion costs** are allocated on a rational and consistent basis, for example, **relative sales values** at the time of separate identification or at the time of completion. If a by-product is immaterial, it may be measured at net realizable value and subtracted from the cost of the main product.

Net Realizable Value (NRV)

4. NRV equals estimated selling price in the ordinary course of business minus estimated completion and selling costs. If the cost of inventories is not recoverable, they are written down to NRV. For example, (a) increases in completion or selling costs, (b) obsolescence, or (c) decreases in selling prices may justify a writedown to NRV.
   a. **Writedowns** are usually on a per-item basis. However, sometimes writedowns for groups of similar or related items, such as a product line, may be proper. For a service provider, writedowns may be proper for each service for which costs are accumulated and a separate price is charged.
   b. **Materials** are not written down if the finished goods will be sold for an amount at least equal to cost. Otherwise, materials may be written down.

c. **NRV** is assessed each period. Accordingly, inventory may be written up to the lower of cost or the revised NRV.

Expensing Inventory

5. Normally, inventory sold is **expensed** when the related revenue is recognized. However, losses and writedowns to NRV are expensed when they occur.
   a. If a **separate expense account is not used** (for example, expense due to decline of inventory to NRV), the ending inventory will be reduced directly. The result will be an increase in cost of goods sold. The effect is to hide the loss in cost of goods sold.
      1) If a **separate expense account is used**, the writedown appears on the income statement as a reduction of gross profit (sales – cost of goods sold). The advantage is that cost of goods sold is not misstated.
   b. A reversal of a writedown to NRV because of an increase in NRV reduces the amount of inventories expensed in the **period of the reversal.**

Inventory On Hand

6. Inventory **quantities** are usually determined by either physical counts at the end of reporting periods or perpetual records. Goods **not physically on hand** may properly be included. For example, goods out on **consignment** are effectively part of the inventory.
   a. Whether goods recently purchased or sold and currently in transit are properly included may be a function of the **shipping terms** in the relevant contract.
      1) The term **FOB shipping point** means that title passes to the buyer at the time and place of shipment.
      2) The term **FOB destination** means that title passes when tender of delivery of the goods is made at the destination.

Inventory Systems

7. A **periodic system** is used by an entity with no need to monitor inventory on a continuous basis.
8. A **perpetual system** is used by an entity that requires continuously accurate balances.
9. **Purchases**
   a. In a **periodic system**, the beginning balance is retained throughout the period. Acquisitions are debited to purchases.
   b. In a **perpetual system**, acquisitions are added to inventory as they occur.

Periodic			Perpetual		
Purchases	x,xxx		Inventory	x,xxx	
Accounts payable		x,xxx	Accounts payable		x,xxx

10. **Sales**
    a. In a **periodic system**, changes in inventory and cost of goods sold are recorded only at the end of the period.
       1) **Cost of goods sold** equals goods available for sale (beginning inventory plus purchases) minus ending inventory.
    b. In a **perpetual system**, inventory and cost of goods sold are adjusted as sales occur.

Periodic			Perpetual		
Accounts receivable	x,xxx		Accounts receivable	x,xxx	
Sales		x,xxx	Sales		x,xxx
No entry			Cost of goods sold	x,xxx	
			Inventory		x,xxx

11. **Closing**

a. A physical inventory count must be taken at specified intervals, regardless of which system is used.

1) In a **periodic system**, the physical count must be taken at the end of each reporting period. It allows adjustment of the inventory balance to the physical count and calculation of cost of goods sold.

Periodic			Perpetual		
Inventory (physical count)	x,xxx		Inventory over-and short (dr, cr)	xx	
Cost of goods sold (residual)	x,xxx		Inventory (correction) (cr, dr)		xx
Purchases (total for period)		x,xxx			
Inventory (beginning balance)		x,xxx			

2) In a **perpetual system**, a physical count at least once a year is needed to detect material misstatements in the perpetual records.

a) **Inventory over-and-short** is debited (credited) when the physical count is less (greater) than the balance in the perpetual records.

b) Inventory over-and-short is either closed to cost of goods sold or reported separately under other revenues or other expenses.

Cost Formulas

12. **Specific identification** assigns the costs of items that are not usually interchangeable and of goods and services segregated for specific projects.

a. The costs of inventories not assigned using specific identification should be accounted for using the **first-in, first-out (FIFO)** method or the **weighted-average** method.

1) The **last-in, first-out (LIFO) method** is **not** permitted.

b. The same formula should be used for all inventories with a similar nature and use.

13. **FIFO** considers the first goods purchased to be the first goods sold. Accordingly, **ending inventory** consists of the latest purchases. **Cost of goods sold** consists of goods purchased at the beginning of the current period and in prior periods.

a. The measurement is the same in a periodic or a perpetual system.

14. **Weighted-average.** This formula divides the total cost of beginning inventory and all purchases by the sum of the number of units in beginning inventory plus those purchased to obtain a weighted-average **unit cost**.

a. The **moving-average method** calculates a **weighted average to date** that can be used only with perpetual inventory records in which inventory costs also are included. After each purchase, a new weighted-average unit cost is calculated for the goods then on hand.

Retail Method

15. Retailers that have many transactions in low-cost goods usually find it less expensive to estimate ending inventory and cost of goods sold using the retail method. They ordinarily price goods soon after acquisition and do not record the cost for each transaction. Moreover, percentage markups within departments are usually similar, which makes it possible to estimate costs.

a. Because cost-retail ratios vary among departments, this method is often applied at the departmental level. The results are added for reporting.

b. Records of the **beginning inventory and net purchases** are maintained at cost and retail. Sales at retail and any other appropriate items are subtracted from goods available for sale at retail (the sum of beginning inventory and net purchases at retail) to provide **ending inventory at retail**.

   1) This amount is adjusted to estimated cost using a **cost-retail ratio**, which is based on actual current costs and retail prices.

c. The following **records** must be available to implement the retail method:

   1) Beginning inventory at cost and retail
   2) Purchases at cost and retail
   3) Markups, markdowns, cancelations, and employee discounts
   4) Other adjustments, such as sales returns and allowances; transportation-in (freight-in); purchase discounts; purchase returns and allowances; and losses on damaged, stolen, obsolete, or deteriorated goods
   5) Sales

d. **Normal spoilage** is anticipated in setting retail prices and is considered in the determination of the cost-retail ratio. However, normal spoilage ultimately is a reduction in the goods available to be sold. Thus, it is subtracted from the retail column in the same manner as sales.

   1) **Abnormal spoilage** is not a cost of good units and is not anticipated in setting retail prices. Accordingly, it is subtracted from both cost and retail in arriving at goods available for sale.

e. Several versions of the retail method may be used. **FIFO cost** is the most straightforward. The cost-retail ratio is computed for **adjusted purchases**. Ending inventory is assumed to include only goods from current purchases. Moreover, to approximate cost, **markups are added** to and **markdowns are subtracted** from purchases at retail to determine the ratio.

f. **Average cost.** The difference between average cost and FIFO cost is that the cost-retail ratio for average cost is based on **goods available for sale** (BI + Pur).

g. **Lower of average cost or NRV** is a popular method known as the conventional retail inventory method. It calculates the cost-retail ratio using **goods available for sale**, with an adjustment for **net markups but not net markdowns**.

COMPARATIVE EXAMPLE

	Cost	Retail
Beginning inventory	US $ 90,000	US $130,000
Purchases	330,000	460,000
Markups		10,000
Markdowns		40,000
Sales		480,000

Ending inventory at retail is US $80,000 ($130,000 + $460,000 + $10,000 – $40,000 – $480,000).

The cost-retail ratio for the average-cost retail method is 420 ÷ 560. Markups and markdowns are included in goods available at retail.

The cost-retail ratio for the **FIFO-cost** retail method is 330 ÷ 430. Markups and markdowns are applied to goods purchased.

The cost-retail ratio for the lower-of-cost-or-NRV retail method is 420 ÷ 600. Markups, not markdowns, are included in the calculation of the percentage. The exclusion of markdowns from the ratio results in a measurement that approximates the lower of average cost or NRV.

Stop and review! You have completed the outline for this subunit. Study multiple-choice questions 23 through 25 beginning on page 154.

3.7 PROPERTY, PLANT, AND EQUIPMENT (PPE) – ACQUISITION AND MEASUREMENT

1. Property, plant, and equipment, also called fixed assets, consist of tangible property expected to benefit the entity for more than one year that are held for
    a. The production or supply of goods or services
    b. Rental to others
    c. Administrative purposes

Initial Cost

2. PPE are **measured initially at cost** if the **recognition criteria** are met. Thus, (a) it must be probable that the entity will receive future economic benefits, and (b) the cost must be reliably measurable.
    a. **Initial cost** includes
        1) The **net purchase price** (minus trade discounts and rebates, plus purchase taxes and import duties).
        2) The **directly attributable costs** of bringing the asset to the **location and condition** needed for its intended operation, such as architects' and engineers' fees, site preparation, delivery and handling, installation, assembly, and testing.
        3) The **estimated costs of eventual decommissioning** of the asset, i.e., for removal and site restoration.
    b. The following are examples of **costs excluded** from the initial measurement of PPE:
        1) Administrative and other general overhead
        2) Preproduction costs, e.g., those for opening a new plant, introducing a new product, or doing business in a new place
        3) Interest **not** associated with a self-constructed asset
    c. **Interest** (borrowing costs) directly attributable to the acquisition, construction, or production of a qualifying asset is included in its initial carrying amount.
        1) **Qualifying assets** are those that require a substantial time to prepare for their intended use or sale.
            a) They do not include
                i) Assets measured at **fair value.**
                ii) Inventories produced repetitively in large quantities that require a substantial time to prepare for sale.
        2) Interest on funds borrowed **specifically** to acquire a qualifying asset, minus **investment income**, are capitalizable.
        3) If funds obtained by **general borrowing** are used for a qualifying asset, the capitalized amount also will include the product of (a) a **weighted-average of general borrowing rates** for the period and (b) the expenditures for the asset.
            a) The capitalized amount may not exceed the periodic amount incurred.
        4) **Capitalization begins** when expenditures for the asset and borrowing costs are being incurred and activities to prepare the asset for its intended use have begun.

5) **Capitalization ends** upon substantial completion of the asset.

EXAMPLE

Lyssa Co. constructed a building for its own use. The capitalization period began on 10/1/Year 1 and ended on 9/30/Year 2. The average accumulated expenditures are based on the following **construction-related expenditures** and the amounts of time they incurred interest:

			AAE
10/1/Year 1	US $500,000 × (12 ÷ 12)	=	US $ 500,000
1/1/Year 2	$400,000 × (9 ÷ 12)	=	300,000
4/1/Year 2	$600,000 × (6 ÷ 12)	=	300,000
7/1/Year 2	$400,000 × (3 ÷ 12)	=	100,000
9/30/Year 2	$900,000 × (0 ÷ 12)	=	0
			US $1,200,000

On 10/1/Year 1, Lyssa **specifically borrowed** US $1,000,000 at a rate of 10% to finance the construction. Its **other borrowings** outstanding during the entire construction period consisted of the following bond issues:

US $2,000,000 principal, 8% interest rate
US $6,000,000 principal, 9% interest rate

All interest is paid at fiscal year-end. Accordingly, the **weighted-average rate on other borrowings** is 8.75%.

		Interest		Principal	Rate
(US $2,000,000 × 8%)	=	US $160,000		US $2,000,000	
(US $6,000,000 × 9%)	=	540,000		6,000,000	
		US $700,000	÷	US $8,000,000	8.75%

Interest incurred for the project is US $117,500.

US $1,000,000 × 10%	=	US $100,000
(US $1,200,000 – $1,000,000) × 8.75%	=	17,500
		US $117,500

Subsequent Costs

d. These are incurred to add to, replace part of, or service an item of PPE. They are added to its carrying amount if the recognition criteria are met.

1) Thus, day-to-day servicing costs are expensed, but costs of replacements and major inspections are included in the carrying amount.

Nonmonetary Exchanges

3. An item(s) of PPE may be obtained for a nonmonetary asset(s) or a combination of nonmonetary and monetary assets. The cost is measured at **fair value** unless the **exchange lacks commercial substance** or the fair value of what is received or given is **not** reliably measurable.

a. An acquired item not recorded at fair value is measured at the carrying amount of what was given.

Subsequent Measurement

4. **Measurement after initial recognition** of an item of PPE is at cost minus accumulated depreciation and impairment losses.

a. However, an item of PPE whose **fair value can be reliably measured** may be carried at a **revalued** amount equal to **fair value at the revaluation date** (minus subsequent accumulated depreciation and impairment losses).

b. **Revaluation** is needed whenever fair value and the asset's carrying amount differ materially. Some assets may be revalued as often as annually.
   1) Accumulated depreciation is restated proportionately or eliminated.
   2) If an item of PPE is revalued, all of the items in its class (e.g., land, buildings, or office equipment) also should be revalued.

c. A **revaluation increase** is credited **directly to equity** (revaluation surplus), but a reversal of a previous decrease is recognized in profit or loss.
   1) A **revaluation decrease** is recognized in **profit or loss** after any revaluation surplus is reduced to zero.
   2) The **revaluation surplus** may be transferred directly to **retained earnings** when the asset is **derecognized**, for example, after disposal of the asset.
      a) Also, the difference between revalued depreciation and original-cost depreciation (if a surplus) may be transferred to retained earnings while the item is in use.

Depreciation

5. Depreciation systematically allocates the depreciable amount of an item of PPE over its useful life. It is **not** a process of valuation.
   a. **Each significant part** of the item is separately depreciated.
   b. The periodic charge for depreciation is offset by a credit to **accumulated depreciation**, a **contra-asset**.
   c. Depreciation does not provide resources for **asset replacement**. Except to the extent that it is tax deductible and reduces cash outlays for taxes, it does not affect cash.
   d. Depreciation is **not always recognized** in **profit or loss**. For example, under the **full-cost method**, depreciation on a factory building and machinery used in production of inventory is charged to overhead, which in turn is applied to work-in-progress.
   e. Residual value and the useful life are **estimates** reviewed at least every year-end.
      1) The **residual value** is the amount (after disposal costs) receivable currently if the item were of the same age and in the same condition as expected at the end of the useful life.
      2) The **useful life** is estimated with regard to the item's utility to the entity, not its economic life.
      3) Periodic review of the **useful life** results in adjustment of current and future depreciation if expectations differ significantly from prior estimates. Periodic review of the **depreciation method** results in a change of method if the expected pattern of economic benefits has changed significantly.
         a) These changes are treated as **changes in estimate**.
   f. The **amount to be depreciated** over the asset's useful life equals the cost, or other financial statement amount, **minus the residual value** estimated at the acquisition date.
      1) But if items of PPE are revalued, a new estimate of the residual value is made.
   g. The **depreciation period** begins when the asset is available for use and ends at the earlier of when it is classified as held for sale or derecognized.

Allocating the Depreciable Amount

h. The method chosen should reflect the **pattern in which economic benefits are consumed**.

1) **Straight-line.** Under this method, depreciation is a **constant amount** (depreciable amount ÷ estimated useful life) for each period. Thus, its effect on profit or loss is constant.

EXAMPLE

An entity paid US $112,000,000 for a new machine that it estimates will produce 8,000,000 brake pads before becoming obsolete. Its estimated useful life is 10 years. At the end of its useful life, the entity estimates that the machine can be sold for US $14,000,000.

Depreciation expense for each year is

$$\frac{\text{US } \$112{,}000{,}000 - \$14{,}000{,}000}{10} = \text{US } \$9{,}800{,}000$$

2) **Accelerated methods** are time-based techniques that result in **decreasing depreciation expense** over the life of the asset. Thus, the effect on profit or loss decreases.

a) **Diminishing-balance (DB)** determines periodic depreciation by multiplying the **carrying amount** (**not** a depreciable amount equal to cost minus residual value) at the beginning of each period by some percentage (e.g., 200%, 150%, or 125%) of the straight-line rate.

$$\text{Carrying amount} \times \text{DB rate}$$

i) The carrying amount decreases by the depreciation recognized. The result is the use of a **constant rate** against a diminishing balance.

ii) **Residual value** is ignored in determining the carrying amount, but the asset is not depreciated below residual value.

EXAMPLE

If the entity chooses the DB method at 200% of the straight-line rate, the DB rate is 20% [(100% ÷ 10-year useful life) x 2].

Year	Carrying Amount	Times: Declining-Balance %	Equals: Depreciation Expense	Accumulated Depreciation
1	US $112,000,000	20%	US $22,400,000	US $22,400,000
2	89,600,000	20%	17,920,000	40,320,000
3	71,680,000	20%	14,336,000	54,656,000
4	57,344,000	20%	11,468,800	66,124,800
5	45,875,200	20%	9,175,040	75,299,840
6	36,700,160	20%	7,340,032	82,639,872
7	29,360,128	20%	5,872,026	88,511,898
8	23,488,102	20%	4,697,620	93,209,518
9	18,790,482	20%	3,758,096	96,967,614
10	15,032,386		1,032,386	98,000,000

Depreciation expense is US $1,032,386 in the last year. The asset is not depreciated below its US $14,000,000 residual value.

b) **Sum-of-the-years'-digits (SYD)** multiplies a **constant depreciable amount** (cost – residual value) by a diminishing fraction. It is a diminishing-rate, diminishing-charge method.

i) The SYD fraction's **numerator** for a given year equals the number of years of remaining useful life.

ii) If n is the total useful life of the asset, the formula to compute the **denominator** is

$$n\frac{(n+1)}{2}$$

EXAMPLE

The denominator of the SYD fraction is 55 given a useful life of 10 years {[10 × (10 + 1)] ÷ 2}. Depreciation expense for the **first year** is calculated as follows:

$$(\text{US }\$112{,}000{,}000 - \$14{,}000{,}000) \times \frac{10}{55} = \text{US }\$17{,}818{,}182$$

Depreciation expense for the **second year** is calculated as follows:

$$(\text{US }\$112{,}000{,}000 - \$14{,}000{,}000) \times \frac{9}{55} = \text{US }\$16{,}036{,}364$$

3) The **units-of-production** method calculates depreciation as a function of an asset's use or output rather than the time it has been held. Thus, its effect on profit or loss is unpredictable.

a) The **depreciable amount** is

Cost – Residual value

b) A **cost driver** must be chosen to measure the asset's productive output.

c) **Periodic depreciation expense** is calculated as follows:

$$\frac{\text{Depreciable amount} \times \text{Cost drive measure for period}}{\text{Estimated lifetime driver units}}$$

EXAMPLE

In its first year of operation, the machine produced 940,000 brake pads. Depreciation expense for the year is calculated as follows:

$$\frac{(\text{US }\$112{,}000{,}000 - \$14{,}000{,}000) \times 940{,}000}{8{,}000{,}000} = \text{US }\$11{,}515{,}000$$

Impairment

6. **IAS 36**, *Impairment of Assets*, states that an asset is impaired when its **carrying amount exceeds its recoverable amount**. The entity assesses at each reporting date whether an indication of impairment exists. Given such an indication, the recoverable amount must be estimated. Moreover, **intangible assets** with indefinite useful lives or those not yet available for use and **goodwill** are tested for impairment annually.

a. The **recoverable amount** of an asset is the greater of its fair value minus cost to sell or value in use.

b. The recognized **impairment loss** is the excess of the asset's carrying amount over its recoverable amount.

Assets Held for Sale

7. According to **IFRS 5**, *Noncurrent Assets Held for Sale and Discontinued Operations*, a noncurrent asset (or disposal group) is **held for sale** if recovery of its carrying amount will be primarily by sale, not use. Sale must be highly probable.
   a. A **disposal group** is a group of assets to be disposed of in one transaction with directly associated liabilities.
   b. Noncurrent assets to be **abandoned** are not classified as held for sale. A temporarily idled asset is not deemed to be abandoned.
   c. Held-for-sale assets or disposal groups are reported at the **lower of their carrying amount or fair value minus costs to sell**.
   d. Held-for-sale assets and assets in disposal groups are **not depreciated or amortized**.
   e. Just before an asset (disposal group) is first classified as held for sale, its carrying amount is measured in accordance with the IFRSs. Any subsequent writedown to fair value minus cost to sell is treated as an **impairment loss**.
      1) A later **increase in fair value minus cost to sell** is recognized as a gain but only to the extent of previously recognized impairment losses.

Stop and review! You have completed the outline for this subunit. Study multiple-choice questions 26 through 28 beginning on page 155.

3.8 INTANGIBLE ASSETS

1. **IAS 38**, *Intangible Assets*, defines an intangible asset as "an identifiable nonmonetary asset without physical substance."
2. An intangible asset is **identifiable** if it is **separable** (able to be divided from the entity and transferred, sold, licensed, etc., alone or with a related contract, asset, or liability) or results from **contractual or legal rights** (even if such rights are not separable).
   a. An **asset** is a resource **controlled** by the entity as a result of past events and from which economic benefits are expected.
3. Examples of intangible assets to which IAS 38 applies include
   a. Licenses
   b. Patents (an exclusive legal right to use or sell an invention, such as a device or process)
   c. Computer software not integral to the related hardware (but an operating system is an item of PPE)
   d. Copyrights (legal protection for tangible expressions of ideas, e.g., novels, songs, and software)
   e. Franchises
   f. Customer lists obtained from others
   g. Mortgage servicing rights

Internally Generated Intangible Assets

4. Internally generated intangible assets may be recognized in certain cases.
   a. **Research** is "original and planned investigation undertaken with the prospect of gaining new scientific or technical knowledge and understanding." Expenditures on research are **expensed** when incurred.
   b. **Development** is "the application of research findings or other knowledge to a plan or design for the production of new or substantially improved materials, devices, products, processes, systems, or services prior to the commencement of commercial production or use."

1) Development results in **recognition of an intangible asset** if the entity can demonstrate the (a) technical feasibility of completion of the asset, (b) intent to complete, (c) ability to use or sell the asset, (d) way in which it will generate probable future economic benefits, (e) availability of resources to complete and use or sell the asset, and (f) ability to measure reliably expenditures attributable to the asset.

c. Intangible assets are not recognized for internally generated brands, mastheads, publishing titles, customer lists, and similar items.

Other Issues

5. **Initial recognition** of an intangible asset is at cost. Recognition is permitted only when it is **probable** that the entity will receive the expected economic benefits, and the **cost** is reliably measurable.
6. **Cost** includes the purchase price (including purchase taxes and import duties) and any **directly attributable costs** to prepare the asset for its intended use, such as legal fees.
   a. If an intangible asset is obtained in a **business combination**, its cost is its fair value at the date of acquisition.
7. **Internally generated goodwill** is not an asset, but goodwill acquired in a **business combination** is considered an asset.
   a. Goodwill is recognized as an asset equal to the excess of the cost of the combination over the acquirer's interest in the fair value of the identifiable assets, liabilities, and contingent liabilities acquired.
8. Items expensed as incurred include expenditures for research and for
   a. Startup activities (unless included in an item of PPE)
   b. Training
   c. Advertising and promotion
   d. Relocating or reorganizing part or all of an entity
9. **Past expenses.** Once expenditures for an intangible item have been expensed, they may not subsequently be capitalized.

Measurement after Recognition

10. An intangible asset is carried at **cost** minus any accumulated amortization and impairment losses, or at a **revalued amount**.
    a. The revaluation model is similar to that for items of PPE (initial recognition of an asset at cost). However, fair value must be determined based on an **active market**.
11. The **useful life** of an intangible asset is finite or indefinite. If it is determined to be **finite**, the entity assesses the number of production (or similar) units in that life.
    a. An **indefinite life** has no foreseeable limit on the period during which the asset will produce net cash inflows.

Amortization

12. Amortization of an intangible asset with a finite useful life begins when it is **available for use**. Its depreciable amount is systematically allocated over its **useful life**.
    a. Amortization is normally recognized in profit or loss.
    b. The **amortization method** for an intangible asset should reflect the pattern of consumption of the economic benefits. But if a reliable determination cannot be made, the straight-line method is used.
    c. The **residual value** is presumed to be zero barring a third-party commitment to purchase or the existence of an active market for the asset that will probably exist at the end of the useful life.

d. The amortization period and method should be **reviewed** at least at each balance sheet date. Any changes should be treated as changes in estimate.

e. An intangible asset with an indefinite useful life is **not amortized**.

Stop and review! You have completed the outline for this subunit. Study multiple-choice questions 29 and 30 on page 156.

3.9 SUMMARY

1. Financial statements provide information about (a) accountability for assets, (b) ability to generate cash, (c) financial position, (d) performance and its variability, and (e) changes in financial position.
2. Information should be readily understandable by reasonably knowledgeable users, but relevant information should not be excluded because of its complexity.
3. Information has relevance if users are able to predict the outcome of future events or confirm or correct their prior expectations.
4. Information is reliable if it is free of material error and bias. Users should be able to depend upon it to represent faithfully the economic transactions or events it purports to represent or could reasonably be expected to represent.
5. Financial statements must be comparable for the same entity over time. They also should be comparable among different entities.
6. Assets are resources "controlled by the entity as a result of past events and from which future economic benefits are expected to flow to the entity."
7. Liabilities are current obligations "of the entity arising from past events, the settlement of which is expected to result in an outflow from the entity of resources embodying economic benefits."
8. "Equity is the residual interest in the assets of the entity after deducting all its liabilities."
9. Income is defined as "increases in economic benefits during the accounting period in the form of inflows or enhancements of assets or decreases of liabilities that result in increases in equity, other than those relating to contributions from equity participants."
10. The usual procedures for income recognition, such as that revenue be earned, reflect the recognition criteria, that is, (a) reliable measurement and (b) a sufficient probability. Thus, income is recognized when an increase in future economic benefits associated with an increase in an asset or a decrease in a liability has arisen that can be reliably measured.
11. The bases for expense recognition are direct association (matching), systematic and rational allocation, and immediate recognition.
12. Measurement bases include (a) historical cost, (b) realizable (settlement) value, and (c) present value.
13. Accrual accounting recognizes the financial effects of transactions and other events in the periods when they occur and records and reports them in the periods to which they relate. Accordingly, accrual accounting also considers (a) noncash exchanges of goods or services, (b) credit transactions, (c) nonreciprocal transfers, (d) price changes, (e) changes in fair values, (f) changes in form of assets or liabilities, etc.
14. The required steps in the accounting cycle are (a) identifying and measuring transactions and events to be recognized, (b) journalization, (c) posting to ledgers, (d) developing a trial balance, (e) making adjustments, (f) statement presentation, and (g) closing the books.
15. Revenue is measured at the fair value of the consideration received or receivable by the entity. This amount is ordinarily determined by the parties to the transaction after due allowance for trade discounts and volume rebates. If the transaction is effectively a financing arrangement, future receipts are discounted at an imputed rate to determine the fair value.

16. The following are the conditions for recognizing revenue for a sale of goods: (a) The entity has transferred the significant risks and rewards of ownership; (b) the entity has neither continuing managerial involvement to an extent associated with ownership nor effective control over the goods; (c) the amount can be reliably measured; (d) it is probable that the economic benefits will flow to the entity; and (e) transaction costs can be reliably measured. In a services transaction, the following are the revenue recognition conditions: (a) Revenue can be reliably measured; (b) it is probable that the economic benefits will flow to the entity; (c) the stage of completion can be reliably measured; and (d) the costs incurred and the costs to complete can be reliably measured.
17. Financial position, financial performance, and cash flows should be fairly presented, and properly applying IFRSs almost always results in fair presentation.
18. Annual statements usually are prepared on a going-concern basis. Presentation and classification should be consistent.
19. Current assets are expected to be realized, or are held for sale or consumption, in the normal course of the operating cycle. Assets also are current if they are unrestricted cash items or cash equivalents or are held for trading purposes or are expected to be realized within 12 months. Current liabilities are (a) expected to be settled in the normal course of the operating cycle, (b) due to be settled within 12 months, (c) held primarily to be traded, or (d) obligations for which the entity does not have an unconditional right to defer payment for 12 months. All other assets and liabilities are noncurrent.
20. Comprehensive income for a period consists of (a) a profit or loss (the bottom line of the income statement) and (b) other comprehensive income (OCI). The following are possible components of OCI: (a) the effective portion of a gain or loss on a hedging instrument in a cash flow hedge; (b) a gain or loss on remeasurement of an available-for-sale financial asset; (c) translation gains and losses for financial statements of foreign operations; (d) changes in revaluation surplus for property, plant, and equipment and intangible assets; and (e) certain actuarial gains and losses of defined employee benefit plans.
21. The components of the statement of changes in equity are (a) total comprehensive income, with separate subtotals for the parent and the noncontrolling interest; (b) the effects of retrospective application of accounting policies or restatement of errors, with separate subtotals for each component of equity; (c) contributions from and distributions to owners; and (d) a reconciliation of the beginning balance for each component of equity to the ending balance that separately discloses each change.
22. In a cash flow statement, cash flows are classified and separately disclosed as from operating, investing, or financing activities. Operating activities are the principal revenue-producing activities of the entity. They also include any other activities that are not investing or financing activities. Investing activities include acquiring, or disposing of, long-term assets and other investments that are not cash equivalents. Financing activities result from changes in contributed equity and borrowing. Cash flows from operating activities are reported using the direct method or the indirect method.
23. Noncash investing and financing transactions are not reported in the cash flow statement.
24. The minimum content of an interim financial report includes condensed versions of the balance sheet, income statement, statement of changes in equity, and cash flow statement. It also includes selected notes. If the interim report includes a complete set of statements, they should meet the requirements for annual statements. If condensed statements are published, they should include the headings and subtotals in the annual statements.
25. Financial assets are (a) cash, (b) contract rights to receive cash or another financial asset, (c) contract rights to exchange financial instruments under potentially favorable conditions, (d) another entity's equity instruments, and (e) certain contracts to be settled in the entity's own equities.

26. Financial liabilities are (a) contract obligations to deliver cash or another financial asset, (b) contract obligations to exchange financial instruments under potentially unfavorable conditions, and (c) certain contracts to be settled in the entity's own equities.
27. An equity instrument is a contract that is evidence of a residual interest in an entity's net assets.
28. The categories of financial instruments include (a) assets or liabilities at fair value through profit or loss, (b) held-to-maturity investments, (c) loans and receivables, and (d) available-for-sale financial assets.
29. A fair value hedge is the exposure to changes in fair value of a recognized asset or liability or unrecognized firm commitment. The exposure must be due to a given risk and be able to affect profit or loss.
30. A cash flow hedge is the exposure to variability in cash flows that (a) is due to a given risk associated with a recognized asset or liability (e.g., interest on variable rate debt) or a highly probable forecast transaction and (b) could affect profit or loss.
31. The allowance method is used to record the impairment (bad debt loss) on receivables.
32. Inventories are assets consisting of (a) items held for sale in the ordinary course of business, (b) work in progress, or (c) materials or supplies to be used in production. Inventories are measured at the lower of cost or net realizable value. Cost includes purchase costs, conversion costs, and other costs of bringing inventories to their current location and condition. Net realizable value (NRV) equals estimated selling price in the ordinary course of business minus estimated completion and selling costs. If the cost of inventories is not recoverable because of increases in completion or selling costs, obsolescence, or decreases in selling prices, they are written down to NRV.
33. Permitted inventory cost formulas are (a) specific identification, (b) FIFO, (c) weighted average, and (d) moving average.
34. Items of PPE are initially measured at cost: (a) purchase price, (b) directly attributable costs, and (c) initially estimated costs of removal and restoration.
35. Depreciation systematically allocates the depreciable amount of an item of PPE over its useful life. Each significant part of the item is separately depreciated. The periodic charge for depreciation is offset by a credit to accumulated depreciation, a contra-asset.
36. An asset is impaired when its carrying amount exceeds its recoverable amount. The recoverable amount of an asset is the greater of its fair value minus cost to sell or value in use.
37. The recognized impairment loss is the excess of the asset's carrying amount over its recoverable amount.
38. An intangible asset is identifiable if it is separable or results from contractual or legal rights.
39. Initial recognition of an intangible asset is at cost. Recognition is permitted only when it is probable that the entity will receive the expected economic benefits, and the cost is reliably measurable.
40. Internally generated goodwill is not an asset. Only goodwill acquired in a business combination is considered an asset. However, internally generated intangible assets may be recognized in certain cases.
41. Amortization of an intangible asset with a finite useful life begins when it is available for use. Its depreciable amount is systematically allocated over its useful life. An intangible asset with an indefinite useful life is not amortized.

QUESTIONS

3.1 Framework for the Preparation & Presentation of Financial Statements

1. The amortization of intangible assets with finite useful lives is justified by the

A. Economic entity assumption.

B. Going concern assumption.

C. Monetary unit assumption.

D. Historical cost assumption.

Answer (B) is correct. *(CIA, adapted)*

REQUIRED: The reason for amortizing intangible assets.

DISCUSSION: Every business is assumed to be a going concern that will continue operating indefinitely. Thus, liquidation values are not important. For example, if an entity is not a going concern, its intangible assets are reported at liquidation values, not at historical cost net of amortization.

Answer (A) is incorrect. The economic entity assumption is that every entity's affairs are separate from those of its owners. Answer (C) is incorrect. The monetary unit assumption provides that all transactions and events can be measured in terms of money. Answer (D) is incorrect. The historical cost principle deems cost to be the most objective and reliable measure.

2. An entity with total assets of US $100,000,000 and profit of US $9,000,000 purchases staplers with an estimated life of 10 years for US $1,000. In connection with the purchase, the company debits miscellaneous expense. This scenario is **most** closely associated with which of the following concepts or principles?

A. Materiality and going concern.

B. Relevance and neutrality.

C. Reliability and comparability.

D. Materiality and the balance between cost and benefit.

Answer (D) is correct. *(CIA, adapted)*

REQUIRED: The concepts or principles most closely associated with the choice of an accounting method.

DISCUSSION: In principle, wasting assets should be capitalized and depreciated. However, the effect on the financial statements of expensing rather than capitalizing and depreciating the staplers is clearly not material given that they cost US $1,000 and the enterprise has total assets of US $100,000,000. The choice of treatment is not likely to influence the decisions of financial statement users. The balance between benefit and cost is a pervasive constraint, not a qualitative characteristic. The benefits should exceed the cost of information. Specifically, the cost of producing the information about depreciation expense over 10 years for the staplers probably is higher than the benefits of the information for decision making. Thus, the expedient procedure of expensing the US $1,000 should be followed.

Answer (A) is incorrect. The going-concern principle relates to circumstances in which there is doubt as to the viability of the enterprise. Answer (B) is incorrect. Relevance and reliability are two of the principal qualitative characteristics of information in financial statements. Information is relevant if it permits users to predict the outcome of future events or confirm or correct their prior expectations. Reliability provides assurance that the information is reasonably free from error and bias and represents what it purports to represent. Thus, reliable information must be neutral, that is, free from error and bias. Answer (C) is incorrect. Comparability is a principal qualitative characteristic. Financial statements must be comparable for the same entity over time and also among different entities. Information is relevant if it permits users to predict the outcome of future events or confirm or correct their prior expectations.

3. To comply with the matching principle, the cost of labor services of an employee who participates in the manufacturing of a product normally should be charged to the income statement in the period in which the

A. Work is performed.

B. Employee is paid.

C. Product is completed.

D. Product is sold.

Answer (D) is correct. *(CIA, adapted)*

REQUIRED: The period when the cost of direct labor should be charged to income.

DISCUSSION: Recognition of expenses occurs concurrently with recognition of increases in liabilities or decreases in assets. Expenses are recognized if the costs are directly associated with the earning of particular income items. This process is often called matching. Matching is simultaneous or combined recognition of the revenues and expenses that result directly and jointly from the same transactions or other events. This direct relationship is exemplified by the sale of a product. This transaction results in revenue (sales revenue) for receipt of cash or a receivable, the recognition of an expense (cost of sales) for the sacrifice of the product to a customer, and a decrease in inventory. The direct labor cost of manufacturing the product is absorbed by the finished goods inventory and is not recognized until sale.

3.2 Accrual Accounting and Time Value of Money

4. Which of the following statements is the **best** description of reversing entries?

A. The recording of reversing entries is a mandatory step in the accounting cycle.

B. Reversing entries are made at the end of the next accounting period, after recording regular transactions of the period.

C. Reversing entries are identical to the adjusting entries made in the previous period.

D. Reversing entries are the exact opposite of the adjustments made in the previous period.

Answer (D) is correct. *(CIA, adapted)*

REQUIRED: The best description of reversing entries.

DISCUSSION: Reversing entries are made at the beginning of a period to reverse the effects of adjusting entries made at the end of the preceding period. They are optional entries made for the sake of convenience in recording the transactions of the period. In order for reversing entries to reverse the prior adjustments, they must be the exact opposite of the adjustments made in the previous period.

Answer (A) is incorrect. Reversing entries are optional. Answer (B) is incorrect. Reversing entries are made at the beginning of the next accounting period. Answer (C) is incorrect. Reversing entries are the exact opposite of the adjustments made in the previous period.

5. The relationship between the present value of a future sum and the future value of a present sum can be expressed in terms of their respective interest factors. If the present value of US $200,000 due at the end of 8 years, at 10%, is US $93,300, what is the approximate future value of US $200,000 invested for the same length of time and at the same rate?

A. US $93,300

B. US $200,000

C. US $293,300

D. US $428,724

Answer (D) is correct. *(CIA, adapted)*

REQUIRED: The approximate future value of an amount.

DISCUSSION: The interest factor for the future value of a present sum is equal to the reciprocal of the interest factor for the present value of a future sum. Thus, the future value is US $428,724 [($200,000 ÷ $93,300) × $200,000].

Answer (A) is incorrect. US $93,300 is the present value of US $200,000 to be received in 8 years. Answer (B) is incorrect. US $200,000 is the present value, not the future value, of US $200,000 invested today. Answer (C) is incorrect. The addition of the present and future values has no accounting meaning.

6. Risoner Company plans to purchase a machine with the following conditions:

- Purchase price = US $300,000.
- The down payment = 10% of purchase price with remainder financed at an annual interest rate of 16%.
- The financing period is 8 years with equal annual payments made every year.
- The present value of an annuity of US $1 per year for 8 years at 16% is 4.3436.
- The present value of US $1 due at the end of 8 years at 16% is .3050.

The annual payment (rounded) is

A. US $39,150

B. US $43,200

C. US $62,160

D. US $82,350

Answer (C) is correct. *(CIA, adapted)*

REQUIRED: The annual payment (rounded).

DISCUSSION: The periodic payment is found by dividing the amount to be accumulated (US $300,000 price – $30,000 down payment = US $270,000) by the interest factor for the present value of an ordinary annuity for 8 years at 16%. Consequently, the payment is US $62,160 ($270,000 ÷ 4.3436).

Answer (A) is incorrect. US $39,150 is based on dividing (US $270,000 × 1.16) by 8 (years). Answer (B) is incorrect. US $43,200 is 16% of US $270,000. Answer (D) is incorrect. US $82,350 reflects multiplication by the present value of a sum due (.305) instead of dividing by the present value of an annuity (4.3436).

3.3 Revenue Recognition

7. An entity had cash receipts from sales of US $175,000 during Year 2, of which US $30,000 was unearned at the end of Year 2. At the end of Year 1, the company had US $40,000 of deferred revenue, all of which was earned in Year 2. The company's sales revenue for Year 2 would be

A. US $145,000

B. US $165,000

C. US $175,000

D. US $185,000

Answer (D) is correct. *(CIA, adapted)*

REQUIRED: The sales revenue for Year 2.

DISCUSSION: The sales revenue earned in Year 2 equals Year 2 cash receipts, minus any receipts in Year 2 for which the revenue was deferred, plus the revenue earned from cash receipts in Year 1, or US $185,000 ($175,000 – $30,000 + $40,000).

Answer (A) is incorrect. US $145,000 equals Year 2 revenue from Year 2 sales. Answer (B) is incorrect. US $165,000 adds, rather than subtracts, the Year 2 deferred revenue and subtracts, rather than adds, the Year 1 receipts for which revenue was earned in Year 2. Answer (C) is incorrect. US $175,000 equals the cash receipts for Year 2.

8. Using the cost-recovery method of revenue recognition, profit on an installment sale is recognized

A. On the date of the installment sale.

B. In proportion to the cash collections.

C. After cash collections equal to the cost of goods sold have been received.

D. On the date the final cash collection is received.

Answer (C) is correct. *(CIA, adapted)*

REQUIRED: The timing of revenue recognition using the cost-recovery method.

DISCUSSION: Under the cost-recovery method, no revenue is recognized until cash payments by the buyer exceed the seller's cost of the merchandise sold. This method is appropriate when collection of the revenue is very uncertain.

Answer (A) is incorrect. The accrual basis recognizes revenue on the date of the installment sale. Answer (B) is incorrect. The installment basis recognizes revenue in proportion to the cash collections. Answer (D) is incorrect. After the cash collections equal the cost of sales, revenue is to be recognized for any further collections.

9. A building contractor has a fixed-price contract to construct a large building. It is estimated that the building will take 2 years to complete. Progress billings will be sent to the customer at quarterly intervals. Which of the following describes the preferable point for revenue recognition for this contract if the outcome of the contract can be estimated reliably?

A. After the contract is signed.

B. As progress is made toward completion of the contract.

C. As cash is received.

D. When the contract is completed.

Answer (B) is correct. *(CIA, adapted)*

REQUIRED: The moment when revenue should be recognized.

DISCUSSION: Under the percentage-of-completion method, revenues and expenses are recognized based on the stage of completion at the balance sheet date if the outcome of the contract can be estimated reliably. For a fixed-price contract, the outcome can be estimated reliably if (1) total revenue can be measured reliably, (2) it is probable that the economic benefits of the contract will flow to the enterprise, (3) contract costs to complete and stage of completion can be measured reliably, and (4) contract costs can be clearly identified and measured reliably so that actual and estimated costs can be compared.

Answer (A) is incorrect. Revenue is not recognized until progress has been made toward completion. Answer (C) is incorrect. The cash basis is inappropriate. An accrual method, that is, the percentage-of-completion method, should be used. Answer (D) is incorrect. The completed-contract method is not a permissible method.

3.4 Financial Statements

10. The comparative balance sheet for an enterprise that had profit of US $150,000 for the year ended December 31, Year 2, and paid US $125,000 of dividends during Year 2 is as follows:

	12/31/Yr 2	12/31/Yr 1
Cash	US $150,000	US $180,000
Accounts receivable	200,000	220,000
Total assets	US $350,000	US $400,000
Payables	US $ 80,000	US $160,000
Share capital	130,000	125,000
Retained earnings	140,000	115,000
Total	US $350,000	US $400,000

If dividends paid are treated as a cost of obtaining financial resources, the amount of net cash from operating activities during Year 2 was

A. US $70,000

B. US $90,000

C. US $150,000

D. US $210,000

Answer (B) is correct. *(CIA, adapted)*

REQUIRED: The amount of net cash from operating activities during Year 2.

DISCUSSION: Profit is adjusted to determine the net cash from operations. The payment of cash dividends is regarded as a cash flow from a financing activity. Hence, it is not a reconciling item. However, the decrease in accounts receivable (US $220,000 – $200,000 = US $20,000) during the period represents a cash inflow (collections of pre-Year 2 receivables) not reflected in Year 2 profit. Moreover, the decrease in payables (US $160,000 – $80,000 = US $80,000) indicates a cash outflow (payment of pre-Year 2 liabilities) that also is not reflected in Year 2 net income. Accordingly, net cash from operations was US $90,000 ($150,000 + $20,000 – $80,000).

Answer (A) is incorrect. US $70,000 fails to add to profit the reduction in accounts receivable. Answer (C) is incorrect. US $150,000 is profit. Answer (D) is incorrect. US $210,000 subtracts the reduction in receivables and adds the reduction in payables.

11. A corporation reported salaries expense of US $190,000 for December of the current year. The following data are from its records:

	Dec. 31	Nov. 30
Prepaid salaries	US $ 46,000	US $ 40,000
Salaries payable	170,000	140,000

The amount of cash payments for salaries during December of the current year was

A. US $154,000

B. US $166,000

C. US $214,000

D. US $226,000

Answer (B) is correct. *(CIA, adapted)*

REQUIRED: The amount of cash payments for salaries during December of the current year.

DISCUSSION: An increase in prepaid salaries indicates that salaries expense is less than the cash paid for salaries. An increase in salaries payable indicates that salaries expense is more than the cash paid for salaries. Thus, the amount of cash payments for salaries was US $166,000 ($190,000 salaries expense + $6,000 increase in prepaid salaries – $30,000 increase in salaries payable).

Answer (A) is incorrect. US $154,000 subtracts the US $6,000 increase in prepaid salaries instead of adding it. Answer (C) is incorrect. US $214,000 subtracts the increase in prepaid salaries instead of adding it and adds the US $30,000 increase in salaries payable instead of subtracting it. Answer (D) is incorrect. US $226,000 adds the US $30,000 increase in salaries payable instead of subtracting it.

12. In reconciling profit on an accrual basis to net cash from operating activities, what adjustment is needed to profit because of (1) an increase during the period in prepaid expenses and (2) the periodic amortization of premium on bonds payable?

	(1) Increase in Prepaid Expenses	(2) Amortization of Premium on Bonds Payable
A.	Add	Add
B.	Add	Deduct
C.	Deduct	Add
D.	Deduct	Deduct

Answer (D) is correct. *(CIA, adapted)*

REQUIRED: The adjustments to reconcile accrual-basis profit to net cash from operating activities.

DISCUSSION: An increase in prepaid expenses indicates that cash outlays for expenses exceeded the related expense incurred; thus, profit exceeded net cash from operating activities, and a deduction is needed in the reconciliation. Also, the amortization of premium on bonds payable causes a reduction of interest expense but does not increase cash; therefore, profit exceeds net cash from operating activities, and a deduction is needed in the reconciliation.

Answer (A) is incorrect. The increase in prepaid expenses requires a deduction from profit in the reconciliation. Answer (B) is incorrect. The increase in prepaid expenses requires a deduction from profit in the reconciliation. Answer (C) is incorrect. Amortization of premium on bonds payable requires a deduction from profit in the reconciliation.

Questions 13 through 15 are based on the following information. Balance sheets on December 31, Year 1, and December 31, Year 2, are presented below:

	Dec. 31, Year 1	Dec. 31, Year 2
Assets:		
Cash	US $ 50,000	US $ 60,000
Accounts receivable	95,000	89,000
Allowance for uncollectible accounts	(4,000)	(3,000)
Inventory	120,000	140,000
Property, plant, and equipment	295,000	340,000
Accumulated depreciation	(102,000)	(119,000)
Total Assets	US $ 454,000	US $ 507,000

	Dec. 31, Year 1	Dec. 31, Year 2
Liabilities and equity:		
Trade accounts payable	US $ 62,000	US $ 49,000
Interest payable	8,000	11,000
Bonds payable	200,000	200,000
Unamortized bond discount	(15,000)	(10,000)
Equity	199,000	257,000
Total liabilities and equity	US $454,000	US $507,000

Additional information for Year 2:

1. Cash payments to suppliers of merchandise were US $180,000.
2. Sales revenue was US $338,000.
3. US $3,000 of accounts receivable was written off.
4. Equipment was acquired for US $65,000.
5. Depreciation expense was US $30,000.
6. Interest expense was US $20,000.

13. Cost of goods sold in Year 2 was

A. US $147,000

B. US $160,000

C. US $167,000

D. US $180,000

Answer (A) is correct. *(CIA, adapted)*

REQUIRED: The cost of goods sold.

DISCUSSION: Cost of goods sold equals beginning inventory, plus purchases, minus ending inventory. To determine cost of goods sold, purchases must be calculated. Purchases equal US $167,000 ($49,000 ending accounts payable + $180,000 payments to suppliers – $62,000 beginning accounts payable). Thus, cost of goods sold equals US $147,000 ($120,000 beginning inventory + $167,000 purchases – $140,000 ending inventory).

Answer (B) is incorrect. US $160,000 results from assuming that US $180,000 of cash payments to suppliers equaled purchases. Answer (C) is incorrect. US $167,000 equals purchases. Answer (D) is incorrect. US $180,000 is the amount of cash payments to suppliers.

14. Cash collections from customers in Year 2 were

A. US $341,000

B. US $338,000

C. US $344,000

D. US $335,000

Answer (A) is correct. *(CIA, adapted)*

REQUIRED: The cash collections from customers.

DISCUSSION: Cash collections from customers equals beginning accounts receivable, plus sales revenue, minus accounts written off, minus ending accounts receivable. In Year 2, cash collections from customers were US $341,000 ($95,000 + $338,000 – $3,000 – $89,000).

Answer (B) is incorrect. US $338,000 is the sales revenue for the year. Answer (C) is incorrect. US $344,000 includes the US $3,000 of accounts written off. Answer (D) is incorrect. US $335,000 is sales revenue minus accounts written off.

15. The carrying amount (cost minus accumulated depreciation) of property, plant, and equipment disposed of in Year 2 was

A. US $7,000

B. US $17,000

C. US $20,000

D. US $32,000

Answer (A) is correct. *(CIA, adapted)*

REQUIRED: The carrying amount of property, plant, and equipment disposed of.

DISCUSSION: The cost of PPE disposed of is US $20,000 ($295,000 beginning PPE + $65,000 acquisitions – $340,000 ending PPE). The accumulated depreciation is US $13,000 ($102,000 beginning accumulated depreciation + $30,000 depreciation expense – $119,000 ending accumulated depreciation). Thus, the carrying amount of PPE disposed of is US $7,000 ($20,000 cost of PPE – $13,000 accumulated depreciation).

Answer (B) is incorrect. US $17,000 is the difference between ending and beginning accumulated depreciation. Answer (C) is incorrect. US $20,000 is the cost of the PPE disposed. Answer (D) is incorrect. US $32,000 results from using the change in the PPE account without acquisitions minus the accumulated depreciation.

3.5 Financial Assets and Liabilities

16. An entity offers its customers credit terms of a 2% discount if paid within 10 days, or the full balance is due within 30 days (2/10, n/30). If some customers take advantage of the cash discount and others do not, which of the following accounts will appear on the income statement if the net method of recording receivables is employed?

	Sales Discounts	Sales Discounts Forfeited
A.	Yes	Yes
B.	Yes	No
C.	No	No
D.	No	Yes

Answer (D) is correct. *(CIA, adapted)*

REQUIRED: The account(s) appearing on the income statement if the net method is used.

DISCUSSION: The gross method accounts for receivables at their face amount. If a discount is taken, a sales discount is recorded and classified as an offset to sales in the income statement to yield net sales. The net method records receivables net of the applicable discount. If the payment is not received during the discount period, an interest revenue account, such as sales discounts forfeited, is credited at the end of the discount period or when the payment is received. Accordingly, the application of the net method requires a sales discount forfeited but not a sales discount account.

17. An internal auditor is deriving cash flow data based on an incomplete set of facts. Bad debt expense was US $2,000. Additional data for this period follows:

Credit sales	US $100,000
Gross accounts receivable -- beginning balance	5,000
Allowance for bad debts -- beginning balance	(500)
Accounts receivable written off	1,000
Increase in net accounts receivable (after subtraction of allowance for bad debts)	30,000

How much cash was collected this period on credit sales?

A. US $64,000

B. US $68,000

C. US $68,500

D. US $70,000

Answer (B) is correct. *(CIA, adapted)*

REQUIRED: The cash collected on accounts receivable.

DISCUSSION: The beginning balance of gross accounts receivable (A/R) was US $5,000 (debit). Thus, net beginning A/R was US $4,500 ($5,000 – $500 credit in the allowance for bad debts). The allowance was credited for the US $2,000 bad debt expense. Accordingly, the ending allowance (credit) was US $1,500 ($500 – $1,000 write-off + $2,000). Given a US $30,000 increase in net A/R, ending net A/R must have been US $34,500 ($4,500 beginning net A/R + $30,000), with ending gross A/R of US $36,000 ($34,500 + $1,500). Collections were therefore US $68,000 ($5,000 beginning gross A/R – $1,000 write-off + $100,000 credit sales – $36,000 ending gross A/R).

Gross A/R			
US $ 5,000	Beg. Bal.	US $ 1,000	Write-off
100,000	Cr. Sales	68,000	Collections
US $ 36,000	End. Bal.		

Answer (A) is incorrect. US $64,000 equals credit sales minus the ending gross accounts receivable. Answer (C) is incorrect. US $68,500 equals credit sales, minus the increase in net accounts receivable, minus the ending allowance. Answer (D) is incorrect. US $70,000 equals credit sales minus the increase in net accounts receivable.

18. At the end of September, an entity has outstanding accounts receivable of US $350 on third-quarter credit sales, composed as follows:

Month	Credit Sales	Still Outstanding at the End of September
July	US $600	US $100
August	900	170
September	500	80

The percentage of receivables in the 31-to-60-day age group at the end of September is

A. 22.86%

B. 28.57%

C. 48.57%

D. 71.43%

Answer (C) is correct. *(CIA, adapted)*

REQUIRED: The percentage of receivables in the 31-to-60-day age group.

DISCUSSION: Receivables from August sales still outstanding at the end of September are in the 31-to-60-day age group. This group represents 48.57% of total receivables [US $170 ÷ ($100 + $170 + $80)].

Answer (A) is incorrect. 22.86% is the proportion of receivables in the 0-to-30-day age group at the end of September. Answer (B) is incorrect. 28.57% is the proportion of receivables in the 61-to-90-day age group at the end of September. Answer (D) is incorrect. 71.43% is the proportion of outstanding receivables that are from 0 to 60 days old at the end of September.

19. When a right of return exists, an entity may recognize revenue from a sale of goods at the time of sale only if

A. The amount of future returns can be reliably estimated.

B. The seller retains the risks and rewards of ownership.

C. The buyer resells the goods.

D. The seller believes returns will not be material.

Answer (A) is correct. *(CIA, adapted)*

REQUIRED: The condition for revenue recognition when a right of return exists.

DISCUSSION: One condition for recognition of revenue from the sale of goods is the transfer of the significant risks and rewards of ownership. Retention of significant risk may occur when, for example, the buyer may rescind the purchase for a reason stipulated in the contract, and the buyer is uncertain about the probability of return. However, if the entity can reliably estimate future returns and recognizes a liability for returns based on experience and other pertinent information, revenue may be recognized at the time of sale if the other conditions for revenue recognition are also met.

Answer (B) is incorrect. The risks and rewards of ownership must be transferred. Answer (C) is incorrect. This contingency is an example of retention of significant risk. Answer (D) is incorrect. Returns may be material if they can be reliably estimated.

20. If receivables transferred with recourse qualify for derecognition, the proceeds from the transfer are

A. Accounted for as a collateralized borrowing.

B. Recorded at fair value for the assets obtained and liabilities incurred.

C. Recorded at the historical cost of the assets obtained.

D. Reduced by the fair value of the recourse obligation.

Answer (D) is correct. *(CMA, adapted)*

REQUIRED: The accounting for the proceeds of the sale of receivables with recourse.

DISCUSSION: The entity derecognizes financial assets if it has transferred substantially all of the risks and rewards of ownership. Derecognition also is appropriate when the entity neither has transferred nor retained substantially all the risks and rewards of ownership, providing the entity does not have control. After derecognition, periodic profit or loss will include the difference between the carrying amount transferred and the proceeds, plus or minus any prior adjustment reflecting the fair value of the asset that had been reported in equity. If a new financial asset is created or a new financial liability is assumed, the calculation is adjusted for the fair value of the asset or liability. Thus, the proceeds of the sale are reduced by the fair value of the recourse obligation (a new financial liability). When the transfer does not meet these criteria, the transfer is accounted for as a collateralized borrowing.

21. Which of the following is **not** a criterion for hedge accounting?

A. The hedge is expected to be highly effective and can be reliably measured.

B. The hedge is assessed only at its inception.

C. A forecast transaction subject to a cash flow hedge must be highly probable.

D. The hedge is formally designated and documented at its inception.

Answer (B) is correct. *(Publisher, adapted)*

REQUIRED: The choice that is not a criterion for hedge accounting.

DISCUSSION: An entity can mitigate a possible loss by using hedges to offset risk. Thus, an entity is said to hedge its financial positions. One of the criteria for hedge accounting is that the hedge be continually assessed and determined to have been effective. Thus, it is not assessed only at its inception.

Answer (A) is incorrect. That the hedge is expected to be highly effective and reliably measurable is one of the criteria for hedge accounting. Answer (C) is incorrect. One of the criteria for hedge accounting is that a forecast transaction subject to a cash flow hedge be highly probable. Also, it must be able to affect profit or loss. Answer (D) is incorrect. One criterion for hedge accounting is that the hedge be formally designated and documented at its inception. The risk management objective and strategy must also be included in this designation and documentation.

22. To mitigate a possible loss and offset risk, an entity can use derivatives or other hedging instruments. Which of the following hedging relationships applies to an unrecognized firm commitment?

	Fair Value Hedge	Cash Flow Hedge
A.	No	No
B.	No	Yes
C.	Yes	Yes
D.	Yes	No

Answer (D) is correct. *(Publisher, adapted)*

REQUIRED: The hedging relationship that applies to an unrecognized firm commitment.

DISCUSSION: A fair value hedge is a hedge of the exposure to changes in fair value of a recognized asset or liability or unrecognized firm commitment. The exposure must be due to a given risk and be able to affect profit or loss. A cash flow hedge is a hedge of the exposure to variability in cash flows that (1) is due to a given risk associated with a recognized asset or liability or a highly probable forecast transaction and (2) could affect profit or loss.

Answer (A) is incorrect. A fair value hedge is a hedge of the exposure to changes in fair value of a recognized asset or liability or unrecognized firm commitment. Answer (B) is incorrect. A fair value hedge applies to an unrecognized firm commitment. Answer (C) is incorrect. A cash flow hedge applies to a highly probable forecast transaction, but not to an unrecognized firm commitment.

3.6 Inventory

Questions 23 and 24 are based on the following information. Illustrated below is a perpetual inventory card for the current year.

Date	Units Purchased	Units Sold	Units Balance
January 1			0
January 12	1,000 @ US $2.00		1,000
March 15		300	700
May 5	500 @ US $2.20		1,200
July 8		500	700
November 24	1,000 @ US $1.65		1,700

Additional information:

- The entity had no opening inventory.
- The items sold on March 15 were purchased on January 12.
- The items sold on July 8 were purchased on May 5.

23. The ending inventory balance under the first-in, first-out (FIFO) method of inventory valuation is

A. US $3,050

B. US $3,150

C. US $3,230

D. US $3,430

Answer (B) is correct. *(CIA, adapted)*

REQUIRED: The ending inventory balance under FIFO.

DISCUSSION: Under the FIFO method, the 1,700 units of ending inventory are valued at the most recent prices. Ending inventory is assumed to include 1,000 units purchased November 24, 500 units purchased May 5, and 200 units purchased January 12. Hence, the ending inventory is US $3,150 [(1,000 × $1.65) + (500 × $2.20) + (200 × $2.00)].

Answer (A) is incorrect. US $3,050 is the ending inventory under the specific identification method. Answer (C) is incorrect. US $3,230 is the ending inventory under the weighted-average method. Answer (D) is incorrect. US $3,430 is the ending inventory under the LIFO method.

24. The cost of goods sold under the specific identification method of inventory valuation is

A. US $1,320

B. US $1,520

C. US $1,600

D. US $1,700

Answer (D) is correct. *(CIA, adapted)*

REQUIRED: The cost of goods sold under the specific identification method.

DISCUSSION: Of the 800 units sold during the period, the 300 units sold on March 15 were purchased on January 12 at a cost of US $2.00 per unit. The remaining 500 units were purchased on May 5 at a cost of US $2.20 per unit. The cost of goods sold under the specific identification method is therefore US $1,700 [(300 units × $2.00) + (500 units × $2.20)].

Answer (A) is incorrect. US $1,320 is the cost of goods sold under the LIFO method. Answer (B) is incorrect. US $1,520 is the cost of goods sold under the weighted-average method. Answer (C) is incorrect. US $1,600 is the cost of goods sold under the FIFO method.

25. A retail entity maintains a markup of 25% based on cost. The entity has the following information for the current year:

Purchases of merchandise	US $690,000
Freight-in on purchases	25,000
Sales	900,000
Ending inventory	80,000

Beginning inventory was

A. US $40,000

B. US $85,000

C. US $110,000

D. US $265,000

Answer (B) is correct. *(CIA, adapted)*

REQUIRED: The beginning inventory.

DISCUSSION: Cost of goods sold equals beginning inventory, plus purchases (including freight-in), minus ending inventory. Given that sales reflect 125% of cost, cost of goods sold must equal US $720,000 ($900,000 sales ÷ 1.25). Consequently, the beginning inventory must have been US $85,000 ($720,000 CGS + $80,000 EI – $690,000 purchases – $25,000 freight-in).

Answer (A) is incorrect. US $40,000 is based on a 25% markup on sales. Answer (C) is incorrect. US $110,000 omits the freight-in from the computation of cost of goods available for sale. Answer (D) is incorrect. US $265,000 uses the sales figure for cost of goods sold.

3.7 Property, Plant, and Equipment (PPE) – Acquisition and Measurement

26. Which of the following is **not** an appropriate basis for measuring the cost of property, plant, and equipment?

A. The purchase price, freight costs, and installation costs of a productive asset should be included in the asset's cost.

B. Proceeds obtained in the process of readying land for its intended purpose, such as from the sale of cleared timber, should be recognized immediately as income.

C. The costs of improvements to equipment incurred after its acquisition should be added to the asset's cost if they increase future service potential.

D. All costs incurred in the construction of a plant building, from excavation to completion, should be considered as part of the asset's cost.

Answer (B) is correct. *(CIA, adapted)*

REQUIRED: The basis that is inappropriate for measuring the cost of property, plant, and equipment.

DISCUSSION: Accordingly, items of property, plant, and equipment (PPE) that meet the recognition criterion are initially measured at cost. The cost includes the purchase price (minus trade discounts and rebates, plus purchase taxes) and the directly attributable costs of bringing the assets to working condition for their intended use. Directly attributable costs include site preparation, installation, initial delivery and handling, architect and equipment fees, costs of removing the assets and restoring the site, etc. Accordingly, the cost of land includes the cost of obtaining the land and readying it for its intended uses, but it is inappropriate to recognize the proceeds related to site preparation immediately in profit or loss. They should be treated as reductions in the price of the land.

Answer (A) is incorrect. The purchase price, freight costs, and installation costs of a productive asset are included in the asset's cost. Answer (C) is incorrect. Subsequent costs are added to the carrying amount of an item of PPE if it is probable that, as a result, future economic benefits will be received, and the costs are reliably measurable. Answer (D) is incorrect. All costs of construction should be included as a part of the asset's cost.

27. A depreciable asset has an estimated 20% residual value. At the end of the asset's estimated useful life, the accumulated depreciation will equal the original cost of the asset under which of the following depreciation methods?

	Diminishing-Balance	Sum-of-the-Years'-Digits (SYD)
A.	Yes	Yes
B.	Yes	No
C.	No	Yes
D.	No	No

Answer (D) is correct. *(CIA, adapted)*

REQUIRED: The depreciation method under which accumulated depreciation equals the original cost of the asset at the end of its estimated useful life.

DISCUSSION: At the end of the estimated useful life of a depreciable asset, the amount of accumulated depreciation should equal the depreciable cost (original cost – estimated residual value), regardless of the depreciation method used. Periodic diminishing-balance depreciation is calculated without regard to residual value, but the asset is not depreciated below its residual value. The SYD method uses a depreciable base equal to cost minus residual value.

28. A theme park purchased a new, exciting ride and financed it through the manufacturer. The following facts pertain:

Purchase price	US $800,000
Delivery cost	50,000
Installation cost	70,000
Cost of trial-runs	40,000
Interest charges for first year	60,000

The straight-line method is to be used. Compute the depreciation on the equipment for the first year assuming an estimated service life of 5 years.

A. US $160,000

B. US $184,000

C. US $192,000

D. US $204,000

Answer (C) is correct. *(CIA, adapted)*
REQUIRED: The depreciation expense.
DISCUSSION: Under the straight-line method, the annual depreciation expense for an asset equals the asset's amount (cost – residual value) divided by the asset's estimated useful life. The cost of the asset includes its price and the directly attributable costs of bringing it to working condition for intended use. Thus, the depreciation expense is US $192,000 [($800,000 purchase price + $50,000 delivery cost + $70,000 installation cost + $40,000 trial-run cost) ÷ 5-year estimated service life]. Borrowing costs incurred after the asset is prepared for its intended use are expensed even if the allowed alternative treatment of such costs is followed, and the asset otherwise satisfies the criteria for capitalization of such expenses.

Answer (A) is incorrect. US $160,000 excludes the delivery, installation, and trial-run costs. Answer (B) is incorrect. US $184,000 excludes the trial-run cost. Answer (D) is incorrect. US $204,000 includes the borrowing costs.

3.8 Intangible Assets

29. Which of the following is **not** considered to be an intangible asset?

A. Goods on consignment.

B. Patents.

C. Copyrights.

D. Trademarks.

Answer (A) is correct. *(CIA, adapted)*
REQUIRED: The item not an intangible asset.
DISCUSSION: IAS 38, *Intangible Assets*, defines an intangible asset as "an identifiable nonmonetary asset without physical substance." Inventory is a tangible asset. Thus, goods on consignment are not intangible assets.

Answer (B) is incorrect. Patents are intangible assets. Answer (C) is incorrect. Copyrights are intangible assets. Answer (D) is incorrect. Trademarks are intangible assets.

30. MNO purchased all of XYZ's 100,000 outstanding ordinary (common) shares for US $40 per share on August 31. On this date, XYZ's balance sheet showed total assets of US $5,000,000 and total liabilities of US $2,000,000. The fair value of XYZ's identifiable assets on this date was US $550,000 greater than their carrying amount. The amount that should be reported on MNO's consolidated balance sheet on August 31 for goodwill is

A. US $0

B. US $450,000

C. US $550,000

D. US $1,000,000

Answer (B) is correct. *(CIA, adapted)*
REQUIRED: The amount of goodwill reported.
DISCUSSION: Goodwill is recognized as an asset equal to the excess of the cost over the acquirer's interest in the fair value of the identifiable assets and liabilities acquired. The cost of US $4,000,000 (100,000 × $40) is in excess of the US $3,550,000 ($5,000,000 + $550,000 – $2,000,000) fair value of the identifiable assets and liabilities by US $450,000. This excess is goodwill.

Answer (A) is incorrect. Cost in excess of fair value of the identifiable assets and liabilities is reported as goodwill. Answer (C) is incorrect. US $550,000 is the excess of fair value over the carrying amount of the identifiable assets and liabilities on the seller's books. Answer (D) is incorrect. The purchase price of US $4,000,000 exceeds the seller's US $3,000,000 carrying amount by US $1,000,000.

STUDY UNIT FOUR
FINANCIAL ACCOUNTING II

(29 pages of outline)

Study Unit 4 is the second of two study units pertaining to financial accounting. It addresses topics listed or suggested in the CSO that were not covered in the preceding study unit.

Core Concepts

- Under a defined postemployment benefit plan, the entity is responsible for providing the agreed benefits and therefore bears actuarial risk and investment risk.
- Under defined postemployment benefit plan accounting, the minimum required income or expense is the sum of (1) current service cost, (2) interest cost, (3) the expected return on plan assets, (4) actuarial gains and losses calculated using the corridor approach, (5) post service cost, and (6) curtailment or settlement effects.
- Employee share options exchanged for services are normally accounted for at the fair value of the equity instruments granted by a debit to expense and a credit to equity.
- A lease is an agreement by which a lessor (owner) conveys the right to a lessee to use an asset for an agreed period in exchange for a payment or series of payments. The accounting for leases is based on the substance of the transaction. A lease may be, in effect, the financing of a purchase or a rental agreement.
- The lessee records a finance lease as an asset and a liability at its inception at the fair value of the leased property. The lessor's basic entry for a finance lease is to debit a receivable, credit an asset, and credit unearned finance income. But if the lessor is a manufacturer/dealer, selling profit or loss is recognized.
- A temporary difference (TD) arises when the carrying amount and the tax base of an asset or liability differ. The effect is that a taxable or deductible TD will occur in future years when the asset is recovered or the liability is settled, respectively.
- A financial liability is a liability that is a contractual obligation "(1) to deliver cash or another financial asset to another entity or (2) to exchange financial assets or financial liabilities with another entity under conditions that are potentially unfavorable to the entity."
- An equity instrument is a contract that is evidence of a residual interest in an entity's net assets.
- A current liability is an obligation that is (1) expected to be settled within the normal operating cycle, (2) held to be traded, or (3) due to be settled within 12 months of the balance sheet date. A liability also is current if the entity has no conditional right to defer settlement for 12 months. Any other liability is noncurrent.
- Examples of provisions are liabilities for violations of environmental law, nuclear plant decommissioning costs, warranties, and restructurings.

- A contingent liability is not recognized. However, it should be disclosed unless the possibility of resource outflows is remote. A contingent asset is not recognized but should be disclosed if an inflow of economic benefits is probable.
- Bonds are debt instruments. If issued at a premium or discount, they are accounted for using the effective interest method.
- Equity consists of share capital; items of income and expense reported directly in equity; retained earnings; and possibly, treasury shares.
- Accounting policies are "specific principles, bases, conventions, rules, and practices adopted by an entity in preparing and presenting financial statements" (IAS 8). A voluntary change in accounting policy is ordinarily accounted for by retrospective application.
- A change in accounting estimate should be reflected in the financial statements prospectively.
- All material prior-period errors must be corrected retrospectively in the first set of financial statements issued after their discovery.
- A functional currency is the currency of an entity's primary economic environment. The presentation currency is the currency in which the statements are reported.
- When a foreign currency transaction is reported in the functional currency, exchange differences ordinarily are recognized in profit or loss when they arise.
- The entity's presentation currency may not be the functional currency. Exchange differences arising from translation into the presentation currency are recognized separately in equity.
- A business combination results when an acquirer obtains control over one or more businesses.
- All business combinations must be accounted for using the acquisition method.
- In a business combination, goodwill is recognized as an asset arising from other assets acquired that are not individually identified and separately recognized.
- An associate is an entity over which the investor exercises significant influence and that is not a subsidiary or a joint venture. An entity usually accounts for an associate using the equity method.
- A parent is an entity that controls at least one other entity (a subsidiary). Ordinarily, it presents consolidated statements. "Control is the power to govern the financial and operating policies of an entity so as to obtain benefits from its activities."

4.1 EMPLOYER ACCOUNTING FOR POSTEMPLOYMENT BENEFITS

Benefit Plans

1. Examples of postemployment benefits are pensions and other retirement benefits, life insurance, and medical care. An arrangement to provide these benefits to employees is a postemployment benefit plan. Such a plan may be a defined contribution plan or a defined benefit plan.
   a. Under a **defined contribution plan**, the entity's maximum obligation equals its agreed contributions to a fund (a separate entity). The benefits to be received by employees are determined by the **contributions made** (including any made by the employees) and by the **investment returns**. Accordingly, actuarial risk and investment risk are borne by the employees.
   b. Under a **defined benefit plan**, the entity is responsible for providing the agreed benefits and therefore bears **actuarial risk and investment risk.**
2. **Vested benefits** are earned postemployment benefits owed to an employee that are not conditional upon future service.

Defined Contribution Plan Accounting

3. The employer recognizes an expense and a liability for the **contribution payable** in exchange for an employee's services performed during the period. The amount is determined after subtracting any contribution already made.

a. However, if the contribution made exceeds the amount due, the excess is treated as a **prepaid expense** (an asset).

Defined Benefit Plan Accounting

4. The employer must estimate the benefits attributable to the current and prior periods as a result of employee services rendered. Thus, it must make **actuarial assumptions** about such variables as (a) employee turnover, (b) mortality, (c) the discount rate, (d) future increases in compensation, (e) increases in medical costs, and (f) the expected rate of return on plan assets.

5. The **defined benefit obligation** (DBO) consists of the **present value of future amounts** required to settle the obligation arising from services provided by employees in the current and prior periods.

   a. **Each service period** results in a unit of benefit, with each unit separately measured to determine the total obligation.

   b. The **measurement** of a postemployment benefit obligation includes (1) estimates of future salary increases, (2) the benefits defined in the plan, (3) the benefits arising from any constructive obligation beyond the terms of the plan, and (4) estimates of future changes in government benefits that affect the level of plan benefits.

6. The amount of the **defined benefit liability (DBL)** recognized equals the following:

	Present value of the DBO at the balance sheet date
±	Unrecognized actuarial gains (losses)
–	Unrecognized past service cost
–	Fair value of plan assets at the balance sheet date
	DBL

   a. If this amount is negative, it is an **asset**.

7. The minimum required **income or expense** is recognized for the sum of the following:

   a. **Current service cost** is the increase in the present value of the DBO arising from services rendered by employees in the current period.

   b. **Interest cost** is the increase in the present value of the DBO because settlement is one period closer.

   c. The **expected return on plan assets** is determined with regard to market expectations for returns on the fair value of plan assets held after allowing for actual contributions paid into, and actual benefits paid out of, the fund.

   d. **Actuarial gains and losses** recognized under the "corridor" approach. Actuarial gains and losses include the effects of changes in actuarial assumptions and adjustments for actual experience different from that previously assumed. Hence, the difference between the actual and expected return on plan assets is an actuarial gain or loss.

      1) The **actual return on plan assets** is the difference between the fair value of plan assets at the beginning and the end of the year adjusted for **contributions and benefits paid.**

   e. **Past service cost** recognized. Past service cost is the change in the present value of the DBO related to prior employee service that arises in the current period from the introduction of, or an amendment to, postemployment benefits. It may be positive (benefits increase) or negative (benefits decrease).

      1) Past service cost is expensed on a **straight-line basis** over the average period until vesting.

f. **Curtailment or settlement** effects. A curtailment arises from a reduction in covered employees or an amendment of the plan to reduce benefits for future service. A settlement is a transaction that eliminates the DBO for part or all of plan benefits.

Stop and review! You have completed the outline for this subunit. Study multiple-choice questions 1 through 3 on page 186.

4.2 SHARE-BASED PAYMENT

SBPTS

1. According to **IFRS 2**, *Share-Based Payment*, **share-based payment transactions (SBPTs)** involve **receipt by the entity of goods or services** in return for
   a. Its **equity instruments** (shares or share options) or
   b. Amounts based on the **price** of its equity instruments.

Settlement

2. The SBPTs are settled by the entity in one of three ways:
   a. **Equity settlement** by issuing equity instruments of the entity (e.g., shares or share options)
   b. **Cash settlement** by incurring liabilities based on the price or value of the entity's equity instruments
   c. **Cash or equity settlement** at the option of the entity or supplier

Recognition

3. **Recognition of goods or services** occurs when they are received.
   a. **Equity** is credited in an equity-settled SBPT, and a **liability** is credited in a cash-settled SBPT.
   b. If the goods or services do not meet the asset recognition criteria, an **expense** is debited.

Equity-Settlement SBPTs

4. The goods or services and the credit to equity are measured at the **fair value** of the goods or services if it is **reliably measurable**. If it is not, the transaction is measured at the **fair value of the equity instruments granted**. The second treatment is normally required for employee share options.
   a. The fair value of equity instruments granted is determined at the **measurement date**. The **grant date for employee awards** is the measurement date. For others, measurement occurs when the entity obtains the goods or receives the services.
      1) **Market prices** are usually the basis for the measurement.
   b. If the equity instruments are **fully vested** immediately, the entity recognizes on the **grant date** the full receipt of services and then credits equity accordingly.
      1) If services are to be received over the **vesting period**, their fair value is recognized as the services are rendered.
   c. Vesting conditions affect the **number of equity instruments** included in the measurement.
      1) Thus, recognition of an amount for goods or services received is based on the **best available estimate** of the **number of equity instruments** expected to vest. This estimate is **revised** as required by subsequent information.
      2) On the **vesting date**, the estimate is revised to reflect the **number actually vested**.

d. The fair value of equity instruments (e.g., share options) may not be reliably measurable at the measurement date. In this rare case, **intrinsic value** (fair value of the entity's shares – exercise price) may be used to measure the SBPT when the goods are received or services are rendered.

1) **Remeasurement** is then necessary at each reporting date and the date of final settlement. Any change in intrinsic value is recognized in **profit or loss**.

Cash-Settled SBPT

5. The **fair value of the liability** is the basis for measurement. Until settlement, the entity remeasures this fair value at each reporting date and at the final settlement date, with changes in fair value recognized in **profit or loss**.

Cash or Equity Settlement

6. The entity accounts for the transaction as a cash-settled SBPT if, and to the extent that, the entity has incurred a liability to settle in cash. Absent such a liability, it accounts for the transaction as **equity settled**.

Stop and review! You have completed the outline for this subunit. Study multiple-choice questions 4 and 5 on page 187.

4.3 LEASES

1. A lease is a **long-term contract** in which the owner of property (the **lessor**) allows another party (the **lessee**) the right to use the property for a stated period in exchange for a stated payment or series of payments.

   a. The accounting treatment of the lease should reflect the **substance of the transaction.**

   b. At its **inception**, a lease is normally classified as a purchase-and-financing arrangement (a **finance lease**) or a long-term rental contract (an **operating lease**).

Finance Lease Classification Criteria

2. A lease is classified as a finance lease if it transfers **substantially all of the risks and rewards of ownership**. The following are examples of circumstances that (individually or combined) ordinarily result in that classification:

   a. The lease **transfers ownership** of the leased asset to the lessee at the end of the lease term.

   b. The lease contains a **bargain purchase option.**

      1) A bargain purchase option exists when the lessee may purchase the leased asset at a price expected to be so far below the fair value at the exercise date that, at the lease's inception, exercise is reasonably certain.

   c. The lease term is for the **major part of the economic life** of the leased asset.

   d. The **present value of the minimum lease payments** is at least substantially all of the fair value of the leased asset at the inception of the lease.

   e. The leased asset is such that it can be used only by the lessee **without major modification.**

3. **Other factors** also may indicate classification as a finance lease.

   a. The lessor's losses from cancelation of the lease are borne by the lessee.

   b. The lessee bears the risk of fluctuations in the fair value of the residual value.

   c. The lessee may renew the lease at a rent substantially below the market rent.

Lessee Accounting for Finance Leases

4. The lessee records a finance lease as an **asset and liability** at **fair value** (not exceeding the present value of the minimum lease payments). The lessee records the asset in PPE (i.e., as a tangible asset).
   a. The **discount factor** used to calculate present value is the lessor's interest rate implicit in the lease (if practicable to determine).
      1) The alternative is to use the **lessee's incremental borrowing rate.**
   b. In subsequent periods, the lessee should depreciate the asset and recognize **finance (interest) expense** on the liability.
   c. **Depreciation** should be consistent with the accounting policy for owned assets. Absent a reasonable certainty that the lessee will own the asset at the end of the lease term, it should be fully depreciated over the **shorter** of the **useful life** or the **lease term.**
5. The lessee's **minimum lease payments** include the minimum rental payments during the lease term and the amount of a bargain purchase option.
   a. **If no bargain purchase option** exists, the minimum lease payments equal the sum of (1) the minimum rental payments over the lease term and (2) any amounts guaranteed by the lessee or by a party related to the lessee.
   b. **From the lessor's perspective**, the minimum lease payments (absent a bargain purchase option) equal the sum of (1) the minimum rental payments over the lease term and (2) any residual value guaranteed by the lessee, a party related to the lessee, or a financially capable third party unrelated to the lessor or lessee.
6. A **periodic lease payment** has two components:
   a. Reduction of the outstanding liability **(principal)**
      1) The portion of the payment greater than the finance expense reduces the liability for the finance lease.
   b. The finance expense **(interest)**
      1) This expense is allocated so that a constant periodic rate of interest is maintained on the diminishing liability balance.
      2) Under the **effective-interest method**, the appropriate interest rate is applied to the carrying amount of the lease liability at the beginning of the interest period to calculate finance expense.

Lessor Accounting for Finance Leases

7. Under a finance lease, the lessor recognizes a net receivable equal to the **net investment** in the lease: **gross investment** (lessor's minimum lease payments + unguaranteed residual value) **discounted at the interest rate implicit in the lease.**
   a. **Unearned finance income** equals the difference between the gross investment and the net investment in the lease.
      1) Finance income is recognized so as to provide a constant periodic rate of return on the carrying amount of the net investment. Thus, lease payments (minus costs for services) are applied to reduce the principal and the unearned finance income.
   b. The **initial direct costs** of entering into a finance lease, e.g., commissions and legal fees, are included in the initial measurement of the lease receivable.
      1) Thus, they must be **allocated** over the lease term, not expensed as incurred. However, this rule does not apply to **manufacturer or dealer lessors.**
      2) Their initial direct costs are **expensed** when **selling profit** is recognized.

8. When a **manufacturer or dealer** lessor accounts for a finance lease, selling profit or loss is recognized as if an outright sale had occurred. If the **interest rate is lower** than the market rate, the selling profit (sales revenue – cost of sale) is limited to the amount resulting from using the **market rate**.
   a. The **initial direct costs** are expensed at the lease's inception.
   b. **Sales revenue** is the fair value of the asset or, if lower, the present value of the minimum lease payments based on a market interest rate.
   c. The **cost of sale** equals the cost or carrying amount of the leased property minus the present value of the unguaranteed residual value.
9. The following are the basic lessor entries:

Lessor not a Manufacturer/Dealer			Manufacturer/Dealer		
Lease payments receivable	XXX		Cost of sale	XXX	
Asset		XXX	Asset		XXX
Unearned finance income		XXX			
			Lease payments receivable	XXX	
			Sales revenue		XXX
			Unearned finance income		XXX

Operating Leases

10. Leases that **do not meet any of the criteria** for classification as finance leases are treated as operating leases. The **lessor retains** substantially all the risks and rewards of ownership.
    a. Under an operating lease, the **lessee records no liability** except for rental expense accrued at the end of an accounting period.
    b. Thus, an operating lease is a form of off-balance-sheet financing. The **lessor continues to** recognize and **depreciate** an asset, and a manufacturer or dealer lessor recognizes no selling profit.
11. **Rent** is reported as expense or income by the lessee or lessor, respectively, on a **straight-line basis**.
    a. However, another systematic basis may be used if it is more representative of, respectively, (1) the time pattern of the user's benefit or (2) the time pattern in which the use benefit from the asset is reduced.
12. If **initial direct costs** are incurred for an operating lease, the **lessor** adds them to the carrying amount of the leased asset.

Stop and review! You have completed the outline for this subunit. Study multiple-choice questions 6 through 8 beginning on page 188.

4.4 INCOME TAXES

Definitions

1. Differences may occur between income reported under **IFRSs** (accrual basis) and income reported for **tax purposes** (modified cash basis). A deferred tax liability or asset ordinarily is recognized to reflect the differences that have tax consequences.
   a. A **temporary difference (TD)** arises when the carrying amount and the tax base of an asset or liability differ. The effect is that a taxable or deductible TD will occur in future years when the asset is recovered or the liability is settled, respectively.
      1) A **deferred tax liability (DTL)** is recognized for a TD that results in **future taxable amounts**.
      2) A **deferred tax asset (DTA)** is recognized for a TD that results in **future deductible amounts**.
      3) TDs have income statement and balance sheet consequences.

b. The **tax base** is the amount attributed for tax purposes to an asset or liability.

1) The tax base of an **asset** is the amount **deductible** against future taxable economic benefits when the asset's carrying amount is recovered.

2) The tax base of a **liability** is the portion of the carrying amount that will **not be deductible** against future taxable economic benefits for tax purposes.

a) The tax base of **revenue received in advance** (a liability) is the portion of the carrying amount taxable in the future.

c. **Income taxes** are all domestic and foreign taxes on taxable profits. **Tax expense or tax income** reported in the income statement for the period consists of **current and deferred** components.

1) **Current tax** is the tax payable or recoverable regarding taxable profit or tax loss.

a) **Taxable profit or tax loss** is calculated based on tax law.

2) **Deferred tax expense or income** is the sum of the changes in the DTAs and DTLs.

Δ DTAs + Δ DTLs

a) For example, this amount reflects changes relating to the origination or reversal of TDs, changes in tax rates, and imposition of new taxes. Thus, the decrease in a DTA or an increase in a DTL increases deferred tax expense.

<u>**Temporary Differences**</u>

2. **Taxable TDs** occur when

a. **Revenues** (including gains) are included in taxable income after they are recognized under IFRSs.

1) An example is income recognized under the **equity method** for financial statement purposes and at the time of distribution in taxable income. Another example is sales revenue **accrued** for financial reporting and recognized on the **installment basis** for tax purposes.

b. **Expenses** (including losses) are deductible for tax purposes before they are recognized under IFRSs.

1) An example is accelerated tax depreciation of property.

c. No **DTL** is recognized when it results from the initial recognition of **goodwill** or goodwill for which amortization is not tax deductible. The reason is that the recognition of a DTL would increase goodwill.

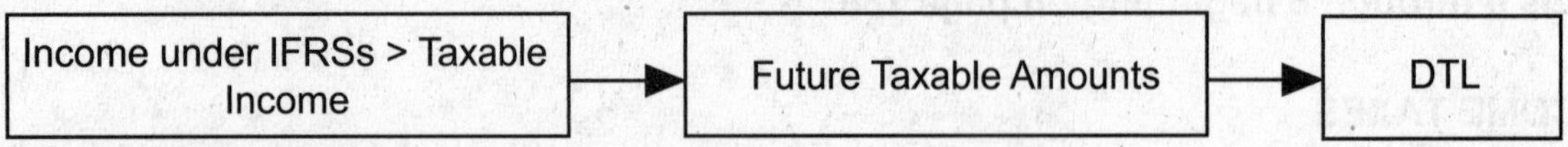

3. **Deductible TDs** occur when

a. **Revenues** (including gains) are included in taxable income before they are recognized under IFRSs.

1) An example is subscription revenue received in advance.

b. **Expenses** (including losses) are deductible for tax purposes after they are recognized under IFRSs.

1) Examples include bad debt expense recognized under the allowance method and warranty costs.

c. A **DTA** is recognized for the **carryforward** of unused tax losses and credits, but only to the extent it is **probable** that taxable profit will be available to permit the use of those amounts.

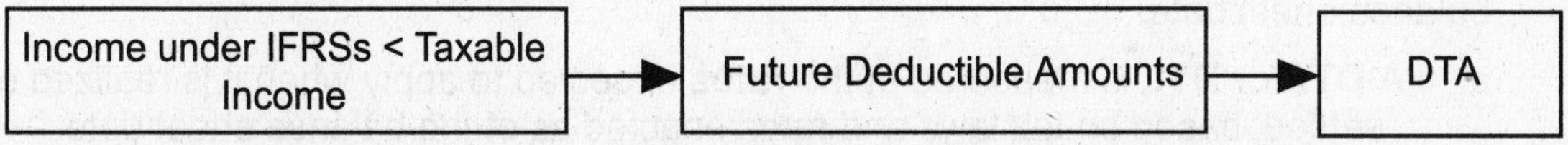

4. In some future period, TDs will reverse. The following are examples:

a. Accelerated tax depreciation

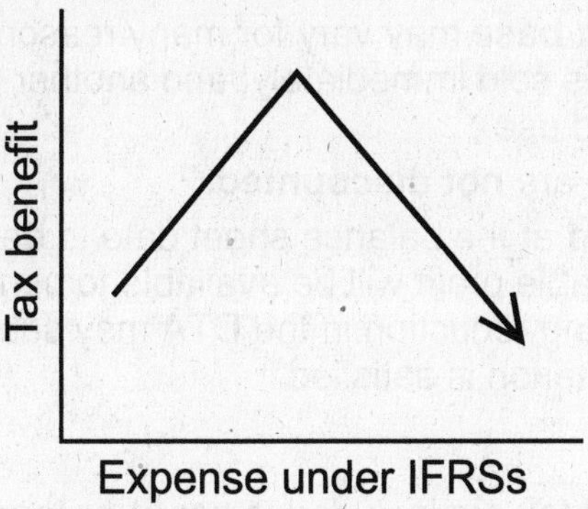

b. Prepaid expenses

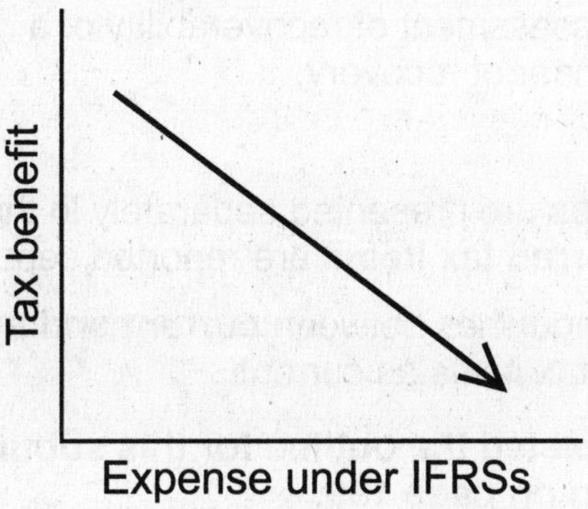

c. Investments accounted for by the equity method

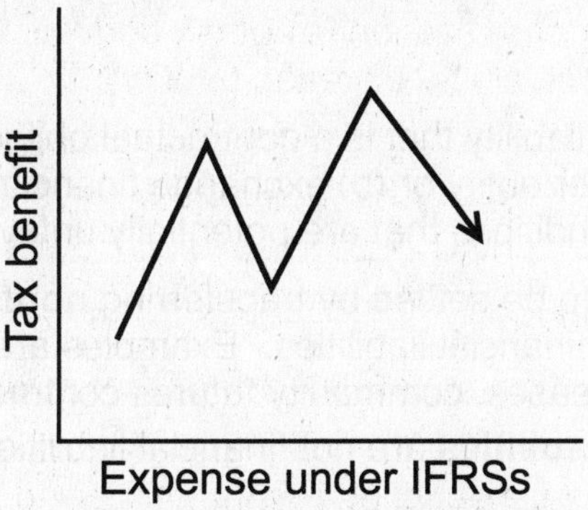

5. **Cash flows** are not affected by the **basis of accounting** used to prepare the financial statements. Accordingly, whether the financial statements are prepared on the tax basis, the cash basis, or a basis generally accepted in a given country, cash flows should be the same.

a. The amount of cash paid in taxes depends on a government's laws, not the basis of accounting an entity uses for its financial statements

Measurement

6. A **current tax liability or asset** for the current and prior periods is the amount to be paid to, or recovered from, the tax authorities, based on tax laws and rates enacted as of the balance sheet date.
   a. A **DTA or DTL** is measured at the **rates** expected to apply when it is realized or settled, based on tax laws and rates enacted as of the balance sheet date.
      1) If different rates apply to different taxable profit levels, a DTA or DTL is measured based on the average rates expected to apply in the periods when the TDs are expected to reverse.
   b. The **tax rate** or **tax base** may vary for many reasons. For example, one tax rate may apply if an asset is sold immediately, and another may apply if it is to be recovered through continued use.
   c. Deferred tax items are **not discounted**.
   d. A **DTA is reviewed** at the balance sheet date to determine **whether it is probable** that sufficient taxable profit will be available to permit the benefit of the DTA to be used. Any resulting reduction in the DTA may subsequently be reversed to the extent the availability criterion is satisfied.

Recognition

7. Current tax and deferred tax are included in **profit or loss** as income or expense.
   a. The **carrying amount** of a deferred tax item may change because of a change in a tax law or rate, a reassessment of recoverability of a deferred tax asset, or a change in the expected manner of recovery.

Presentation

8. **Tax assets and liabilities** are presented separately in the balance sheet from other assets and liabilities, and **deferred tax items** are reported separately from **current tax items**.
   a. An entity that distinguishes between **current and noncurrent items** should **not** classify deferred tax items as current.

Stop and review! You have completed the outline for this subunit. Study multiple-choice questions 9 through 11 beginning on page 189.

4.5 OTHER LIABILITIES

Liability v. Equity

1. A **financial liability** is a liability that is a contractual obligation to (a) deliver cash or another financial asset to another entity or (b) exchange financial assets or financial liabilities with another entity under conditions that are potentially unfavorable.
   a. Liabilities that are to be settled by transferring **nonfinancial assets** or rendering **services** are not financial liabilities. Examples are deferred revenue and liabilities under operating leases, commodity futures contracts, and most warranties.
   b. **Noncontractual liabilities** are not financial liabilities. An example is income taxes payable.
   c. An **equity instrument** is evidence of a **residual interest** in an entity's net assets.

d. Whether a financial instrument is a liability, an asset, or an equity item depends on its **substance**, not its legal form, at the time of initial recognition and on the definitions of those elements.

1) For example, if the issuer must redeem **preference (preferred) shares**, and the amount and date of redemption are fixed, the shares are liabilities.

2) If a financial instrument has **equity and liability components**, they are presented separately in the balance sheet.

a) An example is **convertible debt**.

3) **Interest, dividends, losses, and gains** related to a **financial liability** are reported as income or expense in profit or loss. **Distributions on equity** are debited directly to equity.

a) Accordingly, dividends on shares **classified as liabilities** are items of expense, and gains and losses on their redemption or refinancing also are included in profit or loss.

b) The effects of redemption or refinancing of an **equity instrument**, however, are included directly in equity.

e. Typical financial liabilities include trade accounts payable, notes payable, loans payable, and bonds payable.

f. Financial assets and liabilities usually are **not offset**.

Current Liabilities

2. A current liability is an obligation that is (a) expected to be settled within the normal **operating cycle**, (b) held to be **traded**, or (c) due to be **settled** within 12 months of the balance sheet date.

a. A liability also is current if the entity has **no unconditional right** to defer settlement for 12 months.

b. Any other liability is **noncurrent**.

c. Current liabilities **not settled within the normal operating cycle** include the current part of interest-bearing debt, income taxes, and bank overdrafts.

Refinancing

d. Financial liabilities **due to be settled within 12 months** ordinarily should continue to be classified as current.

1) However, an entity that expects and **has discretion** to refinance or roll over the liability under an **existing** loan agreement classifies it as **noncurrent**.

Obligations Callable Because of Breach

e. A debtor may breach a long-term borrowing agreement, making the debt payable on demand and classifiable as **current**.

3. The most common financial liabilities are **accounts payable** (trade payables). They are usually noninterest-bearing, unsecured obligations to sellers that are incurred when an entity purchases inventory, supplies, or services on credit. These liabilities arise when the goods or services have been received or supplied.

a. The timing of recognition of accounts payable may depend on the **shipping terms**, that is, whether title and risk of loss pass at the point of **shipment** or at the ultimate **destination**.

Accrued Expenses

4. Ordinarily, accrued expenses meet **recognition criteria** in the current period but have **not been paid** as of year-end. They are accounted for using basic accrual entries.

Reversing Entries

5. These may be used to facilitate accounting for accrued expenses in the next period. For example, if wages payable are accrued at year-end, the **entry** is

Wages expense	XXX	
Wages payable		XXX

   a. The **reversing entry** at the beginning of the next period is

Wages payable	XXX	
Wages expense		XXX

      1) In the next period, no allocation of the first wages payment between the liability and the expense is needed. The entry will simply be

Wages expense	XXX	
Cash		XXX

   b. If **reversing entries are not made**, either of the following methods is used in the next period:

      1) The **liability is debited** when the accrued expense is **actually paid**. For example, the entry for the first wages payment of the year is

Wages expense	XXX	
Wages payable	XXX	
Cash		XXX

         a) This entry will differ from later entries recording payment of wages.

      2) Payments are recorded by **debiting expense for the full amounts** paid. At year-end, the liability is adjusted to the balance owed at that date. For example, if the liability for accrued wages has decreased, the **adjusting entry** is

Wages payable	XXX	
Wages expense		XXX

Effects of Nonaccrual

6. If an entity fails to accrue expenses at year-end, **income** is overstated in that period and understated in the next period (when they are paid and presumably expensed).

   a. Moreover, expenses incurred but unpaid and not recorded result in understated **accrued liabilities** and possibly understated assets (for example, if the amounts should be inventoried). In addition, **working capital** (current assets – current liabilities) will be overstated, but **cash flows** will not be affected.

EXAMPLE

Windy Co. must determine the December 31, Year 2, year-end accruals for advertising and rent expenses. A US $500 advertising bill was received January 7, Year 3. It related to costs of US $375 for advertisements in December Year 2 and US $125 for advertisements in January Year 3. A lease, effective December 16, Year 1, calls for fixed rent of US $1,200 per month, payable beginning 1 month from the effective date. In addition, rent equal to 5% of net sales over US $300,000 per calendar year is payable on January 31 of the following year. Net sales for Year 2 were US $550,000.

The US $375 of advertising expense should be accrued in Year 2. This amount can be directly related to events in that period. The US $125 amount is related to events in Year 3 and should not be accrued in Year 2.

The fixed rental is due at mid-month. Thus, the fixed rental for the last half month of Year 2 (US $1,200 ÷ 2 = US $600) and the rental based on annual sales [(US $550,000 – $300,000) × 5% = US $12,500] also should be accrued.

In its December 31, Year 2, balance sheet, Windy should report accrued liabilities of US $13,475 ($375 + $600 + $12,500).

7. **Short-term employee benefits** expected to be paid as a result of service rendered during the period ordinarily should be recognized as an expense and a liability (accrued expense).

   a. For **short-term compensated absences**, the timing of recognition depends on whether the benefits **accumulate**. If they accumulate, the expected cost is recognized when services are rendered that increase the employees' entitlement to future compensated absences.

   b. The obligation is recognized whether it is **vesting** or **not vesting**. It equals the additional amount expected to be paid as a result of the unused accumulated entitlement at the balance sheet date.

Deferred Revenues

8. If the **recognition criteria are not met**, advance receipts (e.g., for rent, deposits, or subscriptions) are treated as **liabilities** (deferred revenues). Recognition is deferred until the obligation is partly or wholly satisfied, that is, when the increase in future **economic benefits** becomes **reliably measurable**.

   a. When the recognition criteria are met, **revenue** is recognized by a debit to deferred revenue and a credit to revenue.

EXAMPLE

The musical group Widget Express is going on a worldwide tour. Its advance ticket sales are US $10,000,000. The journal entry to recognize this deferred revenue as a liability is

Cash	US $10,000,000	
Advance ticket sales		US $10,000,000

After the first concert, Widget Express recognizes revenue:

Advance ticket sales	US $1,000,000	
Revenue		US $1,000,000

Stop and review! You have completed the outline for this subunit. Study multiple-choice questions 12 through 14 beginning on page 190.

4.6 PROVISIONS AND CONTINGENCIES

Provisions

1. These differ from trade payables and accruals because of their greater uncertainty. They differ from contingent liabilities because they are present obligations that meet the recognition criteria.

   a. Provisions are defined in **IAS 37**, *Provisions, Contingent Liabilities, and Contingent Assets*, as liabilities of uncertain timing or amount.

      1) **Examples** of provisions are liabilities for violations of environmental law, nuclear plant decommissioning costs, warranties, restructurings, and premiums offered to customers.

   b. **Recognition** of provisions is appropriate when

      1) The entity has a present obligation resulting from a past event (called an obligating event),

      2) It is probable (more likely than not) that an outflow of economic benefits will be necessary to settle the obligation, and

      3) Its amount can be reliably estimated.

   c. A **past event** leads to a **present obligation** if the entity has no realistic alternative to settlement.

2. **Measurement** of provisions is in accordance with the **best estimate** of the amount needed to settle the obligation.
   a. **Risks and uncertainties** are considered in calculating the best estimate, but they should not result in deliberate overstatement.
   b. The measurement should be at the **present value** of the outflows needed to settle the obligation if the effects of discounting are material.
3. A provision is adjusted at the balance sheet date to the **current best estimate**. If the recognition criteria are no longer met, the provision is reversed.
   a. If a present value measurement has been made, the periodic increase resulting from the reduction in the discount period is treated as a borrowing cost.
4. **Future operating losses** are not an appropriate basis for a provision.

<u>**Contingencies**</u>

5. These are possible obligations or do not meet the recognition criteria.
   a. A **contingent liability** is a **possible obligation** arising from past events. Its existence will be confirmed only by uncertain future events not wholly within the entity's control. A liability also is contingent if it does not meet the recognition criteria.
      1) For example, if the entity and other parties are each potentially liable for the full amount of an obligation, the amount expected to be paid by the other parties is a contingent liability.
      2) A contingent liability is **not recognized** but should be **disclosed.**
   b. A **contingent asset** is a **possible asset** arising from past events and the existence of which will be confirmed only by uncertain future events not wholly within the entity's control. An example is a potential recovery on a legal claim with an uncertain outcome.
      1) A probable contingent asset is **not recognized** but should be **disclosed.**

Stop and review! You have completed the outline for this subunit. Study multiple-choice questions 15 through 17 beginning on page 191.

4.7 BONDS

<u>**Nature of Bonds**</u>

1. Bonds are **debt instruments.**
2. The issue price of a bond is a function of the market interest rate and reflects the bond's fair value.
3. The **proceeds received** from the sale of a bond equal the sum of the **present values** of the **face amount** and the **interest payments** (if the bond is interest-bearing).
   a. When bonds are issued between interest payment dates, the buyer includes **accrued interest** in the purchase price.

Premium or Discount

4. When the **proceeds differ from the face amount**, the difference is a premium or discount.
   a. Bonds are sold at a **premium** when the stated (contract) interest rate exceeds the market (effective) interest rate. The entry is

Cash	XXX	
Premium on bonds payable		XXX
Bonds payable		XXX

   b. Bonds are sold at a **discount** when the stated interest rate is less than the market (effective) interest rate. The entry is

Cash	XXX	
Discount on bonds payable	XXX	
Bonds payable		XXX

5. Bond discount or premium must be amortized using the **effective interest method**, also known as the **interest method** (unless the results of another method are not materially different).
   a. Under the interest method, interest expense changes every period, but the interest rate is constant.
6. **Interest expense** for a period is equal to the **carrying amount** of the bonds at the beginning of the period (face amount – unamortized discount or + unamortized premium) times the yield (market) interest rate.
7. The **cash paid** for periodic interest is equal to the face amount of the bonds times the stated rate. It remains constant over the life of the bonds.
8. The difference between interest expense and cash interest paid is the discount or premium **amortization**.
   a. Discount amortized, total interest expense, and the carrying amount of the bonds **increase** each period when amortizing a **discount**. The journal entry is

Interest expense	XXX	
Discount on bonds payable		XXX
Cash		XXX

   b. Premium amortized, total interest expense, and the carrying amount of the bonds **decrease** each period when amortizing a **premium**. The journal entry is

Interest expense	XXX	
Premium on bonds payable	XXX	
Cash		XXX

EXAMPLE

Amortizing a discount (stated rate less than effective rate). Assume issuance of a 6%, 5-year, US $5,000 bond (interest paid at the end of each annual period) with an 8% effective rate.

Year	Beginning Net Carrying Amount	Times: Effective Rate	Equals: Interest Expense	Minus: Cash Paid	Equals: Discount Amortized	Ending Net Carrying Amount
1	US $4,601	8%	US $ 368	US $ 300	US $ 68	US $4,669
2	4,669	8%	374	300	74	4,743
3	4,743	8%	379	300	79	4,822
4	4,822	8%	386	300	86	4,908
5	4,908	8%	393	300	93	5,000
			US $1,899	US $1,500	US $399	

EXAMPLE

Amortizing a premium (stated rate greater than effective rate). Assume issuance of an 8%, 5-year, US $5,000 bond (interest paid at the end of each annual period) with a 6% effective rate.

Year	Beginning Net Carrying Amount	Times: Effective Rate	Equals: Interest Expense	Minus: Cash Paid	Equals: Premium Amortized	Ending Net Carrying Amount
1	US $5,421	6%	US $ 325	US $ 400	US $ (75)	US $5,346
2	5,346	6%	321	400	(79)	5,267
3	5,287	6%	316	400	(84)	5,183
4	5,183	6%	311	400	(89)	5,094
5	5,094	6%	306	400	(94)	5,000
			US $1,579	US $2,000	US $(421)	

c. At the **maturity date**, the discount or premium will be **fully amortized** to zero, and the net carrying amount of the bonds will equal the face amount.

9. Bond discount or premium is a direct subtraction from or addition to, respectively, the face amount of the bonds payable in the **balance sheet**.

Stop and review! You have completed the outline for this subunit. Study multiple-choice questions 18 and 19 on page 193.

4.8 EQUITY

Elements of Equity

1. Equity consists of share capital; items of income and expense reported directly in equity; retained earnings; and, possibly, treasury shares.

Share capital:			
Preference (preferred) shares	XXX		
Share premium	XXX	XXX	
Ordinary (common) shares	XXX		
Share premium	XXX	XXX	
Total share capital			XXX
Reserves:			
Revaluation surplus		XXX	
Foreign currency translation adjustment		XXX	
Total reserves			XXX
Retained earnings:			
Retained earnings appropriated for...		XXX	
Unappropriated retained earnings		XXX	
Total retained earnings			XXX
Noncontrolling interest			XXX
Treasury shares (at cost)			(XXX)
Total equity			XXX

Share Capital

2. Issued capital represents investments by owners in exchange for shares.
   a. One share capital account shows the **par or stated value** of all shares outstanding (if shares have no par or stated value, the amount received is given).
      1) Amounts for each class of share capital, such as ordinary (common) and preference (preferred) shares, are usually separately listed.
   b. **Share premium** consists of the sources of issued capital in excess of par or stated value.
   c. **Direct transaction costs** are subtracted from equity.
   d. The **number of shares** authorized, issued, and outstanding **must be disclosed**, either on the face of the balance sheet or in the notes.

Reserves

3. The term reserve refers to capital maintenance adjustments (e.g., various revaluations or restatements of assets or liabilities) and appropriations of retained earnings. It also applies to items recognized directly in equity.
   a. Reserves must be presented on the **face of the balance sheet**.
   b. The reserve accounts also report the **cumulative balances** of the items of **other comprehensive income** reported on the statement of comprehensive income.

Retained Earnings

4. This amount is accumulated profit or loss. It is increased by profit and decreased by loss, dividends, and certain transactions in treasury shares.
   a. An entity may **appropriate** retained earnings to, for example, comply with a bond indenture, retain assets, anticipate losses, or meet legal restrictions.
      1) The appropriation limits dividends but does not set aside assets. Moreover, any such transfer is excluded from the determination of profit or loss.

Treasury Shares

5. These are the entity's own equity instruments reacquired for various purposes, e.g., mergers, options, or share dividends.
   a. After treasury shares are reacquired, they are **legally available to be reissued** even if the intention is to cancel them.
   b. The acquisition of treasury shares results in a **direct change in equity**.
      1) **Recognition of income or expense** on treasury share transactions is **not** allowed because they represent a shifting of interests among shareholders.
         a) Thus, the Framework defines **income** to exclude contributions from equity holders and **expense** to exclude distributions to equity holders.

Cost Method v. Par Value Method

   c. Under the **cost method**, the entry to recognize treasury shares is a debit to treasury shares and a credit to cash.
      1) When the treasury shares are subsequently reissued for cash at a price in **excess of acquisition cost**, the difference is credited to **share premium from treasury share transactions**.
      2) If the treasury shares are reissued for **less than acquisition cost**, the difference is debited to **share premium from treasury share transactions**. If this account has a zero balance, the debit is to **retained earnings**.
      3) Treasury shares accounted for at cost reduce total equity.

d. The **par value method** treats the acquisition of treasury shares as the equivalent of a retirement and the resale as a new issuance.

1) Upon acquisition, the original entry to issue shares is reversed by

   a) Offsetting the appropriate share capital account, e.g., ordinary shares, with treasury shares at par value and

   b) Removing the share premium recorded when the shares were originally issued.

2) Any difference between the **original issuance price** and the **reacquisition price** is ordinarily adjusted through share premium accounts and retained earnings.

   a) **Premiums** are credited to share premium from treasury share transactions, and **discounts** are debited to the same account but only to the extent of prior premiums.

      i) If the credit balance in the account is insufficient to absorb the discount, **retained earnings** will be debited for the remainder.

3) **Reissuance** removes the treasury shares at par value and reestablishes share premium for any excess of the reissuance price over par value.

   a) If the reissuance price is less than par, the debit is to a share premium account or to retained earnings.

4) Treasury shares stated at par is a direct reduction of the appropriate **share capital account**.

EXAMPLE

An entity has the following balances in its equity section on December 31, Year 1:

Common shares, US $20 par value, 300,000 outstanding	US $6,000,000
Share premium (US $2 per share)	US $ 600,000
Retained earnings	US $2,000,000

The following transactions occurred in Year 2. The entries (assuming no prior treasury share transactions) are shown below.

1) Reacquired 50,000 shares for US $2,000,000 ($40 per share)
2) Reissued 10,000 shares of treasury stock for US $30 per share
3) Retired the 40,000 remaining treasury shares

Cost

1)	Treasury shares (cost)	US $2,000,000	
	Cash		US $2,000,000
2)	Cash	$300,000	
	Retained earnings	100,000	
	Treasury shares (10,000 × US $40)		US $400,000
3)	Common stock (40,000 × US $20)	US $800,000	
	Share premium (40,000 × US $2)	80,000	
	Retained earnings	720,000	
	Treasury shares (cost) (40,000 × US $40)		US $1,600,000

Par Value

1)	Treasury share, common (par value) (50,000 × US $20)	US $1,000,000	
	Share premium (50,000 × US $2)*	100,000	
	Retained earnings	900,000	
	Cash		US $2,000,000
2)	Cash	$300,000	
	Treasury shares at par value (10,000 × US $20)		US $200,000
	Share premium from treasury shares		100,000
3)	Common stock	US $800,000	
	Treasury shares (par value)		US $800,000

* This entry would differ given a credit balance in share premium from treasury shares.

Issuance of Shares

6. Cash is debited, the appropriate class of share capital is credited for any par or stated value, and the difference is credited to share premium.

   a. Shares may be issued in exchange for **services or property** as well as for cash.

Retirement

7. When shares are retired, cash (or treasury shares) is credited. The appropriate class of share capital account is debited for any par or stated value.

   a. **Share premium** is debited to the extent it exists from the original issuance. Any remainder is debited to retained earnings or credited to **premium from share retirement.**

Cash Dividends

8. **Cash dividends** cannot be rescinded. The following are the entries:

Declaration		
Retained earnings	XXX	
Dividends payable		XXX
Payment		
Dividends payable	XXX	
Cash		XXX

9. If dividends on preference (preferred) shares are **cumulative**, dividends in arrears and the preference dividends for the current period must be paid before ordinary shareholders may receive dividends.

   a. **Dividends in arrears** are not a liability until they are declared and are not recognized in the financial statements.

10. Preference shares also may be **participating**.

   a. For example, they may share equally in a cash dividend after a basic return has been paid to holders of ordinary and preference shares.

Share Dividend and Splits

11. A **share dividend** involves no distribution of cash or other property. Share dividends are accounted for as a reclassification of equity, not as liabilities.

   a. The recipient does **not recognize income**. It has the same proportionate interest in the entity and the same total carrying amount as before the share dividend.

12. **Share splits** are issuances of shares that do not affect any aggregate par value of shares issued and outstanding or total equity.

   a. No entry is made, and no transfer from retained earnings occurs.

Rights

13. In a rights offering, each shareholder is issued a certificate or **warrant** that is a call option to buy a certain number of shares at a fixed price. If the rights are **exercised**, the **issuer** accounts for the proceeds as an increase in share capital at par value or stated value, if any, with any remainder credited to share premium.

   a. However, if rights issued without consideration **lapse**, share capital is unaffected.

   b. The **recipient allocates the carrying amount** of the shares owned between those shares and the rights based on relative fair values. The portion of the price allocated to the rights increases (decreases) the discount (premium) on the investment.

   c. Transaction costs of redeeming share rights reduce equity.

Stop and review! You have completed the outline for this subunit. Study multiple-choice questions 20 through 22 beginning on page 194.

4.9 ACCOUNTING CHANGES

1. According to **IAS 8**, *Accounting Policies, Changes in Estimates, and Errors*, **accounting policies** are "specific principles, bases, conventions, rules, and practices adopted by an entity in preparing and presenting financial statements."
   a. To facilitate comparison, the same accounting policies ordinarily should be followed **consistently**.

Changes in Accounting Policy

2. A change in accounting policy is indicated only if it will result in **reliable and more relevant** information or if it is required.
   a. A change in policy does not occur when a policy is chosen for events or transactions **differing in substance** or transactions or that have **not previously occurred** or that are **not material**.
3. Changes in accounting policy normally are accounted for by **retrospective application**.
   a. The opening balances of all **equity accounts** for the first period presented are adjusted.
   b. All other amounts are adjusted **as if the new policy had been in effect for all periods presented.**
   c. Retrospective application is **not done** if it is impracticable to determine **period-specific effects** or the **cumulative effect**.
      1) **Impracticable** means that the entity cannot apply a requirement after making every reasonable effort.

Changes in Accounting Estimate

4. A **change in accounting estimate** involves adjusting the carrying amount of an asset or liability or the consumption of an asset.
   a. It results from reassessing the status and expected benefits and obligations related to assets and liabilities.
5. A change in estimate is based on new information and is not an error correction.
   a. Its effect is included in **profit or loss** in the period of change (if the change affects that period only) or in the period of change and in future periods (if the change affects both).
   b. If the change in accounting estimate results in changes in **assets, liabilities, or equity**, the change is recognized by adjusting the carrying amount of each related item in the period of change.
   c. **Examples of estimates** are (1) uncollectible receivables, (2) inventory obsolescence, (3) service lives and residual values of depreciable assets, (4) warranty costs, (5) periods benefited by a deferred cost, and (6) recoverable mineral reserves.
   d. If distinguishing between a **change in estimate** and a change in accounting policy is difficult, the change is accounted for as a change in estimate and properly disclosed.

Correction of Errors

6. All **material prior-period errors** must be corrected **retrospectively** in the first set of financial statements issued after their discovery. This is done by restating the comparative amounts for the prior periods when the error occurred.
   a. If the error occurred prior to the first period presented, the **opening balances** for the first period presented are restated.
   b. A **material error** is one that could, individually or collectively, affect the decisions of users of the financial statements.
   c. **Typical errors** are mistakes in mathematical calculations, in the application of accounting policies, or in factual interpretation. Other examples are fraud or simple oversight.
   d. **Comparative information** should be restated **if practicable.**

Error Analysis

7. An **accounting error affecting prior-period statements** may or may not affect profit or loss. For example, misclassifying an item as a gain rather than a revenue does not affect profit or loss and is readily correctable. No adjustment is required.
   a. An error that affects prior-period profit or loss is **counterbalancing** if it self-corrects over two periods.
      1) For example, **understating ending inventory** for one period (and the beginning inventory of the next period) understates the profit and retained earnings of the first period but overstates the profit and retained earnings of the next period by the same amount (assuming no tax changes).
         a) Despite the self-correction, the financial statements **remain misstated.** They should be restated if presented comparatively in a later period.

EXAMPLE

Year 1		Year 2	
Beginning inventory		Beginning inventory	U
+ Purchases		+ Purchases	
− Ending inventory	(U)	− Ending inventory	
= Cost of goods sold	(O)	= Cost of goods sold	(U)
Profit	(U)	Profit	(O)
Retained earnings	(U)	Retained earnings	(O)

      2) An example of a **noncounterbalancing error** is a misstatement of **depreciation**. Such an error does not self-correct over two periods. Thus, an adjustment will be necessary.

Stop and review! You have completed the outline for this subunit. Study multiple-choice questions 23 through 26 beginning on page 195.

4.10 EXCHANGE RATES

1. **IAS 21**, *The Effects of Changes in Foreign Exchange Rates*, applies to (a) foreign currency transactions and balances, (b) translation of the results and financial position of foreign operations included in the entity's statements, and (c) translation of results and financial position into a presentation currency.

Definitions

a. A **functional currency** is the currency of an entity's primary economic environment.
b. A **foreign currency** is any currency that is not the functional currency.
c. A **foreign operation** has activities not in the reporting entity's currency or country.
d. The **presentation currency** is the currency in which the statements are reported.
e. The **closing rate** is the spot exchange rate (rate for immediate delivery) at the balance sheet date.
f. The **spot rate** is the current exchange rate. It is not a future (or forward) rate.

Foreign Currency Transactions

2. A foreign currency transaction is stated, or requires settlement in, a foreign currency.
   a. **Initial recognition** in the **functional currency** is at the spot rate between the functional and foreign currencies at the transaction date
   b. If the monetary aspect of the transaction has not yet occurred at the **balance sheet date**, **monetary items** are translated at the **closing rate**.
      1) **Nonmonetary items measured at historical cost** are **not** retranslated at the balance sheet date. They remain translated at the rate on the **transaction date**.
      2) **Nonmonetary items measured at fair value** are **not** retranslated at the balance sheet date. They remain translated at the rates **when the fair values were measured**.
   c. An **exchange difference** arises when a given amount of one currency is translated into another currency at different exchange rates at different times. This can happen at initial recognition, the balance sheet date, or settlement of monetary items.
      1) Exchange differences ordinarily are recognized **in profit or loss** when they arise.
      2) Certain gains or losses on **nonmonetary items** are recognized in profit or loss and others directly in equity.
         a) For example, if a revaluation gain or loss on PPE is required to be recognized in equity, the exchange component also is recognized in equity.
      3) An exchange difference with respect to a monetary item that is part of a **net investment in a foreign entity** (a share of its net assets) is recorded **directly in equity** in the consolidated statements until disposal of the investment.
3. A **change in the functional currency** is accounted for prospectively.
4. The exchange differences are recognized in a **separate component of equity**.
5. If the functional currency is that of a **hyperinflationary economy**, translation to a different presentation currency is at the **closing rate** for the most recent balance sheet for **all amounts**.
6. **Goodwill** from acquisition of a foreign operation and any **fair value adjustments** to carrying amounts of assets and liabilities are assets and liabilities of the foreign operation. They are stated in the operation's functional currency and translated at the closing rate.

Stop and review! You have completed the outline for this subunit. Study multiple-choice question 27 on page 196.

4.11 BUSINESS COMBINATIONS

Definitions

1. According to **IFRS 3**, *Business Combinations*,
   a. A **business combination** is a transaction or event in which an acquirer obtains control of one or more businesses.
   b. The **acquirer** must be identified in every combination. It is the combining entity that controls one or more businesses. The **acquisition date** is when the acquirer gains control.
   c. **Control** is "the power to govern the financial and operating policies of an entity so as to obtain benefits from its activities."

Acquisition Method

2. This method is used for all business combinations.
3. The acquisition method involves
   a. Identifying the **acquirer**
   b. Determining when the acquirer obtained control of the acquiree (the **acquisition date**)
   c. Recognition and measurement of
      1) Identifiable assets acquired
      2) Liabilities assumed
      3) Any **noncontrolling interest (NCI)**
   d. Recognition and measurement of
      1) **Goodwill** or
      2) Gain from a **bargain purchase**

Measurement

4. Measurement of assets acquired and liabilities assumed is customarily at **acquisition-date fair value**.
   a. **Intangible assets** acquired must be recognized and measured even if they were not recognized by the acquiree.
   b. An **NCI** may be measured at
      1) Fair value or
      2) Its proportionate share of the acquiree's identifiable net assets.

EXAMPLE

Acquirer (AR) obtained 75% of the equity interests of Acquiree (AE) in a forced sale. AR had no prior equity interest in AE. AR determined that the following are appropriate fair value measures to be used in accounting for this combination:

AE's identifiable assets acquired	US $1,000,000
AE's liabilities assumed	200,000

If AR measures the NCI at its proportionate share of the identifiable net assets, it will be reported initially at US $200,000 [(US $1,000,000 – $200,000) × (100% – 75%)].

Goodwill

5. Goodwill is an asset arising from other assets acquired in a business combination that are not individually identified and separately recognized.
   a. The acquirer may recognize goodwill at the acquisition date. Goodwill is the **excess** of 1) over 2):
      1) The sum of
         a) The **consideration** transferred for the acquiree
         b) The amount of an NCI
         c) Any **previously held equity interest** in the acquiree
      2) The **net** of acquisition-date amounts of
         a) Identifiable assets acquired
         b) Liabilities assumed
6. A **bargain purchase** results when the amount in 5.a.2) above exceeds that in 5.a.1). The excess is recognized in **profit or loss** as a **gain**.

EXAMPLE

Acquirer (AR) obtained 75% of the equity interests of Acquiree (AE) in a forced sale. AR had no prior equity interest in AE. AR determined that the following are appropriate fair value measures to be used in accounting for this combination:

Consideration (US $300,000 of cash and US $250,000 of other assets) transferred by AR	US $ 550,000
AE's identifiable assets acquired	1,000,000
AE's liabilities assumed	200,000
NCI in AE	210,000

The gain is US $40,000 [($1,000,000 assets – $200,000 liabilities) – $550,000 consideration – $210,000 NCI]

AR records the following entry in the consolidated statements:

Identifiable assets	US $1,000,000	
Cash		US $300,000
Other assets		250,000
Liabilities		200,000
Equity-NCI (AE)		210,000
Gain-bargain purchase		40,000

If AR had instead transferred US $400,000 in cash, it would have debited goodwill for US $60,000 ($650,000 consideration + $210,000 NCI – $1,000,000 assets + $200,000 liabilities).

Stop and review! You have completed the outline for this subunit. Study multiple-choice questions 28 and 29 on page 197.

4.12 THE EQUITY METHOD AND CONSOLIDATED REPORTING

1. The process for choosing the **accounting method** to be used by an investor begins with an assumption about the **influence** conferred by the **percentage** of the **investee's voting power** held by the investor. The diagram below depicts the possibilities:

% Voting Power	Presumed Influence	Accounting Method
100% – 50%	Control	Consolidation
50% – 20%	Significant	Equity Method
20% – 0%	Little or none	Fair Value or Other Method

Equity Method

2. According to **IAS 28**, *Investments in Associates*, an entity should account for an investment in an **associate** using the equity method.
3. **Definitions**
   a. An **associate** is an entity over which the investor exercises significant influence and that is not a subsidiary or a joint venture.
   b. **Significant influence** is "the power to participate in the financial and operating policy decisions of the investee, but is not control or joint control over those policies."
      1) Significant influence is presumed when the investor holds **at least 20%** of the voting power of the investee.
4. The equity method is **not required** if
   a. The investment is classified as held for sale,
   b. The investment is acquired solely to be disposed of within 12 months, or
   c. Conditions exist similar to those that would exempt an entity from preparing consolidated statements.
5. The equity method involves recognizing both **distributed and undistributed amounts** arising from an investment in an associate.
   a. The investment is **initially recorded at cost** and subsequently adjusted for the investor's undistributed share of the associate's profits or losses.
   b. The **investor's share** of the associate's profit or loss is reported in the investor's profit or loss. **Distributions** from the associate reduce the investment balance.

Consolidation

6. According to **IAS 27(R)**, *Consolidated and Separate Financial Statements*, a parent entity should present consolidated financial statements, i.e., statements that present the parent and all of its subsidiaries as if they were a single economic entity (the economic entity approach).
7. **Definitions**
   a. A **parent** is an entity with one or more subsidiaries
   b. A **subsidiary** is an entity that is controlled by another entity.
   c. **Control** is "the power to govern the financial and operating policies of an entity so as to obtain benefits from its activities."
      1) An entity is presumed to have control when it acquires **more than 50% of the voting power** of a second entity.
      2) But control may be achieved without meeting this condition. For example, an entity may gain control through
         a) An agreement with other investors,
         b) A statute or agreement allowing exercise of power over the other entity's policies,
         c) An ability to appoint directors, or
         d) An ability to cast a majority of votes at a directors' meeting.
8. A parent **need not report consolidated statements when** it
   a. Is a wholly owned subsidiary,
   b. Is not publicly traded, or
   c. Does not file statements with a securities commission.
9. **Consolidation procedures** consist of
   a. Combining like items
   b. Eliminating the investment in each subsidiary and the parent's share of each subsidiary's equity
   c. Identifying noncontrolling interests (NCIs) in profit or loss and net assets of consolidated subsidiaries
   d. Eliminating intragroup balances, transactions, income, and expenses in full
10. NCIs are separately presented in **equity** in the consolidated balance sheet. NCIs in **profit or loss** also are separately reported.

EXAMPLE

Consolidated Income Statement

Revenues	XXX,XXX
Expenses	(XXX,XXX)
Pretax income from continuing operations	XX,XXX
Income tax expense	(XX,XXX)
After-tax income from continuing operations	XX,XXX
Discontinued operations (after tax)	(X,XXX)
Profit or loss	XX,XXX
Minus: Profit or loss – NCI	(X,XXX)
Profit or loss – parent	XX,XXX

EXAMPLE

Consolidated Equity

Equity:	
Parent equity:	
Common stock, par value	XXX,XXX
Share premium	XX,XXX
Retained earnings	XXX,XXX
Accumulated other comprehensive income	XX,XXX
Total parent equity	XXX,XXX
NCI	XX,XXX
Total equity	XXX,XXX

Stop and review! You have completed the outline for this subunit. Study multiple-choice question 30 on page 198.

4.13 SUMMARY

1. Examples of postemployment benefits are pensions and other retirement benefits, life insurance, and medical care. Under a defined contribution plan, the entity's maximum legal or constructive obligation equals its agreed contributions to a fund (a separate entity). Under a defined benefit plan, the entity is responsible for providing the agreed benefits and therefore bears actuarial risk and investment risk.
2. The measurement of a postemployment defined benefit obligation includes (a) estimates of future salary increases, (b) the benefits defined in the plan, (c) the benefits arising from any constructive obligation beyond the terms of the plan, and (d) estimates of future changes in government benefits that affect the level of plan benefits.
3. Equity is credited in an equity-settled share-based payment transaction (SBPT). A liability is credited in a cash-settled SBPT. In an equity-settled SBPT, the goods or services and the credit to equity are measured at the fair value of the goods or services if it is reliably measurable. If it is not, the transaction is measured at the fair value of the equity instruments granted. The second treatment is normally required for employee share options. In a cash-settled SBPT, the fair value of the liability is the basis for measurement. Until settlement, the entity remeasures this fair value at each reporting date and at the final settlement date, with changes in fair value recognized in profit or loss. The debit is usually to expense.
4. A lease is classified as a finance lease if, for example, (a) the lease provides for the transfer of ownership of the leased asset by the end of the lease term, (b) the lease has a bargain purchase option, (c) the lease term is for the major part of the economic life of the leased asset, (d) the present value of the minimum lease payments is at least substantially all of the fair value of the leased asset at the inception of the lease, and (e) the leased asset is such that it can be used only by the lessee without major modification.
5. A lease not treated as a finance lease is classified as an operating lease by lessees and lessors.
6. Income taxes are all domestic and foreign taxes on taxable profits. Tax expense or tax income for the period consists of current and deferred components.
7. A deferred tax liability (DTL) is an amount of income taxes payable in the future with regard to a taxable temporary difference. A deferred tax asset (DTA) is an amount of income taxes recoverable in the future with regard to a deductible temporary difference.
8. The difference between the carrying amount of an asset or liability and its tax base is a temporary difference (TD). A taxable (deductible) TD results in taxable (deductible) amounts in the future when the carrying amount of the asset or liability is recovered or settled.

9. Whether a financial instrument or one of its components is a liability, an asset, or an equity item depends on its substance, not its legal form, at the time of initial recognition and on the definitions of those elements.
10. If a financial instrument has both equity and liability components, they are presented separately in the issuer's balance sheet.
11. Interest, dividends, losses, and gains related to a financial liability are reported as income or expense in profit or loss.
12. Other liabilities include accounts payable, accrued expenses, taxes payable, deferred revenues, and short-term employee benefits.
13. Recognition of provisions is appropriate when (a) the entity has a present obligation resulting from a past event (called an obligating event), (b) it is probable that an outflow of economic benefits will be necessary to settle the obligation, and (c) its amount can be reliably estimated.
14. A contingent liability is a possible obligation arising from past events. Its existence will be confirmed only by uncertain future events not wholly within the entity's control. A liability also is contingent if it does not meet the recognition criteria.
15. Bonds are sold at the sum of the present values of the maturity amount and the interest payments (if interest-bearing). The difference between the nominal amount and the selling price of bonds is either a discount or a premium. Interest expense is equal to the carrying amount of the bond at the beginning of the period times the yield (market) interest rate. Interest paid remains constant and is equal to the nominal amount of the bond, times the stated rate. The difference between interest expense and interest paid is the discount or premium amortization.
16. Share capital (issued capital) represents investments by owners in exchange for shares. Share premium consists of the sources of issued capital in excess of par or stated value. The term reserve is used in the Framework to refer to capital maintenance adjustments (various revaluations or restatements of assets or liabilities) and to appropriations of retained earnings. It also applies to items recognized directly in equity.
17. Retained earnings is increased by profit and decreased by loss, dividends, and certain transactions in treasury shares.
18. Treasury shares are the entity's own equity instruments reacquired for various purposes, e.g., mergers, options, or share dividends. Treasury shares are accounted for using the cost method or the par value method. Treasury shares are subtracted from equity. No income or expense is recognized in profit or loss on transactions in an entity's own equity instruments.
19. Dividends may be in the form of cash, property, or shares. Shareholders also may receive rights. The recipient of share rights must allocate the carrying amount of the shares owned between those shares and the rights based on their relative fair values.
20. To facilitate comparison of an entity's financial information over time, the same accounting policies ordinarily are followed consistently. A change in accounting policy is indicated only if the result will be reliable and provide more relevant information or if it is required by a standard or interpretation. A change in accounting policy under a new standard or interpretation should be accounted for in accordance with its transition provisions. Absent transitional guidance or if a change is voluntary, the change is applied retrospectively.
21. A change in accounting estimate adjusts the carrying amount of an asset or liability or the consumption of an asset. It results from reassessing the status and expected benefits and obligations related to assets and liabilities. A change in accounting estimate should be reflected in the financial statements prospectively.

22. All material prior-period errors must be corrected retrospectively in the first set of financial statements issued after their discovery. This may be done by restating the comparative amounts in the prior periods when the error occurred. If the error occurred prior to the first period presented, the opening balances for the first period presented are restated.
23. A foreign currency transaction is stated in or requires settlement in a foreign currency. Initial recognition in the functional currency is at the spot rate between the functional and foreign currencies at the transaction date. At the balance sheet date, monetary items are translated at the closing rate. Nonmonetary items measured at historical cost are translated at the rate on the transaction date. Nonmonetary items measured at fair value are translated at the rates when the fair values were measured.
24. An exchange difference arises when a given amount of one currency is translated into another currency at different exchange rates. Exchange differences ordinarily are recognized in profit or loss when they arise.
25. If the functional currency is not that of a hyperinflationary economy, translation to a different presentation currency is done as follows: (a) Assets and liabilities for each balance sheet presented are translated at the closing rate as of its date, (b) income and expenses for each income statement presented are translated at the exchange rates at the transaction dates (but an average rate may be used unless rates fluctuate greatly), and (c) the exchange differences are recognized in a separate component of equity.
26. The acquisition method is used for all business combinations. It involves (a) determining the acquirer and the acquisition date and (b) recognizing and measuring (1) identifiable assets acquired, (2) liabilities assumed, (3) any noncontrolling interest, and (4) goodwill or a gain from a bargain purchase.
27. Measurement of assets acquired and liabilities assumed is normally at fair value.
28. The acquirer may recognize goodwill at the acquisition date. Goodwill is the excess of (a) over (b): (a) the sum of (1) the consideration transferred for the acquiree (normally at acquisition-date fair value), (2) the fair value of a noncontrolling interest, and (3) the acquisition-date fair value of a previously held equity interest in the acquiree over (b) the net of acquisition-date amounts of (1) identifiable assets acquired and (2) liabilities assumed.
29. An associate is an entity over which the investor exercises significant influence and that is not a subsidiary or a joint venture. Significant influence is "the power to participate in the financial and operating policy decisions of the investee, but is not control or joint control over those policies." An entity usually accounts for an associate using the equity method.
30. The equity method recognizes both distributed and undistributed amounts arising from an investment in an associate. The investment is recorded initially at cost and is subsequently adjusted for the investor's undistributed share of the associate's profits or losses. The investor's share of the associate's profit or loss is reported in the investor's profit or loss. Distributions from the associate reduce the investment balance.
31. A parent should present consolidated financial statements, which are financial statements of a group under the control of a parent that is reported as one entity.
32. Consolidation procedures include (a) combining like items; (b) eliminating the investment in each subsidiary and the parent's share of each subsidiary's equity; (c) identifying noncontrolling interests in profit or loss and net assets of consolidated subsidiaries; and (d) eliminating intragroup balances, transactions, income, and expense in full.

QUESTIONS

4.1 Employer Accounting for Postemployment Benefits

1. Which of the following statements is true for a defined contribution postemployment benefit plan?

A. The employer is required to contribute a certain amount each period based on the plan's formula.

B. The employer bears the risk of the plan's investment performance.

C. Postemployment benefits received by employees are defined by the plan's formula.

D. The employer and employees are required to contribute equal amounts to the fund.

Answer (A) is correct. *(CIA, adapted)*

REQUIRED: The true statement about a defined contribution plan.

DISCUSSION: A defined contribution plan provides benefits in exchange for services, provides an account for each participant, and specifies how contributions are to be determined. Postemployment benefits depend only on contributions, returns on investment, and allocated forfeitures of other participants' benefits. Thus, employees have the benefit of gain and the risk of loss.

Answer (B) is incorrect. The employees bear the risk of the plan's investment performance. Answer (C) is incorrect. Under a defined benefit plan, the postemployment benefits received by employees are defined by the plan's formula. Answer (D) is incorrect. Equal contributions are not required for a defined contribution plan.

2. The following information relates to the activity of the defined postemployment benefit plan of Twain Publishers, Ltd.:

Current service cost	US $120,000
Expected return on plan assets	30,000
Interest cost on defined benefit obligation	40,000
Amortization of net actuarial loss	10,000
Amortization of past service cost	5,000

Twain's expense recognized in the income statement is

A. US $120,000

B. US $135,000

C. US $140,000

D. US $145,000

Answer (D) is correct. *(Publisher, adapted)*

REQUIRED: The recognized expense related to a defined postemployment benefit plan.

DISCUSSION: Components of the expense are current service cost, interest cost, the expected return on plan assets, past service cost (recognition in full of vested amounts and amortization of nonvested amounts), and amortization of actuarial loss. Current service cost, interest cost, the amortization of actuarial loss, and the past service cost increase the expense. The expected return on plan assets decreases the expense.

Current service cost	US $120,000
Return on plan assets	(30,000)
Interest cost	40,000
Amortization of actuarial loss	10,000
Past service cost	5,000
Expense	US $145,000

Answer (A) is incorrect. US $120,000 includes only the current service cost component. Answer (B) is incorrect. US $135,000 excludes the amortization of the actuarial loss. Answer (C) is incorrect. US $140,000 excludes the past service cost.

3. At the start of its current fiscal year, Emper Corporation amended its defined postemployment benefit plan, resulting in an increase in the present value of the DBO. The benefits become vested after 6 years of service. Past service cost arising from the plan amendment includes US $400,000 of benefits that are already vested and US $200,000 of nonvested benefits. If the average period until vesting is 4 years, the minimum past service cost to be recognized in the first year is

A. US $50,000

B. US $200,000

C. US $450,000

D. US $600,000

Answer (C) is correct. *(Publisher, adapted)*

REQUIRED: The minimum amount of past service cost to be recognized.

DISCUSSION: Past service cost is the increase in the present value of the DBO related to prior employee service that arises in the current period from the introduction of, or an amendment to, postemployment benefits. Accordingly, US $400,000 should be recognized immediately to reflect the vested benefits and amortization of the nonvested benefits equals US $50,000 ($200,000 ÷ 4), a total of US $450,000.

Answer (A) is incorrect. US $50,000 is the periodic amortization of nonvested benefits. Answer (B) is incorrect. US $200,000 is the amount of the nonvested benefits. Answer (D) is incorrect. US $600,000 includes nonvested benefits not yet required to be amortized.

4.2 Share-Based Payment

4. On January 2, Year 1, Kine Co. granted Morgan, its president, share options to buy 1,000 shares of Kine's US $10 par ordinary stock. The options call for a price of US $20 per share and are exercisable for 3 years following the grant date. Morgan exercised the options on December 31, Year 1. The market price of the shares was US $50 on January 2, Year 1, and 70 on the following December 31. If the intrinsic value-based method is followed because the fair value of the options is not reliably measurable, by what net amount should equity increase as a result of the grant and exercise of the options?

A. US $20,000

B. US $30,000

C. US $50,000

D. US $70,000

Answer (A) is correct. *(CIA, adapted)*

REQUIRED: The amount equity increases as a result of the grant and exercise of share options.

DISCUSSION: The measurement date is January 2, Year 1. At that date, the intrinsic value of the options is US $30,000 [1,000 shares × ($50 market price – $20 option price)]. This 30,000 will be recorded as both compensation expense and options outstanding. The net effect on equity is 0. When the options are exercised, the US $20,000 (1,000 shares × $20 exercise price) cash received and the 30,000 options outstanding will be allocated to share capital as US $10,000 ordinary stock and US $40,000 additional paid-in capital. The net effect on equity will be a US $20,000 increase.

Answer (B) is incorrect. US $30,000 is the amount of compensation expense. Answer (C) is incorrect. US $50,000 is the increase in the equity without regard to the compensation expense. Answer (D) is incorrect. US $70,000 results from calculating the increase in equity using the share price on the exercise date.

5. On January 1, Year 1, International Entity entered into an equity-settled share-based payment transaction with its senior executives. This award of 1,000 share options has a 4-year vesting period. The market prices of the options and the related shares on the grant date are US $20 and US $80, respectively. The exercise price is US $85. Assuming that the vesting conditions were **not** met for 100 of the options because of unexpected events in Year 4, the entry to debit option expense at

A. December 31, Year 4, is for US $5,000.

B. December 31, Year 3, is for US $4,500.

C. December 31, Year 2, is for US $5,000.

D. January 1, Year 1, is for US $20,000.

Answer (C) is correct. *(Publisher, adapted)*

REQUIRED: The entry to debit option expense given that vesting conditions were not met for some options.

DISCUSSION: The fair value of each share option is determined at the measurement date, which is the grant date for transactions with employees and others providing similar services. Thus, the fair value of each share option was set at its market price of US $20 on January 1, Year 1. The periodic expense varies only with the expected number of equity instruments expected to vest. Because the events causing 100 options not to vest occurred unexpectedly in Year 4, the entity presumably expected at each balance sheet date for the first 3 years of the vesting period that all options would vest. Total expected expense was therefore US $20,000, and the proportional expense recognized in each of the first 3 years was US $5,000 [(1,000 options × $20) ÷ 4 years].

Answer (A) is incorrect. The Year 4 expense is US $3,000 [$20,000 total expected – $15,000 recognized in Years 1-3 – (100 × $20) not vested]. Answer (B) is incorrect. No retrospective adjustment is made. The Year 3 entry would have been US $5,000 based on a then-expected total expense of US $20,000. Answer (D) is incorrect. US $20,000 would have been recognized at January 1, Year 1, if the options had vested immediately.

4.3 Leases

6. Which of the following leases ordinarily should be classified as a finance lease by the lessee?

	Lease A	Lease B	Lease C	Lease D
Contains a bargain purchase option?	Yes	No	No	No
Lease term is for the major part of the economic life of the leased asset	No	No	Yes	No
Present value of the minimum lease payments is substantially all of the fair value of the leased asset	No	No	No	Yes
Leased asset usable only by lessor without major modification	No	Yes	Yes	No

A. Lease A only.

B. Lease B only.

C. Leases A, C, and D.

D. Leases C and D only.

Answer (C) is correct. *(CIA, adapted)*

REQUIRED: The lease(s) meeting a capitalization criterion.

DISCUSSION: A lease should be classified as a finance lease by a lessee if it transfers substantially all of the risks and rewards of ownership. A lease is classified at its inception. It normally is classified as a finance lease if, for example, (1) the lease provides for the transfer of ownership of the leased asset by the end of the lease term; (2) the lease contains a bargain purchase option, i.e., the lessee has the option to purchase at a price expected to be sufficiently below the fair value of the exercise date that, at the lease's inception, exercise is reasonably certain; (3) the lease term is for the major part of the economic life of the leased asset; (4) the present value of the minimum lease payments is at least substantially all of the fair value of the leased asset at the inception of the lease; or (5) the leased asset is such that it can be used only by the lessee without major modification. Lease A is a finance lease because the terms of the lease include a bargain purchase option. Lease C passes the economic life test, and lease D passes the recovery of investment test.

Answer (A) is incorrect. Leases C and D are also finance leases. Answer (B) is incorrect. B is the only operating lease in the set. If it were usable by the lessee (not the lessor) without major modification, it would normally be classified as a finance lease. Answer (D) is incorrect. Lease A contains a bargain purchase option, so it qualifies as a finance lease.

Questions 7 and 8 are based on the following information.

On January 1, Plantation Partners is planning to enter as the lessee into the two lease agreements described in the opposite column. Each lease is noncancelable, and Plantation does not receive title to either leased property during or at the end of the lease term. All payments required under these agreements are due on January 1 each year.

Lessor	Lease A	Lease B
Type of property	Oven	Computer
Yearly rental	US $15,000	US $4,000
Lease term	10 years	3 years
Economic life	15 years	5 years
Purchase option	None	3,000
Renewal option	None	None
Fair value at inception of lease	US $125,000	US $10,200
Unguaranteed residual value	None	2,000
Lessee's incremental borrowing rate	10%	10%
Executory costs paid by	Lessee	Lessor
Annual executory costs	US $800	US $500
Present value factor at 10% (of an annuity due)	6.76	2.74

7. Plantation should treat Lease A as a(n)

A. Finance lease with an initial asset amount of US $101,400.

B. Operating lease, charging US $14,200 in rental expense and US $800 in executory costs to annual operations.

C. Operating lease, charging the present value of the yearly rental expense to annual operations.

D. Operating lease, charging US $15,000 in rental expense and US $800 in executory costs to annual operations.

Answer (D) is correct. *(CMA, adapted)*

REQUIRED: The true statement about Lease A.

DISCUSSION: Lease A is an operating lease with a US $15,000 annual rental expense with annual executory costs (e.g., maintenance, insurance, and taxes) of US $800 to be paid by the lessee. An operating lease does not transfer the risks and rewards of ownership to the lessee. Lease A is nothing more than a rental arrangement. Circumstances in which the risks and rewards of ownership are normally deemed to be transferred include the following: the lease transfers title to the lessee, the lease has a bargain purchase option, the lease term is for the major part of the useful life of the leased asset, the present value of the minimum lease payments is at least substantially all of the asset's fair value, or the asset is usable only by the lessee without major modification.

Answer (A) is incorrect. Lease A does not qualify as a finance lease. Answer (B) is incorrect. Rental expense is US $15,000. Answer (C) is incorrect. The actual cash outlay for rent, US $15,000, is charged to expense.

8. Plantation should treat Lease B as a(n)

A. Finance lease with an initial asset amount of US $10,960.

B. Finance lease with an initial asset value of US $10,200.

C. Operating lease, charging US $3,500 in rental expense and US $500 in executory costs to annual operations.

D. Finance lease with an initial asset value of US $9,590.

Answer (D) is correct. *(CMA, adapted)*

REQUIRED: The true statement about Lease B.

DISCUSSION: A finance lease is one in which the risks and rewards of ownership are transferred to the lessee. For accounting purposes, the lessee treats a finance lease as similar to the purchase of an asset capitalized at the fair value of the leased asset or, if lower, the present value of the minimum lease payments. The lessee's minimum lease payments include the required payments, excluding contingent rent and executory costs (e.g., taxes and insurance), plus any amounts guaranteed by the lessee or a related party. If a bargain purchase option exists, however, minimum lease payments equal the required payments plus the amount of the option. If the present value of the minimum lease payments (calculated without guaranteed amounts or a bargain purchase option) is substantially all of the asset's fair value, the lease normally is accounted for as a finance lease. Given that the executory costs associated with the lease are to be paid by the lessor, a portion of the lease rental price is for those costs, not for the asset. Consequently, the annual minimum lease payment equals the annual payment minus the executory costs, or US $3,500 ($4,000 yearly rental – $500). The present value of the minimum lease payments is therefore US $9,590 (2.74 × $3,500), which is substantially all of the fair value of the asset. Thus, the lease should be capitalized. The appropriate amount of the initial asset value is the present value of the minimum lease payments calculated above.

Answer (A) is incorrect. The initial asset amount cannot exceed the fair value of the leased asset. Moreover, US $10,960 includes the present value of the executory costs. Answer (B) is incorrect. US $10,200 is the fair value of the leased asset. Answer (C) is incorrect. The lease meets the criteria of a finance lease.

4.4 Income Taxes

9. Which one of the following statements **best** describes the asset-liability method of accounting for deferred income taxes?

A. The amount of deferred tax is based on tax rates in effect when temporary differences originate.

B. The amount of deferred tax is based on the tax rates expected to be in effect during the periods in which the deferred tax liability is settled or the deferred tax asset is realized.

C. The tax effects of temporary differences are not reported separately but are reported as adjustments to the amounts of specific assets and liabilities and the related revenues and expenses.

D. The appropriate tax rate to be reported on the income statement is the tax actually levied in that year, meaning no deferred taxes would be reported.

Answer (B) is correct. *(CIA, adapted)*

REQUIRED: The description of the asset-liability method of accounting for deferred income taxes.

DISCUSSION: A DTA or DTL is measured at the rates expected to apply when it is realized or settled, based on tax laws and rates enacted or substantively enacted as of the balance sheet date. If different rates apply to different taxable profit levels, a DTA or DTL is measured based on the average rates expected to apply in the periods when the TDs are expected to reverse. The tax rate or tax base may vary with the manner of recovery or settlement. For example, one tax rate may apply if an asset is sold immediately and another may apply if it is to be recovered through continued use.

Answer (A) is incorrect. This statement describes the deferred method of accounting for deferred income taxes. Answer (C) is incorrect. This statement describes the net-of-tax method, which recognizes that future taxability and deductibility are important factors in the valuation of individual assets and liabilities. Answer (D) is incorrect. This statement describes the nonallocation or flow-through approach, which does not support the calculation and reporting of deferred income tax.

10. At December 31, SCM Ltd., a calendar-year entity, reported the following accounts for which the carrying amount differed from the tax base:

	Carrying Amount	Tax Base
Depreciable assets (net)	US $150,000	US $80,000
Deferred rental income	40,000	0

What taxable and deductible amounts are related to these temporary differences?

	Taxable Amounts	Deductible Amounts
A.	US $40,000	US $70,000
B.	US $70,000	US $40,000
C.	US $0	US $110,000
D.	US $110,000	US $0

Answer (B) is correct. *(Publisher, adapted)*

REQUIRED: The taxable and deductible amounts arising from the temporary differences.

DISCUSSION: The difference between the carrying amount of an asset or liability and its tax base is a temporary difference (TD). A taxable (deductible) TD results in taxable (deductible) amounts in the future when the carrying amount of the asset or liability is recovered or settled. The tax base is the amount attributed for tax purposes to an asset or liability. The tax base of an asset is the amount deductible against future taxable economic benefits when the asset's carrying amount is recovered. The tax base of a liability is the portion of the carrying amount that will not be deductible against future taxable economic benefits for tax purposes. The tax base of revenue received in advance (a liability) is the portion of the carrying amount taxable in the future. Thus, the US $70,000 temporary difference ($150,000 carrying amount – $80,000 tax base) related to the depreciable assets is classified as a taxable amount. When income, such as rental income, is taxable before being recognized in accounting profit, future sacrifices to provide the rental service or refund amounts paid will result in future tax deductible amounts when the liability is settled. Thus, the US $40,000 temporary difference ($40,000 carrying amount – $0 tax base) related to the deferred rental revenue is classified as a deductible amount.

11. Which of the following results in a tax base of zero?

A. Trade receivables have a carrying amount of US $1,000, and the related revenue has been included in full in the determination of taxable profit.

B. A loan receivable has a carrying amount of US $1,000, and repayment has no tax effects.

C. Unearned interest revenue has a carrying amount of US $1,000, and the related interest revenue was included in full in the determination of taxable profit.

D. Accrued expenses have a carrying amount of US $1,000, and the related expense has been included in full in the determination of taxable profit.

Answer (C) is correct. *(Publisher, adapted)*

REQUIRED: The balance sheet item with a tax base of zero.

DISCUSSION: The difference between the carrying amount of an asset or liability and its tax base is a temporary difference (TD). A taxable (deductible) TD results in taxable (deductible) amounts in the future when the carrying amount of the asset or liability is recovered or settled. The tax base is the amount attributed for tax purposes to an asset or liability. The tax base of an asset is the amount deductible against future taxable economic benefits when the asset's carrying amount is recovered. The tax base of a liability is the portion of the carrying amount that will not be deductible against future taxable economic benefits for tax purposes. The tax base of revenue received in advance (a liability) is the portion of the carrying amount taxable in the future. For unearned interest revenue for which the related interest revenue was taxed on a cash basis, the tax base equals zero (US $1,000 carrying amount – $1,000 not taxable in the future).

4.5 Other Liabilities

12. On December 31, Year 1, XYZ issued 5-year bonds with a face amount of US $1 million. The bonds carry a stated interest rate of 10% and were sold at par. Interest is payable annually on December 31. According to the provisions of the bond indenture, XYZ was to make annual deposits into a bond sinking fund (beginning December 31, Year 2) to accumulate the funds necessary to retire the bonds at their maturity. On December 31, Year 5, all required interest payments and sinking-fund payments due to date had been made on schedule. If the sinking-fund assets are properly classified as noncurrent, how should the balance of bonds payable be classified on the December 31, Year 5, balance sheet?

A. Current liability.

B. Long-term liability.

C. Contra to long-term investments.

D. Deferred credit.

Answer (A) is correct. *(CIA, adapted)*

REQUIRED: The classification of the balance of bonds payable.

DISCUSSION: A current liability is an obligation that is expected to be settled within the normal operating cycle or is due to be settled within 12 months of the balance sheet date. Any other liability is noncurrent. Some current liabilities are included in the working capital employed in the normal operating cycle, e.g., trade payables and accrued employee operating costs. Current liabilities not settled within the normal operating cycle include the current part of interest-bearing debt, dividends, income taxes, and bank overdrafts. Thus, the bonds payable should be classified as current because they are due to be settled within 12 months. Under the Standards, the classification of the sinking-fund assets is irrelevant to the classification of the bond payable.

Answer (B) is incorrect. The bonds should be classified as a current liability. Answer (C) is incorrect. Offsetting assets and liabilities is rarely acceptable. Answer (D) is incorrect. The bonds are a liability and should not be put in an ambiguous category such as deferred credits.

13. At December 31, Year 2, an entity had the following obligations that were expected to be refinanced:

17% note payable	US $140,000
15% note payable	US $200,000

The 17% note payable was issued on October 1, Year 1, and matures on July 1, Year 3. No loan agreement existing at the balance sheet date provides for refinancing. The 15% note payable was issued on May 1, Year 1, and matures on May 1, Year 3. On February 1, Year 3, the entire US $140,000 balance of the 17% note payable was refinanced by issuance of a long-term debt instrument. On February 7, Year 3, the entity entered into a noncancelable agreement with a lender to refinance the 15% note payable on a long-term basis. The financial statements were authorized to be issued on March 1, Year 3. The total amount of obligations that may be properly excluded from current liabilities on the entity's December 31, Year 2, balance sheet is

A. US $0

B. US $140,000

C. US $200,000

D. US $340,000

Answer (A) is correct. *(CIA, adapted)*

REQUIRED: The total amount of obligations that may be properly excluded from current liabilities.

DISCUSSION: Financial liabilities are current if they are due within 12 months even if (1) the original term was for more than 12 months and (2) an agreement to refinance on a long-term basis was completed after the balance sheet date and before the issuance of the financial statements. Thus, both notes are current. The amount excluded from current liabilities is US $0.

Answer (B) is incorrect. The 15% note is also included in current liabilities. Answer (C) is incorrect. The 17% note is also included in current liabilities. Answer (D) is incorrect. Both liabilities should be treated as current at the balance sheet date.

14. An entity allows customers to redeem 20 coupons for a toy (cost US $3.00). Estimates are that 40% of coupons distributed will result in redemption. Since beginning the promotion this year, 4 million coupons were distributed and 1 million coupons redeemed. The adjusting entry to accrue for unredeemed coupons at year-end is

A. Premium expense	US $90,000	
Provision for premiums		US $90,000
B. Sales	US $90,000	
Provision for premiums		US $90,000
C. Premium expense	US $1,800,000	
Provision for premiums		US $1,800,000
D. Sales	US $1,800,000	
Provision for premiums		US $1,800,000

Answer (A) is correct. *(CIA, adapted)*

REQUIRED: The adjusting entry to accrue for unredeemed coupons at year-end.

DISCUSSION: An expense and a provision should be accrued for the coupons still outstanding that are expected to be redeemed. Of the 4 million coupons distributed, 40%, or 1.6 million, are estimated to be redeemable. Of those, 1 million have already been redeemed, and 600,000 more are expected to be redeemed. The promotion requires 20 coupons to receive one toy, so 30,000 (600,000 ÷ 20) more toys will be required. Each toy costs US $3.00, creating a provision of US $90,000 (30,000 × $3.00).

Answer (B) is incorrect. The debit should be to an expense. Answer (C) is incorrect. Although an expense should be accrued, the amount is incorrect. Answer (D) is incorrect. The debit should be to an expense, and the amount is incorrect.

4.6 Provisions and Contingencies

15. An entity introduced a new product that carries a 2-year warranty against defects. It estimates that warranty costs will be 2% of sales in the year of sale and 3% of sales in the year following the year of sale. Sales in Year 1 and Year 2 were US $5 million and US $7 million, respectively. Actual costs of servicing the warranty in Year 1 and Year 2 were US $110,000 and US $260,000, respectively. What provision for warranty costs must the entity recognize in Year 2?

A. US $260,000

B. US $290,000

C. US $350,000

D. US $370,000

Answer (C) is correct. *(CIA, adapted)*

REQUIRED: The warranty provision.

DISCUSSION: The warranty provision must be matched with revenue in the year of sale. Thus, the provision related to Year 2 sales must be recognized in Year 2 even if actual expenditures will not occur until Year 3. The provision related to Year 2 sales equals US $350,000 [$7,000,000 × (2% for the year of sale + 3% for the year after the year of sale)].

Answer (A) is incorrect. US $260,000 is the actual cost of servicing the warranty in Year 2. Answer (B) is incorrect. US $290,000 equals the sum of 2% of Year 2 sales and 3% of Year 1 sales. Answer (D) is incorrect. US $370,000 equals the actual cost of servicing the warranty in Year 1 and Year 2.

16. Because of a defect discovered in its seat belts in December Year 1, an automobile manufacturer believes it is probable that it will be required to recall its products. The final decision on the recall is expected to be made in March Year 2. The cost of the recall is reliably estimated to be US $2.5 million. How should this information be reported in the December 31, Year 1, financial statements?

A. As a loss of US $2.5 million and a provision of US $2.5 million.

B. As an adjustment of the opening balance of retained earnings equal to US $2.5 million.

C. As an appropriation of retained earnings of US $2.5 million.

D. It should not be disclosed because it has not yet happened.

Answer (A) is correct. *(CIA, adapted)*

REQUIRED: The reporting of a probable loss from a product recall.

DISCUSSION: A provision is a liability of uncertain timing or amount. Recognition of provisions is appropriate when the entity has a legal or constructive present obligation resulting from a past event (called an obligating event), it is probable that an outflow of economic benefits will be necessary to settle the obligation, and its amount can be reliably estimated. Consequently, the company must recognize a loss and a liability for US $2.5 million.

Answer (B) is incorrect. Such an adjustment is appropriate for fundamental errors and changes in accounting policies (under the benchmark treatments). Answer (C) is incorrect. An appropriation of retained earnings is permissible although not required, but the entity must still recognize a loss and a provision. Moreover, no part of the appropriation may be transferred to income, and no loss may be charged to an appropriation of retained earnings. Answer (D) is incorrect. If the loss is probable and can be reliably estimated, it should be recognized by a charge to income.

17. An entity has been sued for US $100 million for producing and selling an unsafe product. Attorneys for the entity cannot reliably predict the outcome of the litigation. In its financial statements, the entity should

A. Make the following journal entry, and disclose the existence of the lawsuit in a note.

Estimated loss from litigation	US $100,000,000	
Estimated provision for litigation loss		US $100,000,000

B. Disclose the existence of the lawsuit in a note without making a journal entry.

C. Neither make a journal entry nor disclose the lawsuits in a note because bad publicity will hurt the entity.

D. Make the following journal entry, and disclose the existence of the lawsuit in a note.

Cost of goods sold	US $100,000,000	
Estimated provision for litigation loss		US $100,000,000

Answer (B) is correct. *(CIA, adapted)*

REQUIRED: The financial statement treatment of a loss from pending litigation.

DISCUSSION: In the very rare case in which a reliable estimate of an obligation that otherwise qualifies for treatment as a provision cannot be determined, no liability is recognized. Instead, the existing liability is disclosed as a contingent liability (unless the possibility of any outflow in settlement is remote).

Answer (A) is incorrect. A journal entry is made when the outflow in settlement is probable and can be reliably estimated. Answer (C) is incorrect. A disclosure must be made of a contingent liability. Answer (D) is incorrect. A journal entry is made when the outflow in settlement is probable and can be reliably estimated.

4.7 Bonds

18. If bonds are initially sold at a discount and the effective-interest method of amortization is used,

A. Interest expense in the earlier periods will be less than interest expense in the later periods.

B. Interest expense in the earlier periods will be greater than interest expense in the later periods.

C. Interest expense will equal the cash interest payment each period.

D. Interest expense will be less than the cash interest payment each period.

Answer (A) is correct. *(CIA, adapted)*

REQUIRED: The effect on interest expense if bonds are initially sold at a discount and the effective-interest method of amortization is used.

DISCUSSION: Interest expense equals the carrying amount of the liability at the beginning of the period times the effective interest rate. The carrying amount of the liability equals the face amount of the bond minus the discount. As the discount is amortized over the life of the bond, the carrying amount increases. Consequently, the interest expense increases over the term of the bond.

Answer (B) is incorrect. Interest expense will increase over the term of the bonds. Answer (C) is incorrect. Interest expense exceeds the cash interest payment when bonds are issued at a discount. The reason is that the effective rate is higher than the nominal rate. The excess of interest expense over the cash payment is the amount of discount amortized each period. Answer (D) is incorrect. Interest expense exceeds the cash interest payment when bonds are issued at a discount. The reason is that the effective rate is higher than the nominal rate. The excess of interest expense over the cash payment is the amount of discount amortized each period.

19. On May 1, Year 1, an entity issued, at 103 plus accrued interest, 500 of its 12%, US $1,000 bonds. The bonds are dated January 1, Year 1, and mature on January 1, Year 6. Interest is payable semiannually on January 1 and July 1. The journal entry to record the issuance of the bonds and the receipt of the cash proceeds is

A.

Cash	US $515,000	
Interest payable	20,000	
Bonds payable		US $500,000
Premium on bonds payable		35,000

B.

Cash	US $525,000	
Bonds payable		US $500,000
Premium on bonds payable		15,000
Interest payable		10,000

C.

Cash	US $535,000	
Bonds payable		US $500,000
Premium on bonds payable		15,000
Interest payable		20,000

D.

Cash	US $535,000	
Bonds payable		US $500,000
Premium on bonds payable		35,000

Answer (C) is correct. *(CIA, adapted)*

REQUIRED: The journal entry to record the issuance of a bond at a premium plus accrued interest.

DISCUSSION: The face amount of the 500 bonds is equal to US $500,000 (500 × $1,000). The cash proceeds excluding interest from the issuance of the bonds are US $515,000 ($500,000 × 103%). The US $15,000 premium is the difference between the cash issuance proceeds and the face amount of the bonds. Because the bonds were issued between interest payment dates, the issuer is also entitled to receive accrued interest for the 4 months between the prior interest date and the issuance date. The accrued interest is US $20,000 [500 bonds × $1,000 face value × 12% stated rate × (4 ÷ 12)]. The issuing entity will therefore receive US $535,000 in cash ($515,000 + $20,000). The resulting journal entry includes a US $535,000 debit to cash, a US $500,000 credit to bonds payable, a US $15,000 credit to premium, and a US $20,000 credit to either interest payable or interest expense.

Answer (A) is incorrect. The bond premium is US $15,000 ($500,000 × .03), and interest payable should be credited. Answer (B) is incorrect. Interest payable should be US $20,000 [$500,000 × .12 × (4 ÷ 12)]. Answer (D) is incorrect. The premium on bonds payable should not include interest payable.

4.8 Equity

20. At December 31, Year 1, an entity has the following account balances:

Ordinary shares (US $10 par, 50,000 shares issued)	US $500,000
8% preference shares (US $50 par, 10,000 shares issued)	500,000
Share premium on ordinary shares	640,000
Share premium on preference shares	20,000
Retained earnings	600,000

The preference shares are cumulative and nonparticipating and have a call price of US $55 per share. The journal entry to record the redemption of all preference shares on January 2, Year 2, pursuant to the call provision is

A.

Preference shares	US $500,000	
Share premium: preference	20,000	
Discount on preference shares	30,000	
Cash		US $550,000

B.

Preference shares	US $500,000	
Share premium: preference	20,000	
Loss on redemption of preference shares	30,000	
Cash		US $550,000

C.

Preference shares	US $500,000	
Loss on redemption of preference shares	50,000	
Retained earnings	300,000	
Cash		US $550,000
Share premium: preference		300,000

D.

Preference shares	US $500,000	
Share premium: preference	20,000	
Retained earnings	30,000	
Cash		US $550,000

Answer (D) is correct. *(CIA, adapted)*

REQUIRED: The journal entry to record the redemption of preference shares pursuant to the call provision.

DISCUSSION: The exercise of the call provision resulted in the redemption of the 10,000 preference shares issued and outstanding at the call price of US $550,000 (10,000 shares × $55 call price per share). To eliminate the carrying amount of the preference shares and recognize the cash paid in this transaction, the required journal entry is to debit preference shares for US $500,000, debit share premium: preference for US $20,000, and credit cash for US $550,000. The difference of US $30,000 ($550,000 cash – $520,000 carrying amount of the preference shares) is charged to equity (debit retained earnings). No loss is reported because the recognition of a gain or loss on transactions involving an entity's own shares is prohibited.

Answer (A) is incorrect. The US $30,000 excess of cash paid over the carrying amount of the redeemed shares should be debited to retained earnings. Answer (B) is incorrect. The US $30,000 excess of cash paid over the carrying amount of the redeemed shares should be debited to retained earnings. Answer (C) is incorrect. The premium on the preference shares must be debited for only US $20,000. Moreover, retained earnings must also be debited for the difference of US $30,000.

21. Unlike a share split, a share dividend requires a formal journal entry in the financial accounting records because share

A. Dividends increase the relative carrying amount of an individual's share holding.

B. Splits increase the relative carrying amount of an individual's share holdings.

C. Dividends are payable on the date they are declared.

D. Dividends represent a transfer from retained earnings to share capital.

Answer (D) is correct. *(CIA, adapted)*

REQUIRED: The reason a share dividend requires a formal journal entry and a share split does not.

DISCUSSION: The purpose of a share dividend is to provide evidence to the shareholders of their interest in accumulated earnings without distribution of cash or other property. Share dividends are typically accounted for by a transfer from retained earnings at fair value.

Answer (A) is incorrect. Share dividends have no effect on total equity or on the carrying amount of an individual shareholder's investment. Answer (B) is incorrect. Share splits have no effect on total equity or on the carrying amount of an individual shareholder's investment. Answer (C) is incorrect. Dividends, whether of shares, cash, or property, are usually payable on a date different from the declaration date.

22. Entity UK has 6,000 shares of 5% cumulative, US $100 par value preference shares outstanding and 200,000 ordinary shares outstanding. The board of directors last declared dividends for the year ended May 31, Year 1, and there were no dividends in arrears. For the year ended May 31, Year 3, UK had profit of US $1,750,000. The board of directors is declaring a dividend for ordinary shareholders equivalent to 20% of profit. The total amount of dividends to be paid by UK at May 31, Year 3, is

A. US $350,000

B. US $380,000

C. US $206,000

D. US $410,000

Answer (D) is correct. *(CMA, adapted)*

REQUIRED: The total amount of dividends to be paid given cumulative preference shares.

DISCUSSION: If an entity has cumulative preference shares, all preference dividends for the current and any unpaid prior years must be paid before any dividends can be paid on ordinary shares. The total preference dividends that must be paid equal US $60,000 (6,000 shares × $100 par × 5% × 2 years), and the ordinary dividend is US $350,000 ($1,750,000 × 20%), for a total of US $410,000.

Answer (A) is incorrect. US $350,000 is the ordinary shares dividend. Answer (B) is incorrect. US $380,000 omits the US $30,000 of cumulative dividends for Year 1. Answer (C) is incorrect. US $206,000 is based on a flat rate of US $1 per share.

4.9 Accounting Changes

23. Changes in accounting estimates are viewed as

A. Extraordinary items.

B. Errors in reported amounts in prior periods.

C. Catch-up adjustments related to amounts reported in prior periods.

D. Reassessments of current status and future benefits and obligations.

Answer (D) is correct. *(CIA, adapted)*

REQUIRED: The nature of changes in accounting estimates.

DISCUSSION: A change in accounting estimate adjusts the carrying amount of an asset or liability or the consumption of an asset. It results from reassessing the status and expected benefits and obligations related to assets and liabilities. It is based on new information and is not an error correction.

Answer (A) is incorrect. Items are not classified as extraordinary under IFRSs. Answer (B) is incorrect. Changes in accounting estimates are not errors. Answer (C) is incorrect. Catch-up adjustments to prior reported amounts are retroactive. Changes in accounting estimates are accounted for prospectively.

24. The following financial statement notes are extracts from the audited financial statements of public entities. Which note describes a change in accounting estimate?

A. The entity changed its amortization of capital assets based on a reassessment of the useful lives of the assets. Accordingly, the entity changed its rate of amortization from 5% and 6% to 8% and 10%, for machinery and equipment.

B. Prior to Year 5, plant and equipment (other than customer service replacement parts) were depreciated using the diminishing-balance method. Plant and equipment are now depreciated on a straight-line basis.

C. During the year, the entity changed a method of accounting pursuant to a change in an International Financial Reporting Standard.

D. Effective January 1, Year 5, the entity changed to the LIFO method of inventory valuation. Prior to Year 5, the FIFO method was used.

Answer (A) is correct. *(CIA, adapted)*

REQUIRED: The note describing a change in accounting estimate.

DISCUSSION: Accounting estimates, e.g., service lives, residual values, warranty costs, uncollectible accounts, and inventory obsolescence, are a necessary part of preparing financial statements. However, they inevitably change as new events occur and as additional experience and information are obtained. When altered conditions require a change in estimate, it is accounted for prospectively. Thus, a change in the estimate of the service lives of depreciable assets is a change in accounting estimate.

Answer (B) is incorrect. A change from diminishing-balance depreciation to straight-line depreciation is a change in accounting policy. Answer (C) is incorrect. Changing an accounting method due to a change in an IFRS is a change in accounting policy. Answer (D) is incorrect. LIFO inventory valuation is not permitted under IFRSs.

25. An accounting change requiring retrospective treatment is a change in

A. The residual value of equipment.

B. Depreciation methods from straight-line to diminishing-balance.

C. An accounting policy inseparable from a change in an accounting estimate.

D. A provision for warranty costs.

Answer (B) is correct. *(CMA, adapted)*

REQUIRED: The accounting change requiring retrospective treatment.

DISCUSSION: A change in depreciation methods is reported as a change in accounting policy. A voluntary change in accounting policy is applied retrospectively unless it is impracticable. Retrospective application means adjusting the opening balances of equity for the first period presented and restating other comparative amounts.

Answer (A) is incorrect. The residual value of equipment is a change in estimate that is accounted for on a prospective basis (in the future). Answer (C) is incorrect. If distinguishing between a change in estimate and a change in accounting policy is difficult, the change is accounted for as a change in estimate and properly disclosed. Answer (D) is incorrect. A provision for warranty costs is a change in estimate that is accounted for on a prospective basis (in the future).

26. Which of the following errors is **not** self-correcting over two accounting periods?

A. Failure to record accrued wages.

B. Failure to record depreciation.

C. Overstatement of inventory.

D. Failure to record prepaid expenses.

Answer (B) is correct. *(CIA, adapted)*

REQUIRED: The error not self-correcting over two accounting periods.

DISCUSSION: A failure to record depreciation must be corrected because the effects of the error do not automatically reverse in future periods. Expenses are understated in the year of the error, but no corresponding overstatement of expenses occurs in later years.

Answer (A) is incorrect. Understatement of accrued wages is a self-correcting error. Future wage expense will be overstated, future cost of goods sold will be overstated, and future expenses will be understated, respectively. Answer (C) is incorrect. Overstatement of inventory and the consequent understatement of cost of goods sold is a self-correcting error. Future wage expense will be overstated, future cost of goods sold will be overstated, and future expenses will be understated, respectively. Answer (D) is incorrect. Understatement of prepaid expenses (overstatement of expenses) is a self-correcting error. Future wage expense will be overstated, future cost of goods sold will be overstated, and future expenses will be understated, respectively.

4.10 Exchange Rates

27. On September 22, Year 1, a corporation purchased merchandise from an unaffiliated foreign entity for 10,000 units of the foreign entity's local currency. On that date, the spot rate was US $.55. The corporation paid the bill in full on March 20, Year 2, when the spot rate was US $.65. The closing rate was US $.70 on December 31, Year 1. What amount should the corporation report as a foreign currency transaction loss in its income statement for the year ended December 31, Year 1?

A. US $0

B. US $500

C. US $1,000

D. US $1,500

Answer (D) is correct. *(CPA, adapted)*

REQUIRED: The amount of foreign currency transaction loss to be reported in the income statement.

DISCUSSION: A receivable or payable fixed in a foreign currency is adjusted to its current exchange rate at each balance sheet date. The resulting gain or loss should ordinarily be included in determining profit or loss. It is the difference between the spot rate on the date the transaction originates (or the rate applied in the prior year) and the closing rate. Thus, the Year 1 transaction loss for Yumi Corp. is US $1,500 [10,000 units × ($0.55 – $0.70)].

Answer (A) is incorrect. A loss resulted when the spot rate increased. Answer (B) is incorrect. US $500 results from using the rates at 12/31/Yr 1 and 3/20/Yr 2. Answer (C) is incorrect. US $1,000 results from using the rates at 9/22/Yr 1 and 3/20/Yr 2.

4.11 Business Combinations

28. To effect a business combination initiated on July 1, Year 1, Company P acquired all the outstanding ordinary shares of Company S for cash equal to the carrying amount of Company S's net assets. The carrying amounts of Company S's assets and liabilities approximated their fair values, except that the carrying amount of its building was more than fair value. In preparing Company P's December 31, Year 1, consolidated income statement, what is the effect of recording the assets acquired and liabilities assumed at fair value and should goodwill amortization be recognized?

	Depreciation Expense	Goodwill Amortization
A.	Lower	Yes
B.	Higher	Yes
C.	Lower	No
D.	Higher	No

Answer (C) is correct. *(CPA, adapted)*

REQUIRED: The adjustments made in preparing the consolidated income statement.

DISCUSSION: A business combination is accounted for as an acquisition regardless of the form of consideration given. Thus, assets acquired and liabilities assumed should be recorded at their fair values. The differences between fair values and carrying amounts will affect profit or loss when related expenses are incurred. The effect of recording the building at fair value in the consolidated balance sheet instead of its higher carrying amount on Company S's books will be to decrease future depreciation. If the building is to be used, fair value is its current replacement cost for similar capacity unless expected use indicates a lower value to the acquirer. If the building is to be sold, it should be reported at fair value minus cost to sell. The excess of the sum of the consideration transferred, any noncontrolling interest, and any previously held equity interest over the acquisition-date fair value of the net assets acquired will be recognized as goodwill. This amount will be tested for impairment but not amortized.

Answer (A) is incorrect. Goodwill will be recognized but not amortized. Answer (B) is incorrect. Depreciation will decrease, and goodwill will be recognized but not amortized. Answer (D) is incorrect. Depreciation will decrease.

29. Company P paid US $600,000 for all of the outstanding ordinary stock of Company S in a business combination initiated and completed in the current year. At that time, Company S had the following condensed balance sheet:

	Carrying Amounts
Current assets	US $ 80,000
Plant and equipment, net	760,000
Liabilities	400,000
Equity	440,000

The fair value of the plant and equipment was US $120,000 more than its carrying amount. The fair values and carrying amounts were equal for all other assets and liabilities. What amount of goodwill, related to Company S's acquisition, should Company P report in its consolidated balance sheet?

A. US $40,000

B. US $80,000

C. US $120,000

D. US $160,000

Answer (A) is correct. *(CPA, adapted)*

REQUIRED: The amount of goodwill reported in the consolidated balance sheet.

DISCUSSION: Under the acquisition method, assets acquired and liabilities assumed should be recorded at their acquisition-date fair values. Any excess of the sum of the considerations transferred, any noncontrolling interest, and any previously held equity interest over the fair value of the net assets acquired is recorded as goodwill. After adjusting the net plant and equipment, and given that other items are stated at fair value, the fair value of the net assets acquired is US $560,000 [$80,000 current assets + ($760,000 + $120,000) plant and equipment – $400,000 liabilities]. Hence, goodwill is US $40,000 ($600,000 consideration – $560,000).

Answer (B) is incorrect. US $80,000 is the amount of current assets. Answer (C) is incorrect. US $120,000 is the amount plant and equipment is undervalued. Answer (D) is incorrect. US $160,000 is the difference between the US $600,000 consideration and the US $440,000 carrying amount of the net assets.

4.12 The Equity Method and Consolidated Reporting

30. When the equity method is used to account for the investment in an associate, the recording of the receipt of a cash distribution from the investee will result in

A. The recognition of investment income.

B. A reduction in the investment balance.

C. An increase in a liability account.

D. An increase in a special equity account.

Answer (B) is correct. *(CIA, adapted)*

REQUIRED: The effect under the equity method of the receipt of a cash distribution.

DISCUSSION: When the equity method is used, the investment is initially recorded at cost on the entity's books. The carrying amount is subsequently adjusted to recognize the profits or losses of the associate after the date of acquisition. Dividends received from an associate reduce the carrying amount.

Answer (A) is incorrect. When the equity method is used, investment income (loss) is recognized for the investee's share of the profits or losses of the associate. Dividends received from the investee are recorded as a reduction of the investment account. Answer (C) is incorrect. The investment account is credited. Answer (D) is incorrect. The investment account is credited.

STUDY UNIT FIVE
FINANCE

(40 pages of outline)

The emphasis of this study unit is on the financing of an entity. Sources of funds may be internal or external, short-term or long-term, and debt or equity. Selecting the appropriate types and amounts of available financing sources is necessary to **minimize the entity's cost of capital** and **maximize shareholder value**.

Core Concepts

- The ordinary (common) shareholders are the owners of a corporation.
- Preference (preferred) shares are a hybrid of debt and equity.
- Bonds are long-term debt instruments. They are similar to term loans except that they are usually offered to the public and sold to many investors.
- Share rights evidenced by warrants are options that are distributed with debt or preference (preferred) shares.
- The issuance of rights and a conversion feature delay equity financing when market prices are unfavorable.
- Intermediate-term financing consists of debt issues having approximate maturities of greater than 1 but less than 10 years.
- Short-term credit is debt scheduled to be repaid within 1 year.
- Capital structure consists primarily of long-term debt, preference (preferred) stock, and ordinary (common) equity.
- Leverage is the relative amount of the fixed cost of capital, principally debt, in an entity's capital structure.
- The cost of capital is a weighted average of the various debt and equity components.
- The cost of debt equals the interest rate times one minus the marginal tax rate.
- The cost of retained earnings is an opportunity cost. It is the rate that investors can earn elsewhere on investments of comparable risk.
- The cost of preference (preferred) stock equals the preference (preferred) dividend divided by the net issuance price.
- Standard financial theory states than an optimal capital structure exists.
- The Capital Asset Pricing Model (CAPM) adds the risk-free rate to the product of the beta coefficient and the difference between the market return and the risk-free rate.
- According to the dividend growth model, the required rate of return on retained earnings is the sum of the dividend payout ratio and the dividend growth rate.
- The efficient markets hypothesis states that current share prices immediately and fully reflect all relevant information.

- The cash budget details projected receipts and disbursements, preferably to plan the synchronization of inflows and outflows.
- Cash collections should be expedited. Slowing cash disbursements increases available cash.
- The amount of cash on hand should be determined by cost benefit analysis.
- An entity's excess cash should be placed in an investment with the highest return consistent with low risk.
- Short-term marketable securities are sometimes held as substitutes for cash but are more likely to be acquired as temporary investments.
- The objective of managing accounts receivable is to have both the optimal amount of receivables outstanding and the optimal amount of bad debt.
- Receivables management should maximize the accounts receivable turnover ratio, that is, shorten the average time receivables are held.
- The most fundamental approach to valuing a business combination is capital budgeting analysis. If the net present value (NPV) is positive, the combination is financially sound for the acquirer.
- A derivative is a financial instrument whose value changes with the change in the underlying (a specified interest rate, security price, foreign currency exchange rate, price index, commodity price, etc.).
- A call option is the most common type of option. It gives the owner the right to purchase the underlying asset at a fixed price.
- A put option gives the owner the right to sell the underlying asset for a fixed price.
- A forward contract is an executory (unperformed) contract.
- A futures contract is a specific kind of forward contract. It is a definite agreement that allows a trader to purchase or sell an asset at a fixed price during a specific future month.
- Swaps are contracts to hedge risk by exchanging cash flows.
- The essence of financial statement analysis is the calculation of financial ratios. These ratios establish relationships among financial statement accounts at a moment in time or for a given accounting period.
- Liquidity is an entity's ability to pay its current obligations as they come due and thus remain in business in the short run. Liquidity ratios measure this ability by relating an entity's liquid assets to its current liabilities.
- Activity ratios measure how quickly major noncash assets are converted to cash.
- Solvency is an entity's ability to pay its noncurrent obligations as they come due and thus remain in business in the long run (contrast with liquidity).
- Earnings coverage is a creditor's best measure of an entity's ongoing ability to generate the earnings that will allow it to satisfy its long-term debts and remain solvent.
- Return on investment, or ROI (also called return on invested capital), is a broad measure that reflects how efficiently an entity uses the resources contributed by its shareholders to generate a profit. All forms of ROI are some variation of this ratio: measure of profit or loss ÷ measure of capital.
- Profitability is measured by the profit margin, and the most common valuation measure is book value per share.

5.1 LONG-TERM FINANCING

<u>**Background**</u>

1. An entity may have long-term funding requirements that it cannot, or does not want to, meet using **retained earnings**. It must therefore issue **equity or debt** securities. Certain hybrid forms also are used for long-term financing, e.g., convertible securities.
2. The principal considerations when reviewing financing choices are cost, risk, and the lender's (the investor's) view of the financing device.

Ordinary (Common) Shares

3. The ordinary shareholders are the owners of a corporation, and their rights as owners, although reasonably uniform, depend on the laws where it is incorporated. Equity ownership involves **risk** because holders of ordinary shares are not guaranteed a return and are last in priority in a liquidation. Equity provides the cushion for creditors if any losses occur on liquidation.

   a. **Advantages of ordinary shares to the issuer**

      1) **Dividends are not fixed.** They are paid from profits when available.
      2) There is no fixed **maturity date** for repayment of the capital.
      3) The sale of ordinary shares increases the **creditworthiness** of the entity by providing more equity.
      4) Ordinary shares are frequently more attractive to investors than debt because they **grow in value** with the success of the entity.

         a) The higher the ordinary share value, the more advantageous equity financing is over debt financing.

   b. **Disadvantages of ordinary shares to the issuer**

      1) **Control** (voting rights) of existing ordinary shareholders may be diluted as more ordinary shares are sold.
      2) New ordinary shares **dilute earnings** available to existing shareholders because of the greater number of shares outstanding.
      3) **Underwriting costs** (i.e., cost of issuing shares) are typically higher for ordinary share issues than other forms of financing.
      4) Too much equity may raise the **average cost of capital** of the entity above its optimal level.
      5) Ordinary share **cash dividends** may not be tax deductible as an expense. They are after-tax reductions of cash.

   c. Ordinary shareholders may have **preemptive rights**.

      1) Preemptive rights give ordinary shareholders the right to purchase any additional issuances **in proportion** to their current ownership. Thus, they can maintain their ownership percentages.

Preference (Preferred) Shares

4. Preference shares are a hybrid of debt and equity. They have a fixed charge and increase leverage, but payment of dividends is not a legal obligation. They are less risky for investors than ordinary shares but more risky than bonds. Debt holders have priority over preference shareholders in liquidation.

   a. **Advantages of preference shares to the issuer**

      1) They are a form of equity and therefore build the **creditworthiness** of the entity.
      2) **Control** is still held by ordinary shareholders.
      3) **Superior earnings** are usually still reserved for the ordinary shareholders.

   b. **Disadvantages of preference shares to the issuer**

      1) Cash dividends paid are **not tax deductible** in most countries. The result is a substantially greater cost relative to bonds.
      2) In periods of economic difficulty, **accumulated (past) dividends** may create major managerial and financial problems.

c. **Typical provisions of preference share issues**

1) **Par value.** Par value is the liquidation value, and a percentage of par equals the preference dividend.
2) **Priority** in assets and earnings. If the entity goes bankrupt, the preference shareholders have priority over ordinary shareholders.
3) **Accumulation of dividends.** If preference dividends in arrears are cumulative, they must be paid before any ordinary dividends can be paid.
4) **Convertibility.** Preference share issues may be convertible into ordinary shares at the option of the shareholder.
5) **Participation.** Preference shares may participate with ordinary shares in excess earnings. For example, 8% participating preference shares might pay a dividend each year greater than 8% when the entity is extremely profitable. But nonparticipating preference shares will receive no more than is stated on the face of the share.
6) **Redeemability.** Some preference shares may be redeemed at a given time at the option of the holder, or otherwise at a time not controlled by the entity.
7) **Voting rights.** These may be conferred if preference dividends are in arrears for a stated period.
8) **Callability.** The issuer may have the right to repurchase the shares.
9) **Maturity.** Preference shares may have a sinking fund that allows for the purchase of the outstanding shares.

d. **Advantages of preference shares to the holder**

1) Holding preference shares rather than bonds may provide a **tax advantage**. A portion of dividends received from preference shares may be tax deductible, but all bond interest received normally is taxable.
2) Among the rights typically associated with preference shares are receipt of
   a) **Dividends** at a specified rate before ordinary shareholders
   b) Distributions before ordinary shareholders (but after creditors) upon **liquidation** or bankruptcy.
3) **However**, preference shareholders tend not to have voting rights or receive the same capital gains as the ordinary shareholders when the entity is successful.

Bonds

5. Bonds are long-term debt instruments. They are similar to term loans except that they are usually offered to the public and sold to many investors.

a. **Advantages of bonds to the issuer**

1) Basic **control** of the entity is not shared with the debtholder.
2) **Cost of debt** is limited. Bondholders usually do not participate in the superior earnings of the entity.
3) Ordinarily, the expected **yield** of bonds is lower than the cost of shares.
4) Interest paid on debt is usually **tax deductible**.
5) Debt may add substantial **flexibility** in the financial structure through the use of call provisions.

b. **Disadvantages of bonds to the issuer**

1) Debt has a **fixed charge**. If earnings fluctuate, the risk of insolvency is increased by the fixed interest obligation.
2) Debt **adds risk**. Shareholders will consequently demand higher capitalization rates on equity earnings, which may result in a decline in the market price of shares.
3) Debt usually has a **maturity date**.

4) Debt is a **long-term commitment**, a factor that can affect risk. Debt originally appearing to be profitable may become a burden and drive the entity into bankruptcy.

5) Certain **managerial powers** are usually surrendered in the contractual relationship defined in the **bond indenture**.

   a) For example, **specific financial ratios** may have to remain above a certain level during the term of the loan.

6) The **amount of debt financing** available to the individual entity is limited. Generally accepted investment standards will usually dictate a certain **debt-equity ratio**. Beyond this limit, the cost of debt may rise rapidly, or debt financing may not be available.

c. The **bond indenture** is the contractual arrangement between the issuer and the bondholders. It contains **restrictive covenants** intended to prevent the issuer from taking actions contrary to the interests of the bondholders. A **trustee**, often a bank, is appointed to ensure compliance.

1) **Call provisions** give the right to redeem bonds. If interest rates decline, the entity may call high-interest bonds and replace them with low-interest bonds.

2) Bonds are **puttable** or redeemable if the holder has the right to exchange them for cash.

3) **Sinking fund** requirements provide for the entity to retire a certain portion of its bonds each year or to set aside money for repayment in the future. Such terms increase the probability of repayment for bondholders but require the use of capital by the entity.

4) The issuer may be required to maintain its **financial ratios**, e.g., times-interest-earned, at specified levels.

5) **Dividends** may be limited if earnings do not meet specified requirements.

6) The amount of **new bonds** issued may be restricted to a percentage of bondable property (fixed assets).

d. **Types of bonds**

1) A **mortgage bond** is a pledge of certain assets for a loan. It is less risky for investors than a debenture because it is usually secured by real property as a condition of the loan. A **first mortgage bond** has priority over a **second mortgage bond**.

2) A **debenture** is a long-term bond not secured by specific property. Only borrowers with the best credit ratings can issue debentures because holders will be general creditors. They will have a status inferior to that of secured parties and creditors with priorities in bankruptcy.

3) **Subordinated debentures** normally have a higher yield than secured bonds because they are riskier for investors. They are subordinated (inferior) to the claims of other general creditors, secured parties, and persons with priorities in bankruptcy. The bond indenture specifies the claims (senior debt) to which these bonds are subordinate. They are usually issued only when the entity has some debt instrument outstanding that prohibits the issuance of additional regular bonds.

4) An **income bond** pays interest only if the issuer has earnings. Such bonds are riskier for investors than other bonds. They are correspondingly less risky for the issuer.

5) **Serial bonds** have staggered maturities. These bonds permit investors to choose the maturity dates that meet their needs.

6) **Registered bonds** are issued in the name of the owner. Interest payments are sent directly to the owner. When the owner sells registered bonds, the bond certificates must be surrendered and new certificates issued.

   a) They differ from **coupon (bearer) bonds**, which can be freely transferred and have a detachable coupon for each interest payment.

7) **Participating bonds** participate in excess earnings of the debtor as defined in the indenture.

8) **Indexed bonds** (purchasing power bonds) pay interest that is indexed to a measure of general purchasing power.

9) **Zero-coupon bonds** pay no periodic interest. However, they sell at a deep discount from their face amount.

   a) The need to **reinvest the periodic payments** from normal bonds makes their final return uncertain because future reinvestment rates are uncertain. But investors know the exact return on a zero-coupon bond. Investors might therefore be willing to pay a premium for them, which in turn might lead entities to issue them.

   b) The **lack of interest payments** means the entity has no additional insolvency risk from the issue until it matures.

10) **Junk bonds** are very high-risk, high-yield securities issued to finance leveraged buyouts and mergers. They also are issued by troubled entities. Issuers of junk bonds exploit the large tax deductions for interest paid by entities with high debt ratios.

11) **Convertible bonds** may be exchanged by the holder for equity shares as determined by the bond indenture

   a) Bonds may be issued with **warrants**. Warrants are usually detachable. They are options to purchase equity securities that are separately accounted for. A capital gain results if the share price rises above the option price. The bonds remain outstanding if the warrants are exercised.

12) **International bonds** exist in two forms. **Foreign bonds** are denominated in the currency of the nation in which they are sold. **Eurobonds** are denominated in a currency other than that of the nation where they are sold.

Stop and review! You have completed the outline for this subunit. Study multiple-choice questions 1 through 3 beginning on page 238.

5.2 SHORT-TERM FINANCING

1. Short-term credit is debt scheduled to be **repaid within 1 year.** Three main sources of this credit are trade credit, commercial banks, and commercial paper, but many other sources are available.

Trade Credit

a. The terms of **trade credit** are set by suppliers.

   1) EXAMPLE: If 2/10, net/30 are terms set by a supplier, the buyer has 10 days to take a 2% discount. If it is not taken, the full price must be paid within 30 days. Advantages of this arrangement are that (a) trade credit may be the only source of financing available, and (b) the first 10 days of credit are free. The disadvantage is that the 20 additional days of credit are costly.

2) Payments should be made **within discount periods** if the cost of not taking discounts exceeds the entity's cost of capital.

a) The **cost of not taking discounts** is approximately

$$\frac{360}{(\text{Total pay period} - \text{Discount period})} \times \frac{\text{Discount \%}}{(100\% - \text{Discount \%})}$$

i) In the example on the previous page, the cost of not taking the discount is

$$\frac{360}{(30 - 10)} \times \frac{2}{(100 - 2)} = 36.7\%$$

ii) This equation does not consider the **effects of compounding**. Accordingly, it underestimates the true cost of not taking discounts.

Short-Term Lending

b. **Commercial banks** offer savings (time deposit) and checking (demand deposit) accounts and lend for many purposes. However, other financial institutions perform such functions.

1) **Commercial bank lending** is significant to entities needing short-term financing. It is second only to trade credit as a source of financing.

a) The majority of lending by commercial banks is on a **short-term basis**. Many short-term loans are written for a term of 90 days or less.

b) The loan is obtained by signing a **promissory note**. Repayment is made in a lump sum at the maturity date, or installments are paid.

c) A **line of credit** permits a business to borrow up to a certain amount at any time. This amount is credited to the borrower's checking account for business use.

d) Commercial banks typically require **compensating balances** in checking accounts equal to some percentage of the loan or line of credit. The result is an increase in the effective interest rate.

e) The interest rate at which a bank will lend depends on the borrower's financial strength. The minimum interest rate is the **prime rate**. The prime rate is traditionally the lowest rate charged by banks to borrowers with the strongest credit.

Cost of Borrowing

c. The cost of a bank loan may be determined in several ways. **Simple interest** is based on the borrowed amount and is paid at the end of the loan term.

1) Simple interest rate for a 1-year loan: $\frac{\text{Interest}}{\text{Borrowed amount}}$

d. **Discounted interest** is based on the borrowed amount but is paid in advance. The add-on interest rate for an installment loan equals the interest divided by the average balance.

1) Discounted interest rate for a 1-year loan:

$$\frac{\text{Interest}}{\text{Borrowed amount} - \text{Interest}}$$

e. **Compounding** (periodically adding interest to the carrying amount) increases the effective rate, and the more frequent the compounding, the higher the rate.

f. The **present value and future value formulas** with which accountants should be very familiar illustrate compounding. However, they are not repeated here.

g. Considerations in **choosing a commercial lender**

a) The bank's policy toward risk.

b) The additional services and counseling the bank provides to customers.

c) The support a bank will provide in times of financial distress. Will the bank pressure an entity to repay its loans on time or negotiate extensions?

d) The degree of loan specialization provided by a bank. For example, a bank may specialize in loans to entities in a given line of business.

e) The size of the bank and its lending capacity. Thus, given that a bank cannot lend more than 15% of its capital to one customer, a large entity ordinarily will choose a large bank.

f) The financial strength of the bank.

Intermediate-Term Financing

h. **Commercial paper** consists of short-term, unsecured, notes payable. They are issued in large denominations by large entities with high credit ratings to other entities and institutional investors, such as pension funds, banks, and insurers.

1) The **maturity date** of commercial paper is normally less than 270 days. Commercial paper is traded in **money markets** and thus is highly liquid.

2) Commercial paper is a lower cost source of funds than bank loans. It is usually issued at **below the prime rate**.

3) **Advantages** are that it affords broad and efficient distribution, provides large sums (at a given cost), and avoids costly financing arrangements.

4) **Disadvantages** are that it trades in an impersonal market and that the amount available is limited to the excess liquidity of big corporations.

i. Many **other types of short-term financing** are in use.

1) **Bankers' acceptances** are drafts drawn on deposits at a bank. The acceptance by the bank is a guarantee of payment at maturity.

2) **Repurchase agreements** involve sales by a dealer in government securities who agrees to repurchase at a given time for a specific price. Maturities may be very short-term. This arrangement is in essence a secured loan.

3) **Pledging or assigning receivables** involves securing loans with receivables. A bank often lends up to 80% of outstanding receivables. Receivables may also be **factored** (sold).

4) **Money-market mutual funds** invest in portfolios of short-term securities.

5) **Warehouse financing** uses inventory as security for the loan. A third party, for example, a public warehouse, holds the collateral and serves as the creditor's agent. The creditor receives the warehouse receipts evidencing rights in the collateral. Security for inventory financing also may be in other forms.

a) A **field warehousing arrangement** provides for on-site control and supervision of specified goods by a third party.

6) **Chattel mortgages** are loans secured by movable personal property (e.g., equipment or livestock).

Stop and review! You have completed the outline for this subunit. Study multiple-choice questions 4 through 6 beginning on page 239.

5.3 OPTIMAL CAPITALIZATION

Financial Structure

1. The **financial structure** of an entity is reported in the liability and equity sections of the balance sheet. They describe how assets are financed.

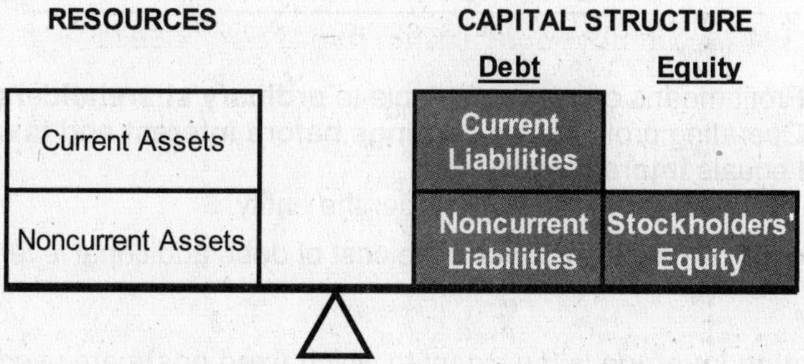

   a. Noncurrent liabilities
      1) **Long-term debt**
         a) Most entities renew (roll over) their long-term obligations. Thus, long-term debt is often effectively permanent.
   b. Stockholders' equity
      1) **Preference shares**
      2) **Ordinary shares**
      3) **Retained earnings**

2. **The following factors influence financial structure:**
   a. Growth rate and stability of future sales
   b. Competitive structures in the industry
   c. Asset composition of the individual entity
   d. Attitude of owners and management toward risk
   e. Control position of owners and management
   f. Lenders' attitudes toward the industry and the entity
   g. Tax considerations

Leverage

3. **Leverage** is the relative amount of the fixed cost of capital, principally debt, in an entity's capital structure. Leverage, by definition, creates **financial risk**, which relates directly to the question of the **cost of capital**. The more leverage, the higher the financial risk, and the higher the cost of debt capital.
   a. The cost of debt is lower than the cost of equity because **interest is tax deductible**. **Earnings per share** ordinarily will be higher if debt is used to raise capital instead of equity, provided that the entity is not over-leveraged. However, the prospect of higher EPS is accompanied by (1) greater risk resulting from required interest costs, (2) creditors' liens on assets, and (3) the possibility of a proportionately lower EPS if earnings does not meet projections.

Degree of Financial Leverage

b. **The degree of financial leverage (DFL)** is the percentage change in earnings available to ordinary shareholders that is associated with a given percentage change in net operating profit. The second formula below can be derived from the first.

c.

$$DFL = \frac{\%\ \Delta\ in\ profit}{\%\ \Delta\ in\ net\ operating\ profit} = \frac{EBIT}{EBIT - I}$$

1) Profit means earnings available to **ordinary shareholders**.
2) Operating profit equals **earnings before interest and taxes (EBIT)**.
3) I equals **interest expense**.
4) The greater the DFL, the riskier the entity.

d. If the return on assets **exceeds** the cost of debt, additional leverage is favorable.

Operating Leverage

e. **Operating leverage** is the extent to which **fixed costs** are used in the production process. An entity with a high percentage of fixed costs is more risky than one in the same industry with a higher ratio of variable costs of production.

1) **The degree of operating leverage (DOL)** is the percentage change in net operating profit associated with a given percentage change in sales. The second formula below can be derived from the first.

2)

$$DOL = \frac{\%\ \Delta\ in\ net\ operating\ profit}{\%\ \Delta\ in\ sales} = \frac{Contribution\ Margin}{Contribution\ Margin\ -\ Fixed\ Costs}$$

a) EXAMPLE: If operating profit increases 20% with a 10% increase in sales, DOL is 2.0.

Degree of Total Leverage

f. **The degree of total leverage (DTL)** combines the DFL and the DOL. It equals the degree of financial leverage times the degree of operating leverage. Thus, it also equals the percentage change in profit that is associated with a given percentage change in sales.

1)

$$DTL = DFL \times DOL = \frac{\%\ \Delta\ in\ profit}{\%\ \Delta\ in\ sales}$$

a) EXAMPLE: If net income increases 15% with a 5% increase in sales, DTL is 3.0.

2) Entities with a **high degree of operating leverage** do not usually employ a high degree of financial leverage and vice versa. One of the most important considerations in the use of financial leverage is operating leverage.

a) EXAMPLE: An entity has a highly automated production process. Because of automation, the degree of operating leverage is 2. If the entity wants a degree of total leverage not exceeding 3, it must restrict its use of debt so that the degree of financial leverage is not more than 1.5. If the entity had committed to a production process that was less automated and had a lower DOL, more debt could be employed, and the entity could have a higher degree of financial leverage.

Cost of Capital

4. **Cost of capital** is the price, in both monetary terms and opportunity cost, of raising funds.

a. Managers must know the entity's cost of capital when making investment (long-term funding) decisions. Investments with a return higher than the cost of capital will increase the value of the entity (shareholders' wealth).

b. The theory underlying the cost of capital applies to new, long-term funding because long-term funds finance **long-term investments**. Long-term investment decisions are typically made using the cost of capital to discount future cash flows.

1) Working capital and other temporary needs are met with short-term funds. Thus, cost of capital is of less concern for short-term funding.

Weighted-Average Cost of Capital

5. The **WACC** weights the cost of each debt and equity component by the percentage of that component in the financial structure.

a. The **cost of debt** is the after-tax interest rate of the debt.

$$\text{Interest rate} \times (1 - \text{Marginal tax rate})$$

1) The after-tax rate is used because interest paid is a tax deduction. Hence, as tax rates increase, debt becomes more favorable.

b. The **cost of preference shares** includes **flotation costs** necessary to offer the stock to the investing public.

$$\text{Dividend per share} \div \text{Net issuance cost per share}$$

1) Because preference dividends paid are not tax deductible, the tax rate is not considered.

c. The **cost of retained earnings** is an opportunity cost, i.e., the rate that investors can earn elsewhere on investments of comparable risk.

1) If the entity is not able to earn a shareholder's required rate of return, retained earnings should be paid out in the form of dividends so that shareholders can find their own, higher-return investments.

d. **Providers of equity capital** are exposed to **more risk** than are lenders because the entity is not obligated to pay them a return. Also, in case of liquidation, equity investors have a lower priority than creditors.

1) Thus, **equity financing is more expensive than debt**. Equity investors require a higher return to compensate for the greater risk assumed.

e. EXAMPLE: **Short-term debt** is not part of the capital structure.

Component	**(1)** Carrying Amount	**(2)** Interest or Dividend Rate	**(3)** After-Tax Rate or Expected Return	**(4)** Fair Value	**(5)** Weight (Proportion of Total Fair Value)	**(3) × (5)** Weighted-Average Cost of Capital
Bonds payable	US $ 2,000,000	8.5%	7.4%	US $ 2,200,000	0.1000	0.7400%
Preference shares	4,000,000	14.0%	10.0%	4,600,000	0.2091	2.0909%
Ordinary equity	12,000,000		16.0%	14,000,000	0.6364	10.1824%
Retained earnings	1,200,000		16.0%	1,200,000	0.0545	0.8720%
Totals	US $19,200,000			US $22,000,000	1.0000	13.8853%

Optimal Capital Structure

6. Standard financial theory provides a model for the **optimal capital structure** of every entity. It states that shareholder wealth is maximized by **minimizing the weighted-average cost of capital**.

a. Thus, the focus of management should **not** be on **maximizing earnings per share**. Increasing debt increases not only EPS but also risk.

1) The optimal capital structure usually involves some debt, but not 100% debt.

b. The relevant relationships are depicted below:

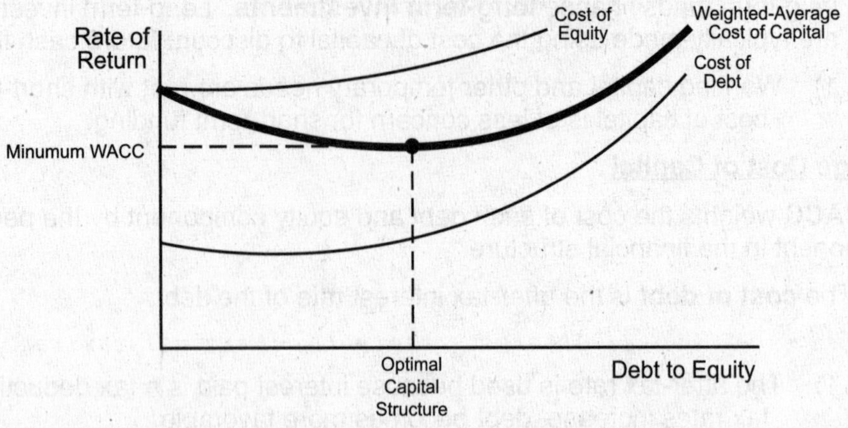

c. Ordinarily, entities cannot identify this optimal point precisely. Thus, they should attempt to find an optimal range for the capital structure.

d. The **required rate of return on equity capital (R)** can be estimated as follows:

1) The **capital asset pricing model (CAPM)** adds the risk-free rate (determined by government securities) to the product of the beta coefficient (a measure of the entity's risk) and the difference between the market return and the risk-free rate. Below is the basic equilibrium equation for the CAPM.

$$R = R_F + \beta(R_M - R_F)$$

a) The **market risk premium** ($R_M - R_F$) is the amount above the risk-free rate required to induce average investors to enter the market.

b) The **beta coefficient (β)** of an individual stock is the correlation between the volatility (price variation) of the stock market and the volatility of the price of the individual stock.

i) EXAMPLE: If an individual stock rises 10% and the stock market 10%, the beta coefficient is 1.0. If the stock rises 15% and the market only 10%, beta is 1.5.

ii) The CAPM is a model that uses just one systematic risk factor to explain the asset's return. That factor is the expected return on the market portfolio, i.e., the market-valued weighted average return for all securities available in the market.

c) EXAMPLE: Assuming a beta of 1.20, a market rate of return of approximately 17%, and an expected risk-free rate of 12%, the required rate of return on equity capital is 18% [12% + 1.2 (17% – 12%)].

d) The graph of this equation (with interest rates plotted on the vertical axis and betas on the horizontal axis) is the **security market line (SML)**. The slope of the SML equals the market risk premium, and the y-intercept is the risk-free rate.

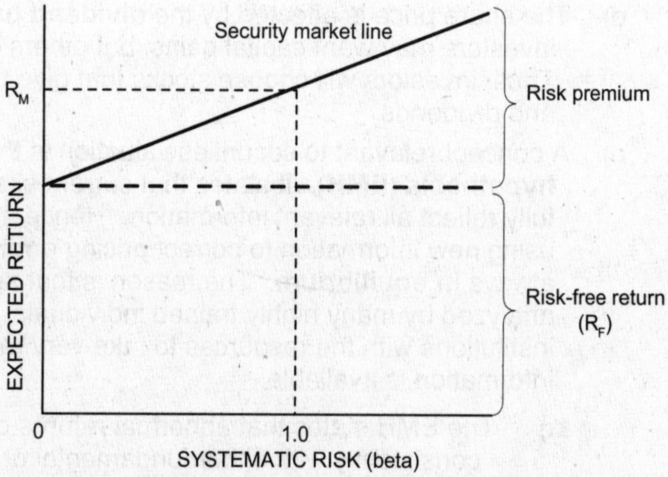

e) The **risk premium** is the difference in expected rates of return on a risky asset and a less risky asset.

2) R also may be estimated by adding a percentage to the entity's long-term cost of debt. A 3% to 5% premium is frequently used.

3) The **economic value** of the entity is expressed by the formula

$$V = \sum_{t=1}^{N} \frac{CF_t}{(1 + k)^t}$$

If: V is value, CF is net cash flow, k is the discount rate (cost of capital), and t is time.

4) The **dividend growth model** estimates the cost of **retained earnings** using the dividends per share, the expected growth rate, and the market price. To justify retention of earnings, management must expect a return at least equal to the dividend yield plus a growth rate.

a) The formula for calculating the cost of retained earnings is

$$R = \frac{D_1}{P_0} + G$$

If: P_0 = current price
D_1 = next dividend
R = required rate of return
G = growth rate in dividends per share (but the model assumes that the dividend payout ratio, retention rate, and therefore the EPS growth rate are constant)

i) EXAMPLE: An entity's dividend is expected to be US $4, the market price is US $50, and the dividend is expected to grow at a constant rate of 6%. Thus, the required rate of return is 14% (US $4 ÷ $50 + 6%).

b) To determine the **cost of new ordinary shares** (external equity), the model is altered to incorporate the flotation cost. As the **flotation cost** rises, R increases accordingly.

$$R = \frac{D_1}{P_0(1 - Flotation\ cost)} + G$$

c) The dividend growth model also is used for **share price evaluation**. The formula can be restated in terms of P_0 as follows:

$$P_0 = \frac{D_1}{R - G}$$

d) The share price is affected by the **dividend payout ratio** because some investors may want capital gains, but others may prefer current income. Thus, investors will choose stocks that give the proper mix of capital gains and dividends.

e) A concept relevant to securities valuation is the **efficient markets hypothesis (EMH)**. It states that current share prices immediately and fully reflect all relevant information. Hence, the market is continuously using new information to correct pricing errors, and securities prices are always **in equilibrium**. The reason is that securities are intensely analyzed by many highly trained individuals. These analysts work for institutions with the resources to take very rapid action when new information is available.

i) The EMH states that abnormal returns cannot be obtained consistently with either fundamental or technical analysis.

ii) Under the EMH, the **expected return** of each security equals the return required by the marginal investor given its risk. The **price** equals its fair value as perceived by investors.

e. An entity cannot raise unlimited amounts of new funds at its historical cost of capital. At some point, the costs of new funds will increase its cost of capital.

1) The **marginal cost of capital (MCC)** is the cost to an entity of the next monetary unit of new capital raised.

2) EXAMPLE: The entity with the capital structure presented in the schedule in item 5.e. on page 209 determined that it requires US $2,000,000 of new funding.

a) The simplest source, retained earnings, is insufficient.

i) If the entity issues US $800,000 of bonds, its debt-to-equity ratio will increase. The increased risk may result in paying a higher rate on the new debt.

ii) If the entity issues new preference shares, the investors will demand a priority dividend.

iii) If the entity issues new stock, issue costs must be paid.

b) The entity's WACC equals its current rate of 13.8853% for the US $1,200,000 of retained earnings. However, the MCC will be higher for new external capital.

3) This phenomenon can be depicted as follows:

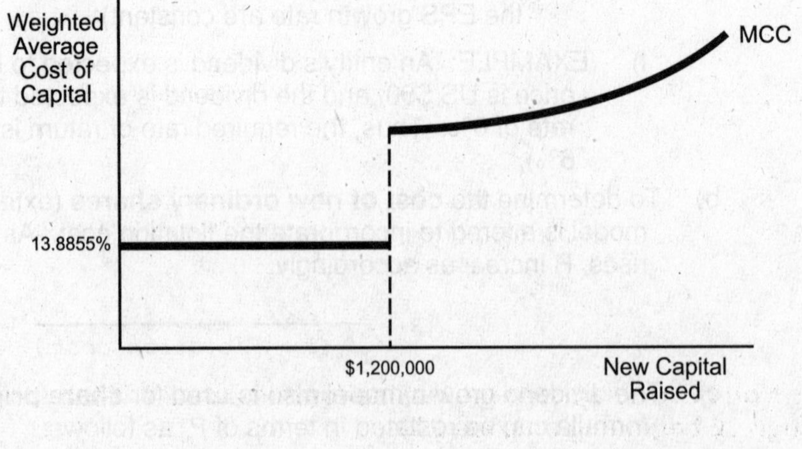

4) The **marginal efficiency of investment (MEI)** is the decrease in return on additional capital investment because the most profitable investments are made initially.

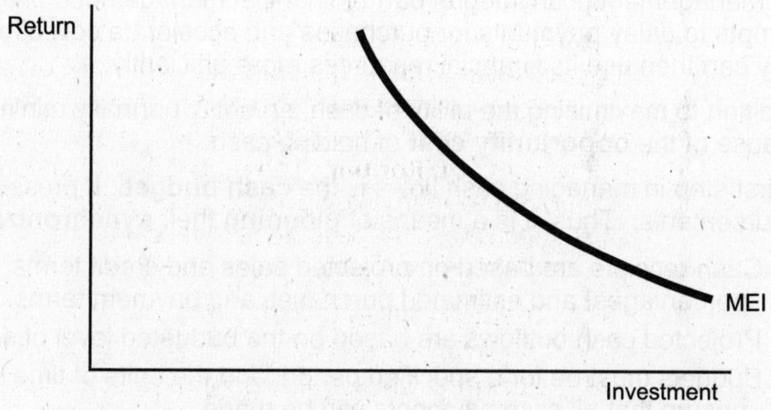

a) The MCC and MEI curves define the equilibrium investment level for the entity (Q*) at a particular interest rate (I) and given capital budget.

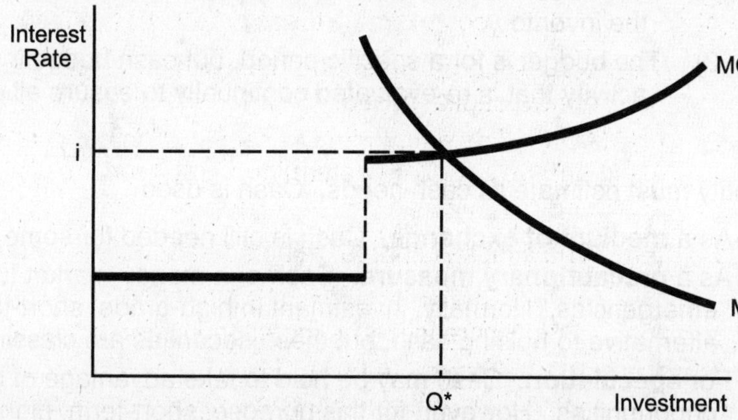

7. To ensure short-term and long-term survival, entities use budgeting and financial forecasts. **Additional funds needed (AFN)** must be calculated to avoid shortages of working capital and provide for capital expansion. **Working capital** is required for sales growth. Furthermore, an entity nearing full capacity must respond to **fixed asset requirements**. If retained earnings is insufficient, it must seek external capital, which will result in an increase of debt or equity.

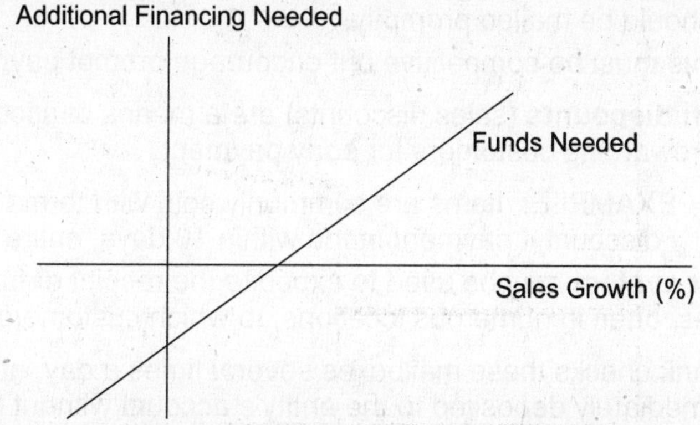

Stop and review! You have completed the outline for this subunit. Study multiple-choice questions 7 through 10 beginning on page 240.

5.4 MANAGEMENT OF CURRENT ASSETS

Cash

1. Cash management is an integral part of financial management. In general, an entity attempts to delay payments for purchases and accelerate collections on credit sales. The entity can then use its financial resources more efficiently.
2. In addition to maximizing the utility of cash, an entity normally minimizes its cash on hand because of the **opportunity cost** of holding cash.
3. The first step in managing cash flows is the **cash budget**. It presents projected receipts and disbursements. Thus, it is a means of **planning** their **synchronization**.
   a. Cash receipts are based on projected sales and credit terms, estimated collection percentages, and estimated purchases and payment terms.
   b. Projected cash outflows are based on the budgeted level of sales.
   c. Budgets must be for a specified period, and the units of time must be short enough to ensure that all cash payments can be made.
      1) The cash budget considers the **cash flow/cash conversion cycle**. It is the time from disbursement for inventory purchases to receipt of cash from the sale of the inventory.
      2) The budget is for a specific period, but cash budgeting is an ongoing, cumulative activity that is re-evaluated continually to ensure all objectives are met.

Uses of Cash

4. An entity must estimate its cash needs. Cash is used
   a. As a **medium of exchange**. Cash is still needed for some business transactions.
   b. As a **precautionary measure**. Cash or a money-market fund can be held for emergencies. Normally, investment in high-grade, short-term securities is a better alternative to holding cash, but these securities are classified as cash under IFRSs.
   c. For **speculation**. Cash may be held to take advantage of bargain-purchase opportunities. However, for this purpose, short-term, highly liquid securities are preferable.
   d. As a **compensating balance** in exchange for a bank's services or loans.

Cash Collections

5. The cash budget also examines **cash collections**. Sound financial management requires that cash collections be expedited.
   a. Invoices should be mailed promptly.
   b. Credit terms must be competitive but encourage prompt payment.
      1) **Cash discounts** (sales discounts) are a means of accelerating cash collection by rewarding customers for early payment.
         a) EXAMPLE: Items are commonly sold with terms of 2/10, n/30 (2% discount if payment made within 10 days, entire balance due in 30 days).
   c. A **lockbox system** may be used to expedite the receipt of funds. An entity maintains mailboxes, often in numerous locations, to which customers send payments.
      1) A bank checks these mailboxes several times a day, and funds received are immediately deposited to the entity's account without first being processed by its accounting system. This practice hastens availability of the funds.
      2) In addition, having several lockboxes reduces the time a payment is in the postal system.

d. **Transfer of funds by wire** expedites cash management. A **wire transfer** is any electronic funds transfer by means of a two-way system, for example, the U.S. Federal Reserve Wire Transfer System (Fedwire).

e. **Electronic funds transfer (EFT)** and customer debit cards expedite cash inflows. With the recent widespread growth of **electronic commerce** (the buying and selling of products and services over the Internet) by individuals, the use of EFT has mushroomed. Entities such as PayPal enable individuals to transfer funds to each other at little or no cost.

6. If the entity is able to slow cash disbursements without increasing costs, it can increase available cash on hand.

   a. Payment beyond normal credit terms, however, creates vendor ill will and may incur interest charges. If these interest charges are higher than alternative lending choices, this practice will not maximize shareholder wealth and should be avoided.

   b. Payments should be made within **discount periods** if the cost of not taking a discount exceeds the entity's cost of capital.

   c. Payment by **draft** (a three-party instrument in which the drawer orders the drawee to pay money to the payee) is a means of slowing cash outflows.

      1) A **check** is the most common draft. **Float** arises from the delay between an expenditure or receipt by check and the clearing of the check.

         a) The effect is an interest-free loan to the payor.

         b) Accordingly, entities attempt to maximize **disbursements float** (the period from when checks are written to when they are subtracted from the bank balance). They also minimize **collections float**, the sum of (1) the time checks are in the mail, (2) internal processing time, and (3) the time required for clearing through the banking system.

7. The cash budget also must consider cash required to be kept on deposit with banks to satisfy compensating balances.

<u>**Cash on Hand**</u>

8. This amount should be determined by cost-benefit analysis. The objective of financial management is to maximize shareholder wealth. Thus, the entity minimizes the cost of holding cash and maximizes the returns on investing cash.

   a. The reduction in average cash times the interest rate (cost of capital or investment yield rate) is the **benefit**.

   b. **Costs** of having insufficient cash include incremental personnel cost, lost discounts, and lost vendor goodwill.

   c. Whenever possible, excess cash should be placed in an investment with a high return and little risk.

   d. An entity with excess cash may be a takeover target.

<u>**Cash Management Models**</u>

9. The **economic order quantity (EOQ)** model applies to cash as well as inventory management.

   a. It can be stated in terms of the following **assumptions**:

      1) A known demand for cash
      2) A given carrying (interest) cost
      3) The flat amount (cost) of converting other assets to cash, such as the broker's fee for sale of marketable securities (assumed to be constant regardless of the transaction size)

b. One such EOQ-type model is the **Baumol Cash Management Model**. It attempts to minimize the total of the costs of securities transactions and the opportunity costs of holding cash (the return forgone by not investing in marketable securities or the cost of borrowing cash). The **formula** is

$$OC = \sqrt{\frac{2bT}{i}}$$

If: OC = the optimal cash level
b = the cost per transaction
T = the total demand for cash for the period
i = the interest rate on marketable equity securities or the cost of borrowing cash

c. The **Miller-Orr cash management model** assumes **uncertain cash flows** that are **random in amount and direction** and are **normally distributed** as the number of periods increases.

1) It derives the most cost efficient cash balance by determining an upper limit and lower limit for cash balances. The target is between these two limits. As long as cash is between the two limits, no transaction to replenish or invest the cash balance occurs.

2) At points A, B, and D in the diagram, the cash balance reaches the upper limit, and the excess over the return point is immediately invested in short-term securities. At point C, the lower limit is reached, and sufficient securities are sold to make the balance of cash equal the return point.

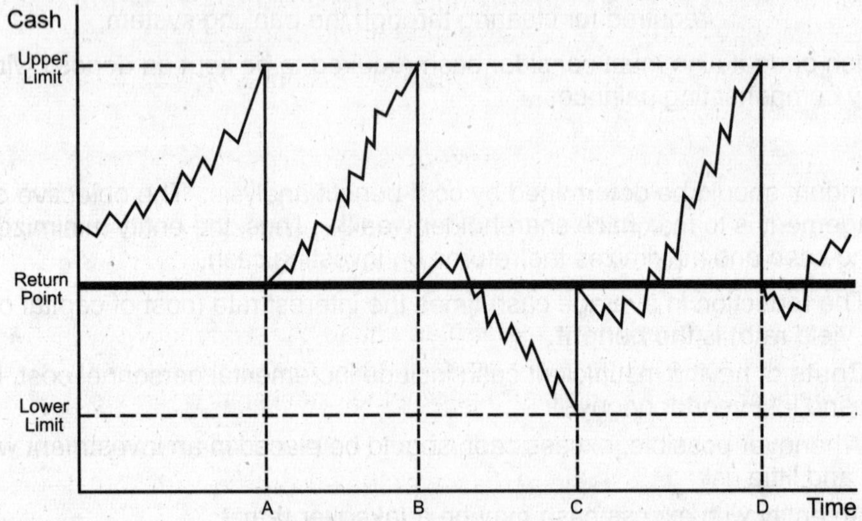

Marketable Securities

10. Short-term marketable securities are sometimes held as **substitutes for cash** but are more likely to be acquired as **temporary investments**. An entity's excess cash should be placed in an investment with the highest return consistent with low risk, such as those listed below and on the next page.

a. Short-term debt securities may be guaranteed explicitly by a government and exempt from local taxation. They may be sold on a discount basis.

b. **Certificates of deposit** are a form of savings deposit that cannot be withdrawn before maturity without a high penalty. However, negotiable CDs are subject to government securities regulation.

c. **Money-market accounts** are similar to checking accounts but pay higher interest.
d. **High-grade commercial paper** consists of unsecured, short-term notes issued by large entities that are very good credit risks. However, commercial paper may yield a higher return than CDs because it is riskier.
e. An entity with excessive cash may be a takeover target.

11. Short-term marketable securities are usually chosen for reasons that make high-yield, high-risk investments unattractive. Hence, a higher return may be forgone in exchange for greater safety. Given the various options available, an entity should have an **investment policy statement** to provide continuing guidance to management regarding the risk-return trade-off.
    a. Thus, speculative tactics, such as **selling short** (borrowing and selling securities in the expectation that their price will decline by the time they must be replaced) and **margin trading** (borrowing from a broker to buy securities) are avoided.

<u>**Accounts Receivable**</u>

12. The **objective** of managing accounts receivable is to have both the **optimal amount of receivables** outstanding and the **optimal amount of bad debts**.
    a. This balance requires a trade-off between the **benefits** of credit sales, such as more sales, and the **costs** of accounts receivable, such as collection, interest, and bad debt costs. The appropriate policy does not seek merely to maximize sales or to minimize default risk.
13. Credit terms, collection policies, etc., are frequently determined by **competitors**. An entity must match such incentives to make sales. Entities often use a statistical technique called **credit scoring** to determine whether to extend credit to a specific customer. Credit scoring assigns numerical values to the elements of credit worthiness, e.g., income, length of time employed in the same job, occupation, and home ownership.
14. Receivables management should maximize the accounts receivable turnover ratio, that is, shorten the average time receivables are held.
    a. The **accounts receivable turnover ratio** equals net credit sales divided by average accounts receivable.
    b. A common analytical tool is an **aging schedule** developed from an entity's accounts receivable ledger. It stratifies the accounts depending on how long they have been outstanding.
    c. The **number of days of receivables** equals the number of days in the year (365, 360, or 300) divided by the receivables turnover ratio. This ratio can be compared with the seller's credit terms to determine whether most customers are paying on time.
        1) It is the average number of days to collect a receivable **(collection period)**.
        2) It also may be computed as average accounts receivable divided by average daily sales (net credit sales ÷ days in a year).
    d. **Average gross receivables** is calculated by multiplying average daily sales by the average collection period.
15. For **inventory management**, see Study Unit 2.

Stop and review! You have completed the outline for this subunit. Study multiple-choice questions 11 through 13 on page 242.

5.5 BUSINESS VALUATION

Capital Budgeting

1. The most fundamental approach to valuing a business is capital budgeting.
   a. For a full outline of this topic, see Subunit 6.4.
2. If the **net present value (NPV) is positive**, that is, if the present value of the estimated incremental cash flows from the acquisition exceeds the present value of the amounts to be paid for the acquiree, the investment is financially sound for the acquirer.
   a. The shareholders of the acquiree should perform a similar analysis and compare the result with the NPV of remaining an independent entity.
3. The analysis must emphasize
   a. Accurate estimates of **expected cash flows**
   b. The effect on the **cost of capital** and the **optimal capital structure** of the acquirer
   c. How the acquisition will be **financed**
   d. The **price** to be paid
      1) An acquisition should be synergistic or otherwise result in the creation of new value. In that case, a **premium** can be paid to the shareholders of the acquiree while still permitting the shareholders of the acquirer to benefit.
         a) However, most of the gain in value usually is paid to the acquiree's shareholders as an inducement to sell.
4. Key variables in valuation analysis are the estimates of the **incremental cash flows** from the acquisition and the **required rate of return** (cost of capital). This rate is the discount rate to be used in calculating the NPV.
   a. Projecting incremental cash flows becomes relatively more difficult when the entities' operations are to be merged or if the acquiree's operations are to be changed.
      1) The analysis also should consider the **transaction costs** involved.
   b. An acquisition often requires consideration of **complex debt arrangements**.
      1) The debt acquired will have different rates from that held by the acquirer.
      2) Debt may be issued to finance the acquisition or expansion of the acquiree.
   c. The projected cash flow analysis should incorporate **interest**. Because the net cash flows will be calculated after subtraction of interest, the valuation will reflect the **equity residual**, i.e., the value to the acquirer.
   d. The **forecast** of the incremental cash flows available to the acquirer should be based on analyses of the **sensitivity** of the NPV to changes in the key variables. It also should consider the range of the probable values of these variables based on their probability distributions.
      1) Consequently, a **computer simulation** may be a useful technique for evaluating the acquisition, assuming probabilities can be estimated for the components of the projected cash flows.
   e. To calculate the net incremental cash flows to the acquirer, the **discount rate** used should be the **cost of equity capital**. Moreover, this rate should reflect the risk associated with the use of funds rather than their source.
      1) The rate therefore should not be the cost of capital of the acquirer but rather the cost of equity of the combined entity after the acquisition. This calculation requires a new estimate of **beta** to be used in the **Capital Asset Pricing Model**.

f. Estimating the value of the acquisition using discounted cash flows should not ignore the **market prices** of comparable investments. If the market is efficient, market prices should equal the values of those investments.

1) This analysis should include the P-E ratio, price-to-book-value ratio, and price-to-sales ratio.

g. The **nature of the bid** for the acquiree (cash, stock, debt, or a combination) has important effects on

1) The combined entity's **capital structure**
2) The **tax position** of the acquirer and the shareholders of the acquiree
3) Whether the **acquiree's shareholders** will benefit from postacquisition gains by the combined entity
4) The extent of governmental **regulatory involvement**

Stop and review! You have completed the outline for this subunit. Study multiple-choice question 14 on page 243.

5.6 DERIVATIVE FINANCIAL INSTRUMENTS

1. A **derivative** is defined informally as an investment transaction in which the buyer purchases the right to a potential gain with a commitment for a potential loss. It is a wager on whether the value of something will go up or down. The purpose of the transaction is either to speculate (incur risk) or to hedge (avoid risk).

a. Thus, a derivative is an unperformed contract that results in cash flow between two **counterparties** based on the change in some underlying indicator of value. Examples of these indicators include (1) prices of financial instruments, such as ordinary shares or government bonds; (2) currency exchange rates; (3) interest rates; (4) commodity prices; or (5) stock indexes.

b. Derivative instruments (derivatives) should be contrasted with such other financial instruments as cash, accounts receivable, notes receivable, bonds, preference shares, and ordinary shares.

<u>**Options**</u>

2. Options and futures are derivatives. They are not claims on business assets, such as those represented by equity securities. Instead, they are contracts by parties who agree to buy, sell, or exchange assets, such as stocks, commodities, or bonds, at a specified price in the future.

a. An **American option** is a contractual arrangement that gives the owner the right to buy or sell an asset at a fixed price at any moment in time before or on a specified date. A **European option** differs from an American option because it is exercisable only at the expiration date.

b. Exercising the option is the act of buying or selling **the underlying**. This is the technical term for the asset to be bought, sold, or traded under the terms of the option. For example, the underlying for a share option on Siemens stock is Siemens stock.

c. An option is a right of the owner or holder of the option. The seller has sold the rights.

d. The **exercise or strike price** is the price at which the owner can purchase or sell the asset underlying the option contract. The **option price**, also called **option premium**, is the amount paid to acquire an option.

1) The **bid-ask spread** is the difference between what a buyer is willing to bid and what a seller is asking.

e. An option usually has an **expiration date** after which it can no longer be exercised.

f. The **longer the time before expiration**, the more valuable the option. The reason is the increased time available for the asset's price to rise or fall.

3. The two types of options are calls and puts.
   a. A **call option** is the most common type. It gives the owner the right to purchase the underlying asset at a fixed price. Thus, it represents a **long position** because the owner gains from a price increase in the underlying. The profit is the difference between the price paid and the value at the closing date, minus the brokerage fee.
      1) Call options usually involve ordinary shares as the underlying. However, any type of asset may underlie an option.
      2) If the value of the asset underlying a call option is less than the exercise price of the option, the option is **out-of-the-money**, or not worth exercising. If the value of the asset underlying the option is greater than the exercise price, it is **in-the-money** and can earn the owner a profit. If the value of the asset is at the strike price, the option is **at-the-money**.
      3) A call option's **expiration value** equals the excess of the current price of the asset over the exercise price. If the exercise price exceeds the current price, the option is worthless.
      4) **Net Gain or Loss on a Call Option**
         a) For the purchaser (long position), the **gain or loss** is the following:

            [(# of shares) × (excess of market price over exercise price)] – amount paid for option

         b) For the seller (short position), the **loss or gain** is the following:

            Amount received for option – [# of shares × (excess of market price over exercise price)]

         c) The call option will not be exercised unless the market price is greater than the exercise price. The **seller** profits only when
            i) The option is not exercised, or
            ii) The price received for the option exceeds the excess of the market price over the exercise price.
         d) EXAMPLE: If the exercise price is US $100, the market price is US $105, and 100 options, each providing for a purchase of one ordinary share, are sold for US $3 each, the results are as follows:

Purchaser's gain:	{[100 shares × (US $105 – $100)] – (100 options × $3)} = US $200
Seller's loss:	{(100 options × US $3) – [100 shares × ($105 – $100)]} = US $(200)

   b. A **put option** gives the owner the right to sell the underlying asset for a fixed price. It represents a **short position** because the owner benefits from a price decrease.
      1) If the value of the **asset underlying a put option** is greater than the option's exercise price, the put option is worthless or out-of-the-money.
      2) If the value of the asset underlying the put option is less than the option's exercise price, the put is in-the-money. Thus, the option has **intrinsic value**. This is the difference between the exercise price and the market price of the underlying security.
      3) Put options also may be referred to as at-the-money and out-of-the-money.
      4) A put option's expiration value equals either zero or the excess of the exercise price over the current market price.
      5) **Net Gain or Loss on a Put Option**
         a) For the purchaser (long position), the **gain or loss** is the following:

            [(# of shares) × (excess of exercise price over market price)] – amount paid for option

         b) For the seller (short position), the **loss or gain** is the following:

            Amount received for option – [# of shares × (excess of exercise price over market price)]

c) The put option will not be exercised unless the exercise price is greater than the market price. The **seller** profits only when

i) The option is not exercised, or

ii) The price received for the option exceeds the excess of the exercise price over the market price.

d) EXAMPLE: If the exercise price is US $105, the market price is US $100, and 100 options were sold for US $3 each, the results are as follows:

Purchaser's gain: {[100 shares × (US $105 – $100)] – (100 options × $3)} = US $200
Seller's loss: {[100 options × US $3) – [100 shares × ($105 – $100)]} = US $(200)

4. Calls and puts may be covered or uncovered.

a. A **covered option** is written against stock held in the option writer's portfolio.

b. A **naked (uncovered) option** is not backed by stock.

c. Thus, an option is naked if the writer is not using it to hedge because (s)he does not own the underlying.

5. Calls and puts also may be classified based on the underlying.

a. A **stock option** is an option to buy a specific stock at some future time.

b. An **index option** is an option whose underlying security is an index. If exercised, settlement is made by cash payment because physical delivery is not possible.

c. **Long-term equity anticipation securities (LEAPS)** are examples of long-term stock options or index options, with expiration dates up to three years away.

d. **Foreign currency options** give the holder the right to buy a specific foreign currency at a designated exchange rate.

6. The value of a call option is based on its exercise price, its expiration date, the price of the underlying asset, the variability of that asset, and the risk-free interest rate. The well-known **Black-Scholes option-pricing model** uses these factors.

a. The CIA exam may ask questions about the volatility of the stock or market and the effect it has on the price of a call or a put.

1) **Volatility** (i.e., variances in daily trading prices) and interest rates vary directly with the prices of puts and calls.

Interest Rate Caps, Floors, and Collars

7. An **interest rate cap** is an option that limits the risk of **interest rate increases**. If interest rates rise above a certain level, the **cap holder** receives the excess of the actual interest rate over a designated interest rate (the strike or cap rate) based on the notional principal amount. The cap holder's loss is limited to the premium paid to the **cap writer**. The cap writer has unlimited risk from potential increases in interest rates above the specified rate.

8. An **interest rate floor** is an option that limits the risk of interest rate decreases. If rates fall below a specified level, the **floor holder** receives cash payments equal to the excess of a designated rate (the strike or floor rate) over the actual rate based on the notional principal amount. The buyer pays the writer a premium to receive this right, and the floor writer faces significant risk from potential decreases in rates below the specified rate.

9. A **collar** is an option that combines the strategies of a cap and a floor. The **buyer acquires a cap and writes a floor**. The writer writes a cap and buys a floor. Collars fix the rate a variable-rate lender will receive or a borrower will pay between the cap and floor rate levels. Collars help reduce the cost of buying outright a cap or floor. Because a borrower or lender is usually only interested in protecting against movements in interest rates in one direction, the premium received for writing a cap or floor serves to reduce the cost of the cap or floor purchased.

Forwards

10. A **forward contract** is an unperformed agreement negotiated between two parties for the purchase and sale of a stated amount of a commodity, foreign currency, or financial instrument at a stated price, with delivery or settlement at a stated future date. Forward contracts are usually specifically negotiated agreements and are not traded on regulated exchanges. Thus, the parties are subject to **default risk** (i.e., that the other party will not perform).

Futures

11. A **futures contract** is a specific kind of **forward contract**. It is a definite agreement that allows a trader to purchase or sell an asset at a fixed price during a specific future month. Futures contracts for agricultural commodities, metals, oil, and financial assets are traded on numerous exchanges.
    a. One characteristic of a futures contract is that it may be **highly leveraged**. The initial **margin** paid may be a very small percentage of the price. Thus, the risk of either gain or loss to a speculator may be great.
    b. A futures contract differs from a forward contract in part because it is **traded on an exchange** and is standardized. The result is a liquid market in futures that permits buyers and sellers to net out their positions. For example, a party who has sold a contract can net out his/her position by buying a futures contract.
    c. Another distinguishing feature of futures contracts is that their prices are **marked to market** every day at the close of the day to each person's account. Thus, the market price is posted at the close of business each day. A mark-to-market provision minimizes a futures contract's **chance of default** because profits and losses on the contracts must be received or paid each day through a clearinghouse. This requirement of **daily settlement** minimizes default and is necessary because futures contracts are sold on margin (they are highly leveraged).
    d. A futures contract is entered into as either a **speculation or a hedge**. A financial manager can protect an entity against adverse changes in prices and interest rates by hedging in the futures market. **Hedging** is the process of using offsetting commitments to minimize or avoid the effect of adverse price movements.
        1) **Long hedges** are futures contracts that are purchased to protect against price increases.
        2) **Short hedges** are futures contracts that are sold to protect against price declines.
        3) EXAMPLE: In the **commodities market**, an entity might have a contract with a farmer to buy soybeans at a future date. The price is agreed upon as the current price. The entity would lose money if soybean prices declined before delivery. To avoid any loss (or gain), the entity could sell soybeans **in the future at today's price**. If the price of soybeans declines before the delivery date, it will lose money on the contract with the farmer, but it will gain money on the futures contract by purchasing cheap soybeans in the future to cover the delivery.
            a) Because commodities can be bought and sold **on margin**, considerable leverage is involved. This high degree of leverage is most beneficial to the speculator who is looking for large returns and is willing to bear the risk to get them. For **hedgers**, however, the small margin requirement is useful only because the risk can be hedged without tying up a large amount of cash.
    e. **Swaps** are contracts to hedge risk by exchanging cash flows. The simplest form, sometimes called a **plain vanilla swap**, is an exchange of interest rates without any change in the initial debt arrangement.

f. **Arbitrage** is the **simultaneous purchase and sale** of identical or equivalent financial instruments or commodity futures to benefit from a discrepancy in their price relationship. This sometimes involves selling in one market while simultaneously buying in another market.

Stop and review! You have completed the outline for this subunit. Study multiple-choice questions 15 through 17 on page 243.

5.7 RATIOS: LIQUIDITY, ACTIVITY, AND SOLVENCY

1. The essence of financial statement analysis is the **calculation of financial ratios**. These ratios establish relationships among financial statement accounts at a **moment in time** or for a given **accounting period**. Once calculated, the entity's ratios can be compared with its **historical data** and with its **projections** for the future. Moreover, ratios also may be evaluated by comparison with those for **other entities** or with **industry averages**. However, users must be aware of the **limitations** of ratio analysis, for example, those arising from differences in the nature of the entities being compared, changes in accounting policies, and the effects of changing price levels. Moreover, ratios must be evaluated in terms of broad economic and strategic factors and from the unique perspectives of particular users.

Liquidity Ratios

2. **Liquidity** is an entity's ability to pay its **current obligations** as they come due and thus remain in business in the **short run**. Liquidity depends on the ease with which current assets can be converted to cash.
   a. Liquidity ratios measure this ability by relating an entity's liquid assets to its current liabilities at a moment in time.
   b. EXAMPLE of a balance sheet:

RESOURCES

	Current Year End	Prior Year End
CURRENT ASSETS:		
Cash and equivalents	US $ 325,000	US $ 275,000
Available-for-sale securities	165,000	145,000
Accounts receivable (net)	120,000	115,000
Notes receivable	55,000	40,000
Inventories	85,000	55,000
Prepaid expenses	10,000	5,000
Total current assets	**US $ 760,000**	**US $ 635,000**
NONCURRENT ASSETS:		
Equity-method investments	US $ 120,000	US $ 115,000
Property, plant, and equipment	1,000,000	900,000
Minus: accum. depreciation	(85,000)	(55,000)
Goodwill	5,000	5,000
Total noncurrent assets	**US $1,040,000**	**US $ 965,000**
Total assets	**US $1,800,000**	**US $1,600,000**

FINANCING

	Current Year End	Prior Year End
CURRENT LIABILITIES		
Accounts payable	US $ 150,000	US $ 75,000
Notes payable	50,000	50,000
Accrued interest on note	5,000	5,000
Current maturities of L.T. debt	100,000	100,000
Accrued salaries and wages	15,000	10,000
Income taxes payable	70,000	35,000
Total current liabilities	**US $ 390,000**	**US $ 275,000**
NONCURRENT LIABILITIES:		
Bonds payable	US $ 500,000	US $ 600,000
Long-term notes payable	90,000	60,000
Employee-related obligations	15,000	10,000
Deferred income taxes	5,000	5,000
Total noncurrent liabilities	**US $ 610,000**	**US $ 675,000**
Total liabilities	**US $1,000,000**	**US $ 950,000**
EQUITY:		
Ordinary shares, US $1 par	US $ 500,000	US $ 500,000
Share premium	100,000	100,000
Preference shares, US $50 par	120,000	0
Share premium on P.S.	10,000	0
Retained earnings	70,000	50,000
Total equity	**US $ 800,000**	**US $ 650,000**
Total liabilities and equity	**US $1,800,000**	**US $1,600,000**

c. **Current assets** are the most liquid. They are expected to be converted to cash, sold, or consumed within 1 year or the operating cycle, whichever is longer. Ratios involving current assets thus measure an entity's ability to continue operating in the short run.

   1) Current assets include, in descending order of liquidity: cash and equivalents; marketable securities; receivables; inventories; and prepaid items.

d. **Current liabilities** are expected to be settled or converted to other liabilities within 1 year or the operating cycle, whichever is longer.

   1) Current liabilities include accounts payable, notes payable, current maturities of long-term debt, deferred revenues, taxes payable, wages payable, and other accruals.

e. **Working capital** consists of the resources the entity must have to continue operating in the short run if it must liquidate all of its current liabilities.

   1) `Current assets - Current liabilities`

      a) EXAMPLE: Current Year: US $760,000 – $390,000 = US $370,000
         Prior Year: US $635,000 – $275,000 = US $360,000

      b) Although current liabilities increased, current assets increased by US $10,000 more.

f. The **current ratio** (working capital ratio) is the most common measure of near-term solvency.

   1) $$\frac{\text{Current assets}}{\text{Current liabilities}}$$

      a) EXAMPLE: Current Year: US $760,000 ÷ $390,000 = 1.949
         Prior Year: US $635,000 ÷ $275,000 = 2.309

      b) Although working capital increased in **absolute** terms (US $10,000), current assets now provide less **proportional** coverage of current liabilities than in the prior year.

   2) A low ratio indicates a possible solvency problem. An overly high ratio indicates that management may not be investing idle assets productively.

   3) The general principle is that the current ratio should be proportional to the operating cycle. Thus, a shorter cycle may justify a lower ratio.

      a) For example, a grocery store has a short operating cycle and can survive with a lower current ratio than could a gold mining entity, which has a much longer operating cycle.

   4) The quality of accounts receivable and merchandise inventory should be considered before evaluating the current ratio. A low receivables turnover (net credit sales ÷ average accounts receivable) and a low inventory turnover (cost of sales ÷ average inventory) indicate a need for a higher current ratio.

g. The **quick (acid-test) ratio** excludes inventories and prepaid items from the numerator because those assets are difficult to liquidate at their stated amounts. The quick ratio is thus a more conservative measure than the basic current ratio.

   1) $$\frac{\text{Cash and equivalents + Marketable securities + Net accounts receivable}}{\text{Current liabilities}}$$

      a) EXAMPLE:

Current Year: (US $325,000 + $165,000 + $120,000 + $55,000) ÷ $390,000 = 1.705
Prior Year: (US $275,000 + $145,000 + $115,000 + $40,000) ÷ $275,000 = 2.455

b) Despite its increase in total working capital, the entity's position in its most liquid assets deteriorated significantly.

2) This ratio measures the ability to pay short-term debts and avoids the problem of inventory valuation.

3) A less conservative variation divides the difference between current assets and inventory by current liabilities.

Activity Ratios

3. **Activity ratios** measure how quickly major noncash assets are converted to cash. These ratios measure results for an accounting period and thus relate information from the **balance sheet** to information from the **income statement**.

a. Example of an income statement:

	Current Year	**Prior Year**
Net Sales	**US $ 1,800,000**	**US $ 1,400,000**
Cost of goods sold	(1,450,000)	(1,170,000)
Gross profit	US $ 350,000	US $ 230,000
SG&A expenses	(160,000)	(80,000)
Operating profit	**US $ 190,000**	**US $ 150,000**
Other income and expenses	(65,000)	(25,000)
Profit bef. int. and taxes	US $ 125,000	US $ 125,000
Interest expense	(15,000)	(10,000)
Profit before taxes	US $ 110,000	US $ 115,000
Income taxes (40%)	(44,000)	(46,000)
Profit	**US $ 66,000**	**US $ 69,000**

b. **Accounts receivable turnover** measures the efficiency of accounts receivable collection.

1) $$\frac{\text{Net credit sales}}{\text{Average trade receivables (net)}}$$

a) EXAMPLE: All of the entity's sales are on credit. Net trade receivables at the balance sheet date of the second prior year were US $105,000.

Current Year: US $1,800,000 ÷ [($120,000 + $115,000) ÷ 2] = 15.3 times
Prior Year: US $1,400,000 ÷ [($115,000 + $105,000) ÷ 2] = 12.7 times

b) The entity turned over its trade receivables balance 2.6 more times during the current year, even as receivables were growing in absolute terms. Thus, the entity's effectiveness at collecting accounts receivable has improved noticeably.

2) If a business is highly seasonal, a simple average of beginning and ending balances is inadequate. The monthly balances should be averaged instead.

3) A high turnover means that customers are paying their accounts promptly.

4) Because sales is in the numerator, higher sales without an increase in receivables will result in better turnover. Because receivables are in the denominator, encouraging customers to pay quickly (thereby lowering the balance in receivables) also results in a higher turnover ratio.

c. **Inventory turnover** measures the efficiency of inventory management.

1) $$\frac{\text{Cost of goods sold}}{\text{Average inventory}}$$

a) EXAMPLE: The balance in inventories at the balance sheet date of the second prior year was US $45,000.

Current Year: US $1,450,000 ÷ [($85,000 + $55,000) ÷ 2] = 20.7 times
Prior Year: US $1,170,000 ÷ [($55,000 + $45,000) ÷ 2] = 23.4 times

b) The entity did not turn over its inventories as many times during the current year. This is to be expected during a period of growing sales (and building inventory level) and so is not necessarily a sign of poor inventory management.

2) As with receivables turnover, if a business is highly seasonal, a simple average of beginning and ending balances is inadequate. The monthly balances should be averaged instead.

3) A high turnover implies that the entity is not carrying excess levels of inventory or inventory that is obsolete.

4) Because cost of goods sold is in the numerator, higher sales without an increase in inventory balances will result in better turnover.

5) Because inventory is in the denominator, keeping inventory levels as low as possible also results in a higher turnover ratio.

d. **Days sales outstanding in receivables** (also called the **average collection period**) measures the average number of days it takes to collect a receivable.

1) $$\frac{365}{\text{Accounts receivable turnover}}$$

a) EXAMPLE:

Current Year: 365 days ÷ 15.3 times = 23.9 days
Prior Year: 365 days ÷ 12.7 times = 28.7 days

b) Because the denominator (calculated above) increased and the numerator is a constant, 50 days' sales will necessarily decrease. In addition to improving its collection practices, the entity also may have become better at assessing the creditworthiness of its customers.

2) Other possible numerators are 360 (for simplicity) and 300 (the number of business days in a year).

3) Days sales outstanding in receivables can be compared with the entity's credit terms to determine whether the average customer is paying within the credit period.

e. Two other important activity ratios are:

1) $$\text{Total assets turnover} = \frac{\text{Net sales}}{\text{Average total assets}}$$

2) $$\text{Fixed assets turnover} = \frac{\text{Net sales}}{\text{Average net fixed assets}}$$

Operating Cycle

4. An entity's operating cycle is the amount of time that passes between the acquisition of inventory and the collection of cash on the sale of that inventory.

a. The (overlapping) steps in the operating cycle are

1) Acquisition of inventory and incurrence of a payable
2) Settlement of the payable
3) Holding of inventory

4) Selling of inventory and incurrence of a receivable
5) Collection of the receivable and acquisition of more inventory

Operating cycle = Days sales in receivables + Days sales in inventory

b. EXAMPLE:

1) Current Year: 23.9 days + 15.5 days = 39.4 days
Prior Year: 28.7 days + 13.7 days = 42.4 days

2) The entity has managed to slightly reduce its operating cycle, even while increasing sales and inventories.

c. The **cash cycle**, also called the **cash conversion cycle**, is that portion of the operating cycle that is not **days purchases in accounts payable**. The cash cycle is the portion of the operating cycle when the entity does **not** have cash, that is, when cash is converted to inventory or accounts receivable.

Cash cycle = Operating Cycle – Days purchases in payables

1) EXAMPLE:

a) Current Year: 39.4 days – 23.4 days = 16.0 days
Prior Year: 42.4 days – 17.7 days = 24.7 days

b) Of the entity's total operating cycle of 39.4 days, cash is held for the 23.4 days that payables are outstanding. The 16.0 days of the cash cycle represent the period when cash is converted to other forms of current assets.

d. The following diagram depicts the interactions between the phases of the operating and cash cycles:

Operating Cycle

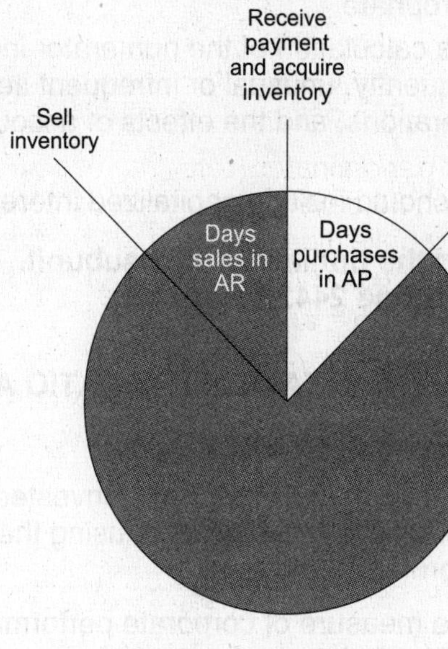

Shaded area = Cash cycle

Days sales in inventory = Operating cycle – Days sales in AR

Solvency Ratios

5. **Solvency** is an entity's ability to pay its noncurrent obligations as they come due and thus remain in business in the long run (contrast with liquidity). The key ingredients of solvency are the entity's capital structure and degree of leverage.

a. **Capital structure ratios** report the relative proportions of debt and equity in the capital structure.

b. The **debt to total assets ratio** (also called the debt ratio) reports the long-term debt burden per monetary unit of equity.

1) $$\frac{\text{Total liabilities}}{\text{Total assets}}$$

a) EXAMPLE: Current Year: US $1,000,000 ÷ $1,800,000 = 0.556
Prior Year: US $950,000 ÷ $1,600,000 = 0.594

b) Although total liabilities increased in absolute terms, this ratio improved because total assets increased even more.

2) Numerically, this ratio is identical to the total debt to total capital ratio.

Earnings Coverage

6. **Earnings coverage** is a creditor's best measure of an entity's ongoing ability to generate the earnings that will allow it to satisfy its long-term debts and remain solvent.

a. The **times interest earned ratio** is an income statement approach to evaluating the ongoing ability to meet interest payments on debt obligations.

1) $$\frac{\text{Earnings before interest and taxes (EBIT)}}{\text{Interest expense}}$$

a) EXAMPLE: Current Year: US $85,000 ÷ $15,000 = 5.67
Prior Year: US $45,000 ÷ $10,000 = 4.50

b) The entity has improved its ability to pay interest expense. In the prior year, EBIT was only four and a half times interest expense, but in the current year, it is more than five and a half times.

2) For the ratio to be meaningful, profit cannot be used in the numerator. What is being measured is the ability to pay interest. Thus, earnings **before** interest and taxes is appropriate.

3) The most accurate calculation of the numerator includes only earnings expected to recur. Consequently, unusual or infrequent items, extraordinary items, discontinued operations, and the effects of accounting changes should be excluded.

4) The denominator should include capitalized interest.

Stop and review! You have completed the outline for this subunit. Study multiple-choice questions 18 through 21 beginning on page 244.

5.8 RATIOS: ROI, PROFITABILITY, AND LIMITATIONS OF RATIO ANALYSIS

Return on Invested Capital

1. **Return on investment**, or **ROI** (also called return on invested capital), is a broad concept for measures that reflect how efficiently an entity is using the resources contributed by its shareholders to generate a profit.

a. ROI is the most effective measure of corporate performance because it **relates the income statement to the balance sheet.** All forms of ROI are some variation on this general ratio:

$$\text{Return on investment (ROI)} = \frac{\text{Measure of profit}}{\text{Measure of capital}}$$

1) Besides reflecting the effectiveness of management decision making and overall entity profitability, ROI also aids in forecasting earnings, planning, budgeting, and control. Each profit center, product line, etc., can be assessed on the basis of ROI.

c. **Net profit margin** is what percentage remains after other gains and losses (including interest expense) and income taxes have been added or deducted.

EXAMPLE:

	Current Year	Prior Year
Net sales	100.0%	100.0%
Cost of goods sold	(80.6%)	(83.6%)
Gross profit margin	**19.4%**	**16.4%**
SG&A expenses	(8.9%)	(5.7%)
Operating profit margin	**10.6%**	**10.7%**
Other income and expense	(3.6%)	(1.8%)
Profit bef. int. and taxes	6.9%	8.9%
Interest expense	(0.8%)	(0.7%)
Profit before taxes	6.1%	8.2%
Income taxes (40%)	(2.4%)	(3.3%)
Net profit margin	**3.7%**	**4.9%**

9. **Book value per share** equals the amount of net assets available to the shareholders of a given type of shares divided by the number of those shares outstanding.

$$\text{Book value per share} = \frac{\text{Total equity - Liquidation value of preference shares}}{\text{Ordinary shares outstanding}}$$

When preference shares are cumulative and in arrears or participating, liquidation value will exceed their carrying amount. Book value per share is ordinarily based on historical cost expressed in nominal units of money. Accordingly, it may be misleading because book values ordinarily differ materially from fair values. Fair value usually is what shares sell for on the open market. Book value may be materially higher or lower.

10. A high **price-earnings (P-E) ratio** reflects the stock market's positive assessment of the entity's earnings quality and persistence. It measures how much an investor must spend to acquire a unit of earnings.

$$\text{Price-earnings ratio} = \frac{\text{Market price per share}}{\text{Diluted earnings per share}}$$

11. **Earnings per share (EPS)** is the most common performance measure used by investors. EPS states the amount of current-period earnings that can be associated with a single ordinary share. Preference shareholders have superior claim to earnings. Thus, amounts associated with preference shares must be removed during the calculation of EPS.

a. **Basic earnings per share (BEPS)**

$$\frac{\text{Profit or loss attributable to ordinary equity holders}}{\text{Weighted-average outstanding ordinary shares}}$$

1) A BEPS amount also is calculated with a numerator equal to **profit or loss from continuing operations** (if presented) attributable to ordinary equity holders.

2) The **numerator** is adjusted for after-tax preference dividends and other effects of preference shares treated as equity.

3) The **denominator** includes shares from the time consideration is receivable, e.g., when cash is receivable or interest on convertible debt no longer accrues.

a) Adjustments are made for events (other than conversion of potential ordinary shares) that change ordinary shares outstanding **without an increase in resources**, e.g., a share split or a capitalization or bonus issue (a stock dividend).

b. **Diluted earnings per share (DEPS)**

1) Calculation of DEPS amounts requires **adjustments of the BEPS numerator and denominator** for the effects of dilutive potential ordinary (common) shares.

a) **Potential ordinary shares (POSs)** are contracts that may entitle holders to ordinary (common) shares.

b) A POS is **dilutive** if it reduces (increases) EPS (loss per share) as a result of assuming the conversion of convertible instruments, exercise of options or warrants, or issue of ordinary shares when conditions are satisfied.

2) The **BEPS numerators** are adjusted for after-tax effects of

a) **Dividends** or other items associated with dilutive POSs that were subtracted in arriving at the BEPS numerator,

b) Recognized **interest** on dilutive POSs, and

c) Other changes in income or expense associated with conversion of POSs.

3) The **BEPS denominator** is adjusted for the weighted-average number of ordinary shares assumed to have been issued upon conversion of all dilutive POSs.

a) Conversion is assumed to have occurred at the earlier of the beginning of the period or issue date of the POSs.

12. **Limitations of Ratio Analysis**

a. Development of ratios for comparison with **industry averages** is more useful for entities that operate within a particular industry than for conglomerates.

b. **Inflation** misstates the balance sheet and income statement because of the effects on fixed assets, depreciation, inventory, long-term debt, and profitability.

c. **Seasonal factors** affect results. For example, inventory and receivables may vary widely, and year-end balances may not reflect the periodic averages.

d. An entity's management has an incentive to **window dress** financial statements.

e. Comparability of financial statement amounts and the ratios derived from them is impaired if different entities choose different **accounting policies**.

f. The ratios that are strong indicators of an entity's **financial position** may vary from one industry, entity, or division to another.

g. Ratios are constructed from **accounting data** subject to estimation.

h. **Trends** may be misinterpreted absent sufficient years of analysis.

i. Ratio analysis may be distorted by failing to use an **average or weighted average**.

j. Misleading conclusions may result if **improper comparisons** are selected.

k. Whether a certain level of a ratio is favorable depends on the **underlying circumstances**.

l. Different ratios may yield opposite conclusions about an entity's financial health. Thus, the **net effects** of a set of ratios should be analyzed.

m. **Industry averages** may include data from capital-intensive and labor-intensive entities and from entities with divergent policies about leverage.

n. Some data may be presented either before or after **taxes**.

o. Comparability among entities may be impaired if they have different **fiscal years**.

p. The **geographical locations** of entities may affect comparability because of differences in labor markets, price levels, regulation, taxation, etc.

q. **Size differentials** among entities affect comparability because of differences in access to and cost of capital, economies of scale, and width of markets.

13. **Comparative analysis** includes horizontal (trend) analysis that compares analytical data over time and vertical analysis that makes comparisons among one year's data.
    a. Comparing an entity's performance with respect to its industry may identify its strengths and weaknesses. Horizontal analysis of the industry may identify industrywide trends and practices.
    b. **Common-size financial statements** compare entities of different sizes by expressing items as percentages of corresponding base-year figures. The base amount is assigned the value of 100%.
        1) The **horizontal** form evaluates trends. The amounts for subsequent years are stated in percentages of a base-year amount.
        2) **Vertical** common-size analysis presents figures for one year expressed as percentages of a base amount on the balance sheet (e.g., total assets) and on the income statement (e.g., sales).

Stop and review! You have completed the outline for this subunit. Study multiple-choice questions 22 through 28 beginning on page 245.

5.9 BUSINESS DEVELOPMENT LIFE CYCLES

1. The **product life cycle** is useful in understanding other cycles. It has the following stages:
    a. **Precommercialization.** The **strategy** is to innovate by conducting R&D, marketing research, and production tests. During product development, the entity has no sales, but it has high investment costs.
    b. In the **introduction stage**, the growth rate and profits are low. The reason is the high cost of **promotion** and selective distribution to generate product awareness and encourage customers to try it. **Competitors** are few, basic versions of the product are produced, and higher-income customers (innovators) are usually targeted. **Cost-plus prices** are charged. They may initially be high to permit cost recovery when unit sales are low. The **strategy** is to (1) infiltrate the market, (2) plan for financing to cope with losses, (3) build supplier relations, (4) increase production and marketing efforts, and (5) plan for competition.
    c. In the **growth stage**, (1) sales and profits increase rapidly, (2) cost per customer decreases, (3) customers are early adopters, (4) new competitors enter an expanding market, (5) new product models and features are introduced, and (6) promotion spending declines or remains stable. The entity enters new market segments and distribution channels and attempts to build brand loyalty and achieve the maximum share of the market. Thus, prices are set to **penetrate the market**, distribution channels are extended, and the mass market is targeted through advertising. The **strategy** is to advance by these means and by achieving economies of productive scale.
    d. In the **maturity stage**, sales peak but growth declines. Competitors are most numerous but may begin to decline in number, and per-customer cost is low. **Profits** are high for large market-share entities. For others, profits may fall because of **competitive price-cutting** and increased R&D spending to develop improved versions of the product. The **strategy** is to defend market share and maximize profits through diversification of brands and models to enter new market segments. The entity also engages in still more intensive distribution, cost cutting, and advertising to encourage **brand switching**. Customer service is emphasized.
        1) Some writers identify a separate stage between growth and maturity. During the **shakeout period**, the overall growth rate falls, price cutting occurs, and weaker entities leave the market.

   e. During the **decline stage**, sales and **profits** drop as **prices are cut**, and some entities leave the market. Customers include late adopters (laggards), and per-customer cost is low. Weak products and unprofitable distribution media are eliminated, and advertising budgets are reduced to the level needed to retain the most loyal customers. The **strategy** is to withdraw by reducing production, promotion, and inventory.

2. The **business life cycle** interacts with product life cycles and the overall economic cycle. For example, successful new product introductions may increase sales and profits during a recession.

   a. In the **formative stage**, the emerging entity most likely relies on the personal resources of its owners, assistance from governmental agencies, and trade credit for its financing needs.

   b. If the entity is successful and enters the stage of **rapid growth**, internal financing becomes feasible, and trade credit continues to be used. Moreover, the entity's performance may enable it to secure bank credit to meet seasonal needs and intermediate-term loans. Such an entity also may attract equity financing from **venture capitalists**.

      1) If the entity is extremely successful, it may be able to issue securities that are **publicly traded**. Thus, the entity may enter the formal capital and money markets. These markets provide financing at lower cost than venture capitalists.

   c. The entity must consider the limitations of the **product life cycle**. Absent the development of new products, growth will not continue, and the entity will enter the **product maturity and decline stage**. The financing pattern at this stage usually includes internal financing, diversification, share repurchases, and mergers.

   d. Another perspective on life cycles compares the entity's **growth rate** with the economy's.

      1) Thus, during the **early stages** of the cycle, the entity's rate is much greater than that of the economy. Later, the rates tend to be about the same. In the **decline stage**, the entity's growth rate is lower than the economy's.

      2) Accordingly, its earnings, dividends, and stock price fall. Entities with growth rates that do not approximate the economy's growth rate are **nonconstant growth** entities. Calculations using the **dividend growth model** are more complicated for such entities.

Stop and review! You have completed the outline for this subunit. Study multiple-choice questions 29 and 30 beginning on page 247.

5.10 SUMMARY

1. The ordinary shareholders are the owners of the corporation, and their rights as owners, although reasonably uniform, depend on the laws where the entity is incorporated. Ordinary shareholders ordinarily have preemptive rights.
2. Preference shares are a hybrid of debt and equity. They have a fixed charge and increase leverage, but payment of dividends is not a legal obligation.
3. Bonds are long-term debt instruments. They are similar to term loans except that they are usually offered to the public and sold to many investors. The bond indenture is the contractual arrangement between the issuer and the bondholders. It contains restrictive covenants intended to prevent the issuer from taking actions contrary to the interests of the bondholders. A trustee, often a bank, is appointed to ensure compliance. Types of bonds are (a) mortgage bonds, (b) debentures, (c) subordinated debentures, (d) income bonds, (e) serial bonds, (f) registered bonds, (g) coupon bonds, (h) participating bonds, (i) indexed bonds, (j) zero-coupon bonds, (k) junk bonds, and (l) international bonds.

4. Share rights and convertibility are among the common financing arrangements used to increase investor interest in corporate securities. The objective is a lower interest rate on bonds or a higher selling price for shares. Share rights evidenced by warrants are options that are distributed with debt or preference shares. Both the issuance of rights and a conversion feature offer a corporation a means of delayed equity financing when market prices are unfavorable. When the market price rises above the conversion price, holders will presumably exercise the rights or convert the securities.
5. Intermediate-term financing refers to debt issues having approximate maturities of greater than 2 but less than 10 years. The principal types of intermediate-term financing are term loans and lease financing. Major lenders under term agreements are commercial banks, life insurance companies, and, to some extent, pension funds.
6. Short-term credit is debt scheduled to be repaid within 1 year. Three main sources of this credit are trade credit, commercial banks, and commercial paper, but many other sources are available.
7. The financial structure of an entity encompasses the right-hand side of the balance sheet, which describes how assets are financed. Capital structure is permanent financing and is represented primarily by long-term debt, preference stock, and ordinary equity.
8. Leverage is the relative amount of the fixed cost of capital, principally debt, in the capital structure. Leverage, by definition, creates financial risk, which relates directly to the question of the cost of capital. The more leverage, the higher the financial risk, and the higher the cost of debt capital.
9. Interest is tax deductible, so EPS ordinarily is higher if debt capital is raised instead of equity, assuming the entity is not over-leveraged.
10. The degree of financial leverage (DFL) is the percentage change in earnings available to ordinary shareholders that is associated with a given percentage change in net operating profit.
11. The degree of operating leverage (DOL) is the percentage change in net operating profit associated with a given percentage change in sales.
12. The degree of total leverage (DTL) combines the DFL and the DOL.
13. The cost of capital is a weighted average of the various debt and equity components. The weighted-average cost of capital weights the percentage cost of each component by the percentage of that component in the financial structure. The cost of debt equals the interest rate times one minus the marginal tax rate because interest is a tax deduction. Hence, an increase in the tax rate decreases the cost of debt. The cost of retained earnings is an opportunity cost. It is the rate that investors can earn elsewhere on investments of comparable risk. The cost of internally generated funds is an imputed cost. The cost of new external ordinary equity is higher than the cost of retained earnings because of stock flotation costs. The cost of preference shares equals the preference dividend divided by the net issuance price. No tax adjustment is necessary because preference dividends paid are not deductible.
14. Standard financial theory states that an optimal capital structure exists. The optimal capital structure minimizes the weighted average cost of capital and thereby maximizes the value of the entity.
15. The Capital Asset Pricing Model (CAPM) adds the risk-free rate (determined by government securities) to the product of the beta coefficient (a measure of the entity's risk) and the difference between the market return and the risk-free rate. Below is the basic equilibrium equation for the CAPM.

$$R = R_F + \beta(R_M - R_F)$$

16. The dividend growth model estimates the cost of retained earnings using the dividends per share, the expected growth rate, and the market price. To justify retention of earnings, management must expect a return at least equal to the dividend yield plus a growth rate.

17. A concept relevant to securities valuation is the efficient markets hypothesis (EMH). It states that current share prices immediately and fully reflect all relevant information. Hence, the market is continuously using new information to correct pricing errors, and securities prices are always in equilibrium.
18. The cash budget details projected receipts and disbursements, preferably to plan the synchronization of inflows and outflows. It is based on the projected sales and credit terms, collection percentages, and estimated purchases and payment terms.
19. Cash collections should be expedited. For this purpose, a lockbox system, concentration banking, wire transfers, and EDI are helpful.
20. Slowing cash disbursements increases available cash. Payment beyond normal credit terms, however, creates vendor ill will and may incur interest charges. Payments should be made within discount periods if the cost of not taking a discount exceeds the entity's cost of capital.
21. The amount of cash on hand should be determined by cost-benefit analysis. The reduction in average cash times the interest rate (cost of capital or investment yield rate) is the benefit. Costs of having insufficient cash include incremental personnel cost, lost discounts, and lost vendor goodwill.
22. Excess cash should be placed in an investment with the highest return consistent with low risk, such as T-bills, CDs, money-market accounts, or high-grade commercial paper.
23. As temporary investments, marketable securities may be purchased with maturities timed to (a) meet seasonal fluctuations, (b) pay off a bond issue, (c) make tax payments, or (d) otherwise satisfy anticipated needs. Marketable securities should be chosen with a view to the risk of default (financial risk). Interest-rate risk should be minimized given the reasons for holding marketable securities.
24. The objective of managing accounts receivable is to have both the optimal amount of receivables outstanding and the optimal amount of bad debts. The balance requires a trade-off between the benefits of credit sales, such as more sales, and the costs of accounts receivable, such as collection, interest, and bad debt costs. The appropriate policy does not seek merely to maximize sales or to minimize default risk.
25. Receivables management should maximize the accounts receivable turnover ratio, that is, shorten the average time receivables are held. The accounts receivable turnover ratio equals net credit sales divided by average accounts receivable.
26. The most fundamental approach to valuing a business is capital budgeting analysis. If the net present value (NPV) is positive, that is, if the present value of the estimated incremental cash flows from the acquisition exceeds the present value of the amounts to be paid for the acquiree, the investment is financially sound. The shareholders of the acquiree should perform a similar analysis and compare the result with the NPV of remaining an independent equity.
27. A derivative is a financial instrument whose value changes with the change in the underlying (a specified interest rate, security price, foreign currency exchange rate, price index, commodity price, etc.).
28. A call option is the most common type of option. It gives the owner the right to purchase the underlying asset at a fixed price. Thus, it represents a long position because the owner gains from a price increase. The profit is the difference between the price paid and the value at the closing date, minus the brokerage fee. A put option gives the owner the right to sell the underlying asset for a fixed price. It represents a short position because the owner benefits from a price decrease.
29. The value of a call option may be viewed as based on its exercise price, its expiration date, the price of the underlying asset, the variability of that asset, and the risk-free interest rate. The well-known Black-Scholes Option-Pricing Model uses these factors.

30. A forward contract is simply an executory (unperformed) contract. The parties agree to the terms of a purchase and sale, but performance, i.e., payment by the buyer and delivery by the seller, is deferred. A futures contract is a specific kind of forward contract. It is a definite, negotiated agreement that allows a trader to purchase or sell an asset at a fixed price during a specific future month. Futures contracts for agricultural commodities, metals, oil, and financial assets are traded on numerous exchanges. One characteristic of a futures contract is that it may be highly leveraged. It is also marked to market daily.
31. Hedging is the process of using offsetting commitments to minimize or avoid the impact of adverse price movements. Long hedges are futures purchased to protect against price increases. Short hedges are futures sold to protect against price declines.
32. Swaps are contracts to hedge risk by exchanging cash flows. The simplest form, sometimes called a plain vanilla swap, is an exchange of interest rates without any change in the initial debt arrangement.
33. The essence of financial statement analysis is the calculation of financial ratios. These ratios establish relationships among financial statement accounts at a moment in time or for a given accounting period. Once calculated, the entity's ratios can be compared with its historical data and with its projections for the future, as well as with those for other entities or with industry averages.
34. Liquidity is an entity's ability to pay its current obligations as they come due and thus remain in business in the short run. Liquidity depends on the ease with which current assets can be converted to cash.
    a. Liquidity ratios measure this ability by relating an entity's liquid assets to its current liabilities.
35. Activity ratios measure how quickly the major noncash assets are converted to cash. They measure results over a period of time and thus related information drawn from the entity's balance sheet to information drawn from the income statement.
36. An entity's operating cycle is the amount of time that passes between the acquisition of inventory and the collection of cash on the sale of that inventory. The (overlapping) steps in the operating cycle are (a) acquisition of inventory and incurrence of a payable, (b) settlement of the payable, (c) holding of inventory, (d) selling of inventory and incurrence of a receivable, and (e) collection on the receivable and acquisition of further inventory.
37. Solvency is an entity's ability to pay its noncurrent obligations as they come due and thus remain in business in the long run (contrast with liquidity). The key ingredients of solvency are capital structure and degree of leverage.
38. Earnings coverage is a creditor's best measure of an entity's ongoing ability to generate the earnings that will allow it to satisfy its long-term debts and remain solvent.
39. Return on investment, or ROI (also called return on invested capital), is a broad concept for measures that reflect how efficiently an entity is using the funds contributed by its shareholders to generate a profit. ROI is the most effective measure of corporate performance because it relates the income statement to the balance sheet.
40. The variety of definitions in use for the terms return and investment creates difficulties in comparability.
41. Three common percentages measure profitability directly from the income statement. Gross profit margin is what percentage of gross revenues remains to the entity after paying for merchandise. Operating profit margin is what percentage remains after selling and general and administrative expenses have been paid. Net profit margin is what percentage remains after other gains and losses (including interest expense) and income taxes have been added or deducted.
42. Book value per share equals the amount of net assets available to the shareholders of a given type of stock divided by the number of those shares outstanding.

43. Earnings per share (EPS) is the most common performance measure used by investors. EPS states the amount of current-period earnings that can be associated with a single ordinary share. EPS is calculated in two forms: basic and diluted (if the entity has dilutive potential ordinary shares).

44. The stages of the product life cycle are (a) precommercialization, (b) introduction, (c) growth, (d) maturity, (e) shakeout, and (f) decline.

45. Businesses have life cycles. These cycles interact with business cycles and product cycles. For example, successful new product introductions may increase sales and profits during a recession. Another perspective on life cycles compares the entity's growth rate with the economy's.

QUESTIONS

5.1 Long-Term Financing

1. Preference shares are securities with characteristics of both ordinary shares and bonds. Preference shares have <List A> like ordinary shares and <List B> like bonds.

	List A	List B
A.	A maturity date	A fixed periodic payment
B.	No maturity date	No fixed periodic payment
C.	A maturity date	No fixed periodic payment
D.	No maturity date	A fixed periodic payment

Answer (D) is correct. *(CIA, adapted)*

REQUIRED: The characteristics of preference shares.

DISCUSSION: Like ordinary shares (but unlike bonds), preference shares have no maturity date, although certain preference shares (transient preference shares) must be redeemed within a short time (e.g., 5 to 10 years). Like bonds (but unlike ordinary shares), preference shares have a fixed periodic payment. The fixed payment is in the form of a stated dividend in the case of the preference shares and interest payments in the case of bonds. However, preference dividends, unlike interest, do not become an obligation unless declared.

Answer (A) is incorrect. Preference shares do not have a maturity date. Answer (B) is incorrect. Preference shares have fixed periodic dividend payments. Answer (C) is incorrect. Preference shares do not have a maturity date but do have fixed periodic dividend payments.

2. Convertible bonds and bonds issued with warrants differ in that

A. Convertible bonds have lower coupon rates than straight bonds, while bonds issued with warrants have higher coupon rates than straight bonds.

B. Convertible bonds have higher coupon rates than straight bonds, while bonds issued with warrants have lower coupon rates than straight bonds.

C. Convertible bonds remain outstanding after the bondholder exercises the right to become an ordinary shareholder, while bonds that are issued with warrants do not.

D. Bonds that are issued with warrants remain outstanding after the bondholder exercises the right to become an ordinary shareholder, while convertible bonds do not.

Answer (D) is correct. *(CIA, adapted)*

REQUIRED: The difference between convertible bonds and bonds issued with warrants.

DISCUSSION: Warrants are usually detachable. They are options to purchase equity securities and should be separately accounted for. A capital gain results if the share price rises above the option price. The bonds remain outstanding if the warrants are exercised. Convertible bonds must be surrendered when the conversion privilege is exercised. Under IFRSs, the equity and debt features of convertible bonds are separately accounted for.

Answer (A) is incorrect. Bonds issued with warrants and convertible bonds have lower coupon rates than conventional bonds. Answer (B) is incorrect. Bonds issued with warrants and convertible bonds have lower coupon rates than conventional bonds. Answer (C) is incorrect. Convertible bonds do not remain outstanding.

3. Which of the following classes of securities are listed in order from lowest risk/opportunity for return to highest risk/opportunity for return?

A. Corporate first mortgage bonds; corporate income bonds; preference shares.

B. Corporate income bonds; corporate mortgage bonds; subordinated debentures.

C. Ordinary shares; corporate first mortgage bonds; corporate second mortgage bonds.

D. Preference shares; ordinary shares; corporate debentures.

Answer (A) is correct. *(CIA, adapted)*

REQUIRED: The correct listing of classes of securities from lowest to highest risk/opportunity for return.

DISCUSSION: The general principle is that risk and return are directly correlated. Corporate first mortgage bonds are less risky than income bonds or shares because they are secured by specific property. In the event of default, the bondholders can have the property sold to satisfy their claims. Holders of first mortgages have rights paramount to those of any other parties, such as holders of second mortgages. Income bonds pay interest only in the event the corporation earns income. Thus, holders of income bonds have less risk than shareholders because meeting the condition makes payment of interest mandatory. Preference shareholders receive dividends only if they are declared, and the directors usually have complete discretion in this matter. Also, shareholders have claims junior to those of debtholders if the entity is liquidated.

Answer (B) is incorrect. The proper listing is mortgage bonds, subordinated debentures, and income bonds. Debentures are unsecured debt instruments. Their holders have enforceable claims against the issuer even if no income is earned or dividends declared. Answer (C) is incorrect. The proper listing is first mortgage bonds, second mortgage bonds, and ordinary shares. The second mortgage bonds are secured, albeit junior, claims. Answer (D) is incorrect. The proper listing is debentures, preference shares, and ordinary shares. Holders of ordinary shares cannot receive dividends unless the holders of preference shares receive the stipulated periodic percentage return, in addition to any arrearages if the preference shares are cumulative.

5.2 Short-Term Financing

4. An entity obtaining short-term financing with trade credit will pay a higher percentage financing cost, everything else being equal, when the

A. Discount percentage is lower.

B. Items purchased have a higher price.

C. Items purchased have a lower price.

D. Supplier offers a longer discount period.

Answer (D) is correct. *(CIA, adapted)*

REQUIRED: The factor resulting in a higher cost of trade credit.

DISCUSSION: If the discount period is longer, the days of extra credit obtained by forgoing the discount are fewer. Assuming other factors are constant, the result is that the cost of trade credit, that is, the cost of not taking the discount, is greater.

Answer (A) is incorrect. The lower the discount percentage, the lower the opportunity cost of forgoing the discount and using the trade credit financing. Answer (B) is incorrect. Percentage financing cost is unaffected by the purchase price of the items. Answer (C) is incorrect. Percentage financing cost is unaffected by the purchase price of the items.

5. An entity has accounts payable of US $5 million with terms of 2% discount within 15 days, net 30 days (2/15 net 30). It can borrow funds from a bank at an annual rate of 12%, or it can wait until the 30th day when it will receive revenues to cover the payment. If it borrows funds on the last day of the discount period in order to obtain the discount, its total cost will be

A. US $51,000 less.

B. US $75,500 less.

C. US $100,000 less.

D. US $24,500 more.

Answer (B) is correct. *(CIA, adapted)*

REQUIRED: The effect on total cost of taking a cash discount.

DISCUSSION: The interest cost of borrowing US $4,900,000 ($5,000,000 × 98%) to take advantage of the discount is US $24,500 [$4,900,000 × 12% × (15 ÷ 360)], and the total cost will be US $4,924,500. The total cost if the discount is not taken will be 5,000,000, a difference of US $75,500.

Answer (A) is incorrect. US $51,000 less is based on a 30-day borrowing period. Answer (C) is incorrect. US $100,000 less does not consider the interest paid. Answer (D) is incorrect. US $24,500 more reflects interest paid but ignores the discounted price.

6. The following forms of short-term borrowing are available to an entity:

- Floating lien
- Factoring
- Revolving credit
- Chattel mortgages
- Bankers' acceptances
- Lines of credit
- Commercial paper

The forms of short-term borrowing that are unsecured credit are

A. Floating lien, revolving credit, chattel mortgage, and commercial paper.

B. Factoring, chattel mortgage, bankers' acceptances, and line of credit.

C. Floating lien, chattel mortgage, bankers' acceptances, and line of credit.

D. Revolving credit, bankers' acceptances, line of credit, and commercial paper.

Answer (D) is correct. *(CMA, adapted)*

REQUIRED: The forms of short-term borrowing that are unsecured credit.

DISCUSSION: An unsecured loan is a loan made by a bank based on credit information about the borrower and the ability of the borrower to repay the obligation. The loan is not secured by collateral, but is made on the signature of the borrower. Unsecured credit is not backed by collateral. Revolving credit, bankers' acceptances, lines of credit, and commercial paper are all unsecured means of borrowing. A chattel mortgage is a loan secured by personal property (movable property such as equipment or livestock). A floating lien is also secured by property, such as inventory, the composition of which may be constantly changing. Factoring is a form of financing in which receivables serve as security.

5.3 Optimal Capitalization

7. An entity has made the decision to finance next year's capital projects through debt rather than additional equity. The benchmark cost of capital for these projects should be the

A. Before-tax cost of new-debt financing.

B. After-tax cost of new-debt financing.

C. Cost of equity financing.

D. Weighted-average cost of capital.

Answer (D) is correct. *(CIA, adapted)*

REQUIRED: The benchmark cost of capital.

DISCUSSION: A weighted average of the costs of all financing sources should be used, with the weights determined by the usual financing proportions. The terms of any financing raised at the time of initiating a particular project do not represent the cost of capital for the entity. When an entity achieves its optimal capital structure, the weighted-average cost of capital is minimized. The cost of capital is a composite, or weighted average, of all financing sources in their usual proportions. The cost of capital should also be calculated on an after-tax basis.

8. If two entities, entity X and entity Y, are alike in all respects except that entity X employs more debt financing and less equity financing than entity Y does, which of the following statements is true?

A. Entity X has more net earnings variability than entity Y.

B. Entity X has more operating earnings variability than entity Y.

C. Entity X has less operating earnings variability than entity Y.

D. Entity X has less financial leverage than entity Y.

Answer (A) is correct. *(CIA, adapted)*

REQUIRED: The true statement regarding an entity's debt and equity financing.

DISCUSSION: Given that entity X is more highly leveraged, it has greater fixed financing charges than entity Y. Interest payments are fixed financing charges, but ordinary share dividends are not. As a result, entity X will be more risky and therefore will have a more volatile net income stream than entity Y, if other factors are constant.

Answer (B) is incorrect. The level of fixed financing charges does not affect operating income variability. Answer (C) is incorrect. The level of fixed financing charges does not affect operating income variability. Answer (D) is incorrect. Entity X has greater, not less, financial leverage than entity Y. Greater use of debt financing means that an entity has greater financial leverage.

Questions 9 and 10 are based on the following information.

An entity has the following three investment projects available:

Project	Cost	Internal Rate of Return
A	US $ 50 million	14%
B	US $ 75 million	12%
C	US $125 million	8%

The entity has a 40% debt and 60% equity capital structure. Each monetary unit of investment funds will be raised in these proportions (.40 of debt and .60 of equity).

The marginal cost of financing increases with the amount of new funds raised, as follows:

Interval	Amount Raised	Weighted-Average Cost of Capital
1	First US $ 75 million	6%
2	Next US $100 million	10%
3	Over US $175 million	12%

These investment opportunities and financing costs are shown in the graph below:

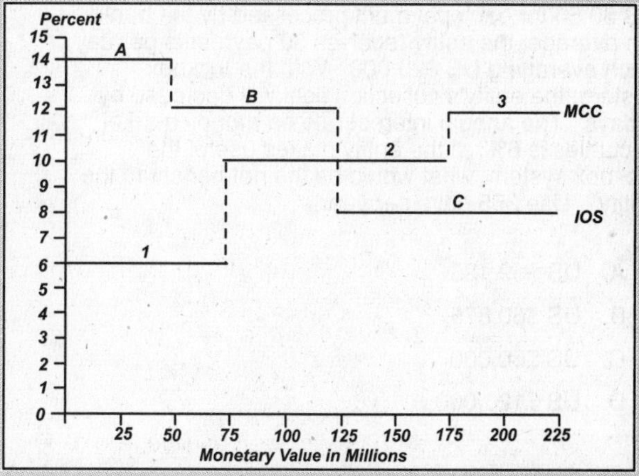

MCC = Marginal cost of capital
IOS = Investment opportunity schedule

9. The investment opportunity schedule (IOS) shows, in rank order, how much money the entity would invest at different rates of return. Such schedules can be drawn only for a set of projects that

A. Have the same investment cost.

B. Are mutually exclusive.

C. Have the same net present value.

D. Are independent.

Answer (D) is correct. *(CIA, adapted)*

REQUIRED: The characteristics of projects on an IOS.

DISCUSSION: An IOS schedule is drawn for a set of independent projects. The decision to be made is whether to accept or reject each project without regard to other investment opportunities. Thus, the cash flows of one independent project are not influenced by those of another. Independence should be distinguished from mutual exclusivity. Projects are mutually exclusive if acceptance of one requires rejection of the other.

Answer (A) is incorrect. IOS schedules do not require that all projects have the same investment cost. The steps of the schedule can be of varying lengths. Answer (B) is incorrect. IOS schedules cannot be drawn for mutually exclusive projects. Answer (C) is incorrect. IOS schedules do not require that all projects have the same NPV. The NPV of each project depends on the investment cost and on the present value of the expected cash flows. Both costs and cash flows can vary for projects on an IOS.

10. The entity should invest in Project(s) <List A> and has an optimal capital budget of <List B> million.

	List A	List B
A.	B only	75
B.	A and B only	125
C.	A and C only	175
D.	C only	125

Answer (B) is correct. *(CIA, adapted)*

REQUIRED: The project(s) in which the entity should invest and its optimal capital budget.

DISCUSSION: The intersection of the IOS and MCC schedules determines the cost of capital and the optimal capital budget. The entity should begin with the project having the highest return and continue accepting projects as long as the IRR exceeds the MCC. The highest ranked project is A, with a US $50 million cost and a 14% IRR. The MCC is only 6% over this range of financing. The next highest ranked project is B, with a US $75 million cost and a 12% IRR. When US $125 million has been invested, the marginal cost of the next unit of capital is 10%, so Project B is also acceptable, bringing the optimal capital budget to US $125 million. Project C is not acceptable because it has an 8% return. The MCC is 10% for the first US $50 million invested in this project and 12% for the remaining US $75 million.

Answer (A) is incorrect. Both A and B should be undertaken. Answer (C) is incorrect. A is acceptable, but C is not. Answer (D) is incorrect. C is not acceptable. It offers an IRR less than the marginal cost of financing the project.

5.4 Management of Current Assets

11. An entity has a majority of its customers located in states A and B. A major west coast bank has agreed to provide a lockbox system to the entity at a fixed fee of US $50,000 per year and a variable fee of US $0.50 for each payment processed by the bank. On average, the entity receives 50 payments per day, each averaging US $20,000. With the lockbox system, the entity's collection float will decrease by 2 days. The annual interest rate on money market securities is 6%. If the entity makes use of the lockbox system, what would be the net benefit to the entity? Use 365 days per year.

A. US $59,125

B. US $60,875

C. US $50,000

D. US $120,000

Answer (B) is correct. *(CMA, adapted)*

REQUIRED: The net benefit to the entity if a lockbox system is adopted.

DISCUSSION: If payments are collected 2 days earlier, the entity can earn US $120,000 ($20,000 × 50 payments per day × 2 days × .06) at a cost of US $59,125 [$50,000 + (50 payments × 365 days × $.50)], a gain of US $60,875.

Answer (A) is incorrect. US $59,125 is the annual lockbox cost. Answer (C) is incorrect. US $50,000 is the annual fixed fee. Answer (D) is incorrect. US $120,000 is the annual savings without regard to costs.

12. A retail mail order entity currently uses a central collection system that requires all checks to be sent to its headquarters. An average of 6 days is required for mailed checks to be received, 3 days for the entity to process them, and 2 days for the checks to clear through the bank. A proposed lockbox system would reduce the mailing and processing time to 2 days and the check clearing time to 1 day. The entity has an average daily collection of US $150,000. How much will the average cash balance increase by if the entity adopts the lockbox system?

A. US $1,200,000

B. US $750,000

C. US $600,000

D. US $450,000

Answer (A) is correct. *(Publisher, adapted)*

REQUIRED: The average increase in cash after the adoption of a lockbox system.

DISCUSSION: Checks are currently tied up for 11 days (6 for mailing, 3 for processing, and 2 for clearing). If that period were reduced to 3 days, the entity's cash balance would increase by US $1,200,000 ($150,000 per day × 8 days).

Answer (B) is incorrect. The decrease is 8 days, not 5. Answer (C) is incorrect. US $600,000 represents only a 4-day savings. Answer (D) is incorrect. The lockbox system will result in an additional 8 days of savings, not 3.

13. An entity uses the following formula in determining its optimal level of cash.

$$OC = \sqrt{\frac{2bT}{i}}$$

If: b = fixed cost per transaction
T = total demand for cash over a period of time
i = interest rate on marketable securities

This formula is a modification of the economic order quantity (EOQ) formula used for inventory management. Assume that the fixed cost of selling marketable securities is US $10 per transaction and the interest rate on marketable securities is 6% per year. The entity estimates that it will make cash payments of US $12,000 over a one-month period. What is the average cash balance (rounded to the nearest dollar)?

A. US $1,000

B. US $2,000

C. US $3,464

D. US $6,928

Answer (C) is correct. *(CMA, adapted)*

REQUIRED: The average cash balance.

DISCUSSION: The EOQ for inventory is a function of ordering cost per order, inventory demand, and carrying cost. In the cash model, the fixed cost per sale of securities is equivalent to the ordering cost, the demand for cash is similar to the demand for inventory, and the interest rate is effectively the cost of carrying a dollar of cash for the period. Substituting in the formula yields an optimal cash balance of about US $6,928. Thus, the average cash balance is US $3,464 ($6,928 ÷ 2).

$$\sqrt{\frac{2bT}{i}} = \sqrt{\frac{2 \times \text{US } \$10 \times \$12{,}000}{6\% \div 12 \text{ months}}} = \sqrt{\frac{\text{US } \$240{,}000}{.005}} = \text{US } \$6{,}928$$

Answer (A) is incorrect. US $1,000 results from using 24% in the denominator. Answer (B) is incorrect. US $2,000 results from using 6% in the denominator. Answer (D) is incorrect. US $6,928 is the optimal cash balance.

5.5 Business Valuation

14. A common mistake in valuing the entity to be acquired in a business combination is

A. Using market values in the valuation.

B. Including incremental cash flows in the valuation.

C. Using the acquirer's discount rate when valuing the incremental cash flows.

D. Including all related transaction costs associated with an acquisition.

Answer (C) is correct. *(Publisher, adapted)*

REQUIRED: The common mistake in valuing the acquiree.

DISCUSSION: If the net incremental cash flows to the acquirer's shareholders are to be valued, the discount rate used should be the cost of equity capital. Moreover, this rate should reflect the risk associated with the use of funds rather than their source. The rate therefore should not be the cost of capital of the acquirer but rather the cost of equity of the combined entity after the combination. This calculation requires a new estimate of beta to be used in the Capital Asset Pricing Model.

5.6 Derivative Financial Instruments

15. An entity has recently purchased some stock of a competitor as part of a long-term plan to acquire the competitor. However, it is somewhat concerned that the market price of this stock could decrease over the short run. The entity could hedge against the possible decline in the stock's market price by

A. Purchasing a call option on that stock.

B. Purchasing a put option on that stock.

C. Selling a put option on that stock.

D. Obtaining a warrant option on that stock.

Answer (B) is correct. *(CIA, adapted)*

REQUIRED: The means of hedging against the possible decline in the stock's market price.

DISCUSSION: A put option is the right to sell stock at a given price within a certain period. If the market price falls, the put option may allow the sale of stock at a price above market, and the profit of the option holder will be the difference between the price stated in the put option and the market price, minus the cost of the option, commissions, and taxes. The entity that issues the stock has nothing to do with put (and call) options.

Answer (A) is incorrect. A call option is the right to purchase shares at a given price within a specified period. Answer (C) is incorrect. Selling a put option could force the entity to purchase additional stock if the option is exercised. Answer (D) is incorrect. A warrant gives the holder a right to purchase stock from the issuer at a given price (it is usually distributed along with debt).

16. The use of derivatives to either hedge or speculate results in

A. Increased risk regardless of motive.

B. Decreased risk regardless of motive.

C. Offset risk when hedging and increased risk when speculating.

D. Offset risk when speculating and increased risk when hedging.

Answer (C) is correct. *(Publisher, adapted)*

REQUIRED: The effects of hedging and speculating on risk.

DISCUSSION: Derivatives, including options and futures, are contracts between the parties who contract. Unlike stocks and bonds, they are not claims on business assets. A futures contract is entered into as either a speculation or a hedge. Speculation involves the assumption of risk in the hope of gaining from price movements. Hedging is the process of using offsetting commitments to minimize or avoid the impact of adverse price movements.

Answer (A) is incorrect. Hedging decreases risk by using offsetting commitments that avoid the impact of adverse price movements. Answer (B) is incorrect. Speculation involves the assumption of risk in the hope of gaining from price movements. Answer (D) is incorrect. Speculating increases risk while hedging offsets risk.

17. The activity of trading futures with the objective of reducing or controlling risk is called

A. Insuring.

B. Hedging.

C. Short-selling.

D. Factoring.

Answer (B) is correct. *(CIA, adapted)*

REQUIRED: The name for the activity of trading futures with the objective of reducing or controlling risk.

DISCUSSION: Hedging is the use of offsetting commitments to minimize the effect of adverse future price movements. Thus, a financial manager may limit many risk exposures by trading in futures markets.

Answer (A) is incorrect. Insurance is a contract in which the insurer undertakes to guarantee the insured against loss from specified contingencies or perils up to a specified amount. Answer (C) is incorrect. Short-selling is the sale of commodities or stocks that are not owned in anticipation of a price decline. Answer (D) is incorrect. Factoring is the sale of accounts receivable.

5.7 Ratios: Liquidity, Activity, and Solvency

18. The following account balances represent the December 31 balance sheet of an entity

Accounts payable	US $ 67,000
Accounts receivable (net)	115,000
Accumulated depreciation -- building	298,500
Accumulated depreciation -- equipment	50,500
Cash	27,500
Ordinary shares (US $10 par value)	100,000
Deferred income taxes payable (expected to reverse more than one year from now)	37,500
Equipment	136,000
Income taxes payable	70,000
Inventory	257,000
Land and building	752,000
Long-term notes payable	123,000
Financial assets held for trading	64,000
Notes payable within 1 year	54,000
Other current liabilities	22,500
Share premium	150,000
Prepaid expenses	27,000
Retained earnings	403,500

The quick ratio for this year is

A. 1.42

B. 1.08

C. 0.97

D. 0.82

Answer (C) is correct. *(CIA, adapted)*

REQUIRED: The quick ratio.

DISCUSSION: The acid test (quick) ratio equals quick assets (cash, financial assets held for trading, and accounts receivable) divided by current liabilities. Quick assets total US $206,500 ($27,500 cash + $64,000 financial assets held for trading + $115,000 net accounts receivable). Given current liabilities of US $213,500 ($67,000 accounts payable + $54,000 current notes payable + $70,000 income taxes payable + $22,500 other current liabilities), the quick ratio is 0.967 (US $206,500 ÷ $213,500).

Answer (A) is incorrect. Excluding the income taxes payable from the current liabilities results in 1.42. Answer (B) is incorrect. Including prepaid expenses in the quick assets and excluding income taxes payable in the current liabilities results in 1.08. Answer (D) is incorrect. Including deferred income taxes payable in the current liabilities results in 0.82.

Questions 19 and 20 are based on the following information. An entity has a current ratio of 1.4, a quick, or acid test, ratio of 1.2, and the following partial summary balance sheet:

Cash	US $ 10	Current liabilities	______
Accounts receivable	______	Long-term liabilities	US $40
Inventory	______	Equity	30
Fixed assets	______	Total liabilities and equity	______
Total assets	100		

19. The entity has an accounts receivable balance of

A. US $12

B. US $26

C. US $36

D. US $66

Answer (B) is correct. *(CIA, adapted)*

REQUIRED: The accounts receivable balance.

DISCUSSION: Total assets equal total liabilities and equity. Hence, if total assets equal US $100, total liabilities and equity must equal US $100, and current liabilities must equal US $30 ($100 – $40 – $30). Because the quick ratio equals the quick assets (cash + accounts receivable) divided by current liabilities, the quick assets must equal US $36 ($30 × 1.2 quick ratio), and the accounts receivable balance is US $26 ($36 – $10 cash).

Answer (A) is incorrect. Current assets minus current liabilities equals US $12. Answer (C) is incorrect. The quick assets equals US $36. Answer (D) is incorrect. The sum of the quick assets and current liabilities equals US $66.

20. The entity has a fixed assets balance of

A. US $0

B. US $16

C. US $58

D. US $64

Answer (C) is correct. *(CIA, adapted)*

REQUIRED: The fixed assets balance.

DISCUSSION: Total assets (given as US $100) equals the sum of cash (given as US $10), accounts receivable (US $26), inventory, and fixed assets. Inventory can be determined because it is included in current, but not quick, assets, and the current and quick ratios are known. Current assets equal US $42 (1.4 current ratio × $30 current liabilities), and the quick assets equal US $36 (1.2 quick ratio × $30 current liabilities). Thus, inventory, which is the only difference in this question between current and quick assets, equals US $6 ($42 – $36). Fixed assets must then equal US $58 ($100 total assets – $10 cash – $26 accounts receivable – $6 inventory).

Answer (A) is incorrect. The sum of cash, accounts receivable, and inventory is less than US $100. Answer (B) is incorrect. The result of neglecting to subtract the equity balance when calculating the current liability balance is US $16. Answer (D) is incorrect. Improperly assuming that inventory is US $0 results in US $64.

21. Given an acid-test ratio of 2.0, current assets of US $5,000, and inventory of US $2,000, the value of current liabilities is

A. US $1,500

B. US $2,500

C. US $3,500

D. US $6,000

Answer (A) is correct. *(CIA, adapted)*

REQUIRED: The value of current liabilities given the acid-test ratio, current assets, and inventory.

DISCUSSION: The acid-test or quick ratio equals the ratio of the quick assets (cash, net accounts receivable, and marketable securities) divided by current liabilities. Current assets equal the quick assets plus inventory and prepaid expenses. This question assumes that the entity has no prepaid expenses. Given current assets of US $5,000, inventory of US 2,000, and no prepaid expenses, the quick assets must be US 3,000. Because the acid-test ratio is 2.0, the quick assets are double the current liabilities. Current liabilities therefore are equal to US 1,500 (US 3,000 quick assets ÷ 2.0).

Answer (B) is incorrect. Dividing the current assets by 2.0 results in US $2,500. Current assets includes inventory, which should not be included in the calculation of the acid-test ratio. Answer (C) is incorrect. Adding inventory to current assets rather than subtracting it results in US $3,500. Answer (D) is incorrect. Multiplying the quick assets by 2 instead of dividing by 2 results in US $6,000.

5.8 Ratios: ROI, Profitability, and Limitations of Ratio Analysis

22. The following ratios relate to an entity's financial situation compared with that of its industry:

	The Entity	Industry Average
Return on assets (ROA)	7.9%	9.2%
Return on equity (ROE)	15.2%	12.9%

What conclusion could a financial analyst validly draw from these ratios?

A. The entity's product has a high market share, leading to higher profitability.

B. The entity uses more debt than does the average entity in the industry.

C. The entity's profits are increasing over time.

D. The entity's shares have a higher market value to carrying amount than does the rest of the industry.

Answer (B) is correct. *(CIA, adapted)*

REQUIRED: The conclusion from comparing ROA and ROE with industry averages.

DISCUSSION: The use of financial leverage has a multiplier effect on the return on assets. The extended Du Pont formula illustrates this point by showing that the return on equity equals the return on assets times the leverage factor, also called the equity multiplier (total assets ÷ ordinary equity). Thus, greater use of debt increases the equity multiplier and the return on equity. In this example, the equity multiplier is 1.92 (15.2% ROE ÷ 7.9% ROA), and the industry average is 1.40 (12.9% ROE ÷ 9.2% ROA). The higher equity multiplier indicates that the entity uses more debt than the industry average.

Answer (A) is incorrect. The question gave no information about market share. Answer (C) is incorrect. This comparison is with an industry average, not over time. Answer (D) is incorrect. Share valuation is a response to many factors. The higher-than-average return on equity does not mean that the entity has a more favorable market-to-carrying-amount ratio.

Questions 23 through 25 are based on the following information. An entity's financial statements for the current year are presented below:

Balance Sheet

Cash	US $100
Accounts receivable	200
Inventory	50
Net fixed assets	600
Total	US $950
Accounts payable	US $140
Long-term debt	300
Share capital	260
Retained earnings	250
Total	US $950

Statement of Income and Retained Earnings

Sales	US $3,000
Cost of goods sold	1,600
Gross profit	1,400
Operations expenses	970
Operating profit	430
Interest expense	30
Profit before tax	400
Income tax	200
Profit	200
Plus Jan. 1 retained earnings	150
Minus dividends	100
Dec. 31 retained earnings	US $ 250

23. The entity has a dividend-payout ratio of

A. 19.6%

B. 28.6%

C. 40.0%

D. 50.0%

Answer (D) is correct. *(CIA, adapted)*
REQUIRED: The dividend-payout ratio.
DISCUSSION: The dividend-payout ratio is the ratio of dividends paid to profit for the period. Hence, it equals 50.0% (US $100 dividends ÷ $200 profit).
Answer (A) is incorrect. The ratio of dividends paid to the December 31 carrying amount of ordinary equity is 19.6%. Answer (B) is incorrect. The ratio of dividends paid to the sum of beginning retained earnings and profit is 28.6%. Answer (C) is incorrect. The ratio of dividends paid to the December 31 retained earnings is 40.0%.

24. The entity has return on assets of

A. 21.1%

B. 39.2%

C. 42.1%

D. 45.3%

Answer (A) is correct. *(CIA, adapted)*
REQUIRED: The return on assets.
DISCUSSION: The return on assets is the ratio of profit to total assets. It equals 21.1% (US $200 profit ÷ $950 total assets).
Answer (B) is incorrect. The ratio of profit to ordinary equity is 39.2%. Answer (C) is incorrect. The ratio of profit before tax to total assets is 42.1%. Answer (D) is incorrect. The ratio of profit before interest and tax to total assets is 45.3%.

25. The entity has a profit margin of

A. 6.67%

B. 13.33%

C. 14.33%

D. 46.67%

Answer (A) is correct. *(CIA, adapted)*
REQUIRED: The profit margin.
DISCUSSION: The profit margin is the ratio of profit to sales. It equals 6.67% (US $200 profit ÷ $3,000 sales).
Answer (B) is incorrect. The ratio of profit before tax to sales is 13.33%. Answer (C) is incorrect. The ratio of profit before interest and taxes to sales is 14.33%. Answer (D) is incorrect. The ratio of gross profit to sales is 46.67%.

26. In the computation of DEPS, which of the following are potential ordinary shares?

	Nonconvertible Preference Shares	Share Options
A.	Yes	No
B.	Yes	Yes
C.	No	Yes
D.	No	No

Answer (C) is correct. *(CPA, adapted)*
REQUIRED: The potential ordinary shares.
DISCUSSION: Potential ordinary shares are contracts that may entitle holders to obtain ordinary shares. They include options, warrants, convertible preference shares, convertible debt, and contingently issuable shares. Unlike an option, nonconvertible preference shares are never potential ordinary shares.

27. In computing the loss per share of ordinary shares, cumulative preference dividends **not** earned should be

A. Deducted from the loss for the year.

B. Added to the loss for the year.

C. Deducted from income in the year paid.

D. Added to income in the year paid.

Answer (B) is correct. *(Publisher, adapted)*

REQUIRED: The effect of unearned cumulative preference dividends on the loss-per-share calculation.

DISCUSSION: When preference shares are cumulative, the dividend, whether earned or not, is deducted from profit or loss from continuing operations and profit or loss, or added to any loss for the year, in computing earnings or loss. When preference shares are noncumulative, an adjustment is made for dividends declared. If the dividend is cumulative only if earned, no adjustment is necessary except to the extent of available income; that is, the preference dividends accumulate only to the extent of profit or loss.

Answer (A) is incorrect. The effect is to reduce loss per share. Answer (C) is incorrect. Preference dividends are an adjustment when they accumulate. Answer (D) is incorrect. Preference dividends are an adjustment when they accumulate.

28. In a diluted earnings-per-share computation, outstanding options issued by the reporting entity are assumed to be exercised. If the exercise price of these options exceeds the average market price, the computation would

A. Fairly present diluted earnings per share on a prospective basis.

B. Fairly present the maximum potential dilution of diluted earnings per share on a prospective basis.

C. Reflect the excess of the number of shares assumed issued at the average market price over the number of shares assumed issued at the exercise price.

D. Be antidilutive.

Answer (D) is correct. *(CPA, adapted)*

REQUIRED: The effect on DEPS of an exercise price above the average market price for options.

DISCUSSION: Options and warrants (instruments that give the holders the right to purchase ordinary shares of the entity) issued by the reporting entity are assumed to be exercised at the beginning of the period or at time of issuance, if later. The proceeds are assumed to be from an issuance at the average market price for the period. The difference between (1) the shares issued and (2) the shares that would have been issued at the average market price is an issue for no consideration. If the options are in the money (exercise price is less than average market price), they are dilutive because (1) exceeds (2), and the excess will be added to the BEPS denominator. However, when the exercise price exceeds the average market price, the result is antidilutive.

Answer (A) is incorrect. When the exercise price exceeds the average market price, the result is antidilutive. Answer (B) is incorrect. When the exercise price exceeds the average market price, the result is antidilutive. Answer (C) is incorrect. If an option is not in the money, it is antidilutive.

5.9 Business Development Life Cycles

29. In a product's life cycle, the first symptom of the decline stage is a decline in the

A. Entity's inventory levels.

B. Product's sales.

C. Product's production cost.

D. Product's prices.

Answer (B) is correct. *(CIA, adapted)*

REQUIRED: The initial symptom of the decline stage in a product's life cycle.

DISCUSSION: The sales of most product types and brands eventually decrease permanently. This decline may be slow or rapid. This first symptom of the decline stage of a product's life cycle triggers such other effects as price cutting, narrowing of the product line, and reduction in promotion budgets.

Answer (A) is incorrect. A decline in the entity's purchases, resulting in a decline in the entity's inventory levels, is not the first symptom. It will occur only when production declines as a result of a drop in sales. Answer (C) is incorrect. A decline in production costs may be due to many factors, e.g., new plant technology or the increased availability of raw materials. Moreover, production costs may decrease in any stage of a product's life cycle and not specifically in the decline stage. Answer (D) is incorrect. A change in prices is a marketing decision. It is an action that may be taken in the maturity stage to compete in the market. Moreover, a decrease in the product's prices is a response to a permanent decline in sales.

30. While auditing a marketing department, the internal auditor discovered that the product life cycle model was used to structure the marketing mix. Under such a philosophy, the price charged on a consistent basis for a specific product would probably be lowest during which life cycle stage?

A. Introduction stage.

B. Growth stage.

C. Maturity stage.

D. Decline stage.

Answer (C) is correct. *(CIA, adapted)*

REQUIRED: The product life cycle stage during which the price charged on a consistent basis for a specific product is likely to be the lowest.

DISCUSSION: During the maturity stage, competition is at its greatest and costs are at their lowest. Moreover, entities are engaged in competitive price-cutting measures, resulting in some of the lowest prices seen during a product's life cycle.

Answer (A) is incorrect. During the introduction stage, per-unit costs of production are high and little competition exists. Hence, prices are at their highest. Answer (B) is incorrect. During the growth stage, prices will be lower than during the introduction stage, but not as low as during the maturity stage. In the growth stage, costs are dropping and competitors are being added, but costs are not at their minimum and competitors are not at their maximum. Answer (D) is incorrect. During the decline stage, price-cutting predominates as entities struggle to maintain sales volume in the face of a permanent decrease in demand. However, late in the decline stage, there are few competitors, so prices can be raised. In addition, per-unit costs are on the rise because volume is declining, resulting in higher prices.

STUDY UNIT SIX
MANAGERIAL ACCOUNTING

(50 pages of outline)

Study Unit 6 covers basic concepts of managerial accounting. One basic concept is **cost behavior**, that is, whether costs are fixed, variable, or some combination. Cost behavior must be understood to plan for firm profitability. This study unit also addresses **cost allocation methods**. These methods are used to assign indirect costs to cost objects. Other subunits apply to costing systems, budgeting, marginal analysis, transfer pricing, and responsibility systems.

Core Concepts

- A cost object is any entity to which costs can be attached. A cost driver is the basis used to assign costs to a cost object. The cost driver is the cause of the cost.
- Product costs (also called inventoriable costs) are capitalized as part of finished goods inventory. They eventually become a component of cost of goods sold. Period costs are expensed as incurred, i.e., they are not capitalized in finished goods inventory and are thus excluded from cost of goods sold.
- Variable cost per unit remains constant in the short run regardless of the level of production. Variable costs in total, on the other hand, vary directly and proportionally with changes in volume. Fixed costs in total remain unchanged in the short run regardless of production level. Fixed cost per unit, on the other hand, varies indirectly with the activity level. Mixed (semivariable) costs combine fixed and variable elements.
- Under absorption costing (sometimes called full or full absorption costing), the fixed portion of manufacturing overhead is “absorbed” into the cost of each product. Product cost thus includes all manufacturing costs, both fixed and variable. Variable costing (sometimes called direct costing) is more appropriate for internal reporting. Product cost includes only variable manufacturing costs.
- The net present value (NPV) method for projecting the profitability of an investment expresses a project’s return in dollar terms. NPV nets the expected cash streams related to a project (inflows and outflows), then discounts them at the hurdle rate, also called the desired rate of return.
- The internal rate of return (IRR) method expresses a project’s return in percentage terms. The IRR of an investment is the discount rate at which the investment’s NPV equals zero. In other words, it is the rate that makes the present value of the expected cash inflows equal the present value of the expected cash outflows.
- In the operating budget, the emphasis is on obtaining and using current resources. It contains the sales budget, production budget, direct materials budget, direct labor budget, manufacturing overhead budget, ending finished goods inventory budget, cost of goods sold budget, nonmanufacturing budget, and pro forma income statement.

- Budget systems include: project budget, activity-based budgeting, zero-based budgeting (ZBB), continuous (rolling) budgeting, kaizen budgeting, static budgeting, flexible budgeting, and life-cycle budgeting.
- Transfer prices are the amounts charged by one segment of an organization for goods and services it provides to another segment of the same organization. Transfer pricing should motivate managers by encouraging goal congruence and managerial effort. Three basic methods for determining transfer prices are in common use: cost plus pricing, market pricing, and negotiated pricing.
- Cost-volume-profit analysis (also called breakeven analysis) is a tool for understanding the interaction of revenues with fixed and variable costs. The breakeven point is the level of output at which total revenues equal total expenses; that is, the point at which operating income is zero.
- The typical problem for which marginal (differential or incremental) analysis can be used involves choices among courses of action. The focus is on incremental revenues and costs, not the totals of all revenues and costs for the given option. A special order that might at first be rejected could turn out to be profitable after marginal analysis. Marginal analysis emphasizes incremental costs, highlighting the ability of marginal revenue to cover fixed costs.
- Job-order costing is concerned with accumulating costs by specific job. This method is appropriate when producing products with individual characteristics or when identifiable groupings are possible (e.g., yachts and jewelry).
- Process cost accounting is used to assign costs to relatively homogeneous products that are mass produced on a continuous basis (e.g., petroleum products, thread, and computer monitors).
- Activity-based costing (ABC) is a response to the significant increase in the incurrence of indirect costs resulting from the rapid advance of technology. ABC is a refinement of an existing costing system (job-order or process).
- A life-cycle approach to budgeting estimates a product's revenues and expenses over its entire sales life cycle beginning with research and development, proceeding through the introduction and growth stages into the maturity stage, and finally into the harvest or decline stage. Accordingly, life-cycle costing takes a long-term view of the entire cost life cycle, also known as the value chain.
- Operation costing is a hybrid of job-order costing and process costing that emphasizes physical processes (operations) for cost management and control purposes. Operation costing is appropriate when similar products are produced in different models or styles or otherwise have distinctive traits.
- Backflush costing is often used by firms that have adopted a just-in-time (JIT) production philosophy. A JIT system treats carrying inventory as a nonvalue-adding activity. Hence, components are made available just in time to be used in the production process. Backflush costing complements JIT because it simplifies costing.
- A well-designed responsibility accounting system establishes responsibility centers (also called strategic business units).
- A cost center, e.g., a maintenance department, is responsible for costs only. A revenue center, e.g., a sales department, is responsible for revenues only. A profit center, e.g., an appliance department in a retail store, is responsible for revenues and expenses. An investment center, e.g., a branch office, is responsible for revenues, expenses, and invested capital.
- Performance measures are means of revealing how efficiently an investment center is deploying the capital that has been invested in it to produce income for the owners. Return on investment (ROI) is the key performance measure of an investment center. Residual income is a dollar measure rather than a percentage rate. The target rate is ordinarily the weighted-average cost of capital, but it may be an arbitrary hurdle rate.

6.1 COST MANAGEMENT TERMINOLOGY

Basic Definitions

1. Three essential definitions:
   a. A **cost** is the measure of a resource used up for some purpose.
      1) For financial reporting, a cost can either be **capitalized** as an asset or **expensed**.
   b. A **cost object** is any entity to which costs can be attached.
      1) Examples are products, processes, employees, departments, and facilities.
   c. A **cost driver** is the basis used to assign costs to a cost object.
      1) Cost driver is defined by the IMA as "a measure of activity, such as direct labor hours, machine hours, beds occupied, computer time used, flight hours, miles driven, or contracts, that is a causal factor in the incurrence of cost to an entity."

Manufacturing vs. Nonmanufacturing

2. Costs can be classified as manufacturing or nonmanufacturing.
   a. The **costs of manufacturing** a product can be classified as one of three types:
      1) **Direct materials** are those tangible inputs to the manufacturing process that can practicably be traced to the product, e.g., sheet metal welded together for a piece of heavy equipment.
         a) All costs of bringing raw materials to the production line, e.g., transportation-in, are included in the cost of direct materials.
      2) **Direct labor** is the cost of human labor that can practicably be traced to the product, e.g., the wages of the welder.
      3) **Manufacturing overhead** consists of all costs of manufacturing that are not direct materials or direct labor.
         a) **Indirect materials** are tangible inputs to the manufacturing process that cannot practicably be traced to the product, e.g., the welding compound used to put together a piece of heavy equipment.
         b) **Indirect labor** is the cost of human labor connected with the manufacturing process that cannot practicably be traced to the product, e.g., the wages of assembly line supervisors and janitorial staff.
         c) **Factory operating costs**, such as utilities, real estate taxes, insurance, depreciation on factory equipment, etc.
   b. Manufacturing costs are often grouped into the following classifications:
      1) **Prime cost** equals direct materials plus direct labor, i.e., those costs directly attributable to a product.
      2) **Conversion cost** equals direct labor plus manufacturing overhead, i.e., the costs of converting raw materials into the finished product.
   c. Operating a manufacturing concern requires the incurrence of **nonmanufacturing costs:**
      1) **Selling (marketing) costs** are those costs incurred in getting the product from the factory to the consumer, e.g., sales personnel salaries and product transportation.
      2) **Administrative expenses** are those costs incurred by a company not directly related to producing or marketing the product, e.g., executive salaries and depreciation on the headquarters building.

Product vs. Period

3. Costs can also be classified as product costs or period costs.
   a. One of the most important classifications a managerial accountant can make is whether to capitalize a cost as part of finished goods inventory or to expense it as incurred.
      1) **Product costs** (also called inventoriable costs) are capitalized as part of finished goods inventory. They eventually become a **component of cost of goods sold**.
      2) **Period costs** are expensed as incurred, i.e., they are not capitalized in finished goods inventory and are thus **excluded from cost of goods sold.**
   b. This distinction is crucial because of the required treatment of manufacturing costs for external financial reporting purposes.
      1) **Under GAAP**, all manufacturing costs (direct materials, direct labor, variable overhead, and fixed overhead) must be treated as product costs, and all selling and administrative (S&A) costs must be treated as period costs.
         a) This approach is called **absorption costing** (also called full costing).
      2) For **internal reporting**, a more informative accounting treatment is often to capitalize only variable manufacturing costs as product costs, and treat all other costs (variable S&A and the fixed portion of both production and S&A expenses) as period costs.
         a) This approach is called **variable costing** (also called direct costing).
      3) The following table summarizes these two approaches:

<table>
<tr><th></th><th>Absorption Costing
(Required under GAAP)</th><th>Variable Costing
(For internal reporting only)</th></tr>
<tr><td rowspan="2">Product Costs
(Included in Cost of Goods Sold)</td><td colspan="2">Variable production costs</td></tr>
<tr><td>Fixed production costs</td><td></td></tr>
<tr><td rowspan="3">Period Costs
(Excluded from Cost of Goods Sold)</td><td></td><td>Fixed production costs</td></tr>
<tr><td colspan="2">Variable S&A expenses</td></tr>
<tr><td colspan="2">Fixed S&A expenses</td></tr>
</table>

         a) These treatments are explained more fully in Subunit 3.

Direct vs. Indirect

4. Costs can be classified by how they are assigned to cost objects.
   a. **Direct costs** are ones that can be associated with a particular cost object in an economically feasible way, i.e., they can be **traced** to that object.
      1) Examples are the direct materials and direct labor inputs to a manufacturing process discussed in item 2.a.
   b. **Indirect costs** are ones that cannot be associated with a particular cost object in an economically feasible way and thus must be **allocated** to that object.
      1) Examples are the indirect materials and indirect labor inputs to a manufacturing process discussed in item 2.a.3) on the previous page.
      2) To simplify the allocation process, indirect costs are often collected in cost pools.
         a) A **cost pool** is an account into which a variety of similar cost elements with a common cause are accumulated.
         b) Manufacturing overhead is a commonly used cost pool into which various untraceable costs of the manufacturing process are accumulated prior to being allocated.

c. **Common costs** are another notable type of indirect cost. A common cost is one shared by two or more users.

1) The key to common costs is that, since they cannot be directly traced to the users that generate the costs, they must be **allocated** using some systematic and rational basis.

2) An example is depreciation on the headquarters building. This is a direct cost when treating the building as a whole but is a common cost of the departments located in the building and thus must be allocated when treating the individual departments.

Stop and review! You have completed the outline for this subunit. Study multiple-choice questions 1 and 2 beginning on page 298.

6.2 COST BEHAVIOR AND RELEVANT RANGE

1. The **relevant range** defines the limits within which per-unit variable costs remain constant and fixed costs are not changeable. It is synonymous with the **short run**.

a. The relevant range is established by the efficiency of a company's current manufacturing plant, its agreements with labor unions and suppliers, etc.

<u>**Variable vs. Fixed Cost Behavior**</u>

2. **Variable Costs**

a. **Variable cost per unit** remains constant in the short run regardless of the level of production.

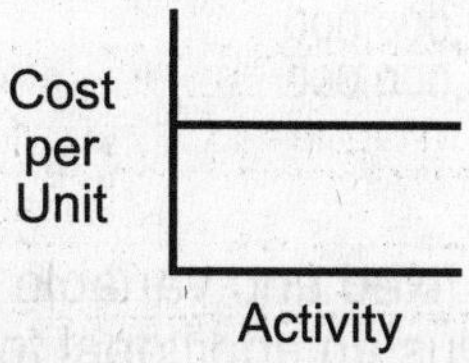

b. **Variable costs in total**, on the other hand, vary directly and proportionally with changes in volume.

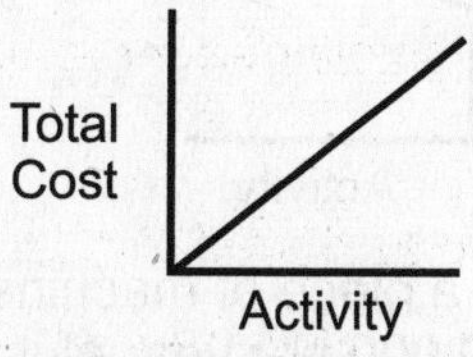

c. EXAMPLE: A company requires one unit of direct material to be used in each finished good it produces.

Number of outputs produced	Input cost per unit	Total cost of inputs
0	US $10	US $ 0
100	10	1,000
1,000	10	10,000
5,000	10	50,000
10,000	10	100,000

3. **Fixed Costs**

   a. **Fixed costs in total** remain unchanged in the short run regardless of production level, e.g., the amount paid for an assembly line is the same even if production is halted entirely.

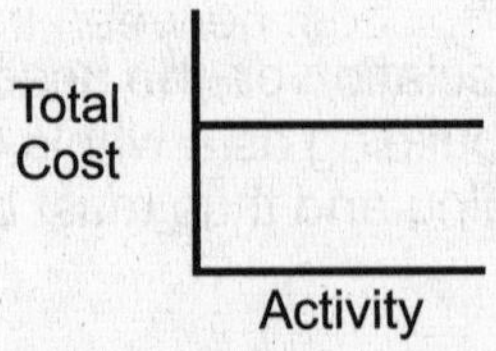

   b. **Fixed cost per unit**, on the other hand, varies indirectly with the activity level.

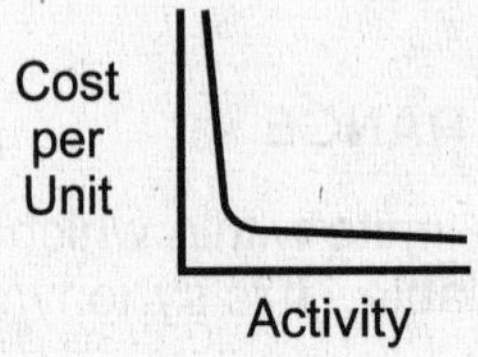

   c. EXAMPLE: The historical cost of the assembly line is settled, but its cost per unit decreases as production increases.

Number of outputs produced	Cost of assembly line	Per unit cost of assembly line
0	US $1,000,000	US $1,000,000
100	1,000,000	10,000
1,000	1,000,000	1,000
5,000	1,000,000	200
10,000	1,000,000	100

Other Cost Behaviors

4. **Mixed (semivariable) costs** combine fixed and variable elements, e.g., rental expense on a car that carries a flat fee per month plus an additional fee for each mile driven.

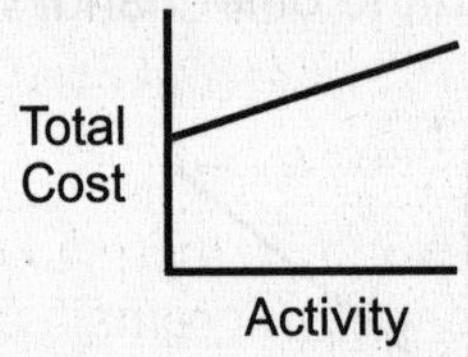

   a. EXAMPLE: The company rents a piece of machinery to make its production line more efficient. The rental is US $150,000 per year plus US $1 for every unit produced.

Number of outputs produced	Fixed cost of extra machine	Variable cost of extra machine	Total cost of extra machine
0	US $150,000	US $ 0	US $150,000
100	150,000	100	150,100
1,000	150,000	1,000	151,000
5,000	150,000	5,000	155,000
10,000	150,000	10,000	160,000

b. Sometimes the fixed and variable portions of a mixed cost are not set by contract as in the above example and thus must be **estimated**. Two methods of estimating mixed costs are in general use:

1) The **high-low method** is the less accurate but the quicker of the two methods.

a) The difference in cost between the highest and lowest levels of activity is divided by the difference in the activity level to arrive at the variable portion of the cost.

b) EXAMPLE: A company has the following cost data:

Month	Machine Hours	Maintenance Costs
April	1,000	US $2,275
May	1,600	3,400
June	1,200	2,650
July	800	1,900
August	1,200	2,650
September	1,000	2,275

c) The numerator can be derived by subtracting the cost at the lowest level (July) from the cost at the highest level (May) [US $3,400 – $1,900 = US $1,500].

d) The denominator can be derived by subtracting the lowest level of activity (July) from the highest level (May) [1,600 – 800 = 800].

e) The variable portion of the cost is therefore US $1.875 per machine hour (US $1,500 ÷ 800).

f) The fixed portion can be calculated by inserting the appropriate values for either the high or low month in the range:

Fixed portion = Total cost – Variable portion
= US $1,900 – ($1.875 × 800 hours)
= US $1,900 – $1,500
= US $400

2) The **regression (scattergraph) method** is considerably more complex and determines the average rate of variability of a mixed cost rather than the variability between the high and low points in the range.

5. **Linear vs. Nonlinear Cost Functions**

a. Four of the five costs described on the previous pages are **linear-cost functions**, i.e., they change at a constant rate (or remain unchanged) over the short run.

b. Fixed cost per unit, however, is an example of a **nonlinear-cost function**.

1) Note that fixed cost per unit has an asymptotic character with respect to the x axis, approaching it closely while never intersecting it (it does intersect the y axis at the zero level of activity). The function shows a high degree of variability over its range taken as a whole (see item 3.b.).

2) Another type of nonlinear-cost function is a **step-cost function**, one that is constant over small ranges of output but increases by steps (discrete amounts) as levels of activity increase.

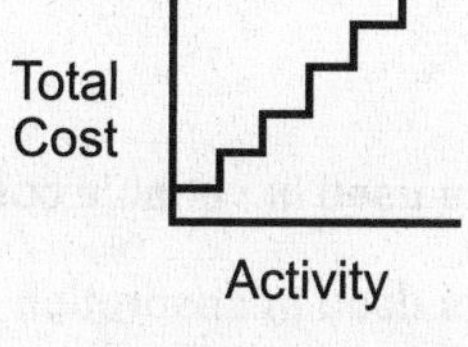

a) Both fixed and variable costs can display step-cost characteristics. If the steps are relatively narrow, these costs are usually treated as variable. If the steps are wide, they are more akin to fixed costs.

Relevant Range and Marginal Cost

6. Relevant range and marginal cost are related concepts.
   a. **Marginal cost** is the cost incurred by a one-unit increase in the activity level of a particular cost driver.
      1) Necessarily then, **marginal cost remains constant across the relevant range.**
   b. Management accountants capture the concept of relevant range when they say, **"All costs are variable in the long run."**
      1) Investment in new, more productive equipment results in higher total fixed costs but may result in lower total and per-unit variable costs.

Stop and review! You have completed the outline for this subunit. Study multiple-choice question 3 on page 299.

6.3 ABSORPTION (FULL) VS. VARIABLE (DIRECT) COSTING

Overview

1. Under **absorption costing** (sometimes called full or full absorption costing), the fixed portion of manufacturing overhead is "absorbed" into the cost of each product.
   a. **Product cost** thus includes **all manufacturing costs, both fixed and variable.**
   b. Absorption-basis cost of goods sold is subtracted from sales to arrive at gross margin.
   c. Total selling and administrative (S&A) expenses (i.e., both fixed and variable) are then subtracted from gross margin to arrive at operating income.
   d. This method is **required under GAAP** for external reporting purposes **and under the Internal Revenue Code** for tax purposes. The justification is that, for external reporting, product cost should include all manufacturing costs.
2. **Variable costing** (sometimes called direct costing) is more appropriate for internal reporting.
   a. The term "direct costing" is somewhat misleading because it suggests traceability, which is not what is meant in this context. "Variable costing" is more suitable.
   b. **Product cost** includes **only variable manufacturing costs.**
   c. Variable-basis cost of goods sold and the variable portion of S&A expenses are subtracted from sales to arrive at **contribution margin.**
      1) This figure (sales – total variable costs) is an important element of the variable costing income statement because it is the amount available for **covering fixed costs** (both manufacturing and S&A).
      2) For this reason, some accountants call the method **contribution margin reporting.**
      3) This is an important metric internally but is generally irrelevant to outside financial statement users.

Calculations

3. EXAMPLE: A firm, during its first month in business, produced 100 units and sold 80 while incurring the following costs:

Direct materials	US $1,000
Direct labor	2,000
Variable overhead	1,500
Manufacturing costs used in variable costing	**US $4,500**
Fixed overhead	3,000
Manufacturing costs used in absorption costing	**US $7,500**

a. The impact on the financial statements from using one method over the other can be seen in these calculations:

	Manufacturing costs	Divided by: Units produced	Equals: Per unit cost	Times: Units in ending inventory	Equals: Value of ending inventory
Absorption basis	US $7,500	100	US $75	20	US $1,500
Variable basis	4,500	100	45	20	900

b. The per-unit selling price of the finished goods was US $100, and the company incurred US $200 of variable selling and administrative expenses and US $600 of fixed selling and administrative expenses.

c. The following are partial income statements prepared using the two methods:

		Absorption Costing (Required under GAAP)		Variable Costing (For internal reporting only)	
	Sales		**US $ 8,000**		**US $ 8,000**
	Beginning finished goods inventory	US $ 0		US $ 0	
Product Costs	Plus: variable production costs	4,500 (a)		4,500 (a)	
	Plus: fixed production costs	3,000 (b)			
	Goods available for sale	US $7,500		US $4,500	
	Less: ending finished goods inventory	(1,500)		(900)	
	Cost of goods sold		**US $(6,000)**		**US $(3,600)**
Period Costs	Less: variable S&A expenses				(200) (c)
	Gross margin (abs.) / Contribution margin (var.)		**US $ 2,000**		**US $ 4,200**
	Less: fixed production costs				(3,000) (b)
	Less: variable S&A expenses		(200) (c)		
	Less: fixed S&A expenses		(600) (d)		(600) (d)
	Operating income		**US $ 1,200**		**US $ 600**

d. The US $600 difference in operating income (US $1,200 – US $600) is the **difference between the two ending inventory values** (US $1,500 – US $900).

1) In essence, the absorption method carries 20% of the fixed overhead costs (US $3,000 × 20% = US $600) on the balance sheet as an asset because 20% of the month's production (100 available – 80 sold = 20 on hand) is still in inventory.

Implications

4. As production and sales levels change, the two methods have varying impacts on **operating income.**

a. When **everything produced** during a period **is sold** that period, the two methods report the **same operating income.**

1) Total fixed costs budgeted for the period are charged to sales revenue in the period under both methods.

b. When **production and sales are not equal** for a period, the two methods report **different** operating income.

1) ILLUSTRATION:

When production	**When production**
⌂⌂⌂⌂⌂⌂⌂⌂	⌂⌂⌂
exceeds sales,	**is less than sales,**
⌂⌂⌂	⌂⌂⌂⌂⌂⌂⌂⌂⌂
ending inventory expands.	**ending inventory contracts.**
↑↑↑↑↑↑↑↑↑↑↑↑↑↑↑	↓↓↓↓↓↓
Under absorption costing, some fixed costs are still embedded in ending inventory.	**Under absorption costing,** fixed costs embedded in beginning inventory get expensed.
Under variable costing, all fixed costs have been expensed.	**Under variable costing,** only the current period's fixed costs are expensed.
Therefore,	Therefore,
operating income is higher under <u>absorption</u> costing.	**operating income is higher under <u>variable</u> costing.**

c. The diagram above illustrates the **perverse incentive inherent to absorption costing** and reveals why many companies prefer variable costing for internal reporting.

1) Operating income increases whenever production exceeds sales.
2) A production manager can thus increase absorption-basis operating income merely by increasing production, whether there is any customer demand for the additional product or not.
   a) The company must also deal with the increased carrying costs resulting from swelling inventory levels.
3) This practice, called **producing for inventory**, can be effectively discouraged by using variable costing for performance reporting and consequent bonus calculation.

d. EXTENDED EXAMPLE: A company has the following sales and cost data:

	Year 1	Year 2	Year 3
Production in units	40,000	50,000	0
Sales in units	30,000	30,000	30,000
Ending inventory in units (FIFO)	10,000	30,000	0

Unit sales price	US $1.00
Unit variable cost	0.50
Fixed manufacturing costs per year	4,000
Variable S&A expenses per unit	0.03333
Fixed S&A expenses per year	1,000

1) Compare the 3-year income statements prepared under the two methods:

Absorption Costing (Required under GAAP)				Variable Costing (For internal reporting only)			
	Year 1	Year 2	Year 3		Year 1	Year 2	Year 3
Sales	**US $30,000**	**US $30,000**	**US $30,000**	**Sales**	**US $30,000**	**US $30,000**	**US $30,000**
Beginning inventory	US $ 0	US $ 6,000	US $17,400	Beginning inventory	US $ 0	US $ 5,000	US $15,000
Variable mfg. costs	20,000	25,000	0	Variable mfg. costs	20,000	25,000	0
Fixed mfg. costs	4,000	4,000	4,000				
Goods available for sale	US $24,000	US $35,000	US $21,400	Goods avail. for sale	US $20,000	US $30,000	US $15,000
Less: ending inventory	(6,000)	(17,400)	0	Less: ending inventory	(5,000)	(15,000)	0
Absorption CGS	**US $18,000**	**US $17,600**	**US $21,400**	**Variable CGS**	**US $15,000**	**US $15,000**	**US $15,000**
				Variable S&A exps.	(1,000)	(1,000)	(1,000)
Gross margin	**US $12,000**	**US $12,400**	**US $ 8,600**	**Contribution margin**	**US $14,000**	**US $14,000**	**US $14,000**
				Fixed mfg. costs	(4,000)	(4,000)	(4,000)
Variable S&A expenses	(1,000)	(1,000)	(1,000)				
Fixed S&A expenses	(1,000)	(1,000)	(1,000)	Fixed S&A expenses	(1,000)	(1,000)	(1,000)
Operating income	**US $10,000**	**US $10,400**	**US $ 6,600**	**Operating income**	**US $ 9,000**	**US $ 9,000**	**US $ 9,000**

2) Note that, assuming zero inventory at the beginning of Year 1 and at the end of Year 3, the **total operating income for the 3-year period is the same** under either costing method.

	Absorption Costing	Variable Costing
Year 1	US $10,000	US $ 9,000
Year 2	10,400	9,000
Year 3	6,600	9,000
3-Year Total	**US $27,000**	**US $27,000**

3) Absorption costing shows a higher operating income than variable costing in Years 1 and 2 because fixed overhead has been capitalized and does not get expensed until Year 3.

a) Variable costing, on the other hand, treats fixed overhead as an expense of the period in which the cost is incurred.

b) In Year 2, despite the same cash flow, there is a US $1,400 difference between the final operating income figures. There is an even greater difference in Year 3.

4) If fixed costs increase relative to variable costs, the differences become more dramatic (here, 50% of the selling price is variable manufacturing cost, and fixed overhead is no more than 20% of the variable manufacturing cost).

5) From an internal point of view, a manager can manipulate absorption income by changing production levels. But, with variable costing, a manager cannot manipulate simply by changing production levels.

Stop and review! You have completed the outline for this subunit. Study multiple-choice questions 4 and 5 on page 300.

6.4 CAPITAL BUDGETING

Overview

1. **Capital budgeting** is the process of planning and controlling investments for **long-term projects**.
   a. It is this long-term aspect of capital budgeting that presents the management accountant with specific challenges.
      1) Most financial and management accounting topics, such as calculating allowance for doubtful accounts or accumulating product costs, concern tracking and reporting activity for a **single accounting or reporting cycle**, such as 1 month or 1 year.
      2) By their nature, capital projects affect **multiple accounting periods** and will constrain the organization's financial planning well into the future. Once made, capital budgeting decisions tend to be relatively inflexible.
   b. Capital budgeting applications include:
      1) Buying equipment
      2) Building facilities
      3) Acquiring a business
      4) Developing a product or product line
      5) Expanding into new markets
   c. A firm must accurately **forecast future changes in demand** in order to have the necessary production capacity when demand for its product is strong, without having excess idle capacity when demand slackens.
   d. A capital project usually involves **substantial expenditures**.
      1) Planning is crucial because of possible **changes in capital markets, inflation, interest rates, and the money supply**.
2. A dollar received in the future is worth less than a dollar received today. Thus, when analyzing capital projects, the management accountant must discount the relevant cash flows using the **time value of money**.
   a. A firm's goal is for its **discount rate** to be **as low as possible**.
      1) The lower the firm's discount rate, the lower the "hurdle" the company must clear to achieve profitability. For this reason, the rate is sometimes called the **hurdle rate**.
   b. The **two most widely used rates** in capital budgeting are
      1) The firm's weighted-average cost of capital and
      2) The shareholders' opportunity cost of capital.
   c. A **common pitfall** in capital budgeting is the tendency to use the company's current rate of return as the benchmark. This can lead to rejecting projects that should be accepted.
      1) EXAMPLE: A firm's current rate of return on all projects is 12%. Its shareholders' opportunity cost of capital is 10%. The company incorrectly rejects a project earning 11%.
   d. The **two principal methods** for projecting the profitability of an investment are net present value and internal rate of return.

Two Principal Methods

3. The **net present value (NPV) method** expresses a project's return in **dollar terms**.
   a. NPV **nets the expected cash streams** related to a project (inflows and outflows), then discounts them at the hurdle rate, also called the **desired rate of return**.
      1) If the NPV of a project is **positive**, the project is **desirable** because it has a higher rate of return than the company's desired rate.

b. EXAMPLE:

1) The company discounts the relevant net cash flows using a hurdle rate of 6% (its desired rate of return).

Period	Net Cash Flow	6% PV Factor	Discounted Cash Flows
Initial Investment	US $(501,000)	1.00000	US $(501,000)
Year 1	77,000	0.94340	72,642
Year 2	77,000	0.89000	68,530
Year 3	77,000	0.83962	64,651
Year 4	77,000	0.79209	60,991
Year 5	85,000	0.74726	63,517
Year 6	85,000	0.70496	59,922
Year 7	85,000	0.66506	56,530
Year 8	101,800	0.62741	63,870
Net Present Value			**US $ 9,653**

2) Because the project has net present value > US $0, it is profitable given the company's hurdle rate.

4. The **internal rate of return (IRR)** expresses a project's return in **percentage terms**.

a. The IRR of an investment is the **discount rate** at which the investment's **NPV equals zero**. In other words, it is the rate that makes the present value of the expected cash inflows equal the present value of the expected cash outflows.

1) If the IRR is **higher** than the company's desired rate of return, the investment is **desirable**.

b. EXAMPLE:

1) The discounted cash flows used in the NPV exercise above can be recalculated using a higher discount rate (a higher rate will drive down the present value) in an attempt to get the solution closer to US $0.

Period	Net Cash Flow	7% PV Factor	Discounted Cash Flows
Initial Investment	US $(501,000)	1.00000	US $(501,000)
Year 1	77,000	0.93458	71,963
Year 2	77,000	0.87344	67,255
Year 3	77,000	0.81630	62,855
Year 4	77,000	0.76290	58,743
Year 5	85,000	0.71299	60,604
Year 6	85,000	0.66634	56,639
Year 7	85,000	0.62275	52,934
Year 8	101,800	0.58201	59,249
Net Present Value			**US $ (10,759)**

2) The higher hurdle rate causes the NPV to be negative. Thus, the IRR of this project is somewhere around 6.5%.

3) Because the company's desired rate of return is 6%, the project should be accepted, the same decision that was arrived at using the net present value method.

5. **Cash Flows and Discounting**

a. Conceptually, net present value is calculated using the following formula:

$$NPV = \frac{Cash\ Flow_0}{(1 + r)^0} + \frac{Cash\ Flow_1}{(1 + r)^1} + \frac{Cash\ Flow_2}{(1 + r)^2} + \frac{Cash\ Flow_3}{(1 + r)^3} + etc.$$

1) The subscripts and exponents represent the discount periods. The variable *r* is the discount rate.

b. Present value tables are available as a convenient way to discount cash flows.

Pitfalls of IRR

6. IRR used in isolation is seldom the best route to a sound capital budgeting decision.
   a. **Direction of cash flows.** When the direction of the cash flows changes, focusing simply on IRR can be misleading.
      1) EXAMPLE: Below are the net cash flows for two potential capital projects.

	Initial	Period 1
Project X	US $(222,222)	US $ 240,000
Project Y	222,222	(240,000)

The cash flow amounts are the same in absolute value, but the directions differ. In choosing between the two, a decision maker might be tempted to select the project that has a cash inflow earlier and a cash outflow later.

      2) The IRR for both projects is 8%, which can be proved as follows:

Project X				Project Y			
US $(222,222)	×	1.000	= US $(222,222)	US $222,222	×	1.000	= US $ 222,222
240,000	×	0.926	= 222,222	(240,000)	×	0.926	= (222,222)
			US $ -0-				**US $ -0-**

      3) Discounting the cash flows at the company's hurdle rate of 6% reveals a different picture.

Project X				Project Y			
US $(222,222)	×	1.000	= US $(222,222)	US $222,222	×	1.000	= US $ 222,222
240,000	×	0.943	= 226,415	(240,000)	×	0.943	= (226,415)
			US $ 4,193				**US $ (4,193)**

         a) It turns out that, given a hurdle rate lower than the rate at which the two projects have the same return, the project with the positive cash flow earlier is by far the less desirable of the two.
         b) Clearly, a decision maker can be seriously misled if (s)he uses the simple direction of the cash flows as the tiebreaker when two projects have the same IRR.
      4) This effect is known as the **multiple IRR problem**. Essentially, there are **as many solutions** to the IRR formula as there are **changes in the direction** of the net cash flows.
   b. **Mutually exclusive projects.** As with changing cash flow directions, focusing only on IRR when capital is limited can lead to unsound decisions.
      1) EXAMPLE: Below are the cash flows for two potential capital projects.

	Initial	Period 1	IRR
Project S	US $(178,571)	US $200,000	12%
Project T	(300,000)	330,000	10%

      2) If capital is available for only one project, using IRR alone would suggest that Project S be selected.
      3) Once again, however, discounting both projects' net cash flows at the company's hurdle rate suggests a different decision.

Project S				Project T			
US $(178,571)	×	1.000	= US $(178,571)	US $(300,000)	×	1.000	= US $(300,000)
200,000	×	0.943	= 188,679	330,000	×	0.943	= 311,321
			US $ 10,108				**US $ 11,321**

         a) While Project S has the distinction of giving the company a higher internal rate of return, Project T is in fact preferable because it adds more to shareholder value.

c. **Varying rates of return.** A project's NPV can easily be determined using different desired rates of return for different periods. The IRR is limited to a single summary rate for the entire project.

d. **Multiple investments.** NPV amounts from different projects can be added, but IRR rates cannot. The IRR for the whole is not the sum of the IRRs for the parts.

Comparing Cash Flow Patterns

7. Often a decision maker must choose between two mutually exclusive projects.

   a. One project's **inflows are higher in the early years** but fall off drastically later, and the other project's **inflows are steady** throughout the project's life.

      1) The **higher a firm's hurdle rate**, the more quickly a project must pay off.
      2) Firms with **low hurdle rates** prefer a slow and steady payback.

   b. EXAMPLE: Consider the net cash flows of these two projects:

	Initial	Year 1	Year 2	Year 3	Year 4
Project K	US $(200,000)	US $140,000	US $100,000	–	–
Project L	(200,000)	65,000	65,000	US $65,000	US $65,000

      1) A graphical representation of the two projects at various discount rates helps to illustrate the factors a decision maker must consider in such a situation.

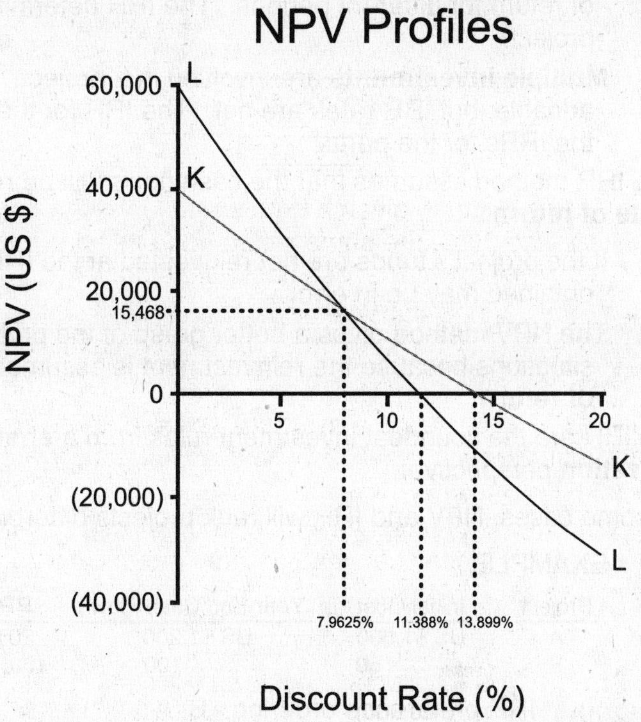

   c. The NPV profile can be of great practical use to managers trying to make investment decisions. It gives the manager a clear insight into the following questions:

      1) How sensitive is a project's profitability to changes in the discount rate?

         a) At a hurdle rate of **exactly** 7.9625%, a decision maker is indifferent between the two projects. The net present value of both is US $15,468 at that discount rate.
         b) At hurdle rates **below** 7.9625%, the project whose **inflows last longer** into the future is the better investment (L).
         c) At hurdle rates **above** 7.9625%, the project whose **inflows are "front-loaded"** is the better choice (K).

2) At what discount rates is an investment project still a profitable opportunity?

a) At any hurdle rate **above** 13.899%, Project K **loses money**. This is its IRR, i.e., the rate at which its NPV = US $0 (Project L's is 11.388%).

Comparing NPV and IRR

8. The **reinvestment rate** becomes critical when choosing between the NPV and IRR methods. NPV assumes the cash flows from the investment can be reinvested at the particular project's discount rate, that is, the **desired rate of return**.

a. The NPV and IRR methods give the same accept/reject decision if projects are independent. **Independent projects** have unrelated cash flows. Hence, all acceptable independent projects can be undertaken.

1) However, if projects are **mutually exclusive**, the NPV and IRR methods may rank them differently if

a) The **cost** of one project is greater than the cost of another.

b) The timing, amounts, and directions of **cash flows** differ among projects.

c) The projects have **different useful lives.**

d) The **cost of capital** or **desired rate of return** varies over the life of a project. The NPV can easily be determined using different desired rates of return for different periods. The IRR determines one rate for the project.

e) **Multiple investments** are involved in a project. NPV amounts are addable, but IRR rates are not. The IRR for the whole is not the sum of the IRRs for the parts.

2) The IRR method assumes that the cash flows will be **reinvested at the internal rate of return.**

a) If the project's funds are not reinvested at the IRR, the ranking calculations obtained may be in error.

b) The NPV method gives a better grasp of the problem in many decision situations because the reinvestment is assumed to be in the **desired rate of return.**

b. NPV and IRR are the soundest investment rules from a **shareholder wealth maximization** perspective.

1) In some cases, NPV and IRR will rank projects differently.

a) EXAMPLE:

Project	Initial Cost	Year-End Cash Flow	IRR	NPV (k=10%)
A	US $1,000	US $1,200	20%	US $91
B	50	100	100%	41

i) IRR preference ordering: B, A

ii) NPV preference ordering: A, B

c. If one of two or more **mutually exclusive projects** is accepted, the others must be rejected.

1) EXAMPLE: The decision to build a shopping mall on a piece of land eliminates placing an office building on the same land.

2) When choosing between mutually exclusive projects, the ranking differences between NPV and IRR become very important. In the example above, a firm using IRR would accept B and reject A. A firm using NPV would make exactly the opposite choice.

Nondiscounting Methods

9. The **payback period** is the **number of years** required to return the original investment; that is, the time necessary for a new asset to pay for itself. Note that **no accounting is made for the time value of money** under this method.

   a. Companies using the payback method set a maximum length of time within which projects must pay for themselves to be considered acceptable.

   b. **If the cash flows are constant**, the formula is

   $$\text{Payback period} = \frac{\text{Initial net investment}}{\text{Annual expected cash flow}}$$

      1) EXAMPLE: A project is being considered that will require an outlay of US $200,000 immediately and will return a steady cash flow of US $52,000 for the next 4 years. The company requires a 4-year payback period on all capital projects.

         a) Payback period = US $200,000 ÷ US $52,000 = 3.846 years

         b) The project's payback period is less than the company's maximum, and the project is thus acceptable.

   c. **If the cash flows are not constant**, the calculation must be in cumulative form.

      1) EXAMPLE: Instead of the smooth inflows predicted above, the project's cash stream is expected to vary. The payback period is calculated as follows:

End of Year	Cash Inflow	Remaining Initial Investment
Year 0	US $ 0	US $200,000
Year 1	48,000	152,000
Year 2	54,000	98,000
Year 3	54,000	44,000
Year 4	42,000	2,000

         a) At the end of 4 years, the original investment has still not been recovered, so the project is rejected.

   d. The **strength** of the payback method is its simplicity.

      1) The payback method is sometimes used for foreign investments if foreign expropriation of firm assets is feared. Even in these circumstances, it is most often used in addition to a more sophisticated method.

      2) To some extent, the payback period measures risk. The longer the period, the more risky the investment.

   e. The payback method has two significant **weaknesses**:

      1) It disregards all cash inflows after the payback cutoff date. Applying a single cutoff date to every project results in accepting many marginal projects and rejecting good ones.

      2) It disregards the time value of money. Weighting all cash inflows equally ignores the fact that money has a cost.

10. The **discounted payback method** is sometimes used to overcome the second of the drawbacks inherent in the basic payback method.
    a. The net cash flows in the denominator are discounted to calculate the period required to recover the initial investment.

Period	Cash Inflow	6% PV Factor	Discounted Cash Flow	Remaining Initial Investment
Initial Investment	US $ 0	1.00000	US $ 0	US $200,000
Year 1	48,000	0.94340	45,283	154,717
Year 2	54,000	0.89000	48,060	106,657
Year 3	54,000	0.83962	45,339	61,317
Year 4	42,000	0.79209	33,268	28,050

1) After 4 years, the project is much further from paying off than under the basic method.
2) Clearly then, this is a **more conservative** technique than the traditional payback method.

b. The discounted payback method's advantage is that it acknowledges the time value of money.

1) Its drawbacks are that it loses the simplicity of the basic payback method and still ignores cash flows after the arbitrary cutoff date.

Other Payback Methods

11. The **bailout payback method** incorporates the salvage value of the asset into the calculation. It measures the length of the payback period when the periodic cash inflows are combined with the salvage value.
    a. The **payback reciprocal** (1 ÷ payback) is sometimes used as an estimate of the internal rate of return.
    b. The **breakeven time** is the period required for the discounted cumulative cash inflows on a project to equal the discounted cumulative cash outflows (usually but not always the initial cost).

1) Thus, it is the time necessary for the present value of the discounted cash flows to equal zero. This period begins at the outset of a project, not when the initial cash outflow occurs.
2) An alternative that results in a longer breakeven time is to consider the time required for the present value of the cumulative cash inflows to equal the present value of all the expected future cash outflows.

Capital Rationing

12. Capital rationing exists when a firm sets a limit on the amount of funds to be invested during a given period. In such situations, an entity cannot afford to undertake all profitable projects.
    a. Another way of stating this is that the entity cannot invest the entire amount needed to fund its theoretically optimal capital budget.

1) Only those projects that will return the **greatest NPV** for the limited capital available in the **internal capital market** can be undertaken.

b. **Reasons** for capital rationing include

1) A lack of nonmonetary resources (e.g., managerial or technical personnel)
2) A desire to control estimation bias (overly favorable projections of a project's cash flows)
3) An unwillingness to issue new equity (e.g., because of its cost or a reluctance to reveal data in regulatory filings)

Post-Investment Audits

13. Post-investment audits should be conducted to serve as a control mechanism and to deter managers from proposing unprofitable investments.
    a. Actual-to-expected cash flow comparisons should be made, and unfavorable variances should be explained. The reason may be an inaccurate forecast or implementation problems.
    b. Individuals who supplied unrealistic estimates should have to explain differences. Knowing that a post-investment audit will be conducted may cause managers to provide more realistic forecasts in the future.
    c. The temptation to evaluate the outcome of a project too early must be overcome. Until all cash flows are known, the results can be misleading.
    d. Assessing the receipt of expected nonquantitative benefits is inherently difficult.

Stop and review! You have completed the outline for this subunit. Study multiple-choice questions 6 and 7 on page 301.

6.5 BUDGET SYSTEMS

1. The **master budget**, also called the comprehensive budget or **annual profit plan**, encompasses the organization's **operating** and **financial plans** for a specified period (ordinarily a year or single operating cycle).
    a. The importance of carefully drafting the budget calendar is illustrated here. The information contained in the lower-numbered budgets feeds the higher-numbered budgets.
    b. In the **operating budget**, the emphasis is on obtaining and using current resources.
        1) Sales budget
        2) Production budget
        3) Direct materials budget
        4) Direct labor budget
        5) Manufacturing overhead budget
        6) Ending finished goods inventory budget
        7) Cost of goods sold budget
        8) Nonmanufacturing budget
            a) Research and development budget
            b) Design budget
            c) Marketing budget
            d) Distribution budget
            e) Customer service budget
            f) Administrative budget
        9) **Pro forma income statement**
    c. In the **financial budget**, the emphasis is on obtaining the funds needed to purchase operating assets. It contains the
        1) Capital budget (completed before operating budget is begun)
        2) Projected cash disbursement schedule
        3) Projected cash collection schedule
        4) Cash budget
        5) **Pro forma balance sheet**
        6) **Pro forma statement of cash flows**

2. A **project budget** consists of all the costs expected to attach to a particular project, such as the design of a new airliner or the building of a single ship.
   a. While the project is obviously part of the company's overall line of business, the costs and profits associated with it are significant enough to be tracked separately.
   b. A project will typically use resources from many parts of the organization, e.g., design, engineering, production, marketing, accounting, and human resources.
      1) All of these aspects of the project budget must align with those of the firm's master budget.
3. **Activity-based budgeting** applies activity-based costing principles (see Subunit 10) to budgeting.
   a. It focuses on the numerous activities necessary to produce and market goods and services and requires analysis of cost drivers. Budget line items are related to activities performed.
      1) This approach contrasts with the traditional emphasis on functions or spending categories.
      2) The costs of non-value-added activities are quantified.
   b. Activity-based budgeting provides greater detail than traditional functional or spending-category budgeting, especially regarding indirect costs, because it permits the isolation of numerous cost drivers.
      1) A **cost pool** is established for each activity, and a cost driver is identified for each pool.
      2) The budgeted cost for each pool is determined by multiplying the demand for the activity by the estimated cost of a unit of the activity.
4. **Zero-based budgeting (ZBB)** is a budget and planning process in which each manager must justify his/her department's entire budget every budget cycle.
   a. The concept originated in the U.S. Department of Agriculture in the early 1960s but was abandoned. Texas Instruments Corporation began using it in the late 1960s and early 1970s, as did the state of Georgia under Governor Jimmy Carter. Carter also tried to introduce the concept into the federal budget system when he served as president (1977–1980).
   b. ZBB differs from the traditional concept of **incremental budgeting**, in which the current year's budget is simply adjusted to allow for changes planned for the coming year.
      1) The managerial advantage of incremental budgeting is that the manager has to put forth less effort to justify changes in the budget.
   c. Under ZBB, a manager must build the budget every year from a base of zero. All expenditures must be justified regardless of variance from previous years.
      1) The objective is to encourage periodic reexamination of all costs in the hope that some can be reduced or eliminated.
   d. ZBB begins with the deepest budgetary units of the entity.
      1) It requires determination of objectives, operations, and costs for each activity and the alternative means of carrying out that activity.
      2) Different levels of service (work effort) are evaluated for each activity, measures of work and performance are established, and activities are ranked according to their importance to the entity.

3) For each budgetary unit, a decision package is prepared that describes various levels of service that may be provided, including at least one level of service lower than the current one.

a) Accordingly, ZBB requires managers to justify each expenditure for each budget period and to review each cost component from a cost-benefit perspective.

e. The major limitation of ZBB is that it requires more time and effort to prepare than a traditional budget.

5. A **continuous (rolling) budget** is one that is revised on a regular (continuous) basis.

a. Typically, a company continuously extends such a budget for an additional month or quarter in accordance with new data as the current month or quarter ends.

1) For example, if the budget cycle is one year, a budget for the next 12 months will be available continuously as each month ends.

b. The principal advantage of a rolling budget is that it requires managers always to be thinking ahead.

1) The disadvantage is the amount of time managers must constantly spend on budget preparation.

6. The Japanese term **kaizen** means continuous improvement, and **kaizen budgeting** assumes the continuous improvement of products and processes.

a. It requires estimates of the effects of improvements and the costs of their implementation.

b. Accordingly, kaizen budgeting is based not on the existing system but on changes yet to be made.

c. Budget targets, for example, **target costs**, cannot be reached unless those improvements occur.

7. A **static budget** is based on only one level of sales or production.

a. The level of production and the containment of costs are, though related, two separate managerial tasks.

1) EXAMPLE: A company has the following information for the period:

	Actual	Static Budget	Static Variance
Production in units	1,000	1,200	200 U
Direct materials (units × US $6)	US $ 6,000	US $ 7,200	US $1,200 F
Direct labor (units × US $10)	10,000	12,000	2,000 F
Variable overhead (units × US $5)	5,000	6,000	1,000 F
Total variable costs	US $21,000	US $25,200	US $4,200 F

From these results, it appears that, although the production manager failed to achieve his/her production quota, (s)he did a good job of cost control.

b. Contrast this with a **flexible budget**, which is a series of budgets prepared for many levels of activity.

1) At the end of the period, management can compare actual performance with the appropriate budgeted level in the flexible budget.

8. A **life-cycle budget** estimates a product's revenues and expenses over its entire life cycle beginning with research and development and ending with the withdrawal of customer support.
   a. Life-cycle budgeting is intended to account for the costs at all stages of the **value chain** (R&D, design, production, marketing, distribution, and customer service). This information is important for pricing decisions because revenues must cover costs incurred in each stage of the value chain, not just production.
   b. Life-cycle budgeting emphasizes the relationships among costs incurred at different value-chain stages, e.g., the effect of reduced design costs on future customer-service costs.
   c. Life-cycle budgeting also highlights the distinction between **incurring costs** (actually using resources) and **locking in (designing in) future costs.**
   d. Life-cycle concepts are also helpful in **target costing** and **target pricing**.
   e. See also Subunit 10.

Stop and review! You have completed the outline for this subunit. Study multiple-choice questions 8 through 11 beginning on page 301.

6.6 OPERATING BUDGET COMPONENTS

1. The **sales budget**, also called the revenue budget, is the **starting point** for the massive cycle that produces the annual profit plan (i.e., the master budget).
   a. The sales budget is an outgrowth of the **sales forecast**. The sales forecast distills recent sales trends, overall conditions in the economy and industry, market research, activities of competitors, and credit and pricing policies.
      1) For example,
         a) The company may determine that demand is highly elastic for its mature products and that growth will come only from new product introductions and from cost savings on existing products.
         b) At the same time, the company determines that a tight monetary policy on the Fed's part must cause the firm to tighten its credit standards.
         c) Simultaneously, a competitor that the firm knows is a low-cost producer is also considering moving into the markets that the budgeting company is considering.
      2) All of these factors must be taken into account when forming expectations about product sales for the coming budget cycle.
   b. The sales budget must specify both **projected unit sales and dollar revenues.**
   c. EXAMPLE of a sales budget. The demand for this firm's product is elastic, so the price cut in the third month is expected to boost sales.

	April	May	June	2nd Quarter Totals	Ref.
Projected sales in units	1,000	1,200	1,800	4,000	**SB1**
Selling price	× US $400	× US $400	× US $380		
Projected total sales	**US $400,000**	**US $480,000**	**US $684,000**	**US $1,564,000**	**SB2**

2. The **production budget** follows directly from the sales budget.
   a. The production budget is concerned with **units only**. Product pricing is not a consideration since the goal is purely to plan output and inventory levels and the necessary manufacturing activity.
   b. To minimize finished goods carrying costs and obsolescence, the levels of production are dependent upon the projections contained in the sales budget.

c. EXAMPLE of a production budget.

	Source	April	May	June	2nd Quarter Totals	Ref.
Projected sales in units	SB1	1,000	1,200	1,800	4,000	
Add: desired ending inventory (10% of next month's sales)		120	180	200		
Total needed		1,120	1,380	2,000	4,500	
Less: beginning inventory		(100)	(120)	(180)		
Units to be produced		**1,020**	**1,260**	**1,820**	**4,100**	**PB**

3. The **direct materials and direct labor budgets** follow directly from the production budget.

   a. The direct materials budget is concerned with both **units and input prices.**

      1) To minimize raw materials carrying costs and obsolescence, the purchasing of inputs is tied closely to the projections contained in the production budget.

      2) EXAMPLES of two direct materials budgets. Note that in the third month,

         a) The process is expected to experience improved efficiency with regard to Raw Material A.

         b) A price break on Raw Material B is expected.

Raw Material A	Source	April	May	June	2nd Quarter Totals	Ref.
Units to be produced	PB	1,020	1,260	1,820		
Raw material per finished product		× 4	× 4	× **3**		**DMB1**
Total units needed for production		4,080	5,040	5,460		
Raw material cost per unit		× US $12	× US $12	× **US $12**		**DMB2**
Cost of units used in production		US $48,960	US $60,480	US $65,520	**US $174,960**	**DMB3**
Add: desired units in ending inventory (20% of next month's need)		1,008	1,092	1,600		
Total needs		5,088	6,132	7,060		
Less: beginning inventory		(400)	(1,008)	(1,092)		
Raw material to be purchased		4,688	5,124	5,968		
Raw material cost per unit		× US $12	× US $12	× US $12		
Cost of raw material to be purchased		**US $56,256**	**US $61,488**	**US $71,616**		**DMB4**

Raw Material B	Source	April	May	June	2nd Quarter Totals	Ref.
Units to be produced	PB	1,020	1,260	1,820		
Raw material per finished product		× 2	× 2	× **2**		**DMB5**
Total units needed for production		2,040	2,520	3,640		
Raw material cost per unit		× US $10	× US $10	× **US $ 8**		**DMB6**
Cost of units used in production		US $20,400	US $25,200	US $29,120	**US $74,720**	**DMB7**
Add: desired units in ending inventory (20% of next month's need)		504	728	900		
Total needs		2,544	3,248	4,540		
Less: beginning inventory		(200)	(504)	(728)		
Raw material to be purchased		2,344	2,744	3,812		
Raw material cost per unit		× US $10	× US $10	× US $ 8		
Cost of raw material to be purchased		**US $23,440**	**US $27,440**	**US $30,496**		**DMB8**

b. The **direct labor budget** depends on wage rates, amounts and types of production, numbers and skill levels of employees to be hired, etc.

1) EXAMPLE of a direct labor budget. No new efficiencies are expected, and the wage rate is set by contract with the union.

	Source	April	May	June	2nd Quarter Totals	Ref.
Units to be produced	PB	1,020	1,260	1,820	4,100	
Direct labor hours per unit		× 2	× 2	× **2**		**DLB1**
Projected total direct labor hours		2,040	2,520	**3,640**	8,200	**DLB2**
Direct labor cost per hour		× US $18.641	× US $18.641	× US $18.641		
Total projected direct labor cost		**US $38,027**	**US $46,975**	**US $67,852**	**US $152,854**	**DLB3**

4. The **cost of fringe benefits** must be derived once the cost of wages has been determined.

a. EXAMPLE of an employee fringe benefit projection.

	Source	April	May	June	2nd Quarter Totals	Ref.
Projected direct labor wages	DLB3	US $38,027	US $46,975	US $67,852	US $152,854	
Employer FICA match (7.65%)		2,909	3,594	5,191	11,693	
Health insurance (12.1%)		4,601	5,684	8,210	18,495	
Life insurance (5%)		1,901	2,349	3,393	7,643	
Pension matching (4%)		1,521	1,879	2,714	6,114	
Total projected direct labor cost		**US $48,960**	**US $60,480**	**US $87,360**	**US $196,800**	**DLB4**

b. The **full per-hour cost of labor** can now be determined. This will be used in determining the costs embedded in units remaining in ending finished goods inventory.

1) Since a first-in, first-out (FIFO) assumption is used for all inventories, and only units produced in June are expected to remain at the end of June, the calculation is only necessary for June's data.

Total projected direct labor cost	÷	Total projected direct labor hours	=	Full direct labor cost per hour	Ref.
US $87,360	÷	3,640	=	**US $24**	**DLB5**

c. Whether employee fringes are included in direct labor costs or treated as overhead, the **effect on cost of goods sold is the same**. Both ways include the amounts in variable manufacturing costs.

5. The **manufacturing overhead budget** reflects the nature of overhead as a **mixed cost**, i.e., one that has a variable component and a fixed component (for a fuller discussion of mixed costs, see Subunit 2).

a. **Variable overhead** contains those elements that **vary** with the level of production.

1) Indirect materials
2) Some indirect labor
3) Variable factory operating costs (e.g., electricity)

b. EXAMPLE of a variable overhead budget. Note that variable overhead will be applied to finished goods on the basis of direct labor hours.

Variable overhead	Source	April	May	June	2nd Quarter Totals	Ref.
Projected total direct labor hours	DLB2	2,040	2,520	3,640	8,200	
Variable OH rate per direct labor hour		× US $2	× US $2	× US $2		**MOB1**
Projected variable overhead		**US $4,080**	**US $5,040**	**US $7,280**	**US $16,400**	**MOB2**

c. **Fixed overhead** contains those elements that remain **the same regardless** of the level of production.
   1) Real estate taxes
   2) Insurance
   3) Depreciation

d. EXAMPLE of a fixed overhead budget. Note that fixed overhead will be applied based on the number of units produced.

Fixed overhead	Source	April	May	June	2nd Quarter Totals	Ref.
Projected fixed overhead		**US $9,000**	**US $9,000**	**US $9,000**	**US $27,000**	**MOB3**
Divided by: projected output	SB1	1,000	1,200	1,800		
Equals: Fixed OH applied per unit		US $ 9.00	US $ 7.50	**US $ 5.00**		**MOB4**

6. The **ending finished goods inventory budget** can be prepared now that the components of finished goods cost have been projected.

   a. The end result will have a direct impact on the pro forma balance sheet. The higher the amount of costs capitalized in finished goods, the higher will be the firm's projected asset balance at year-end.

   b. EXAMPLE of a unit-cost calculation. Since a first-in, first-out (FIFO) assumption is used for all inventories, and only units produced in June are expected to remain at the end of June, this calculation uses June's data.

	Source	Qty.	Source	Input cost	Cost per finished unit
Production costs in ending inventory:					
Direct materials – raw material A	DMB1	3	DMB2	US $12.00	US $ 36.00
Direct materials – raw material B	DMB5	2	DMB6	8.00	16.00
Direct labor	DLB1	2	DLB5	24.00	48.00
Variable overhead	DLB1	2	MOB1	2.00	4.00
Fixed overhead	--	1	MOB4	5.00	5.00
Finished goods cost					US $109.00

   c. Now the total amount of cost embedded in ending inventory can be derived.

Total FIFO cost per finished unit	×	Projected units at June 30	=	Projected ending inventory	Ref.
US $109.00	×	200	=	**US $21,800**	**EFGIB**

7. The **cost of goods sold budget** combines the results of the projections for the three major inputs (materials, labor, overhead). The end result will have a direct impact on the pro forma income statement. Cost of goods sold is the single largest reduction to revenues for a manufacturer.

   a. EXAMPLE of a cost of goods sold budget for the quarter.

	Source			Ref.
Beginning finished goods inventory			US $ 16,200	
Manufacturing costs:				
Direct materials used – A	DMB3	US $174,960		
Direct materials used – B	DMB7	74,720		
Direct labor employed	DLB4	196,800		
Variable overhead	MOB2	16,400		
Fixed overhead	MOB3	27,000		
Cost of goods manufactured			489,880	
Cost of goods available for sale			US $506,080	
Ending finished goods inventory	EFGIB		(21,800)	
Cost of goods sold			**US $484,280**	**CGSB**

1) The schedule on the previous page was prepared using **absorption (full) costing**, i.e., it includes all manufacturing costs, both variable and fixed, in cost of goods sold. This will be used to arrive at **GAAP-based gross margin** on the pro forma income statement.

2) For internal reporting, **variable (direct) costing** is more useful than absorption costing. It includes only variable manufacturing costs in the calculation of cost of goods sold and is used to arrive at **contribution margin**.

a) While impermissible for GAAP-based reporting, contribution margin is more useful to management accountants for projecting profitability (for a fuller discussion of absorption and variable costing, see Subunit 3).

Sales		X,XXX
Beginning inventory	X,XXX	
Variable manufacturing costs	X,XXX	
Goods available for sale	X,XXX	
Less: ending inventory	(XXX)	
Variable cost of goods sold		(X,XXX)
Variable nonmanufacturing expenses		(XXX)
Contribution margin		X,XXX

b) Contribution margin **per unit** is useful in projecting the **breakeven point**, i.e., the level of production at which all variable costs have been covered and everything extra is available for "contributing" to the covering of fixed costs and providing a profit.

$$\frac{\text{Budgeted contribution margin}}{\text{Budgeted units to be produced}} = \text{Budget contribution margin per unit}$$

8. The **nonmanufacturing budget** consists of the individual budgets for **R&D, design, marketing, distribution, customer service,** and **administrative costs**.

a. The development of separate R&D, design, marketing, distribution, customer service, and administrative budgets reflects a **value chain** approach.

1) An alternative is to prepare a single **selling and administrative budget** for nonproduction costs.

b. The **variable and fixed portions** of selling and administrative costs must be treated **separately**.

1) Some S&A costs vary directly and proportionately with the level of sales. As more product is sold, sales representatives must travel more miles and serve more customers.

2) Other S&A expenses, such as sales support staff, are fixed; they must be paid no matter the level of sales.

3) As the variable portion of S&A costs increases, contribution margin, i.e., the amount available for covering fixed costs, is decreased.

c. EXAMPLE of a nonmanufacturing costs budget. Note the separate treatment of the variable and fixed portions.

	Source	April	May	June	2nd Quarter Totals	Ref.
Variable nonmanufacturing costs:						
Projected sales in units	SB1	1,000	1,200	1,800	4,000	
Variable S&A expenses (3 per unit sold)		× US $3	× US $3	× US $3		
Total variable nonmanufacturing costs		US $ 3,000	US $ 3,600	US $ 5,400	US $ 12,000	
Fixed nonmanufacturing costs:						
Research and development		US $ 8,000	US $ 8,000	US $ 8,000	US $ 24,000	
Design		4,000	4,000	4,000	12,000	
Marketing		7,000	7,000	7,000	21,000	
Distribution		10,000	10,000	10,000	30,000	
Customer service		11,000	11,000	11,000	33,000	
Administrative		50,000	50,000	50,000	150,000	
Total fixed nonmanufacturing costs		US $90,000	US $90,000	US $90,000	US $270,000	
Total nonmanufacturing costs		**US $93,000**	**US $93,600**	**US $95,400**	**US $282,000**	**NMB**

d. Note that management can make **tradeoffs** among elements of selling and administrative expenses that can **affect contribution margin.**

1) For example, use of fixed advertising expense will increase contribution margin, while the same sales level might be reached using variable sales commissions, a method that would reduce contribution margin.

9. The **pro forma income statement** is the **culmination** of the operating budget process.

a. **Pro forma** is a Latin phrase meaning literally "according to form." It can be loosely translated "as if." Financial statements are referred to as pro forma when they reflect projected, rather than actual, results.

b. The pro forma income statement is used to decide whether the budgeted activities will result in an acceptable level of income. If the initial pro forma income shows a loss or an unacceptable level of income, adjustments can be made to the component parts of the master budget.

	Source	
Sales	SB2	US $1,564,000
Cost of goods sold	CGSB	(484,280)
Gross margin		1,079,720
Nonmanufacturing costs	NMB	(282,000)
Operating income		**US $ 797,720**

Stop and review! You have completed the outline for this subunit. Study multiple-choice questions 12 and 13 beginning on page 303.

6.7 TRANSFER PRICING

Overview

1. **Transfer prices** are the amounts charged by **one segment** of an organization for goods and services it provides **to another segment** of the same organization. Transfer pricing is used by profit and investment centers (a cost center's costs are allocated to producing departments).
   a. **Upper management's challenge** is to set transfer pricing policy such that division managers achieve the company's overall goals by pursuing their own narrow divisional goals.
   b. Thus, transfer pricing should motivate managers by encouraging **goal congruence** and **managerial effort**.
      1) **Goal congruence** takes place when a manager's individual goals align with those of the organization.
      2) **Managerial effort** is the extent to which a manager attempts to accomplish a goal.
2. **Three basic methods** for determining transfer prices are in common use:
   a. **Cost plus pricing** sets price at the selling division's full cost of production plus a reasonable markup.
   b. **Market pricing** uses the price the selling division could obtain on the open market.
   c. **Negotiated pricing** gives the divisions the freedom to bargain between themselves and come to their own agreement regarding price.

Calculations

3. **EXAMPLE:** A conglomerate refines nitrogen and manufactures fertilizer. Upper management is considering the factors involved in setting transfer pricing policy. External markets exist for both products.
   a. The Fertilizer Division would like to pay only the Nitrogen Division's cost plus 10%. The Nitrogen Division wants to sell at the market price. When forced to compromise, management of the two divisions settled on a price in between.
   b. The Nitrogen Division's results under the three alternatives are calculated as follows:

Nitrogen Division	**Full Cost Plus 10%**	**Market Price**	**Negotiated Price**
Revenues:			
Revenue per cubic foot	US $ 3.30	US $ 4.00	US $ 3.65
Times: cubic feet	× 10,000	× 10,000	× 10,000
Total division revenue	**US $ 33,000**	**US $ 40,000**	**US $ 36,500**
Costs (for all three prices):			
Purchase cost per cubic foot	US $ 2.00		
Division variable costs	0.25		
Division fixed costs	0.75		
Per-cubic foot division costs	US $ 3.00		
Times: cubic feet	× 10,000		
Total division costs	**US $ 30,000**		
Operating income:			
Total division revenue	US $ 33,000	US $ 40,000	US $ 36,500
Total division costs	(30,000)	(30,000)	(30,000)
Division operating income	**US $ 3,000**	**US $ 10,000**	**US $ 6,500**

c. The Fertilizer Division's results under the three alternatives are calculated as follows:

Fertilizer Division	
Revenues:	
Revenue per pound	US $ 14.00
Times: pounds	× 5,000
Total division revenue	**US $ 70,000**
Costs:	
Division variable costs	US $ 4.00
Division fixed costs	0.50
Per-pound division costs	US $ 4.50
Times: pounds	× 5,000
Total division costs	**US $ 22,500**

	Full Cost Plus 10%	**Market Price**	**Negotiated Price**
Operating income:			
Total division revenue	US $ 70,000	US $ 70,000	US $ 70,000
Transferred-in costs	(33,000)	(40,000)	(36,500)
Total division costs	(22,500)	(22,500)	(22,500)
Division operating income	**US $ 14,500**	**US $ 7,500**	**US $ 11,000**

d. The divisions' motivation to set price differently is clear. However, as far as the firm as a whole is concerned, the following calculation shows that the choice between the three methods is irrelevant to the bottom line. Motivating division management is the paramount concern.

	Full Cost Plus 10%	**Market Price**	**Negotiated Price**
Nitrogen Division operating income	US $ 3,000	US $10,000	US $ 6,500
Fertilizer Division operating income	14,500	7,500	11,000
Combined operating incomes	**US $17,500**	**US $17,500**	**US $17,500**

Applicability

4. **Factors Involved in Setting Transfer Pricing Policy**

a. The **minimum price** that a selling division is willing to accept is calculated as follows:

$$\text{Minimum transfer price} = \text{Incremental cost so far} + \text{Opportunity cost of selling internally}$$

The opportunity cost of selling internally varies depending on two factors: the existence of an external market for the product and whether the selling division has excess capacity.

b. **An external market exists and the selling division has no excess capacity**

1) The opportunity cost to sell internally is the contribution margin the division would have received selling on the external market.

2) The selling division can sell everything it produces on the open market, so this margin must be included in the transfer price to make selling internally worthwhile.

c. **An external market exists and the selling division has excess capacity**

1) Both divisions will find acceptable any price between the floor of the incremental cost so far and a ceiling of the market price.

2) The selling division cannot demand the full contribution margin because the open market may not absorb everything if it ramps up to full production.

d. **No external market exists**

1) The selling division cannot demand anything above its incremental cost so far.

5. **Multinational Considerations**

   a. When divisions are located in different countries, taxes and tariffs may override any other considerations when setting transfer prices.

   b. EXAMPLE: The Nitrogen Division is located in Canada, which imposes a combined tax and tariff burden of 45%, while the Fertilizer Division located in the U.S. is only subject to a 20% income tax.

	Full Cost Plus 10%	Market Price	Negotiated Price
Nitrogen Division operating income	US $ 3,000	US $10,000	US $ 6,500
Fertilizer Division operating income	14,500	7,500	11,000
Combined operating incomes	**US $17,500**	**US $17,500**	**US $17,500**
Canadian taxes and tariffs (45%)	US $ 1,350	US $ 4,500	US $ 2,925
U.S. income tax (20%)	2,900	1,500	2,200
Combined tax liability	**US $ 4,250**	**US $ 6,000**	**US $ 5,125**

   If tax minimization is the firm's overall goal, upper management is no longer unconcerned about which transfer pricing policy to select.

   c. Exchange rate fluctuations, threats of expropriation, and limits on transfers of profits outside the host country are additional concerns.

      1) Thus, because the best transfer price may be a low one because of the existence of tariffs or a high one because of the existence of foreign exchange controls, the effect may be to skew the performance statistics of management.

      2) The high transfer price may result in foreign management appearing to show a lower return on investment than domestic management, but the ratio differences may be negated by the fact that a different transfer pricing formula is used.

Stop and review! You have completed the outline for this subunit. Study multiple-choice questions 14 and 15 on page 304.

6.8 COST-VOLUME-PROFIT (CVP) ANALYSIS

__Overview__

1. **Cost-volume-profit (CVP) analysis** (also called breakeven analysis) is a tool for understanding the interaction of revenues with fixed and variable costs. It illuminates how changes in assumptions about cost behavior and the relevant ranges in which those assumptions are valid may affect the relationships among revenues, variable costs, and fixed costs at various production levels. Thus, CVP analysis allows management to discern the probable effects of changes in sales volume, sales price, product mix, etc.

2. The inherent simplifying **assumptions** of CVP analysis are the following:

   a. Cost and revenue relationships are predictable and linear. These relationships are true over the **relevant range** of activity and specified time span. For example, reductions in prices are not necessary to increase revenues, and no learning curve effect operates to reduce unit variable labor costs at higher output levels.

   b. Total **variable costs** change proportionally with volume, but unit variable costs are constant over the relevant range. Raw materials and direct labor are typically variable costs.

   c. Changes in inventory are insignificant in amount.

d. **Fixed costs** remain constant over the relevant range of volume, but unit fixed costs vary indirectly with volume. The classification of fixed versus variable can be affected by the time frame being considered.
e. Unit selling prices and market conditions are constant.
f. Production equals sales.
g. The **revenue (sales) mix** is constant, or the firm makes and sells only one product.
h. All costs are either fixed or variable relative to a given cost object for a given time span. The longer the time span, the more likely the cost is variable.
i. Technology and productive efficiency are constant.
j. Revenues and costs vary only with changes in physical unit volume. Hence, volume is the sole revenue driver and cost driver.
k. The breakeven point is directly related to costs and inversely related to the budgeted margin of safety and the contribution margin.
l. The time value of money is ignored.

3. The assumptions under which CVP analysis operates primarily hinge on **certainty**. However, many decisions must be made even though uncertainty exists. Assigning probabilities to the various outcomes and sensitivity ("what-if") analysis are important approaches to dealing with uncertainty.

4. **Definitions**

a. The **breakeven point** is the level of output at which total revenues equal total expenses, that is, the point at which operating income is zero.
b. The **margin of safety** is a measure of risk. It is the excess of budgeted revenues over breakeven revenues (or budgeted units over breakeven units).
c. **Mixed costs (or semivariable costs)** are costs with both fixed and variable elements.
d. The **revenue (sales) mix** is the composition of total revenues in terms of various products, i.e., the percentages of each product included in total revenues. It is maintained for all volume changes.
e. **Sensitivity analysis** examines the effect on the outcome of not achieving the original forecast or of changing an assumption.
f. **Unit contribution margin (UCM)** is the unit selling price minus the unit variable cost. It is the contribution from the sale of one unit to cover fixed costs (and possibly a targeted profit).
   1) It is expressed as either a percentage of the selling price **(contribution margin ratio)** or a dollar amount.
   2) The UCM is the slope of the total cost curve plotted so that volume is on the x-axis and dollar value is on the y-axis.

<u>Calculations</u>

5. The general formula for operating income can be stated as follows:

```
Operating income = Sales - Variable costs - Fixed costs
```

a. The **breakeven point** can be determined by setting **operating income equal to zero** and solving the equation.

b. EXAMPLE: A product is sold for US $.60 per unit, with variable costs of US $.20 per unit and fixed costs of US $10,000. What is the breakeven point?

Operating income = Sales – Variable costs – Fixed costs
US $0 = ($.60 × Q) – ($.20 × Q) – US $10,000
US $.40 × Q = US $10,000
Q = 25,000 units

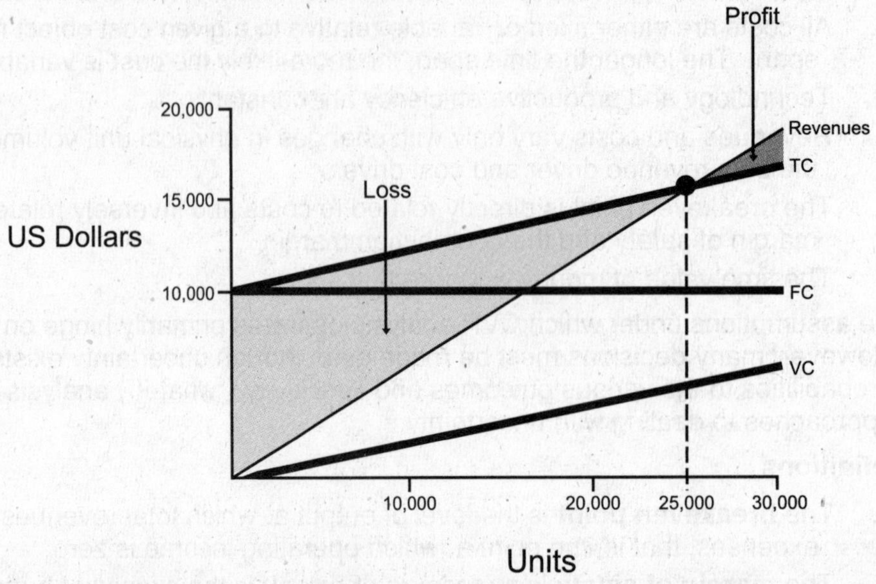

c. A simpler calculation is to divide fixed costs by the unit contribution margin (the unit contribution to coverage of fixed costs).

$$\textit{Breakeven point in units} = \frac{\textit{Fixed costs}}{\textit{UCM}}$$

1) The UCM is US $.40 (US $.60 sales price – US $.20 variable cost). Thus, to cover US $10,000 of fixed costs, 25,000 units (US $10,000 ÷ US $.40 UCM) must be sold to break even.

d. The breakeven point in dollars can be calculated by dividing fixed costs by the contribution margin ratio {[US $10,000 ÷ ($.40 ÷ $.60)] = US $15,000}.

6. The **contribution income statement with per unit amounts** is an integral part of breakeven analysis.

a. EXAMPLE:

	In Total	Per Unit	Percent
Sales (40,000 units)	US $ 24,000	US $ 0.60	100%
Less: variable costs	(8,000)	(0.20)	(33%)
Contribution margin	US $ 16,000	US $ 0.40	67%
Less: fixed costs	(10,000)		
Operating income	US $ 6,000		

b. Every unit sold **contributes** a certain percentage of its sales revenue to **covering fixed costs**, in this case 67%. Management can conclude that every unit sold in the relevant range will contribute US $.40 to covering fixed costs.

c. Once fixed costs are fully covered, all additional revenue becomes **profit**.

Stop and review! You have completed the outline for this subunit. Study multiple-choice questions 16 through 19 beginning on page 305.

6.9 RELEVANT COSTS

Overview

1. The typical problem for which **marginal (differential or incremental) analysis** can be used involves choices among courses of action.
   a. **Quantitative analysis** emphasizes the ways in which revenues and costs vary with the option chosen. Thus, the focus is on **incremental revenues and costs**, not the totals of all revenues and costs for the given option.
   b. EXAMPLE: A firm produces a product for which it incurs the following unit costs:

Direct materials	US $2.00
Direct labor	3.00
Variable overhead	.50
Fixed overhead	.50
Total cost	US $6.00

      1) The product normally sells for US $10 per unit. An application of marginal analysis is necessary if a foreign buyer, who has never before been a customer, offers to pay US $5.60 per unit for a **special order** of the firm's product.
         a) The immediate reaction might be to refuse the offer because the selling price is less than the average cost of production.
      2) However, **marginal analysis** results in a different decision. Assuming that the firm has idle capacity, only the additional costs should be considered.
         a) In this example, the only marginal costs are for direct materials, direct labor, and variable overhead. No additional fixed overhead costs would be incurred.
         b) Because **marginal revenue** (the US $5.60 selling price) **exceeds marginal costs** (US $2 materials + $3 labor + $.50 variable OH = US $5.50 per unit), accepting the special order will be profitable.
      3) **If a competitor bids** US $5.80 per unit, the firm can still profitably accept the special order while underbidding the competitor by setting a price below US $5.80 per unit but above US $5.50 per unit.
2. Caution always must be used in applying marginal analysis because of the many qualitative factors involved.
   a. **Qualitative factors** include
      1) Special price concessions place the firm in violation of the **price discrimination** provisions of the Robinson-Patman Act of 1936.
      2) Government contract pricing regulations apply.
      3) Sales to a special customer affect sales in the firm's regular market.
      4) Regular customers learn of a special price and demand equal terms.
      5) Disinvestment, such as by dropping a product line, will hurt sales in the other product lines (e.g., the dropped product may have been an unintended loss leader).
      6) An outsourced product's quality is acceptable and the supplier is reliable.
      7) Employee morale may be affected. If employees are laid off or asked to work too few or too many hours, morale may be affected favorably or unfavorably.

Applicability

3. **Make-or-Buy Decisions** (Insourcing vs. Outsourcing)
   a. The firm should use **available resources** as efficiently as possible before outsourcing. Often, an array of products can be produced efficiently if production capacity is available.
      1) If not enough capacity is available to produce all products, those that are produced **least efficiently should be outsourced** (or capacity should be expanded).
      2) Support services, such as computer processing, legal work, accounting, and training, may also be outsourced.
      3) Moreover, both products and services may be outsourced internationally. Thus, computer programming, information processing, customer service via telephone, etc., as well as manufacturing tasks, may be not only outsourced but outsourced offshore.
   b. In a **make-or-buy** decision, the manager considers only the costs relevant to the investment decision. If the total relevant costs of production are less than the cost to buy the item, it should be insourced.
      1) The **key variable** is **total relevant costs**, not all total costs.
      2) **Sunk costs are irrelevant.** Hence, a production plant's cost of repairs last year is irrelevant to this year's make-or-buy decision. The carrying amount of old equipment is another example.
      3) **Costs that do not differ** between two alternatives should be **ignored** because they are not relevant to the decision being made.
      4) **Opportunity costs** must be considered when **idle capacity** is not available. They are of primary importance because they represent the forgone opportunities of the firm.
   c. EXAMPLE: Should a company make or buy an item?

	Make	Buy
Total variable cost	US $10	
Allocation of fixed cost	5	
Total unit costs	US $15	US $13

      1) If the plant has excess capacity, the decision should be to produce the item. Total variable cost (US $10) is less than the purchase price.
         a) However, if the plant is running at capacity, the opportunity cost of displaced production becomes a relevant cost that might alter the decision in favor of purchasing the item from a supplier.
      2) The firm also should consider the qualitative aspects of the decision. For example, will product quality be as high if a component is outsourced than if produced internally? Also, how reliable are the suppliers?

4. **Capacity Constraints and Product Mix**
   a. Marginal analysis also applies to decisions about which products and services to sell and in what quantities given the known demand and resource limitations.
      1) For example, if the firm can sell as much as it can produce and has a single resource constraint, the decision rule is to **maximize the contribution margin per unit** of the constrained resource.
         a) However, given multiple constraints, the decision is more difficult. In that case, sophisticated techniques such as **linear programming** must be used.

5. **Disinvestment** decisions are the opposite of capital budgeting decisions, i.e., to terminate an operation, product or product line, business segment, branch, or major customer rather than start one.
   a. In general, if the **marginal cost** of a project **exceeds the marginal revenue**, the firm should disinvest.
   b. **Four steps** should be taken in making a disinvestment decision:
      1) **Identify fixed costs** that will be eliminated by the disinvestment decision, e.g., insurance on equipment used.
      2) Determine the **revenue needed to justify continuing operations**. In the short run, this amount should at least equal the variable cost of production or continued service.
      3) Establish the **opportunity cost of funds** that will be received upon disinvestment (e.g., salvage value).
      4) Determine whether the **carrying amount of the assets** is equal to their economic value. If not, reevaluate the decision using current fair value rather than the carrying amount.
   c. When a firm disinvests, excess capacity exists unless another project uses this capacity immediately. The **cost of idle capacity** should be treated as a **relevant** cost.
6. **Sell-or-Process Decisions**
   a. In determining whether to sell a product at the split-off point or process the item further at additional cost, the **joint cost** of the product is **irrelevant** because it is a sunk cost.
   b. The sell-or-process decision should be based on the relationship between the **incremental costs** (the cost of additional processing) and the **incremental revenues** (the benefits received).

Stop and review! You have completed the outline for this subunit. Study multiple-choice questions 20 through 23 beginning on page 307.

6.10 COST ACCUMULATION SYSTEMS

Actual, Normal, and Standard Costing

1. **Actual costing** is the most accurate method of accumulating costs. However, it is also the least timely and most volatile method.
   a. After the end of the production period, all actual costs incurred for a cost object are totaled; indirect costs are allocated.
   b. Because per-unit costs depend on the level of production in a period, large fluctuations arise from period to period. This volatility can lead to the reporting of misleading financial information.
2. **Normal costing** charges actual direct materials and direct labor to a cost object but applies overhead on the basis of budgeted (normalized) rates. This compensates for the fluctuations in unit cost inherent in actual costing.
   a. **Extended normal costing** extends the use of normalized rates to direct materials and direct labor, so that all three major input categories use normalized rates.
3. **Standard costing** is a system designed to alert management when the actual costs of production differ significantly from target ("standard") costs.
   a. Standard costs are predetermined, attainable unit costs. A standard cost is not just an average of past costs, but an objectively determined estimate of what a cost should be.
   b. Standard costs can be used with both job-order and process-costing systems.

Six Principal Accumulation Systems

4. **Job-order costing** is appropriate when producing products with individual characteristics or when identifiable groupings are possible.
   a. Costs are attached to specific "jobs." Each job will result in a single, identifiable end product.
   b. Examples are any industry that generates custom-built products, such as shipbuilding.
5. **Process costing** is used when similar products are mass produced on a continuous basis.
   a. Costs are attached to specific departments or phases of production. Examples are automobile and candy manufacturing.
   b. Since costs are attached to streams of products rather than individuals, process costing involves calculating an average cost for all units. The two widely used methods are weighted-average and first-in, first-out (FIFO).
   c. Some units remain unfinished at the end of the period. For each department to adequately account for the costs attached to its unfinished units, the units must be restated in terms of equivalent units of production (EUP).

   For a fuller explanation, see Subunit 6.11.
6. **Activity-based costing (ABC)** attaches costs to activities rather than to physical goods.
   a. ABC is a response to the distortions of product cost information brought about by peanut-butter costing, which is the inaccurate averaging or spreading of costs like peanut butter over products or service units that use different amounts of resources.
      1) A major cause of peanut-butter costing is the significant increase in indirect costs brought about by the increasing use of technology.
   b. The difference between traditional (that is, volume-based) costing systems and ABC can be summarized as follows:
      1) Under volume-based systems, a single pool collects all indirect costs and the total cost in the pool is then allocated to production.
      2) Under ABC, by contrast, every activity that bears on the production process has its own cost pool. The costs in each pool are assigned based on a cost driver specific to the activity.
7. **Life-cycle costing** emphasizes the need to price products to cover all the costs incurred over the lifespan of a product, not just the costs of production.
   a. Costs incurred before production, such as R&D and product design, are referred to as upstream costs.
   b. Costs incurred after production, such as marketing and customer service, are called downstream costs.
8. **Operation costing** is a hybrid of job-order and process costing and is used by companies whose manufacturing processes involve some similar and some dissimilar operations.
   a. Direct materials costs are charged to specific products (as in job-order systems).
   b. Conversion costs are accumulated and a unit conversion cost for each operation is derived (as in process costing).
9. **Backflush costing** delays the assignment of costs until the goods are finished.
   a. After production is finished for the period, standard costs are flushed backward through the system to assign costs to products. The result is that detailed tracking of costs is eliminated.
   b. Backflush costing is best suited to companies that maintain low inventories because costs can flow directly to cost of goods sold. It is often used with just-in-time (JIT) inventory, one of the goals of which is the maintenance of low inventory levels.

Stop and review! You have completed the outline for this subunit. Study multiple-choice questions 24 and 25 on page 309.

6.11 PROCESS COSTING

Overview

1. Process cost accounting is used to assign costs to inventoriable goods or services. It is applicable to **relatively homogeneous products** that are mass produced on a continuous basis (e.g., petroleum products, thread, computer monitors).
   a. Where job-order costing uses subsidiary ledgers to keep track of specific jobs, process costing typically has a **work-in-process account for each department** through which the production of output passes.
   b. Process costing is an averaging process that calculates the average cost of all units:
      1) Costs are accumulated for a cost object that consists of a large number of similar units of goods or services;
      2) Work-in-process is stated in terms of equivalent units;
      3) Unit costs are established.

Journal Entries

2. The accumulation of costs under a process costing system is **by department rather than by project**. This reflects the continuous, homogeneous nature of the manufacturing process.
   a. As in job-order costing, the physical inputs required for the production process are obtained from suppliers.

Raw materials	XXX	
Accounts payable		XXX

   b. **Direct materials** are used by the first department in the process.

Work-in-process -- Department A	XXX	
Raw materials		XXX

   c. **Conversion costs** are the sum of direct labor and manufacturing overhead. The nature of process costing makes this accounting treatment more efficient (the implications of this for the calculation of unit quantities are covered in item 4. on page 287).

Work-in-process -- Department A	XXX	
Wages payable (direct and indirect labor)		XXX
Manufacturing supplies (indirect materials)		XXX
Property taxes payable		XXX
Prepaid insurance		XXX
Accumulated depreciation -- factory equipment		XXX

   d. The products **move from one department** to the next.

Work-in-process -- Department B	XXX	
Work-in-process -- Department A		XXX

   e. The **second department adds** more direct materials and more conversion costs.

Work-in-process -- Department B	XXX	
Raw materials		XXX

Work-in-process -- Department B	XXX	
Wages payable (direct and indirect labor)		XXX
Manufacturing supplies (indirect materials)		XXX
Property taxes payable		XXX
Prepaid insurance		XXX
Accumulated depreciation -- factory equipment		XXX

f. Because manufacturing overhead is assigned to work-in-process as part of conversion costs, there is **rarely an overhead control or overhead applied account** under process costing, and the issue of over- or underapplied overhead does not arise.

   1) The exception is when a standard costing system is used. Under standard costing, a predetermined overhead rate (as in job-order costing) is used to assign overhead costs.

g. When processing is finished in the last department, all the costs are transferred to **finished goods.**

Finished goods	X,XXX	
Work-in-process -- Department B		X,XXX

h. As **products are sold**, the costs are transferred to cost of goods sold.

Cost of goods sold	X,XXX	
Finished goods		X,XXX

3. The following diagram depicts the **flow of cost accumulation** in a process costing system:

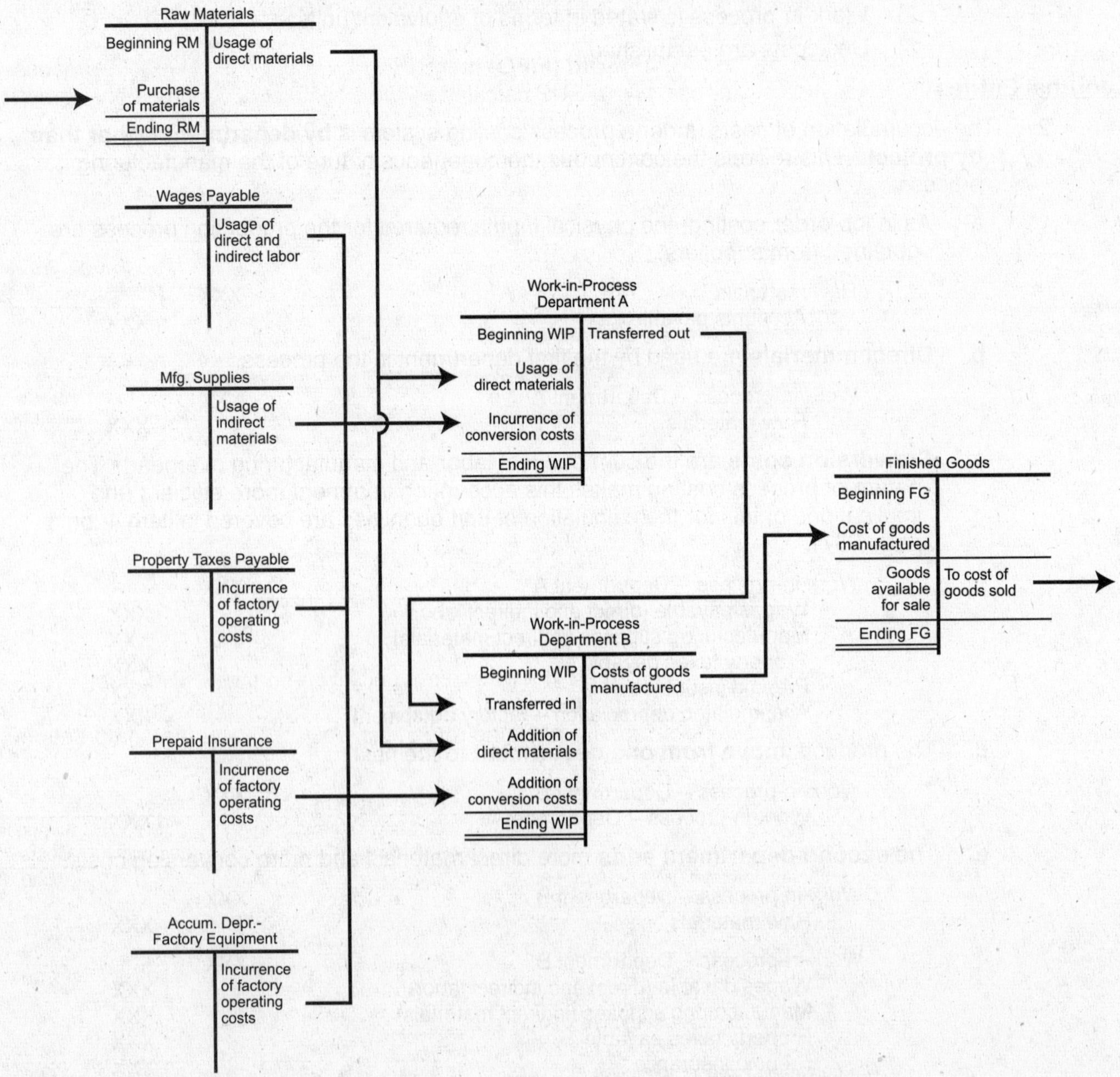

Equivalent Units of Production

4. Some units remain unfinished at the end of the period. For each department to account adequately for the costs attached to its unfinished units, the units must be restated in terms of equivalent units of production.

   a. **Equivalent units of production (EUP)** is the number of complete goods that could have been produced using the inputs consumed during the period.

      1) The EUP conversion is a two-phase process: First, the **equivalent units** are determined, then the **per-unit cost** is calculated.

      2) The two calculations are made separately for direct materials and conversion costs (transferred-in costs are by definition 100% complete). Conversion costs are assumed to be uniformly incurred.

   b. Two methods of calculating EUP are in common use: weighted-average and FIFO.

      1) Under the **weighted-average method**, units in beginning work-in-process inventory are treated as if they were started and completed during the current period. Beginning work-in-process is therefore not separately accounted for in the EUP calculation.

      2) Under the **first-in, first-out (FIFO) method**, units in beginning work-in-process inventory are part of the EUP calculation. The calculation is thus more complex than weighted-average but tends to be more accurate.

   c. EXAMPLE: A department of a manufacturing concern is preparing its cost reports for the month.

      1) The first step is to prepare a quantity schedule:

	Units	Completed for Direct Materials	Completed for Conversion Costs
Beginning work-in-process	2,000	80%	40%
Units started during period	8,000		
Units to account for	10,000		
Units transferred to next department	9,000		
Ending work-in-process	1,000	90%	70%
Units accounted for	10,000		

      2) The costs to be allocated are presented in this table:

	Direct Materials	Conversion Costs
Beginning work-in-process	US $25,000	US $10,000
Added during the month	55,000	50,000

      3) The next step is to calculate the equivalent units of production. This table illustrates the different outcomes of applying the two methods. Note that beginning work-in-process plays no role in the weighted-average computation but is backed out under FIFO.

	Weighted-Average		FIFO	
	Direct Materials	Conversion Costs	Direct Materials	Conversion Costs
Units transferred to next department	9,000	9,000	9,000	9,000
Add: ending work-in-process EUP				
Direct materials: 1,000 units × 90%	900		900	
Conversion costs: 1,000 units × 70%		700		700
Total completed units			9,900	9,700
Less: beginning work-in-process EUP				
Direct materials: 2,000 units × 80%			(1,600)	
Conversion costs: 2,000 units × 40%				(800)
Equivalent units of production	9,900	9,700	8,300	8,900

4) Once the equivalent units have been calculated, the per-unit costs under each of the two methods can be derived.

a) Under the **weighted-average** method, **all direct materials and conversion costs** are averaged in, both those incurred in the current period and those in beginning work-in-process.

Direct materials:	$\frac{\text{US \$25,000 + \$55,000}}{\text{9,900 EUP}}$	=	US $ 8.08
Conversion costs:	$\frac{\text{US \$10,000 + \$50,000}}{\text{9,700 EUP}}$	=	6.19
Total unit cost under weighted-average			US $14.27

b) Under the **FIFO** method, **only the costs incurred in the current period** are included in the calculation, because only the work performed in the current period is included in EUP.

Direct materials:	$\frac{\text{US \$55,000}}{\text{8,300 EUP}}$	=	US $ 6.63
Conversion costs:	$\frac{\text{US \$50,000}}{\text{8,900 EUP}}$	=	5.62
Total unit cost under first-in, first-out			US $12.24

Spoilage in Process Costing

5. As with job-order costing, the cost of a **normal** level of spoilage is left in cost of goods sold; **abnormal** spoilage is recognized separately as a loss.

a. Recognizing the loss resulting from abnormal spoilage under process costing is a multi-step process.

1) The manufacturer establishes **inspection points**, that is, the places in the production process where those goods not meeting specifications are pulled from the process. This is in contrast to job-order costing, in which a unit can be judged to be spoiled at any time.

a) The typical arrangement is to inspect units as they are being transferred from one department to the next. This way, **each department** has its own amount of spoilage, calculated using its own equivalent-unit costs.

2) The loss is equal to the number of units of abnormal spoilage multiplied by the department's equivalent-units costs, whether weighted-average or FIFO.

Loss on abnormal spoilage	XXX	
Work-in-process -- Department A		XXX

3) The following calculations serve as a check that all costs have been accounted for.

Weighted-Average

Costs in beginning WIP:				
Direct materials	XX,XXX			
Conversion costs	XX,XXX			
Total costs in beginning WIP		XX,XXX		
Costs added in current period:			Cost of good units transferred out	XXX,XXX
Direct materials	XX,XXX		Normal spoilage	XX,XXX
Conversion costs	XX,XXX		Abnormal spoilage	XX,XXX
Total costs added in current period		XX,XXX	Ending WIP	XX,XXX
Total costs to account for		XXX,XXX	Total costs accounted for	XXX,XXX

FIFO

Costs in beginning WIP		XX,XXX	Total from beginning WIP	XX,XXX
Costs added in current period:			Started and completed	XX,XXX
Direct materials	XX,XXX		Normal spoilage	XX,XXX
Conversion costs	XX,XXX		Abnormal spoilage	XX,XXX
Total costs added in current period		XX,XXX	Ending WIP	XX,XXX
Total costs to account for		XXX,XXX	Total costs accounted for	XXX,XXX

Stop and review! You have completed the outline for this subunit. Study multiple-choice questions 26 and 27 on page 310.

6.12 ACTIVITY-BASED COSTING

Overview

1. **Activity-based costing (ABC)** is a response to the significant increase in the incurrence of indirect costs resulting from the rapid advance of technology.
   a. ABC is a **refinement of an existing costing system** (job-order or process)
      1) Under a traditional (volume-based) costing system, overhead is simply dumped into a single cost pool and spread evenly across all end products.
      2) Under ABC, indirect costs are attached to activities that are then rationally allocated to end products.
   b. ABC may be used by manufacturing, service, or retailing entities.

Problems of Volume-Based Costing

2. The inaccurate averaging or spreading of indirect costs over products or service units that use different amounts of resources is called **peanut-butter costing**.
   a. Peanut-butter costing results in **product-cost cross-subsidization**, the condition in which the miscosting of one product causes the miscosting of other products.
   b. The peanut-butter effect of using a **traditional (i.e., volume-based) costing system** can be summarized as follows:
      1) Direct labor and direct materials are traced to products or service units.
      2) A single pool of indirect costs (overhead) is accumulated for a given organizational unit.
      3) Indirect costs from the pool are assigned using an allocative (rather than a tracing) procedure, such as using a single overhead rate for an entire department, e.g., US $3 of overhead for every direct labor hour.
         a) The effect is an averaging of costs that may result in significant inaccuracy when products or service units do not use similar amounts of resources.

3. EXAMPLE: The effect of product-cost cross-subsidization can be illustrated as follows:

   a. A company produces two similar products.

      1) Both products require one unit of raw material and one hour of direct labor. Raw materials costs are US $14 per unit, and direct labor is US $70 per hour.

   b. During the month just ended, the company produced 1,000 units of Product A and 100 units of Product B. Manufacturing overhead for the month totaled US $20,000.

   c. Using direct labor hours as the overhead allocation base, per-unit costs and profits are calculated as follows:

	Product A	Product B	Total
Raw materials	US $ 14,000	US $ 1,400	
Direct labor	70,000	7,000	
Overhead {US $20,000 × [$70,000 ÷ ($70,000 + $7,000)]}	18,182		
Overhead {US $20,000 × [$7,000 ÷ ($70,000 + $7,000)]}		1,818	
Total costs	**US $102,182**	**US $ 10,218**	**US $112,400**
Selling price	US $ 119.99	US $ 119.99	
Cost per unit	(102.18)	(102.18)	
Profit per unit	**US $ 17.81**	**US $ 17.81**	

   d. The company's management accountants have determined that overhead consists almost entirely of production line setup costs, and that the two products require equal setup times. Allocating overhead on this basis yields vastly different results.

	Product A	Product B	Total
Raw materials	US $14,000	US $ 1,400	
Direct labor	70,000	7,000	
Overhead (US $20,000 × 50%)	10,000		
Overhead (US $20,000 × 50%)		10,000	
Total costs	**US $94,000**	**US $18,400**	**US $112,400**
Selling price	US $119.99	US $119.99	
Cost per unit	(94.00)	(184.00)	
Profit per unit	**US $ 25.99**	**US $ (64.01)**	

   e. Rather than the comfortable profit the company believed it was making on both products using peanut-butter costing, it becomes clear that the company is losing money on every unit of Product B that it sells. The high-volume Product A has been heavily subsidizing the setup costs for the low-volume Product B.

4. The previous example assumed a single component of overhead for clarity. In reality, overhead is made up of many components.

   a. The **peanut-butter effect** of traditional overhead allocation is illustrated in the following diagram. US dollars are used here, but any currency can be substituted.

Overhead Allocation in a Traditional (Volume-Based) Cost Accumulation System

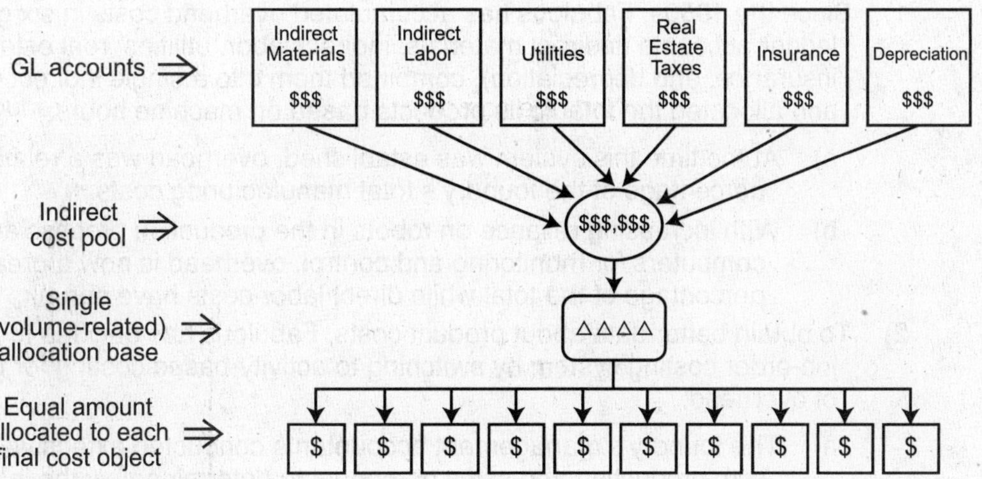

Volume-Based vs. Activity-Based

5. Volume-based systems were appropriate throughout the decades when direct costs were the bulk of manufacturing costs. With **increasing automation**, however, overhead became an ever greater percentage of the total. ABC was developed to deal with this increasing complexity of overhead costs.
   a. **Volume-based systems**, as illustrated above, involve
      1) Accumulating costs in **general ledger accounts** (utilities, taxes, etc.).
      2) Using a **single cost pool** to combine the costs in all the related accounts.
      3) Selecting a **single driver** to use for the entire indirect cost pool.
      4) Allocating the indirect cost pool to **final cost objects**.
   b. **Activity-based systems**, by contrast, involve
      1) Identifying organization **activities** that constitute overhead.
      2) Assigning the costs of **resources** consumed by the activities.
      3) Assigning the costs of the activities to **final cost objects**.

ABC Process

6. **Step 1 – Activity Analysis**
   a. An **activity** is a set of work actions undertaken within the entity, and a **cost pool** is established for each activity.
   b. Activities are classified in a **hierarchy** according to the level of the production process at which they take place.
      1) **Unit-level activities** are performed for each unit of output produced. Examples are using direct materials and using direct labor.
      2) **Batch-level activities** occur for each group of outputs produced. Examples are materials ordering, materials handling, and production line setup.
      3) **Product-sustaining** (or service-sustaining) **activities** support the production of a particular product (or service), irrespective of the level of production. Examples are product design, engineering changes, and testing.
      4) **Facility-sustaining activities** concern overall operations and therefore cannot be traced to products at any point in the production process. Examples are accounting, human resources, maintenance of physical plant, and safety/security arrangements.

c. EXAMPLE: Fabulous Foundry uses a job-order system to accumulate costs for the custom pipe fittings of all sizes that it produces.

1) Since the 1950s, Fabulous has accumulated overhead costs in six general ledger accounts (indirect materials, indirect labor, utilities, real estate taxes, insurance, and depreciation), combined them into a single indirect cost pool, and allocated the total to its products based on machine hours.

a) At the time this system was established, overhead was a relatively small percentage of the foundry's total manufacturing costs.

b) With increasing reliance on robots in the production process and computers for monitoring and control, overhead is now a greater percentage of the total while direct labor costs have shrunk.

2) To obtain better data about product costs, Fabulous has decided to refine its job-order costing system by switching to activity-based costing for the allocation of overhead.

a) The foundry's management accountants conducted extensive interviews with production and sales personnel to determine how the incurrence of indirect costs can be viewed as activities that consume resources.

b) The accountants identified five activities and created a cost pool for each to capture the incurrence of indirect costs:

Activity	Hierarchy
Product design	Product-sustaining
Production setup	Batch-level
Machining	Unit-level
Inspection & testing	Unit-level
Customer maintenance	Facility-sustaining

7. **Step 2 – Assign Resource Costs to Activities**

a. Once the activities are designated, the next step in enacting an ABC system is to **assign the costs of resources** to the activities. This is termed **first-stage allocation**.

b. **Identifying resource costs** is not the simple matter it is in volume-based overhead allocation (where certain GL accounts are designated for combination into a single cost pool).

1) A **separate accounting system** may be necessary to track resource costs separately from the general ledger.

c. Once the resources have been identified, resource drivers are designated to allocate resource costs to the activity cost pools.

1) **Resource drivers** are measures of the resources consumed by an activity.

d. EXAMPLE: Fabulous Foundry's management accountants identified the following resources used by its indirect cost processes:

Resource	Driver
Computer processing	CPU cycles
Production line	Machine hours
Materials management	Hours worked
Accounting	Hours worked
Sales & marketing	Number of orders

8. **Step 3 – Allocate Activity Cost Pools to Final Cost Objects**
   a. The final step in enacting an ABC system is **allocating the activity cost pools** to final cost objects. This is termed **second-stage allocation**.
   b. Costs are reassigned to final-stage (or, if intermediate cost objects are used, next-stage) cost objects on the basis of activity drivers.
      1) **Activity drivers** are measures of the demands made on an activity by next-stage cost objects, such as the number of parts in a product used to measure an assembly activity.
      2) EXAMPLE: Fabulous Foundry's management accountants have designated these drivers to associate with their corresponding activities:

Activity	Driver
Product design	Number of products
Production setup	Number of setups
Machining	Number of units produced
Inspection & testing	Number of units produced
Customer maintenance	Number of orders

9. The differences between traditional overhead allocation and activity-based costing are illustrated in the following diagram. US dollars are used here, but any currency can be substituted.

Indirect Cost Assignment in an Activity-Based Costing System

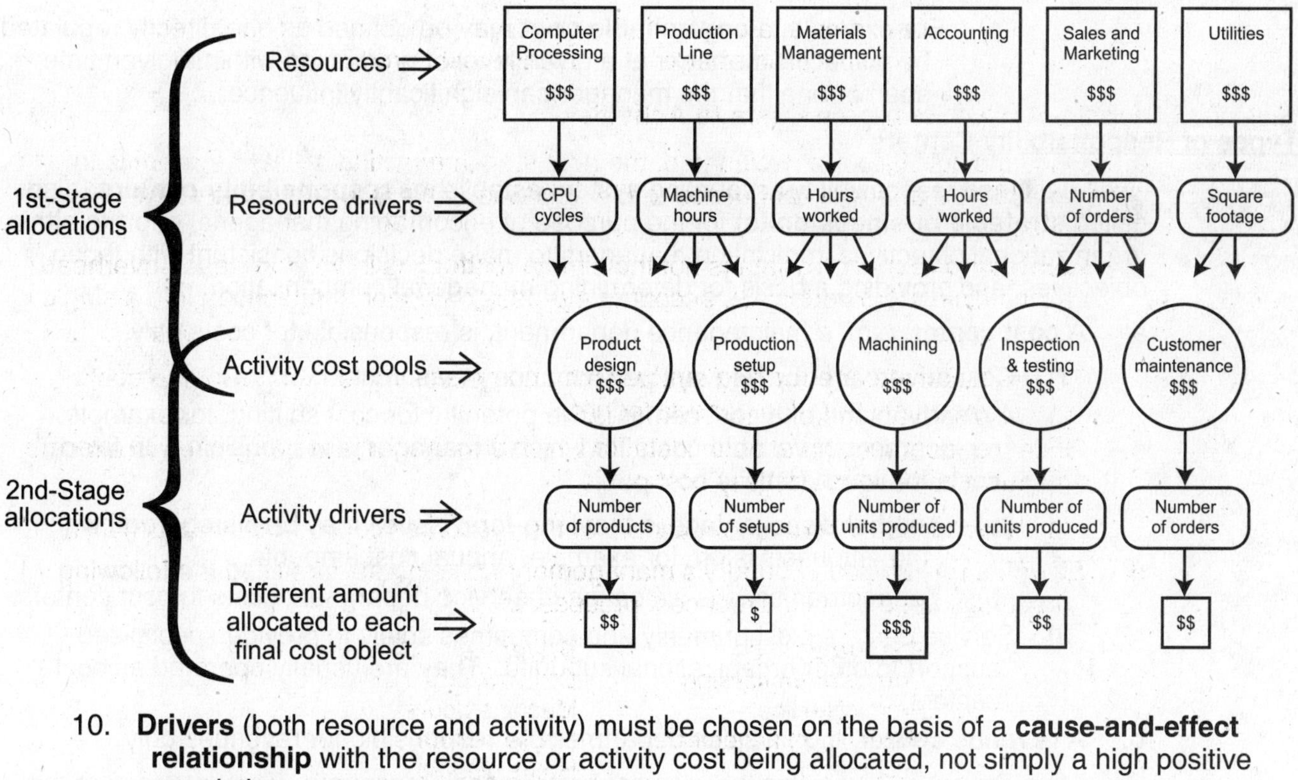

10. **Drivers** (both resource and activity) must be chosen on the basis of a **cause-and-effect relationship** with the resource or activity cost being allocated, not simply a high positive correlation.
    a. A **cost object** may be a job, product, process, activity, service, or anything else for which a cost measure is desired.
    b. **Intermediate cost objects** receive temporary accumulations of costs as the cost pools move from their originating points to the final cost objects.
       1) For example, work-in-process is an intermediate cost object, and finished salable goods are final cost objects.

Stop and review! You have completed the outline for this subunit. Study multiple-choice questions 28 and 29 on page 311.

6.13 RESPONSIBILITY ACCOUNTING

Overview

1. The primary distinction between **centralized and decentralized organizations** is in the degree of **freedom of decision making** by managers at many levels.
   a. Centralization assumes decision making must be consolidated so that activities throughout the organization may be more effectively coordinated.
      1) In decentralization, decision making is at as low a level as possible. The premise is that the local manager can make more informed decisions than a centralized manager.
      2) Decentralization typically reflects larger companies that are divided into multiple segments.
      3) In most organizations, a mixture of these approaches is used.
   b. **Controllability** is the extent to which a manager can influence activities and related revenues, costs, or other items.
      1) In principle, controllability is proportionate to, but not coextensive with, **responsibility.**
      2) Managerial performance ordinarily should be evaluated based on factors **that can be influenced by the manager**, such as revenues, costs, or investments.
         a) For example, a **controllable cost** may be defined as one directly regulated by a specific manager at a given level of production within a given time span or one that the manager can significantly influence.

Types of Responsibility Centers

2. A well-designed responsibility accounting system establishes **responsibility centers** (also called **strategic business units**) for the purpose of encouraging managerial effort to attain organizational objectives, motivating managers to make decisions consistent with those objectives, and providing a basis for determining managerial compensation.
   a. A **cost center**, e.g., a maintenance department, is responsible for costs only.
      1) Cost drivers are the relevant performance measures.
      2) A disadvantage of a cost center is the potential for cost shifting, for example, replacement of variable costs for which a manager is responsible with fixed costs for which (s)he is not.
         a) Another disadvantage is that long-term issues may be disregarded when the emphasis is on, for example, annual cost amounts.
         b) Yet another issue is allocation of service department costs to cost centers.
      3) Service centers exist primarily and sometimes solely to provide specialized support to other organizational subunits. They are usually operated as cost centers.
   b. A **revenue center**, e.g., a sales department, is responsible for revenues only.
      1) Revenue drivers are the relevant performance measures. They are factors that influence unit sales, such as changes in prices and products, customer service, marketing efforts, and delivery terms.
   c. A **profit center**, e.g., an appliance department in a retail store, is responsible for revenues and expenses.

d. An **investment center**, e.g., a branch office, is responsible for revenues, expenses, and invested capital.

1) The advantage of an investment center is that it permits an evaluation of performance that can be compared with that of other responsibility centers or other potential investments on a return on investment basis, i.e., on the basis of the effectiveness of asset usage.

Considerations

3. **Controllability is not the only basis** for responsibility.

a. More than one manager may influence a cost, and responsibility may be assigned based on knowledge about its incurrence rather than ability to control it directly.

b. Accordingly, a successful system is dependent upon the proper delegation of responsibility and the commensurate authority.

4. The purpose of a responsibility system is to **motivate management performance** that adheres to overall company objectives (goal congruence).

a. **Goal congruence** is promoted by encouraging cooperation among organizational functions (production, marketing, and support) by influencing managers to think of their products or services as salable outside the firm, and by encouraging managers to find new methods of earning profits.

b. **Suboptimization** occurs when one segment of a firm takes action that is in its own best interests but is detrimental to the firm as a whole.

Measures

5. **Return on investment**, or **ROI** (also called return on invested capital), is an umbrella concept for measures that reflect how efficiently a company is using the monies contributed by its shareholders to generate a profit.

a. ROI is the most effective measure of corporate performance because it **relates the income statement to the balance sheet**. All forms of ROI are some variation on this general ratio:

$$\text{Return on investment (ROI)} = \frac{\text{Measure of income}}{\text{Measure of capital}}$$

1) Besides reflecting the effectiveness of management decision making and overall firm profitability, ROI also aids in forecasting earnings, planning, budgeting, and control. Each profit center, product line, etc., can be assessed on the basis of ROI.

b. **Inconsistent definitions.** The wide variety of definitions in use for the terms "return" and "investment" creates difficulties in comparability.

1) The **numerator ("return")** may be adjusted by

a) Subtracting preferred dividends to leave only income available to common stockholders

b) Adding back minority interest in the income of a consolidated subsidiary (when invested capital is defined to include the minority interest)

c) Adding back interest expense

d) Adding back both interest expense and taxes so that the numerator is earnings before interest and taxes (EBIT); this results in the basic earning power ratio, which enhances comparability of firms with different capital structures and tax planning strategies.

2) The **denominator ("investment")** may be adjusted by
   a) Excluding nonoperating assets, such as investments, intangible assets, and the other asset category
   b) Excluding unproductive assets, such as idle plant, intangible assets, and obsolete inventories
   c) Excluding current liabilities to emphasize long-term capital
   d) Excluding debt and preferred stock to arrive at equity capital
   e) Stating invested capital at market value

6. **Residual income** is the excess of the return on an investment over a targeted amount equal to an imputed interest charge on invested capital.
   a. The rate is ordinarily the weighted-average cost of capital, but it may be an arbitrary hurdle rate.
   b. Projects with a positive residual income should be accepted, and projects with a negative residual income should be rejected.
   c. Residual income is often touted as superior to ROI. It may be more consistent with maximizing profits.

Stop and review! You have completed the outline for this subunit. Study multiple-choice question 30 on page 312.

6.14 SUMMARY

1. A cost object is any entity to which costs can be attached. A cost driver is the basis used to assign costs to a cost object. The cost driver is the cause of the cost.
2. The costs of manufacturing a product can be classified as one of three types: direct materials, direct labor, and manufacturing overhead. Overhead typically consists of indirect materials, indirect labor, and factory operating costs.
3. Product costs (also called inventoriable costs) are capitalized as part of finished goods inventory. They eventually become a component of cost of goods sold. Period costs are expensed as incurred, i.e., they are not capitalized in finished goods inventory and are thus excluded from cost of goods sold.
4. The relevant range defines the limits within which per-unit variable costs remain constant and fixed costs are not changeable. It is synonymous with the short run.
5. Variable cost per unit remains constant in the short run regardless of the level of production. Variable costs in total, on the other hand, vary directly and proportionally with changes in volume.
6. Fixed costs in total remain unchanged in the short run regardless of production level. Fixed cost per unit, on the other hand, varies indirectly with the activity level.
7. Mixed (semivariable) costs combine fixed and variable elements.
8. Under absorption costing (sometimes called full or full absorption costing), the fixed portion of manufacturing overhead is "absorbed" into the cost of each product. Product cost thus includes all manufacturing costs, both fixed and variable. Absorption-basis cost of goods sold is subtracted from sales to arrive at gross margin. This method is required under GAAP for external reporting purposes and under the Internal Revenue Code for tax purposes.
9. Variable costing (sometimes called direct costing) is more appropriate for internal reporting. Product cost includes only variable manufacturing costs. Variable-basis cost of goods sold and the variable portion of S&A expenses are subtracted from gross margin to arrive at contribution margin.

10. Capital budgeting is the process of planning and controlling investments for long-term projects. By their nature, capital projects affect multiple accounting periods and will constrain the organization's financial planning well into the future. Once made, capital budgeting decisions tend to be relatively inflexible.
11. The net present value (NPV) method for projecting the profitability of an investment expresses a project's return in dollar terms. NPV nets the expected cash streams related to a project (inflows and outflows), then discounts them at the hurdle rate, also called the desired rate of return.
12. The internal rate of return (IRR) method expresses a project's return in percentage terms. The IRR of an investment is the discount rate at which the investment's NPV equals zero. In other words, it is the rate that makes the present value of the expected cash inflows equal the present value of the expected cash outflows.
13. The payback period is the number of years required to return the original investment; that is, the time necessary for a new asset to pay for itself. Note that no consideration is made for the time value of money under this method.
14. The breakeven time is the period required for the discounted cumulative cash inflows on a project to equal the discounted cumulative cash outflows (usually but not always the initial cost).
15. In the operating budget, the emphasis is on obtaining and using current resources. It contains the sales budget, production budget, direct materials budget, direct labor budget, manufacturing overhead budget, ending finished goods inventory budget, cost of goods sold budget, nonmanufacturing budget, and pro forma income statement.
16. Budget systems include: project budget, activity-based budgeting, zero-based budgeting (ZBB), continuous (rolling) budgeting, kaizen budgeting, static budgeting, flexible budgeting, and life-cycle budgeting.
17. Transfer prices are the amounts charged by one segment of an organization for goods and services it provides to another segment of the same organization. Transfer pricing should motivate managers by encouraging goal congruence and managerial effort.
18. Three basic methods for determining transfer prices are in common use: cost plus pricing, market pricing, and negotiated pricing.
19. Cost-volume-profit analysis (also called breakeven analysis) is a tool for understanding the interaction of revenues with fixed and variable costs.
20. The breakeven point is the level of output at which total revenues equal total expenses; that is, the point at which operating income is zero.
21. The typical problem for which marginal (differential or incremental) analysis can be used involves choices among courses of action. The focus is on incremental revenues and costs, not the totals of all revenues and costs for the given option.
22. A special order that might at first be rejected could turn out to be profitable after marginal analysis. Marginal analysis emphasizes incremental costs, highlighting the ability of marginal revenue to cover fixed costs.
23. Job-order costing is concerned with accumulating costs by specific job. This method is appropriate when producing products with individual characteristics or when identifiable groupings are possible (e.g., yachts and jewelry).
24. Process cost accounting is used to assign costs to relatively homogeneous products that are mass produced on a continuous basis (e.g., petroleum products, thread, and computer monitors).
25. Activity-based costing (ABC) is a response to the significant increase in the incurrence of indirect costs resulting from the rapid advance of technology. ABC is a refinement of an existing costing system (job-order or process).

26. A life-cycle approach to budgeting estimates a product's revenues and expenses over its entire sales life cycle beginning with research and development, proceeding through the introduction and growth stages into the maturity stage, and finally into the harvest or decline stage. Accordingly, life-cycle costing takes a long-term view of the entire cost life cycle, also known as the value chain.
27. Operation costing is a hybrid of job-order costing and process costing that emphasizes physical processes (operations) for cost management and control purposes. Operation costing is appropriate when similar products are produced in different models or styles or otherwise have distinctive traits.
28. Backflush costing is often used by firms that have adopted a just-in-time (JIT) production philosophy. A JIT system treats carrying inventory as a nonvalue-adding activity. Hence, components are made available just in time to be used in the production process. Backflush costing complements JIT because it simplifies costing.
29. A well-designed responsibility accounting system establishes responsibility centers (also called strategic business units).
30. A cost center, e.g., a maintenance department, is responsible for costs only. A revenue center, e.g., a sales department, is responsible for revenues only. A profit center, e.g., an appliance department in a retail store, is responsible for revenues and expenses. An investment center, e.g., a branch office, is responsible for revenues, expenses, and invested capital.
31. Performance measures are means of revealing how efficiently an investment center is deploying the capital that has been invested in it to produce income for the owners. Return on investment (ROI) is the key performance measure of an investment center. Residual income is a dollar measure rather than a percentage rate. The target rate is ordinarily the weighted-average cost of capital, but it may be an arbitrary hurdle rate.

QUESTIONS

6.1 Cost Management Terminology

1. Using absorption costing, fixed manufacturing overhead costs are **best** described as

A. Direct period costs.

B. Indirect period costs.

C. Direct product costs.

D. Indirect product costs.

Answer (D) is correct. *(CIA, adapted)*

REQUIRED: The manufacturing overhead costs under absorption costing.

DISCUSSION: Using absorption costing, fixed manufacturing overhead is included in inventoriable (product) costs. Fixed manufacturing overhead costs are indirect costs because they cannot be directly traced to specific units produced.

Answer (A) is incorrect. Fixed manufacturing overhead costs are neither direct nor period costs. Answer (B) is incorrect. Fixed manufacturing overhead costs are not period costs. Answer (C) is incorrect. Fixed manufacturing overhead costs are not direct costs.

2. A company experienced a machinery breakdown on one of its production lines. As a consequence of the breakdown, manufacturing fell behind schedule, and a decision was made to schedule overtime to return manufacturing to schedule. Which one of the following methods is the proper way to account for the overtime paid to the direct laborers?

A. The overtime hours times the sum of the straight-time wages and overtime premium would be charged entirely to manufacturing overhead.

B. The overtime hours times the sum of the straight-time wages and overtime premium would be treated as direct labor.

C. The overtime hours times the overtime premium would be charged to repair and maintenance expense, and the overtime hours times the straight-time wages would be treated as direct labor.

D. The overtime hours times the overtime premium would be charged to manufacturing overhead, and the overtime hours times the straight-time wages would be treated as direct labor.

Answer (D) is correct. *(CIA, adapted)*

REQUIRED: The proper way to account for the overtime paid to the direct laborers.

DISCUSSION: Direct labor costs are wages paid to labor that can feasibly be specifically identified with the production of finished goods. Factory overhead consists of all costs, other than direct materials and direct labor, that are associated with the manufacturing process. Thus, straight-time wages would be treated as direct labor; however, because the overtime premium cost is a cost that should be borne by all production, the overtime hours times the overtime premium should be charged to manufacturing overhead.

Answer (A) is incorrect. The straight-time wages times the overtime hours should still be treated as direct labor. Answer (B) is incorrect. Only the straight-time wages times the overtime hours is charged to direct labor. Answer (C) is incorrect. Labor costs are not related to repairs and maintenance expense.

6.2 Cost Behavior and Relevant Range

3. An assembly plant accumulates its variable and fixed manufacturing overhead costs in a single cost pool, which is then applied to work in process using a single application base. The assembly plant management wants to estimate the magnitude of the total manufacturing overhead costs for different volume levels of the application activity base using a flexible budget formula. If there is an increase in the application activity base that is within the relevant range of activity for the assembly plant, which one of the following relationships regarding variable and fixed costs is true?

A. The variable cost per unit is constant, and the total fixed costs decrease.

B. The variable cost per unit is constant, and the total fixed costs increase.

C. The variable cost per unit and the total fixed costs remain constant.

D. The variable cost per unit increases, and the total fixed costs remain constant.

Answer (C) is correct. *(CIA, adapted)*

REQUIRED: The effect on variable and fixed costs of a change in activity within the relevant range.

DISCUSSION: Total variable cost changes when changes in the activity level occur within the relevant range. The cost per unit for a variable cost is constant for all activity levels within the relevant range. Thus, if the activity volume increases within the relevant range, total variable costs will increase. A fixed cost does not change when volume changes occur in the activity level within the relevant range. If the activity volume increases within the relevant range, total fixed costs will remain unchanged.

6.3 Absorption (Full) vs. Variable (Direct) Costing

Questions 4 and 5 are based on the following information. A company manufactures and sells a single product. Planned and actual production in its first year of operation was 100,000 units. Planned and actual costs for that year were as follows:

	Manufacturing	Nonmanufacturing
Variable	US $600,000	US $500,000
Fixed	400,000	300,000

The company sold 85,000 units of product at a selling price of US $30 per unit.

4. Using absorption costing, the company's operating profit was

A. US $750,000

B. US $900,000

C. US $975,000

D. US $1,020,000

Answer (B) is correct. *(CIA, adapted)*

REQUIRED: The absorption costing operating profit.

DISCUSSION: Under absorption costing, product costs include fixed and variable manufacturing costs. The unit product cost under absorption costing is US $10 [($600,000 + $400,000) ÷ 100,000 units produced]. All nonmanufacturing costs are expensed in the period incurred. Thus, operating profit is US $900,000.

Revenue (85,000 units × US $30)	US $2,550,000
Cost of goods sold (85,000 units × US $10)	(850,000)
Nonmanufacturing costs (US $500,000 + $300,000)	(800,000)
Operating profit	US $ 900,000

Answer (A) is incorrect. US $750,000 equals absorption costing profit minus ending inventory (15,000 units × US $10). Answer (C) is incorrect. US $975,000 treats the variable nonmanufacturing costs as manufacturing costs. Answer (D) is incorrect. US $1,020,000 assumes that all costs are manufacturing costs.

5. Using variable costing, the company's operating profit was

A. US $750,000

B. US $840,000

C. US $915,000

D. US $975,000

Answer (B) is correct. *(CIA, adapted)*

REQUIRED: The variable costing operating profit.

DISCUSSION: Under variable costing, the product cost includes only variable manufacturing costs. All fixed costs are expensed in the period incurred. Unit product cost under variable costing is US $6 (US $600,000 ÷ 100,000 units produced).

Revenue (85,000 units × US $30)	US $2,550,000
Variable cost of goods sold (85,000 units × US $6)	(510,000)
Variable nonmanufacturing costs	(500,000)
Contribution margin	US $1,540,000
Fixed costs	(700,000)
Operating profit	US $ 840,000

Answer (A) is incorrect. US $750,000 equals variable costing profit minus ending inventory (15,000 units × US $6). Answer (C) is incorrect. US $915,000 treats all variable costs as manufacturing costs. Answer (D) is incorrect. US $975,000 treats all variable costs and fixed manufacturing costs as product costs.

6.4 Capital Budgeting

6. Which one of the following is the **best** characteristic concerning the capital budget? The capital budget is a(n)

A. Plan to ensure that there are sufficient funds available for the operating needs of the company.

B. Exercise that sets the long-range goals of the company including the consideration of external influences caused by others in the market.

C. Plan that results in the cash requirements during the operating cycle.

D. Plan that assesses the long-term needs of the company for plant and equipment purchases.

Answer (D) is correct. *(CMA, adapted)*

REQUIRED: The true statement about the capital budget.

DISCUSSION: Capital budgeting is the process of planning expenditures for long-lived assets. It involves choosing among investment proposals using a ranking procedure. Evaluations are based on various measures involving rate of return on investment.

Answer (A) is incorrect. Capital budgeting involves long-term investment needs, not immediate operating needs. Answer (B) is incorrect. Strategic planning establishes long-term goals in the context of relevant factors in the firm's environment. Answer (C) is incorrect. Cash budgeting determines operating cash flows. Capital budgeting evaluates the rate of return on specific investment alternatives.

7. Everything else being equal, the internal rate of return (IRR) of an investment project will be lower if

A. The investment cost is lower.

B. Cash inflows are received later in the life of the project.

C. Cash inflows are larger.

D. The project has a shorter payback period.

Answer (B) is correct. *(CIA, adapted)*

REQUIRED: The true statement about the IRR.

DISCUSSION: The IRR is the discount rate at which the net present value is zero. Because the present value of a dollar is higher the sooner it is received, projects with later cash flows will have lower net present values for any given discount rate than will projects with earlier cash flows, if other factors are constant. Hence, projects with later cash flows will have a lower IRR.

Answer (A) is incorrect. The present value of the cash inflows is inversely related to the discount rate; that is, if the discount rate is higher, the present value of the cash inflows is lower. If the investment cost is lower, a higher discount rate (the IRR) will be required to set the net present value equal to zero. Answer (C) is incorrect. The larger the cash inflows, the higher the IRR will be. Higher cash inflows have a higher present value at any given discount rate. A higher discount rate will be required to set the net present value equal to zero. Answer (D) is incorrect. Projects with shorter payback periods have higher cash inflows early in the life of the project. Projects with earlier cash inflows have higher IRRs.

6.5 Budget Systems

8. The major appeal of zero-based budgeting is that it

A. Solves the problem of measuring program effectiveness.

B. Relates performance to resource inputs by an integrated planning and resource-allocation process.

C. Reduces significantly the time required to review a budget.

D. Deals with some of the problems of the incremental approach to budgeting.

Answer (D) is correct. *(CIA, adapted)*

REQUIRED: The major appeal of zero-based budgeting.

DISCUSSION: The traditional approach to budgeting is to merely increase last year's figures by a given percentage or increment. Zero-based budgeting divides programs into packages of goals, activities, and required resources. The cost of each package is then calculated afresh, without regard to previous performance.

Answer (A) is incorrect. Zero-based budgeting is not primarily a measurement tool for program effectiveness. Answer (B) is incorrect. The relationship of performance to resource inputs by integrated planning and resource allocation is part of the PPBS, or planning-programming-budgeting system. Answer (C) is incorrect. Zero-based budgeting generally increases the time required to review a budget rather than reduces it; i.e., it consists of a determination of resources needed rather than an extrapolation of resources used in prior periods.

9. The major objectives of any budget system are to

A. Define responsibility centers, provide a framework for performance evaluation, and promote communication and coordination among organization segments.

B. Define responsibility centers, facilitate the fixing of blame for missed budget predictions, and ensure goal congruence between superiors and subordinates.

C. Foster the planning of operations, provide a framework for performance evaluation, and promote communication and coordination among organization segments.

D. Foster the planning of operations, facilitate the fixing of blame for missed budget predictions, and ensure goal congruence between superiors and subordinates.

Answer (C) is correct. *(CIA, adapted)*

REQUIRED: The major objectives of any budget system.

DISCUSSION: A budget is a realistic plan for the future expressed in quantitative terms. The process of budgeting forces a company to establish goals, determine the resources necessary to achieve those goals, and anticipate future difficulties in their achievement. A budget is also a control tool because it establishes standards and facilitates comparison of actual and budgeted performance. Because a budget establishes standards and accountability, it motivates good performance by highlighting the work of effective managers. Moreover, the nature of the budgeting process fosters communication of goals to company subunits and coordination of their efforts. Budgeting activities by entities within the company must be coordinated because they are interdependent. Thus, the sales budget is a necessary input to the formulation of the production budget. In turn, production requirements must be known before purchases and expense budgets can be developed, and all other budgets must be completed before preparation of the cash budget.

Answer (A) is incorrect. Responsibility centers are determined prior to budgeting. Answer (B) is incorrect. Responsibility centers are determined prior to budgeting, budgets do not fix blame but rather measure performance, and goal congruence is promoted but not ensured by budgets. Answer (D) is incorrect. Budgets do not fix blame but rather measure performance, and goal congruence is promoted but not ensured by budgets.

10. A company prepares a flexible budget each month for manufacturing costs. Formulas have been developed for all costs within a relevant range of 5,000 to 15,000 units per month. The budget for electricity (a semivariable cost) is US $19,800 at 9,000 units per month, and US $21,000 at 10,000 units per month. How much should be budgeted for electricity for the coming month if 12,000 units are to be produced?

A. US $26,400

B. US $25,200

C. US $23,400

D. US $22,200

Answer (C) is correct. *(CIA, adapted)*

REQUIRED: The amount that should be budgeted for electricity given desired units of production.

DISCUSSION: A flexible budget consists of a fixed cost component and a variable cost component. The fixed cost component can be expected to remain constant throughout the budget's relevant range. The variable cost component, however, will change at a constant rate within the budget's range. The increase in budgeted cost of US $1,200 ($21,000 – $19,800) per 1,000 units of production can therefore be calculated as the variable cost per unit of US $1.20 [($21,000 – $19,800) ÷ 1,000] and the total fixed costs of US $9,000 [$21,000 – (10,000 × $1.20)]. These costs can then be used to determine the total cost of using 12,000 units of electricity [US $9,000 FC + (12,000 × $1.20)].

Answer (A) is incorrect. The flexible budget for 12,000 units should be computed by determining the variable cost per unit of US $1.20 [($21,000 – $19,800) ÷ 1,000] and the total fixed costs of US $9,000 [$21,000 – (10,000 × $1.20)]. These costs can then be used to determine the total cost of using 12,000 units of electricity [US $9,000 FC + (12,000 × US $1.20)]. Answer (B) is incorrect. The flexible budget for 12,000 units should be computed by determining the variable cost per unit of US $1.20 [($21,000 – $19,800) ÷ 1,000] and the total fixed costs of US $9,000 [$21,000 – (10,000 × $1.20)]. These costs can then be used to determine the total cost of using 12,000 units of electricity [US $9,000 FC + (12,000 × $1.20)]. Answer (D) is incorrect. US $22,200 is arrived at by subtracting the increase in budgeted cost of US $1,200.

11. The major feature of zero-based budgeting (ZBB) is that it

A. Takes the previous year's budgets and adjusts them for inflation.

B. Questions each activity and determines whether it should be maintained as it is, reduced, or eliminated.

C. Assumes all activities are legitimate and worthy of receiving budget increases to cover any increased costs.

D. Focuses on planned capital outlays for property, plant, and equipment.

Answer (B) is correct. *(CIA, adapted)*

REQUIRED: The major feature of ZBB.

DISCUSSION: ZBB is a planning process in which each manager must justify his/her department's full budget for each period. The purpose is to encourage periodic reexamination of all costs in the hope that some can be reduced or eliminated.

Answer (A) is incorrect. Traditional or incremental budgeting takes the previous year's budgets and adjusts them for inflation. Answer (C) is incorrect. ZBB is a planning process in which each manager must justify his/her department's full budget for each period. The purpose is to encourage periodic reexamination of all costs in the hope that some can be reduced or eliminated. Answer (D) is incorrect. It is a definition of a capital budget.

6.6 Operating Budget Components

Questions 12 and 13 are based on the following information.

The Raymar Company is preparing its cash budget for the months of April and May. The firm has established a US $200,000 line of credit with its bank at a 12% annual rate of interest on which borrowings for cash deficits must be made in US $10,000 increments. There is no outstanding balance on the line of credit loan on April 1. Principal repayments are to be made in any month in which there is a surplus of cash. Interest is to be paid monthly. If there are no outstanding balances on the loans, Raymar will invest any cash in excess of its desired end-of-month cash balance in U.S. Treasury bills. Raymar intends to maintain a minimum balance of US $100,000 at the end of each month by either borrowing for deficits below the minimum balance or investing any excess cash. Expected monthly collection and disbursement patterns are shown in the columns to the right.

- *Collections.* 50% of the current month's sales budget and 50% of the previous month's sales budget.
- *Accounts Payable Disbursements.* 75% of the current month's accounts payable budget and 25% of the previous month's accounts payable budget.
- All other disbursements occur in the month in which they are budgeted.

Budget Information

	March	April	May
Sales	US $40,000	US $50,000	US $100,000
Accounts payable	30,000	40,000	40,000
Payroll	60,000	70,000	50,000
Other disbursements	25,000	30,000	10,000

12. In May, Raymar will be required to

A. Repay US $20,000 principal and pay US $1,000 interest.

B. Repay US $90,000 principal and pay US $100 interest.

C. Pay US $900 interest.

D. Borrow an additional US $20,000 and pay US $1,000 interest.

Answer (D) is correct. *(CMA, adapted)*

REQUIRED: The transaction required in May.

DISCUSSION: The company will have to borrow US $100,000 in April, which means that interest will have to be paid in May at the rate of 1% per month (12% annual rate). Consequently, interest expense is US $1,000 ($100,000 × 1%). May receipts are US $75,000 [($100,000 May sales × 50%) + ($50,000 April sales × 50%)]. Disbursements in May are US $40,000 [($40,000 May payables × 75%) + ($40,000 April payables × 25%)]. In addition to the May accounts payable disbursements, payroll and other disbursements are US $60,000, bringing total disbursements to US $101,000 ($60,000 + $40,000 + $1,000). Thus, disbursements exceed receipts by US $26,000 ($101,000 – $75,000). However, cash has a beginning surplus balance of US $7,500 ($100,000 April loan – $92,500 negative cash flow for April). As a result, the company needs to borrow an additional US $18,500 to eliminate its cash deficit. Given the requirement that loans be in US $10,000 increments, the May loan must be for US $20,000.

Answer (A) is incorrect. No funds are available to repay the loan. May receipts are less than May disbursements. Answer (B) is incorrect. The 1% interest is calculated on a US $100,000 loan, not a US $90,000 loan. Answer (C) is incorrect. The 1% interest is calculated on a US $100,000 loan, not a US $90,000 loan.

13. Refer to the information on the preceding page(s). In April, Raymar's budget will result in

A. US $45,000 in excess cash.

B. A need to borrow US $50,000 on its line of credit for the cash deficit.

C. A need to borrow US $100,000 on its line of credit for the cash deficit.

D. A need to borrow US $90,000 on its line of credit for the cash deficit.

Answer (C) is correct. *(CMA, adapted)*

REQUIRED: The effect on cash by the end of April.

DISCUSSION: Assuming Raymar maintained a US $100,000 cash balance at the end of March, the amount to be borrowed or invested in April is the difference between cash receipts and disbursements. April's cash collections are US $45,000 [($50,000 April sales × 50%) + ($40,000 March sales × 50%)]. Disbursements for accounts payable are US $37,500 [($40,000 April payables × 75%) + ($30,000 March payables × 25%)]. In addition to the accounts payable disbursements, payroll and other disbursements will require an additional US $100,000. Hence, total disbursements are estimated to be US $137,500. The net negative cash flow (amount to be borrowed to reach the required minimum cash balance of US $100,000) is US $92,500 ($137,500 – $45,000). Because the line of credit must be drawn upon in US $10,000 increments, the loan must be for US $100,000.

Answer (A) is incorrect. US $45,000 equals cash receipts. Answer (B) is incorrect. The cash deficit will be US $92,500 without borrowing. Answer (D) is incorrect. A loan of only US $90,000 would still leave a negative cash balance of US $2,500.

6.7 Transfer Pricing

14. A limitation of transfer prices based on actual cost is that they

A. Charge inefficiencies to the department that is transferring the goods.

B. Can lead to suboptimal decisions for the company as a whole.

C. Must be adjusted by some markup.

D. Lack clarity and administrative convenience.

Answer (B) is correct. *(CIA, adapted)*

REQUIRED: The limitation of transfer prices based on actual cost.

DISCUSSION: The optimal transfer price of a selling division should be set at a point that will have the most desirable economic effect on the firm as a whole while at the same time continuing to motivate the management of every division to perform efficiently. Setting the transfer price based on actual costs rather than standard costs would give the selling division little incentive to control costs.

Answer (A) is incorrect. Inefficiencies are charged to the buying department. Answer (C) is incorrect. By definition, cost-based transfer prices are not adjusted by some markup. Answer (D) is incorrect. Cost-based transfer prices provide the advantages of clarity and administrative convenience.

15. Division Z of a company produces a component that it currently sells to outside customers for US $20 per unit. At its current level of production, which is 60% of capacity, Division Z's fixed cost of producing this component is US $5 per unit and its variable cost is US $12 per unit. Division Y of the same company would like to purchase this component from Division Z for US $10. Division Z has enough excess capacity to fill Division Y's requirements. The managers of both divisions are compensated based upon reported profits. Which of the following transfer prices will maximize total company profits and be **most** equitable to the managers of Division Y and Division Z?

A. US $12 per unit.

B. US $18 per unit.

C. US $20 per unit.

D. US $22 per unit.

Answer (B) is correct. *(CIA, adapted)*

REQUIRED: The transfer price that will maximize total company profits and be most equitable to the managers of the divisions.

DISCUSSION: A unit price of US $18 is less than Division Y's cost of purchase from an outside supplier but exceeds Division Z's production cost. Accordingly, both Y and Z benefit.

Answer (A) is incorrect. US $12 per unit merely allows Division Z to recover its unit variable cost. Answer (C) is incorrect. At US $20 per unit, Division Y may be indifferent as to whether it purchases internally or externally. Buying from an outside source for US $20 per unit is contrary to the company's interests given idle capacity available for the component's manufacture and an incremental unit cost of US $20. Answer (D) is incorrect. At US $22 per unit, Division Y would have incentive to purchase from an external supplier (i.e., market price is US $20).

6.8 Cost-Volume-Profit (CVP) Analysis

16. Presented below is a cost-volume-profit chart for a firm. Various reference points are marked on the chart with letters.

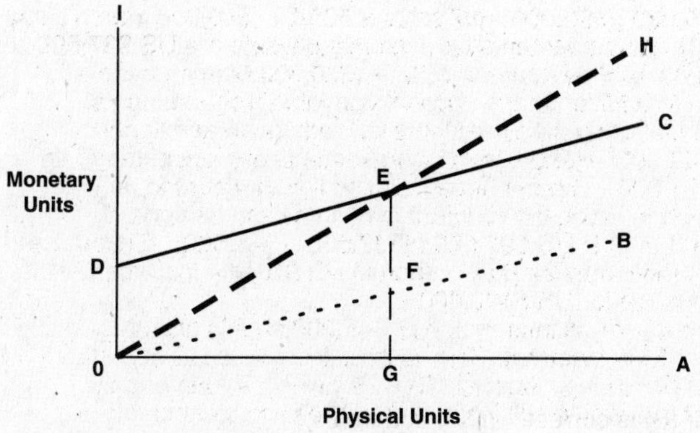

The letters CEH on the chart represent the

A. Total sales.
B. Total expenses.
C. Area of the chart where total sales exceed total expenses.
D. Area of the chart where total expenses exceed total sales.

Answer (C) is correct. *(CIA, adapted)*
REQUIRED: The meaning of the letters CEH on the chart.
DISCUSSION: A cost-volume-profit chart contains elements (lines, points, axes) that identify variable cost, fixed cost, the breakeven point, total revenue, profit, and volume in units. When the total sales revenue line rises above the total expense line, a company will have positive net income.
Answer (A) is incorrect. Line HEO represents total sales. Answer (B) is incorrect. Line CED represents total expenses. Answer (D) is incorrect. The loss area, i.e., the area of the chart where total expenses exceed sales, is represented by the area OED.

17. A retail company determines its selling price by marking up variable costs 60%. In addition, the company uses frequent selling price markdowns to stimulate sales. If the markdowns average 10%, what is the company's contribution margin ratio?

A. 27.5%
B. 30.6%
C. 37.5%
D. 41.7%

Answer (B) is correct. *(CIA, adapted)*
REQUIRED: The contribution margin ratio.
DISCUSSION: The contribution margin equals revenues minus variable costs. The CMR equals the UCM divided by the selling price. For example, if variable costs average US $10 per unit, the average selling price is US $16 ($1.60 × $10). However, the 10% markdown implies that the actual average selling price is US $14.40 (.90 × $16). The CMR is therefore 30.6% [(US $14.40 – $10.00) ÷ $14.40].
Answer (A) is incorrect. Improperly omitting markdowns from the denominator results in 27.5%. Answer (C) is incorrect. Improperly omitting markdowns results in 37.5%. Answer (D) is incorrect. Improperly omitting markdowns from the numerator results in 41.7%.

Questions 18 and 19 are based on the following information. A company manufactures and sells a single product. It takes two machine hours to produce one unit. Annual sales are expected to be 75,000 units. Annual production capacity is 200,000 machine hours. Expected selling price is US $10 per unit. Cost data for manufacturing and selling the product are as follows:

Variable costs (per unit)	
Direct materials	US $3.00
Direct labor	1.00
Variable manufacturing overhead	0.80
Variable selling	2.00
Fixed costs (per year)	
Fixed manufacturing overhead	US $90,000
Fixed selling	60,000

18. The company receives a special order for 10,000 units at US $7.60. Variable selling cost for each of these 10,000 units will be US $1.20. This special order will not affect regular sales of 75,000 units. If the company accepts this special order, its profit will

A. Increase by US $8,000.

B. Increase by US $16,000.

C. Decrease by US $4,000.

D. Decrease by US $12,000.

Answer (B) is correct. *(CIA, adapted)*

REQUIRED: The change in profit resulting from a special order.

DISCUSSION: If the company accepts the special order, its revenue will increase by US $76,000 ($7.60 × 10,000 units). However, its incremental cost will include only the variable costs because fixed manufacturing and selling costs will be unchanged. The increase in cost from accepting the special order is US $60,000 [($3.00 + $1.00 + $0.80 + $1.20) × 10,000 units]. Thus, acceptance of the special order will increase profits by US $16,000 ($76,000 – $60,000).

Answer (A) is incorrect. An increase of US $8,000 assumes unit variable selling cost is US $2.00. Answer (C) is incorrect. Profit will increase. Answer (D) is incorrect. Profit will increase.

19. The company estimates that by reducing its selling price to US $9.30 per unit, it can increase sales to 90,000 units annually. Fixed costs per year and unit variable costs will remain unchanged. If the company reduces its selling price to US $9.30 per unit, its profit will

A. Decrease by US $5,000.

B. Decrease by US $15,000.

C. Decrease by US $45,000.

D. Increase by US $15,000.

Answer (B) is correct. *(CIA, adapted)*

REQUIRED: The effect on profit if selling price is reduced.

DISCUSSION: Because total fixed costs are unaffected, the change in profit is the change in the contribution margin. The contribution margin at the current selling price is US $240,000 [($10 – $3 – $1 – $0.80 – $2) × 75,000 units]. The contribution margin at the US $9.30 selling price is US $225,000 [($9.30 – $3 – $1 – $0.80 – $2) × 90,000 units]. Hence, profit will be reduced by US $15,000 ($240,000 – $225,000) if the selling price is lowered to US $9.30.

6.9 Relevant Costs

Questions 20 and 21 are based on the following information.

A business needs a computer application that can be either developed internally or purchased. Suitable software from a vendor costs US $29,000. Minor modifications and testing can be conducted by the systems staff as part of their regular workload.

If the software is developed internally, a systems analyst would be assigned full time, and a contractor would assume the analyst's responsibilities. The hourly rate for the regular analyst is US $25. The hourly rate for the contractor is US $22. The contractor would occupy an empty office. The office has 100 square feet, and occupancy cost is US $45 per square foot.

Other related data follows. Computer time is charged using predetermined rates. The organization has sufficient excess computer capacity for either software development or modification/testing of the purchased software.

	Internal Development	Purchased Software
Systems analyst time in hours:		
Development	1,000	N/A
Modifications and testing	N/A	40
Computer charges	US $800	US $250
Additional hardware purchases	US $3,200	N/A
Incidental supplies	US $500	US $200

20. When applying the cost-benefit approach to a decision, the primary criterion is how well management goals will be achieved in relation to costs. Costs include all expected

A. Variable costs for the courses of action but not expected fixed costs because only the expected variable costs are relevant.

B. Incremental out-of-pocket costs as well as all expected continuing costs that are common to all the alternative courses of action.

C. Future costs that differ among the alternative courses of action plus all qualitative factors that cannot be measured in numerical terms.

D. Historical and future costs relative to the courses of action including all qualitative factors that cannot be measured in numerical terms.

Answer (C) is correct. *(CIA, adapted)*

REQUIRED: The costs included in the cost-benefit approach.

DISCUSSION: The analysis of a make-or-buy decision is based on relevant costs. If costs do not vary with the option chosen, they are irrelevant. Moreover, the decision may be based on nonquantitative factors, for example, the desire to maintain a relationship with a vendor or to assume control over development of a product.

Answer (A) is incorrect. Variable and fixed costs may be relevant or irrelevant. Answer (B) is incorrect. Expected incremental out-of-pocket expenses should be considered, but common costs should not. Answer (D) is incorrect. Historical costs are not relevant to cost-benefit analysis because they are sunk costs.

21. Based solely on the cost figures presented, the cost of developing the computer application will be

A. US $3,500 less than acquiring the purchased software package.

B. US $500 less than acquiring the purchased software package.

C. US $1,550 more than acquiring the purchased software package.

D. US $3,550 more than acquiring the purchased software package.

Answer (A) is correct. *(CIA, adapted)*

REQUIRED: The comparison of the costs of developing and purchasing software.

DISCUSSION: Development cost equals the cost of the outside contractor plus the costs for hardware and supplies. Computer charges are transfer prices and do not require additional expenditures, given idle capacity. The relevant cost of supplies is US $300 ($500 – $200 cost if the software is purchased). The contractor's use of an otherwise idle office is not relevant. Thus, the relevant cost of development is US $25,500 [(1,000 hours × $22 hourly cost of the contractor) + $3,200 hardware purchases + $300 incremental cost of supplies]. This amount is US $3,500 less than the US $29,000 cost of purchase. A systems analyst's work on the new software is not relevant. It is part of the regular workload.

Answer (B) is incorrect. The contractor is not paid US $25 per hour. Answer (C) is incorrect. US $550 in computer charges and US $4,500 in occupancy charges should not be included. Answer (D) is incorrect. The contractor is not paid US $25 per hour, and 40 hours of modification and testing, US $550 of the computer charges, and the occupancy costs are irrelevant.

Questions 22 and 23 are based on the following information. The segmented income statement for a retail company with three product lines is presented below:

	Total Company	Product Line 1	Product Line 2	Product Line 3
Volume (in units)		20,000	28,000	50,000
Sales revenue	US $2,000,000	US $800,000	US $700,000	US $500,000
Costs & expenses:				
Administrative	US $ 180,000	US $ 60,000	US $ 60,000	US $ 60,000
Advertising	240,000	96,000	84,000	60,000
Commissions	40,000	16,000	14,000	10,000
Cost of sales	980,000	360,000	420,000	200,000
Rent	280,000	84,000	140,000	56,000
Salaries	110,000	54,000	32,000	24,000
Total costs & expenses	US $1,830,000	US $670,000	US $750,000	US $410,000
Operating income (loss)	US $ 170,000	US $130,000	US $ (50,000)	US $ 90,000

The company buys the goods in the three product lines directly from manufacturers' representatives. Each product line is directed by a manager whose salary is included in the administrative expenses. Administrative expenses are allocated to the three product lines equally because the administration is spread evenly among the three product lines. Salaries represent payments to the workers in each product line and therefore are traceable costs of each product line. Advertising promotes the entire company rather than the individual product lines. As a result, the advertising is allocated to the three product lines in proportion to the sales revenue. Commissions are paid to the salespersons in each product line based on 2% of gross sales. Rent represents the cost of the retail store and warehouse under a lease agreement with 5 years remaining. The product lines share the retail and warehouse space, and the rent is allocated to the three product lines based on the square footage occupied by each of the product lines.

22. The company has an opportunity to promote one of its product lines by making a one-time US $7,000 expenditure. The company can choose only one of the three product lines to promote. The incremental sales revenue that would be realized from this US $7,000 promotion expenditure in each of the product lines is estimated as follows:

	Increase in Sales Revenue
Product Line 1	US $15,000
Product Line 2	20,000
Product Line 3	14,000

In order to maximize profits, the promotion expenditure should be spent on <List A>, resulting in an increase in operating income of <List B>.

	List A	List B
A.	Product Line 2	US $13,000
B.	Product Line 2	US $ 5,000
C.	Product Line 3	US $ 1,400
D.	Product Line 3	US $ 1,120

Answer (D) is correct. *(CIA, adapted)*

REQUIRED: The product line to be promoted by a one-time advertising expenditure and the resulting income increase.

DISCUSSION: Fixed costs should be ignored. Thus, the increase in sales revenue should be multiplied by the contribution margin ratio for each product line. The incremental promotion cost (US $7,000) is subtracted from this amount to determine the marginal benefit of promoting each product line. Hence, Product Line 3 has an increased profit of US $1,120.

Calculation of Contribution Margin

	Total Company	Product Line 1	Product Line 2	Product Line 3
Sales revenue	US $2,000,000	US $800,000	US $700,000	US $500,000
Variable costs				
Commissions	$ 40,000	$ 16,000	$ 14,000	$ 10,000
Cost of sales	980,000	360,000	420,000	200,000
Total	$1,020,000	$376,000	$434,000	$210,000
CM	$ 980,000	$424,000	$266,000	$290,000
CMR	49%	53%	38%	58%
Revenue		$ 15,000	$ 20,000	$ 14,000
CMR		.53	.38	.58
CM		$ 7,950	$ 7,600	$ 8,120
Promotion cost		7,000	7,000	7,000
Increased profits		US $ 950	US $ 600	US $ 1,120

Answer (A) is incorrect. Product Line 2 has an increased profit of US $600. Answer (B) is incorrect. Product Line 2 has an increased profit of US $600. Answer (C) is incorrect. US $1,400 omits the commissions from the calculation.

23. A customer, operating in an isolated foreign market, has approached the head salesperson for Product Line 1 and offered to purchase 4,000 units of a special-order product over the next 12 months. This product would be sold in the same manner as Product Line 1's other products except that the customer is hoping for a price break. Product Line 1's cost to purchase this product (cost of sales) would be US $14.70. Product Line 1 has excess capacity, meaning that the rate or amount of the remaining operating costs would not change as a consequence of the purchase and sale of this special-order product. The minimum selling price for this special-order product would be

A. US $15.00

B. US $17.30

C. US $27.50

D. US $30.20

Answer (A) is correct. *(CIA, adapted)*

REQUIRED: The minimum selling price for a special-order product.

DISCUSSION: Product Line 1 needs to cover its variable out-of-pocket costs as a minimum on this special-order product; therefore, any selling price greater than the variable cost will contribute towards profits. Thus, the minimum selling price of the special-order product is the variable cost divided by 1 minus the commission rate, or US $15 [$14.70 ÷ (1.0 – .02)].

Answer (B) is incorrect. US $17.30 includes the average cost of salaries (at the new volume level of 24,000 units) as a cost that needs to be covered when determining the minimum selling price. Answer (C) is incorrect. US $27.50 is calculated based on a full cost approach. Answer (D) is incorrect. US $30.20 adds all costs and expenses (except cost of sales) and divides them by the original volume level of 20,000 units to determine the average operating costs. The new cost of sales is added to the average operating costs to determine the minimum selling price.

6.10 Cost Accumulation Systems

24. In a company, products pass through some or all of the production departments during manufacturing, depending upon the product being manufactured. Direct material and direct labor costs are traced directly to the products as they flow through each production department. Manufacturing overhead is assigned in each department using separate departmental manufacturing overhead rates. The inventory costing method that the manufacturing company is using in this situation is

A. Absorption costing.

B. Activity-based costing.

C. Backflush costing.

D. Variable costing.

Answer (A) is correct. *(CIA, adapted)*

REQUIRED: The appropriate inventory costing method.

DISCUSSION: Absorption costing inventories all direct manufacturing costs and both variable and fixed manufacturing overhead (indirect) costs.

Answer (B) is incorrect. Activity-based costing develops cost pools for activities and then allocates those costs to cost objects based on the drivers of the activities. Answer (C) is incorrect. A backflush costing system applies costs based on output. Answer (D) is incorrect. Variable costing excludes fixed manufacturing overhead costs from inventoriable costs and treats them as period costs.

25. Three commonly employed systems for product costing are termed job-order costing, operations costing, and process costing. Match the type of production environment with the costing method used.

	Job-Order Costing	Operations Costing	Process Costing
A.	Auto repair	Clothing manufacturer	Oil refining
B.	Loan processing	Drug manufacturing	Custom printing
C.	Custom printing	Paint manufacturing	Paper manufacturing
D.	Engineering design	Auto assembly	Motion picture production

Answer (A) is correct. *(CIA, adapted)*

REQUIRED: The match of the types of production environments with the costing methods.

DISCUSSION: Job-order costing is appropriate when producing products with individual characteristics and/or when identifiable groupings are possible. Process costing should be used to assign costs to similar products that are mass produced on a continuous basis. Operations costing is a hybrid of job order and process costing systems. It is used by companies that manufacture goods that undergo some similar and some dissimilar processes. Thus, job-order costing would be appropriate for auto repair, operations costing for clothing manufacturing, and process costing for oil refining.

Answer (B) is incorrect. Custom printing would not use process costing. Answer (C) is incorrect. Paint manufacturing would not use operations costing. Answer (D) is incorrect. Motion picture production would not use process costing.

6.11 Process Costing

Questions 26 and 27 are based on the following information. A company harvests, packs, and ships all of its own produce. The company operates three packing lines. A summary of completed inventory costs is as follows:

Packing-line employee salary expense	US $150,000
Packing-line supervision salary expense	90,000
Quality control salary expense	30,000
Packing crates expense	15,000
Electricity expense	3,000
Depreciation expense	66,000

26. Costs for the packing lines would be accumulated in part by

A. Recording payroll expense by employee job category.

B. Computing depreciation expense.

C. Producing monthly financial statements.

D. Forecasting monthly material shortages.

Answer (A) is correct. *(CIA, adapted)*

REQUIRED: Identify how costs for the packing line would be accumulated.

DISCUSSION: Cost accumulation is performed by accounting systems that organize data by an appropriate catalog. Actual costs, rather than predicted costs, are accumulated.

Answer (B) is incorrect. Computing depreciation expense would not organize date into categories. Answer (C) is incorrect. Producing financial statements would not organize data into categories. Answer (D) is incorrect. Forecasting material shortages would not organize data into categories.

27. At the end of the reporting period, 600,000 units had been packed and shipped. No inventory remained on hand. If the company used process costing, the cost per unit would be

A. US $0.197

B. US $0.275

C. US $0.315

D. US $0.590

Answer (D) is correct. *(CIA, adapted)*

REQUIRED: Calculate the cost per unit if the company used process costing.

DISCUSSION: Process costing is used to assign costs to products or services. It is applicable to relatively homogeneous items that are mass produced on a continuous basis. Process costing is the average cost per unit produced, or total cost divided by the number of units. US $150,000 + $90,000 + $30,000 + $15,000 + $3,000 + $66,000 = US $354,000 ÷ 600,000 = US $0.59.

Answer (A) is incorrect. Process costing does not allocate costs per packing line. (US $150,000 + $90,000 + $30,000 + $15,000 + $3,000 + $66,000 = US $354,000 ÷ 600,000 = .59 ÷ 3 = US $0.197). Answer (B) is incorrect. Process costing includes all costs. (US $150,000 + $15,000 = US $165,000 ÷ 600,000 = US $0.275). Answer (C) is incorrect. Process costing includes all costs. (US $90,000 + $30,000 + $3,000 + $66,000 = US $189,000 ÷ 600,000 = US $0.315).

6.12 Activity-Based Costing

Questions 28 and 29 are based on the following information. Believing that its traditional cost system may be providing misleading information, an organization is considering an activity-based costing (ABC) approach. It now employs a full cost system and has been applying its manufacturing overhead on the basis of machine hours.

The organization plans on using 50,000 direct labor hours and 30,000 machine hours in the coming year. The following data show the manufacturing overhead that is budgeted.

Activity	Cost Driver	Budgeted Activity	Budgeted Cost
Material handling	No. of parts handled	6,000,000	US $ 720,000
Setup costs	No. of setups	750	315,000
Machining costs	Machine hours	30,000	540,000
Quality control	No. of batches	500	225,000
		Total manufacturing overhead cost:	US $1,800,000

Cost, sales, and production data for one of the organization's products for the coming year are as follows:

Prime costs:	
Direct material cost per unit	US $4.40
Direct labor cost per unit .05 DLH @ US $15.00/DLH	.75
Total prime cost	US $5.15
Sales and production data:	
Expected sales	20,000 units
Batch size	5,000 units
Setups	2 per batch
Total parts per finished unit	5 parts
Machine hours required	80 MH per batch

28. If the organization uses the traditional full cost system, the cost per unit for this product for the coming year will be

A. US $5.39

B. US $5.44

C. US $6.11

D. US $6.95

Answer (C) is correct. *(CIA, adapted)*

REQUIRED: The unit cost under traditional full costing.

DISCUSSION: Given that manufacturing overhead is applied on the basis of machine hours, the overhead rate is US $60 per hour ($1,800,000 ÷ 30,000) or US $.96 per unit [(80 machine hours per batch × $60) ÷ 5,000 units per batch]. Accordingly, the unit full cost is US $6.11 ($5.15 unit price cost + $.96).

Answer (A) is incorrect. US $5.39 assumes that 80 machine hours are required for the total production of 20,000 units. Answer (B) is incorrect. US $5.44 is based on the machining overhead rate (US $18). Answer (D) is incorrect. US $6.95 is based on the direct labor hour manufacturing overhead rate.

29. If the organization employs an activity-based costing system, the cost per unit for the product described for the coming year will be

A. US $6.00

B. US $6.08

C. US $6.21

D. US $6.30

Answer (D) is correct. *(CIA, adapted)*

REQUIRED: The unit cost under the ABC system.

DISCUSSION: Materials handling cost per part is US $.12 ($720,000 ÷ 6,000,000), cost per setup is US $420 ($315,000 ÷ 750), machining cost per hour is US $18 ($540,000 ÷ 30,000), and quality cost per batch is US $450 ($225,000 ÷ 500). Hence, total manufacturing overhead applied is US $22,920 [(5 parts per unit) × 20,000 units × $.12) + (4 batches × 2 setups per batch × $420) + (4 batches × 80 machine hours per batch × $18) + (4 batches × $450)]. The total unit cost is US $6.296 [$5.15 prime cost + ($22,920 ÷ 20,000 units) overhead].

Answer (A) is incorrect. US $6.00 assumes one setup per batch and 80 total machine hours. Answer (B) is incorrect. US $6.08 assumes that only 80 machine hours were used. Answer (C) is incorrect. US $6.21 assumes one setup per batch.

6.13 Responsibility Accounting

30. Which of the following techniques would be **best** for evaluating the management performance of a department that is operated as a cost center?

A. Return on assets ratio.

B. Return on investment ratio.

C. Payback method.

D. Variance analysis.

Answer (D) is correct. *(CIA, adapted)*

REQUIRED: The best method for evaluating a cost center.

DISCUSSION: A cost center is a responsibility center that is responsible for costs only. Of the alternatives given, variance analysis is the only one that can be used in a cost center. Variance analysis involves comparing actual costs with predicted or standard costs.

Answer (A) is incorrect. Return on assets cannot be computed for a cost center. The manager is not responsible for revenue (return) or the assets available. Answer (B) is incorrect. Return on investments cannot be computed for a cost center. The manager is not responsible for revenue (return) or the assets available. Answer (C) is incorrect. The payback method is a means of evaluating alternative investment proposals.

STUDY UNIT SEVEN
REGULATORY, LEGAL, AND ECONOMIC ISSUES

(24 pages of outline)

This study unit discusses the impact of government regulation and the economic environment on business. The first subunit concerns such matters as environmental law, consumer protection, securities regulation, antitrust law, the money supply and interest rates, and criminal law. The second subunit covers international trade issues, such as comparative advantage, foreign currency exchange rates, and trade barriers. The next subunit discusses various tax structures and their effects on business. The fourth subunit describes key economic indicators such as the gross domestic product and other national income concepts, inflation indexes, and the balance of payments. Other key indicators are classified as leading, lagging, and coincident. The fifth subunit outlines the legal rules of evidence. The final subunit addresses the nature and essential elements of contract-based agreements.

Core Concepts

- Agencies and commissions may have the functions of investigation, enforcement, rule making, and adjudication.
- Securities law requires complete and fair disclosure to potential investors, although some securities and transactions are exempt. It also imposes penalties for fraud and prohibits insider trading on the basis of nonpublic information.
- Antitrust law makes restraints of trade illegal and prohibits actions that lessen competition substantially or tend to create a monopoly.
- Much consumer protection legislation has been enacted to, for example, (1) maintain the safety of drugs and food, (2) protect the public from hazardous consumer products, (3) regulate product warranties, and (4) require truth in lending.
- Environmental law may (1) establish air and water quality standards, (2) regulate hazardous waste, (3) provide for cleanup of pollution, and (4) require government agencies to consider the environmental effects of their actions.
- A central bank (1) controls the nation's money supply, (2) affects interest rates, (3) supervises the banking system, (4) holds the reserves of member banks, (5) oversees check collection, and (6) serves as the government's fiscal agent.
- A nation has a comparative advantage when it has a lower opportunity cost (output forgone) of producing a product.
- The exchange rate is the price of one country's currency in terms of another country's currency.
- Equilibrium exchange rates in floating markets are determined by supply and demand for currencies.
- A seller ordinarily wants to be paid in its own currency. Thus, when the demand for a country's products rises, demand for its currency also rises.
- Protectionism is any measure taken by a government to protect domestic producers. Protectionism takes many forms.
- Advocates of trade barriers advance three basic arguments: (1) Reducing imports protects domestic jobs, (2) certain industries are essential to national security, and (3) infant industries need protection.

- Protectionist measures have the effect of shifting workers from relatively efficient export industries into less efficient protected industries.
- The WTO Agreement is a permanent set of commitments by more than 120 nations designed to prohibit trade discrimination among member nations and between imported and domestic products.
- The study of business cycles focuses on the periodic cycles in the economy, most of which involve changes in price levels and rates of employment. A cycle's stages are trough, recovery, peak, and recession.
- Economic indicators are variables that in the past have been highly correlated with economic activity.
- Government, at all levels, finances its expenditures by taxation. Thus, taxes generate government revenues. National governments also use taxation as a means of implementing fiscal policy regarding inflation, full employment, economic growth, etc.
- The gross domestic product is the total market value of all final goods and services produced within the boundaries of a country, whether by domestic or foreign-owned sources, during a specified period (usually one year).
- The balance of payments includes all international payments made by one nation to another, including those for imports, exports, investments, unilateral transfers, and capital movements. The principal accounts are the current account and the capital account.
- The legal rules of evidence are found in statutes, case law, and constitutions. Their essential purpose is to govern the admissibility of evidence in legal proceedings, but they are drafted with a view to protecting the parties as well as ascertaining the truth.
- A contract is a promise or an agreement that the law recognizes as establishing a duty of performance. It is enforceable by applying a remedy for its breach.

7.1 REGULATION OF BUSINESS

1. A topic tested at the awareness level is the **impact of government legislation and regulation on business** (Content Outline, Part III). To address this broad subject, Subunit 7.1 provides an overview of some of the major areas of governmental activity.

<u>**Agencies and Commissions**</u>

2. An administrative agency is any public officer or body that makes rules and renders decisions.
   a. An agency or commission may regulate a specific industry or one area affecting all industries.
   b. Agencies and commissions may have the functions of investigation, enforcement, rule making, and adjudication. They do not impose criminal sanctions.
   c. They must act within the authority granted by the **enabling statutes**.
   d. **Administrative agency rules and regulations**
      1) Should not go beyond the scope of the delegated authority of its **enabling statutes**.
      2) May be issued under a **general grant of authority** to an agency to regulate an industry.
      3) May be issued under a **specific grant of authority** to an agency to make detailed rules carrying out objectives of a statute.
   e. **Courts** interpret statutes, regulations, and the actions of agencies when a dispute develops and one or both parties wish a judicial determination.
   f. Some rules and regulations, agencies, and legislation have **sunset provisions** that require periodic review and reenactment or they terminate.

Economic Regulation

3. Such regulation usually concerns price and service to the public and is ordinarily industry specific.

Social Regulation

4. This type of regulation has broader objectives and more pervasive effects. It addresses quality of life issues that are difficult for market forces to remedy, such as workplace and product safety, pollution, and fair employment practices. It applies to most industries.
   a. Social regulation has been criticized on the grounds that it (1) is costly, (2) contributes to overregulation, (3) may inhibit innovation, (4) increases inflation, and (5) may place a disproportionate burden on small entities, thereby having an anticompetitive effect.
   b. Another criticism is that regulators are perceived to have little concern for the relation of marginal benefits and costs.

Securities Law

5. **One purpose** is to provide complete and fair **disclosure** to potential investors in an **initial issuance** of securities.
   a. Disclosure is through a filing with a government agency. Potential investors may be required to receive a disclosure document, the contents of which may be highly regulated.
   b. **Exemptions.** Certain securities and transactions may be exempt, for example, transactions by a person not an issuer, underwriter, or a dealer. Other exemptions also may be available.
   c. **Civil liability** may be imposed on parties associated with a filing that contains a misstatement or omission of a material fact.
      1) Liability also may be imposed for failing to make a required filing or to deliver a required disclosure document to investors or for making a sale prior to a required filing.
   d. **Antifraud liability** may be imposed on sellers in an initial issuance of securities. Liability also may result from selling a security using a communication containing an untrue statement, or an omission, of a material fact.
6. **Other purposes** are to regulate trading of securities **after initial issuance**, provide adequate information to investors, and prevent insiders from unfairly using nonpublic information.
   a. **Registration** may be necessary for securities exchanges, brokers and dealers, securities traded on exchanges, and high-volume securities traded over the counter. Moreover, issuers may be required to file reports.
   b. Insiders (officers, directors, and certain shareholders) may be required to surrender to the entity any **short-swing profits** earned on purchases and sales. They also may be prohibited from buying or selling stock based on inside information not available to the public.
      1) **Insider trading** is buying or selling securities of an entity by individuals with access to nonpublic material information. These individuals have a fiduciary obligation to shareholders or potential shareholders.
      2) **Civil and criminal penalties** for insider trading may be imposed.
   c. Antifraud provisions related to subsequent trading may make unlawful any fraudulent scheme.
   d. In some countries, legislation prohibits secret payments to persons in foreign countries for purposes contrary to public policy. Examples are **corrupt payments** to foreign officials, political parties, or candidates for office for the purpose of obtaining or retaining business.

Antitrust Law

7. **Competition** controls private economic power, increases output, and lowers prices. It promotes
   a. Efficient allocation of resources (resulting in lower prices)
   b. Greater choice by consumers
   c. Greater business opportunities
   d. Fairness in economic behavior
   e. Avoidance of concentrated political power resulting from economic power
8. **Restraints of trade** in domestic or foreign commerce may be prohibited.
   a. But only unreasonable restraints may be illegal.
   b. Some restraints may be automatically treated as violations.
      1) **Price fixing** is usually the most prosecuted violation.
9. Other antitrust laws may prohibit the acquisition of stock or assets of another entity if the effect may be to **lessen competition substantially** or **tend to create a monopoly**.
   a. The following are other actions that may be prohibited by antitrust laws:
      1) **Tying or tie-in sales** (sales in which a buyer must take other products to buy the first product)
      2) **Exclusive dealing** (a requirement by the seller that a buyer not deal with the seller's competitors)
      3) **Price discrimination**
         a) Sellers may not be allowed to grant, and buyers may not induce, unfair discounts and other preferences. However, price discrimination may be justified by cost savings or the need to meet competition.
   b. **Interlocking directorates** also could be prohibited if the entities ceased to be competitors.
10. Unfair methods of competition and unfair or deceptive acts in commerce, including false or misleading advertising, are antitrust violations in some countries.

Consumer Protection

11. A government agency may help to maintain the **safety of drugs, food, cosmetics, etc.**, and also may enforce laws requiring the labeling of hazardous substances.
    a. New drugs may be required to be thoroughly tested before they are marketed. But the premarket review is usually based upon research supplied by the manufacturers.
12. Other consumer protection laws may
    a. Prohibit deceptive **packaging and labeling**.
    b. Give consumers the right to obtain the information reported by **credit agencies**.
    c. Protect the public from **unreasonable risk of injury** from consumer products. They may emphasize safety standards for new products.
    d. Prohibit **discrimination** in providing **credit** and
       1) Provide consumers with rights in contesting billing errors,
       2) Prohibit mailing of unsolicited credit cards, or
       3) Limit a consumer's liability for unauthorized use of lost or stolen credits cards.
    e. Regulate **written warranties** on consumer products.
    f. Prohibit abuses of consumers' rights by **collection agencies**.
    g. Require **disclosure** of the terms and conditions of **consumer credit**.

Environmental Protection

13. An **agency** may be created to centralize environmental control functions of the national government.
14. A **national environmental policy** may be established, and the consideration of environmental issues by government agencies may be promoted.
    a. Thus, agencies may be required to consider the adverse environmental effects of their actions, proposals, legislation, and regulations.
15. **Air quality standards** may be established for listed pollutants. The law may determine emission standards for stationary and mobile sources of pollution.
16. The law also may establish national **water quality standards** and pollution standards for each industry.
    a. It also may provide for a discharge permit program and grants and loans for publicly owned treatment plants.
    b. Additional provisions may apply to oil spills and toxic chemicals.
17. Still other laws may be designed to control **hazardous waste**.
    a. Management requirements may be imposed on generators, transporters, and owners of hazardous waste and on operators of treatment, storage, and disposal facilities.

Money Supply and Interest Rates

18. The **central bank** (a group of regional banks) controls the **money supply**. Any policy designed to affect the money supply, and thus the economy, is **monetary policy**.
    a. Control of the growth of the money supply is essential to control spending, inflation, and the availability of credit. One reason is that the economic health of the nation requires the money supply to grow at the same rate as the economy.
19. The **functions of a central bank** include
    a. Control of the money supply
    b. Check collection
    c. Serving as the fiscal agent of the government
    d. Supervision of the entire banking system
    e. Holding deposits (reserves) for member institutions
20. A **commercial bank** must have on reserve a certain percentage of its total deposits. These **fractional reserve requirements** are required by law to
    a. Ensure that money will be on hand to carry out transactions
    b. Control the total supply of money
21. If a bank's actual reserves exceed the reserves required by law, it has **excess reserves** with which it can (and will, if it is a profit-maximizing bank) extend loans.
    a. An individual bank creates money equal to a multiple of its excess reserves when it lends the excess reserves rather than investing in securities.
    b. **Money multiplier.** For the banking system as a whole, assuming **no leakage** (that is, assuming that all the money in the economy is in banks), money creation is measured by a multiple of excess reserves, as follows:

       $D = 1 \div r$ If: D = the money multiplier
       r = the legal reserve requirement

       1) EXAMPLE: Assume the banking system's excess reserves increase by US $100. Using the formula above (and assuming the reserve requirement is 20%), the money supply is multiplied by 5.

          $D = 1 \div .2 = 5$
          (US $100 × 5) = US $500

c. A **market** exists for the lending by **member banks** of their reserves to each other. Member banks are affiliated with the central bank. (But the distinction between member and nonmember banks may not be meaningful because the central bank may regulate the whole banking system.)

   1) Thus, if one bank has **excess reserves**, it can earn additional interest by lending to another member bank that needs additional reserves. These are very short-term loans.

22. A central bank uses **monetary policy tools**.

   a. **Open-market operations.** Purchase and sale of government securities is a primary mechanism of monetary control.

      1) **Purchases are expansionary.** They increase bank reserves and the money supply.
      2) **Sales are contractional.** Paying money into the central bank takes the money out of circulation, reduces bank reserves, and contracts the money supply.
      3) **Interest rate** changes may be used. Changes in the target for the rate charged by member banks for short-term loans to each other is one tool of monetary policy.

         a) For example, to lower the rate, the central bank buys government securities, putting more reserves into the system and exerting downward pressure on the rate. This process has the same effect as changing the money supply.

   b. **Reserves.** The legal reserve requirement is the percentage of deposits that must be kept on hand.

      1) **Lowering the percentage is expansionary** (allowing banks to put more of their excess reserves into circulation through loans).
      2) **Raising the percentage has the opposite effect.**
      3) This tool is not often used because of its powerful effects.

   c. **Changing the rate** at which member banks may borrow from the central bank.

      1) **Lowering the rate** encourages borrowing and increases the money supply.
      2) **Raising the rate** discourages borrowing, increases saving, and decreases the money supply.

Stop and review! You have completed the outline for this subunit. Study multiple-choice questions 1 through 5 beginning on page 337.

7.2 INTERNATIONAL TRADE

Comparative Advantage

1. The laws of **supply and demand** affect imports and exports in the same way that they affect domestic goods. For example, a decrease in petroleum production in a single country can raise the world price of oil.

   a. **Net exports** is the amount of a country's exports minus its imports. A nation has **net imports** if its imports exceed its exports.

2. **The exchange ratio (terms of trade)** is the ratio of a country's export price index to its import price index, multiplied by 100.

   a. EXAMPLE: Kenya's entire exports for the year consist of US $800,000 worth of coffee to Spain. Spain's entire exports consist of US $1,000,000 worth of concrete to Kenya.

      1) Kenya's terms of trade are thus 80 [(US $800,000 ÷ $1,000,000) × 100]. Spain's terms of trade are 125 [(US $1,000,000 ÷ $800,000) × 100].

b. When the ratio falls, a country is said to have deteriorating terms of trade. When the ratio is less than 100, the country is an overall loser in terms of world trade.

3. **Countries vary greatly in their efficiency** in producing certain goods because of differences in such factors as
   a. Climatic and geographical conditions
   b. Human capacities
   c. Supply and type of capital accumulation
   d. Proportions of resources
   e. Political and social climates

4. Given these differences, countries can **mutually benefit from trade.**
   a. The greatest advantage from trade is obtained **when each nation specializes** in producing what it can produce most efficiently or, more precisely, least inefficiently.
      1) If nations specialize and then exchange with others, **more is produced and consumed** than if each nation tries to be self-sufficient.
   b. Specialization of labor is beneficial for individuals. The same principle applies to nations.
   c. The reason for this phenomenon is **comparative advantage.**
      1) Comparative advantage is based on the principle of **relative opportunity costs.**
      2) A country has a comparative advantage in the production of a good when it has a lower opportunity cost than another producer. That is, it has to **sacrifice fewer units** of another good to generate an additional unit of the first good.
   d. EXAMPLE: Stellonia and Lumpen can produce the following output with one year of labor. Labor is the only input:

	Stellonia	Lumpen
Food (tons)	100	40
Cars	100	90

      1) Stellonia has an **absolute advantage** regarding both products. It is a more efficient producer of food and cars because its output of each is greater with the same input.
      2) However, Lumpen has a **comparative advantage** in production of one product.
         a) Stellonia is 2.5 times as efficient at producing food (100 ÷ 40), but only 1.1 times as efficient at producing cars (100 ÷ 90).
         b) If Lumpen devoted a year of labor to food, the world output of food would only increase by 40 tons. But if it devoted that same year of labor to cars, world car output would increase by 90.
            i) Stellonia gains one car by forgoing 1.0 ton of food (100 ÷ 100). However, Lumpen gains one car by forgoing just .44 ton of food (40 ÷ 90). Thus, Lumpen's comparative advantage arises because its **opportunity cost is lower** than that of Stellonia for cars with respect to food.
      3) If the two countries specialize and engage in trade, the world has more of both food and cars. Thus, specialization and trade **enhance world output without changing total input.**
         a) Moreover, the greater abundance of affordable goods means that workers in **both countries** experience **higher real wages.**
      4) A nation theoretically **exports** goods in which it has a **comparative advantage** and **imports** goods in which it has a **comparative disadvantage.**

Foreign Currency Rates and Markets

5. When a person buys **something from a party in a foreign country**, whether it is merchandise, a capital asset, or a financial instrument, the seller wishes to be paid in its domestic currency.
   a. For the buyer and seller to execute this transaction efficiently, the two currencies must be convertible to one another in an **exchange market** at an easily determinable rate.

Fixed Exchange Rates

6. One unit of a currency is set equal to a given number of units of another currency by law.
   a. EXAMPLE: In July 1986, the **Saudi** riyal was fixed at a ratio of 3.75 riyals to 1 US dollar. Because the U.S. buys a large quantity of petroleum from Saudi Arabia, this fixed currency has the advantage of adding stability to the U.S. oil market.

Floating Exchange Rates

7. The market is allowed to determine the exchange rate of two currencies.
   a. Thus, **supply and demand functions** exist for currencies.
   b. The rate at which the supply and demand for a currency in terms of another currency are equal is the **equilibrium exchange rate**.
      1) EXAMPLE: Given the supply and demand curves below, domestic parties can exchange 20 local currency units (LCUs) for one foreign currency unit (FCU).

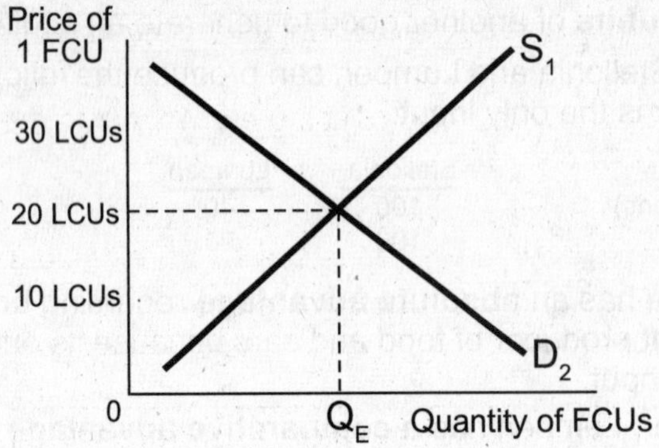

8. A seller normally wants to be paid in its own currency. Thus, when the **demand for a foreign country's products** rises, **demand for its currency** also rises.
   a. EXAMPLE: Assuming a fixed supply of FCUs, the equilibrium price of FCUs increases. This relationship is depicted by the rightward shift of the demand curve below:

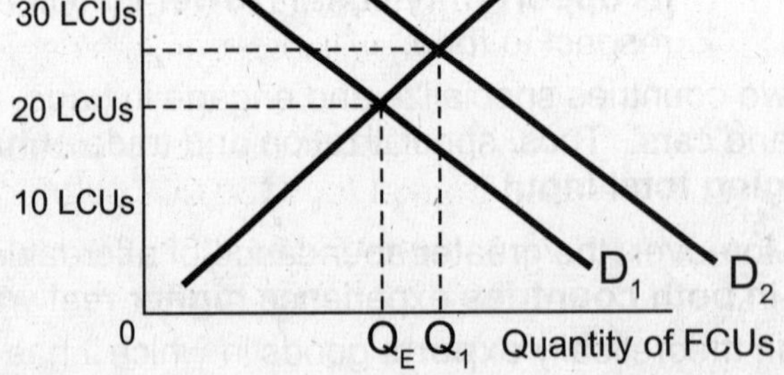

      1) If a domestic buyer wants one FCU, it must pay 27.5 LCUs. Thus, LCUs have lost purchasing power **(depreciated)**, and FCUs have gained purchasing power **(appreciated)**.

2) In general, **the purchasing power of a currency moves in tandem with demand for that country's output**.

9. Domestic **incomes** also affect the **demand** for a foreign currency.

   a. When **incomes rise**, buyers demand more goods and services, including those originating in other countries.

   b. The result is **depreciation of the local currency**. Incomes have risen, so the supply of LCUs also has risen, reducing their value. Moreover, the foreign currency has appreciated relative to the local currency.

10. Relative **interest rates** affect the **supply** of a foreign currency.

   a. When **the real interest rate in a foreign country** is higher than that in the domestic economy, investors will tend to demand more of that foreign currency to take advantage of the higher rate.

      1) This principle does not apply, however, if the high interest rate in the foreign country is due to high inflation.

Interaction in Foreign Currency Markets

11. Exchange rates are set in the spot market and the forward market. The relevant market depends on when the transaction will be settled.

   a. The relevant exchange rates are the spot rate and the forward rate.

      1) The **spot rate** is the exchange rate in effect today to settle a transaction today.

      2) The **forward rate** is the exchange rate in effect today for a transaction that will be settled in the future.

   b. A rate can be **locked in** by purchasing a **contract** in the forward market at a definite rate.

      1) The spot and forward **rates are calculated** using the ratio **FCU ÷ LCU**. The ratio states how many FCUs can be purchased for one LCU.

      2) Discount or premium is determined by the following:

	LCU	FCU
Forward rate > spot rate	Premium	Discount
Spot rate > forward rate	Discount	Premium

12. An entity can **manage the risk** inherent in currency exchange rates by hedging, that is, by purchasing or selling **foreign currency futures**.

   a. EXAMPLE: Robespierre Gauge and Meter (RGM), a French corporation, has sold sophisticated electronic scales to a Japanese pharmaceutical business.

      1) The sales price is fixed at ¥130,000,000 due in 90 days.

         a) The entity holding the receivable (RGM) wants to **hedge the risk** that the foreign currency (yen) will lose purchasing power against the domestic currency (euro).

      2) Based on the spot rate in effect on the day of the sale, RGM **buys a futures contract** on the open market for ¥130,000,000 to be received in 90 days.

      3) In 90 days, the yen has depreciated slightly against the euro, so the ¥130,000,000 RGM receives from the Japanese entity is worth fewer euros than RGM expected.

      4) RGM sends a wire transfer to exchange the ¥130,000,000 for euros, receiving fewer than originally expected.

      5) RGM also **sells the futures contract** it had purchased 90 days earlier.

6) The loss in purchasing power of the yen and the gain in the value of the futures contract offset each other. Accordingly, the value of the hedged transaction in euros is approximately the same as on the day of the sale.

Trade Barriers

13. Even though individuals (as a whole) are best off under free trade, **governments** often establish policies designed to **interfere** in the workings of the marketplace.

a. **Protectionism** is any measure taken by a government to protect domestic producers. Protectionism takes many forms.

1) **Tariffs** are consumption taxes designed to restrict imports, e.g., a tax on German beer. Governments raise tariffs to discourage consumption of imported products. Domestic producers are not subject to the tariff and will therefore have a price advantage over their foreign competitors. However, absent such competition, the domestic price of the item will be higher. Domestic producers will sell more at a higher price, and domestic consumers will consume less following the price increase.

a) **Revenue tariffs** are usually applied to products that are not produced domestically. Their purpose is to provide the government with tax revenue.

2) **Import quotas** set fixed limits on different products, e.g., French wine.

a) In the short run, import quotas will help a country's balance of payments position by increasing domestic employment, but the prices of the products produced also will increase.

b) An **embargo** is a total ban on some kinds of imports. It is an extreme form of the import quota.

3) **Domestic content rules** require that at least a portion of any imported product be constructed from parts manufactured in the importing nation.

a) This rule is sometimes used by **capital-intensive nations**. Parts can be produced using idle capacity and then sent to a labor-intensive country for final assembly.

4) **Voluntary export restrictions** are agreements entered into by exporters to reduce the number of products made available in a foreign country in an attempt to avoid official sanctions.

a) These restrictions can be counterproductive. Because the supply of the product desired by consumers in the importing country is held artificially low, the exporter sometimes can charge a price high enough to earn profits greater than normal.

5) A **trigger price mechanism** automatically imposes a tariff barrier against unfairly cheap imports by levying a duty (tariff) on all imports below a particular reference price (the price that activates the tariff).

6) **Antidumping rules** prevent foreign producers from selling excess goods on the domestic market at less than cost to eliminate competitors and gain control of the market.

7) **Exchange controls** limit foreign currency transactions and set exchange rates. The purpose is to limit the ability of an entity selling in a country to **repatriate** its earnings.

8) **Export subsidies** are payments by the government to producers in certain industries in an attempt to increase exports.

a) A government may impose **countervailing duties** on imported goods if those goods were produced in a foreign country with the aid of a governmental subsidy.

9) **Special tax benefits to exporters** are an indirect form of export subsidy. However, the WTO has ruled some of these tax benefits to be illegal.

10) Certain exports may require **licenses**. For example, sales of technology with military applications are limited by western nations that are members of the Coordinating Committee for Multilateral Export Controls.

11) An extreme form of protectionism is **expropriation** of the assets of a foreign entity. It is also the greatest **political risk** of doing business abroad.

b. The **economic effects of tariffs and quotas** can be summarized as follows:

1) **Workers** are shifted from relatively efficient export industries into **less efficient** protected industries. **Real wages decline** as a result, as does total world output.

2) Under a **tariff**, the excess paid by the customer for an imported good goes into the **government treasury** where it can be spent for any purpose.

a) Under a **quota**, prices also are driven up (by the induced shortage), but the excess goes to the **exporter** in the foreign country.

3) A **tariff** is imposed on all importers equally. Thus, the more efficient ones will still be able to set their **prices lower** than the less efficient ones.

a) An import **quota**, on the other hand, does not affect foreign importers equally. Import licenses may be assigned as much for **political favoritism** as on any other grounds.

c. Advocates of trade barriers advance three basic **arguments in favor of protectionism**:

1) Reducing imports **protects domestic jobs**.
2) Certain industries are **essential to national security**.
3) Infant industries need protection in the **early stages of development**.

d. **Special-interest groups** are strong and well-organized. They **lobby** effectively to pass legislation that restricts free trade.

Stop and review! You have completed the outline for this subunit. Study multiple-choice questions 6 through 14 beginning on page 338.

7.3 METHODS OF TAXATION

1. Government, at all levels, finances its expenditures by taxation. Thus, taxes generate **government revenues**. National governments also use taxation as a means of implementing fiscal policy regarding inflation, full employment, economic growth, etc.

2. One reason for taxation is that individuals should pay tax based on the **benefits received** from the services (e.g., paying for the use of a public park or swimming pool). Another view is that consumers should pay taxes based on their **ability to pay** (e.g., taxes on income and wealth).

__Tax Rate Structures__

3. **Progressive.** Higher income persons pay a higher percentage of their income in taxes.

a. **Indexing** is a means of avoiding the unfairness that results when inflation increases nominal but not real taxable income, subjecting it to higher tax rates. Adjusting tax bracket, deduction, and exemption amounts by reference to some index of inflation avoids this problem.

4. **Proportional.** At all levels of income, the percentage paid in taxes is constant (e.g., a flat tax on income).

5. **Regressive.** As income increases, the percentage paid in taxes decreases (e.g., sales, payroll, property, or excise taxes). For example, an **excise tax** is regressive because its burden falls disproportionately on lower-income persons. As personal income increases, the percentage of income paid declines because an excise tax is a flat amount per quantity of the good or service purchased.
   a. An excise tax increases the selling price of the product. This **price** increase will have a less negative effect on sales volume for products with less **elastic demand**. Examples of products with low elasticity of demand include gasoline, tobacco, and alcohol. The tax revenue generated by an increase in excise taxes is therefore higher if the tax is levied on products with less elastic demand.
      1) Demand is price elastic if a given percentage change in price results in a greater percentage change in revenues in the opposite direction.

Tax Rates

6. The **marginal tax rate** is the rate applied to the last unit of taxable income.
   a. The **average tax rate** is the total tax liability divided by the amount of taxable income.
   b. The **effective tax rate** is the total tax liability divided by total economic income (includes amounts that do not have tax consequences).

Direct vs. Indirect

7. **Direct taxes** are imposed upon the taxpayer and paid directly to the government, e.g., the personal income tax.
   a. **Indirect taxes** are levied against others and therefore only indirectly on the individual taxpayer, e.g., corporate income taxes.

Tax Credits

8. Tax credits, e.g., the **investment tax credit**, are deductions on the income tax return that lower investment cost and increase a project's net present value.

Incidence of Taxation

9. Who actually bears a particular tax is not always obvious. Accordingly, the person who actually bears an indirect tax may not be the one who pays the tax to the government.
   a. The incidence of taxation is important when a government wants to change the tax structure. Because taxation is a form of **fiscal policy**, the government needs to know who will actually bear the burden of a tax, not just who will statutorily pay it.
   b. Taxes such as the **corporate income tax** and corporate **property and excise taxes** are often shifted to customers in the form of higher prices.
      1) However, sellers ordinarily must bear part of the burden. Passing on the entire tax might reduce unit sales unacceptably by raising the price too high. Thus, the effect of the tax is to reduce supply (because suppliers' costs increase) and quantity demanded by buyers (because the price increases). The combined loss of sellers and buyers is called the **deadweight loss** or excess burden of taxation.
   c. Taxes such as **windfall profits taxes** are not shifted to customers via higher prices. This type of one-time-only tax levied on part of the output produced does not increase the equilibrium price of the taxed good.
   d. **Supply-side economists** use the **Laffer Curve** to attempt to explain how people react to varying rates of income taxation. For example, if the income tax rate is 0%, zero revenue will be raised. Similarly, if the tax rate is 100%, income tax revenue will probably be zero because an earner who faces a tax rate of 100% will not work.
      1) The **optimal income tax rate** will bring in the most revenue possible. A rate that is either too high or too low will generate less than optimal tax revenues.

2) Supply-side economists do not state that lowering income tax rates will produce more revenue. Instead, they claim that, **if the rates are too high**, lowering rates will produce more revenue because output and national income will increase. This result, in theory, should follow because of increased incentives to work, invest, and save.

3) However, economic policy should not be confused with **political considerations**. There are obvious political reasons for having higher or lower tax rates on certain income levels. Thus, the theory underlying the Laffer Curve does not address questions of redistributionist politics.

4) A criticism of the Laffer Curve is that it does not prescribe the **optimal tax rate**. The only way to know whether the current tax rates are too high or too low is to change them and see whether revenues increase.

a) Critics also have observed that the incentives provided by tax cuts may have relatively small supply-side effects and that those effects may be felt only in the very long run.

b) Still another potential problem is that cutting taxes in an **expanding economy** may overstimulate demand, thereby increasing inflation.

<u>**International Tax Considerations**</u>

10. **Multinational corporations** frequently derive income from several countries. The government of each country in which a corporation does business may enact statutes imposing one or more types of tax on the corporation.

11. **Treaties.** To avoid double taxation, two or more countries may adopt treaties to coordinate or synchronize the effects of their taxing statutes.

a. Treaties also are used integrate other governmental goals, e.g., providing incentives for desired investment.

b. A treaty might modify the rules in a country's statutes that designate the source country of income or the domicile of an entity.

12. **Multinational Corporations**

a. Most countries tax only the **income sourced to that country**.

b. But some countries tax **worldwide income** (from whatever source derived) of a domestic corporation. Double taxation is avoided by allowing a credit for income tax paid to foreign countries or by treaty provisions.

c. In the case of **foreign corporations**, a country may tax only income sourced to it. Ordinarily, such income is effectively connected with engaging in a trade or business of the country. Certain source income, e.g., gain on the sale of most stock, may not be taxed.

d. **Transfer pricing** is an important aspect of the tax calculation for multinational corporations that transfer inventories between branches in different countries.

1) For example, laws may limit the amount of profit that can be transferred from a local parent to a foreign subsidiary or branch.

2) The basic transfer pricing rules also may limit the amount of taxable income that can be claimed by the foreign subsidiary.

3) Thus, transfer prices charged to foreign subsidiaries may differ substantially from those charged to domestic subsidiaries.

e. Transfer pricing has **nontax aspects**. For example, limitations on taking profits out of a foreign country, or **currency restrictions**, can be avoided by charging the foreign subsidiary a higher transfer price than that charged to domestic subsidiaries.

1) Entities in developing countries are allowed to pay their accounts payable to foreign vendors, but they may not be allowed to distribute profits to foreign owners.

f. The existence of **tariffs** in the foreign country may necessitate a lower transfer price to reduce a tariff based on the inventory value.

Value-Added Tax (VAT)

13. Many major industrial nations have already adopted a **value-added tax (VAT)**.

    a. The tax is levied on the **value added to goods by each business unit in the production and distribution chain**. The amount of value added is the difference between sales and purchases. Each entity in the chain collects the tax on its sales, takes a credit for taxes paid on purchases, and remits the difference to the government.

    b. The consumer ultimately bears the incidence of the tax through higher prices.

    c. A VAT encourages consumer savings because taxes are paid only on consumption, not on savings. Because the VAT is based on consumption, people in the lower income groups spend a greater proportion of their income on this type of tax. Thus, the VAT is regressive.

    d. Only those businesses that make a profit have to pay income taxes. The VAT, however, requires all businesses to pay taxes, regardless of income.

    e. The VAT tax is not a useful tool for fiscal policy purposes.

Stop and review! You have completed the outline for this subunit. Study multiple-choice questions 15 through 18 beginning on page 340.

7.4 ECONOMIC INDICATORS

Business Cycles

1. The study of business cycles focuses on the periodic cycles in the economy, most of which involve changes in price levels and rates of employment.

    a. A business cycle has four stages: trough, recovery, peak, and recession.

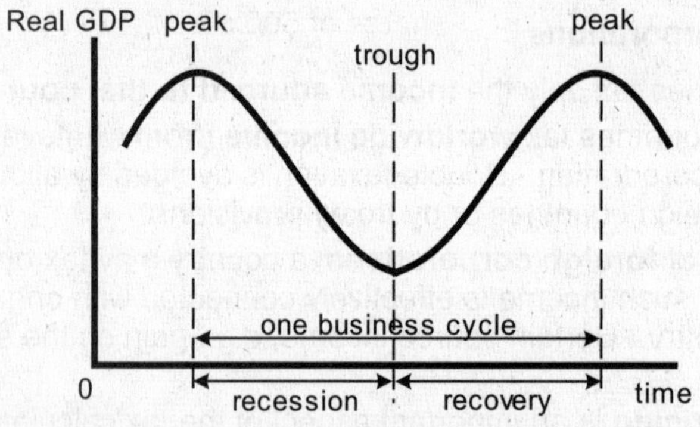

1) A **trough** has low levels of economic activity and underuse of resources. Sales and profits of most entities are depressed.

2) **Recovery** is the stage of increasing economic activity. Sales and profits of most entities rise.

3) At the **peak**, economic activity is at a high level. Sales and profits are at the maximum for most entities.

4) **Recession** means economic activities and employment levels contract. Sales and profits decline.

    a) During the recessionary phase of a business cycle, society's resources are underused. Because of the underuse of resources, potential national income will exceed actual national income.

5) A **depression** is a major, long-lasting downturn in the economy. Conditions are similar to that of a recession, but more severe and less easily adjusted.

a) If businesses reduce their spending too severely and too quickly, their suppliers are forced to lay off employees in large numbers. If unemployment becomes widespread, it creates a cycle leading to more unemployment.

b) Causes of a depression include (1) overextension of credit during prosperity, (2) inventories in excess of consumer demand, (3) overspeculation in stocks and commodities, and (4) failure of new investments to match savings.

b. Business cycles are a natural phenomenon, at least under classical economic theory. In recent decades, **fiscal and monetary policy** have been used to minimize the negative effects of business cycles.

1) Although the specific causes of cycles have never been definitively identified, **consumer confidence** seems to be one factor. When consumers become pessimistic about future economic events, they spend less. The result is an increase in inventory levels. Businesses respond to the increase in inventory by reducing production and laying off workers.

<u>**Economic Indicators**</u>

2. Economists use economic indicators to forecast changes in the business cycle. They are variables that in the past have had a high correlation with aggregate economic activity. The best known are the composite indexes calculated by **The Conference Board**, a private research group with many corporate and other members worldwide. Indicators may lead, lag, or coincide with economic activity. A leading indicator is a forecast of future economic trends, and a lagging indicator changes after the economic activity has occurred.

a. **Leading indicators** include

1) Average workweek for production workers
2) Prices of the ordinary shares of 500 companies
3) Average weekly initial unemployment insurance claims
4) New orders for consumer goods and materials
5) New orders for nondefense capital goods
6) Building permits for homes
7) Vendor performance (slower deliveries diffusion index)
8) Money supply
9) Index of consumer expectations
10) Interest rate spread

b. **Lagging indicators** include

1) Average duration of unemployment in weeks
2) Change in index of labor cost per unit of output
3) Average prime rate charged by banks
4) Ratio of manufacturing and trade inventories to sales
5) Commercial and industrial loans outstanding
6) Ratio of consumer installment credit outstanding to personal income
7) Change in consumer price index for services

c. **Coincident indicators** include

1) Employees on nonagricultural payrolls
2) Personal income minus transfer payments
3) Industrial production (based on value added and physical output)
4) Manufacturing and trade sales

Investment Expenditure

3. This factor is often used by economists to explain business cycles.
   a. The **accelerator theory** gives a model for volatility of investment and the subsequent effects on gross domestic product (GDP), the broadest measure of national economic activity.
      1) The accelerator theory states that **capital investment** is related to the rate of change in GDP.
      2) It assumes a particular level of **capital equipment** needed to produce a given level of output.
   b. Given an economy producing at capacity and a subsequent increase in **product demand**, an increase in capital investment is required to meet the increased demand. The demand for capital goods then creates an additional increase in demand, which in turn requires an additional investment in capital goods. In this way, the process of investing to meet **demand continues to accelerate**.
   c. A **positive net investment** occurs when the additions to capital goods exceed the amount of depreciation on existing capital goods.
      1) **Negative net investment** occurs when depreciation exceeds the additions to capital stock.

National Income Accounting

4. National income accounting measures the output and performance of the economy. The **gross domestic product (GDP)** is the principal measure. It is the total market value of all final goods and services produced within the boundaries of a country, whether by domestic or foreign-owned sources, during a specified period of time (usually a year). GDP is calculated without regard to the **ownership of productive resources**. Thus, the value of the output of a factory abroad is excluded regardless of its ownership, but the output of a foreign-owned factory is included in the host country's GDP.
   a. **Income (resource cost) approach.** GDP equals the sum of the items below.
      1) Employee compensation, interest, and rents
      2) Self-employment income
      3) Depreciation (consumption of fixed capital)
      4) Indirect business taxes (e.g., sales taxes)
      5) Rents, interest income, and corporate profits
      6) Net income of foreigners (a positive number if the amount earned domestically by foreigners exceeds the amount earned abroad by citizens)
   b. **Expenditure approach.** GDP is also the sum of
      1) Personal consumption expenditures
      2) Gross private domestic investment
      3) Government purchases
      4) Net exports
   c. To **avoid double counting**, the value added to each good or service at each stage of production over the period must be summed. Alternatively, the total market value of all final goods and services may be added.
   d. **GDP is not an ideal measure** of economic well-being.
      1) GDP is a **monetary measure**. Accordingly, comparing GDP over a period of time requires adjustment for changes in the price level. The **GDP deflator** is a price index used to convert nominal GDP to real GDP.
      2) Increases in GDP often involve **environmental damage** such as noise, congestion, or pollution.

3) GDP is not adjusted for **changes in the population** (which changes per capita income).
4) Changes in the value of **leisure time** are not considered.
5) Some **nonmarket transactions** are excluded, e.g., the value of homemakers' work.
6) **Military expenditures** are included at cost, not incremental total value.

e. **Other National Income Concepts**

1) The **Gross National Product (GNP)** measures the output of a country's production, including factors of production located outside the boundaries of the country. The GNP differs from the GDP because GNP includes the output of a country's workers located in another country. It also equals GDP minus net income of foreigners (a positive or negative amount).
2) **Net domestic product (NDP)** = GDP – depreciation.
3) **National income (NI)** = NDP + net income earned abroad – indirect business taxes (e.g., sales taxes).
   a) NI is the income earned by a nation's resources, whether located at home or abroad.
   b) NI plus depreciation and indirect business taxes equals GNP.
4) **Personal income (PI)** = NI – corporate income taxes and undistributed profits – required contributions to governmental social security programs + transfer payments (public and private).
5) **Disposable income** = PI – personal income taxes.

f. **Real per capita output** is GDP divided by population, adjusted for inflation. It is used as a measure of the standard of living.

Measuring Inflation

5. One type of index measures inflation by a monthly pricing of items on a typical **household shopping list**.
   a. The current index uses a base year as a reference point. The price in the current year of a market basket of goods and services is determined relative to the same basket for the base year.
   b. $$\frac{\text{Price of market basket in a given year}}{\text{Price of the same market basket in the base year}} \times 100$$
6. Another type of index measures increases in prices at the **wholesale level**. It is often accepted as a proxy for future inflation.
7. The **GDP deflator** is a price index that includes every item produced in the economy at the price at which it entered the GDP account. **Nominal GDP** is stated at the actual prices at time of measurement. **Real GDP**, after application of the deflator, is stated in base-year dollars.
   a. Real GDP increases when resource inputs and their productivity increase. For example, to the extent that real GDP depends on labor inputs, real GDP equals total worker hours (labor input) times labor productivity (real output per worker per hour).
8. The distinction between nominal income and real income is crucial for understanding the effects of inflation.
   a. **Nominal income** is the **amount in money** received by a consumer as wages, interest, rent, and profits.
   b. **Real income** is the **purchasing power** of the income received, regardless of how it is denominated. Purchasing power relates directly to the consumer's standard of living.
   c. **Real income shrinks when nominal income does not match inflation.**

Unemployment

9. **Frictional unemployment** is the amount of unemployment caused by the normal workings of the labor market.
   a. This group can include those moving to another city, those ceasing work temporarily to pursue further education and training, and those who are simply between jobs.
   b. This definition acknowledges that a "normal" amount of unemployment exists at any given time in a dynamic economy.
10. **Structural unemployment** results when the composition of the workforce does not match the need. It is the result of changes in consumer demand, technology, and geographical location.
   a. As consumers' desires shift, certain skills become obsolete.
   b. For example, the computer revolution has drastically changed the skills required for many jobs and completely eliminated others.
11. **Cyclical unemployment** is directly related to the level of an economy's output. For this reason, it is sometimes called **deficient-demand unemployment**.
   a. As consumers slow their spending, entities cut back production and lay off workers.
12. **Full Employment**
   a. The **natural rate of unemployment** consists of the sum of frictional and structural unemployment.
      1) Economists consider the economy to be at **full employment** when all unemployed workers are in these categories.
      2) The rate varies over time because of demographic and institutional changes in the economy.
   b. The **economy's potential output** is the real (inflation-adjusted) domestic output that could be achieved if the economy sustained full employment.
      1) This concept illustrates the importance of providing all interested workers with productive jobs.

Stop and review! You have completed the outline for this subunit. Study multiple-choice questions 19 through 22 beginning on page 341.

7.5 LEGAL RULES OF EVIDENCE

Sources

1. The legal rules of evidence are found in **statutes, case law, and constitutions**. Their essential purpose is to govern the admissibility of evidence in legal proceedings, but they are drafted with a view to protecting the parties as well as ascertaining the truth.
   a. **Exclusionary rules** prevent the admission of evidence whose value as proof is offset by its possible prejudicial effect. An internal auditor, however, need not be limited by the legal and constitutional safeguards imposed in court.
      1) The internal auditor may examine and evaluate any information until, in his/her professional judgment, sufficient, reliable, relevant, and useful information has been collected.
      2) In this text, the word **evidence** is used strictly in the legal context. The word **information** is used to signify the support for the internal auditor's observations, conclusions, and recommendations.

Internal Audit

2. Nevertheless, **legal and internal auditing concepts** share much common ground. Information in the internal auditing context and evidence in the legal context are intended to provide a basis for belief, to prove or disprove something.

3. The legal rules of evidence may be most obviously relevant to internal auditors when they participate in **fraud investigations** or provide **litigation-support services**, but such knowledge also may be beneficial in ordinary engagement work.

Types of Evidence

4. The following are types of evidence:
   a. **Best evidence** or **primary evidence** constitutes the most satisfactory and reliable method of proving the matter asserted.
      1) The most frequent application of the best evidence rule is to **documentary evidence**.
      2) To prove the **content of a writing**, the original contract, deed, business record, or other document must be produced if it is available.
         a) The purpose of preventing the admission of testimonial evidence to prove the content of a writing is to avoid misinterpretation.
            i) However, oral evidence may be admissible to explain the terms of a writing when it is subject to more than one reasonable interpretation.
   b. **Secondary evidence** is less reliable than primary evidence because it may consist of copies of original documents or oral evidence regarding their content.
      1) Nevertheless, **copies** may be admissible when the originals
         a) Have been lost or destroyed without wrongful intent by the party proffering the copies
         b) Cannot be obtained through legal or other reasonable means by the party proffering the copies
         c) Are within the control of a public entity
      2) Copies are preferable to **written summaries** of, or **oral testimony** about, original writings. However, these types of evidence may be admitted when the originals
         a) Are very voluminous
         b) Cannot be considered by the court within a reasonable time
         c) Are available to be produced for inspection at the court's discretion
      3) Secondary evidence also may be admitted when **production of the originals**, such as the accounting records of a business, and their possession by the court for a long time might cause undue hardship on a party.
   c. **Direct evidence** is proof without presumption or inference.
      1) Examples are original documents and testimony about what a witness him/herself did, saw, or heard.
   d. **Circumstantial evidence** is indirect evidence because it proves **intermediate facts** from which a primary fact that is material to the matter in dispute may be deduced.
      1) For example, an alteration of online accounting data protected by password access constitutes circumstantial evidence that an authorized person was responsible. However, this inference may be unsound if an unauthorized person has been able to obtain the necessary password.
   e. **Conclusive evidence** is so powerful that it permits only one reasonable conclusion and needs no additional corroboration.
   f. **Corroborative evidence** supports other evidence.
      1) For example, the testimony of a second eyewitness to an event may strengthen and confirm the account of the first witness.

g. **Opinion evidence** is usually excluded because of its potentially prejudicial effect.

1) **Witnesses** ordinarily are allowed to testify only as to factual matters within their direct experience.

2) An exception is made for **expert opinion**. Such testimony is allowed when it

a) Concerns matters beyond the knowledge of lay people

b) Is offered by someone whose special expertise and objectivity will assist the court and the jury in the truth ascertainment process

h. **Hearsay evidence** is a statement other than one made by the declarant while testifying at the trial or hearing, offered in evidence to prove the truth of the matter asserted.

1) For example, if Employee A states that Employee B said that she saw Employee C steal from petty cash, Employee A's statement, if offered to prove that Employee C stole from petty cash, is hearsay.

2) Hearsay is **normally inadmissible** because it cannot be tested by cross-examination. Thus, in the example above, Employee A merely heard what B said and therefore cannot be asked questions testing the truth of the matter asserted in the declaration made out of court (or out of the internal auditor's hearing).

3) Various **exceptions** to the hearsay rule exist based on circumstances promoting the reliability of the assertions.

a) For example, documents effectively are hearsay, but documents created in the ordinary course of business are admissible if properly authenticated.

Stop and review! You have completed the outline for this subunit. Study multiple-choice questions 23 through 26 beginning on page 342.

7.6 CONTRACTS

1. No part of commercial law is more pervasive than **contract law**. Billions of contract-based agreements to transfer property and services are negotiated daily by individuals, businesses, and governments.

a. Promise keeping is essential for planning in a modern complex society. Without a legal system committed to **enforcement of private contractual agreements**, everyday transactions in a free-enterprise economy would be impossible. Contemporary contract law allows parties to enter into private agreements with assurance that these agreements are enforceable against a party that fails to perform.

2. A **contract** is a promise or an agreement that the law recognizes as establishing a duty of performance. It is enforceable by applying a remedy for its breach.

Elements

3. The most basic element of a contract is a voluntary agreement by the parties. **Agreement** requires the mutual assent of the contracting parties reached through an offer by the offeror and acceptance by the offeree.

a. An **offer** is a statement or other communication that, if not terminated, confers upon the offeree the power of acceptance. An offer need not be in any particular form to be valid. It must

1) Be communicated to an offeree,
2) Indicate an intent to enter into a contract, and
3) Be sufficiently definite and certain.

b. **Communication** of an offer may be done in various ways and may occur over time. However, at some moment in the formation of a contract, each party expresses an intent to enter into a legally binding and enforceable agreement.

1) Whether an offer has been made is determined by an **objective standard** that uses the following test: Would a reasonable person assume that the power of acceptance had been conferred upon him/her? An offer must be made with serious intent, not in anger, great excitement, or jest.

2) Language constituting an offer should be distinguished from that merely **soliciting or inviting offers**. Communications between parties may simply be preliminary negotiations concerning a possible contract. A party may initiate negotiations by suggesting the general nature of a possible contract.

c. An offer also must be **definite and certain**. If an offer is indefinite or vague or lacking an essential provision, no agreement arises from an attempt to accept it because the courts cannot tell what the parties are bound to do.

1) However, minor details left for future determination do not make an agreement too vague to be an offer.

d. An offer does not remain effective forever. The **offer will terminate** under any of the following circumstances:

1) Revocation by the offeror,
2) Rejection or counteroffer by the offeree,
3) Death or incompetency of either the offeror or offeree,
4) Destruction of the specific subject matter to which the offer relates,
5) Subsequent illegality of the offer, or
6) Lapse of a specified or reasonable time.

e. **Acceptance** of an offer is essential to the formation of a contract. An agreement consists of an offer and an acceptance.

1) To be effective, an acceptance must relate to the terms of the offer. The acceptance must be positive, unequivocal, and unconditional. It may not change, subtract from, add to, or qualify in any way the terms of the offer.

4. **Consideration** is the primary basis for the enforcement of agreements in contract law. It is what is given to make a promise enforceable. Ordinarily, if a promise is not supported by consideration, it is not enforceable.

a. One requirement of consideration is **mutuality of obligation**. Both parties must give consideration. Consequently, something of legal value must be given in a bargained-for exchange when the parties intend an exchange.

b. The second required element of consideration is **legal sufficiency** (something of legal value). Consideration is legally sufficient to render a promise enforceable if the promisor receives a legal benefit or the promisee incurs a legal detriment.

1) To incur a legal detriment, the promisee must do (or promise to do) something that (s)he is not legally obligated to do or not do (or promise not to do) something (s)he is legally entitled to do. A cause-and-effect relationship must exist between the promise made by one party and the detriment incurred by the other.

5. Parties to a contract must possess legal capacity. **Capacity** is the mental ability to make a rational decision, which includes the ability to perceive and appreciate all relevant facts. Three classes of parties are legally limited in their capacity to contract: minors (also known as infants), mentally incompetent persons, and intoxicated parties.

a. For **public policy reasons**, parties in these three groups are protected from the enforcement of most contracts against them.

6. **Legality** is an essential requirement for an agreement to be valid and enforceable. Formation or performance of an agreement may violate a criminal law, constitute a civil wrong upon which a suit may be filed, or be determined by a court to be contrary to public policy. In these instances, the agreement is illegal and unenforceable.
   a. An agreement that is **contrary to public policy** has a negative impact on society at large that outweighs the interests of the parties. This principle reflects a balancing by the courts of freedom of contract and the public interest. Examples of agreements that may violate public policy are
      1) Agreements to unduly restrain competition;
      2) Clauses that excuse one of the parties from any liability;
      3) Contracts calling for immoral acts; and
      4) Agreements found to be unfair, oppressive, or unconscionable.

Written Contracts

7. An oral contract is as enforceable as a written contract. However, a statute may require that some contracts be **in writing** to be enforceable. For example, statutes may require the following to be in writing:
   a. Contracts involving an interest in land
   b. Contracts that by their terms cannot possibly be performed within 1 year (e.g., some employment contracts)
   c. Collateral promises by which a person promises to answer for the debt or duty of another (e.g., a guarantee)
   d. Contracts for the sale of goods for more than a stated amount

Stop and review! You have completed the outline for this subunit. Study multiple-choice questions 27 through 30 beginning on page 343.

7.7 SUMMARY

1. An administrative agency is any public officer or body that makes rules and renders decisions. An agency or commission may regulate a specific industry or one area affecting all industries. Agencies and commissions may have the functions of investigation, enforcement, rule making, and adjudication. They do not impose criminal sanctions.
2. One purpose of securities law is to provide complete and fair disclosure to potential investors in an initial issuance of securities. Disclosure may be through a filing with the designated regulator. Certain securities and transactions may be exempt, for example, transactions by a person not an issuer, underwriter, or a dealer. Other exemptions also may be available.
3. Other purposes of securities law are to regulate trading of securities after initial issuance, provide adequate information to investors, and prevent insiders from unfairly using nonpublic information.
4. Insider trading is buying or selling securities of an entity by individuals with access to nonpublic material information. These individuals have a fiduciary obligation to shareholders or potential shareholders.
5. Antifraud provisions related to subsequent trading make unlawful any fraudulent scheme.
6. Restraints of trade in domestic or foreign commerce may be prohibited. But only unreasonable restraints may be illegal. Some restraints also may be automatic violations. These may include (a) price fixing (agreement by sellers to a maximum or minimum price), (b) division of markets by competitors, (c) group boycotts (agreeing not to deal with another), and (d) resale price maintenance (limiting a buyer's resale price).

7. Other antitrust laws may prohibit the acquisition of stock or assets of another corporation if the effect may be to lessen competition substantially or tend to create a monopoly in any line of commerce in any part of the country. The following also may be prohibited: tie-in sales, exclusive dealing, and price discrimination.
8. Consumer protection law addresses (a) the safety of food, drugs, cosmetics, etc.; (b) deceptive packaging and labeling; (c) product safety; (d) credit discrimination; (e) written warranties on consumer products; (f) fair credit billing (credit cards); (g) debt collection; and (h) truth in lending.
9. One government agency may oversee the environmental control functions of the national government. A national environmental policy and the consideration of environmental issues by government agencies may be promoted. Thus, agencies may have to consider the adverse environmental effects of their actions, proposals, legislation, and regulations.
10. A central bank controls the money supply. Any policy designed to affect the money supply, and thus the economy, is known as monetary policy. Control of the growth of the money supply is viewed as essential to control the availability of credit, spending, and inflation. One reason is that the economic health of the nation requires the money supply to grow at the same rate as the economy.
11. If a bank's actual reserves exceed the reserves required by law, it has excess reserves with which it can (and will, if it is a profit-maximizing bank) extend loans. An individual bank creates money equal to a multiple of its excess reserves when it lends the excess reserves rather than investing in securities.
12. The laws of supply and demand affect imports and exports in the same way that they affect domestic goods.
13. The exchange ratio (terms of trade) is the ratio of a country's export price index to its import price index, multiplied by 100.
14. The greatest advantage from trade is obtained when each nation specializes what it can produce most efficiently.
15. As exchange rates fluctuate, buying power rises and falls. Currency appreciates when it can buy more units of another currency. Currency depreciates when it can purchase fewer units of another currency. Equilibrium exchange rates in floating markets are determined by the supply of and demand for the currencies.
16. Trade barriers cause resources to be misallocated in the country that established the barrier because inputs are used to produce products that could be produced more economically in other countries.
17. In general, when the demand for a country's merchandise, capital assets, and financial instruments rises, demand for its currency rises.
18. Most currencies operate under a system of floating exchange rates, meaning the equivalent amount of another currency can change under the influence of market forces.
19. An entity may minimize the risk of exchange rate fluctuations by purchasing or selling futures contracts, a practice called hedging.
20. Protectionism is any measure taken by a government to protect domestic producers. Protectionism takes many forms. Examples are (a) tariffs, (b) import quotas, (c) domestic content rules, (d) voluntary export restrictions, (e) trigger pricing, (f) antidumping rules, (g) exchange controls, (h) export subsidies, (i) tax benefits to exporters, and (j) licensing.
21. Protectionism reduces economic efficiency, real wages, and world output.
22. Multinational corporations frequently derive income from several countries. The government of each country in which a corporation does business may enact statutes imposing one or more types of tax on the corporation. To avoid double taxation, two or more countries may adopt treaties to coordinate or synchronize the effects of their taxing statutes.

23. Transfer pricing is an important aspect of the tax calculation for multinational corporations that transfer inventories between branches in different countries.
24. Government, at all levels, finances its expenditures by taxation. Thus, taxes generate government revenues. National governments also use taxation as a means of implementing fiscal policy regarding inflation, full employment, economic growth, etc.
25. Tax structures may be progressive, proportional, or regressive. Taxes also may be direct or indirect.
26. The incidence of taxation refers to who actually bears a particular tax. Accordingly, the person who actually bears an indirect tax may not be the one who pays the tax to the government.
27. Many major industrial nations have already adopted a value-added tax (VAT).
28. The study of business cycles focuses on the periodic cycles in the economy, most of which are characterized by changes in price levels and in rates of employment. A cycle's stages are trough, recovery, peak, and recession. A trough is marked by low levels of economic activity and underuse of resources. Sales and profits of most entities are depressed. Recovery is marked by increasing economic activity. Sales and profits of most entities rise. The peak is that period when economic activity is booming. Sales and profits are at the maximum for most entities. Recession means economic activities and employment levels contract. Sales and profits decline.
29. Economists use economic indicators to forecast turns in the business cycle. They are variables that in the past have had a high correlation with aggregate economic activity. The best known are the composite indexes calculated by The Conference Board, a private research group with many corporate and other members worldwise. Indicators may lead, lag, or coincide with economic activity. A leading indicator is a forecast of future economic trends, and a lagging indicator changes after the economic activity has occurred.
30. National income accounting measures the output and performance of the economy. The gross domestic product (GDP) is the principal measure. It is the total market value of all final goods and services produced within the boundaries of a country, whether by domestic or foreign-owned sources, during a specified period of time (usually a year). GDP is calculated without regard to the ownership of productive resources. Thus, the value of the output of a factory abroad is excluded regardless of its ownership, but the output of a foreign-owned factory is included in the host country's GDP.
31. GDP may be calculated using an income (resource cost) or an expenditure approach.
32. Other national income concepts are (a) gross national product, (b) net domestic product, (c) national income, (d) personal income, and (e) disposable income.
33. The GDP deflator measures inflation using a price index that includes every item produced in the economy at the price at which it entered the GDP account.
34. The legal rules of evidence are found in statutes, case law, and constitutions. Their essential purpose is to govern the admissibility of evidence in legal proceedings, but they are drafted with a view to protecting the parties as well as ascertaining the truth.
35. Exclusionary rules prevent the admission of evidence whose value as proof is offset by its possible prejudicial effect. An internal auditor, however, need not be limited by the legal and constitutional safeguards imposed in court. The types of evidence are (a) best or primary, (b) secondary, (c) direct, (d) circumstantial, (e) conclusive, (f) corroborative, (g) opinion, and (h) hearsay.
36. A contract is a promise or an agreement that the law recognizes as establishing a duty of performance. It is enforceable by applying a remedy for its breach.
37. The elements of a contract are (a) an offer, (b) acceptance, (c) consideration, (d) capacity of each party to enter into contracts, and (e) legality.

QUESTIONS

7.1 Regulation of Business

1. Regulatory agencies usually do **not** have power to

A. Impose agency taxes on private industry.

B. Issue rules and regulations.

C. Investigate violations of statutes and rules.

D. Conduct hearings and decide whether violations have occurred.

Answer (A) is correct. *(CMA, adapted)*

REQUIRED: The true statement about the powers that regulatory agencies do not have.

DISCUSSION: A regulatory agency may regulate some aspect of all industries or may regulate a specific industry in accordance with power delegated by the enabling legislation. Agency functions include executive, adjudicatory, and rule-making activities. Such agencies, however, may not impose taxes.

Answer (B) is incorrect. Regulatory agencies have the power to issue rules and regulations. Answer (C) is incorrect. Regulatory agencies have the power to investigate violations of statutes and rules. Answer (D) is incorrect. Regulatory agencies have the power to conduct hearings and decide whether violations have occurred.

2. The basic purpose of **most** national securities laws is to regulate the issue of investment securities by

A. Providing a regulatory framework for those local governments that do not have their own securities laws.

B. Requiring disclosure of all relevant facts so that investors can make informed decisions.

C. Prohibiting the issuance of securities that the government determines are not of investment grade.

D. Channeling investment funds into uses that are economically most important.

Answer (B) is correct. *(CMA, adapted)*

REQUIRED: The means of regulating the issue of investment securities.

DISCUSSION: The basic purpose of the securities laws is to provide disclosure of adequate information so that investors can evaluate investments. This is accomplished through reporting requirements concerning the issuance and subsequent trading of securities. However, the government does not assess the merits of these securities.

Answer (A) is incorrect. National law applies in all parts of a country. Answer (C) is incorrect. The government does not determine the merits of securities. It evaluates whether sufficient information is provided. Answer (D) is incorrect. The securities laws generally are not intended to influence the investment of capital in more socially or economically beneficial ways.

3. An antifraud law that prohibits trading on the basis of inside information about a business corporation's stock **most** likely applies to

A. Officers and directors.

B. All officers, directors, and shareholders.

C. Officers, directors, and holders of a large amount of the corporation's stock.

D. Anyone who bases his/her trading activities on the inside information.

Answer (D) is correct. *(CMA, adapted)*

REQUIRED: The person(s) most likely prohibited from trading securities based on inside information.

DISCUSSION: Such antifraud provisions typically prohibit any person from engaging in manipulative or deceptive acts in the purchase or sale of any security. It prohibits trading on the basis of inside information and applies to anyone who has not made a full disclosure of the inside information. It may apply not only to officers, directors, and shareholders, but also to tippees, i.e., those who receive inside information from insiders.

4. Antitrust laws are intended to

A. Establish set profit percentages for entities in regulated industries.

B. Prohibit entities in the same industry from engaging in joint ventures.

C. Require entities in regulated industries to share any patent rights with other entities in that industry.

D. Ensure a free and competitive market in which consumer demand dictates prices.

Answer (D) is correct. *(Publisher, adapted)*

REQUIRED: The intent of antitrust laws.

DISCUSSION: Antitrust laws are designed to promote more efficient allocation of resources, greater choice for consumers, greater business opportunities, fairness in economic behavior, and avoidance of concentrated political power resulting from economic power. Competition results in greater output and lower prices than other market structures.

Answer (A) is incorrect. Profit percentages are not set by antitrust laws other than to the extent that price discrimination is prohibited. Answer (B) is incorrect. Entities may enter into joint ventures. Answer (C) is incorrect. Patents are available to all inventors, regardless of size.

5. Which one of the following examples of corporate behavior would **most** clearly represent a violation of antitrust law?

A. A retailer offers quantity discounts to large institutional buyers.

B. The members of a labor union meet and agree not to work for a specific entity unless the starting wage is at least a specified amount per hour.

C. Two entities that are in different, unrelated industries merge.

D. Two entities in the same industry agree in a telephone conversation to submit identical bids on a government contract.

Answer (D) is correct. *(CMA, adapted)*

REQUIRED: The item that would most clearly represent a violation of antitrust law.

DISCUSSION: Antitrust law addresses restraints of trade. Some types of arrangements are considered automatic violations. These violations may include price fixing, division of markets, group boycotts, and resale price maintenance. Agreeing to submit identical bids on a government contract is a form of price fixing.

Answer (A) is incorrect. Quantity discounts are not prohibited. Answer (B) is incorrect. Antitrust laws usually do not apply to labor unions. Answer (C) is incorrect. Only mergers that could lead to restraint of trade are outlawed.

7.2 International Trade

6. The total exports of Vietnam are US $20,000,000 worth of rice to Greece, and the total exports of Greece are US $18,000,000 worth of olives to Vietnam. The terms of trade are

	Greece	Vietnam
A.	90	111
B.	120	180
C.	111	90
D.	97	103

Answer (A) is correct. *(CIA, adapted)*

REQUIRED: The terms of trade given the value of two countries' exports.

DISCUSSION: A country's terms of trade are calculated by dividing its export price index by its import price index and multiplying by 100. Greece's total exports (US $18,000,000) divided by its total imports (US $20,000,000) equals 0.9 × 100 = 90. Vietnam's total exports (US $20,000,000) divided by its total imports (US $18,000,000) equals 1.11 × 100 = 111.

7. The economic reasoning dictating that each nation specialize in the production of goods that it produces relatively more efficiently than other nations and import those goods that are produced relatively more efficiently by other nations is called the doctrine of

A. Efficient trade.

B. Diminishing returns.

C. Relative competition.

D. Comparative advantage.

Answer (D) is correct. *(CMA, adapted)*

REQUIRED: The reason each nation should specialize in those goods it produces relatively more efficiently than other nations.

DISCUSSION: The doctrine of comparative advantage relates to comparative costs within one country. It holds that a country should produce those products in which it has a comparative advantage, not necessarily those products in which it has an absolute advantage. The doctrine suggests that a country should produce those products for which the greatest efficiencies are attainable even if it could also produce other goods more efficiently than another nation. In the long run, importing a product in which a country has an absolute advantage but not a comparative advantage will result in an overall increase in global production.

Answer (A) is incorrect. Efficient trade is not meaningful in this context. Answer (B) is incorrect. Diminishing returns is not meaningful in this context. Answer (C) is incorrect. Relative competition is not meaningful in this context.

8. If the value of the U.S. dollar in foreign currency markets changes from US $1 = .95 euros to US $1 = .90 euros,

A. The euro has depreciated against the dollar.

B. Products imported from Europe to the U.S. will become more expensive.

C. U.S. tourists in Europe will find their dollars will buy more European products.

D. U.S. exports to Europe should decrease.

Answer (B) is correct. *(CMA, adapted)*

REQUIRED: The effect of a depreciation in the value of the dollar.

DISCUSSION: The dollar has declined in value relative to the euro. If an American had previously wished to purchase a European product that was priced at 10 euros, the price would have been about US $10.53. After the dollar's decline in value, the price of the item has increased to about US $11.11. Hence, imports from Europe should decrease and exports increase.

Answer (A) is incorrect. The euro has appreciated (increased in value) relative to the dollar. Answer (C) is incorrect. Dollars will buy fewer European products. Answer (D) is incorrect. U.S. exports should increase.

9. Two countries have flexible exchange rate systems and an active trading relationship. If incomes <List A> in country 1, everything else being equal, then the currency of country 1 will tend to <List B> relative to the currency of country 2.

	List A	List B
A.	Rise	Remain constant
B.	Fall	Depreciate
C.	Rise	Depreciate
D.	Remain constant	Appreciate

Answer (C) is correct. *(CIA, adapted)*
REQUIRED: The effect of a change in incomes in one nation on its currency.
DISCUSSION: If incomes in country 1 rise, consumers in country 1 will increase their imports from country 2. The resulting increase in the supply of currency 1 will result in a tendency for it to depreciate relative to the currency of country 2.
Answer (A) is incorrect. If incomes in country 1 rise, the result will be a tendency for it to devalue relative to the currency of country 2. Answer (B) is incorrect. If incomes in country 1 fall, consumers in country 1 will reduce their imports. The resulting decrease in the supply of currency 1 will result in a tendency for it to appreciate relative to the currency of country 2. Answer (D) is incorrect. If incomes in country 1 remain constant, the currency of country 1 will not tend to appreciate or depreciate relative to the currency of country 2.

10. An entity has a foreign-currency-denominated trade payable, due in 60 days. To eliminate the foreign currency exchange-rate risk associated with the payable, the entity could

A. Sell foreign currency forward today.

B. Wait 60 days and pay the invoice by purchasing foreign currency in the spot market at that time.

C. Buy foreign currency forward today.

D. Borrow foreign currency today, convert it to domestic currency on the spot market, and invest the funds in a domestic bank deposit until the invoice payment date.

Answer (C) is correct. *(CIA, adapted)*
REQUIRED: The means of eliminating exchange-rate risk.
DISCUSSION: The entity can arrange to purchase the foreign currency today rather than in 60 days by buying the currency in the forward market. This hedging transaction will eliminate the exchange-rate risk associated with the trade payable.
Answer (A) is incorrect. A forward market sale of foreign currency is appropriate to hedge a receivable denominated in a foreign currency. Answer (B) is incorrect. Waiting to buy the currency in 60 days does not eliminate the risk of an adverse exchange-rate movement. Answer (D) is incorrect. This strategy would be comparable to a future sale of the foreign currency at a rate known today, which would not provide the currency needed to pay the invoice. However, the opposite strategy would be an effective money market hedge. If the entity converted domestic currency to foreign currency in the spot market today and invested in a foreign bank deposit or treasury bill, it could then use the proceeds from the foreign investment to pay the invoice in 60 days.

11. Which of the following is a tariff?

A. Licensing requirements.

B. Consumption taxes on imported goods.

C. Unreasonable standards pertaining to product quality and safety.

D. Domestic content rules.

Answer (B) is correct. *(CIA, adapted)*
REQUIRED: The example of a tariff.
DISCUSSION: Tariffs are excise taxes on imported goods imposed either to generate revenue or protect domestic producers. Thus, consumption taxes on imported goods are tariffs.
Answer (A) is incorrect. Licensing requirements limit exports, e.g., of militarily sensitive technology. Answer (C) is incorrect. Unreasonable standards pertaining to product quality and safety are nontariff trade barriers. Answer (D) is incorrect. Domestic content rules require that a portion of an imported good be made in the importing country.

12. Which of the following is an economic rationale for government intervention in trade?

A. Maintaining spheres of influence.

B. Protecting infant industries.

C. Preserving national identity.

D. Dealing with friendly countries.

Answer (B) is correct. *(Publisher, adapted)*
REQUIRED: The best economic rationale for government intervention in trade.
DISCUSSION: The infant-industry argument contends that protective tariffs are needed to allow new domestic industries to become established. Once such industries reach a maturity stage in their life cycles, the tariffs can supposedly be removed.

13. Governments most likely restrict trade in the long run to

I. Help foster new industries.
II. Protect declining industries.
III. Increase tax revenues.
IV. Foster national security.

A. I only.
B. I and II only.
C. II and III only.
D. I, II, and IV only.

Answer (B) is correct. *(CIA, adapted)*
REQUIRED: The reason(s) governments restrict trade in the long run.
DISCUSSION: Governmental impediments to global competition are generally imposed for the announced purpose of protecting local entities and jobs and developing new industries. They also may have the effect of raising revenue in the short run. In the long run, tax and revenues will decline because of reduced trade. Examples of governmental impediments are tariffs; duties; quotas; domestic content rules; preferences for local entities regarding procurement, taxes, R&D, labor regulations, and other operating rules; and laws (e.g., anti-bribery or tax) enacted by a national government that impede national entities from competing globally. These impediments are most likely when industries are viewed as crucial.
Answer (A) is incorrect. Governments often impose impediments to global competition to protect declining industries. Answer (C) is incorrect. Restrictions on global trade, e.g., tariffs, may increase tax revenues in the short run. However, in the long run, the effect of reduced trade is to decrease tax revenues. Answer (D) is incorrect. Tax revenues will decrease in the long run if trade is restricted. Moreover, restricting trade for national security reasons is often not necessary in the long run. For example, a ban on export of sensitive technology is no longer needed when it becomes obsolete.

14. Which of the following statements is true with respect to international transfer pricing?

A. Transfer prices charged to foreign subsidiaries must be the same as those charged to domestic subsidiaries.
B. The existence of tariffs in the foreign country may necessitate that a higher transfer price be charged a foreign subsidiary.
C. Limitations on taking profits out of a foreign country can be avoided by charging the foreign subsidiary a higher transfer price.
D. Currency restrictions prohibit payments to foreign vendors.

Answer (C) is correct. *(Publisher, adapted)*
REQUIRED: The true statement about international transfer prices.
DISCUSSION: Transfer pricing is an important aspect of the tax calculation for multinational corporations that transfer inventories between branches in different countries. Transfer prices charged to foreign subsidiaries may differ substantially from those charged to domestic subsidiaries for a variety of reasons. Limitations on taking profits out of a foreign country can be avoided by charging the foreign subsidiary a higher transfer price so that little or no profit exists to be repatriated.
Answer (A) is incorrect. Transfer prices charged to foreign subsidiaries are often quite different from those charged domestic subsidiaries. Answer (B) is incorrect. The existence of tariffs in the foreign country would necessitate that a lower transfer price be charged to avoid a high tariff. Answer (D) is incorrect. Currency restrictions may limit transfer of profits to foreign vendors.

7.3 Methods of Taxation

15. An individual had taxable income of US $23,000 per year and paid US $8,000 in income tax. The individual's taxable income then increased to US $30,000 per year resulting in a US $10,000 income tax liability. The personal tax system being applied to this individual is

A. Progressive.
B. Regressive.
C. Marginal.
D. Proportional.

Answer (B) is correct. *(CIA, adapted)*
REQUIRED: The nature of the personal tax system.
DISCUSSION: The average tax rate of the individual has decreased from 34.8% (US $8,000 ÷ $23,000) to 33.3% (US $10,000 ÷ $30,000). Under a regressive tax system, the average tax rate falls as income rises, although the amount of tax paid may rise.
Answer (A) is incorrect. Under a progressive tax system, both the amount of tax and the percentage of income paid in tax (the average tax rate) rise as income increases. In the case described, the individual pays a higher amount of tax but a lower percentage of income in tax. Answer (C) is incorrect. Marginal is not a type of tax system but a type of tax rate. The marginal tax rate is the tax rate paid on incremental income. Answer (D) is incorrect. Under a proportional income tax system, the average tax rate is the same for all levels of income. The average tax rate of this individual falls as income rises.

16. In most countries <List A> taxes tend to be <List B> with respect to income.

	List A	List B
A.	General sales	Proportional
B.	Property	Regressive
C.	Personal income	Proportional
D.	Personal income	Regressive

Answer (B) is correct. *(CIA, adapted)*

REQUIRED: The correct match of a tax and its proportion of a taxpayer's income.

DISCUSSION: Property taxes tend to be regressive. Taxpayers with lower incomes must pay a higher portion of their incomes for necessities, such as housing.

Answer (A) is incorrect. General sales taxes tend to be regressive. The lower the taxpayer's income, the higher the proportion that is usually paid in sales taxes, which are collected at a flat rate per dollar. Low-income taxpayers are unable to save as high a portion of their income as high-income taxpayers. Thus, the latter are less exposed to general sales taxes because they avoid the tax on the amount saved. Answer (C) is incorrect. Personal income taxes tend to be progressive. Higher tax rates are charged on higher incomes. Answer (D) is incorrect. Personal income taxes tend to be progressive. Higher tax rates are charged on higher incomes.

17. On what basis is value-added tax collected?

A. The difference between the value of an entity's sales and the value of its purchases from other domestic entities.

B. The difference between the selling price of a real estate property and the amount the entity originally paid for the property.

C. The value of an entity's sales to related companies.

D. The profit earned on an entity's sales.

Answer (A) is correct. *(CIA, adapted)*

REQUIRED: The basis for collecting a value-added tax.

DISCUSSION: A value-added tax (VAT) is collected on the basis of the value created by the entity. This tax is measured by the difference between the value of the entity's sales and the value of its purchases. A VAT is in effect a retail sales tax. Because a consumer can avoid the tax by not purchasing, a VAT encourages saving and discourages consumption.

Answer (B) is incorrect. The difference between the selling price of a real estate property and the amount the entity originally paid for the property is a capital gain. Answer (C) is incorrect. The value of an entity's sales to related companies is the internal transfer price. Answer (D) is incorrect. The profit earned on an entity's sales is subject to the income tax.

18. Which of the following designations refers to taxes that will **not** necessarily take a larger absolute amount of income as income rises?

A. Progressive.

B. Proportional.

C. Regressive.

D. Regenerative.

Answer (C) is correct. *(CIA, adapted)*

REQUIRED: The taxes that will not necessarily take a larger absolute amount of income as income rises.

DISCUSSION: Regressive taxes are those for which the average tax rate falls as income rises. They take a smaller percentage of income as income rises, so they will not necessarily take a larger absolute amount of income as income rises.

Answer (A) is incorrect. Progressive taxes, for which the average tax rate rises as income rises, take both a larger percentage of income and a larger absolute amount of income as income rises. Answer (B) is incorrect. Proportional taxes, for which the average tax rate is constant for all income levels, always take a larger absolute amount of income as income rises. Answer (D) is incorrect. Regenerative is not a term used to designate types of taxes.

7.4 Economic Indicators

19. The trough of a business cycle is generally characterized by

A. Shortages of essential raw materials and rising costs.

B. Increasing purchasing power and increasing capital investments.

C. Rising costs and an unwillingness to risk new investments.

D. Unused productive capacity and an unwillingness to risk new investments.

Answer (D) is correct. *(CMA, adapted)*

REQUIRED: The characteristic of the trough of a business cycle.

DISCUSSION: There are four phases of a business cycle: trough, recovery, peak, and recession. The trough is marked by low levels of economic activity and underuse of resources. Investors are unwilling to risk new investments in productive capacity.

Answer (A) is incorrect. The trough of a business cycle is characterized by excess resources and a lack of demand-pull inflation; thus, prices are more apt to be stable or decline during the trough. Answer (B) is incorrect. Investors are unwilling to risk new investments during the trough. Answer (C) is incorrect. Costs ordinarily do not rise during the trough.

20. Which of the following may provide a leading indicator of a future increase in gross domestic product?

A. A reduction in the money supply.

B. A decrease in the issuance of building permits.

C. An increase in the timeliness of delivery by vendors.

D. An increase in the average hours worked per week of production workers.

Answer (D) is correct. *(CIA, adapted)*

REQUIRED: The leading indicator.

DISCUSSION: An economic indicator is highly correlated with changes in aggregate economic activity. A leading indicator changes prior to a change in the direction of the business cycle. The leading indicators included in the Conference Board's index are average weekly hours worked by manufacturing workers, unemployment claims, consumer goods orders, stock prices, orders for fixed assets, building permits, timeliness of deliveries, money supply, consumer confidence, and the spread between the yield on 10-year Treasury bonds and the federal funds rate. An increase in weekly hours worked by production workers is favorable for economic growth.

Answer (A) is incorrect. A falling money supply is associated with falling GDP. Answer (B) is incorrect. A decline in the issuance of building permits signals lower expected building activity and a falling GDP. Answer (C) is incorrect. An increase in the timeliness of delivery by vendors indicates slacking business demand and potentially falling GDP.

21. The two main variables that contribute to increases in real gross domestic product (GDP) derived from labor inputs are labor productivity and

A. The potential labor force.

B. The inflation rate.

C. Quality of output.

D. Total worker hours.

Answer (D) is correct. *(CIA, adapted)*

REQUIRED: The other main variable contributing to increased real GDP derived from labor inputs.

DISCUSSION: Real GDP increases when resource inputs and their productivity increase. Thus, to the extent that real GDP depends on labor inputs, real GDP equals total worker hours (labor input) times labor productivity (real output per worker per hour).

Answer (A) is incorrect. The potential labor force is not a factor in the calculation. Rather, real GDP is determined by actual inputs and their productivity. Answer (B) is incorrect. Real GDP is adjusted for inflation. Answer (C) is incorrect. National income accounting does not address the quality of output.

22. Net domestic product is composed of the total market value of all

A. Final goods and services produced in the economy in 1 year.

B. Goods and services produced in the economy in 1 year.

C. Final goods and services produced in the economy in 1 year minus the capital consumption allowance.

D. Goods and services produced in the economy in 1 year minus the capital consumption allowance.

Answer (C) is correct. *(CIA, adapted)*

REQUIRED: The composition of net domestic product.

DISCUSSION: Net domestic product is the market value of all final goods and services produced within the boundaries of a country within 1 year minus the capital consumption allowance.

Answer (A) is incorrect. Net domestic product is calculated net of the capital consumption allowance. Answer (B) is incorrect. Net domestic product includes only final goods. The inclusion of intermediate goods would involve double counting. Also, net domestic product is calculated net of the capital consumption allowance. Answer (D) is incorrect. Net domestic product does not include intermediate goods.

7.5 Legal Rules of Evidence

23. A contract dispute has arisen between an organization and a major supplier. To resolve the dispute, the **most** competent evidence is

A. Oral testimony of contracting parties.

B. The original contract.

C. Actions by parties to the contract.

D. A letter from the supplier's attorney.

Answer (B) is correct. *(CIA, adapted)*

REQUIRED: The most competent evidence to resolve a contract dispute between an entity and a major supplier.

DISCUSSION: The best (primary) evidence is the most persuasive evidence. Reliability and the best evidence rule are closely related. The best evidence rule is ordinarily applied only to documentary evidence, especially to proof of the content of a writing. If the original writing is available, the best evidence rule prohibits a party from proving the content of a writing through oral testimony. Therefore, the original writing is the most competent evidence.

Answer (A) is incorrect. If the original writing is available, oral testimony cannot contradict the content of the writing. Answer (C) is incorrect. The contract itself is the best evidence. Answer (D) is incorrect. The contract itself is the best evidence.

24. Which of the following statements describes an internal control questionnaire? It

A. Provides detailed evidence regarding the substance of the control system.

B. Takes less of the engagement client's time to complete than other control evaluation devices.

C. Requires that the internal auditor be in attendance to properly administer it.

D. Provides indirect evidence that might need corroboration.

Answer (D) is correct. *(CIA, adapted)*

REQUIRED: The statement that describes an internal control questionnaire.

DISCUSSION: An internal control questionnaire consists of a series of questions about the controls designed to prevent or detect errors or irregularities. Answers to the questions help the internal auditor to identify specific internal control policies and procedures relevant to specific assertions and to design tests of controls to evaluate the effectiveness of their design and operation. The questionnaire provides a framework to assure that specific concerns are not overlooked, but it is not a sufficient means of understanding the entire system. Thus, the evidence obtained is indirect and requires corroboration by means of observation, interviews, flowcharting, examination of documents, etc.

Answer (A) is incorrect. Questionnaires usually provide for yes/no responses and therefore provide less detailed evidence than some other procedures. Answer (B) is incorrect. Questionnaires tend to be lengthy, and their completion is time-consuming. Answer (C) is incorrect. An auditor need not be present.

25. During interviews with the inventory management personnel, an internal auditor learned that salespersons often order inventory for stock without receiving the approval of the vice president of sales. Also, detail testing showed that there are no written approvals on purchase orders for replacement parts. The detail testing is a good example of

A. Indirect evidence.

B. Circumstantial evidence.

C. Corroborative evidence.

D. Subjective evidence.

Answer (C) is correct. *(CIA, adapted)*

REQUIRED: The evidence of which detail testing is a good example.

DISCUSSION: Corroborative evidence is evidence from a different source that supplements and confirms other evidence. For example, oral testimony that a certain procedure was not performed may be corroborated by the absence of documentation.

Answer (A) is incorrect. Detail testing provides direct evidence that the approvals were not received. Indirect evidence establishes immediately collateral facts from which the main fact may be inferred. Answer (B) is incorrect. Circumstantial evidence tends to prove a fact by proving other events or circumstances that afford a basis for a reasonable inference of the occurrence of the fact. Thus, it is also indirect evidence. Answer (D) is incorrect. Subjective evidence is opinion-oriented and is not dependable for reaching engagement conclusions. No subjective evidence is present in this situation.

26. Much of the internal auditor's work involves accumulation of engagement information. A duplicate of a contract rather than the original is an example of what kind of evidence?

A. Secondary.

B. Circumstantial.

C. Hearsay.

D. Opinion.

Answer (A) is correct. *(CIA, adapted)*

REQUIRED: The type of evidence exemplified by the duplicate of a contract.

DISCUSSION: Secondary evidence according to the legal view is acceptable if primary evidence (the strongest evidence, e.g., original documents) has been destroyed or is not reasonably procurable. Secondary evidence must be a proper representation of primary evidence, e.g., copies of a contract.

Answer (B) is incorrect. Circumstantial evidence inferentially establishes one fact by proving another collateral fact. Answer (C) is incorrect. Hearsay is an out-of-court statement offered in evidence to prove the truth of the matter asserted. Answer (D) is incorrect. Except for testimony by experts, witnesses may normally testify as to facts only.

7.6 Contracts

27. Which of the following is **not** a required element of a contract?

A. Legality.

B. Consideration.

C. Legal capacity.

D. A writing.

Answer (D) is correct. *(Publisher, adapted)*

REQUIRED: The element not required in a contract.

DISCUSSION: The four essential elements of a contract are an agreement (offer and acceptance), consideration, legal capacity of the parties to contract, and a legal objective or purpose. A writing is not required to enter into a contract. However, some contracts are not enforceable unless a writing evidences the contract.

Answer (A) is incorrect. Legality is a required element of a contract. Answer (B) is incorrect. Consideration is a required element of a contract. Answer (C) is incorrect. Legal capacity is a required element of a contract.

28. The necessary elements of a contract include

A. Some form of writing, equal consideration, and legal capacity.

B. Formal execution, definite terms, and a valid offer and acceptance.

C. Offer and acceptance, consideration, legal capacity, and mutual assent.

D. Bilateral promises, legal capacity, and legality of purpose.

Answer (C) is correct. *(Publisher, adapted)*

REQUIRED: The element of a contract that is not necessary.

DISCUSSION: Contracts require each of the following:

1. Offer and acceptance
2. Mutual assent (meeting of the minds)
3. Consideration (bargained-for exchange)
4. Legality (legal purpose)
5. Capacity of parties (legal ability)

Answer (A) is incorrect. An oral contract is usually enforceable. Consideration must be legally sufficient and must be bargained for but need not have equal market value. Answer (B) is incorrect. Most contracts are informal (simple), and if a term is missing, it can be implied by the court, with the exception of a quantity term. Answer (D) is incorrect. Promises can be unilateral or divisible.

29. Consideration consists of

A. Something with monetary value.

B. Each party's receiving an actual benefit only.

C. Two promises.

D. Legal sufficiency and bargained-for exchange.

Answer (D) is correct. *(Publisher, adapted)*

REQUIRED: The elements of consideration.

DISCUSSION: Consideration must be legally sufficient and intended as a bargained-for exchange. A promisee has provided legally sufficient consideration if (s)he incurs a legal detriment or if the promisor receives a legal benefit. An essential aspect of consideration is that it be bargained for, and given in exchange for, the consideration provided by the other party. That is, consideration is mutual.

Answer (A) is incorrect. A promise satisfies the element of legal sufficiency. Monetary value is relatively unimportant. Answer (B) is incorrect. Consideration is an exchange of legal benefit that may not have actual benefit. Answer (C) is incorrect. Contracts can be unilateral, which involves only one promise.

30. Lamar became homeless at a very young age and was taken in by Aunt and Uncle. Many years later, Lamar became a detective in the city police department. When Aunt disappeared and was not heard from for a month, the case was assigned to Lamar. Uncle also came to Lamar and asked him to promise to find Aunt in return for the years of support. Lamar agreed to Uncle's request. Which of the following is true?

A. Lamar's contractual duty to find Aunt is based on past consideration.

B. Lamar has no contractual duty to find Aunt.

C. If Uncle had also promised Lamar US $1,000 for finding Aunt, he would be liable when Lamar found her.

D. Lamar will be liable for breach of contract if he does not find Aunt.

Answer (B) is correct. *(Publisher, adapted)*

REQUIRED: The true statement regarding Lamar's contractual duty.

DISCUSSION: Lamar has a preexisting legal duty to find Aunt. Consideration does not exist if an existing duty was imposed by law or a person is already under a contractual agreement to render a specified performance. Lamar will suffer no new legal detriment by finding Aunt; thus, no contractual obligation exists.

Answer (A) is incorrect. Past consideration does not satisfy the consideration requirement for the formation of a contract. Answer (C) is incorrect. Lamar has a preexisting legal duty to find Aunt. Answer (D) is incorrect. Lamar has not made a valid contract with Uncle.

STUDY UNIT EIGHT
INFORMATION TECHNOLOGY I

(23 pages of outline)

This study unit addresses the control frameworks commonly used in designing internal control systems over IT, the nature and modes of computer processing, and basic IT control concepts. It continues with a treatment of computer communications and concludes with discussions of electronic funds transfer, electronic commerce, and electronic data interchange.

Core Concepts

- A control framework is a model for establishing a system of internal control, including controls over IT. The most prominent ones are COSO, eSAC, COBIT, and GTAG.
- Data can be processed in one of two basic modes: batch or online, real-time. Each has its own set of appropriate input controls.
- An organization must establish appropriate IT controls at three levels: the executive management level, the business process level, and the IT support level.
- Computer controls can be classified into two basic categories: general controls and application controls.
- A network consists of multiple connected computers at multiple locations. Computers that are electronically linked permit an organization to assemble and share transaction and other information among different physical locations.
- Electronic funds transfer (EFT) is a service provided by financial institutions worldwide that is based on electronic data interchange technology. EFT transaction costs are lower than for manual systems. A typical consumer application of EFT is the direct deposit of payroll checks.
- Electronic data interchange (EDI) is the communication of electronic documents directly from a computer in one entity to a computer in another entity, for example, to order goods from a supplier or to transfer funds.
- Electronic commerce (e-commerce) is the purchase and sale of goods and services by electronic means. Security issues for e-commerce include authentication, authorization, and verification.

8.1 CONTROL FRAMEWORKS

1. A **control framework** is a model for establishing a system of internal control.
   a. The framework does not prescribe the actual controls themselves, but it does force management to focus on risk areas and design controls accordingly.
   b. Often, a control framework describes "families" of controls, that is, conceptual groupings of controls that attempt to address a particular type of risk exposure.

COSO

2. Probably the most well-known control framework in the U.S. is ***Internal Control – Integrated Framework***, published in 1992 by the Committee of Sponsoring Organizations of the Treadway Commission (COSO). The document is commonly referred to as "the COSO Framework."

   a. The COSO Framework defines **internal control** as

      A process, effected by an organization's board of directors, management, and other personnel, designed to provide reasonable assurance regarding the achievement of objectives in the following categories:

      - ***Effectiveness and efficiency*** *of operations*
      - ***Reliability*** *of financial reporting*
      - ***Compliance*** *with applicable laws and regulations*

      1) COSO's simple and straightforward definition has proved extremely useful. Also, these principles are as applicable to an organization's IT function as they are to any other.

   b. COSO further describes five components of an internal control system:

      1) **Control environment**
      2) **Risk assessment**
      3) **Control activities**
      4) **Information and communication**
      5) **Monitoring**
         a) This part of the model also can easily be used in an IT context.

   c. The importance and durability of the COSO Framework was reinforced when the **U.S. Securities and Exchange Commission** acknowledged it as an appropriate model for designing internal controls under the requirements of the Sarbanes-Oxley Act of 2002.

eSAC

3. ***Electronic Systems Assurance and Control (eSAC)*** is a publication of The IIA.

   a. In the eSAC model, the organization's internal processes accept inputs and produce outputs.

      1) **Inputs:** Mission, values, strategies, and objectives
      2) **Outputs:** Results, reputation, and learning

   b. The eSAC model's broad control objectives are influenced by those in the COSO Framework:

      1) Operating **effectiveness and efficiency**
      2) **Reporting** of financial and other management information
      3) **Compliance** with laws and regulations
      4) **Safeguarding** of assets

   c. eSAC's IT business assurance objectives fall into five categories:

      1) **Availability.** The organization must assure that information, processes, and services are available at all times.
      2) **Capability.** The organization must assure reliable and timely completion of transactions.
      3) **Functionality.** The organization must assure that systems are designed to user specifications to fulfill business requirements.
      4) **Protectability.** The organization must assure that a combination of physical and logical controls prevents unauthorized access to system data.
      5) **Accountability.** The organization must assure that transactions are processed under firm principles of data ownership, identification, and authentication.

COBIT

4. Specifically for IT controls, the best-known framework is ***Control Objectives for Information and Related Technology (COBIT)***. Version 4.0 of this document was published in 2005 by the IT Governance Institute.
   a. Automated information systems have been woven into every function of the modern organization, making **IT governance** an integral part of overall organizational governance. The COBIT model for IT governance contains five focus areas:
      1) **Strategic alignment**
      2) **Value delivery**
      3) **Resource management**
      4) **Risk management**
      5) **Performance measurement**
   b. The COBIT framework embodies four characteristics:
      1) **Business-focused**
      2) **Process-oriented**
      3) **Controls-based**
      4) **Measurement-driven**
   c. Each characteristic contains multiple components.
      1) **Business-focused**
         a) This characteristic lists seven distinct but overlapping **information criteria**: effectiveness, efficiency, confidentiality, integrity, availability, compliance, and reliability.
         b) **Business goals** must feed **IT goals**, which in turn allow the organization to design the appropriate **enterprise architecture** for IT.
         c) **IT resources** include applications, information, infrastructure, and people.
      2) **Process-oriented.** This part of the model contains four domains:
         a) **Plan and organize**
         b) **Acquire and implement**
         c) **Deliver and support**
         d) **Monitor and evaluate**
      3) **Controls-based.** "An IT control objective is a statement of the desired result or purpose to be achieved by implementing control procedures in a particular IT activity." COBIT describes controls in three areas:
         a) **Process controls.** "Operational management uses processes to organize and manage ongoing IT activities."
         b) **Business controls.** These impact IT at three levels: the executive management level, the business process level, and the IT support level.
         c) **IT general controls and application controls.** This dichotomy for IT controls is of very long standing.
            i) "General controls are those controls embedded in IT processes and services ... Controls embedded in business process applications are commonly referred to as application controls."
      4) **Measurement-driven**
         a) The centerpiece of the COBIT framework in this area is the **maturity model**.
            i) "The organization must rate how well managed its IT processes are. The suggested scale employs the rankings of non-existent, initial, repeatable, defined, managed, and optimized."

b) **Performance measurement**

Goals and metrics are defined in COBIT at three levels:

- *IT goals and metrics that define what the business expects from IT*
- *Process goals and metrics that define what the IT processes must deliver to support IT's objectives*
- *Process performance metrics*

GTAG

5. Beginning in 2005, The IIA replaced its Practice Advisories on IT topics with an extremely detailed series of documents known collectively as the ***Global Technology Audit Guide (GTAG)***.
   a. The control model discussed in GTAG 1, *Information Technology Controls*, is very useful for this discussion.
   b. GTAG 1 recognizes three "families" of controls:
      1) **General and application controls**, described in the COBIT framework in item 4.c.3) on the previous page.
      2) Preventive, detective, and corrective controls.
         a) **Preventive controls** "prevent errors, omissions, or security incidents from occurring."
         b) **Detective controls** "detect errors or incidents that elude preventive controls."
         c) **Corrective controls** "correct errors, omissions, or incidents once they have been detected."
      3) Governance, management, and technical controls.
         a) "**Governance controls** ... are linked with the concepts of corporate governance, which are driven both by organizational goals and strategies and by outside bodies such as regulators."
         b) **Management controls** "are deployed as a result of deliberate actions by management to recognize risks to the organization, its processes, and assets; and enact mechanisms and processes to mitigate and manage risks."
         c) **Technical controls** "are specific to the technologies in use within the organization's IT infrastructures."

Stop and review! You have completed the outline for this subunit. Study multiple-choice questions 1 through 3 on page 368.

8.2 ASPECTS OF AUTOMATED INFORMATION PROCESSING

Characteristics of Automated Processing

1. The use of computers in business information systems has **fundamental effects** on the nature of business transacted, the procedures followed, the risks incurred, and the methods of mitigating those risks. These effects flow from the characteristics that distinguish computer-based from manual processing.
   a. **Transaction trails.** A complete trail useful for audit and other purposes might exist for only a short time or only in computer-readable form. The nature of the trail is often dependent on the transaction processing mode, for example, whether transactions are batched prior to processing or whether they are processed immediately as they happen.

b. **Uniform processing of transactions.** Computer processing uniformly subjects like transactions to the same processing instructions and thus virtually eliminates clerical error, but programming errors (or other similar systematic errors in either the hardware or software) will result in all like transactions being processed incorrectly when they are processed under the same conditions.

c. **Segregation of functions.** Many controls once performed by separate individuals may be concentrated in computer systems. Hence, an individual who has access to the computer may perform incompatible functions. As a result, other controls may be necessary to achieve the control objectives ordinarily accomplished by segregation of functions.

d. **Potential for errors and fraud.** The potential for individuals, including those performing control procedures, to gain unauthorized access to data, to alter data without visible evidence, or to gain access (direct or indirect) to assets may be greater in computer systems. Decreased human involvement in handling transactions can reduce the potential for observing errors and fraud. Errors or fraud in the design or changing of application programs can remain undetected for a long time.

e. **Potential for increased management supervision.** Computer systems offer management many analytical tools for review and supervision of operations. These additional controls may enhance internal control. For example, traditional comparisons of actual and budgeted operating ratios and reconciliations of accounts are often available for review on a more timely basis. Furthermore, some programmed applications provide statistics regarding computer operations that may be used to monitor actual processing.

f. **Initiation or subsequent execution of transactions by computer.** Certain transactions may be automatically initiated or certain procedures required to execute a transaction may be automatically performed by a computer system. The authorization of these transactions or procedures may not be documented in the same way as those in a manual system, and management's authorization may be implicit in its acceptance of the design of the system.

g. **Dependence of controls in other areas on controls over computer processing.** Computer processing may produce reports and other output that are used in performing manual control procedures. The effectiveness of these controls can be dependent on the effectiveness of controls over the completeness and accuracy of computer processing. For example, the effectiveness of a manual review of a computer-produced exception listing is dependent on the controls over the production of the listing.

<u>**Processing Modes**</u>

2. Data can be processed in one of **two basic modes**:

   a. **Batch processing.** In this mode, transactions are accumulated and submitted to the computer as a single "batch." In the early days of computers, this was the only way a job could be processed.

      1) In batch processing, the user cannot influence the process once the job has begun (except to ask that it be aborted completely). (S)he must wait until the job is finished running to see if any transactions in the batch were rejected and failed to post.

      2) Despite huge advances in computer technology, this accumulation of transactions for processing on a delayed basis is still widely used. It is very efficient for such applications as payroll, where large numbers of routine transactions must be processed on a regular schedule.

b. **Online, real-time processing.** In some systems, having the latest information available at all times is crucial to the proper functioning of the system. An airline reservation system is a common example.

1) In an online, real-time system, the database is updated immediately upon entry of the transaction by the operator. Such systems are referred to as **online transaction processing**, or **OLTP**, systems.

Stop and review! You have completed the outline for this subunit. Study multiple-choice questions 4 through 9 beginning on page 369.

8.3 IT CONTROLS

Classification of Controls

1. The COBIT framework provides the following discussion about the business controls mentioned on page 347:

   *At the **executive management level**, business objectives are set, policies are established and decisions are made on how to deploy and manage the resources of the enterprise to execute the enterprise strategy.*

   *At the **business process level**, controls are applied to specific business activities. Most business processes are automated and integrated with IT application systems, resulting in many of the controls at this level being automated as well. These controls are known as application controls.*

   *To **support the business processes**, IT provides IT services, usually in a shared service to many business processes, as many of the development and operational IT processes are provided to the whole enterprise, and much of the IT infrastructure is provided as a common service (e.g., networks, databases, operating systems and storage). The controls applied to all IT service activities are known as IT general controls.*

   a. The organization must implement **appropriate controls at each of the three levels** described in the COBIT model.

      1) For example, at the executive level, an **IT steering committee** should be established, composed of senior managers from both the IT function and the end-user functions. The committee approves development projects, assigns resources, and reviews their progress.

      2) The steering committee also ensures that requests for new systems are **aligned with the overall strategic plan** of the organization.

   b. The interaction between the last two types of controls described above (general and application) is crucial in an **audit context**. As COBIT goes on to specifically state:

      The reliable operation of these general controls is necessary for reliance to be placed on application controls.

      1) In other words, because general controls affect the organization's entire processing environment, the auditor must achieve satisfaction about their proper operation before relying on application controls.

   c. The COBIT model divides **general controls** into **four basic areas**: systems development, change management, security, and computer operations. These general controls are discussed in Subunits 9.7, 9.8, 10.3, and 9.1 respectively.

   d. The COBIT model gives the following as examples of types of **application controls**: completeness, accuracy, validity, authorization, and segregation of duties.

      1) Note the similarity between these controls and the management assertions about financial statements in the standard audit model.

2) This similarity highlights the fact that a computer application is merely the automation of a business process and the objectives of internal control are the same.

Application Controls

2. Application controls relate to the business tasks performed by a particular system. They should provide reasonable assurance that the recording, processing, and reporting of data are properly performed.
   a. The most economical point for correcting input errors in an application is the time at which the data are entered into the system.
      1) For these reasons, **input controls** are the focus of an internal auditor's activity. Each of the two major types of processing modes has its own controls.
   b. **Batch Input Controls**
      1) **Financial totals** summarize dollar amounts in an information field in a group of records. The total produced by the system after the batch has been processed is compared to the total produced manually beforehand.
      2) **Record counts** track the number of records processed by the system for comparison to the number that the user expected to be processed.
      3) **Hash totals** are control totals without a defined meaning, such as the total of vendor numbers or invoice numbers, that are used to verify the completeness of the data.
   c. **Online Input Controls**
      1) **Preformatting** of data entry screens, i.e., to make them imitate the layout of a printed form, can aid the operator in keying to the correct fields.
      2) **Field checks** are tests of the characters in a field to verify that they are of an appropriate type for that field. For example, the system is programmed to reject alphabetic characters entered in the field for Social Security Number.
      3) **Validity checks** compare the data entered in a given field with a table of valid values for that field. For example, the vendor number on a request to cut a check must match the table of current vendors, and the invoice number must match the approved invoice table.
      4) **Limit and range checks** are based on known limits for given information. For example, hours worked per week must be between 0 and 100, with anything outside that range requiring management authorization.
      5) **Self-checking digits** are used to detect incorrect identification numbers. The digit is generated by applying an algorithm to the ID number. During the input process, the check digit is recomputed by applying the same algorithm to the code actually entered.
   d. An important detective control is **user review** of output. Users should be able to determine when output is incomplete or not reasonable, particularly when the user prepared the input. Thus, users as well as computer personnel have a quality assurance function.

Stop and review! You have completed the outline for this subunit. Study multiple-choice questions 10 through 14 beginning on page 370.

8.4 DATA COMMUNICATIONS, NETWORKS, AND CLIENT-SERVER SYSTEMS

Background to Networking

1. Large **mainframe computers** dominated the electronic data processing field in its first decades.
   a. Mainframes were arranged so that all processing and data storage were done in a single, central location.
   b. Communication with the mainframe was accomplished with the use of **dumb terminals**, simple keyboard-and-monitor combinations with no processing power (i.e., no CPU) of their own.
2. The next stage in the evolution of networking was to connect computers not in different rooms of a building, but in separate buildings and eventually separate countries.
   a. This required converting the **digital signal** used internally by the computer into an **analog signal** suitable for transmission over ordinary telephone lines.

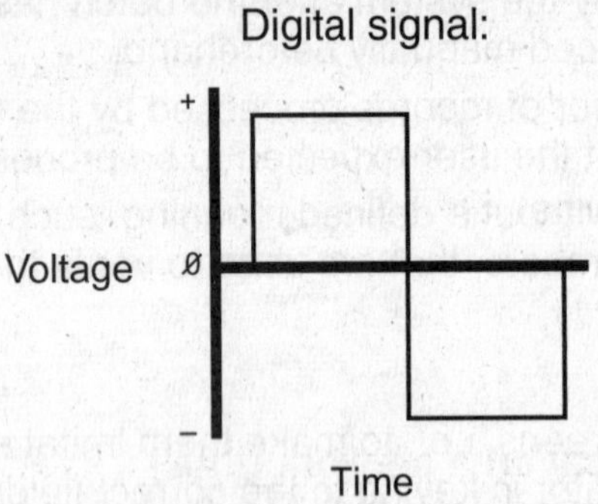

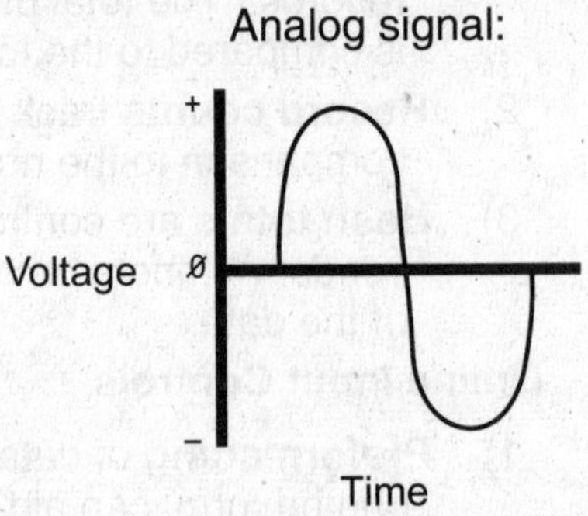

      1) This conversion is necessary because when a digital signal travels more than about 10 feet, it starts to lose its shape and eventually resembles an analog signal. By that point it has become completely unusable.
   b. In all-digital networks, such as LANs (see item 4. on the next page) and connections between dumb terminals and mainframes, **repeaters** are placed every so often to revive the digital signal and return it to its full square-wave shape.
      1) This is obviously not an option with the existing telephone network and its hundreds of thousands of miles of wire.
      2) The solution is simply to convert the computer's digital signal into an analog signal **(modulation)**, send it over the phone line, then reconvert it to a digital signal at the other end **(demodulation)**.
      3) The device that performs these conversion and reconversion functions is a **modem** (short for modulator-demodulator).
   c. The introduction of the modem allowed organizations to begin moving information between locations in purely electronic format, eliminating the need for the passage of physical documents. The potential for **cost savings** in this technology was obvious.
3. Improvements in technology have led to increasing **decentralization** of information processing.
   a. The mainframe-style computer was the only arrangement available in the early days of data processing. International Business Machines (now called IBM) dominated the marketplace.
      1) **Mainframes are still in use** at large institutions, such as governments, banks, insurance companies, and universities.
         a) However, remote connections to them are usually through desktop computers rather than through dumb terminals. This is known as **terminal emulation**.

2) In the 1980s, the **minicomputer** gave organizations the ability to perform data processing without the high cost and large dedicated facilities of a mainframe. Digital Equipment Corporation (DEC) and Hewlett-Packard (HP) dominated this market.

3) As minicomputers evolved, the concept of distributed processing arose.

a) **Distributed processing** involves the decentralization of processing tasks and data storage and assigning these functions to multiple computers, often in separate locations.

b) This allowed for a drastic reduction in the amount of communications traffic because data that were needed locally could reside locally.

4) In 1981, IBM introduced the **Personal Computer (PC)**. This designation quickly lost its status as a brand name and became a generic term for almost any computer smaller than a minicomputer.

b. During the 1980s, desktop computers, and the knowledge needed to build information systems, became widespread throughout the organization.

1) In the early part of this period, the only means of moving data from one computer to another was the laborious process of copying the data to a diskette and physically carrying it to the destination computer. This method of connecting computers was called **sneakernet**, after the footwear involved.

2) It was clear that a reliable way of wiring office computers together would lead to tremendous gains in productivity.

LANs and Client-Server

4. This need led to the development of the **local area network (LAN)**. A LAN is any interconnection between devices in a single office or building.

a. Very small networks with few devices can be connected using a **peer-to-peer** arrangement, where every device is directly connected to every other.

1) Peer-to-peer networks become increasingly difficult to administer with each added device.

b. The most cost-effective and easy-to-administer arrangement for LANs uses the client-server model.

1) **Client/server networks** differ from peer-to-peer networks in that the devices play more specialized roles. Client processes (initiated by the individual user) request services from server processes (maintained centrally).

2) In a client/server arrangement, **servers** are centrally located and devoted to the functions that are needed by all network users.

a) Examples include mail servers (to handle electronic mail), application servers (to run application programs), file servers (to store databases and make user inquiries more efficient), Internet servers (to manage access to the Internet), and web servers (to host websites).

b) Whether a device is **classified as a server** is not determined by its hardware configuration but rather by the **function it performs**. A simple desktop computer can be a server.

3) Technically, a **client** is any object that uses the resources of another object. Thus, a client can be either a device or a software program.

a) In common usage, however, "client" refers to a device that requests services from a server. This understanding of the term encompasses anything from a powerful graphics workstation to a personal data assistant (PDA), such as a Palm Pilot or a Blackberry.

b) A client device normally displays the user interface and enables data entry, queries, and the receipt of reports. Moreover, many applications, e.g., word processing and spreadsheet software, run on the client computer.

4) The key to the client/server model is that **it runs processes on the platform most appropriate to that process while attempting to minimize traffic over the network.**

5) **Security** for client-server systems may be more difficult than in a highly centralized system because of the numerous access points.

OSI 7-Layer Model

5. The **Open Systems Interconnection (OSI) Reference Model** provides a perspective for categorizing the functions that must be performed by any computer network

a. Originally, it was devised by the International Organization for Standardization (ISO) as the basis for an actual family of protocols. Many nations and companies in Europe and Asia began adopting these protocols as they became standardized.

1) However, the OSI protocols were eventually overwhelmed worldwide by the spread of the Internet and its accompanying TCP/IP set of protocols [see item 8.c.2)a)].

2) Although the protocols did not survive, the reference model portion of the overall OSI project has proven useful for the study of networks.

b. The OSI reference model depicts any computer network as required to perform certain functions. The functions are grouped in **seven layers**.

1) Each layer provides "services" to the next higher layer. This can be depicted by the diagram below:

OSI 7-Layer Network Reference Model

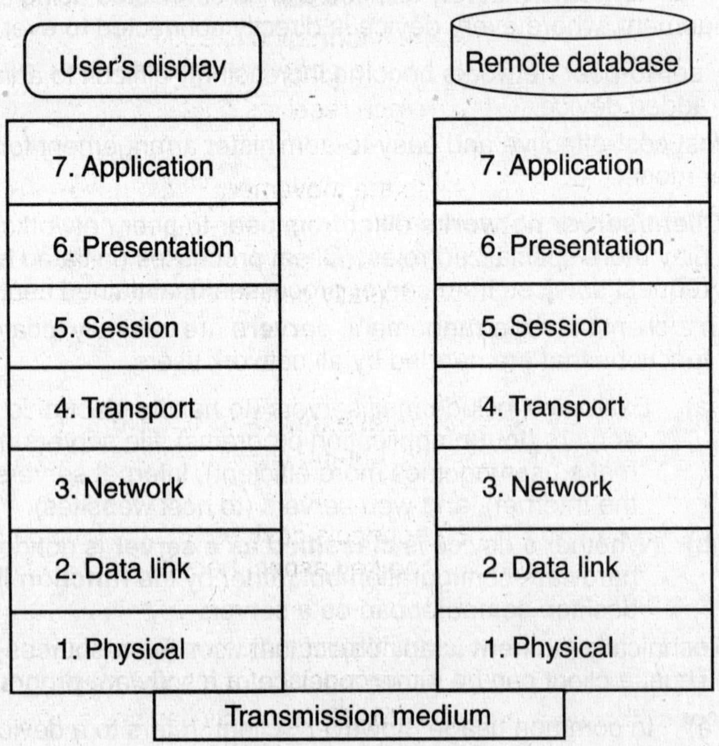

c. The functions performed by the layers can be summarized as follows:
   1) The **physical layer (layer 1)** describes how the bits must be organized to flow over the medium being used (copper wire, fiber optic, microwave, etc.).
   2) The **data link layer (layer 2)** ensures that errors in the stream of data are detected and corrected.
   3) The **network layer (layer 3)** ensures the "packets" of data on the network move to the correct destination.
   4) The **transport layer (layer 4)** establishes a "class of service" between the two communicating parties (such as batch or interactive) and ensures that sufficient resources are available to maintain it.
   5) The **session layer (layer 5)** ensures a continuous session between the two communicating parties, such that the users experience no interruptions taking place on the transport layer beneath.
   6) The **presentation layer (layer 6)** negotiates "syntax" differences between the two communicating parties. This refers to the various ways digital bits are arranged to represent letters and numbers (ASCII and EBCDIC are the best known).
   7) The **application layer (layer 7)** interacts with the user's hardware, operating system, and application to make data entry and display possible.

d. The following **analogy** can be useful for understanding how the OSI reference model depicts the management of a data stream:
   1) At the highest layer, a person writes a letter. The person then proceeds to fold the letter, insert it in an envelope, seal the envelope, address it, apply a stamp, and place it in the custody of the Postal Service.
      a) The process just described corresponds to the movement of a data packet down the layers. The Postal Service is the transmission medium.
      b) At each layer, some information is added to the packet, wrapping it in more and more extra data to perform the necessary functions.
   2) The recipient of the envelope receives it, opens it, pulls out the letter, unfolds it, and reads it.
      a) This corresponds to the movement of the data packet up the layers on the destination computer.
      b) At each layer, the network strips away the extra data applied at that layer by the sender, eventually getting the message into a form understandable by the recipient.

<u>Types of Networks I</u>

6. **Classifying networks by geographical extent and function.** The range of networking has expanded from the earliest form (two computers in the same room) to the global reach of the Internet.

   a. A **local area network (LAN)** connects devices within a single office or home or among buildings in an office park. The key aspect here is that a LAN is **owned entirely by a single organization**.
      1) The LAN is the network familiar to office workers all over the world. In its simplest conception, it can consist of a few desktop computers and a printer.

   b. A **metropolitan area network (MAN)** connects devices across an urban area, for instance, two or more office parks.
      1) This conception had limited success as a wire-based network but may make a comeback using microwaves [see item 8.d.3)].

c. A **wide area network (WAN)** consists of a conglomerate of LANs over widely separated locations. The key aspect here is that a WAN can be either **publicly or privately owned**.

1) WANs come in **many configurations**. In its simplest conception, it can consist of a lone desktop computer using a slow dialup line to connect to an Internet service provider.

2) **Publicly owned** WANs, such as the public telephone system and the Internet, are available to any user with a compatible device. The assets of these networks are paid for by means other than individually imposed user fees.

a) **Public-switched networks** use public telephone lines to carry data. This arrangement is economical, but the quality of data transmission cannot be guaranteed and security is highly questionable.

3) **Privately owned** WANs are profit-making enterprises. They offer fast, secure data communication services to organizations that do not wish to make their own large investments in the necessary infrastructure.

a) **Value-added networks (VANs)** are private networks that provide their customers with reliable high-speed, secure transmission of data.

i) To compete with the Internet, these third-party networks add value by providing their customers with error detection and correction services, electronic mailbox facilities for EDI purposes, EDI translation, and security for email and data transmissions.

b) **Virtual private networks (VPNs)** emerged as a relatively inexpensive way to solve the problem of the high cost of leased lines.

i) A company connects each office or LAN to a local Internet service provider and routes data through the shared, low-cost public Internet.

ii) The success of VPNs depends on the development of secure encryption products that protect data while in transit.

c) A **private branch exchange (PBX)** is a specialized computer used to handle both voice and data traffic.

i) A PBX can switch digital data among computers and office equipment, e.g., printers, copiers, and fax machines. A PBX uses telephone lines, so its data transmission capacity is limited.

<u>**Network Equipment**</u>

7. **Equipment used in networks.** Networks consist of (a) the hardware devices being connected and (b) the medium through which the connection is made.

a. **Client devices.** Devices of all sizes and functions (mainframes, laptop computers, personal digital assistants, MP3 players, printers, scanners, cash registers, ATMs, etc.) can be connected to networks.

1) Connecting a device to a network requires a **network interface card (NIC)**. The NIC allows the device to speak that particular network's "language," that is, its protocol (see item 8.).

2) A development in the late 1990s called the **thin client** explicitly mimics the old mainframe-and-terminal model.

a) A typical thin client consists merely of a monitor, a keyboard, and a small amount of embedded memory. The key is that it has **no local hard drive.**

b) Essentially all **processing and data storage** is done on the **servers**. Just enough of an application is downloaded to the client to run it.

c) An advantage of this architecture is the large amount of IT staff time and effort saved that formerly went to configuring and troubleshooting desktop machines. A disadvantage is that there must be 100% server availability for any work to be done by users.

d) The thin client architecture has not met with widespread use because the cost of hard drives has continued to steadily decrease, defying predictions.

b. **Types of media.** The medium that connects the devices on a network can take many forms.

1) **Bandwidth** is the signal-carrying capacity of a transmission medium. It is a rough indication of the highest "speed" that data can attain when traveling through it.

a) A medium that can carry only one signal is called **baseband**. A medium that can carry multiple signals is called **broadband**.

2) On a **wired LAN**, the choice of cabling depends on speed requirements.

a) **Twisted pair** wiring is graded into categories, each of which denotes a different bandwidth. Twisted pair is fundamentally a **baseband** medium.

i) Twisted pair takes its name from the continuous weaving of the strands of wire around each other within the cable.

- A magnetic field is produced around any wire through which current is passed. These fields can disrupt the transmission of electrical signals, a phenomenon known as **electromagnetic interference**.
- Twisting the strands of copper around each other within a cable has the effect of canceling the magnetic fields.
- Twisted pair comes in shielded (STP) and unshielded (UTP) varieties. Shielded twisted pair carries extra protection against electromagnetic interference.

ii) **Category 1** twisted pair is unshielded. It is usually referred to as regular telephone wire.

iii) **Category 3** comes in both shielded and unshielded varieties and can support a higher bandwidth than Category 1.

iv) **Category 5** also comes in both shielded and unshielded varieties and can support a higher bandwidth than Category 3.

b) **Coaxial cable** is a commonly used medium for LANs. Coax (pronounced *COE-ax*), as it is called, is also the familiar transmission medium of cable TV.

i) Generally, coax is necessary when **broadband** transmission is desired.

ii) This cable design is named coaxial because one signal conductor surrounds the other, giving them a common "axis."

3) Wired LANs depend on two basic types of **networking devices** to connect the cabling:

a) **Hubs** are, in computing terms, very simple ("dumb") and serve only to broadcast messages to every other device on the network.

i) The device for which the message is intended will keep it and process it. The other devices will discard it.

b) **Bridges** improve traffic flow by dividing LANs into **segments**. Bridges are more "intelligent" than hubs.

i) Instead of simply broadcasting messages as hubs do, bridges read the destination address and isolate the message to the segment where the destination device is located, greatly reducing unnecessary traffic on the network.

c) Separate LANs are connected by either specialized bridges, called **remote bridges**, or by **gateways**.

4) On a **wireless LAN**, the NIC uses an antenna instead of a cable to connect to the hub or router through the air. The differences in wireless networks are best discussed in the context of communication protocols (see item 8.d.).

5) **WANs**, with their greater traffic requirements, need higher-capacity media.

a) **Fiber-optic cable** consists of extremely fine threads of glass or plastic.

i) The electrical signal is converted to **pulses of light**, which are sent through the optical medium at much higher speeds than electrical signals can travel through copper wire.

ii) The light pulses do not travel straight down the fiber. They are deliberately aimed into the fiber at an angle with respect to the cable's insulation (called cladding).

- This angling causes the light pulses to **continuously bounce** from one side of the fiber to the other as they travel down the length of the cable.
- This bouncing phenomenon is an aid in separating the various signals when they arrive at the other end.

iii) Fiber optics has **two major advantages** over wire in addition to drastically greater bandwidth:

- The light pulses used in fiber optics are not subject to electromagnetic interference.
- Interception by unauthorized parties is impossible because the light pulses cannot be "tapped" as electrical signals can. Also, the cut end of an optical fiber becomes a mirror, immediately alerting the administrator that there is a problem with the cable.

b) **Microwave transmission** involves propagating electrical signals through air and space instead of through metal wire or optical fiber.

i) **Satellite relay** involves transmitting the microwave signal to a satellite in orbit, which retransmits the signal to the destination back on Earth. This medium offers very high speeds and wide geographic coverage.

ii) **LOS (line-of-sight) microwave** transmission is an older technology still in use in some places. It consists of beaming the signals from one tower to another from horizon to horizon.

- Almost all long-distance voice telephone calls in the United States were transmitted by LOS microwave between the 1960s and the advent of fiber-optic cable in the 1980s.

iii) Both satellite relay and LOS microwave systems have the advantage of not having to secure rights-of-way for the laying of physical cable over long distances.

Types of Networks II

8. **Classifying networks by protocol.** A protocol is a set of standards for message transmission among the devices on the network.
   a. **LAN Protocols**
      1) **Ethernet** has been the most successful protocol for LAN transmission. The Ethernet (capitalized because it is a trademark) design breaks up the flow of data between devices into discrete groups of data bits called "frames."
         a) ANALOGY: Ethernet follows the "polite conversation" method of communicating.
            i) Each device "listens" to the network to determine whether another conversation is taking place, that is, whether the network is busy moving another device's message.
            ii) Once the network is determined to be free of traffic, the device sends its message.
         b) Inevitably, frames collide on Ethernet networks constantly. When this happens, the two contending devices wait a random (and extremely brief) length of time, then transmit again. Eventually, both messages will hit the network at a moment when it is free.
         c) This design, while seemingly inefficient in accepting such a high number of collisions and retransmissions, has been extraordinarily successful. Over the years, Ethernet has proven to be secure, adaptable, and expandable.
      2) The **token ring** protocol originally had a much higher speed than Ethernet.
         a) Each device is directly connected to the next device in a ring configuration. A special frame called the token is passed continuously around the ring from one device to the next.
         b) When a device wishes to send a message, it attaches the message to the token. The token drops off the message when it arrives at the destination device.
         c) Token ring, though heavily promoted by IBM, is expensive and difficult to expand, and its early speed advantage has been eclipsed by advances in Ethernet.
   b. **Switched Networks**
      1) As described in item 6.a., in a **LAN**, all the devices and all the transmission media belong to **one organization**.
         a) This single ownership of infrastructure assets plus the ability to unify all communication on a single protocol make for great **efficiency and security**.
      2) When communication must **cross organizational boundaries** or travel **beyond a limited geographical range**, this single ownership principle no longer applies. A WAN is the applicable model.
         a) A WAN, with its hundreds of users and much greater distances, could never function using the collision-detection-and-retransmission method of Ethernet. To overcome this, the technique called **switching** is used.

3) Switching takes two basic forms:
   a) In **circuit switching**, a single physical pathway is established in the public telephone system, and that pathway is reserved for the full and exclusive use of the two parties for the duration of their communication.
      i) An example is an ordinary landline telephone call or a dialup connection from a modem. This is obviously a slow and insecure alternative for data transmission.
   b) In **packet switching**, the data bits making up a message are broken up into "packets" of predefined length. Each packet has a header containing the electronic address of the device for which the message is intended.
4) **Switches** are the networking devices that read the address on each packet and send it along the appropriate path to its destination.
   a) ANALOGY: The machinery for a new plant is mounted on several 18-wheelers for transport to the plant site. The trucks leave the machinery vendor's factory headed to the destination.
      i) As each truck arrives at a traffic light, it stops while vehicles going in other directions pass through the intersection.
      ii) As the trucks arrive at the plant site, they are unloaded and the machinery is installed.
5) By allowing message flow from many different organizations to pass through common points, switches **spread the cost** of the WAN infrastructure.
   a) **Frame relay** and **ATM (asynchronous transfer mode)** are examples of fast packet switched network protocols.

c. **Routed Networks**
1) **Routers** have more intelligence than hubs, bridges, or switches.
   a) Routers have **tables** stored in memory that tell them the **most efficient path** along which each packet should be sent.
   b) ANALOGY: The trucks leave the machinery vendor's factory with the same destination.
      i) As the trucks stop at each intersection, traffic cops redirect them down different routes depending on traffic conditions.
      ii) As the trucks arrive in unknown sequence at the plant site, they are held until the machinery can be unloaded in the correct order.
2) Routing is what makes the **Internet** possible.
   a) **Transmission Control Protocol/Internet Protocol (TCP/IP)** is the suite of routing protocols that makes it possible to interconnect many thousands of devices from dozens of manufacturers all over the world through the Internet.
      i) TCP/IP operates on layers 4 and 3 of the OSI reference model.
   b) **IP addressing** (also called dotted decimal addressing) is the heart of Internet routing. It allows any device anywhere in the world to be recognized on the Internet through the use of a standard-format IP address.
      i) Each of the four decimal-separated elements of the IP address is a numeral between 0 and 255.

         EXAMPLE: 128.67.111.25

c) **Dynamic host configuration protocol (DHCP)** allows tremendous flexibility on the Internet by enabling the constant reuse of IP addresses.

i) Routers generally have their IP addresses hardcoded when they are first installed. However, the individual client devices on most organizational networks are assigned an IP address by DHCP from a pool of available addresses every time they boot up.

d. **Wireless Networks**

1) The **Wi-Fi** family of protocols supports client devices within a radius of about 300 feet around a wireless router. This usable area is called a **hotspot**.

a) Wi-Fi **avoids the collisions** inherent in Ethernet by constantly searching for the best frequency within its assigned range to use.

b) Security was a problem in early incarnations of Wi-Fi. Later versions alleviated some of these concerns with encryption.

2) The **Bluetooth** standard operates over a much smaller radius than Wi-Fi, about 30 feet. This distance permits the creation of what has come to be called the **personal area network** or **PAN** (i.e., a network of devices for a single user).

a) A prominent example is the in-ear device that allows the wearer to make telephone calls hands-free or to listen to a personal music player in wireless mode. Wireless keyboards and mice also employ the Bluetooth standard.

b) Bluetooth is considerably slower than Wi-Fi.

3) The **WiMax** standard uses microwaves to turn an entire city into a hotspot, reviving the old MAN model. The radius is about 10 miles and the speed is quite fast.

a) Providers of wired networks can bill individual customers for use of the network. However, since anyone with the right device could access a WiMax network, the initial investment in infrastructure would have to be financed through a means other than user fees, making WiMax's widespread deployment unlikely in the near future.

4) **Radio-frequency identification (RFID)** technology involves the use of a combined microchip with antenna to store data about a product, pet, vehicle, etc. Common applications include

a) Inventory tracking
b) Lost pet identification
c) Tollbooth collection

Stop and review! You have completed the outline for this subunit. Study multiple-choice questions 15 through 18 beginning on page 372.

8.5 ELECTRONIC FUNDS TRANSFER (EFT)

1. **Electronic funds transfer (EFT)** is a service provided by financial institutions worldwide that is based on electronic data interchange (EDI) technology.

a. EFT transaction costs are lower than for manual systems because documents and human intervention are eliminated from the transaction process. Moreover, transfer customarily requires less than a day.

b. A typical consumer application of EFT is the **direct deposit** of payroll checks in employees' accounts or the automatic withdrawal of payments for cable and telephone bills, mortgages, etc.

2. The most important application of EFT is **check collection**. To reduce the enormous volume of paper, the check-collection process has been computerized.
   a. The result has been to reduce the significance of paper checks because EFT provides means to make payments and deposit funds without manual transfer of negotiable instruments. Thus, wholesale EFTs among financial institutions and businesses (commercial transfers) are measured in the trillions of dollars.
      1) The two major systems for these "wire" or nonconsumer transfers are Fedwire (Federal Reserve wire transfer network) and CHIPS (New York Clearing House Interbank Payment System). Private systems also are operated by large banks.

Stop and review! You have completed the outline for this subunit. Study multiple-choice questions 19 and 20 beginning on page 373.

8.6 E-COMMERCE

<u>**Overview**</u>

1. **Electronic commerce (e-commerce)** is the purchase and sale of goods and services by electronic means. **E-business** is a more comprehensive term defined as all methods of conducting business electronically.
   a. E-commerce may occur via online transactions on public networks, electronic data interchange (EDI), and email.
2. **Security issues** for e-commerce include
   a. The correct identification of the transacting parties **(authentication)**
   b. Determination of who may rightfully make decisions, such as entering into contracts or setting prices **(authorization)**
   c. Methods for protecting the confidentiality and integrity of information, providing evidence of the transmission and receipt of documents, and guarding against repudiation by the sender or recipient
   d. The trustworthiness of listed **prices** and the confidentiality of **discounts**
   e. The confidentiality and integrity of orders, payments, delivery addresses, and confirmations
   f. The proper extent of **verification** of payment data
   g. The best **method of payment** to avoid wrongdoing or disagreements
   h. Lost or duplicated transactions
   i. Determining who bears the risk of fraud
3. **Responses to security issues** include
   a. Encryption and the associated authentication methods
   b. Adherence to legal requirements, such as privacy statutes
   c. Documenting trading agreements, especially the terms of trade and methods of authorization and authentication
   d. Agreements for end-to-end security and availability with providers of information services and VANs
   e. Disclosure by public trading systems of their terms of business
   f. The capacity of the host computer to avoid downtime and repel attacks

Practice Advisory

4. The IIA's former Practice Advisory 2100-6, *Control and Audit Implications of E-commerce Activities*, contains much useful information concerning engagements to audit electronic commerce activities.

   a. **Electronic commerce (e-commerce)** means "conducting commercial activities over the Internet." These activities can be business-to-business **(B2B)**, business-to-consumer **(B2C)**, and business to employee **(B2E)**. Technology not only supports these e-commerce strategies but also is an integral part. **Web-based and other technology changes** have had a pervasive impact. Such changes and the dramatic growth of e-commerce create significant control and management challenges.

   b. In **understanding and planning** an e-commerce engagement, the auditor should understand the changes in business and information systems, the related risks, and the alignment of strategies with design and market requirements. The auditor reviews **strategic planning** and **risk assessment** and management's decisions about risks, controls, and monitoring.

   c. The auditor (1) assesses **control** and whether there is reasonable assurance that **objectives** are achievable, (2) determines **risk acceptability**, (3) understands **information flow**, (4) reviews **interfaces**, and (5) evaluates **disaster recovery plans**.

   d. The CAE's concerns are the **competency and capacity** of the IAA. **Limiting factors** are (1) the sufficiency of skills, (2) the need for training and other resources, (3) long-term and short-term staffing levels, and (4) deliverability of the expected audit plan.

   e. The auditor considers many factors during the **risk assessment**, such as (1) the existence of a **business plan**; (2) its coverage of the integration of the planning, design, and implementation of the e-commerce system with the strategies of the organization; (3) the effect on the **system**; (4) whether **users' needs** will be met; (5) consideration of **regulatory** issues; (6) the **security** of hardware and software and whether they prevent or detect harmful effects and losses; (7) transaction **processing** integrity and accuracy; (8) strength of the **control environment**; (9) **completeness** of the risk assessment; (10) **inherent risks** associated with the Internet and Internet provider; (11) implications of dealing with **outside vendors**, e.g., whether a going concern evaluation has conducted by a trusted, qualified third party, and if vendors provide hosting services, they have a tested business contingency plan; and (12) legal matters, e.g., issues involving taxes, contract enforcement in other countries, privacy, intellectual property, defamation, copyrights, trademarks, fraud, and electronic signatures.

   f. **Risk** is the uncertainty of an event's occurrence that could adversely affect the achievement of objectives. Risk is inherent. **Opportunity risks** assumed by management are drivers of activities. Beyond them may be threats and other dangers not clearly understood and fully evaluated and too easily accepted. **Managing risk** requires an understanding of **risk elements** and an awareness of **new threats and changes in technology** affecting information security. **Seven key questions** identify organizational risk and possible ways of controlling or mitigating the exposures. The following are the questions and the related risk elements: (1) What adverse events could happen **(threat events)**, (2) what will be the financial effect **(single loss exposure value)**, (3) how often **(frequency)**, (4) how probable are the preceding answers **(uncertainty)**, (5) what can be done by way of risk management **(safeguards and controls)**, (6) what is the cost **(cost of safeguards and controls)**, and (7) how efficient is risk management **(cost/benefit or ROI analysis)**.

   g. The auditor should address the **critical risk and control issues**, such as (1) general project management, (2) specific security threats, (3) transaction integrity in a complex network, (4) website content changes, (5) technology change, (6) legal concerns, and (7) changes in business processes and structures.

h. The **overall audit objective** is effective control. Management of e-commerce should be **documented** in an approved **strategic plan**. **Specific audit objectives** for an e-commerce engagement should be defined, for example, (1) evidence of transactions, (2) availability and reliability of security, (3) effective interface with financial systems, (4) security of monetary transactions, (5) effectiveness of customer authentication, (6) adequacy of business continuity processes, (7) compliance with security standards, (8) use and control of digital signatures, (9) adequacy of control of public key certificates, (10) adequacy and timeliness of operating data, and (11) documentation of effective control.

i. The **e-commerce audit program** will vary with the organization. The following are the components of a general e-commerce **audit protocol** for key areas: (1) e-commerce organization, (2) fraud conditions (red flags), (3) authentication of transactions and evaluation of controls, (4) evaluation of controls over data integrity, (5) review of the continuity plan for coping with business interruptions, and (6) evaluation of how well business units are managing e-commerce.

Stop and review! You have completed the outline for this subunit. Study multiple-choice questions 21 through 25 beginning on page 374.

8.7 ELECTRONIC DATA INTERCHANGE (EDI)

Overview

1. **Electronic data interchange (EDI)** is the communication of electronic documents directly from a computer in one entity to a computer in another entity, for example, to order goods from a supplier or to transfer funds. EDI was the first step in the evolution of e-business.
   a. EDI was developed to enhance JIT (just-in-time) inventory management.
   b. **Advantages of EDI** include reduction of clerical errors, speed of transactions, and elimination of repetitive clerical tasks. EDI also eliminates document preparation, processing, and mailing costs.
   c. **Risks of EDI** include
      1) Security of information
         a) End-to-end data encryption is a security procedure that protects data during transmission.
      2) Loss of data
   d. An extension of EDI is computer-stored records, which can be less expensive than traditional physical file storage.
2. **EDI Terms and Components**
   a. **Standards** concern procedures to convert written documents into a standard electronic document-messaging format to facilitate EDI.
      1) In the U.S., the American National Standards Institute's Accredited Standards Committee **X.12** provides standards.
      2) Many international entities use **UN/EDIFACT** (United Nations EDI for Administration, Commerce, and Transport).
   b. **Conventions** are the procedures for arranging data elements in specified formats for various accounting transactions, e.g., invoices, materials releases, and advance shipment notices.
   c. A **data dictionary** prescribes the meaning of data elements, including specification of each transaction structure.

d. **Transmission protocols** are rules to determine how each electronic envelope is structured and processed by the communications devices.
    1) Normally, a group of transactions is combined in an electronic envelope and transmitted into a communications network.
    2) Rules are required for transmission and the separation of envelopes.

e. Because EDI formats and elements vary, a large entity may gain a competitive advantage by forcing trading partners to adopt its standards. Other entities will need to negotiate EDI standards.

Methods of EDI Communication

3. Originally, point-to-point connections were used in which both parties had fixed, dedicated computer connections.
    a. Third-party **value-added networks (VANs)** are private mailbox-type services in which the sender's and receiver's computers are never directly connected to each other. Instead, both parties to the EDI arrangement subscribe to a third-party VAN provider.
        1) Because of the third-party buffer, the VAN users are not required to conform to the same standards, conventions, and protocols. Also, VANs can store messages (in a mailbox), so the parties can batch outgoing and incoming messages.
        2) Encryption, preferably by physically secure hardware rather than software, is a critical control.
    b. Cost advantages are leading to increased use of the **Internet** as a means of conducting business directly with a trading partner. It can be used in a more open environment in which one firm transmits documents to another.
        1) This approach is based on less formal agreements between the trading partners than in EDI and requires the sending firm to format the documents into the format of the receiving firm.

Implications for Internal Auditors

4. EDI eliminates the paper documents, both internal and external, that are the traditional basis for many procedures performed in substantive testing and in tests of controls.
    a. An organization that has **reengineered** its procedures and processes to take full advantage of EDI may have eliminated even the electronic equivalents of paper documents.
        1) For example, the buyer's **point-of-sale (POS) system** may directly transmit information to the seller, which delivers on a JIT basis. Purchase orders, invoices, and receiving reports are eliminated and replaced with
            a) A long-term contract establishing quantities, prices, and delivery schedules;
            b) Production schedules;
            c) Advance ship notices;
            d) Evaluated receipts settlements (periodic payment authorizations transmitted to the trading partner with no need for matching purchase orders, invoices, and receiving reports); and
            e) Payments by EFT.

2) Internal auditors must seek new forms of evidence to support assertions about EDI transactions, whether the evidence exists at the client organization, the trading partner, or a third party, such as a VAN. Examples of such evidence are
   a) The authorized paper purchase contract,
   b) An electronic completed production schedule image, and
   c) Internal and external evidence of evaluated receipts settlements sent to the trading partner.
3) Internal auditors must evaluate digital signatures and reviews when testing controls.
4) Internal auditors may need to consider other subsystems when testing a particular subsystem. For example, production cycle evidence may be needed to test the expenditure cycle.

5. **EDI controls** will vary with the organization's objectives and applications.
   a. Authorized users with independent access may include
      1) The people initiating transactions
      2) The people authorizing transactions
      3) Other authorizing parties
      4) Senders for exceptional transactions
   b. **Message authentication** may be accomplished using smart cards and other hardware and software techniques. Protection of message integrity by authentication is especially important for such EDI applications as EFT and ordering.
   c. Messages also must be protected from interception or tampering while in transit. Controls include
      1) Encryption
      2) Numerical **sequencing** to identify missing or false messages
      3) **Nonrepudiation** methods
         a) **Digital certificates** are used to prove origination and delivery so that parties cannot disclaim responsibility for sending or receiving a message.
         b) E-commerce sellers and buyers routinely provide acknowledgments and confirmations, respectively, in a website dialogue to avoid later disputes.
         c) In an EDI application, control over nonrepudiation is achieved by sequencing, encryption, and authentication.

Stop and review! You have completed the outline for this subunit. Study multiple-choice questions 26 through 30 beginning on page 375.

8.8 SUMMARY

1. A control framework is a model for establishing a system of internal control, including controls over IT. The most prominent ones are COSO, eSAC, COBIT, and GTAG.
2. The characteristics that distinguish computer-based from manual processing are volatility of transaction trails, uniform processing of transactions, lack of segregation of functions, potential for errors and fraud, potential for increased management supervision, initiation or subsequent execution of transactions by computer, and dependence of controls in other areas on controls over computer processing.
3. Data can be processed in one of two basic modes: In batch processing, transactions are accumulated and submitted to the computer as a single "batch." In online, real-time processing, the database is updated immediately upon entry of the transaction by the operator.

4. The COBIT model describes IT controls at three levels: the executive management level, the business process level (application controls), and the IT support level (general controls).
5. General controls are those that affect all automated processing. They are systems development, change management, security, and computer operations. Application controls are particular to individual computer applications. Examples of application controls are those ensuring completeness, accuracy, validity, authorization, and segregation of duties.
6. The most economical point for correcting input errors in an application is the time at which the data are entered into the system. Input controls for batch systems include financial totals, record counts, and hash totals. Online input controls include preformatting, field checks, validity checks, limit and range checks, and self-checking digits.
7. Electronic funds transfer, or EFT, is a service provided by financial institutions worldwide that is based on EDI technology. EFT transaction costs are lower than for manual systems because documents and human intervention are eliminated.
8. E-commerce is the purchase and sale of goods and services by electronic means. E-business is a more comprehensive term defined as all methods of conducting business electronically. E-commerce may occur via online transactions on public networks, electronic data interchange, and email.
9. Security issues for e-commerce include authentication, authorization, confidentiality and integrity, prices and discounts, evidence of transmission, nonrepudiation, verification of payment, method of payment, lost or duplicated transactions, and risk of fraud.
10. Responses to security issues include encryption, numerical sequencing, avoiding downtime and repelling attacks, digital certificates, adherence to legal requirements, documenting trading agreements, agreements for end-to-end security, and disclosure by public trading systems of their terms of business.
11. Electronic data interchange, or EDI, is the communication of electronic documents directly from a computer in one entity to a computer in another entity. Advantages of EDI include reduction of clerical errors, speed of transactions, and elimination of repetitive clerical tasks. EDI also eliminates document preparation, processing, and mailing costs. Risks of EDI include security of information and loss of data.
12. EDI requires standards for converting written documents into a standard electronic document-messaging format. A large entity may gain a competitive advantage by forcing trading partners to adopt its standards. Other entities will need to negotiate EDI standards.
13. EDI conventions are the procedures for arranging data elements in specified formats for various accounting transactions. Transmission protocols are rules to determine how each electronic envelope is structured and processed by the communications devices.
14. Telephone lines and modems are typically used in EDI. Point-to-point is the most traditional EDI connection. Both parties have fixed, dedicated computer connections. However, a third-party VAN has many advantages. VAN users are not required to conform to the same standards, conventions, and protocols. Also, VANs can store messages.

QUESTIONS

8.1 Control Frameworks

1. Control objectives regarding effectiveness and efficiency, reliability, and compliance are the basis of which control framework?

A. GTAG.

B. eSAC.

C. COBIT.

D. COSO.

Answer (D) is correct. *(Publisher, adapted)*

REQUIRED: The appropriate control framework.

DISCUSSION: Probably the most well-known control framework in the U.S. is *Internal Control – Integrated Framework*, published in 1992 by the Committee of Sponsoring Organizations of the Treadway Commission (COSO). The document is commonly referred to as "the COSO Framework." The COSO Framework defines internal control as

A process, effected by an organization's board of directors, management, and other personnel, designed to provide reasonable assurance regarding the achievement of objectives in the following categories:

- *Effectiveness and efficiency of operations*
- *Reliability of financial reporting*
- *Compliance with applicable laws and regulations*

Answer (A) is incorrect. GTAG, The IIA's *Global Technology Audit Guide*, is not the source of these three control objectives. Answer (B) is incorrect. The IIA's *Electronic Systems Assurance and Control*, eSAC, is not the source of these three control objectives. Answer (C) is incorrect. COBIT, the ITGI's *Control Objectives for Information and Related Technology*, is not the source of these three control objectives.

2. Which of the following control frameworks groups IT business assurance objectives into the five categories of availability, capability, functionality, protectability, and accountability?

A. COBIT.

B. COSO.

C. eSAC.

D. GTAG.

Answer (C) is correct. *(Publisher, adapted)*

REQUIRED: The control framework to which five business assurance objectives apply.

DISCUSSION: eSAC's IT business assurance objectives fall into these five categories: availability, capability, functionality, protectability, and accountability.

Answer (A) is incorrect. These five control objectives are not put forth by COBIT. Answer (B) is incorrect. These five control objectives are not put forth by COSO. Answer (D) is incorrect. These five control objectives are not put forth by GTAG.

3. Which of the following types of controls is not described in the IT Governance Institute's *Control Objectives for Information and Related Technology* (COBIT)?

A. General controls.

B. Exchange controls.

C. Business controls.

D. Process controls.

Answer (B) is correct. *(Publisher, adapted)*

REQUIRED: The type of control not described in COBIT.

DISCUSSION: COBIT describes controls in three areas: process controls, business controls, and IT general and application controls.

8.2 Aspects of Automated Information Processing

4. Which of the following statements accurately describes the impact that automation has on the controls normally present in a manual system?

A. Transaction trails are more extensive in a computer-based system than in a manual system because there is always a one-for-one correspondence between data entry and output.

B. Responsibility for custody of information assets is more concentrated in user departments in a computer-based system than it is in a manual system.

C. Controls must be more explicit in a computer-based system because many processing points that present opportunities for human judgment in a manual system are eliminated.

D. The quality of documentation becomes less critical in a computer-based system than it is in a manual system because data records are stored in machine-readable files.

Answer (C) is correct. *(CIA, adapted)*

REQUIRED: The impact that automation has on the controls normally present in a manual system.

DISCUSSION: Using a computer does not change the basic concepts and objectives of control. However, the use of computers may modify the control techniques used. The processing of transactions may be combined with control activities previously performed separately, or control function may be combined within the information system activity.

Answer (A) is incorrect. The "paper trail" is less extensive in an automated system. Combining processing and controls within the system reduces documentary evidence. Answer (B) is incorrect. Information assets are more likely to be under the control of the information system function. Answer (D) is incorrect. Documentation is more important in an information system. This is because information is more likely to be stored in machine-readable form than in hard copy, requiring specialized knowledge for retrieval.

5. A firm has recently converted its purchasing cycle from a manual process to an online computer system. Which of the following is a probable result associated with conversion to the new automatic system?

A. Processing errors are increased.

B. The firm's risk exposures are reduced.

C. Processing time is increased.

D. Traditional duties are less segregated.

Answer (D) is correct. *(CIA, adapted)*

REQUIRED: The probable result associated with conversion to the new automatic system.

DISCUSSION: In a manual system with appropriate internal control, separate individuals are responsible for authorizing transactions, recording transactions, and custody of assets. These checks and balances prevent fraud and detect inaccurate or incomplete transactions. In a computer environment, however, this segregation of duties is not always feasible. For example, a computer may print checks, record disbursements, and generate information for reconciling the account balance.

Answer (A) is incorrect. A computer system decreases processing errors. Answer (B) is incorrect. The conversion to a new system does not reduce the number of risk exposures. Answer (C) is incorrect. Processing time is decreased.

6. A small client recently put its cash disbursements system on a server. About which of the following internal control features would an auditor **most** likely be concerned?

A. Programming of the applications are in Visual Basic rather than Java.

B. The server is operated by employees who have cash custody responsibilities.

C. Only one employee has the password to gain access to the cash disbursement system.

D. There are restrictions on the amount of data that can be stored and on the length of time that data can be stored.

Answer (B) is correct. *(CPA, adapted)*

REQUIRED: The control feature of most concern to an auditor.

DISCUSSION: Segregation of duties is a basic category of control activities (AU 319). Functions are incompatible if a person is in a position both to perpetrate and conceal fraud or errors. Hence, the duties of authorizing transactions, recording transactions, and custody of assets should be assigned to different people. Those employees that operate the server may be able to override the controls to change records to conceal a theft of cash.

Answer (A) is incorrect. The choice of language would have little effect on internal control. Answer (C) is incorrect. The limitation on access would be considered a strength. Answer (D) is incorrect. Restrictions on the amount of data that can be stored and on the length of time that data can be stored do not constitute a control weakness.

7. A small company has changed from a system of recording time worked on clock cards to a computerized payroll system in which employees record time in and out with magnetic cards. The computer system automatically updates all payroll records. Because of this change,

A. A generalized computer audit program must be used.

B. Part of the audit trail is altered.

C. The potential for payroll-related fraud is diminished.

D. Transactions must be processed in batches.

Answer (B) is correct. *(CPA, adapted)*

REQUIRED: The effect of computerization of a payroll system.

DISCUSSION: In a manual payroll system, a paper trail of documents is created to provide audit evidence that controls over each step in processing are in place and functioning. One element of a computer system that differentiates it from a manual system is that a transaction trail useful for auditing purposes might exist only for a brief time or only in computer-readable form.

Answer (A) is incorrect. Use of generalized audit software is only one of many ways of auditing a computer-based system. Answer (C) is incorrect. Conversion to a computer system may actually increase the chance of fraud by eliminating segregation of incompatible functions and other controls. Answer (D) is incorrect. Automatic updating indicates that processing is not in batch mode.

8. Batch processing

A. Is not used by most businesses because it reduces the audit trail.

B. Allows users to inquire about groups of information contained in the system.

C. Accumulates transaction records into groups for processing against the master file on a delayed basis.

D. Can only be performed on a centralized basis.

Answer (C) is correct. *(CMA, adapted)*

REQUIRED: The true statement about batch processing.

DISCUSSION: Batch processing is the accumulation and grouping of transactions for processing on a delayed basis. The batch approach is suitable for applications that can be processed against the master file at intervals and involve large volumes of similar items, such as payroll, sales, inventory, and billing.

Answer (A) is incorrect. Batch processing provides as much of an audit trail as any computerized operation. Answer (B) is incorrect. Batch processing refers to the input of data, not inquiry. Answer (D) is incorrect. Batch processing can also be performed on a decentralized basis.

9. What type of computer processing system is characterized by data that are assembled from more than one location and records that are updated immediately?

A. Personal computer systems.

B. Data compression systems.

C. Batch processing systems.

D. Online, real-time systems.

Answer (D) is correct. *(CPA, adapted)*

REQUIRED: The system allowing data entry from multiple locations and immediate updating.

DISCUSSION: Real-time processing involves processing an input record and receiving the output soon enough to affect a current decision-making process. In a real-time system, the user interacts with the system to control an ongoing activity. Online indicates that the decision maker is in direct communication with the computer. Online, real-time systems usually permit access to the main computer from multiple remote terminals.

Answer (A) is incorrect. Access from multiple locations is more typical of larger computer systems than of personal computer systems. Answer (B) is incorrect. Data compression systems encode data to take up less storage space. Answer (C) is incorrect. Batching of transactions requires assembly of data at one place and a delay in updating.

8.3 IT Controls

10. The two broad groupings of information systems control activities are general controls and application controls. General controls include controls

A. Relating to the correction and resubmission of faulty data.

B. For developing, modifying, and maintaining computer programs.

C. Designed to assure that only authorized users receive output from processing.

D. Designed to ensure that all data submitted for processing have been properly authorized.

Answer (B) is correct. *(Publisher, adapted)*

REQUIRED: Identify the characteristics of general controls in relation to information systems control activities.

DISCUSSION: General controls are policies and procedures that relate to many information systems application and support the effective functioning of application controls by helping to ensure the continued proper operation of information systems. General controls include controls over (1) data center and network operations; (2) systems software acquisition and maintenance; (3) access security; and (4) application systems acquisition, development, and maintenance (AU 319).

11. The purpose of input controls is to ensure the

A. Authorization of access to data files.

B. Authorization of access to program files.

C. Completeness, accuracy, and validity of updating.

D. Completeness, accuracy, and validity of input.

Answer (D) is correct. *(CIA, adapted)*

REQUIRED: The purpose of input controls.

DISCUSSION: Input controls provide reasonable assurance that data received for computer processing have been properly authorized and are in a form suitable for processing, i.e., complete, accurate, and valid. Input controls also relate to rejection, correction, and resubmission of data that were initially incorrect.

Answer (A) is incorrect. Access controls authorize access to data files. Answer (B) is incorrect. Access controls authorize access to program files. Answer (C) is incorrect. Processing controls ensure the completeness, accuracy, and validity of updating.

12. Which of the following computerized control procedures would be **most** effective in ensuring that data uploaded from desktop computers to a server are complete and that no additional data are added?

A. Self-checking digits to ensure that only authorized part numbers are added to the database.

B. Batch control totals, including control totals and hash totals.

C. Passwords that effectively limit access to only those authorized to upload the data to the mainframe computer.

D. Field-level edit controls that test each field for alphanumerical integrity.

Answer (B) is correct. *(CIA, adapted)*

REQUIRED: The control over completeness of data uploaded from personal computers.

DISCUSSION: Batch control totals for the data transferred can be reconciled with the batch control totals in the existing file. This comparison provides information on the completion of the data transfer. Batch totals may include record counts, totals of certain critical amounts, or hash totals. A hash total is a control total without a defined meaning, such as the total of employee numbers or invoice numbers, that is used to verify the completeness of data. Thus, the hash total for the employee listing by the personnel department could be compared with the total generated during the payroll run.

Answer (A) is incorrect. Self-checking digits detect inaccurate identification numbers. They are an effective control to ensure that the appropriate part has been identified. However, the control objective is to ensure that data transfer is complete. Answer (C) is incorrect. Passwords help ensure that only authorized personnel make the transfer, not that data transfer is complete. Answer (D) is incorrect. Field checks are effective input controls, but they do not ensure completeness of data transfer.

13. When assessing application controls, which one of the following input controls or edit checks is **most** likely to be used to detect a data input error in the customer account number field?

A. Limit check.

B. Validity check.

C. Control total.

D. Hash total.

Answer (B) is correct. *(CIA, adapted)*

REQUIRED: The input control or edit check most likely to be used to detect a data input error in the customer account number field.

DISCUSSION: Validity checks are tests of identification numbers or transaction codes for validity by comparison with items already known to be correct or authorized. For example, Social Security numbers on payroll input records can be compared with Social Security numbers authorized by the personnel department.

Answer (A) is incorrect. Reasonableness, limit, and range checks are based upon known limits for given information. For example, the hours worked per week is not likely to be greater than 45. Answer (C) is incorrect. A record count is a control total of the number of records processed during the operation of a program. Financial totals summarize dollar amounts in an information field in a group of records. Answer (D) is incorrect. A hash total is the number obtained from totaling the same field value for each transaction in a batch. The total has no meaning or value other than as a comparison with another hash total.

14. The online data entry control called preformatting is

A. A program initiated prior to regular input to discover errors in data before entry so that the errors can be corrected.

B. A check to determine if all data items for a transaction have been entered by the person entering the data.

C. A series of requests for required input data that requires an acceptable response to each request before a subsequent request is made.

D. The display of a document with blanks for data items to be entered by the person entering the data.

Answer (D) is correct. *(CMA, adapted)*

REQUIRED: The definition of preformatting.

DISCUSSION: To avoid data entry errors in online systems, a preformatted screen approach may be used. It is a screen prompting approach that involves the display on a monitor of a set of boxes for entry of specified data items. The format may even be in the form of a copy of a transaction document. This technique is best suited to conversion of data from a source document.

Answer (A) is incorrect. An edit routine is a program initiated prior to regular input to discover errors in data before entry so that the errors can be corrected. Answer (B) is incorrect. A completeness check tests whether all data items for a transaction have been entered by the person entering the data. Answer (C) is incorrect. The dialogue approach is another screen prompting method for data entry. It is most appropriate when information is received orally, e.g., by phone.

8.4 Data Communications, Networks, and Client-Server Systems

15. When two devices in a data communications system are communicating, there must be agreement as to how both data and control information are to be packaged and interpreted. Which of the following terms is commonly used to describe this type of agreement?

A. Asynchronous communication.

B. Synchronous communication.

C. Communication channel.

D. Communication protocol.

Answer (D) is correct. *(CIA, adapted)*

REQUIRED: The agreement as to how both data and control information are to be packaged and interpreted.

DISCUSSION: A protocol is a set of formal rules or conventions governing communication between a sending and a receiving device. It prescribes the manner by which data are transmitted between these communications devices. In essence, a protocol is the envelope within which each message is transmitted throughout a data communications network.

Answer (A) is incorrect. Asynchronous communication is a mode of transmission. Communication is in disjointed segments, typically character by character, preceded by a start code and ended by a stop code. Answer (B) is incorrect. Synchronous communication is a mode of transmission in which a continuous stream of blocks of characters result in faster communications. Answer (C) is incorrect. A communication channel is a transmission link between devices in a network. The term is also used for a small processor that controls input-output devices.

16. Large organizations often have their own telecommunications networks for transmitting and receiving voice, data, and images. Very small organizations, however, are unlikely to be able to make the investment required for their own networks and are more likely to use

A. Public switched lines.

B. Fast-packet switches.

C. Standard electronic mail systems.

D. A WAN.

Answer (A) is correct. *(CIA, adapted)*

REQUIRED: The telecommunications networks likely to be used by small organizations.

DISCUSSION: Companies can use public switched lines (phone lines) on a per-transmission basis. This option is the most cost-effective way for low-volume users to conduct telecommunications.

Answer (B) is incorrect. Fast-packet switches receive transmissions from various devices, break the data into packets, and route them over a network to their destination. They are typically installed by telecommunication utility companies and other large companies that have their own networks. Answer (C) is incorrect. Electronic mail systems do not allow for voice transmissions. Answer (D) is incorrect. Large organizations would use a wide area network.

17. A local area network (LAN) is **best** described as a(n)

A. Computer system that connects computers of all sizes, workstations, terminals, and other devices within a limited proximity.

B. System to allow computer users to meet and share ideas and information.

C. Electronic library containing millions of items of data that can be reviewed, retrieved, and analyzed.

D. Method to offer specialized software, hardware, and data-handling techniques that improve effectiveness and reduce costs.

Answer (A) is correct. *(CMA, adapted)*

REQUIRED: The best description of a local area network (LAN).

DISCUSSION: A LAN is a local distributed computer system, often housed within a single building. Computers, communication devices, and other equipment are linked by cable. Special software facilitates efficient data communication among the hardware devices.

Answer (B) is incorrect. A LAN is more than a system to allow computer users to share information; i.e., it is an interconnection of a computer system. Answer (C) is incorrect. A LAN is not a library. Answer (D) is incorrect. A LAN does not require specialized hardware.

18. Using a telecommunications provider affects in-house networks. To prepare for changes resulting from enhanced external network services, management should

A. Optimize in-house networks to avoid bottlenecks that would limit the benefits offered by the telecommunications provider.

B. Plan for rapid implementation of new capabilities in anticipation of ready acceptance of the new technology.

C. Downsize the company's disaster recovery plan to recognize the increasing role of the telecommunications provider.

D. Enhance the in-house network management to minimize dependence on the tele communications provider for network management.

Answer (A) is correct. *(CIA, adapted)*

REQUIRED: The appropriate action to prepare for changes resulting from enhanced external network services.

DISCUSSION: To prepare the company for changes resulting from the enhanced external network services, management should take appropriate action. A number of bottlenecks may limit the benefits that can be derived from the external network. For example, conversion from analog to digital technology is necessary to achieve rapid improvements in bandwidth and speed and to improve access to telecommunications services. Furthermore, applications, systems software, and communications protocols must be able to process information in a format and in a manner acceptable to end users. Communications security also has heightened importance as greater amounts of data are transmitted from remote sites.

Answer (B) is incorrect. Resistance to change, inflexible organizational structures, and skepticism about the technology should be expected and must be successfully managed if the company is to reap the benefits. Answer (C) is incorrect. A company's disaster recovery plan should be enhanced to ensure the reliability of the network. Answer (D) is incorrect. Network management may now be primarily a function, yet it will become more of a partnership arrangement with the communications carrier.

8.5 Electronic Funds Transfer (EFT)

19. Which of the following risks is **not** greater in an electronic funds transfer (EFT) environment than in a manual system using paper transactions?

A. Unauthorized access and activity.

B. Duplicate transaction processing.

C. Higher cost per transaction.

D. Inadequate backup and recovery capabilities.

Answer (C) is correct. *(CIA, adapted)*

REQUIRED: The risk not greater in an EFT environment than in a manual system using paper transactions.

DISCUSSION: EFT is a service provided by financial institutions worldwide that is based on EDI technology. EFT transaction costs are lower than for manual systems because documents and human intervention are eliminated from the transactions process.

Answer (A) is incorrect. Unauthorized access and activity is a risk specific to EFT. Answer (B) is incorrect. Inaccurate transaction processing (including duplication) is a risk specific to EFT. Answer (D) is incorrect. Inadequate backup and recovery capabilities is a risk specific to EFT.

20. Which of the following is usually a benefit of using electronic funds transfer (EFT) for international cash transactions?

A. Improvement of the audit trail for cash receipts and disbursements.

B. Creation of self-monitoring access controls.

C. Reduction of the frequency of data entry errors.

D. Off-site storage of source documents for cash transactions.

Answer (C) is correct. *(CPA, adapted)*

REQUIRED: The benefit of using EFT for international cash transactions.

DISCUSSION: The processing and transmission of electronic transactions, such as EFTs, virtually eliminates human interaction. This process not only helps eliminate errors but also allows for the rapid detection and recovery from errors when they do occur.

Answer (A) is incorrect. The audit trail is typically less apparent in an electronic environment than in a manual environment. Answer (B) is incorrect. A key control is management's establishment and monitoring of access controls. Answer (D) is incorrect. Source documents are often eliminated in EFT transactions.

8.6 E-Commerce

21. All of the following are potential security issues for e-commerce **except**

A. Correct identification of transacting parties.

B. Proliferation of computer viruses.

C. Determining who may rightfully make transaction decisions.

D. Verification of payment data.

Answer (B) is correct. *(Publisher, adapted)*

REQUIRED: The process that is not a potential security issue for e-commerce.

DISCUSSION: E-commerce is the purchase and sale of goods and services by electronic means. E-commerce may occur via online transactions on public networks, electronic data interchange (EDI), and email. E-commerce security issues include the correct identification of transacting parties (authentication), determining who may rightfully make decisions (authorization), and verification of payment data. While proliferation of computer viruses is a general security issue with regard to information systems, it is not a specific risk associated with e-commerce.

Answer (A) is incorrect. Authentication is a security issue related to e-commerce. Answer (C) is incorrect. Authorization is a security issue related to e-commerce. Answer (D) is incorrect. Verification of payment data is a security issue related to e-commerce.

22. When performing an e-commerce engagement, the greatest two concerns about the internal audit activity are

A. Independence and competency.

B. Capacity and objectivity.

C. Competency and objectivity.

D. Capacity and competency.

Answer (D) is correct. *(Publisher, adapted)*

REQUIRED: The greatest concerns about performing an e-commerce engagement.

DISCUSSION: The chief audit executive's (CAE's) concerns about performing an e-commerce engagement are the competency and capacity of the internal audit activity. Among the possible factors that may limit the internal audit activity are the following:

- Does the internal audit activity have sufficient skills? If not, can the skills be acquired?
- Are training or other resources necessary?
- Is the staffing level sufficient for the near term and long term?
- Can the expected audit plan be delivered?

Answer (A) is incorrect. Independence is not a primary concern related to the internal audit activity in an e-commerce engagement. Answer (B) is incorrect. Objectivity is not a primary concern related to the internal audit activity in an e-commerce engagement. Answer (C) is incorrect. Objectivity is not a primary concern related to the internal audit activity in an e-commerce engagement.

23. Which of the following is **not** a major component of an audit of e-commerce activities?

A. Make certain that goals and objectives can be achieved.

B. Assess the internal control structure.

C. Review the interface issues.

D. Evaluate the business continuity and disaster recovery plans.

Answer (A) is correct. *(Publisher, adapted)*

REQUIRED: The item that is not a major component of an audit of e-commerce activities.

DISCUSSION: Auditing e-commerce activities should provide reasonable assurance – not ensure or make certain – that goals and objectives can be achieved. An auditor cannot be absolutely certain that goals and objectives will be achieved. The following are other major components of an audit of e-commerce activities:

- Assess the internal control structure, including the tone set by senior management,
- Determine whether the risks are acceptable,
- Understand the information flow,
- Review the interface issues (such as hardware to hardware, software to software, and hardware to software), and
- Evaluate the business continuity and disaster recovery plans.

24. Which type of risks assumed by management are often drivers of organizational activities?

A. Opportunity risks.

B. Inherent risks.

C. General project management risks.

D. Control risks.

Answer (A) is correct. *(Publisher, adapted)*

REQUIRED: The type of risks assumed by management that are often drivers of organizational activities.

DISCUSSION: Risk can be defined as the uncertainty of an event occurring that could have a negative impact on the achievement of objectives. Risk is inherent to every business or government entity. Opportunity risks assumed by management are often drivers of organizational activities. Beyond these opportunities may be threats and other dangers that are not clearly understood or fully evaluated and are too easily accepted as part of doing business.

25. What is the overall audit objective when auditing an e-commerce activity?

A. To ensure that all e-commerce processes have efficient internal controls.

B. To ensure that all e-commerce processes have effective internal controls.

C. To ensure that all e-commerce processes are adequate to fulfill their intended objectives.

D. To ensure that all e-commerce processes meet the functionality requirements of the end users.

Answer (B) is correct. *(Publisher, adapted)*

REQUIRED: The overall audit objective when auditing an e-commerce activity.

DISCUSSION: According to PA 2100-6, when auditing e-commerce activities, the overall audit objective should be to ensure that all e-commerce processes have effective internal controls.

Answer (A) is incorrect. The overall audit objective is not about ensuring the efficiency of internal controls. It is about ensuring the effectiveness of internal controls. Answer (C) is incorrect. Adequacy of processes should be considered during the internal auditor's risk assessment. Answer (D) is incorrect. Meeting functional requirements should be considered during the internal auditor's risk assessment.

8.7 Electronic Data Interchange (EDI)

26. Companies now can use electronic transfers to conduct regular business transactions. Which of the following terms **best** describes a system in which an agreement is made between two or more parties to electronically transfer purchase orders, sales orders, invoices, and/or other financial documents?

A. Electronic mail (email).

B. Electronic funds transfer (EFT).

C. Electronic data interchange (EDI).

D. Electronic data processing (EDP).

Answer (C) is correct. *(CIA, adapted)*

REQUIRED: The term best describing electronic transfer of documents.

DISCUSSION: Electronic data interchange is the electronic transfer of documents between businesses. EDI was developed to enhance just-in-time (JIT) inventory management. Advantages include speed, reduction of clerical errors, and elimination of repetitive clerical tasks and their costs.

Answer (A) is incorrect. Email can send text or document files, but the term encompasses a wide range of transfers. EDI specifically applies to the system described in the question. Answer (B) is incorrect. Electronic funds transfer (EFT) refers to the transfer of money. Answer (D) is incorrect. Electronic data processing (EDP) is a generic term for computerized processing of transaction data within organizations.

27. Which of the following is usually a benefit of transmitting transactions in an electronic data interchange (EDI) environment?

A. A compressed business cycle with lower year-end receivables balances.

B. A reduced need to test computer controls related to sales and collections transactions.

C. An increased opportunity to apply statistical sampling techniques to account balances.

D. No need to rely on third-party service providers to ensure security.

Answer (A) is correct. *(CPA, adapted)*

REQUIRED: The benefit of EDI.

DISCUSSION: EDI transactions are typically transmitted and processed in real time. Thus, EDI compresses the business cycle by eliminating delays. The time required to receive and process an order, ship goods, and receive payment is greatly reduced compared with that of a typical manual system. Accordingly, more rapid receipt of payment minimizes receivables and improves cash flow.

Answer (B) is incorrect. Use of a sophisticated processing system would increase the need to test computer controls. Answer (C) is incorrect. Computer technology allows all transactions to be tested rather than just a sample. Answer (D) is incorrect. EDI often uses a VAN (value-added network) as a third-party service provider, and reliance on controls provided by the VAN may be critical.

28. The emergence of electronic data interchange (EDI) as standard operating practice increases the risk of

A. Unauthorized third-party access to systems.

B. Systematic programming errors.

C. Inadequate knowledge bases.

D. Unsuccessful system use.

Answer (A) is correct. *(CIA, adapted)*

REQUIRED: The risk increased by the emergence of EDI as standard operating practice.

DISCUSSION: EDI is the communication of electronic documents directly from a computer in one entity to a computer in another entity. EDI for business documents between unrelated parties has the potential to increase the risk of unauthorized third-party access to systems because more outsiders will have access to internal systems.

Answer (B) is incorrect. Systematic programming errors are the result of misspecification of requirements or lack of correspondence between specifications and programs. Answer (C) is incorrect. Inadequate knowledge bases are a function of lack of care in building them. Answer (D) is incorrect. A benefit of EDI is to improve the efficiency and effectiveness of system use.

29. Which of the following are essential elements of the audit trail in an electronic data interchange (EDI) system?

A. Network and sender/recipient acknowledgments.

B. Message directories and header segments.

C. Contingency and disaster recovery plans.

D. Trading partner security and mailbox codes.

Answer (A) is correct. *(CPA, adapted)*

REQUIRED: The essential element in an EDI audit trail.

DISCUSSION: An audit trail allows for the tracing of a transaction from initiation to conclusion. Network and sender/recipient acknowledgments relate to the transaction flow and provide for the tracking of transactions.

Answer (B) is incorrect. Message directories and header segments provide information controlling the message, such as originating and destination stations, message type and priority level, which are part of the message and not the audit trail. Answer (C) is incorrect. Although contingency and disaster recovery plans are important controls, they do not relate to the audit trail. Answer (D) is incorrect. Although maintaining control over security and mailbox codes is an important control, it does not relate to the audit trail.

30. Which of the following statements is true concerning internal control in an electronic data interchange (EDI) system?

A. Preventive controls generally are more important than detective controls in EDI systems.

B. Control objectives for EDI systems generally are different from the objectives for other information systems.

C. Internal controls in EDI systems rarely permit control risk to be assessed at below the maximum.

D. Internal controls related to the segregation of duties generally are the most important controls in EDI systems.

Answer (A) is correct. *(CPA, adapted)*

REQUIRED: The true statement about EDI controls.

DISCUSSION: In general, preventive controls are more important than detective controls because the benefits typically outweigh the costs. In electronic processing, once a transaction is accepted, there is often little opportunity to apply detective controls. Thus, it is important to prevent errors or frauds before they happen.

Answer (B) is incorrect. The basic control objectives are the same regardless of the nature of the processing: to ensure the integrity of the information and to safeguard the assets. Answer (C) is incorrect. To gather sufficient evidence in a sophisticated computer system, it is often necessary to rely on the controls. Control risk may be assessed at below the maximum if relevant controls are identified and tested and if the resulting evidential matter provides the degree of assurance necessary to support the assessed level of control risk. Answer (D) is incorrect. The level of segregation of duties achieved in a manual system is usually not feasible in a computer system.

STUDY UNIT NINE
INFORMATION TECHNOLOGY II

(24 pages of outline)

This study unit addresses the roles of IT personnel, the use of encryption to increase the security of data transmission, the protection of data from viruses and other threats, and an organization's investment in IT. It continues with a treatment of enterprise-wide resource planning and concludes with discussions of systems software (operating systems and utility programs), application development, program change control, and end-user computing.

Core Concepts

- Controls should ensure the efficiency and effectiveness of IT operations. They include proper segregation of the duties within the IT environment.
- Encryption technology converts data into a code. Unauthorized users may still be able to access the data, but without the encryption key, they will be unable to decode the information.
- The business assurance objective in the SAC model that is most concerned with malicious software (malware) is protectability. Thus, IT assets should be protected from "unauthorized access, use, or harm."
- Hardware and software are significant assets that require careful management. Among the decisions to be made are resource requirements, evaluation of the full costs of the investment, and choosing whether to own or lease technology.
- Enterprise-wide resource planning (ERP) is intended to integrate information systems across the organization by creating one database linked to all of the entity's applications.
- Access to powerful software, such as utility programs, must be restricted.
- The systems development life-cycle (SDLC) approach is the traditional methodology applied to the development of large, highly structured application systems. It consists of five major phases: definition, design, development, implementation, and maintenance.
- The process of managing changes to existing information systems is referred to as systems maintenance, and the relevant controls are called program change controls.
- End-user computing involves user-created or user-acquired systems that are maintained and operated outside of traditional information systems controls.

9.1 FUNCTIONAL AREAS OF IT OPERATIONS

1. Controls should ensure the efficiency and effectiveness of IT operations. They include proper segregation of the duties within the IT environment. Thus, the responsibilities of systems analysts, programmers, operators, file librarians, the control group, and others should be assigned to different individuals, and proper supervision should be provided.
   a. **Segregation of duties.** This general control is vital because a traditional segregation of responsibilities for authorization, recording, and access to assets may not be feasible in an IT environment.

1) For example, a computer may print checks, record disbursements, and generate information for reconciling the account balance, which are activities customarily segregated in a manual system.

a) If the same person provides the input and receives the output for this process, a significant control weakness exists. Accordingly, certain tasks should not be combined.

2. **Responsibilities of IT Personnel**

a. **Systems analysts** are specifically qualified to analyze and design computer information systems. They survey the existing system, analyze the organization's information requirements, and design new systems to meet those needs. The design specifications will guide the preparation of specific programs by computer programmers.

1) Systems analysts should not have access to the computer operations center, production programs, or data files.

b. The **database administrator (DBA)** is the individual who has overall responsibility for developing and maintaining the database and for establishing controls to protect its integrity.

1) Thus, only the DBA should be able to update **data dictionaries**.

2) In small systems, the DBA may perform some functions of a **database management system (DBMS)** (see Subunit 10.4). In larger applications, the DBA uses a DBMS as a primary tool.

c. **Programmers** design, write, test, and document the specific programs according to specifications developed by the analysts.

1) Programmers as well as analysts may be able to modify programs, data files, and controls. Thus, they should have no access to the computer operations center or to production programs or data.

d. The **webmaster** is responsible for the content of the organization's website. (S)he works closely with programmers and network technicians to ensure that the appropriate content is displayed and that the site is reliably available to users.

e. **Operators** are responsible for the day-to-day functioning of the computer center, whether the organization runs a mainframe, servers, or anything in between.

1) Operators load data, mount storage devices, and operate the equipment. Operators should not be assigned programming duties or responsibility for systems design. Accordingly, they also should have no opportunity to make changes in programs and systems as they operate the equipment.

a) Ideally, computer operators should not have programming knowledge or access to documentation not strictly necessary for their work.

f. **Help desks** are usually a responsibility of computer operations because of the operational nature of their functions. Help desk personnel log reported problems, resolve minor problems, and forward more difficult problems to the appropriate information systems resources, such as a **technical support unit** or **vendor assistance**.

g. **Network technicians** maintain the bridges, hubs, routers, switches, cabling, and other devices that interconnect the organization's computers. They are also responsible for maintaining the organization's connection to other networks such as the Internet.

h. **End users** must be able to change production data, but not programs.

Stop and review! You have completed the outline for this subunit. Study multiple-choice questions 1 through 5 beginning on page 401.

9.2 ENCRYPTION

Overview

1. Encryption technology converts data into a code. A program codes data prior to transmission. Another program decodes it after transmission. Unauthorized users may still be able to access the data, but, without the encryption key, they will be unable to decode the information.
2. Encryption software uses a fixed algorithm to manipulate **plaintext** and an encryption key to introduce variation. The information is sent in its manipulated form **(cyphertext)**, and the receiver translates the information back into plaintext. Although data may be accessed by tapping into the transmission line, the encryption key is necessary to understand the data being sent. The machine instructions necessary to code and decode data can constitute a 20-to-30% increase in system overhead.
   a. Encryption technology may be either hardware- or software-based. Two major types of encryption software exist.

Two Types of Encryption

3. **Public-key**, or asymmetric, encryption requires two keys: The public key for coding messages is widely known, but the private key for decoding messages is kept secret by the recipient. Accordingly, the parties who wish to transmit coded messages must use algorithmically related **pairs** of public and private keys. The sender searches a directory for the recipient's public key, uses it to encode the message, and transmits the message to the recipient. The latter uses the public key and the related private (secret) key to decode the message.
   a. One advantage of public-key encryption is that the message is encoded using one key and decoded using another. In contrast, private-key encryption requires both parties to know and use the secret key.
   b. A second advantage is that neither party knows the other's private key. The related public-key and private-key pair is issued by a **certificate authority** (a third-party fiduciary, e.g., VeriSign or Thawte). However, the private key is issued only to one party.
      1) Thus, **key management** in a public-key/private-key system is more secure than in a secret-key system because the parties do not have to agree on, transmit, and handle the one secret key.
   c. **RSA**, named for its developers (Rivest, Shamir, and Adelman), is the most commonly used public-key/private-key method.
   d. A public-key/private-key system is used to create **digital signatures (fingerprints)**.
      1) A digital signature is a means of **authentication** of an electronic document, for example, of the validity of a purchase order, acceptance of a contract, or financial information.
         a) The sender uses its private key to encode all or part of the message, and the recipient uses the sender's public key to decode it. Hence, if that key decodes the message, the sender must have written it.
         b) One variation is to send the message in both plaintext and cyphertext. If the decoded version matches the plaintext version, no alteration has occurred.

2) A **digital certificate** is another means of authentication used in e-business. The certificate authority issues a coded electronic certificate that contains the holder's name, a copy of its public key, a serial number, and an expiration date. The certificate verifies the holder's identity.

a) The recipient of a coded message uses the certificate authority's public key (available on the Internet) to decode the certificate included in the message. The recipient then determines that the certificate was issued by the certificate authority. Moreover, the recipient can use the sender's public key and identification data to send a coded response.

i) Such methods might be used for transactions between sellers and buyers using credit cards.

b) A certificate also may be used to provide assurance to customers that a website is genuine.

c) The **public key infrastructure** permits secure monetary and information exchange over the Internet. Thus, it facilitates e-business.

d) Protocols commonly used for coding and decoding functions on the Internet are **SSL** (Secure Sockets Layer) and **S-HTTP** (Secure Hypertext Transport Protocol).

e) **Digital time stamping services** verify the time (and possibly the place) of a transaction. For example, a document may be sent to a service, which applies its digital stamp and then forwards the document.

4. **Private-key**, or symmetric, encryption requires only a single key for each pair of parties that want to send each other coded messages.

a. **Data Encryption Standard (DES)**, a shared private-key method developed by the U.S. government, is the most prevalent secret-key method. It is based on numbers with 56 binary digits.

b. The **Advanced Encryption Standard (AES)** is a recently adopted cryptographic algorithm for use by U.S. government organizations to protect sensitive information. The AES will be widely used on a voluntary basis by organizations, institutions, and individuals as well as by the U.S. government.

Stop and review! You have completed the outline for this subunit. Study multiple-choice questions 6 through 9 beginning on page 402.

9.3 INFORMATION PROTECTION

Business Objective

1. The business assurance objective in the SAC model that is most concerned with malicious software (malware) is **protectability**. Thus, IT assets should be protected from "unauthorized access, use, or harm."

a. Control, e.g., over access and change management, should be in place to achieve the objective of protectability.

b. Moreover, **security awareness** by all concerned should be heightened. Consequently, the business assurance objective of **accountability** is also pertinent. The roles, actions, and responsibilities for security should be defined.

Malicious Software and Controls

2. Malicious software may exploit a known hole or weakness in an application or operating system program to evade security measures. Such a vulnerability may have been caused by a programming error. It also may have been intentionally (but not maliciously) created to permit a programmer simple access (a back door) for correcting the code.

a. Having bypassed security controls, the intruder can do immediate damage to the system or install malicious software.

1) A **Trojan horse** is an apparently innocent program (e.g., a spreadsheet) that includes a hidden function that may do damage when activated.

a) For example, it may contain a **virus**, which is a program code that copies itself from file to file. The virus may destroy data or programs. A common way of spreading a virus is by email attachments and downloads.

b) A **worm** copies itself not from file to file but from computer to computer, often very rapidly. Repeated replication overloads a system by depleting memory or disk space.

c) A **logic bomb** is much like a Trojan horse except it activates only upon some occurrence, e.g., on a certain date.

d) A maliciously created **back door** can be used for subsequent high-level access to data, computers, and networks.

e) Malware may create a **denial of service** by overwhelming a system or website with more traffic than it can handle.

i) In other cases, malware infection may have little or no effects noticeable by users.

3. **Controls** to prevent or detect infection by malware are particularly significant for file servers in large networks. The following are broad control objectives:

a. A policy should require use only of authorized software.

b. A policy should require adherence to licensing agreements.

c. A policy should create accountability for the persons authorized to maintain software.

d. A policy should require safeguards when data or programs are obtained by means of external media.

e. Antivirus software should continuously monitor the system for viruses (or worms) and eradicate them. It should also be immediately upgraded as soon as information about new threats becomes available.

f. Software and data for critical systems should be regularly reviewed.

g. Investigation of unauthorized files or amendments should be routine.

h. Email attachments and downloads (and files on unauthorized media or from networks that are not secure) should be checked.

i. Procedures should be established and responsibility assigned for coping with malware.

1) Procedures should reflect an understanding that another organization that has transmitted malware-infected material may have done so unwittingly and may need assistance. If such events occur repeatedly, however, termination of agreements or contracts may be indicated.

2) Procedures and policies should be documented, and employees must understand the reasons for them.

j. Business continuity (recovery) plans should be drafted, e.g., data and software backup.

k. Information about malware should be verified and appropriate alerts given.

l. Responsible personnel should be aware of the possibility of hoaxes, which are false messages intending to create fear of a malware attack. For example, a spurious email message may be received instructing users to delete supposedly compromised files.

m. Qualified personnel should be relied upon to distinguish **hoaxes** from malware.

4. The following are **specific controls**:
   a. All computer media (incoming or outgoing) may be scanned by **sheep dip** (dedicated) computers.
   b. Nonscreened media should not be allowed on the organization's computers.
   c. Scanning may be done of standalone computers or those on networks as another line of defense if media control fails.
   d. Software may reside in memory to scan for malware communicated through a network.
   e. Email gateways may have software to scan attachments.
   f. Network servers may have software to detect and erase or store malware.
   g. Scanning software on a standalone device should be upgraded when it is networked.
5. Use of external rather than internal expertise for coping with malware problems may be more costly and time consuming but less risky.
   a. **External service providers** should be subject to the terms of a contract, and access and other controls should be in place.
6. Off-site computers and media of employees should be subject to malware controls, such as screening.
7. Response to threats via **covert channels** and **Trojan horse** programs include the following:
   a. Purchases should be of evaluated products from trusted suppliers.
   b. Purchases should be in source code so that it is verifiable. This code should be inspected and tested prior to use.
   c. Access to and changes in code should be restricted after it is put in use.
   d. The availability of security patches for bugs in programs should be monitored constantly, especially regarding such items as network operating systems, email servers, routers, and firewalls. Patches should be tested and installed promptly.
   e. Trusted employees should be assigned to key systems.
   f. Known Trojan horses can be detected by scanning.
   g. Reviewing data outflows, for example, through the firewall, may detect suspicious activity meriting investigation.
8. **Hosts** are the most common targets in a network because they furnish services to other requesting hosts.
   a. Protective measures include promptly installing the most recent patches, fixes, and updates.
      1) How they affect other elements of the system should be considered.
      2) Updates should be tested before installation.

<u>Types of Attacks</u>

9. **Password Attacks**
   a. A number of methods may be used.
      1) A **brute-force attack** uses password-cracking software to try large numbers of letter and number combinations to access a network.
         a) A simple variation is the use of password-cracking software that tries all the words in a dictionary.
      2) Passwords (and user accounts) also may be discovered by Trojan horses, IP spoofing, and packet sniffers.
         a) **Spoofing** is identity misrepresentation in cyberspace, for example, by using a false website to obtain information about visitors.

b) **Sniffing** is use of software to eavesdrop on information sent by a user to the host computer of a website.

b. Once an attacker has access, (s)he may do anything the rightful user could have done.

1) If that user has privileged access, the attacker may create a back door to facilitate future entry despite password and status changes.
2) The attacker also may be able to leverage the initial access to obtain greater privileges than the rightful user.

c. If a user has the same password for multiple hosts, cracking that password for one compromises all.

d. Expressive methods of thwarting password attacks are one-time password and cryptographic authentication.

e. Optimal passwords are randomly generated, 8-character or longer combinations of numbers, uppercase and lowercase letters, and special symbols.

1) A disadvantage is that users often write down passwords that are hard to remember. However, software has been developed that encrypts passwords to be kept on a handheld computer. Thus, the user only needs to know one password.

10. A **man-in-the-middle attack** takes advantage of networking packet sniffing and routing and transport protocols.

a. These attacks may be used to

1) Steal data
2) Obtain access to the network during a rightful user's active session
3) Analyze the traffic on the network to learn about its operations and users
4) Insert new data or modify the data being transmitted
5) Deny service

b. Cryptography is the effective response to man-in-the-middle attacks. The encrypted data will be useless to the attacker unless it can be decrypted.

11. A **denial-of-service (DOS) attack** is an attempt to overload a system (e.g., a network or Web server) with false messages so that it cannot function (a system crash).

a. A distributed DOS attack comes from multiple sources, for example, the machines of innocent parties infected by Trojan horses. When activated, these programs send messages to the target and leave the connection open.

b. A DOS may establish as many network connections as possible to exclude other users, overloading primary memory, or corrupting file systems.

c. **Responses**

1) Firewalls should not permit use of **Internet relay chat** channels or other TCP/IP ports unless for business purposes. Thus, the organization should determine what relay kits have been installed, e.g., by employees connected to virtual private networks via cable or DSL.

a) These methods, intrusion detection systems, and penetration testing may prevent a system from being used to make a DOS attack.

2) The best protection by the target is the Internet service provider (ISP). The ISP can establish rate limits on transmissions to the target's website.

a) Thus, only a defined amount of message packets with certain characteristics are allowed to reach the site.

Countermeasures

12. **Intrusion Detection Systems (IDS)**
    a. If an organization's computer system has external connections, an IDS is needed to respond to security breaches.
        1) The IDS complements the computer system's firewalls. It responds to attacks on
            a) The **network infrastructure** (protected by the network IDS component)
                i) Routers
                ii) Switches
                iii) Bandwidth
            b) **Servers** (protected by the host IDS component)
                i) Operating systems
                ii) Applications
        2) An IDS responds to an attack by
            a) Taking action itself
            b) Alerting the management system
    b. A **host IDS** provides maximum protection only when the software is installed on each computer. It may operate in the following ways:
        1) The aggressive response is to monitor every call on the operating system and application as it occurs.
        2) A less effective method of preventing attacks is analysis of access log files.
        3) A host IDS may also identify questionable processes and verify the security of system files.
    c. A **network IDS** works by using sensors to examine packets traveling on the network. Each sensor monitors only the segment of the network to which it is attached. A packet is examined if it matches a **signature**.
        1) **String signatures** (certain strings of text) are potential signs of an attack.
        2) **Port signatures** alert the IDS that a point subject to frequent intrusion attempts may be under attack.
            a) A **port** in this sense (as opposed to the physical serial and parallel ports on a personal computer) is a logical connection to the system.
                i) A **port number** included in the message header stipulates how the message will be handled. Because many port numbers are widely known, an attacker may be able to send messages to determine whether ports are open and therefore vulnerable.
        3) A **header signature** is a suspicious combination in a packet header.
    d. The preferable IDS combines host IDS and network IDS components.
        1) A host IDS has greater potential for preventing a specific attack, but the network IDS provides a necessary overall perspective. Thus, a host IDS should be in place for each host, with a network IDS for the whole system.
    e. **Knowledge-based detection** is based on information about the system's weaknesses and searches for intrusions that take advantage of them.
        1) This type of IDS depends on frequent and costly updating of information about intrusion methods. It is also specialized with respect to those methods and operating system methods.
            a) Problems are compounded when different versions of the operating system (or different operating systems) are in place.

f. **Behavior-based detection** presumes that an attack will cause an observable anomaly. Actual and normal system behavior (a model of expected operations) are compared. A discrepancy results in an alert.

1) This approach is more complete than the knowledge-based approach because every attack should be detected. However, the level of accuracy is lower. False alarms may be generated, so the model must be updated whenever operational changes are made.

2) The advantages of behavior-based detection are that

a) Knowledge of specific new intrusion techniques is not necessary.

b) It is less specific to particular operating systems.

g. **Responses to detection of an intrusion** normally include an automatic component. Continuous monitoring and response by individuals may not be feasible or sufficiently rapid.

1) An **automatically acting IDS** provides continuous security. It responds without the presence of humans. Responses may include

a) Disconnecting the entire network from outside access

b) Locking access to all or part of the system

c) Slowing the system's activity to reduce injury

d) Validating the external user

e) Sending console, email, pager, or phone messages to appropriate personnel

2) **Alarmed systems resources** are dummy files or accounts, for example, a default administrator account with a default password set. They are traps for an intruder.

a) Access to a dummy resource results in automatic action or notice to appropriate employees.

b) The advantage of this method is that it is uncomplicated and inexpensive.

c) The disadvantage is that authorized persons may inadvertently cause an alarm.

Stop and review! You have completed the outline for this subunit. Study multiple-choice questions 10 through 13 on page 404.

9.4 INVESTMENT IN IT

1. Hardware and software are significant assets that require careful management. Among the decisions to be made are resource requirements, evaluation of the full costs of the investment, and choosing whether to own or lease the technology.

2. The growth of e-business means that greater resources are needed for transactions within the organization and with outside parties, for example, as a result of hosting websites with many users.

a. **Capacity planning** should be undertaken by management and IT specialists. It determines whether the organization's current and future hardware resources relative to its priorities are, and will continue to be, sufficient. Among the issues are

1) The maximum volume of transactions that can be simultaneously processed by the system

2) The effect of software developments

3) Performance measures, e.g., response time

4) Changes in capacity needs resulting from business combinations, increased demand for the organization's products and services, and new applications

b. **Scalability** is the characteristic of a system that permits its capacity to be increased to meet greater demands without a system failure.

1) For example, a website should be supported by adequate processing, storage, and network assets to cope with peak demand.

3. The **costs of ownership** of IT assets include indirect as well as direct costs. Thus, rational economic decisions about hardware and software acquisition require an analysis of the true or full costs of all factors involved. Failing to consider total long-term costs may seriously underestimate the economic effects of IT decisions.

a. The **total cost of ownership (TCO) model** will vary with the organization's unique needs. The following are typical factors to be considered:

1) Capital costs of hardware, such as computers, terminals, storage devices, printers, and upgrades
2) Capital costs of software, including purchase price or licensing cost per user, with upgrades
3) Installation costs of hardware and software
4) Training costs for IT specialists and end users
5) Support costs incurred for help desks, other technical support labor, documentation, R&D, development of configuration standards, and review
6) Maintenance costs for hardware and software upgrades
7) Infrastructure costs of obtaining, supporting, and maintaining networks, back-up storage, etc.
8) Costs of unproductive time (downtime) resulting from hardware or software failure
9) Utility and real property costs of computer installations
10) Costs of nonstandard personal computer configurations

a) A standard configuration scheme for a given category of end users reduces costs by facilitating upgrades and support. However, new applications and updates of hardware may cause a loss of standardization.

11) Costs of transferring end users

a) An end user is customarily restricted to a given personal computer with needed applications and access. Hence, transfer of an end user results in incurrence of costs for reinstallation and testing.

b. **Managed systems** are less costly to maintain and administer because **hidden (indirect) costs** are understood and minimized.

1) A centralized mainframe may be cheaper than a client-server architecture despite higher initial costs because of lower network administration and support costs.
2) In large entities, centralized acquisition policies save costs because organizational subunits are not allowed to purchase incompatible or redundant hardware and software. Standardized IT resources improve operations and decrease costs of administration.
3) Management of systems should include **tracking** IT resources and configuration changes. Tracking permits measurement of the cost of a configuration change in terms of personnel, money, time, and other resources. The cost can then be compared with the benefit.

c. The **Systems Assurance and Control (SAC) model** provides the following framework for determining TCO for an IT installation:
   1) Cost of the **standard configuration** times the number of **workstations**
   2) Sum of the **technical infrastructure** costs (hardware and software costs of servers, printers, routers, bridges, cables, supplier support, utility software, help desks, taxes, shipping, and upgrades over the productive life cycle of the configuration and infrastructure)
   3) The sum of **staff costs** for full-time equivalent positions directly involved during the productive life cycle, plus **administrative costs** (e.g., for developing procedures and standards, capacity planning, and change control)
   4) A percentage of the foregoing costs to reflect **hidden costs**, including such intangibles as end-user help provided by coworkers rather than the help desk
   5) Costs of facilities, turnover, travel, and transportation

Stop and review! You have completed the outline for this subunit. Study multiple-choice questions 14 and 15 on page 405.

9.5 ENTERPRISE-WIDE RESOURCE PLANNING (ERP)

__Overview__

1. **Enterprise-wide resource planning (ERP)** is the latest phase in the development of computerized systems for managing organizational resources. ERP is intended to **integrate** enterprise-wide information systems across the organization by creating **one database** linked to all of the entity's applications.
   a. ERP connects all functional subsystems (human resources, the financial accounting system, production, marketing, distribution, purchasing, receiving, order processing, shipping, etc.) and also connects the organization with its suppliers and customers.
      1) Thus, ERP facilitates demand analysis and materials requirements planning.
      2) By decreasing lead times, it improves just-in-time inventory management.
      3) Even more importantly, ERP's coordination of all operating activities permits flexible responses to shifts in supply and demand.
   b. The disadvantages of ERP are its extent and complexity, which make customization of the software difficult and costly.
   c. The leading comprehensive product in the field is **SAP R/3**. Other ERP products are marketed by Oracle, PeopleSoft, and J. D. Edwards.
   d. Because ERP software is costly and complex, it is usually installed only by the largest enterprises. However, mid-size organizations are increasingly likely to buy ERP software.
   e. The benefits of ERP may significantly derive from the required **business process reengineering**.
      1) Using ERP software that reflects the **best practices** forces the linked subunits in the organization not only to redesign and improve their processes but also to conform to one standard.
      2) An organization may wish to undertake a reengineering project before choosing ERP software. The project should indicate what best practices already exist in the organization's processes. This approach may be preferable for a unique enterprise in a highly differentiated industry.
         a) Carrying out a reengineering project before installing an ERP system defines what process changes are needed and which vendor software should be used.

b) If the organization is not especially unique, vendor software probably is already based on industry best practices. In these circumstances, a preliminary reengineering project may not be needed. Thus, the organization should simply conform its processes to the software.

3) The processes reflected in the ERP software may differ from the organization's. In this case, the better policy is usually to change the organization's processes. **Customizing** the ERP software is expensive and difficult, and it may result in bugs and awkwardness in adopting upgrades.

a) Implementing an ERP system is likely to encounter significant resistance because of its comprehensiveness. Most employees will have to change ingrained habits and learn to use new technology. Hence, successful implementation requires effective **change management**.

Evolution

2. **Materials requirements planning (MRP)** was an early attempt to create an integrated computer-based information system. It was designed to plan and control materials used in a production setting.

   a. MRP was a push system. It assumed that the demand for materials is typically dependent upon some other factor, which can be programmed. Thus, the timing of deliveries is vital to avoid production delays.

   b. For example, an auto manufacturer need only tell the system how many autos of each type are to be manufactured. The MRP system then generates a complete list of every part and component needed. MRP, in effect, creates schedules of when items on inventory will be needed in the production departments.

      1) If parts are not in stock, the system will automatically generate a purchase order on the proper date (considering lead times) so that deliveries will arrive on time. Hence, effective application of MRP necessitates the generation of accurate data about costs and amounts of inventory, set-up costs, and costs of downtime.

3. **Manufacturing resource planning (MRP II)** continued the evolution begun with MRP. It is a closed-loop manufacturing system that integrates all facets of a manufacturing business, including production, sales, inventories, schedules, and cash flows. The same system is used for the accounting, finance, and directing functions, which use the same transactions and numbers.

   a. MRP II includes forecasting and planning capacities for generating cash and other budgets.

   b. MRP II uses an MPS (master production schedule), which is a statement of the anticipated manufacturing schedule for selected items for selected periods. MRP also uses the MPS. Thus, MRP is a component of an MRP II system.

4. The **traditional ERP system** is one in which subsystems share data and coordinate their activities.

   a. Thus, if marketing receives an order, it can quickly verify that inventory is sufficient to notify shipping to process the order.

      1) Otherwise, production is notified to manufacture more of the product, with a consequent automatic adjustment of output schedules.

      2) If materials are inadequate for this purpose, the system will issue a purchase order.

      3) If more labor is needed, human resources will be instructed to reassign or hire employees.

4) The foregoing business processes (and others) should interact seamlessly in an ERP system. Moreover, the current generation of ERP software also provides the capability for smooth (and instant) interaction with the business processes of external parties.

b. The subsystems in a traditional ERP system are internal to the organization. Hence, they are often called **back-office** functions. The information produced is principally (but not exclusively) intended for internal use by the organization's managers.

Current Generation

5. The current generation of ERP software **(ERP II)** has added **front-office** functions. These connect the organization with customers, suppliers, shareholders or other owners, creditors, and strategic allies (e.g., the members of a trading community or other business association). Accordingly, an ERP II system has the following interfaces with its back-office functions:

a. **Supply-chain management** applications for an organization focus on relationships extending from its suppliers to its final customers. Issues addressed include distribution channels, warehousing and other logistical matters, routing of shipments, and sales forecasting.

1) In turn, one organization's supply chain is part of a **linked chain** of multiple organizations. This chain stretches from the producers of raw materials, to processors of those materials, to entities that make intermediate goods, to assemblers of final products, to wholesalers, to retailers, and lastly, to ultimate consumers.

2) Supply chain management involves a **two-way exchange of information**. For example, a customer may be able to track the progress of its order, and the supplier may be able to monitor the customer's inventory. Thus, the customer has better information about order availability, and the supplier knows when the customer's inventory needs replenishment.

3) An **advanced planning and scheduling system** may be an element of a supply chain management application for a manufacturer. It controls the flow of material and components within the chain. Schedules are created given projected costs, lead times, and inventories.

b. **Customer relationship management** applications extend to customer service, finance-related matters, sales, and database creation and maintenance.

1) Integrated data is helpful in better understanding customer needs, such as product preference or location of retail outlets. Thus, the organization may be able to optimize its sales forecasts, product line, and inventory levels.

a) **Business intelligence** software is used to analyze customer data.

c. **Partner relationship management** applications connect the organization not only with such partners as customers and suppliers but also with owners, creditors, and strategic allies (for example, other members of a joint venture).

1) **Collaborative business partnerships** may arise between competitors or arise between different types of organizations, such as a manufacturer partnering with an environmental group. Special software may be helpful to the partners in sharing information, developing a common strategy, and measuring performance.

Configuration

6. The following are the main elements of the **architecture** of an ERP:
   a. Current ERP systems have a **client-server configuration** with possibly scores or hundreds of client (user) computers.
      1) So-called **thin clients** have little processing ability, but **fat clients** may have substantial processing power.
      2) The system may have multiple servers to run applications and contain databases.
      3) The network architecture may be in the form of a **local area network** or **wide-area network**, or users may connect with the server(s) via the **Internet**.
      4) An ERP system may use almost any of the available **operating systems** and **database management systems**.
   b. An advantage of an ERP system is the elimination of data redundancy through the use of a **central database**. In principle, information about an item of data is stored once, and all functions have access to it.
      1) Thus, when the item (such as a price) is updated, the change is effectively made for all functions. The result is reliability **(data integrity)**.
         a) If an organization has separate systems for its different functions, the item would have to be updated whenever it was stored. Failure of even one function to update the item would cause loss of data integrity. For example, considerable inefficiency may arise when different organizational subunits (IT, production, marketing, accounting, etc.) have different data about prices and inventory availability.
   c. An organization may not have the resources, desire, or need for an ERP system with the greatest degree of integration (e.g., SAP R/3).
      1) An alternative to a comprehensive system is a **best-of-breed approach**. Thus, an organization might install a traditional ERP system from one vendor and add e-commerce and other extended applications from separate niche vendors.
         a) An organization that adopts this approach needs to use **middleware**, that is, software that permits different applications to communicate and exchange data. This type of middleware is called an **extended application interface**.
   d. An ERP system that extends to customers, suppliers, and others uses **Internet portals**. In this case, a portal is a website through which authorized external users may gain access to the organization's ERP.
      1) Portals provide links to related websites and services (e.g., newsletters, email, and e-commerce capabilities).

Other Considerations

7. **Implementation of ERP** may take years and cost millions. Moreover, a poor implementation may cause the project to fail regardless of the quality of the software.
   a. However, more rapid and less costly implementation may be possible if no customization is done.
   b. The initial step is to do **strategic planning** and to organize a **project team** that is representative of affected employee groups.
   c. The second step is to **choose ERP software** and a **consulting firm**.
      1) One possibility is to choose the software before the consultants because the first decision may affect the second.

2) Another option is to hire consultants to help with the selection of the software.

a) The organization may then hire other consultants to help with implementation.

d. The third and longest step is **preimplementation**.

1) The length of the **process design** phase is a function of the extent of

a) Reengineering

b) Customization of the software

2) **Data conversion** may be delayed because of disagreements about the means of defining every data field, for example, whether codes should have independent meaning.

3) The ERP system and its interfaces must be **tested**.

e. **Implementation** ("going live") is not the final step. **Follow-up** is necessary to monitor the activities of the numerous employees who have had to change their routines. For example, a mistake caused by reverting to the old method of entering a sales order may have pervasive consequences in a new integrated system: a credit check, rescheduling of production, and ordering of materials.

f. **Training** should be provided during implementation not only regarding technical matters but also to help employees understand the reasons for process changes. For example, the employees who enter sales orders should know what the effects will be throughout the system.

1) Other **change management** techniques include effective communication to allay employee fears and the creation of user-friendly documents and interfaces.

8. The **costs** of an ERP system include

a. Losses from an unsuccessful implementation, e.g., sales declines

b. Purchasing hardware, software, and services

c. Data conversion from legacy systems to the new integrated system (but conversion software may help)

d. Training

e. Design of interfaces and customization

f. Software maintenance and upgrades

g. Salaries of employees working on the implementation

9. The **benefits** of an ERP system may be hard to quantify. They include

a. Lower inventory costs

b. Better management of liquid assets

c. Reduced labor costs and greater productivity

d. Enhanced decision making

e. Elimination of data redundancy and protection of data integrity

f. Avoidance of the costs of other means of addressing needed IT changes

g. Increased customer satisfaction

h. More rapid and flexible responses to changed circumstances

i. More effective supply chain management

j. Integration of global operations

Stop and review! You have completed the outline for this subunit. Study multiple-choice questions 16 and 17 on page 406.

9.6 SYSTEMS SOFTWARE

1. Systems software performs the fundamental tasks needed to manage computer resources. The most basic piece of systems software is the operating system.
   a. An **operating system** acts as an interface between users, application software, and the computer's hardware (CPU, disk drives, printers, communications devices, etc.).
      1) z/OS is the most recent operating system for the very successful IBM **mainframe**.
      2) **Server** operating systems include Unix, Microsoft Windows Server, and Apple MacOS X Server. Inherent networking capabilities are an important part of server operating systems.
      3) Microsoft Windows and Apple MacOS are operating systems for **desktop computers**.
   b. **Utility programs** are the other important type of systems software.
      1) Utilities perform basic data maintenance tasks, such as
         a) Sorting, e.g., arranging all the records in a file by invoice number.
         b) Merging, meaning combining the data from two files into one.
         c) Copying and deleting entire files.
      2) Utilities are **extremely powerful**. Their use should be **restricted** to appropriate personnel, and each occurrence should be **logged**.

Stop and review! You have completed the outline for this subunit. Study multiple-choice questions 18 and 19 beginning on page 406.

9.7 APPLICATION DEVELOPMENT

Build or Buy

1. When an organization acquires a new system by purchasing from an **outside vendor**, contract management personnel oversee the process. The future end-users of the system as well as IT personnel are also involved, drawing up specifications and requirements.
   a. However, when a new system is to be **created in-house**, planning and managing the development process is one of the IT function's most important tasks.
      1) The needs of the end users must be balanced with budget and time constraints; the decision to use existing hardware vs. the purchase of new platforms must be weighed.
   b. Because so much time and so many resources are devoted to the creation of a new application (and because, generally, the more important the business function being automated, the more complex the application is), having a **well-governed methodology** for overseeing the development process is vital.
   c. Both the end users who specified the new system's functionality and IT management who are overseeing the development process **must approve progress** toward the completion of the system at the end of each of the stages described below. This requirement for ongoing review and approval of the project is a type of **implementation control**.

Systems Development Life Cycle (SDLC)

2. The systems development life-cycle approach is the traditional methodology applied to the development of large, highly structured application systems.
   a. A major advantage of the life-cycle approach is **enhanced management and control** of the development process.

b. Once the need for a new system has been recognized, the **five phases** (each with multiple steps) of the SDLC proceed as depicted in the diagram below (portions of the phases can overlap).

Systems Development Life Cycle

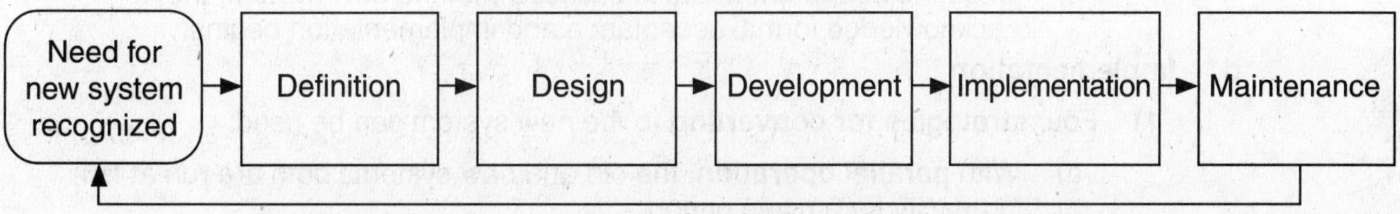

c. Note that the feedback gathered during the maintenance of a system provides information for developing the next generation of systems, hence the name life **cycle**.

3. The phases and component steps of the traditional SDLC can be described as follows:

a. **Definition**

1) A **proposal** for a new system is submitted to the IT steering committee describing the need for the application and the business function(s) that it will affect.

2) **Feasibility studies** are conducted to determine

a) What **technology** the new system will require
b) What **economic resources** must be committed to the new system
c) How the new system will affect current **operations**

3) The **steering committee** gives its go-ahead for the project.

b. **Design**

1) **Logical design** consists of mapping the flow and storage of the data elements that will be used by the new system and the new program modules that will constitute the new system.

a) Data flow diagrams (DFDs) and structured flowcharts are commonly used in this step.

b) Some data elements may already be stored in existing databases. Good logical design ensures that they are not duplicated.

2) **Physical design** involves planning the specific interactions of the new program code and data elements with the hardware platform (existing or planned for purchase) on which the new system will operate.

a) Systems analysts are heavily involved in these two steps.

c. **Development**

1) The actual **program code and database structures** that will be used in the new system are written.

2) **Testing** is the most crucial step of the process.

a) The programmers thoroughly test each new program module of the system, both alone and in concert with other modules.

i) The data used in testing new programs is never the organization's actual production data; such testing would be far too risky to the organization's business.

ii) Instead, a carefully designed **test database** is filled with both **good and bad data** to test how well the new system deals with bad input.

3) **User acceptance testing** is the final step before placing the system in live operation.

a) IT must demonstrate to the user department that submitted the original request that the system performs the functionality that was desired.

b) Once the user department is satisfied with the new system, they acknowledge formal acceptance and implementation begins.

d. **Implementation**

1) Four **strategies for converting** to the new system can be used:

a) With **parallel operation**, the old and new systems both are run at full capacity for a given period.

i) This strategy is the safest since the old system is still producing output (in case there are major problems with the new system), but it is also the most expensive and time-consuming.

b) With **cutover conversion**, the old system is shut down and the new one takes over processing at once.

i) This is the least expensive and least time-consuming strategy, but it is also the riskiest.

c) Under **pilot conversion**, one branch, department, or division at a time is fully converted to the new system.

i) Experience gained from each installation is used to benefit the next one. One disadvantage of this strategy is the extension of the conversion time.

d) In some cases, **phased conversion** is possible. Under this strategy, one function of the new system at a time is placed in operation.

i) For instance, if the new system is an integrated accounting application, accounts receivable could be installed, then accounts payable, cash management, materials handling, etc.

ii) The advantage of this strategy is allowing the users to learn one part of the system at a time.

2) **Training and documentation** are critical.

a) The users must be made to feel comfortable with the new system and have plenty of guidance available, either hardcopy or online.

b) Documentation consists of more than just operations manuals for the users. Layouts of the program code and database structures must also be available for the programmers who must modify and maintain the system.

3) **Systems follow-up or post-audit evaluation** is a subsequent review of the efficiency and effectiveness of the system after it has operated for a substantial time (e.g., 1 year).

e. **Maintenance**, the final phase of the SDLC, is discussed in Subunit 9.8.

<u>**Other Topics**</u>

4. **Prototyping** is an **alternative approach** to application development.

a. Prototyping involves creating a **working model** of the system requested, demonstrating it for the user, obtaining feedback, and making changes to the underlying code.

1) This process repeats through **several iterations** until the user is satisfied with the system's functionality.

b. Formerly, this approach was derided as being wasteful of resources and tending to produce unstable systems, but with vastly increased processing power and high-productivity development tools, prototyping can, in some cases, be an efficient means of systems development.

5. **Application authentication** is a means of taking a user's identity from the operating system on which the user is working and passing it to an authentication server for verification. This can be designed into an application from its inception.

Application Development Tools

6. **Computer-aided software engineering (CASE)** applies the computer to software design and development.
   a. It provides the capacity to maintain on the computer all of the system documentation, e.g., data flow diagrams, data dictionaries, and pseudocode (structured English); to develop executable input and output screens; and to generate program code in at least skeletal form.
   b. Thus, CASE facilitates the creation, organization, and maintenance of documentation and permits some automation of the coding process.

7. **Object-oriented programming** combines data and the related procedures into an object. Thus, an object's data can be operated on only within the object.
   a. If the procedures (called methods) for manipulating the data in an object are changed, no other parts of the program are affected. The idea of limiting code that operates on an object to its own source code unit is called encapsulation.
      1) The basic concepts of object-oriented programming are class and inheritance. Programs are written by describing the creation and interaction of objects. One class of objects can inherit the characteristics of a more general class. Thus, a basic advantage of object-oriented programming is that the code is reusable.
      2) In object-oriented programming, every object has attached to it two sets of characteristics, called **attributes** and **methods**.
      3) EXAMPLE:
         a) A company's programmers have created an **object** named "order."
         b) "order" has the following **attributes**: order_number, order_date, customer_number, part_number, qty_ordered, unit_price, bin_number.
         c) "order" is given the following **methods**:
            i) extended_price (qty_ordered × unit_price)
            ii) three_month_history (every order with the same customer_number and order_date less than three months old is retrieved)
            iii) quantity_remaining (uses bin_number to determine current quantity on hand and subtracts qty_ordered)
         d) The object "order" can now be **reused** by the programmers without all of its attributes and methods having to be recreated in every application that uses it.

8. **Rapid application development (RAD)** is a software development process involving iterative development, the construction of prototypes, and the use of CASE tools.
   a. The RAD process usually involves **compromises** in usability, features, and/or execution speed; increased speed of development occurs through rapid prototyping, virtualization of system related routines, and other techniques. However, there is usually decreased end-user utility.

b. RAD **tools** include requirements-gathering tools, data-modeling tools, and code-generation tools.

1) **Requirements-gathering tools.** All stages of the RAD methodology, particularly the requirements planning stage, specify that requirements should be captured in a tool rather than an unstructured document.

a) For this reason, and because the unified modeling language (UML) is the only language for this task, tools that support writing in the UML support RAD. Among the numerous tools that support UML notation is Microsoft Visio.

2) **Code-generation tools.** RAD was designed in large part to take advantage of CASE technology, which involves aspects of requirements gathering and data modeling, but most especially of code generation.

a) Code generation involves taking some input (and transforming it to the source code that a developer might otherwise have to write according to templates.

Stop and review! You have completed the outline for this subunit. Study multiple-choice questions 20 through 23 beginning on page 407.

9.8 PROGRAM CHANGE CONTROL

1. Over the life of an application, users are constantly asking for **changes**. The process of managing these changes is referred to as **systems maintenance**, and the relevant controls are called **program change controls**.

a. Once a change to a system has been approved, the programmer should save a **copy of the production program** in a test area of the computer, sometimes called a "sandbox."

1) Except in emergencies, and then only under close supervision, should a change be made directly to the production version of a computer program.

b. The programmer **makes the necessary changes** to this copy of the program.

1) The program appears on the programmer's screen, not as digital bits and bytes, but as English-like statements and commands. A computer program in this form, i.e., readable by humans, is called **source code**.

c. The programmer **transforms the changed program** into a form that the computer can execute. The resulting machine-ready program is referred to as object code, or more precisely, **executable code.**

1) Program languages that are transformed from source into executable one line of code at a time are said to be **interpreted**. Program languages that are transformed in entire modules of code are said to be **compiled**.

d. Once the programmer has the executable version of the changed program, (s)he **tests** it to see if it performs the new task as expected.

1) This testing process must absolutely not be run against production data. A special set of **test data** must be available for running test programs against.

e. The programmer **demonstrates** the new functionality for the user who made the request.

1) The user either accepts the new program, or the programmer can go back and make further changes.

f. Once the program is in a form acceptable to the user, the programmer moves it to a **holding area**.

   1) Programmers (except in emergencies) should never be able to put programs directly into production.

g. The programmer's supervisor reviews the new program, approves it, and **authorizes its move into production**, generally carried out by operations personnel.

   1) The compensating control is that operators generally lack the programming knowledge to put fraudulent code into production.

Stop and review! You have completed the outline for this subunit. Study multiple-choice questions 24 through 26 beginning on page 408.

9.9 END-USER COMPUTING (EUC)

<u>End-User vs. Centralized Computing</u>

1. End-user computing involves **user-created or user-acquired systems** that are maintained and operated outside of traditional information systems controls.

   a. **Environmental control risks** that are more likely in an EUC environment include copyright violations that occur when unauthorized copies of software are made or when software is installed on multiple computers.

   b. **Access** to application programs and related data by unauthorized persons is another concern because of lack of physical access controls, application-level controls, and other controls found in mainframe or networked environments.

   c. Moreover, an EUC environment may be characterized by inadequate **backup, recovery, and contingency planning** that may result in an inability to re-create the system or its data.

   d. **Program development, documentation, and maintenance** may also suffer from the lack of centralized control found in larger systems.

      1) The risk of allowing end users to develop their own **applications** is decentralization of control. End-user-developed applications may not be subject to an independent outside review by systems analysts and are not created in the context of a formal development methodology. These applications may lack appropriate standards, controls, and quality assurance procedures.

      2) Moreover, when end users create their own applications and files, **private information systems** may proliferate in which data are largely uncontrolled. Systems may contain the same information, but end-user applications may update and define the data in different ways. Thus, determining the location of data and ensuring data consistency become more difficult.

      3) The auditors should determine that the EUC applications contain **controls** that allow users to rely on the information produced. Identification of applications is more difficult than in a traditional centralized computing environment because few people know about and use them. The auditor's first concern is to discover their existence and their intended functions. One approach is to take an organization-wide inventory of major EUC applications. An alternative is to review major EUC applications in concert with the function or department that is the major user.

         a) The next step is **risk assessment**. The EUC applications that represent high-risk exposures are chosen for audit, for example, because they support critical decisions or are used to control cash or physical assets.

         b) The third step is to review the controls included in the applications chosen in the second phase.

e. In a personal computer setting, the user is often the programmer and operator. Thus, the protections afforded by segregation of duties are eliminated.

f. The **audit trail** is diminished because of the lack of history files, incomplete printed output, etc.

g. In general, available security features for stand-alone machines are limited compared with those in a network configuration.

Basic Architectures for Desktop Computing

2. Three types of end-user computing environments are in common use:

   a. **Client-server model.** A client-server system divides processing of an application between a client machine on a network and a server. This division depends on which tasks each is best suited to perform.

      1) However, **user interaction** is ordinarily restricted to the client part of the application. This portion normally consists of the user interface, data entry, queries, and receipt of reports.

      2) The **server** customarily manages peripheral hardware and controls access to shared databases. Thus, a client-server application must be designed as separate software components that run on different machines but appear to be one application.

      3) **Security** for client-server systems may be more difficult than in a mainframe-based system because of the numerous access points. They also use distributed processing methods that result in heightened risk of unauthorized access to data and processing. New methods of accessing data and processing, such as remote procedure calls, are also available.

   b. **Dummy terminal model.** In this architecture, desktop machines that lack stand-alone processing power have access to remote computers in a network. To run an application, programs are downloaded to the terminal. These machines are relatively inexpensive because they have no disk drives.

   c. The **application server model** involves a three-tiered or distributed network application. The middle (application) tier translates data between the database (back-end) server and the user's (front-end) server. The application server also performs business logic functions, transaction management, and load balancing.

      1) **Business logic functions** interpret transactions and determine how they will be processed, e.g., applicable discounts, shipping methods, etc. Mainly performed by the application server in contrast to the presentation logic performed by the user's front end server.

      2) **Transaction management** keeps track of all of the steps in transaction processing to ensure completion, editing, and/or deletion.

      3) **Load balancing** is a process to distribute data and data processing among available servers, e.g., evenly to all servers or to the next available server.

Stop and review! You have completed the outline for this subunit. Study multiple-choice questions 27 through 30 beginning on page 409.

9.10 SUMMARY

1. Controls should ensure the efficiency and effectiveness of IT operations. They include proper segregation of the duties within the IT environment. Roles and responsibilities within the IT function are designed to promote segregation of duties. Roles that should be separated include systems analysts, database administrators, programmers, the webmaster, operators, help desk personnel, network technicians, and end-users.
2. Encryption technology may be either hardware- or software-based. Two major types of encryption software exist. Public-key, or asymmetric encryption, is the more secure of the two and requires two keys; the public key for coding messages is widely known, but the private key for decoding messages is kept secret by the recipient. A public-key system is used to create digital signatures and certificates. Private-key, or symmetric encryption, is less secure because it requires only a single key for each pair of parties that want to send each other coded messages.
3. IT assets should be protected from unauthorized access, use, or harm. Malicious software (malware) may exploit a known hole or weakness in an application or operating system to evade security measures. Such a vulnerability may have been caused by a programming error. It also may have been intentionally, but not maliciously, created to permit a programmer simple access for correcting the code.
4. Having bypassed security controls, an intruder can do immediate damage to the system or install malware. A Trojan horse is an apparently innocent program that includes a hidden function that may do damage when activated. It may contain a virus, worm, logic bomb, or maliciously created back door access to data, computers, and networks. Also, malware may create a denial of service by overwhelming a system or website with more traffic than it can handle.
5. Controls to prevent or detect infection by malware are particularly significant for file servers in large networks. Antivirus software should continuously monitor the system for viruses or worms and eradicate them. Email attachments, downloads, files on unauthorized media, and files from networks that are not secured should be checked. Furthermore, procedures should be established and responsibility assigned for coping with malware.
6. Hardware and software are significant assets that require careful management. Among the decisions to be made are resource requirements, evaluation of the full costs of the investment, and choosing whether to own or lease the technology.
7. Capacity planning should be undertaken by management and IT specialists. It determines whether the organization's current and future hardware resources relative to its priorities are, and will continue to be, sufficient.
8. Among the issues are scalability and the cost of ownership. Scalability is the characteristic of a system that permits its capacity to be increased to meet greater demands without a system failure. The costs of ownership of IT assets include indirect as well as direct costs. Thus, rational economic decisions about hardware and software acquisition require an analysis of the true or full costs of all factors involved. Failing to consider total long-term costs may seriously underestimate the economic effects of IT decisions. Remember, aside from the initial costs of purchasing hardware and software, you have other costs to consider, such as installation, training, support, maintenance, and more.
9. Enterprise-wide resource planning, or ERP, is the latest phase in the development of computerized systems for managing organizational resources. ERP is intended to integrate enterprise-wide information systems by creating one database linked to all of an organization's applications. ERP connects all functional subsystems and also connects the organization with its suppliers and customers.

10. Thus, ERP facilitates demand analysis and materials requirements planning. By decreasing lead times, it improves just-in-time inventory management. Even more importantly, ERP's coordination of all operating activities permits flexible responses to shifts in supply and demand. The disadvantages of ERP are its scope and complexity, which make customization of the software difficult and costly.
11. The benefits of ERP may significantly derive from the required business process reengineering. Using ERP software that reflects the best practices forces the linked subunits in the organization not only to redesign and improve their processes but also to conform to one standard.
12. The traditional enterprise resource planning system is one in which subsystems share data and coordinate their activities. These subsystems are internal to the organization and are often called back-office functions.
13. The current generation of ERP software, called ERP II, has added front-office functions. These connect the organization with customers, suppliers, owners, creditors, and strategic allies. Accordingly, an ERP II system must have interfaces with its back-office functions.
14. Supply-chain management applications for an organization focus on relationships extending from its suppliers to its final customers. Customer relationship management applications in an ERP II system extend to customer service, finance-related matters, sales, and database creation and maintenance. Partner relationship management applications in an ERP II system connect the organization not only with such partners as customers and suppliers but also with owners, creditors, and strategic allies.
15. Finally, an ERP system that extends to customers, suppliers, and others uses Internet portals. In this case, a portal is a website through which authorized external users may gain access to the organization's ERP. Portals provide links to related websites and services, such as newsletters, email, and e-commerce capabilities.
16. Systems software performs the fundamental tasks needed to manage computer resources. The most basic piece of systems software is the operating system, which acts as an interface between users, application software, and the computer's hardware. Utility programs perform basic data maintenance tasks, such as sorting, merging, copying and deleting data files. Utilities are extremely powerful. Their use should be restricted to appropriate personnel and each occurrence should be logged.
17. When a new system is to be created in-house, planning and managing development process is one of the IT function's most important tasks. The systems development life-cycle (SDLC) approach is the traditional methodology applied to the development of large, highly structured application systems.
18. The five phases of the traditional SDLC are definition (consisting of a proposal and feasibility studies), design (consisting of a logical and a physical design), development (consisting of program code generation and testing), implementation (consisting of installation and training), and maintenance.
19. Over the life of an application, users are constantly asking for changes. The process of managing these changes is referred to as systems maintenance, and the relevant controls are called program change controls. The programmer should make the changes to a copy of the program, thoroughly test it, and demonstrate it for the user. The changed program should be moved into production only after the programming supervisor's approval and authorization.
20. End-user computing (EUC) involves user-created or user-acquired systems that are maintained and operated outside of traditional information systems controls. Strict standards are necessary because an EUC environment may be characterized by inadequate backup, recovery, and contingency planning that may result in an inability to re-create the system or its data.

QUESTIONS

9.1 Functional Areas of IT Operations

1. The practice of maintaining a test program library separate from the production program library is an example of

A. An organizational control.

B. Physical security.

C. An input control.

D. A concurrency control.

Answer (A) is correct. *(CIA, adapted)*

REQUIRED: The type of control represented by separating the test and production program libraries.

DISCUSSION: This separation is an organizational control. Organizational controls concern the proper segregation of duties and responsibilities within the information systems department. Although proper segregation is desirable, functions that would be considered incompatible if performed by a single individual in a manual activity are often performed through the use of an information systems program or series of programs. Thus, compensating controls may be necessary, such as library controls, effective supervision, and rotation of personnel. Segregating test programs makes concealment of unauthorized changes in production programs more difficult.

Answer (B) is incorrect. Physical security (e.g., climate control and restrictions on physical access) is another aspect of organizational control. Answer (C) is incorrect. Input controls validate the completeness, accuracy, and appropriateness of input. Answer (D) is incorrect. Concurrency controls manage situations in which two or more programs attempt to use a file or database at the same time.

2. An organization's computer help-desk function is usually a responsibility of the

A. Applications development unit.

B. Systems programming unit.

C. Computer operations unit.

D. User departments.

Answer (C) is correct. *(CIA, adapted)*

REQUIRED: The entity in charge of a computer help desk.

DISCUSSION: Help desks are usually a responsibility of computer operations because of the operational nature of their functions. A help desk logs reported problems, resolves minor problems, and forwards more difficult problems to the appropriate information systems resources, such as a technical support unit or vendor assistance.

Answer (A) is incorrect. Applications development is responsible for developing systems, not providing help to end-users. Answer (B) is incorrect. The responsibility of systems programming is to implement and maintain system-level software, such as operating systems, access control software, and database systems software. Answer (D) is incorrect. User departments usually lack the expertise to solve computer problems.

3. When a new application is being created for widespread use in a large organization, the principal liaison between the IT function and the rest of an organization is normally a(n)

A. End user.

B. Application programmer.

C. Maintenance programmer.

D. Systems analyst.

Answer (D) is correct. *(CIA, adapted)*

REQUIRED: The principal liaison between the information systems (IS) department and the rest of the organization.

DISCUSSION: Systems analysts are specifically qualified to analyze and design computer information systems. They survey the existing system, analyze the organization's information requirements, and design new systems to meet those needs. Systems analysts communicate with the entire organization and act as a liaison between the organization and the IT function.

Answer (A) is incorrect. End users make up the rest of the organization. Answer (B) is incorrect. Programmers design, write, test, and document the specific programs developed by systems analysts. It is not the responsibility of an application programmer to act as a liaison between the IS department and the rest of the organization. Answer (C) is incorrect. Programmers design, write, test, and document the specific programs developed by systems analysts. It is not the responsibility of a maintenance programmer to act as a liaison between the IS department and the rest of the organization.

4. In the organization of the IT function, the **most** important separation of duties is

A. Not allowing the data librarian to assist in data processing operations.

B. Assuring that those responsible for programming the system do not have access to data processing operations.

C. Having a separate information officer at the top level of the organization outside of the accounting function.

D. Using different programming personnel to maintain utility programs from those who maintain the application programs.

Answer (B) is correct. *(CMA, adapted)*

REQUIRED: The most important separation of duties in the information systems function.

DISCUSSION: Separation of duties is a general control that is vital in a computerized environment. Some separation of duties common in noncomputerized environments may not be feasible in a computer environment. However, certain tasks should not be combined. Systems analysts and programmers should be separate from computer operators. Both programmers and analysts may be able to modify programs, files, and controls and should therefore have no access to those programs nor to computer equipment. Operators should not be assigned programming duties or responsibility for systems design and should have no opportunity to make changes in programs and systems.

Answer (A) is incorrect. Librarians maintain control over documentation, programs, and data files; they should have no access to equipment, but they can assist in data processing operations. Answer (C) is incorrect. A separate information officer outside of the accounting function would not be as critical a separation of duties as that between programmers and processors. Answer (D) is incorrect. Programmers usually handle all types of programs.

5. The duties properly assigned to an information security officer could include all of the following **except**

A. Developing an information security policy for the organization.

B. Maintaining and updating the list of user passwords.

C. Commenting on security controls in new applications.

D. Monitoring and investigating unsuccessful access attempts.

Answer (B) is correct. *(CIA, adapted)*

REQUIRED: The duty not properly assigned to an information security office.

DISCUSSION: The information security officer should not know user passwords. They are normally stored on a computer in encrypted format, and users change them directly.

Answer (A) is incorrect. Developing an information security policy for the organization is an appropriate duty of the information security officer. Answer (C) is incorrect. Commenting on security controls in new applications is an appropriate duty of the information security officer. Answer (D) is incorrect. Monitoring and investigating unsuccessful access attempts is an appropriate duty of the information security officer.

9.2 Encryption

6. A controller became aware that a competitor appeared to have access to the company's pricing information. The internal auditor determined that the leak of information was occurring during the electronic transmission of data from branch offices to the head office. Which of the following controls would be **most** effective in preventing the leak of information?

A. Asynchronous transmission.

B. Encryption.

C. Use of fiber-optic transmission lines.

D. Use of passwords.

Answer (B) is correct. *(CIA, adapted)*

REQUIRED: The most effective control over electronic transmission of data.

DISCUSSION: Encryption software uses a fixed algorithm to manipulate plain text and an encryption key (a set of random data bits used as a starting point for application of the algorithm) to introduce variation. Although data may be accessed by tapping into the transmission line, the encryption key is necessary to understand the data being sent.

Answer (A) is incorrect. Asynchronous transmission is a method of data transmission, not a means of safeguarding data. It is used for slow, irregular transmissions, such as from a keyboard terminal. Each character is marked by a start and stop code. Answer (C) is incorrect. Although fiber-optic transmission lines are difficult to tap, their use will not prevent theft of unencrypted data by someone who has access to them. Answer (D) is incorrect. The use of passwords will control access at the sending location and the head-office computer. However, passwords will not prevent someone from tapping the transmission line.

7. The use of message encryption software

A. Guarantees the secrecy of data.

B. Requires manual distribution of keys.

C. Increases system overhead.

D. Reduces the need for periodic password changes.

Answer (C) is correct. *(CIA, adapted)*

REQUIRED: The effect of message encryption software.

DISCUSSION: Encryption software uses a fixed algorithm to manipulate plain text and an encryption key (a set of random data bits used as a starting point for application of the algorithm) to introduce variation. The machine instructions necessary to encrypt and decrypt data constitute system overhead. As a result, processing speed may be slowed.

Answer (A) is incorrect. No encryption approach absolutely guarantees the secrecy of data. Answer (B) is incorrect. Keys may also be distributed electronically via secure key transporters. Answer (D) is incorrect. Periodic password changes are needed. Passwords are the typical means of validating users' access to unencrypted data.

8. Which of the following is an encryption feature that can be used to authenticate the originator of a document and ensure that the message is intact and has **not** been tampered with?

A. Heuristic terminal.

B. Perimeter switch.

C. Default settings.

D. Digital signatures.

Answer (D) is correct. *(CPA, adapted)*

REQUIRED: The encryption feature used to authenticate the originator of a document and ensure that the original message is intact.

DISCUSSION: Businesses and others require that documents sent over the Internet be authentic. To authenticate a document, a company or other user may transmit a complete plaintext document along with an encrypted portion of the same document or another standard text that serves as a digital signature. If the plaintext document is tampered with, the two will not match.

Answer (A) is incorrect. The term "heuristic terminal" is not meaningful in this context. Answer (B) is incorrect. The term "perimeter switch" is not meaningful in this context. Answer (C) is incorrect. In a computer program, a default setting is a value that a parameter will automatically assume unless specifically overridden.

9. The encryption technique that requires two keys, a public key that is available to anyone for encrypting messages and a private key that is known only to the recipient for decrypting messages, is

A. Rivest, Shamir, and Adelman (RSA).

B. Data encryption standard (DES).

C. Modulator-demodulator.

D. A cypher lock.

Answer (A) is correct. *(CIA, adapted)*

REQUIRED: The encryption technique requiring two keys.

DISCUSSION: RSA is an encryption standard licensed to hardware and software vendors. Public-key encryption requires management of fewer keys for a given client-server environment than does private-key encryption. However, compared with DES, RSA entails more complex computations and therefore has a higher processing overhead. RSA requires two keys: The public key for encrypting messages is widely known, but the private key for decrypting messages is kept secret by the recipient.

Answer (B) is incorrect. DES is a shared private-key method developed by the U.S. government. It encrypts data into 64-bit blocks using a 56-bit key. DES requires only a single key for each pair of parties that want to send each other encrypted messages. DES is being replaced by AES, Advanced Encryption Standard, as the method of choice by the U.S. government. Answer (C) is incorrect. A modem is used for telecommunications. Answer (D) is incorrect. A cypher lock is a physical device.

9.3 Information Protection

10. Which of the following is a computer program that appears to be legitimate but performs some illicit activity when it is run?

A. Hoax virus.

B. Web crawler.

C. Trojan horse.

D. Killer application.

Answer (C) is correct. *(CPA, adapted)*

REQUIRED: The apparently legitimate computer program that performs an illicit activity.

DISCUSSION: A Trojan horse is a computer program that appears friendly, for example, a game, but that actually contains an application destructive to the computer system.

Answer (A) is incorrect. A hoax virus is a false notice about the existence of a computer virus. It is usually disseminated through use of distribution lists and is sent by email or via an internal network. Answer (B) is incorrect. A web crawler (a spider or bot) is a computer program created to access and read information on websites. The results are included as entries in the index of a search engine. Answer (D) is incorrect. A killer application is one that is so useful that it may justify widespread adoption of a new technology.

11. The **best** preventive measure against a computer virus is to

A. Compare software in use with authorized versions of the software.

B. Execute virus exterminator programs periodically on the system.

C. Allow only authorized software from known sources to be used on the system.

D. Prepare and test a plan for recovering from the incidence of a virus.

Answer (C) is correct. *(CIA, adapted)*

REQUIRED: The best preventive measure against a computer virus.

DISCUSSION: Preventive controls are designed to prevent errors before they occur. Detective and corrective controls attempt to identify and correct errors. Preventive controls are usually more cost beneficial than detective or corrective controls. Allowing only authorized software from known sources to be used on the system is a preventive measure. The authorized software from known sources is expected to be free of viruses.

Answer (A) is incorrect. Comparing software with authorized versions is a detective control used to determine whether only authorized versions of the software are being used on the system. Answer (B) is incorrect. Executing virus exterminator programs is a corrective control against a computer virus. Answer (D) is incorrect. Preparing and testing a plan for virus recovery is a corrective control against a computer virus.

12. Which of the following is an indication that a computer virus is present?

A. Frequent power surges that harm computer equipment.

B. Unexplainable losses of or changes to data.

C. Inadequate backup, recovery, and contingency plans.

D. Numerous copyright violations due to unauthorized use of purchased software.

Answer (B) is correct. *(CIA, adapted)*

REQUIRED: The indicator of a computer virus.

DISCUSSION: The effects of computer viruses range from harmless messages to complete destruction of all data within the system. A symptom of a virus would be the unexplained loss of or change to data.

Answer (A) is incorrect. Power surges are caused by hardware or power supply problems. Answer (C) is incorrect. Inadequate backup, recovery, and contingency plans are operating policy weaknesses. Answer (D) is incorrect. Copyright violations represent policy or compliance problems.

13. Which of the following operating procedures increases an organization's exposure to computer viruses?

A. Encryption of data files.

B. Frequent backup of files.

C. Downloading public-domain software from websites.

D. Installing original copies of purchased software on hard disk drives.

Answer (C) is correct. *(CIA, adapted)*

REQUIRED: The procedure that increases exposure to viruses.

DISCUSSION: Viruses are spread through shared data. Downloading public-domain software carries a risk that contaminated data may enter the computer.

Answer (A) is incorrect. Viruses are spread through the distribution of contaminated programs. Answer (B) is incorrect. Backing up files does not increase the chances of a virus entering the computer system. Answer (D) is incorrect. Original copies of purchased software on hard disk drives should be free of viruses.

9.4 Investment in IT

14. Inefficient use of excess computer equipment can be controlled by

A. Contingency planning.

B. System feasibility studies.

C. Capacity planning.

D. Exception reporting.

Answer (C) is correct. *(CIA, adapted)*

REQUIRED: The control over inefficient use of excess computer equipment.

DISCUSSION: Planning is as important for the information systems function as for any other part of the organization. The master plan for this function should be consistent with the strategic plan for the organization and include goals and objectives, an inventory of current capacity, and a forecast of future needs. The plan is the basis for determining hardware needs.

Answer (A) is incorrect. Contingency planning concerns the arrangements for alternative processing facilities in the event of equipment failure. Answer (B) is incorrect. A feasibility study is one of the phases in the systems development life cycle. Answer (D) is incorrect. Exception reports are meant to list errata and bring them to the attention of management.

15. An automobile and personal property insurer has decentralized its information processing to the extent that headquarters has less processing capacity than any of its regional processing centers. These centers are responsible for initiating policies, communicating with policyholders, and adjusting claims. The company uses leased lines from a national telecommunications company. Initially, the company thought there would be little need for interregion communication, but that has not been the case. The company underestimated the number of customers that would move between regions and the number of customers with claims arising from accidents outside their regions. The company has a regional center in an earthquake-prone area and is planning how to continue processing if that center, or any other single center, were unable to perform its processing.

The company considered mirroring the data stored at each regional center at another center. A disadvantage of such an arrangement is

A. Lack of awareness at headquarters of the state of processing.

B. Increased cost and complexity of network traffic.

C. Interference of the mirrored data with original source data.

D. Confusion on the part of insurance agents about where customer data are stored.

Answer (B) is correct. *(CIA, adapted)*

REQUIRED: The disadvantage of mirroring data across centers.

DISCUSSION: If data stored at one regional center is to mirror the data stored at another center, the most efficient method to ensure each center has the most current data is to transfer data across a network. Consequently, the cost of network traffic would increase dramatically. The complexity of the network would also increase as the network would need to provide a great deal of security when transferring data.

Answer (A) is incorrect. Headquarters could monitor the network on a real-time basis and have complete awareness of the state of processing. Answer (C) is incorrect. Adequate controls will ensure that the mirrored data will not affect the source data. Answer (D) is incorrect. The location of the data is not relevant to the insurance agents. The agents will retrieve customer data through the network.

9.5 Enterprise-Wide Resource Planning (ERP)

16. An enterprise resource planning (ERP) system integrates the organization's computerized subsystems and may also provide links to external parties. An advantage of ERP is that

A. The reengineering needed for its implementation should improve business processes.

B. Customizing the software to suit the unique needs of the organization will facilitate upgrades.

C. It can be installed by organizations of all sizes.

D. The comprehensiveness of the system reduces resistance to change.

Answer (A) is correct. *(Publisher, adapted)*

REQUIRED: The advantage of ERP.

DISCUSSION: The benefits of ERP may significantly derive from the business process reengineering that is needed for its implementation. Using ERP software that reflects the best practices forces the linked subunits in the organization not only to redesign and improve their processes but also to conform to one standard.

Answer (B) is incorrect. The disadvantages of ERP are its extent and complexity, which make customization of the software difficult and costly. Answer (C) is incorrect. ERP software is costly and complex. It is usually installed only by the largest enterprises. Answer (D) is incorrect. Implementing an ERP system is likely to encounter significant resistance because of its comprehensiveness.

17. A manufacturing resource planning (MRP II) system

A. Performs the same back-office functions for a manufacturer as an ERP system.

B. Uses a master production schedule.

C. Lacks the forecasting and budgeting capabilities typical of an ERP system.

D. Performs the same front-office functions for a manufacturer as an ERP system.

Answer (B) is correct. *(Publisher, adapted)*

REQUIRED: The true statement about MRP II.

DISCUSSION: Manufacturing resource planning (MRP II) continued the evolution begun with MRP. It is a closed-loop manufacturing system that integrates all facets of manufacturing, including production, sales, inventories, schedules, and cash flows. The same system is used for accounting and finance functions, which use the same transactions and numbers. MRP II uses an MPS (master production schedule), a statement of the anticipated manufacturing schedule for selected items for selected periods. MRP also uses the MPS. Thus, MRP is a component of an MRP II system.

Answer (A) is incorrect. An MRP II system does not integrate all the subsystems internal to the organization (back-office functions), such as human resources and customer service. Answer (C) is incorrect. MRP II includes forecasting and planning capacities for generating cash and other budgets. Answer (D) is incorrect. MRP, MRP II, and traditional ERP do not provide for front-office functions, that is, connections with customers, suppliers, owners, creditors, and strategic allies.

9.6 Systems Software

18. Auditors often make use of computer programs that perform routine processing functions, such as sorting and merging. These programs are made available by computer companies and others and are specifically referred to as

A. Compiler programs.

B. Supervisory programs.

C. Utility programs.

D. User programs.

Answer (C) is correct. *(CPA, adapted)*

REQUIRED: The term for programs used to perform routine functions.

DISCUSSION: Utility programs are provided by manufacturers of equipment to perform routine processing tasks required by both clients and auditors, such as extracting data, sorting, merging, and copying. Utility programs are pretested, are independent of the client's own programming efforts, and furnish useful information without the trouble of writing special programs for the engagement.

Answer (A) is incorrect. Compiler programs convert source programs written in a higher-level language into computer-readable object programs, i.e., into machine language. Answer (B) is incorrect. Supervisory programs, also termed operating systems, are master programs responsible for controlling operations within a computer system. Answer (D) is incorrect. User programs are those prepared for a particular application.

19. In general, mainframe or server production programs and data are adequately protected against unauthorized access. Certain utility software may, however, have privileged access to software and data. To compensate for the risk of unauthorized use of privileged software, IT management can

A. Prevent privileged software from being installed on the mainframe.

B. Restrict privileged access to test versions of applications.

C. Limit the use of privileged software.

D. Keep sensitive programs and data on an isolated machine.

Answer (C) is correct. *(CIA, adapted)*

REQUIRED: The best alternative information systems management can take to minimize unauthorized use of privileged software.

DISCUSSION: Since certain utility software may have privileged access to software and data stored on the mainframe or server, management must control the use of this utility software. Management should limit the use of this software to only those individuals with appropriate authority.

Answer (A) is incorrect. Privileged software may be needed to modify programs and data. Answer (B) is incorrect. Privileged access may be necessary to modify the final versions of applications. Answer (D) is incorrect. Authorized users must access sensitive programs and data through their workstations that are connected to the mainframe or server.

9.7 Application Development

20. Effective internal control for application development should provide for which of the following?

I. A project steering committee to initiate and oversee the system

II. A technical systems programmer to evaluate systems software

III. Feasibility studies to evaluate existing systems

IV. The establishment of standards for systems design and programming

A. I and III only.

B. I, II, and IV only.

C. I, III, and IV only.

D. II, III, and IV only.

Answer (C) is correct. *(CISA, adapted)*

REQUIRED: The components of effective internal control for application development.

DISCUSSION: Effective systems development requires participation by top management. This can be achieved through a steering committee composed of higher-level representatives of system users. The committee approves or recommends projects and reviews their progress. Studies of the economic, operational, and technical feasibility of new applications necessarily entail evaluations of existing systems. Another necessary control is the establishment of standards for system design and programming. Standards represent user and system requirements determined during systems analysis.

Answer (A) is incorrect. Standards must be established. Answer (B) is incorrect. A technical systems programmer has a role in the development and modification of the operating system but not necessarily in applications development. The technical support in this area would be provided by systems analysts rather than programmers. Answer (D) is incorrect. A technical systems programmer has a role in the development and modification of the operating system but not necessarily in applications development.

21. A benefit of using computer-aided software engineering (CASE) technology is that it can ensure that

A. No obsolete data fields occur in files.

B. Users become committed to new systems.

C. All programs are optimized for efficiency.

D. Data integrity rules are applied consistently.

Answer (D) is correct. *(CIA, adapted)*

REQUIRED: The benefit of CASE.

DISCUSSION: CASE is an automated technology (at least in part) for developing and maintaining software and managing projects. A benefit of using CASE technology is that it can ensure that data integrity rules, including those for validation and access, are applied consistently across all files.

Answer (A) is incorrect. Obsolete data fields must be recognized by developers or users. Once recognized, obsolete data fields can be treated consistently in CASE procedures. Answer (B) is incorrect. Using CASE will not ensure user commitment to new systems if they are poorly designed or otherwise do not meet users' needs. Answer (C) is incorrect. Although it has the potential to accelerate system development, CASE cannot ensure that all programs are optimized for efficiency. In fact, some CASE-developed modules may need to be optimized by hand to achieve acceptable performance.

22. User acceptance testing is more important in an object-oriented development process than in a traditional environment because of the implications of the

A. Absence of traditional design documents.

B. Lack of a tracking system for changes.

C. Potential for continuous monitoring.

D. Inheritance of properties in hierarchies.

Answer (D) is correct. *(CIA, adapted)*

REQUIRED: The reason user acceptance testing is more important in an object-oriented development process.

DISCUSSION: In object-oriented development, all objects in a class inherit the properties of higher classes in the hierarchy. Thus, changes in one object may affect many other objects, and the extent and effects of errors significantly increase. Testing one object provides no assurance that the objects are properly coordinated. Accordingly, user acceptance testing to verify correct functioning of the whole system becomes more important.

Answer (A) is incorrect. Instead of traditional design documents, items such as the business model, narratives of process functions, iterative development screens, computer processes and reports, and product descriptions guides are produced in object-oriented development. Answer (B) is incorrect. In general, object-oriented development systems include tracking systems for changes made in objects and hierarchies. Answer (C) is incorrect. Object-oriented systems are usually developed in client-server environments, so the potential exists for continuous monitoring of system use. However, continuous monitoring typically occurs during system operation, not during development.

23. A systems development approach used to quickly produce a model of user interfaces, user interactions with the system, and process logic is called

A. Neural networking.

B. Prototyping.

C. Reengineering.

D. Application generation.

Answer (B) is correct. *(CIA, adapted)*

REQUIRED: The approach used to produce a model of user interfaces, user interactions with the system, and process logic.

DISCUSSION: Prototyping produces the first model(s) of a new system. This technique usually employs a software tool for quick development of a model of the user interface (such as by report or screen), interaction of users with the system (for example, a menu-screen approach or data entry), and processing logic (the executable module). Prototyping stimulates user participation because the model allows quick exploration of concepts and development of solutions with quick results.

Answer (A) is incorrect. Neural networking involves hardware or software that imitates the processing activities of the human brain. Answer (C) is incorrect. Reengineering salvages reusable components of existing systems and restructures them to develop new systems or to improve the old systems. Answer (D) is incorrect. An application generator is software that can be used to develop an application simply by describing its requirements to the computer rather than by writing a procedural program.

9.8 Program Change Control

24. The process of monitoring, evaluating, and modifying a system as needed is referred to as systems

A. Analysis.

B. Feasibility study.

C. Maintenance.

D. Implementation.

Answer (C) is correct. *(CMA, adapted)*

REQUIRED: The term for the process of monitoring, evaluating, and modifying a system.

DISCUSSION: Systems maintenance must be undertaken by systems analysts and applications programmers continually throughout the life of a system. Maintenance is the redesign of the system and programs to meet new needs or to correct design flaws. These changes should be part of a regular program of preventive maintenance.

Answer (A) is incorrect. Systems analysis is the process of determining user problems and needs, surveying the organization's present system, and analyzing the facts. Answer (B) is incorrect. A feasibility study determines whether a proposed system is technically, operationally, and economically feasible. Answer (D) is incorrect. Implementation involves training and educating users, testing, conversion, and follow-up.

25. Change control typically includes procedures for separate libraries for production programs and for test versions of programs. The reason for this practice is to

A. Promote efficiency of system development.

B. Segregate incompatible duties.

C. Facilitate user input on proposed changes.

D. Permit unrestricted access to programs.

Answer (B) is correct. *(CIA, adapted)*

REQUIRED: The reason for having separate libraries for production programs and for test versions of programs.

DISCUSSION: Separating production and test versions of programs facilitates restricting access to production programs to the individuals, such as computer operators, who need access. The effect is to separate the incompatible functions of operators and programmers.

Answer (A) is incorrect. Production and test programs can be separated only if a specific procedure exists for placing programs in production libraries. Thus, maintaining the separation requires its own procedure, which may decrease development efficiency. Answer (C) is incorrect. Separating production and test versions of programs is independent of facilitating user input on proposed changes. Answer (D) is incorrect. Separating production and test versions of programs restricts access to programs.

26. A company often revises its production processes. The changes may entail revisions to processing programs. Ensuring that changes have a minimal impact on processing and result in minimal risk to the system is a function of

A. Security administration.

B. Change control.

C. Problem tracking.

D. Problem-escalation procedures.

Answer (B) is correct. *(CIA, adapted)*

REQUIRED: The approach to ensure changes have a minimal impact on processing.

DISCUSSION: Change control is the process of authorizing, developing, testing, and installing coded changes so as to minimize the impact on processing and the risk to the system.

Answer (A) is incorrect. Security administration is concerned with access to data. Answer (C) is incorrect. Problem tracking is concerned with collecting data to be analyzed for corrective action. Answer (D) is incorrect. Problem escalation-procedures are a means of categorizing problems so that the least skilled person can address them.

9.9 End-User Computing (EUC)

27. The marketing department's proposal was finally accepted, and the marketing employees attended a class in using the report writer. Soon, the marketing analysts found that it was easier to download the data and manipulate it on their own desktop computers in spreadsheets than to perform all the data manipulation on the server. One analyst became highly skilled at downloading and wrote downloading command sequences for the other employees. When the analyst left the company for a better job, the department had problems making modifications to these command sequences. The department's problems are **most** likely due to inadequate

A. Documentation.

B. Data backup.

C. Program testing.

D. Anti-virus software.

Answer (A) is correct. *(CIA, adapted)*

REQUIRED: The reason for difficulties in modifying the command sequences.

DISCUSSION: One risk of end-user computing is that documentation may be poor and that important knowledge may be limited to one person. The command sequences should have been documented so that other analysts could use and modify them readily.

Answer (B) is incorrect. The inability of other analysts to understand the command sequences is not a function of inadequate data backup procedures. Answer (C) is incorrect. The inability of other analysts to understand the command sequences is not a function of inadequate testing. Answer (D) is incorrect. The inability of other analysts to understand the command sequences is not a function of inadequate use of anti-virus software.

28. Traditional information systems development procedures that ensure proper consideration of controls may not be followed by users developing end-user computing (EUC) applications. Which of the following is a prevalent risk in the development of EUC applications?

A. Management decision making may be impaired due to diminished responsiveness to management's requests for computerized information.

B. Management may be less capable of reacting quickly to competitive pressures due to increased application development time.

C. Management may place the same degree of reliance on reports produced by EUC applications as it does on reports produced under traditional systems development procedures.

D. Management may incur increased application development and maintenance costs for EUC systems, compared with traditional (mainframe) systems.

Answer (C) is correct. *(CIA, adapted)*

REQUIRED: The risk in development of EUC applications.

DISCUSSION: End-user developed applications may not be subject to an independent outside review by systems analysts and are not created in the context of a formal development methodology. These applications may lack appropriate standards, controls, quality assurance procedures, and documentation. A risk of end-user applications is that management may rely on them as much as traditional applications.

Answer (A) is incorrect. EUC systems typically increase flexibility and responsiveness to management's information requests. Such systems are more easily modified. Answer (B) is incorrect. EUC systems typically reduce application development cycle time. Answer (D) is incorrect. EUC systems typically result in reduced application development and maintenance costs.

29. Traditional information systems development and operational procedures typically involve four functional areas. The systems analysis function focuses on identifying and designing systems to satisfy organizational requirements. The programming function is responsible for the design, coding, testing, and debugging of computer programs necessary to implement the systems designed by the analysis function. The computer operations function is responsible for data preparation, program/job execution, and system maintenance. The user function provides the input and receives the output of the system. Which of these four functions is often poorly implemented or improperly omitted in the development of a new end-user computing (EUC) application?

A. Systems analysis function.

B. Programming function.

C. Computer operations function.

D. User function.

Answer (A) is correct. *(CIA, adapted)*

REQUIRED: The function often omitted in development of a new EUC application.

DISCUSSION: Systems analysis is one step that is not absolutely required in the development of a system. The desire to produce a system quickly may result in this step being eliminated or poorly implemented. A system is often produced and then analyzed to see if it will satisfy the needs of the organization. In an EUC application, the systems analysis is often incomplete or omitted.

Answer (B) is incorrect. Without programming, there would be no system. Answer (C) is incorrect. Without computer operations, the system would not be able to do anything. Answer (D) is incorrect. Without users, there would be no need for the system.

30. Responsibility for the control of end-user computing (EUC) exists at the organizational, departmental, and individual user level. Which of the following should be a direct responsibility of the individual users?

A. Acquisition of hardware and software.

B. Taking equipment inventories.

C. Strategic planning of end-user computing.

D. Physical security of equipment.

Answer (D) is correct. *(CIA, adapted)*

REQUIRED: The direct responsibility of an individual user.

DISCUSSION: EUC involves user-created or user-acquired systems that are maintained and operated outside of traditional information systems controls. In this environment, an individual user is ordinarily responsible for the physical security of the equipment (s)he uses.

Answer (A) is incorrect. The acquisition of hardware and software is an organizational- and departmental-level responsibility. Answer (B) is incorrect. Taking equipment inventories is an organizational-level responsibility. Answer (C) is incorrect. Strategic planning is an organizational- and departmental-level responsibility.

STUDY UNIT TEN
INFORMATION TECHNOLOGY III

(17 pages of outline)

This study unit addresses voice communications, planning for contingencies (i.e., interruptions of normal processing), and systems security. It continues with a treatment of databases and concludes with discussions of software licensing and web infrastructure.

Core Concepts

- It is important in any information processing environment not to lose or otherwise destroy data. For this reason, the organization must undertake contingency planning and risk analysis.
- Systems security is the process of maintaining data integrity. Systems security consists of access control software, physical security controls, and logical security controls.
- A database is a series of related files combined to eliminate redundancy of data items. A single integrated system allows for improved data accessibility.
- Software is copyrightable, but a substantial amount is in the public domain. Networks of computer users may share such software. Software piracy is a problem for vendors.
- The Internet is a network of networks all over the world. With the explosive growth of the World Wide Web in the 1990s, whole new distribution channels opened up for businesses.

10.1 VOICE COMMUNICATIONS

1. **Voice communications channels** differ from the data channels connecting the CPU and peripheral equipment. They are the communications media for transmitting voice signals and are classified according to their capacity.
   a. An example of a voiceband channel is a telephone line.
   b. **Internet telephony**, known as **voice over IP (VoIP)**, is any transmission of two-way voice communication that uses the Internet for all or part of its path. This can be performed with traditional telephone devices, desktop computers equipped with a sound card, microphone, and speakers, or terminals dedicated to this function.
2. **Voice recognition** input devices are still another alternative to keyboard input. These systems compare the speaker's voice patterns with prerecorded patterns. Advanced systems now have large vocabularies and shorter training periods. They allow for dictation and are not limited to simple commands.
3. A **voice output device** converts digital data into speech using prerecorded sounds.
4. **Pagers** have long been used to alert the recipient of a message, but newer systems now permit transmission of brief text messages.
5. A **cell phone** uses radio waves to transmit voice and data through antennas in a succession of cells or defined geographic areas.

6. **Personal communications services (PCS)** is a cellular technology based on lower-power, higher-frequency radio waves. Cells must be smaller and more numerous, but the phones should be smaller and less expensive and be able to operate where other such devices cannot.

Stop and review! You have completed the outline for this subunit. Study multiple-choice questions 1 and 2 on page 427.

10.2 CONTINGENCY PLANNING

Overview

1. The information security goal of data availability is primarily the responsibility of the IT function.
   a. **Contingency planning** is the name commonly given to this activity.
      1) **Disaster recovery** is the process of resuming normal information processing operations after the occurrence of a major interruption.
      2) **Business continuity** is the continuation of business by other means during the period in which computer processing is unavailable or less than normal.
   b. Two major types of contingencies must be planned for: those in which the data center is physically available and those in which it is not.
      1) Examples of the first type of contingency are power failure, random intrusions such as viruses, and deliberate intrusions such as hacking incidents. The organization's physical facilities are sound, but immediate action is required to keep normal processing going.
      2) The second type of contingency is much more serious. This type is caused by disasters such as floods, fires, hurricanes, earthquakes, etc. An occurrence of this type necessitates the existence of an alternate processing facility [see item 5.a) on the next page].

Backup and Rotation

2. Periodic backup and offsite rotation of computer files is the **most basic part** of any disaster recovery/business continuity plan.
   a. It is a truth seldom grasped by those who are not computer professionals that an organization's **data is more valuable than its hardware**. Hardware can be replaced for a price, but each organization's data bundle is unique and is indispensable to carrying on business. If it is ever destroyed, it cannot be replaced. For this reason, periodic backup and rotation are essential.
   b. A **typical backup routine** involves duplicating all data files and application programs once a month. Incremental changes are then backed up and taken to the offsite location once a week. (Application files must be backed up in addition to data since programs change too.)
   c. The **offsite location** must be temperature- and humidity-controlled and guarded against physical intrusion. Just as important, it must be geographically remote enough from the site of the organization's main operations that it would not be affected by the same natural disaster. It does the organization no good to have adequate backup files if the files are not accessible or have been destroyed.
   d. In case of an interruption of normal processing, the organization's systems can be restored such that at most seven days of business information is lost. This is not an ideal situation, but it is a far cry from a complete loss of a company's files, which could essentially put it out of business.

3. The **risk assessment** that forms the core of contingency planning involves
   a. Identifying and prioritizing the organization's critical applications
      1) Not all of an organization's systems are equally important. The firm must decide which vital applications it simply cannot do business without and in what order they should be brought back into operation.
   b. Determining the minimum recovery time frames and minimum hardware requirements
      1) How long will it take to reinstall each critical application and what platform is required? If the interruption has been caused by an attack, such as a virus or hacker, how long will it take to isolate the problem and eliminate it from the system?
   c. Developing a recovery plan
      1) Each type of contingency requires its own specific recovery procedures (see items 4. and 5. below).

Two Types of Contingencies

4. **Data Center Available**
   a. **Power failures** can be guarded against by the purchase of backup electrical generators. These can be programmed to automatically begin running as soon as a dip in the level of electric current is detected. This is a widespread practice in settings such as hospitals where 24-hour system availability is crucial.
   b. Attacks such as **viruses** and denial-of-service call for a completely different response. The system must be brought down "gracefully" to halt the spread of the infection. The IT staff must be well trained in the nature of the latest virus threats to know how to isolate the damage and bring the system back to full operation.
5. The most extreme contingency is when the organization's **main facility** is rendered **uninhabitable** by flood, fire, earthquake, etc. It is to prepare for these cases that organizations contract for alternate processing facilities.
   a. An **alternate processing facility** is a physical location maintained by an outside contractor for the express purpose of providing processing facilities for customers in case of disaster.
      1) The recovery center, like the offsite storage location for backup files, must be far enough away that it will likely be unaffected by the same natural disaster that forced the abandonment of the main facility. Usually, companies contract for backup facilities in another city.
      2) Once the determination is made that processing is no longer possible at the principal site, the backup files are retrieved from the secure storage location and taken to the recovery center.
   b. Recovery centers take two basic forms. Organizations determine which facility is best by calculating the tradeoff between the cost of the contract and the cost of downtime.
      1) A **hot site** is a fully operational processing facility that is immediately available. Usually, the organization enters into a contract with a service provider.
         a) For a set fee, the service provider agrees to have a hardware platform and communication lines substantially identical to the organization's ready for use 24 hours a day, 365 days a year.
         b) This is the least risky and most expensive solution.

2) A **cold site** is simply a shell facility with sufficient electrical power, environmental controls, and communication lines to permit the organization to install its own newly acquired equipment.

a) On an ongoing basis, this is a much less expensive solution.

b) However, the time to procure replacement equipment can be weeks or months. Also, emergency procurements from equipment vendors can be very expensive.

c. Any contract for a hot site must include a **provision for annual testing**.

1) The service provider agrees to a window of time in which the organization can declare a fake disaster, load its backup files onto the equipment at the hot site, and determine how long it takes to resume normal processing.

Other Technologies

6. Other technologies that can assist in recovery from an interruption in processing:

a. **Fault-tolerant computer systems** (formerly called **fail-soft systems**) have additional hardware and software as well as a backup power supply. A fault-tolerant computer has additional chips and disk storage. This technology is used for mission-critical applications that cannot afford to suffer downtime.

1) The enabling technology for fault-tolerance is the redundant array of inexpensive discs, or RAID. It is a grouping of multiple hard drives with special software that allows for data delivery along multiple paths. If one drive fails, the other discs can compensate for the loss.

b. **High-availability computing** is used for less-critical applications because it provides for a short recovery time rather than the elimination of recovery time.

Stop and review! You have completed the outline for this subunit. Study multiple-choice questions 3 through 8 beginning on page 428.

10.3 SYSTEMS SECURITY

Data Integrity

1. The difficulty of maintaining the integrity of the data is the most significant limitation of computer-based audit tools.

a. Electronic evidence is difficult to authenticate and easy to fabricate.

b. Internal auditors must be careful not to treat computer printouts as traditional paper evidence. The data security factors pertaining to electronic evidence must be considered.

c. The degree of reliance on electronic evidence by the auditor depends on the effectiveness of the controls over the system from which such evidence is taken.

d. The most important control is to enact an **organization-wide network security policy**. This policy should promote the following objectives:

1) **Availability.** The intended and authorized users should be able to access data to meet organizational goals.

2) **Security, privacy, and confidentiality.** The secrecy of information that could adversely affect the organization if revealed to the public or competitors should be ensured.

3) **Integrity.** Unauthorized or accidental modification of data should be prevented.

2. Many controls once performed by separate individuals may be concentrated in computer systems. Hence, an individual who has access to the computer may perform incompatible functions. As a result, other control procedures may be necessary to achieve the control objectives ordinarily accomplished by segregation of functions.
   a. These controls can be classified as one of **two broad types**, physical controls and logical controls. Physical controls are further divided into two subcategories.

Physical Controls

3. **Physical access controls** limit who can physically enter the data center.
   a. **Keypad devices** allow entry of a password or code to gain entry to a physical location or computer system.
   b. **Card reader controls** are based on reading information from a magnetic strip on a credit, debit, or other access card. Controls can then be applied to information about the cardholder contained on the magnetic strip.
   c. **Biometric technologies.** These are automated methods of establishing an individual's identity using physiological or behavioral traits. These characteristics include fingerprints, retina patterns, hand geometry, signature dynamics, speech, and keystroke dynamics.
4. **Environmental controls** are also designed to protect the organization's physical information assets. The most important are
   a. Temperature and humidity control
   b. Gaseous fire-suppression system (not water)
   c. Data center not located on an outside wall
   d. Building housing data center not located in a flood plain

Logical Controls

5. **Logical security controls** are needed because of the use of communications networks and connections to external systems. User identification and authentication, restriction of access, and the generation of audit trails are required in this environment. Thus, access controls have been developed to prevent improper use or manipulation of data files and programs. They ensure that only those persons with a bona fide purpose and authorization have access to computer systems.
   a. **Access control software** (1) protects files, programs, data dictionaries, processing, etc., from unauthorized access; (2) restricts use of certain devices (e.g., terminals); and (3) may provide an audit trail for both successful and unsuccessful access attempts. For example, a **firewall** separates internal from external networks.
   b. **Passwords and ID numbers.** The use of passwords and identification numbers is an effective control in an online system to prevent unauthorized access to computer files. Lists of authorized persons are maintained in the computer. The entry of passwords or identification numbers; a prearranged set of personal questions; and the use of badges, magnetic cards, or optically scanned cards may be combined to avoid unauthorized access.
      1) A **security card** may be used with a personal computer so that users must sign on with an ID and a password. The card controls the machine's operating system and records access data (date, time, duration, etc.).
      2) Proper **user authentication** by means of a password requires password-generating procedures to ensure that valid passwords are known only by the proper individuals. Thus, a password should not be displayed when entered at a keyboard.

3) Password security may also be compromised in other ways. For example, **log-on procedures** may be cumbersome and tedious. Thus, users often store log-on sequences on their personal computers and invoke them when they want to use mainframe facilities. A risk of this practice is that anyone with access to the personal computers could log on to the mainframe.

4) To be more effective, passwords should consist of random letters, symbols, and numbers. They should not contain words or phrases.

c. **File attributes** can be assigned to control access to and the use of files. Examples are read/write, read only, archive, and hidden.

d. A **device authorization table** restricts file access to those physical devices that should logically need access. For example, because it is illogical for anyone to access the accounts receivable file from a manufacturing terminal, the device authorization table will deny access even when a valid password is used.

1) Such tests are often called **compatibility tests** because they ascertain whether a code number is compatible with the use to be made of the information. Thus, a user may be authorized to enter only certain kinds of data, have access only to certain information, have access but not updating authority, or use the system only at certain times. The lists or tables of authorized users or devices are sometimes called **access control matrices**.

e. A **system access log** records all attempts to use the system. The date and time, codes used, mode of access, data involved, and operator interventions are recorded.

f. **Encryption** involves using a fixed algorithm to manipulate plaintext.

g. **Controlled disposal of documents.** One method of enforcing access restrictions is to destroy data when they are no longer in use. Thus, paper documents may be shredded and magnetic media may be erased.

h. **Automatic log-off** (disconnection) of inactive data terminals may prevent the viewing of sensitive data on an unattended data terminal.

i. **Security personnel.** An organization may need to hire security specialists. For example, developing an information security policy for the organization, commenting on security controls in new applications, and monitoring and investigating unsuccessful access attempts are appropriate duties of the information security officer.

Internet Security

6. Connection to the Internet presents security issues.

a. Thus, the organization-wide network security policy should at the very least include

1) A user account management system
2) Installation of an Internet firewall
3) Methods such as encryption to ensure that only the intended user receives the information and that the information is complete and accurate

b. **User account management** involves installing a system to ensure that

1) New accounts are added correctly and assigned only to authorized users.
2) Old and unused accounts are removed promptly.
3) Passwords are changed periodically, and employees are educated on how to choose a password that cannot be easily guessed (e.g., a password of at least six diverse characters that do not form a word).

c. A **firewall** separates an internal network from an external network (e.g., the Internet) and prevents passage of specific types of traffic. It identifies names, Internet Protocol (IP) addresses, applications, etc., and compares them with programmed access rules.

1) A firewall may have any of the following features:

   a) A **packet filtering system** examines each incoming network packet and drops (does not pass on) unauthorized packets.

   b) A **proxy server** maintains copies of Web pages to be accessed by specified users. Outsiders are directed there, and more important information is not available from this access point.

   c) An **application gateway** limits traffic to specific applications.

   d) A **circuit-level gateway** connects an internal device, e.g., a network printer, with an outside TCP/IP port. It can identify a valid TCP session.

   e) **Stateful inspection** stores information about the state of a transmission and uses it as background for evaluating messages from similar sources.

2) Firewall systems ordinarily produce **reports** on organization-wide Internet use, unusual usage patterns, and system penetration attempts. These reports are very helpful to the internal auditor as a method of continuous monitoring, or logging, of the system.

   a) Firewalls do not provide adequate protection against **computer viruses.** Thus, an organization should include one or more antivirus measures in its network security policy.

d. Data traveling across the network can be encoded so that it is indecipherable to anyone except the intended recipient.

e. **Other Controls**

1) **Authentication** measures verify the identity of the user, thus ensuring that only the intended and authorized users gain access to the system.

   a) Most firewall systems provide authentication procedures.

   b) Access controls are the most common authentication procedures.

2) **Checksums** help ensure the integrity of data by checking whether the file has been changed. The system computes a value for a file and then proceeds to check whether this value equals the last known value for this file. If the numbers are the same, the file has likely remained unchanged.

<u>Data Storage</u>

7. Storing all related data on one storage device creates security problems.

a. If hardware or software malfunctions occur, or unauthorized access is achieved, the results could be disastrous.

b. Greater emphasis on security is required to provide backup and restrict access to the database.

1) For example, the system may employ **dual logging**, that is, use of two transaction logs written simultaneously on separate storage media. It may also use a snapshot technique to capture data values before and after transaction processing. The files that store these values can be used to reconstruct the database in the event of data loss or corruption.

c. The responsibility for creating, maintaining, securing, and restricting access to the database belongs to the **Database Administrator (DBA)**.

d. A **database management system (DBMS)** includes security features. Thus, a specified user's access may be limited to certain data fields or logical views depending on the individual's assigned duties.

Stop and review! You have completed the outline for this subunit. Study multiple-choice questions 9 through 14 beginning on page 429.

10.4 DATABASES

Overview

1. A **database** is a series of related files combined to eliminate redundancy of data items.
   a. A single integrated system allows for improved data accessibility.
   b. When systems within the organization are not integrated, they not only may contain different data but also may define and update data in inconsistent ways. Thus, determining the location of data and ensuring their consistency are more difficult.
   c. EXAMPLE: The various files related to human resources in the conventional record systems of most organizations include payroll, work history, and permanent personnel data.
      1) An employee's name must appear in each of these files when they are stored and processed separately. The result is redundancy. When data are combined in a database, each data item is usually stored only once.
   d. The data are stored physically on **direct-access storage devices** (e.g., magnetic disks). They are also stored for efficient access.
      1) The most frequently accessed items are placed in the physical locations permitting the fastest access.
      2) When these items were stored in separate files under older file-oriented systems, the physical locations were usually similar to the logical structure of the data. Items that logically belonged together were stored in physical proximity to one another.
      3) A **logical data model** is a user view. It is the way a user describes the data and defines their interrelationships based on the user's needs, without regard to how the data are physically stored.

Database Structures

2. To understand the vast improvement in performance brought about by database technology, it is helpful to review the development of file structures.
   a. The early mainframe computers used **flat files**, meaning that all the records and all the data elements within each record followed one behind the other. Much early mainframe storage was on magnetic tape, which naturally stored data in this fashion.
   b. EXAMPLE: Here are two records excerpted from a tape file:

Record	Customer	Street	City	Order_Nbr	Part_Nbr_1	Qty_1	Price_1	Ext_1	Part_Nbr_2	Qty_2	Price_2	Ext_2
116385	Zeno's Paradox Hardware	10515 Prince Avenue	Athens, GA	19742133	A316	3	$0.35	$1.05	G457	12	$1.15	$13.80

(Many intervening records)

Record	Customer	Street	City	Order_Nbr	Part_Nbr_1	Qty_1	Price_1	Ext_1
122406	Zeno's Paradox Hardware	10515 Prince Avenue	Athens, GA	19742259	A316	4	$0.35	$1.40

   c. Two inefficiencies are apparent at once in this method of accessing data:
      1) The customer's address has to be stored with every order the customer places, taking up much unnecessary storage.
      2) All intervening records must be read and skipped over in order to find both records pertaining to this customer.

3. Database technology overcame these two difficulties. There are three main ways of organizing a database:

   a. A **tree** or **hierarchical structure** arranges data in a one-to-many relationship in which each record has one antecedent but may have an unlimited number of subsequent records.

      1) EXAMPLE: One customer, many orders; one order, many parts:

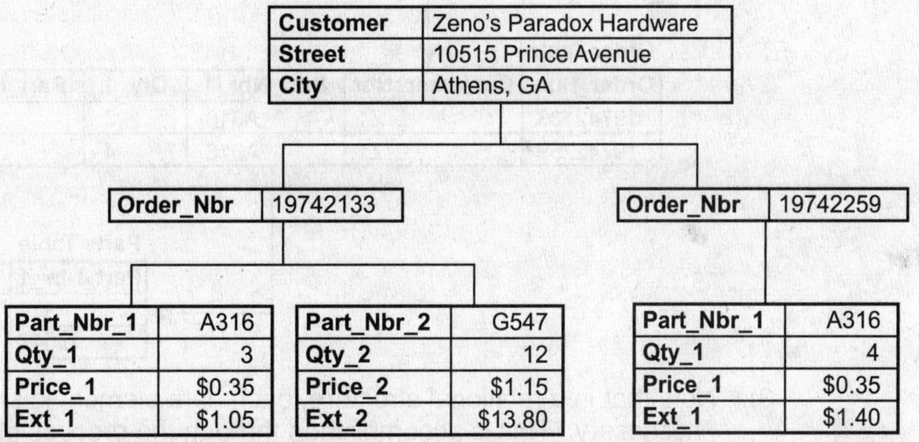

      2) Because the records are not stored one after the other, a tree database structure stores a **pointer** with each record. The pointer is the storage address of the next record.

      3) The tree structure cuts down on data redundancy but retains the necessity of searching every record to fulfill a query. Thus, like the flat file, adding new records is awkward and ad hoc queries are inefficient.

   b. The **network structure** connects every record in the database with every other record.

      1) This was an attempt to make queries more efficient. However, the huge number of cross-references inherent in this structure makes maintenance far too complex.

   c. A **relational structure** organizes data in a conceptual arrangement.

      1) An individual data item is called a **field** or **column** (e.g., name, date, amount).

         a) Related fields are brought together in a **record** or **row** (e.g., for a single sales transaction).

         b) Multiple records make up a **file** or **table** (e.g., sales).

         c) Tables can be **joined** or **linked** based on common fields rather than on high-overhead pointers or linked lists as in other database structures.

         d) Every record in a table has a field (or group of fields) designated as the **key**. The value (or combination of values) in the key uniquely identifies each record.

2) EXAMPLE:

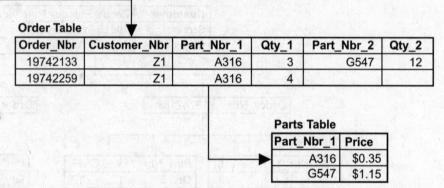

Customer Table

Customer_Nbr	Customer	Street	City
X1	Xylophones To Go	3846 N Lamar Blvd	Oxford, MS
Y1	Yellow Dog Software	1012 E Tennessee St	Tallahassee, FL
Z1	Zeno's Paradox Hardware	10515 Prince Avenue	Athens, GA

Order Table

Order_Nbr	Customer_Nbr	Part_Nbr_1	Qty_1	Part_Nbr_2	Qty_2
19742133	Z1	A316	3	G547	12
19742259	Z1	A316	4		

Parts Table

Part_Nbr_1	Price
A316	$0.35
G547	$1.15

3) Note that in a relational structure, each data element is stored as few times as necessary. This is accomplished through the process of **normalization**. Normalization prevents inconsistent deletion, insertion, and updating of data items.

4) The relational structure requires careful planning, but it is easy to maintain and it processes queries efficiently.

5) The three **basic operations** in the relational model are selecting, joining, and projecting.

   a) **Selecting** creates a subset of records that meet certain criteria.

   b) **Joining** is the combining of relational tables based on a common field or combination of fields.

   c) **Projecting** results in the requested subset of columns from the table. This operation creates a new table containing only the required information.

6) **Cardinality** expresses the bounds (a minimum and a maximum) of the association between related entities. For example, a college class must have a minimum of three students and can have a maximum of 59. The student-class relationship has a cardinality limit expressed as (3, 59).

d. The data in a database are subject to the constraint of **referential integrity**. This means that if data are collected about something, e.g., a payment voucher, all reference conditions regarding it must be met; thus, for a voucher to exist, a vendor must also exist.

e. A **distributed database** is stored in two or more physical sites using either replication or partitioning.

1) The **replication** or **snapshot** technique makes duplicates to be stored at multiple locations.

   a) Changes are periodically copied and sent to each location. If a database is small, storing multiple copies may be cheaper than retrieving records from a central site.

2) **Fragmentation** or **partitioning** stores specific records where they are most needed.

a) For example, a financial institution may store a particular customer's data at the branch where (s)he usually transacts his or her business. If the customer executes a transaction at another branch, the pertinent data are retrieved via communication lines.

b) One variation is the **central index**. A query to this index obtains the location in a remote database where the complete record is to be found.

c) Still another variation is the **ask-the-network distributed database**. In this system, no central index exists. Instead, the remote databases are polled to locate the desired record.

3) Updating data in a distributed system may require special protocols.

a) Thus, a **two-phase commit** disk-writing protocol is used. If data are to be updated in two places, databases in both locations are cleared for updating before either one performs (commits) the update.

b) In the first phase, both locations agree to the update. In the second phase, both perform the update.

f. A **deadly embrace** (deadlock) occurs when each of two transactions has a lock on a single data resource.

1) When deadly embraces occur, the DBMS must have an algorithm for undoing the effects of one of the transactions and releasing the data resources it controls so that the other transaction can run to completion. Then, the other transaction is restarted and permitted to run to completion.

2) If deadly embraces are not resolved, response time worsens or the system eventually fails.

Database Terminology

4. A **database management system (DBMS)** is an integrated set of computer programs that create the database, maintain the elements, safeguard the data from loss or destruction, and make the data available to applications programs and inquiries.

a. The DBMS allows programmers and designers to work independently of the logical structure of the database.

1) Before the development of DBMSs, programmers and systems designers needed to consider the logical structure of the database with the creation of every new application. This was extremely time consuming and therefore expensive.

b. The **schema** is a description of the overall logical structure of the database using **data-definition language**, which is the connection between the logical and physical structures of the database.

1) A **subschema** describes a particular user's (application's) view of a part of the database using data definition language.

c. A fundamental characteristic of databases is that applications are independent of the database structure; when writing programs or designing applications to use the database, only the name of the desired item is necessary.

d. A data item is identified using the **data manipulation language**, after which the DBMS locates and retrieves the desired item(s).

1) The data manipulation language is used to add, delete, retrieve, or modify data or relationships.

e. The physical structure of the database can be completely altered without having to change any of the programs using the data items. Thus, different users may define different views of the data (subschemas).

5. **Other Database Definitions**
   a. The **database administrator (DBA)** is the individual who has overall responsibility for developing and maintaining the database and for establishing controls to protect its integrity.
      1) Thus, only the DBA should be able to update data dictionaries. In small systems, the DBA may perform some functions of a DBMS. In larger applications, the DBA uses a DBMS as a primary tool.
   b. The **data dictionary** is a file, either computer or manual, that describes both the physical and logical characteristics of every data element in a database.
      1) The data dictionary includes, for example, the name of the data element (e.g., employee name, part number), the amount of disk space required to store the data element (in bytes), and what kind of data is allowed in the data element (e.g., alphabetic, numeric).
         a) The data dictionary also provides a mapping from the data element to every application where it is updated and vice versa.
      2) Thus, the data dictionary contains the size, format, usage, meaning, and ownership of every data element as well as what persons, programs, reports, and functions use the data element.
      3) In an advanced data dictionary, a change in a data element automatically changes related programs.
   c. The **database mapping facility** is software that is used to evaluate and document the structure of the database.
   d. The **data control language** specifies the privileges and security rules governing database users.
   e. **Data command interpreter languages** are symbolic character strings used to control the current state of DBMS operations.
6. Storing all related data on one storage device creates **security problems**.
   a. Should hardware or software malfunctions occur, or unauthorized access be achieved, the results could be disastrous.
   b. Greater emphasis on security is required to provide backup and restrict access to the database.
      1) For example, the system may employ **dual logging**, that is, use of two transaction logs written simultaneously on separate storage media.
      2) It may also use a snapshot technique to capture data values before and after transaction processing.
      3) The files that store these values can be used to reconstruct the database in the event of data loss or corruption.
   c. The responsibility for creating, maintaining, securing, and restricting access to the database belongs to the database administrator.
   d. A DBMS includes security features. Thus, a specified user's access may be limited to certain data fields or logical views depending on the individual's assigned duties.
7. Databases and the associated DBMS permit efficient storage and retrieval of data for formal system applications.
   a. They also permit increased ad hoc accessing of data (e.g., to answer inquiries for data not contained in formal system outputs) as well as updating of files by transaction processing.

b. These increased capabilities, however, result in increased cost because they require
   1) The use of sophisticated hardware (direct-access devices)
   2) Sophisticated software (the DBMS)
   3) Highly trained technical personnel (database administrator, staff)
   4) Increased security controls

8. An **object-oriented database** is a response to the need to store not only numbers and characters but also graphics and multimedia applications.
   a. Translating these data into tables and rows is difficult. However, in an object-oriented database, they can be stored, along with the procedures acting on them, within an object.

9. In a **hypermedia database**, blocks of data are organized into nodes that are linked in a pattern determined by the user so that an information search need not be restricted to the predefined organizational scheme. A node may contain text, graphics, audio, video, or programs.
   a. Hybrid systems containing object-oriented and relational database capabilities have also been developed.

10. Advanced database systems provide for **online analytical processing (OLAP)**, also called multidimensional data analysis, which is the ability to analyze large amounts of data from numerous perspectives.
    a. OLAP is an integral part of the data warehouse concept.

11. A **data warehouse** contains not only current operating data but also historical information from throughout the organization. Thus, data from all operational systems is integrated, consolidated, and standardized into an organization-wide database into which data is copied periodically. This data is maintained on one platform and can be read but not changed. Graphics and query software and analytical tools assist users. Accordingly, **data mining** is facilitated by a data warehouse.

Stop and review! You have completed the outline for this subunit. Study multiple-choice questions 15 through 20 beginning on page 431.

10.5 SOFTWARE LICENSING

1. Software is **copyrightable**, but a substantial amount is in the public domain. Networks of computer users may share such software.
   a. **Shareware** is software made available for a fee (usually with an initial free trial period) by the owners to users through a distributor (or websites or electronic bulletin board services).
   b. **Software piracy** is a problem for vendors. The best way to detect an illegal copy of application software is to compare the serial number on the screen with the vendor's serial number.
      1) Use of unlicensed software increases the risk of introducing computer viruses into the organization. Such software is less likely to have been carefully tested.
      2) To avoid legal liability, controls also should be implemented to prevent use of unlicensed software that is not in the public domain. A **software licensing agreement** permits a user to employ either a specified or an unlimited number of copies of a software product at given locations, at particular machines, or throughout the organization. The agreement may restrict reproduction or resale, and it may provide subsequent customer support and product improvements.

3) Software piracy can expose an organization's people to both **civil** and **criminal** penalties. The **Business Software Alliance (BSA)** is a worldwide trade group that coordinates software vendors' efforts to prosecute the illegal duplication of software.

c. Diskless workstations increase security by preventing the copying of software to a floppy disk from a workstation. This control not only protects the company's interests in its data and proprietary programs but also guards against theft of licensed third-party software.

d. To shorten the installation time for revised software in a network, an organization may implement **electronic software distribution (ESD)**, which is the computer-to-computer installation of software on workstations. Instead of weeks, software distribution can be accomplished in hours or days and can be controlled centrally. Another advantage of ESD is that it permits the tracking of PC program licenses.

Stop and review! You have completed the outline for this subunit. Study multiple-choice questions 21 and 22 on page 433.

10.6 WEB INFRASTRUCTURE

1. The **Internet** is a **network of networks** all over the world.

a. The Internet is descended from the original ARPANet, a product of the Defense Department's Advanced Research Projects Agency (ARPA), introduced in 1969.

1) The idea was to have a network that could not be brought down during an enemy attack by bombing a single central location. ARPANet connected computers at universities, corporations, and government. In view of the growing success of the Internet, ARPANet was retired in 1990.

b. The Internet facilitates inexpensive communication and information transfer among computers, with gateways allowing mainframe computers to interface with personal computers.

1) Very high-speed **Internet backbones** carry signals around the world and meet at **network access points**.

c. Most Internet users obtain connections through **Internet service providers (ISPs)** that in turn connect either directly to a backbone or to a larger ISP with a connection to a backbone.

1) The topology of the backbone and its interconnections may once have resembled a spine with ribs connected along its length but is now almost certainly more like a fishing net wrapped around the world with many circular paths.

d. The three main parts of the Internet are the **servers** that hold information, **clients** that view the information, and the **transmission control protocol/Internet protocol (TCP/IP)** suite of protocols that connect the two.

e. The Internet was initially restricted to email and text-only documents.

1) In the 1980s, English computer scientist Tim Berners-Lee conceived the idea of allowing users to click on a word or phrase (a **hyperlink**) on their screens and having another document automatically be displayed.

2) Berners-Lee created a simple coding mechanism called **hypertext markup language (HTML)** to perform this function. He also created a set of rules called **hypertext transfer protocol (HTTP)** to allow hyperlinking across the Internet rather than on just a single computer. He then created a piece of software, called a **browser**, that allowed users to read HTML from any brand of computer. The result was the **World Wide Web** (often simply called the Web).

a) As the use of HTML and its successor languages spread, it became possible to display rich graphics and streaming audio and video in addition to text.

b) **Extensible markup language (XML)** was developed by an international consortium and released in 1998 as an open standard usable with many programs and platforms.

i) XML codes all information in such a way that a user can determine not only **how it should be presented** but also **what it is**, i.e., all computerized data may be tagged with identifiers.

ii) Unlike HTML, XML uses **codes that are extensible, not fixed**. Thus, if an industry can agree on a set of codes, software for that industry can be written that incorporates those codes.

f. **Extensible markup language (XML)** was developed by an international consortium and released in 1998 as an open standard usable with many programs and platforms. XML is a variation of HTML (hypertext markup language), which uses fixed codes (tags) to describe how webpages and other hypermedia documents should be presented. XML codes all information in such a way that a user can also determine what it is. Thus, all computerized data may be tagged with identifiers. Also, unlike HTML, XML uses tags that are extensible, not fixed. Accordingly, if an industry can agree on a set of codes, software for that industry can be written that incorporates those codes. For example, XML allows the user to label the Uniform Product Code (UPC), price, color, size, etc., of goods so that other systems will know exactly what the tag references mean. In contrast, HTML tags would only describe how items are placed on a page and provide links to other pages and objects.

1) Standard setters and other entities are attempting to find ways to incorporate XML with EDI.

2) **Extensible business reporting language (XBRL)** for Financial Statements is the specification developed by an AICPA-led consortium for commercial and industrial entities that report in accordance with U.S. GAAP. It is a variation of XML that is expected to decrease the costs of generating financial reports, reformulating information for different uses, and sharing business information using electronic media.

g. With the explosive growth of the World Wide Web in the 1990s, whole **new distribution channels** opened up for businesses. Consumers can browse a vendor's catalog using the rich graphics of the web, initiate an order, and remit payment, all from the comfort of their homes.

1) An organization's **presence** on the Web is constituted in its **website**. The website consists of a **home page**, the first screen encountered by users, and subsidiary **web pages** (screens constructed using HTML or a similar language).

2) Every page on the World Wide Web has a unique address, recognizable by any web-enabled device, called a **universal resource locator (URL)**. However, just because the address is recognizable does not mean it is accessible to every user -- security is a major feature of any organization's website.

h. An **intranet** permits sharing of information throughout an organization by applying Internet connectivity standards and web software (e.g., browsers) to the organization's internal network.

1) An intranet addresses the connectivity problems of an organization with many types of computers. It is ordinarily restricted to those within the organization and to outsiders after appropriate identification.

2) An **extranet** consists of the linked intranets of two or more organizations, for example, of a supplier and its customers. It typically uses the public Internet as its transmission medium but requires a password for access.

Stop and review! You have completed the outline for this subunit. Study multiple-choice questions 23 through 25 beginning on page 433.

10.7 SUMMARY

1. Voice communications channels differ from the data channels connecting the CPU and peripheral equipment. Internet telephony, known as voice over IP (VoIP), is any transmission of two-way voice communication that uses the Internet for all or part of its path.
2. It is important in any information processing environment not to lose or otherwise destroy data. For this reason, the organization must undertake contingency planning and risk analysis.
3. A computer center should have a reconstruction and recovery plan that will allow it to regenerate important programs and database files. The center should create backup (duplicate) copies of data files, databases, programs, and documentation; store backup copies offsite; and plan for auxiliary processing on alternate systems or at another site.
4. A hot site is a service bureau. It is a fully operational processing facility that is immediately available. A cold site is a shell facility where the user can quickly install computer equipment.
5. Systems security is the process of maintaining data integrity. Systems security consists of access control software, physical security controls, and logical security controls.
6. Access control software protects files, programs, data dictionaries, processing, etc., from unauthorized access. Physical security controls limit physical access and protect against environmental risks and natural catastrophes, such as fire and flood. The most widely used logical security controls consist of user identification and authentication.
7. Connection to the Internet presents security issues. Thus, the organization-wide network security policy should at the very least include a user account management system; an Internet firewall; and methods, such as encryption, to ensure that only the intended user receives the information.
8. A database is a series of related files combined to eliminate redundancy of data items. A single integrated system allows for improved data accessibility. A relational structure organizes data in a conceptual arrangement, consisting of individual data items called fields, related fields brought together (records), and groups of records (files or tables).
9. A database management system (DBMS) is an integrated set of computer programs that allows programmers and designers to work independently of the physical and logical structure of the database. The schema is a description of the overall logical structure of the database using a data-definition language (DDL).

10. Software is copyrightable, but a substantial amount is in the public domain. Networks of computer users may share such software. Software piracy is a problem for vendors. To avoid legal liability, controls should be implemented to prevent use of unlicensed software that is not in the public domain. A software licensing agreement permits a user to employ either a specified or an unlimited number of copies of a software product at given locations, at particular machines, or throughout the organization.
11. The Internet is a network of networks all over the world. With the explosive growth of the World Wide Web in the 1990s, whole new distribution channels opened up for businesses. The three main parts of the Internet are the servers that hold information, the clients that view the information, and the transmission control protocol/Internet protocol (TCP/IP) suite of protocols that connect the two.
12. Hypertext markup language (HTML) and Extensible Markup Language (XML) make it possible to display rich graphics and streaming audio and video in addition to text on the Web.
13. An intranet permits sharing of information throughout an organization by applying Internet connectivity standards and web software (e.g., browsers) to the organization's internal network.

QUESTIONS

10.1 Voice Communications

1. An electronic meeting conducted between several parties at remote sites is referred to as

A. Teleprocessing.

B. Interactive processing.

C. Telecommuting.

D. Teleconferencing.

Answer (D) is correct. *(CMA, adapted)*

REQUIRED: The process of holding an electronic meeting between several parties at remote sites.

DISCUSSION: Conducting an electronic meeting among several parties at remote sites is teleconferencing. It can be accomplished by telephone or electronic mail group communication software. Videoconferencing permits the conferees to see each other on video screens. The practice has grown in recent years as companies have attempted to cut their travel costs.

Answer (A) is incorrect. Teleprocessing refers to connections in an online system. Answer (B) is incorrect. Interactive processing allows users to converse directly with the system. It requires online processing and direct access to stored information. Answer (C) is incorrect. Telecommuting refers to the practice of individuals working out of their homes by communicating with their office via the computer.

2. Which of the following statements about voice communications is true?

A. Modern voice recognition input devices have large vocabularies and short training periods.

B. A voice output device converts speech into digital data.

C. Cell phones and PCS services use the same frequency radio waves.

D. Pagers can alert users to the receipt of messages but cannot transmit text.

Answer (A) is correct. *(Publisher, adapted)*

REQUIRED: The true statement about voice communications.

DISCUSSION: Voice recognition input devices provide an alternative to keyboard input. These systems compare the speaker's voice patterns with prerecorded patterns. Advanced systems now have large vocabularies and shorter training periods. They allow for dictation and are not limited to simple commands.

Answer (B) is incorrect. A voice output device converts digital data into speech using prerecorded sounds. Answer (C) is incorrect. PCS services use lower-power, higher-frequency radio waves than cell phones. Answer (D) is incorrect. Newer pager systems permit transmission of text messages.

10.2 Contingency Planning

3. Contingency plans for information systems should include appropriate backup agreements. Which of the following arrangements would be considered too vendor-dependent when vital operations require almost immediate availability of computer resources?

A. A "hot site" arrangement.

B. A "cold site" arrangement.

C. A "cold and hot site" combination arrangement.

D. Using excess capacity at another data center within the organization.

Answer (B) is correct. *(CIA, adapted)*

REQUIRED: The contingency plan that is too vendor-dependent.

DISCUSSION: Organizations should maintain contingency plans for operations in the case of a disaster. These plans usually include off-site storage of important backup data and an arrangement for the continuation of operations at another location. A "cold site" has all needed assets in place except the needed computer equipment and is vendor-dependent for timely delivery of equipment.

Answer (A) is incorrect. A "hot site" has all needed assets in place and is not vendor-dependent. Answer (C) is incorrect. A "cold and hot site" combination allows the "hot site" to be used until the "cold site" is prepared and is thus not too vendor-dependent. Answer (D) is incorrect. Excess capacity would ensure that needed assets are available and would not be vendor-dependent.

4. Each day, after all processing is finished, a bank performs a backup of its online deposit files and retains it for 7 days. Copies of each day's transaction files are not retained. This approach is

A. Valid, in that having a week's worth of backups permits recovery even if one backup is unreadable.

B. Risky, in that restoring from the most recent backup file would omit subsequent transactions.

C. Valid, in that it minimizes the complexity of backup/recovery procedures if the online file has to be restored.

D. Risky, in that no checkpoint/restart information is kept with the backup files.

Answer (B) is correct. *(CIA, adapted)*

REQUIRED: The true statement about retention of backup files but not each day's transaction files.

DISCUSSION: At appropriate intervals, the disk files should be copied on magnetic tape so that restart procedures can begin at those points if data are lost or destroyed. However, not retaining each day's transaction files is risky because information processed since the last backup file was created will be lost.

Answer (A) is incorrect. The practice of not retaining daily transaction data is unsound in that the bank loses a day's transactions for each backup that is unreadable. Answer (C) is incorrect. The practice of not retaining daily transaction data certainly minimizes complexity but at the expense of losing transaction data if the online file must be restored from the backup. Answer (D) is incorrect. Checkpoint/restart information is not needed. The backups are created after all processing is finished for the day.

5. A company updates its accounts receivable master file weekly and retains the master files and corresponding update transactions for the most recent 2-week period. The purpose of this practice is to

A. Verify run-to-run control totals for receivables.

B. Match internal labels to avoid writing on the wrong volume.

C. Permit reconstruction of the master file if needed.

D. Validate groups of update transactions for each version.

Answer (C) is correct. *(CIA, adapted)*

REQUIRED: The purpose of periodic retention of master files and transaction data.

DISCUSSION: The grandfather-father-son approach normally employs magnetic tapes to furnish backup in a batch processing system. The procedure involves creation and retention of three generations of master files so that lost or destroyed data may be regenerated from the remaining master files and transaction data. In this case, a master file (the grandfather) and the first week's transactions are used to generate a second master file (the father). This file and the second week's transactions are the basis for the current master file (the son). Online systems employ rollback and recovery procedures; i.e., the master file is periodically dumped onto a storage medium. Reconstruction is then possible using the backup copy and the transactions log.

Answer (A) is incorrect. Comparison of batch totals is a control over the completeness of processing, not a recovery procedure. Answer (B) is incorrect. Internal labels may avoid destruction of data but do not aid in recovery. Answer (D) is incorrect. Validation may avoid destruction of data but does not aid in recovery.

6. Good planning will help an organization restore computer operations after a processing outage. Good recovery planning should ensure that

A. Backup/restart procedures have been built into job streams and programs.

B. Change control procedures cannot be bypassed by operating personnel.

C. Planned changes in equipment capacities are compatible with projected workloads.

D. Service level agreements with owners of applications are documented.

Answer (A) is correct. *(CIA, adapted)*

REQUIRED: The condition ensured by good recovery planning.

DISCUSSION: The disaster plan should embrace data center recovery, critical application recovery, and network recovery. It should be updated and current with regard to recent test results and new applications, equipment, and network configurations. The plan should also ensure that backup facilities are still able to process critical applications and that end-user responsibility is established. Another essential component of a disaster recovery plan is that backup/restart procedures have been anticipated and provided for in the application systems.

Answer (B) is incorrect. Whether change control procedures can be bypassed is not usually a consideration in disaster recovery planning. Answer (C) is incorrect. Planned rather than actual changes in equipment capacities are not relevant in disaster recovery planning. Answer (D) is incorrect. Ensuring that service level agreements with owners of critical applications are adequate is not a function of disaster recovery planning.

7. In an online, real-time system, which of the following is **most** likely to be used as backup for an application's master file maintained on magnetic disk?

A. At specified periods, the disk files are dumped to (copied on) magnetic tape; a transaction log is maintained as inputs are received and processed.

B. A duplicate disk file is maintained and all activity is copied on magnetic tape continuously.

C. The grandfather-father-son technique is employed to retain disk files.

D. All source documents for transactions are retained.

Answer (A) is correct. *(CMA, adapted)*

REQUIRED: The backup procedure most likely to be used in an online, real-time system.

DISCUSSION: When an application's master file is maintained on magnetic disk in an online, real-time system, the backup procedure most likely to be used is the rollback and recovery method. This method involves the dumping of the master file's contents and associated data structures onto a backup file. In the event of a loss of data, the dump is used together with the transaction log or file to reconstruct the master file.

Answer (B) is incorrect. It describes dual logging. Answer (C) is incorrect. The grandfather-father-son technique is used as a backup procedure in batch-processing systems. Answer (D) is incorrect. It is not a sufficient backup procedure for an online, real-time system. Often, tangible source documents do not exist in an online system.

8. A checkpoint/restart procedure is primarily designed to recover from

A. Programming errors.

B. Data input errors.

C. Computer operator errors.

D. Hardware failures.

Answer (D) is correct. *(CMA, adapted)*

REQUIRED: The primary purpose of a checkpoint/restart procedure.

DISCUSSION: Checkpoint/restart procedures involve capturing all the values of data and program indicators at specified points and storing these values in another file. If processing is interrupted, it can be resumed at the last checkpoint rather than at the beginning of the run.

Answer (A) is incorrect. A checkpoint/restart procedure is not primarily designed to recover from programming errors. Answer (B) is incorrect. A checkpoint/restart procedure is not primarily designed to recover from data input errors. Answer (C) is incorrect. A checkpoint/restart procedure is not primarily designed to recover from computer operator errors.

10.3 Systems Security

9. Which of the following would **not** be appropriate to consider in the physical design of a data center?

A. Evaluation of potential risks from railroad lines and highways.

B. Use of biometric access systems.

C. Design of authorization tables for operating system access.

D. Inclusion of an uninterruptible power supply system and surge protection.

Answer (C) is correct. *(CIA, adapted)*

REQUIRED: The inappropriate consideration in the physical design of a data center.

DISCUSSION: Authorization tables for operating system access address logical controls, not physical controls.

Answer (A) is incorrect. External risks should be evaluated to determine the center's location. Answer (B) is incorrect. Biometric access systems control physical access to the data center. These devices identify such unique physical qualities as fingerprints, voice patterns, and retinal patterns. Answer (D) is incorrect. Power supply systems and surge protection are included in data center design. Thus, two separate power lines, line conditioning equipment, and backup power are typical elements in the design.

10. Application control objectives do **not** normally include assurance that

A. Authorized transactions are completely processed once and only once.

B. Transaction data are complete and accurate.

C. Review and approval procedures for new systems are set by policy and adhered to.

D. Processing results are received by the intended user.

Answer (C) is correct. *(CISA, adapted)*

REQUIRED: The assurance not provided by an application control.

DISCUSSION: Application controls provide reasonable assurance that the recording, processing, and reporting of data are properly performed. Review and approval procedures for new systems are among the general controls known as system software acquisition and maintenance controls.

Answer (A) is incorrect. An objective of application controls is that authorized transactions are completely processed once and only once. Answer (B) is incorrect. An objective of application controls is that transaction data is complete and accurate. Answer (D) is incorrect. An objective of application controls is that processing results are received by the intended user.

11. Authentication is the process by which the

A. System verifies that the user is entitled to enter the transaction requested.

B. System verifies the identity of the user.

C. User identifies him/herself to the system.

D. User indicates to the system that the transaction was processed correctly.

Answer (B) is correct. *(CISA, adapted)*

REQUIRED: The definition of authentication.

DISCUSSION: Identification is the process of uniquely distinguishing one user from all others. Authentication is the process of determining that individuals are who they say they are. For example, a password may identify but not authenticate its user if it is known by more than one individual.

Answer (A) is incorrect. Authentication involves verifying the identity of the user. This process does not necessarily confirm the functions the user is authorized to perform. Answer (C) is incorrect. User identification to the system does not imply that the system has verified the identity of the user. Answer (D) is incorrect. This procedure is an application control for accuracy of the transaction.

12. Which of the following issues would be of **most** concern to an auditor relating to an organization's Internet security policy?

A. Auditor documentation.

B. System efficiency.

C. Data integrity.

D. Rejected and suspense item controls.

Answer (C) is correct. *(Publisher, adapted)*

REQUIRED: The item of most concern to the auditor relating to Internet security.

DISCUSSION: Controls are intended to ensure the integrity, confidentiality, and availability of information. An auditor relies on the integrity of the system's data and programs in making critical decisions throughout the audit process.

Answer (A) is incorrect. Auditor documentation is not as crucial as data integrity. Answer (B) is incorrect. Efficiency does not affect the basis for critical auditor decisions using information provided by the system. Answer (D) is incorrect. Rejected and suspense item controls represent a portion of the techniques used to ensure data integrity.

13. Passwords for personal computer software programs are designed to prevent

A. Inaccurate processing of data.

B. Unauthorized access to the computer.

C. Incomplete updating of data files.

D. Unauthorized use of the software.

Answer (D) is correct. *(CIA, adapted)*

REQUIRED: The function of passwords.

DISCUSSION: The use of passwords is an effective control in an online system to prevent unauthorized access to computer files. Lists of authorized users are maintained in the computer. The entry of passwords or ID numbers; a prearranged act of personal questions; and use of badges, magnetic cards, or optically scanned cards may be combined to avoid unauthorized access.

Answer (A) is incorrect. Passwords concern authorization, not accuracy of data. Answer (B) is incorrect. Passwords do not prevent physical access to the computer. Answer (C) is incorrect. Passwords concern authorization, not completeness of data.

14. As organizations become more computer integrated, management is becoming increasingly concerned with the quality of access controls to the computer system. Which of the following provides the **most** accountability?

	Option I	Option II	Option III	Option IV
Restrict access by:	Individuals	Groups	Individuals	Departments
Identify computer data at:	Field level	Workstation	Workstation	Individual record level
Restrict access:	Need to know	Right to know	Normal processing by employee type	Items identified as processed by department
Identify users by:	Password	Password	Key access to workstation, or password on workstation	Departmental password
Limit ability to:	Delete, add, or modify data	Add or delete files	Add, delete, or modify data stored at workstation	Add, delete, or modify data normally processed by department

A. Option I.

B. Option II.

C. Option III.

D. Option IV.

Answer (A) is correct. *(CIA, adapted)*

REQUIRED: The access control option providing the most accountability.

DISCUSSION: Access should be limited to those whose activities necessitate access to the computer system. Moreover, the degree of access allowed should be consistent with an individual's responsibilities. Restricting access to particular individuals rather than groups or departments clearly establishes specific accountability. Not everyone in a group will need access or the same degree of access. Thus, passwords assigned to individuals should be required for identification of users by the system. Furthermore, data should be restricted at the field level, not the workstation level. It may be possible to limit access to a workstation, but most workstations are connected to larger mainframe or network databases. Thus, the security at the workstation level only would be insufficient.

10.4 Databases

15. Of the following, the greatest advantage of a database (server) architecture is

A. Data redundancy can be reduced.

B. Conversion to a database system is inexpensive and can be accomplished quickly.

C. Multiple occurrences of data items are useful for consistency checking.

D. Backup and recovery procedures are minimized.

Answer (A) is correct. *(CIA, adapted)*

REQUIRED: The greatest advantage of a database architecture.

DISCUSSION: Data organized in files and used by the organization's various applications programs are collectively known as a database. In a database system, storage structures are created that render the applications programs independent of the physical or logical arrangement of the data. Each data item has a standard definition, name, and format, and related items are linked by a system of pointers. The programs therefore need only to specify data items by name, not by location. A database management system handles retrieval and storage. Because separate files for different applications programs are unnecessary, data redundancy can be substantially reduced.

Answer (B) is incorrect. Conversion to a database is often costly and time consuming. Answer (C) is incorrect. A traditional flat-file system, not a database, has multiple occurrences of data items. Answer (D) is incorrect. Given the absence of data redundancy and the quick propagation of data errors throughout applications, backup and recovery procedures are just as critical in a database as in a flat-file system.

16. In an inventory system on a database management system (DBMS), one stored record contains part number, part name, part color, and part weight. These individual items are called

A. Fields.

B. Stored files.

C. Bytes.

D. Occurrences.

Answer (A) is correct. *(CIA, adapted)*

REQUIRED: The term for the data elements in a record.

DISCUSSION: A record is a collection of related data items (fields). A field (data item) is a group of characters representing one unit of information.

Answer (B) is incorrect. A file is a group or set of related records ordered to facilitate processing. Answer (C) is incorrect. A byte is a group of bits (binary digits). It represents one character. Answer (D) is incorrect. Occurrences is not a meaningful term in this context.

17. An inventory clerk, using a computer terminal, views the following on screen: part number, part description, quantity on hand, quantity on order, order quantity, and reorder point for a particular inventory item. Collectively, these data make up a

A. Field.

B. File.

C. Database.

D. Record.

Answer (D) is correct. *(CIA, adapted)*

REQUIRED: The term for the collection of data described.

DISCUSSION: A record is a collection of related data items (fields). A field (data item) is a group of characters representing one unit of information. The part number, part description, etc., are represented by fields.

Answer (A) is incorrect. Field refers to a single data item. Answer (B) is incorrect. File refers to multiple records. Answer (C) is incorrect. Database refers to multiple files.

18. Which of the following is the elementary unit of data storage used to represent individual attributes of an entity?

A. Database.

B. Data field.

C. File.

D. Record.

Answer (B) is correct. *(CIA, adapted)*

REQUIRED: The elementary unit of data storage that is used to represent individual attributes of an entity.

DISCUSSION: A data item (or field) is a group of characters. It is used to represent individual attributes of an entity, such as an employee's address. A field is an item in a record.

Answer (A) is incorrect. A database is an organized collection of files. Answer (C) is incorrect. A file is a collection of records. Answer (D) is incorrect. A record is a collection of data items.

19. A file-oriented approach to data storage requires a primary record key for each file. Which of the following is a primary record key?

A. The vendor number in an accounts payable master file.

B. The vendor number in a closed purchase order transaction file.

C. The vendor number in an open purchase order master file.

D. All of the answers are correct.

Answer (A) is correct. *(CIA, adapted)*

REQUIRED: The item(s) used as a primary record key.

DISCUSSION: The primary record key uniquely identifies each record in a file. Because there is only one record for each vendor in an accounts payable master file, the vendor number would be the appropriate key.

Answer (B) is incorrect. Purchase order files can have multiple purchase orders made out to the same vendor. The primary key in purchase order files would be the purchase order number because it is the only unique identifier for the record. Answer (C) is incorrect. Purchase order files can have multiple purchase orders made out to the same vendor. The primary key in purchase order files would be the purchase order number because it is the only unique identifier for the record. Answer (D) is incorrect. Not all of the answer choices are correct.

20. A business is designing its storage for accounts receivable information. What data file concepts should be used to provide the ability to answer customer inquiries as they are received?

A. Sequential storage and chains.

B. Sequential storage and indexes.

C. Record keys, indexes, and pointers.

D. Inverted file structure, indexes, and internal labels.

Answer (C) is correct. *(CIA, adapted)*

REQUIRED: The data file concepts needed to answer customer inquiries as they are received.

DISCUSSION: A record key is an attribute that uniquely identifies or distinguishes each record from the others. An index is a table listing storage locations for attributes, often including those other than the unique record key attribute. A pointer is a data item that indicates the physical address of the next logically related record.

Answer (A) is incorrect. The ability to respond immediately to customers requires direct access. Answer (B) is incorrect. The ability to respond immediately to customers requires direct access. Answer (D) is incorrect. Internal labels are used to indicate various things to the computer, such as the contents of various types of data storage media, the beginning of each file (with identification information), and the end of each file. However, they do not provide information for locating specific records in a file. An inverted file structure (inverted list) is an index based on a secondary key, for example, years of experience rather than an employee number (the primary key).

10.5 Software Licensing

21. Which of the following would be the **most** appropriate starting point for a compliance evaluation of software licensing requirements for an organization with more than 15,000 computer workstations?

A. Determine if software installation is controlled centrally or distributed throughout the organization.

B. Determine what software packages have been installed on the organization' s computers and the number of each package installed.

C. Determine how many copies of each software package have been purchased by the organization.

D. Determine what mechanisms have been installed for monitoring software usage.

Answer (A) is correct. *(CIA, adapted)*

REQUIRED: The most appropriate starting point for a compliance evaluation of software licensing requirements in a large entity.

DISCUSSION: The logical starting point is to determine the point(s) of control. Evidence of license compliance can then be assessed. For example, to shorten the installation time for revised software in a network, an organization may implement electronic software distribution (ESD), which is the computer-to-computer installation of software on workstations. Instead of weeks, software distribution can be accomplished in hours or days and can be controlled centrally. Another advantage of ESD is that it permits tracking or metering of PC program licenses.

Answer (B) is incorrect. Before taking this step, an auditor should first determine whether installation is controlled centrally. This determination affects how the auditor will gather information about the installed software. Answer (C) is incorrect. This procedure helps an auditor determine whether software was legitimately purchased. However, a better starting point is determining where the software is installed. Answer (D) is incorrect. Monitoring usage is not as important as determining installation procedures when evaluating licensing compliance.

22. Use of unlicensed software in an organization

I. Increases the risk of introducing viruses into the organization

II. Is not a serious exposure if only low-cost software is involved

III. Can be detected by software checking routines that run from a network server

A. I only.

B. I and II only.

C. I, II, and III.

D. I and III only.

Answer (D) is correct. *(CIA, adapted)*

REQUIRED: The true statement(s) about unlicensed software.

DISCUSSION: Antivirus measures should include strict adherence to software acquisition policies. Unlicensed software is less likely to have come from reputable vendors and to have been carefully tested. Special software is available to test software in use to determine whether it has been authorized.

10.6 Web Infrastructure

23. The Internet consists of a series of networks that include

A. Gateways to allow personal computers to connect to mainframe computers.

B. Bridges to direct messages through the optimum data path.

C. Repeaters to physically connect separate local area networks (LANs).

D. Routers to strengthen data signals between distant computers.

Answer (A) is correct. *(CIA, adapted)*

REQUIRED: The composition of the Internet.

DISCUSSION: The Internet facilitates information transfer between computers. Gateways are hardware or software products that allow translation between two different protocol families. For example, a gateway can be used to exchange messages between different email systems.

Answer (B) is incorrect. Routers are used to determine the best path for data. Answer (C) is incorrect. Bridges connect LANs. Answer (D) is incorrect. Repeaters strengthen signals.

24. Which of the following is true concerning HTML?

A. The acronym stands for HyperText Material Listing.

B. The language is among the most difficult to learn.

C. The language is independent of hardware and software.

D. HTML is the only language that can be used for Internet documents.

Answer (C) is correct. *(Publisher, adapted)*

REQUIRED: The true statement concerning HTML.

DISCUSSION: HTML is the most popular language for authoring Web pages. It is hardware and software independent, which means that it can be read by several different applications and on many different kinds of computer operating systems. HTML uses tags to mark information for proper display on Web pages.

Answer (A) is incorrect. HTML is the acronym for HyperText Markup Language. Answer (B) is incorrect. The language is relatively easy to learn. Almost anyone can learn and use HTML, not just computer programmers. Answer (D) is incorrect. A number of other languages can be used for Internet transmissions, including JAVA and XML.

25. Which of the following is a false statement about XBRL?

A. XBRL is freely licensed.

B. XBRL facilitates the automatic exchange of information.

C. XBRL is used primarily in the U.S.

D. XBRL is designed to work with a variety of software applications.

Answer (C) is correct. *(Publisher, adapted)*

REQUIRED: The false statement about XBRL.

DISCUSSION: XBRL stands for eXtensible Business Reporting Language. It is being developed for business and accounting applications. It is an XML-based application used to create, exchange, and analyze financial reporting information and is being developed for worldwide use.

Answer (A) is incorrect. The AICPA-led consortium that developed XBRL has promoted the application as a freely licensed product. Answer (B) is incorrect. XBRL will facilitate the exchange of information. Answer (D) is incorrect. XBRL will allow exchange of data across many platforms and will soon be integrated into accounting software applications and products.

APPENDIX A
THE IIA CONTENT SPECIFICATION OUTLINES (CSOs) AND CROSS-REFERENCES

For your convenience, we have reproduced verbatim The IIA's Content Specification Outline (CSO), also known as a Content Syllabus, for this CIA exam part from their website (www.theiia.org). We also have provided cross-references to the study units and subunits in this book that correspond to The IIA's more detailed CSO coverage. If one entry appears above a list, it applies to all items. Please visit The IIA's website for updates and more information about the exam. Rely on the Gleim materials to pass each part of the exam. We have researched and studied The IIA's CSOs as well as questions from prior exams to provide you with an excellent review program.

PART III – BUSINESS ANALYSIS AND INFORMATION TECHNOLOGY

A. **BUSINESS PROCESSES (15 - 25%)**

1. Quality management (e.g., TQM) (awareness level) (1.1)
2. The International Organization for Standardization (ISO) framework (awareness level) (1.3)
3. Forecasting (awareness level) (1.4)
4. Project management techniques (proficiency level) (1.5)
5. Business process analysis (e.g., workflow analysis and bottleneck management, theory of constraints) (proficiency level) (1.6)
6. Inventory management techniques and concepts (proficiency level) (2.1)
7. Marketing -- pricing objectives and policies (awareness level) (2.3)
8. Marketing -- supply chain management (awareness level) (2.2)
9. Human resources (individual performance management and measurement, supervision, environmental factors that affect performance, facilitation techniques, personnel sourcing/staffing, training and development, and safety) (proficiency level) (2.4)
10. Balanced scorecard (awareness level) (1.2)

B. **FINANCIAL ACCOUNTING AND FINANCE (15 - 25%)**

1. Basic concepts and underlying principles of financial accounting (statements, terminology, relationships) (proficiency level) (3.1-3.4)
2. Intermediate concepts of financial accounting (e.g., bonds, leases, pensions, intangible assets, R&D) (awareness level) (3.5-3.8, 4.1-4.9)
3. Advanced concepts of financial accounting (e.g., consolidation, partnerships, foreign currency transactions) (awareness level) (4.10-4.13)
4. Financial statement analysis (proficiency level) (5.7, 5.8)
5. Cost of capital evaluation (awareness level) (5.3)
6. Types of debt and equity (awareness level) (4.7, 4.8, 5.1, 5.2)
7. Financial instruments (e.g., derivatives) (awareness level) (3.5, 5.5, 5.8)
8. Cash management (treasury functions) (awareness level) (5.4)
9. Valuation models (awareness level)
   a. Inventory valuation (3.6)
   b. Business valuation (5.5)
10. Business development life cycles (awareness level) (5.9)

C. **MANAGERIAL ACCOUNTING (10 - 20%)**

1. Cost concepts (e.g., absorption, variable, fixed) (proficiency level) (6.1-6.3)
2. Capital budgeting (awareness level) (5.5)
3. Operating budget (proficiency level) (6.5, 6.6)
4. Transfer pricing (awareness level) (6.7)
5. Cost-volume-profit analysis (awareness level) (6.8)
6. Relevant cost (awareness level) (6.9)
7. Costing systems (e.g., activity-based, standard) (awareness level) (6.10-6.12)
8. Responsibility accounting (awareness level) (6.13)

D. **REGULATORY, LEGAL, AND ECONOMICS (5 - 15%)** (awareness level)

1. Impact of government legislation and regulation on business (7.1)
2. Trade legislation and regulations (7.2)
3. Taxation schemes (7.3)
4. Contracts (7.6)
5. Nature and rules of legal evidence (7.5)
6. Key economic indicators (7.4)

E. **INFORMATION TECHNOLOGY (IT) (30 - 40%)** (awareness level)

1. Control frameworks (e.g., SAC, COBIT) (8.1)
2. Data and network communications/connections (e.g., LAN, VAN, and WAN) (8.4)
3. Electronic funds transfer (EFT) (8.5)
4. E-Commerce (8.6)
5. Electronic data interchange (EDI) (8.7)
6. Functional areas of IT operations (e.g., data center operations) (9.1)
7. Encryption (9.2)
8. Information protection (e.g., viruses, privacy) (9.3)
9. Evaluate investment in IT (cost of ownership) (9.4)
10. Enterprise-wide resource planning (ERP) software (e.g., SAP R/3) (9.5)
11. Operating systems (9.6)
12. Application development (9.7-9.9)
13. Voice communications (10.1)
14. Contingency planning (10.2)
15. Systems security (e.g., firewalls, access control) (10.3)
16. Databases (10.4)
17. Software licensing (10.5)
18. Web infrastructure (10.6)

APPENDIX B
THE IIA EXAMINATION BIBLIOGRAPHY

The Institute has prepared a listing of references for the CIA exam, reproduced below. These publications have been chosen by the Board of Regents as reasonably representative of the common body of knowledge for internal auditors. However, all of the information in these texts will not be tested. When possible, questions will be written based on the information contained in the suggested reference list. This bibliography for Part III is listed to give you an overview of the scope of the exam. The IIA also indicates that the examination scope includes

1. Articles from *Internal Auditor* (The IIA periodical)
2. IIA research reports
3. IIA pronouncements, e.g., The IIA Code of Ethics and SIASs
4. Past published CIA examinations

The IIA bibliography is reproduced for your information only. The texts you will need to acquire (use) to prepare for the CIA exam will depend on many factors, including

1. Innate ability
2. Length of time out of school
3. Thoroughness of your undergraduate education
4. Familiarity with internal auditing due to relevant experience

SUGGESTED REFERENCES FOR PART III OF THE CIA EXAM

Part III: Business Analysis and Information Technology

Practice Guides of *International Professional Practices Framework (IPPF)*, including Global Technology Audit Guide (GTAG) and Guides to the Assessment of IT Risk (GAIT) series, 2009, The Institute of Internal Auditors, Inc., www.theiia.org/guidance/standards-and-guidance/.

Sawyer's Internal Auditing, 5th Ed., L.B. Sawyer, et al., 2003, The Institute of Internal Auditors, Inc., www.theiia.org/bookstore/.

Internal Auditing Manual, 2004 Ed., Stephen Head, WG&L Financial Reporting & Management, ria.thomsonreuters.com/estore/.

Management, 10th Ed., Robert Kreitner, 2007, Houghton Mifflin Co., www.cengage.com/southwestern/.

Accounting Principles, with CD, 9th Ed., Jerry J. Weygandt, Donald E. Kieso, Paul D. Kimmel, 2008, John Wiley & Sons, www.wiley.com.

International Financial Reporting Standards (IFRS), 2008, International Accounting Standards Board (IASB), www.iasb.org.

Information Systems Control and Audit, Ron A. Weber, 1998, Prentice Hall, www.mypearsonstore.com.

Internal Auditing: An Integrated Approach, 2nd Ed., Richard Cascarino and Sandy van Esch, 2005, Juta and Co. Ltd., www.theiia.org/bookstore/.

AVAILABILITY OF PUBLICATIONS

The listing above presents only some of the current technical literature available, and The IIA does not carry all of the reference books. Quantity discounts are provided by The IIA. Request a current catalog by mail, call, or visit www.theiia.org/bookstore/.

The IIARF Bookstore
1650 Bluegrass Lakes Pkwy
Alpharetta, GA 30004-7714
iiapubs@pbd.com
(877) 867-4957 (toll-free) or (770) 280-4183

Contact the publisher directly if you cannot obtain the desired texts from The IIA or your local bookstore. Begin your study program with Gleim *CIA Review*, which most candidates find sufficient. If you need additional reference material, borrow books from colleagues, professors, or a library.

APPENDIX C
CURRENT LIST OF FINANCIAL ACCOUNTING STANDARDS

The following is a list of current Standards.

International Accounting Standards (IASs)

IAS 1 *Presentation of Financial Statements*
IAS 2 *Inventories*
IAS 7 *Cash Flow Statements*
IAS 8 *Accounting Policies, Changes in Accounting Estimates and Errors*
IAS 10 *Events After the Balance Sheet Date*
IAS 11 *Construction Contracts*
IAS 12 *Income Taxes*
IAS 16 *Property, Plant and Equipment*
IAS 17 *Leases*
IAS 18 *Revenue*
IAS 19 *Employee Benefits*
IAS 20 *Accounting for Government Grants and Disclosure of Government Assistance*
IAS 21 *The Effects of Changes in Foreign Exchange Rates*
IAS 23 *Borrowing Costs*
IAS 24 *Related Party Disclosures*
IAS 26 *Accounting and Reporting by Retirement Benefit Plans*
IAS 27 *Consolidated and Separate Financial Statements*
IAS 28 *Investments in Associates*
IAS 29 *Financial Reporting in Hyperinflationary Economies*
IAS 31 *Interests in Joint Ventures*
IAS 32 *Financial Instruments: Presentation*
IAS 33 *Earnings Per Share*
IAS 34 *Interim Financial Reporting*
IAS 36 *Impairment of Assets*
IAS 37 *Provisions, Contingent Liabilities and Contingent Assets*
IAS 38 *Intangible Assets*
IAS 39 *Financial Instruments: Recognition and Measurement*
IAS 40 *Investment Property*
IAS 41 *Agriculture*

International Financial Reporting Standards (IFRSs)

IFRS 1 *First-time Adoption of International Financial Reporting Standards*
IFRS 2 *Share-Based Payment*
IFRS 3 *Business Combinations*
IFRS 4 *Insurance Contracts*
IFRS 5 *Noncurrent Assets Held for Sale and Discontinued Operations*
IFRS 6 *Exploration for and Evaluation of Mineral Resources*
IFRS 7 *Financial Instruments: Disclosures*
IFRS 8 *Operating Segments*

INDEX

PASS THE CIA EXAM. GUARANTEED.
GLEIM
CIA REVIEW SYSTEM
SYSTEM INCLUDES:
18 MO. PRODUCT REPLACEMENT
PERSONAL COUNSELOR
TEST PREP for POCKET PC
TEST PREP CD-ROM
GLEIM ONLINE
AUDIO CDs
BOOKS
GLEIM KNOWLEDGE TRANSFER SYSTEMS®
GLEIM.COM/CIA
800.874.5346

Online CPE
Try
FREE
4 hr. Course
as low as
$4/hour
• Easy-to-Complete
• Informative
• Effective
GLEIM is an approved sponsor of QAS and Registry CPE.
QAS
QUALITY ASSURANCE SERVICE
Gleim Publications, Inc. is registered with the National Association of State Boards of Accountancy (NASBA), as a Quality Assurance Service (QAS) sponsor of continuing professional education. Participating state boards of accountancy have final authority on the acceptance of individual courses for CPE credit. Complaints regarding QAS program sponsors may be addressed to NASBA, 150 Fourth Avenue North, Suite 700, Nashville, TN, 37219-2417. Web site: www.nasba.org
CPE
SPONSORS
Gleim Publications, Inc. is registered with the National Association of State Boards of Accountancy (NASBA), as a sponsor of continuing professional education on the National Registry of CPE Sponsors. State boards of accountancy have final authority on the acceptance of individual courses for CPE credit. Complaints regarding registered sponsors may be addressed to the National Registry of CPE Sponsors, 150 Fourth Avenue North, Suite 700, Nashville, TN, 37219-2417. or by visiting the web site: www.nasba.org

GLEIM CPA REVIEW SYSTEM

All 4 sections, including Gleim Online, books*, *Test Prep CD-Rom*, *Test Prep for Pocket PC*, Audio CDs, plus bonus book bag. ☐ $989.95

Also available by exam section @ $274.95 (does not include book bag).

*Fifth book: *CPA Review: A System for Success*

$________

GLEIM CMA REVIEW SYSTEM

Includes: Gleim Online, books*, *Test Prep CD-Rom*, *Test Prep for Pocket PC*, Audio CDs, plus bonus book bag. ☐ $739.95

Also available by exam part @ $213.95 (does not include book bag).

*Fifth book: *CMA Review: A System for Success*

$________

GLEIM CIA REVIEW SYSTEM

Includes: Gleim Online, books*, *Test Prep CD-Rom*, *Test Prep for Pocket PC*, Audio CDs, plus bonus book bag. ☐ $824.95

Also available by exam part @ $224.95 (does not include book bag).

*Fifth book: *CIA Review: A System for Success*

$________

GLEIM EA REVIEW SYSTEM

Includes: Gleim Online, books, *Test Prep CD-Rom*, *Test Prep for Pocket PC*, Audio CDs, plus bonus book bag. ☐ $629.95

Also available by exam part @ $224.95 (does not include book bag).

$________

"THE GLEIM SERIES" EXAM QUESTIONS AND EXPLANATIONS

Includes: 5 books, *Test Prep CD-Rom,* and *Test Prep for Pocket PC*. ☐ $187.25

Also available by part @ $49.90.

$________

GLEIM ONLINE CPE

Try a FREE 4 hour course at gleim.com/cpe

- Easy-to-Complete
- Informative
- Effective

Contact **GLEIM PUBLICATIONS** for further assistance:

gleim.com
800.874.5346
sales@gleim.com

SUBTOTAL $________

Complete your order on the next page

TOLL FREE:	800.874.5346	Customer service is available (Eastern Time):
LOCAL:	352.375.0772	8:00 a.m. - 7:00 p.m., Mon. - Fri.
FAX:	352.375.6940	9:00 a.m. - 2:00 p.m., Saturday
INTERNET:	gleim.com	Please have your credit card ready, or save time by ordering online!
E-MAIL:	sales@gleim.com	

SUBTOTAL (from previous page) $ ______

Add applicable sales tax for shipments within Florida. ______

Shipping (nonrefundable) 25.00

TOTAL $ ______

Fax or write for prices/instructions on shipments outside the 48 contiguous states, or simply order online.

NAME (please print) ______________________

ADDRESS ______________________ Apt. ______
(street address required for UPS)

CITY ______________________ STATE ______ ZIP ______

____ MC/VISA/DISC ____ Check/M.O. Daytime Telephone (   ) ______

Credit Card No. ______ - ______ - ______ - ______

Exp. ____ / ____ Signature ______________________
Month / Year

E-mail address ______________________

1. We process and ship orders daily, within one business day over 98.8% of the time. Call by 3:00 pm for same day service.
2. Gleim Publications, Inc. guarantees the immediate refund of all resalable texts, unopened and un-downloaded Test Prep CD-Roms, and unopened audios returned within 30 days. Online courses may be canceled within 30 days if no more than the first study unit or lesson has been accessed. In addition, Online CPE courses may be canceled within 30 days if no more than the Introductory Study Questions have been accessed. This only applies to products that are purchased directly from Gleim Publications, Inc. No refunds will be provided on opened or downloaded Test Prep CD-Rom or audios, partial returns of package sets, or shipping and handling charges. Any freight charges incurred for returned or refused packages will be the customer's responsibility.
3. Please PHOTOCOPY this order form for others.
4. No CODs. Orders from individuals must be prepaid.
5. Shipping and handling charges are nonrefundable.

Prices subject to change without notice.
05/09

For updates and other important information, visit our website.

GLEI[M]
KNOWLE[DGE]
TRANS[FER]
SYST[EMS]

Please forward your suggestions, corrections, and comments concerning typographical errors, etc., to **Irvin N. Gleim • c/o Gleim Publications, Inc. • P.O. Box 12848 • University Station • Gainesville, Florida • 32604.** Please include your name and address so we can properly thank you for your interest.

1. ______________________________

2. ______________________________

3. ______________________________

4. ______________________________

5. ______________________________

6. ______________________________

7. ______________________________

8. ______________________________

9. ______________________________

10. ______________________________

Please complete and mail to us pages 465 and 466 the week following the CIA exam.

11. ____

12. ____

13. ____

14. ____

15. ____

16. ____

17. ____

18. ____

Remember, for superior service: Mail, email, or fax questions about our materials.
Telephone questions about orders, prices, shipments, or payments.

Name: ________________________________

Address: ________________________________

City/State/Zip: ________________________________

Telephone: Home: ____________ Work: ____________ Fax: ____________

Email: ________________________________